**AQA**
**A-level**

# Business
# for A-level

Ian Marcousé ▪ Andrew Hammond
▪ Nigel Watson

**Approval message from AQA**

This textbook has been approved by AQA for use with our qualification. This means that we have checked that it broadly covers the specification and we are satisfied with the overall quality. Full details of our approval process can be found on our website.

We approve textbooks because we know how important it is for teachers and students to have the right resources to support their teaching and learning. However, the publisher is ultimately responsible for the editorial control and quality of this book.

Please note that when teaching the *AQA A-level Business* course, you must refer to AQA's specification as your definitive source of information. While this book has been written to match the specification, it cannot provide complete coverage of every aspect of the course.

A wide range of other useful resources can be found on the relevant subject pages of our website: aqa.org.uk.

**HODDER**
EDUCATION
AN HACHETTE UK COMPANY

## Acknowledgements

Every effort has been made to trace the copyright holders of material reproduced here. The authors and publishers would like to thank the following for permission to reproduce copyright illustrations.

Fig. 1.6 © Philippe Huguen/AFP/Getty Images; Fig. 6.1 © Fotum – Fotolia; Fig. 10.2 © Suzanne Kreiter/ The Boston Globe via Getty Images; Fig. 11.3 © innocent drinks; Fig. 11.5 © Clynt Garnham Food & Drink/ Alamy; Fig. 12.1 © Tomohiro Ohsumi/Bloomberg via Getty Images; Fig. 12.3 © Robert Wilkinson/Alamy; Fig. 14.2 © Jeanette Dietl – Fotolia; Fig.15.1 © Asife – Fotolia; Fig. 16.6 © Tom Bourdon/Alamy; Fig. 17.2 © Henry Schmitt – Fotolia; Fig. 17.4 © Oli Scarff/Getty Images; Fig. 17.5 © Newscast-Online Limited/Alamy; Fig. 18.1 © Photoshot; Fig. 19.5 © Sonu Mehta/Hindustan Times via Getty Images; Fig. 20.5 courtesy of Taisun Foods & Marketing Co. Ltd; Fig. 22.5 © Richard Levine/Demotix/Press Association Images; Fig. 23.4 © Bernardo De Niz/Bloomberg via Getty Images; Fig. 23.5 © Sunil Saxena/Hindustan Times via Getty Images; Fig. 24.3 © Eranga Jayawardena/AP/Press Association Images; Fig. 27.2 © WavebreakMediaMicro – Fotolia; Fig. 27.4 © Photofusion/REX; Fig. 28.2 © Denis Doyle/Bloomberg via Getty Images; Fig. 30.1 © Oleksiy Maksymenko/ Alamy; Fig. 30.2 © Martina Berg – Fotolia; Fig. 30.4 © Bas Czerwinski/EPA/Corbis; Fig. 30.6 © Piero Cruciatti/ Alamy; Fig. 33.4 © Viktor - Fotolia; Fig. 35.1 © Silvia Olsen/REX; Fig. 42.2 © WavebreakMediaMicro – Fotolia; Fig. 43.3 © Chivote; Fig. 44.2 © ACORN 1/Alamy; Fig. 44.3 © Simon Dawson/Bloomberg via Getty Images; Fig. 44.5 © Michael Blann/Getty Images; Fig. 50.2 © INSADCO Photography/Alamy; Fig. 51.1 © Picture-Factory – Fotolia; Fig. 53.1 © FOX via Getty Images; Fig. 54.5 © stephen searle / Alamy; Fig. 55.2 © SIPA/REX Shutterstock; Fig. 56.4 © Antony SOUTER / Alamy; Fig 57.1 © snapchat; Fig. 63.2 © Zeljko Bozic/Hemera/ Thinkstock; Fig. 63.3 © Fuse/Thinkstock; Fig. 64.2 © Imaginechina/REX Shutterstock; Fig 65.2 First published by the Institute of Economic Affairs, London in 2014; Fig 67.2 © silkwayrain/iStock/Thinkstock; Fig. 73.3 © JCB; Fig. 76.2 © uckyo - Fotolia; 76.4 © amc / Alamy; Fig. 77.5 © Imaginechina/REX Shutterstock; Fig. 78.1 © Bhaskar Paul/The India Today Group/Getty Images; 79.5 © Mark Richardson / Alamy; Fig. 83.4 © ddp USA/ REX Shutterstock; Fig. 84.2 © Little Valley Brewery; Fig. 86.2 © Medioimages/Photodisc/Thinkstock; Fig. 88.4 © Andrew Woodley / Alamy; Fig. 93.6 © Donald Weber/VII/Corbis

Crown copyright material is licensed under the Open Government Licence v1.0

Every effort has been made to trace all copyright holders, but if any have been inadvertently overlooked, the Publishers will be pleased to make the necessary arrangements at the first opportunity.

Although every effort has been made to ensure that website addresses are correct at time of going to press, Hodder Education cannot be held responsible for the content of any website mentioned in this book. It is sometimes possible to find a relocated web page by typing in the address of the home page for a website in the URL window of your browser.

Hachette UK's policy is to use papers that are natural, renewable and recyclable products and made from wood grown in sustainable forests. The logging and manufacturing processes are expected to conform to the environmental regulations of the country of origin.

Orders: please contact Bookpoint Ltd, 130 Milton Park, Abingdon, Oxon OX14 4SB. Telephone: (44) 01235 827720. Fax: (44) 01235 400454. Email education@bookpoint.co.uk Lines are open from 9 a.m. to 5 p.m., Monday to Saturday, with a 24-hour message answering service. You can also order through our website: www.hoddereducation.co.uk

© Ian Marcouse, Andrew Hammond, Nigel Watson, 2015

First published in 2015 by
Hodder Education,
An Hachette UK Company
Carmelite House
50 Victoria Embankment
London EC4Y 0DZ
www.hoddereducation.co.uk

Impression number    5

Year                 2018

Cover photo © Sergey Nivens - Fotolia

Typeset in India

Printed in Italy

A catalogue record for this title is available from the British Library.

ISBN: 978 1471 835698

# Contents

# Understanding the nature and purpose of business

**Linked to:** Issues in understanding forms of business, Chapter 3; Understanding the role and importance of stakeholders, Chapter 10; Decision-making to improve financial performance, Chapter 44.

## Definition

According to business guru Peter Drucker, business is the creation of a customer; in other words, conceiving a product or service that people will pay enough for to generate a profit.

## 1.1 An overview of the subject

Business is best looked at from the boss's point of view. The boss (perhaps the founder or entrepreneur) has an idea or mission. The chief executive of Sainsbury's may decide that a chain of supermarkets in India represents the next big step forward. This is the mission – Sainsbury's succeeding in India. This can then form the basis for setting targets or objectives, such as to open the first ten Sainsbury's supermarkets in India by the end of 2018.

'Business is like a bicycle. Either you keep moving or you fall down.' John David Wright, U.S. businessman

After the chief executive has set that objective, Sainsbury's senior managers must then figure out how to make this happen. What will be needed is a strategy that leads to a plan of action, that is, to set out exactly what needs to happen, and by when. That strategy will have to involve the four main sections of the business (known as the business functions). These are marketing, people, finance and operations (see Table 1.1).

**Table 1.1** Introduction to business functions

| Marketing | This department advises the business on consumer trends, and on the attitudes and purchasing habits of customers – and decides how to advertise and promote new and existing brands. |
|---|---|
| People (Human Resources) | Managers of the firm's staff (human resources or HR) plan for and deal with recruitment, training, financial incentives, equal opportunities and also redundancy and dismissals. |
| Finance | Finance helps to identify what can be afforded and therefore what budgets to set for each of the other functions; it also monitors the spending levels to make sure that costs are kept under control. |
| Operations | Operations manages the supply chain that starts with buying materials and components, then manufactures a finished product and delivers it to the customer. Service businesses also need to plan the flow of work, so operations management is relevant in a bank or a shop as well as in a factory. |

The chief executive will expect the leaders of each of these four functions to come up with their own plan for meeting the overall objective, so there will be a marketing plan, a financial plan and so on. How these things relate to each other can be seen in Figure 1.1.

**Figure 1.1** How business works

Having established their own plans, the four functional leaders will now need to meet to make sure that everything fits together. It is no good if marketing decides on an image of Sainsbury's Super-value (a kind of Aldi/Lidl idea) while operations chooses to build stores targeting India's rich elite. Each of the functions must talk to each other and trust each other (see Figure 1.2). This is also the way you are likely to learn this subject. First you study each business function in turn, then you study how the departments work together (and the problems caused if they fail to do so).

**Figure 1.2** How business works (2)

Important though it is to understand the internal workings of a business as shown in Figure 1.2, there are many added complications. Much as a chief executive may wish to set optimistic objectives, a series of outside factors can get in the way of success. Most obviously, competitors may have their own ideas; if Sainsbury's finds that the massive Walmart is fighting for every suitable property site in India, opening ten stores will become a lot harder. Figure 1.3 gives an overview of the process of running a business, taking into account external as well as internal factors.

**Figure 1.3** How business works (3)

Sainsbury's plc is one of the UK's leading companies, with a 16.5 per cent share of the market for groceries. In 2014 its sales revenue was £26,353 million and profits came to £798 million. Despite these impressive-sounding numbers, the chart below shows how they compare with one of the world's monster businesses – Walmart (which owns Asda). As you can see, Walmart makes more than twenty times more profit per year than Sainsbury's. If Sainsbury's chooses to develop in India, it will probably end up head-to-head with Walmart. That would be tricky.

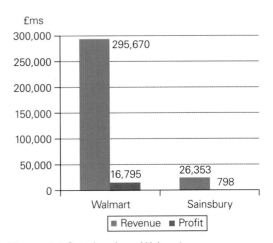

**Figure 1.4** Sainsbury's vs. Walmart

*2014 figures; Walmart dollars converted at $1.60 to the £*

## 1.2 Why businesses exist

Businesses exist because human spirit and a sense of adventure lead people to 'show what they can do' and to want to find a way to create family income that is not dependent on a specific outside force: a company or a boss. Hundreds of years ago this could be done by being a farmer, running a shop or having independence as a skilled tradesman. Today, starting a business can be the path to riches or to long hours and meagre rewards – but the lure of 'being your own boss' remains powerful.

Figure 1.5 below shows the huge rise in business start-ups in recent years, as shown by the 61.5 per cent growth in company formation between 2008/9 and 2013/14. Part of the spur may have been the recent recession, but it is also testimony to the attractions today of running your own business.

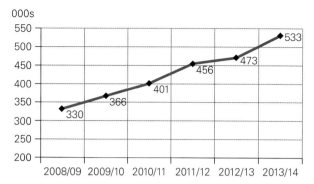

000s

**Figure 1.5** UK company start-ups
Source: www.companieshouse.gov.uk

'Entrepreneur: a high-rolling risk taker who would rather be a spectacular failure than a dismal success.' Anon

Businesses exist because a complex modern world needs more than simply a buyer, a seller and a market for them to meet. A company such as Rolls Royce Aerospace employs over 20,000 people to design, engineer, build, fit and service more than £5,000 million of sales of engines every year, 75 per cent of which are exports from the UK. Managing this requires huge skills of co-ordination and motivation, all within the Rolls Royce mission 'to provide the finest, most technologically advanced power systems'.

## 1.3 Mission and objectives

Mission is the aim for the business that is settled upon by the boss (in a small firm) or by the board of directors in a large one. An aim is a general statement of where the business is heading; mission usually takes that statement and makes it sound more evangelical or motivational. An aim might be 'to be No. 1 in the market for advanced engines'. When dressed up as a mission, this becomes: 'to provide the finest, most technologically advanced power systems' (Rolls Royce).

The reason to turn the aim into a motivational statement is to try to excite customers and staff alike – to make them feel part of the project, just as customers once felt that buying innocent smoothies was helping 'to make the world a little fruitier'. Without doubt, if a business has an exciting aim it is great to express it as a motivating mission. Often, though, dull aims are jazzed up as mission statements that mean little or nothing.

From the aims or mission will come the objectives. These will usually be SMART, that is, Specific,

**Table 1.2** Good and bad mission statements

| Meaningful mission statement | Meaningless mission statement (Would this motivate staff?) |
|---|---|
| 'To become the world's No. 1 online fashion destination for twenty-somethings.' ASOS 2014 (neatly, they call this 'Our Ambition' rather than 'Our Mission') | 'We want Tesco to be the most highly valued business by: the customers we serve, the communities in which we operate, our loyal and committed colleagues and of course, our shareholders.' Tesco 2014 |
| 'Maintaining a global viewpoint, we are dedicated to supplying products of the highest quality, yet at a reasonable price, for worldwide customer satisfaction. Dreams inspire us to create innovative products that enhance mobility and benefit society.' Honda UK 2014 | 'To be the world leader in food ingredients and flavours serving the food and beverage industry, and a leading supplier of added value brands and customer branded foods to the Irish and UK markets.' Kerry Foods 2014 |
| 'Our product mission drives us to make fantastic ice cream – for its own sake.' Ben & Jerry's 2014 | 'We create outstanding places which make a positive difference to people's everyday lives.' British Land, 2014 |

Measurable, Achievable, Realistic and Timebound. For ASOS, an example of a SMART objective might be 'to become one of the Top 3 online clothing sellers in China by January 1st 2017'. Ideally this objective would seem challenging but achievable – and should sit neatly as a stepping stone towards the mission of becoming the world's No. 1.

## 1.4 Why businesses set objectives

Objectives are set because if you're the boss of 21,300 people running Rolls Royce, you cannot make every decision. Therefore you have to give more junior staff the authority to get on and make middle-ranking decisions, perhaps without letting you know. If managers are clear on the overall objectives they can feel confident in making decisions that contribute towards achieving those goals.

Other benefits from setting objectives include:

● It's motivating to have a clear goal to aim towards – for managers and for staff
● The objectives are the basis for devising the strategy: the medium–long term plan for meeting the objectives.

The plan can be costed both in manpower and money, to know what resources are going to be needed to achieve the objectives.

> 'Objectives are not fate; they are direction. They are not commands; they are commitments. They do not determine the future; they are means to mobilise the resources and energies of the business for the making of the future.' Peter Drucker, business guru

## 1.5 Common business objectives

Business objectives are sometimes called corporate objectives because they set targets for the whole organisation, not just one function. Common business objectives include the following:

1. Profit optimisation in the medium-long term. Profit is vital to the long-term health of every company. Profit provides the capital to fund business growth. It also provides the safety blanket that allows a business to take a risk, knowing that even if it flops, the business will not go under. Optimisation means getting the right balance between two or more possibilities: neither so much profit as to risk exploiting the customer, nor so little as to threaten the firm's viability. Good companies appreciate that their long-term position will be helped if their customers believe they are getting value for money.

2. Profit maximisation, that is the attempt by a business to make as much profit as possible, probably as fast as possible. Big companies may follow this approach when they suspect a rival is about to try to buy them out. The higher the profit they can show, the higher the price the company will fetch. The same is likely to be the case for companies about to 'float' their shares onto the stock market.

   Small firms may also be trying to make as much profit as possible, with no concern for their long-term future and therefore no regard for their reputation. Such businesses may end up on investigative TV programmes such as the BBC's *Watchdog*.

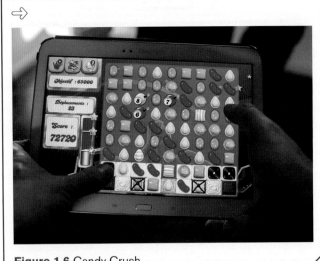
**Figure 1.6** Candy Crush

3. Growth. The importance of online business has placed growth as one of the most common business objectives. The logic is often to say 'there can only be one giant in this market, so we must make sure it's us'. Therefore decisions are made that focus on rising customer/user numbers instead of rising profits. The assumption is often made that if you get the growth today, the profits will come tomorrow. This is famously true in the console business, in which selling hardware rarely makes a profit – it's the software and the add-ons that bring profits later.

> 'Growth is a by-product of the pursuit of excellence and is not itself a worthy goal.' Robert Townsend, Avis chief executive and business author.

4. Cash flow. This is rarely a consideration for large firms, but is important for small ones, especially business start-ups. If the objective of a new firm is to ensure that cash flow remains positive, it will be vital that everyone in the business is practising the same approach. So even quite junior staff who have been given some decision-making power (had authority delegated to them) should be clear that they must not risk creating negative cash flow.

### Real business

When Candy Crush owner King Digital Entertainment decided to float the business, it had nine months to maximize its profit before the flotation took place. Therefore when the Spring 2014 float happened, it was possible to claim such high profits that a very high share price was justified. The final price of $22.50 per share valued the company at $7 billion. Within six months of the float the shares had lost 40 per cent of their value as King announced that revenues from Candy Crush were lower than expected. The share buyers were certainly crushed.

**Figure 1.7** Logic chain: from mission to decision-making

5. Survival. This relates strongly to the previous point about cash flow. If times are tough, survival may be the key objective; and in that case survival will rely on keeping cash flow high enough. This will be a priority for new, start-up businesses aware that one third of new businesses fail to survive three years.

6. Social and ethical objectives are easy to find on company websites; whether they have any significant influence over business decisions is less clear. All through the period that banks were mis-selling service after service to customers, their websites boasted about their ethical purity. Ultimately, social and ethical objectives only mean something if the business is willing to sacrifice some profit or some market share. Arguably Tesco did just this in May 2014 when it volunteered to remove sweets from near its checkouts (though perhaps it was following Lidl's example, as the German firm did the same earlier in the year). The evidence is that it is fair to be sceptical about whether social and ethical objectives are ever much more than image-related add-ons. Financial objectives remain the overwhelming priority for most businesses.

## Five Whys and a How

| Question | Answer |
|---|---|
| Why study business anyway? | Because although some entrepreneurs have no business education, most have quite a lot – and so have most of the world's high-earning chief executives. |
| Why might a company aim be better expressed as a mission? | If more vibrant, motivating language makes staff care more and work harder, a mission will have paid for itself. |
| Why do objectives need to be SMART? | Vaguely worded 'objectives' will be too woolly to allow anyone to measure whether they have been achieved or not, so they'd have no motivating force. |
| Why do new firms struggle with cash flow? | Because retail customers expect generous credit terms (delaying cash inflows) while suppliers demand cash on delivery. |
| Why may social objectives be easy to boast about but hard to carry through? | Boasts about doing good sit well on a website, but may be ignored by bosses intent on high profits and therefore high bonuses. |
| How should bosses decide on their company objectives? | By talking to their staff they'll find out what's wrong at the moment and what's possible in the future. |

## Key terms

**Budgets:** an agreed ceiling on the monthly spending by any department or manager.

**Corporate objectives:** targets for the whole business, such as profits to rise by 20 per cent a year for the next three years.

**Delegated:** having passed authority down the hierarchy so that the local or more expert person makes the decision.

**Entrepreneur:** a person with the initiative and drive to make a business idea happen.

**Mission:** a business aim expressed to make it seem especially purposeful and motivating.

**Mission statement:** a short, powerfully-expressed sentence or two that explains the business aims clearly yet motivationally.

**Objectives:** targets precise enough to allow praise or blame for the person in charge.

**Profit optimisation:** that the surplus of revenue over costs should be just right: neither too high in the short term nor too low to finance long-term success.

**Strategy:** a medium-long term plan for meeting your objectives.

## Evaluation: Understanding the nature and purpose of business

Business is like watching live football. You simply couldn't make it up. The twists and turns for large firms like Tesco or small local firms are remarkably dramatic. One week all is well and the next week there's a crisis.

Both for football managers and company executives, it isn't supposed to be that way. Most football managers want 'a good performance and a clean sheet'. A dull one-nil performance is superior to a frantic 4-3 skirmish. And company bosses yearn for predictability and stability. That's why they set clear objectives and hold managers to account for meeting them. Happily, no matter how much they seek stability, managers are constantly being upset by unexpected results and performances. Studying business should never be boring.

'Entrepreneurs are needed not only to start new business ventures … but also to put life into existing companies, especially large ones.' Anders Wall, Swedish chief executive

# Workbook

## A. Revision questions

(25 marks; 25 minutes)

1. Explain two differences between mission and objectives. (4)

2. State whether each of the following statements is a mission or an objective.
   a) To become the world's favourite car rental business.
   b) To bring healthy eating to Wigan.
   c) To achieve a 40 per cent market share by the end of 2018. (3)

3. Outline two possible risks if a business such as Sainsbury's sets itself the objective of rapid growth. (4)

4. Outline why 'survival' might be the wisest objective for a brand new start-up business. (3)

5. Why might a business suffering bad publicity emphasise a new set of ethical objectives? (3)

6. Read John David Wright's quotation (see page 1). Explain its meaning in your own words. (4)

7. Outline one strength and one weakness of a business such as Aston Villa FC setting itself objectives for the coming season. (4)

## B. Revision exercises
### DATA RESPONSE

Snapchat

In late Autumn 2013 two 23-year-old Californians were each offered $750 million in cash by Facebook's Mark Zuckerberg. And they turned it down. Evan Spiegel and Bobby Murphy launched Snapchat in July 2011. Now Facebook wanted to buy the business for $3,000 million. The founders had each retained a 25 per cent stake in the business, hence the $750 m figure.

Snapchat began late one night at Stanford University when Reggie Brown stepped into fellow-student Spiegel's room groaning about a photo he regretted sending. He then said something like 'I wish there was an app to send disappearing photos'. Spiegel saw the potential, calling Brown's remark 'a million dollar idea'. This conversation is now part of a billion dollar lawsuit, as Brown claims his share of the Snapchat goldmine.

Spiegel developed the app as part of a University project. When he presented it, the feedback was, roughly, who wants a disappearing photo? And when it debuted (under the brand name Picaboo) in the Apple App Store on 13 July 2011, no one noticed. Luckily, a bust-up over the share split in August 2011 made Spiegel and Murphy cut Brown out – including the Picaboo name that Brown had put forward. The new name was Snapchat. User uptake remained painfully slow until high school students in California started using it at school – as Facebook had been banned. Then the take-off was spectacular, as shown in Table 1.3

**Table 1.3** Growth of Snapchat

| | Snapchat users/usage | Snapchat funding |
|---|---|---|
| **August 2011** | 127 | |
| **October 2011** | 1,000 | |
| **December 2011** | 2,250 | |
| **January 2012** | 20,000 | |
| **April 2012** | 100,000 | $485,000 |
| **February 2013** | 60,000,000 | $13,500,000 |
| **November 2013** | 400,000,000 | $50,000,000 |
| **June 2014** | 1,000,000,000 | |

Having turned $3 billion down in 2013, it was perhaps a relief to the founders that Chinese web giant Alibaba talked in August 2014 about an investment that would value Snapchat at $10 billion. This would be an amazing valuation as Snapchat had, at that time, never generated a dollar of revenue. But Snapchat's huge appeal came from demography. Facebook users were now an average of nearly 40 years old, whereas Snapchat's core market was 12–24 year olds, with an average age below 18. Facebook might be the present but Snapchat looked like the future.

The other huge issue for Spiegel and Murphy was Brown's huge lawsuit, demanding his fair share of the company. A similar thing happened with Facebook, making it easy to forecast that lawyers will get rich arguing this case – but it will probably be settled out of court for a very large sum.

### Questions (25 marks; 30 minutes)

1. Why do you think that the Snapchat business exists? Explain your answer. (4)

2. With no income, Snapchat's cash flow was dependent entirely on capital investment from outside sources. Analyse the effect this may have on Spiegel and Murphy's ability to run the business. (9)

3. From your own knowledge of Snapchat, do you think the business could ever generate advertising or other revenue to make it worth billions of dollars? Justify your answer. (12)

## C. Extend your understanding

1. You have been appointed Chief Executive of Marks & Spencer. Your mission is 'to restore M&S as the clothing store of choice for women over the age of 30'. Discuss how you will set about this task. (20)

2. When faced with crisis in early 2015, a commentator suggested that Morrisons 'might not survive the coming three years'. To what extent do you agree with this statement? (20)

# Chapter 2
# Different business forms

**Linked to:** Understanding the nature and purpose of business, Chapter 1; Issues in understanding forms of business, Chapter 3; Understanding the role and importance of stakeholders, Chapter 10.

## Definition

The legal structure of a business determines the financial impact on the business owners if things go wrong. It also affects the ease with which the business can finance growth.

## 2.1 Businesses with unlimited liability

Unlimited liability means that the finances of the business are treated as inseparable from the finances of the business owner(s). So if the business loses £1 million, the people owed money (the creditors) can get the courts to force the individual owners to pay up. If that means selling their houses, cars, and so on, so be it. If the owner(s) cannot pay, they can be made personally bankrupt. Two types of business organisation have unlimited liability: sole traders and partnerships.

### Sole traders

A sole trader is an individual who owns and operates his or her own business. Although there may be one or two employees, this person makes the final decisions about the running of the business. A sole trader is the only one who benefits financially from success, but must face the burden of any failure. In the eyes of the law the individual and the business are the same. This means that the owner has unlimited liability for any debts that result from running the firm. If a sole trader cannot pay his or her bills, the courts can allow personal assets to be seized by creditors in order to meet outstanding debts. For example, the family home or car may be sold. If insufficient funds can be raised in this way the person will be declared bankrupt.

Despite the financial dangers involved, the sole trader is the most common form of legal structure adopted by UK businesses. In some areas of the economy this kind of business dominates, particularly where little finance is required to set up and run the business and customers demand a personal service. Examples include trades such as builders and plumbers, and many independent shopkeepers.

There are no formal rules to follow when establishing as a sole trader, or administrative costs to pay. Complete confidentiality can be maintained because accounts are not published. As a result many business start-ups adopt this structure.

The main disadvantages facing a sole trader are the limited sources of finance available, long hours of work involved and the difficulty of running the business during periods of ill health (plus unlimited liability).

### Partnerships

Partnerships exist when two or more people start a business without forming a company. Like a sole trader, the individuals have unlimited liability for any debts run up by the business. Because people are working together but are unlimitedly liable for any debts, it is vital that the partners trust each other. As a result, this legal structure is often found in the professions, such as medicine and law.

The main difference between a sole trader and a partnership is the number of owners.

## 2.2 Businesses with limited liability

Limited liability means that the legal duty to pay debts run up by a business stays with the business itself, not its owner/shareholders. If a company has £1 million of debts that it lacks the cash to repay, the courts can force the business to sell all its assets (cars, computers, etc.). If there is still not enough money, the company is closed down, but the owner/shareholders have no personal liability for the remaining debts.

To gain the benefits of limited liability, the business must go through a legal process to become a company. The process of incorporation creates a separate legal identity for the organisation. In the eyes of the law the owners of the business and the company itself are now two different things. The business can take legal action against others and have legal action taken against it. In order to gain separate legal status a company must be registered with the Registrar of Companies.

The key advantages and disadvantages that result from forming a limited company are set out below.

Advantages of forming a limited company:

● Shareholders experience the benefits of limited liability, including the confidence to expand.

● A limited company is able to gain access to a wider range of borrowing opportunities than a sole trader or partnership.

Disadvantages of forming a limited company:

● Limited companies must make financial information available publicly at Companies House. Small firms are not required to make full disclosure of their company accounts, but they have to reveal more than would be the case for a sole trader or partnership.

● Limited companies have to follow more, and more expensive, rules than unlimited liability businesses, for example producing audited accounts and holding

**Figure 2.1** Logic chain: sole trader or Ltd?

an annual general meeting of shareholders. These things add several thousands of pounds to annual overhead costs.

## 2.3 Private limited companies

A small business can be started up as a sole trader, a partnership or as a private limited company. For a private limited company, the start-up capital will often be £100, which can be wholly owned by the entrepreneur, or other people can be brought in as investors. The shares of a private limited company cannot be bought and sold without the agreement of the other directors. This means the company cannot be listed on the stock market. As a result it is possible to maintain close control over the way the business is run. This form of business is often run by a family or small group of friends. It may be very profit focused or, like Global Ethics Ltd, have wholly different objectives than maximising profit.

A legal requirement for private companies is that they must state 'Ltd' after the company name. This warns those dealing with the business that the firm is relatively small and has limited liability. Remember, limited liability protects shareholders from business debts, so there is a risk that 'cowboy' businesspeople might start a company, run it into the ground and then walk away from its debts. Therefore the cheques of a limited company are not as secure as ones from an unlimited liability business. This is why many petrol stations have notices saying 'No company cheques allowed'.

Some of the factors that may determine when a business should start up as a sole trader and when as a private limited company are outlined in Table 2.1.

### Real business

#### One Water

In 2003, Duncan Goose quit his job and founded One Water. He wanted to finance water projects in Africa from profits made selling bottled water in Britain. The particular water project was 'Playpumps': children's roundabouts plumbed into freshly dug water wells. As the children play, each rotation of the roundabout brings up a litre of fresh, clean water.

Duncan thought of forming a charity, but felt that the regulations governing charities might force them to be inefficient. So, for the sum of £125 he founded a limited company, Global Ethics Ltd. This enabled him to set the rules, for instance that the shareholders receive no dividends and the directors receive no fees. But, of course, it ensured that he and other volunteers who put time into One Water are protected, should something go wrong and big debts build up. Today One Water is a major business trading internationally. It has raised more than £10 million, funding more than 900 Playpumps and providing clean water to more than 2 million people, permanently.

**Table 2.1** Factors influencing choice between starting a new business as a sole trader or private limited company

| Sole trader | Private limited company |
|---|---|
| When the owner has no intention of expanding, e.g. just wants to run one local restaurant | When the owner has ambitions to expand quickly, therefore needs it to be easier to raise extra finance |
| When there is no need for substantial bank borrowing, i.e. start-up costs are low | When large borrowings mean significant chances of large losses if things go wrong |
| When the business will be small enough to mean that one person can make all the big decisions | When the business may require others to make decisions, e.g. when the entrepreneur is on holiday or unwell |

## 2.4 Public limited companies

When a private limited company expands to the point of having share capital of more than £50,000, it can convert to a public limited company. Then it can be floated on the stock market, which allows any member of the general public to buy shares. This increases the company's access to share capital, which enables it to expand considerably. The term 'plc' will appear after the company name, for example Marks & Spencer plc or Tesco plc.

The principal differences between private and public limited companies are:

- A public company can raise capital from the general public, while a private limited company is prohibited from doing so.
- The minimum capital requirement of a public company is £50,000. There is no minimum for a private limited company.
- Public companies must publish far more detailed accounts than private limited companies.

Most large businesses are plcs. Yet the process of converting from a private to a public company can be difficult. Usually, successful small firms grow steadily, perhaps at a rate of 10 or 15 per cent a year. Even that pace of growth causes problems, but good managers can cope. The problem of floating onto the stock market is that it provides a sudden, huge injection of cash. This sounds great, but it forces the firm to try to grow more quickly (otherwise the new shareholders will say: what are you doing with our cash?). Note that the media increasingly uses the U.S. term IPO (Initial Public Offering) instead of the British term 'flotation'.

'I couldn't be more thrilled to have control over my own destiny in a way that is not possible as a public company'. Michael Dell, after paying $25 billion to take Dell Computers private in 2013.

**Real business**

### Poundland

From its origins as a Lincolnshire market stall in the 1990s, on 12 March 2014 Poundland was floated onto the London stock market at a valuation of £750 million. The sellers of the shares included a private equity investor and Poundland's senior management, which reduced its combined holding from 24 per cent to 10 per cent of the shares. One person who gained no benefit was Poundland's founder, Steve Smith, who sold his entire stake in the business for £50 million in 2004. If he felt aggrieved at missing out on the flotation riches, at least he could do so from the comfort of his 13-bedroom mansion.

## 2.5 Other forms of business organisation

### Co-operatives

These can be worker owned, such as JohnLewis/Waitrose, or customer owned, such as the retail Co-op. Co-operatives have the potential to offer a more united cause for the workforce than the profit of shareholders. Workers at John Lewis can enjoy annual bonuses of 20 per cent of their salary, as their share of the company's profits. The Co-op has been less successful, though its focus on ethical trading has made it more relevant to today's shoppers.

### Not-for-profit organisations
#### Mutual businesses

Mutual businesses, including many building societies and mutual life assurance businesses, have no shareholders and no owners. They exist solely for the best interests of members: its customers. In the 1980s and 1990s traditional mutual societies such as Abbey National and the Halifax were turned into private companies. Not one of these businesses survived the 2007–09 credit crunch without being bailed out or taken over. Nationwide now says it is 'proud to be different', as it is still a true building society in that it has no shareholders pressuring it for profits.

'Too many companies, especially large ones, are driven more and more narrowly by the need to ensure that investors get good returns and to justify executives' high salaries. Too often, this means they view employees as costs.' Hilary Clinton, US politician

## Charities

Many important organisations have charitable status. These include pressure groups such as Greenpeace and Friends of the Earth. They also include conventional charities such as Oxfam and Save The Children. Charitable status ensures that those who fund the charity are not liable for any debts. It also provides significant tax benefits.

## 2.6 Private and public sector organisations

All the organisations mentioned above operate in the private sector. This means that they are not owned by the state; neither by national nor local government. Public sector organisations are different. They are owned by the state and therefore may have different obligations and also pressures.

## Types of public sector organisation:
### Public corporations

These are government-owned organisations that trade mainly with the private sector. There used to be many of these, from British Rail to British Telecom. Now most have been sold to the private sector, often forming a private monopoly such as Thames Water or Virgin West Coast Rail. Among the few remaining public corporations is the Crown Estate, which earns rental income for the government from publicly owned forests, seabeds, farming land and buildings – and also Manchester Airport, which is owned by ten councils around Manchester.

### Local authority services

Until recently all local authorities ran services such as care homes for the elderly, even though there was alternative provision from the private sector. The rationale was that the public sector provision of health care was priced below the private-sector level or might even be free. In keeping with other local authorities, hit by spending cuts, Durham County Council closed its last five care homes in April 2014.

## Five Whys and a How

| Question | Answer |
| --- | --- |
| Why might an entrepreneur choose to be a sole trader instead of forming a private limited company? | To minimise administration costs – and presumably on the assumption that there will be very few risks involved in the business |
| Why would anyone sell goods on credit to a limited liability business? | Because they trust that the proprietors will not close the business down and shelter behind limited personal liability (some have regretted that trust) |
| Why might a growing business turn itself into a plc and then float its shares on the stock market? | To raise extra capital for expansion – and/or to allow the early-stage investors to sell part of their own holding (perhaps making them millionaires) |
| Why might 'the divorce of ownership and control' matter to an investor? | It may mean that senior management are more interested in money/power for themselves than building up the business in the long term |
| Why may a 'mutual' prove no more ethically sound than a profit-seeking company? | Ethics are partly a consequence of personal morality; it may be wrong to assume that those working for mutuals are any different from those working for companies |
| How do you form a company? | To achieve incorporation you need to complete the memorandum and the articles of association and send them, plus fee, to the Registrar of Companies |

## Private-public partnerships

Recent governments have promoted the idea that public services will be more efficient if run in partnership with the private sector. This led to the Private Finance Initiative, in which private sector finance was used to initiate public sector investment in hospitals, schools or transport. Although these schemes were supposed to provide better value to taxpayers, House of Commons committee reports show that the record of these schemes is patchy.

### Key terms

**Bankrupt:** when an individual is unable to meet personal liabilities, some or all of which can be as a consequence of business activities.

**Creditors:** those owed money by a business, for example, suppliers and bankers.

**Incorporation:** establishing a business as a separate legal entity from its owners, and therefore giving the owners limited liability.

**Limited liability:** owners are not liable for the debts of the business; they can lose no more than the sum they invested.

**Monopoly:** where the sales of one business have a dominant share of its marketplace.

**Registrar of Companies:** the government department which can allow firms to become incorporated. It is located at Companies House, where Articles of Association, Memorandums of Association and the annual accounts of limited companies are available for public scrutiny.

**Sole trader:** a one-person business with unlimited liability.

**Unlimited liability:** owners are liable for any debts incurred by the business, even if it requires them to sell all their assets and possessions and become personally bankrupt.

### Evaluation: Different business forms

Business organisation is a dry, technical subject. It does contain some important business themes, however, two of which are particularly valuable sources of evaluative comment.

1. The existence of limited liability has had huge effects on business. Some have been unarguably beneficial. How could firms become really big if the owners felt threatened by equally big debts? Limited liability helps firms to take reasonable business risks. It also, however, gives scope for dubious business practices. For example, it is possible to start a firm, live a great lifestyle, go into liquidation leaving the customers/creditors out of pocket and then start again. All too often this is the story told by programmes such as the BBC's *Watchdog*. Companies Acts lay down legislation that tries to make this harder to do, but it still happens. Such unethical behaviour is why government intervention to protect the consumer can always be justified.

2. Short-termism is a curse for effective business decision-making. There is no proof that a stock exchange listing leads to short-termism, only the suspicion that in many cases it does. Massive companies such as Unilever, Nestle and Shell may be above the pressures for short-term performance. In many other cases, though, it seems that British company directors focus too much on the short-term share price. Could this be because their huge bonuses depend on how high the share price is? Worries about shareholder pressures or takeover bids may distract managers from building a long-term business in the way that companies such as BMW and Toyota have done.

'When the operations of capitalism come to resemble the casino, ill fortune will be the lot of many.' John Maynard Keynes, economist

# Workbook
## A. Revision questions

(25 marks; 25 minutes)

1. Explain two differences between a sole trader and a partnership. (4)

2. In your own words, try to explain the importance of establishing a separate legal entity to separate the business from the individual owner. (4)

3. You can start a business today. All you have to do is tell HM Revenue & Customs (the taxman). Outline two risks of starting in this way. (4)

4. Briefly explain whether each of the following businesses should start as a sole trader, a partnership or a private limited company.

   a) A clothes shop started by Claire Wells with £40,000 of her own money plus £10,000 from the bank. It is located close to her home in Wrexham. (3)

   b) A builders started by Jim Barton and Lee Clark, who plan to become 'No. 1' for loft extensions in Sheffield. They have each invested £15,000 and are borrowing £30,000 from the bank. (3)

5. Explain the risks to a company of moving from a private to a public limited company by floating its shares on the stock market. (5)

6. In what way may the type of business organisation affect the image of the business? (2)

## B. Revision exercises
### DATA RESPONSE 1

#### UK business categories

In 2013 the Federation of Small Businesses estimated that there were 5 million businesses in the UK. Use this information plus the pie chart to answer the questions below.

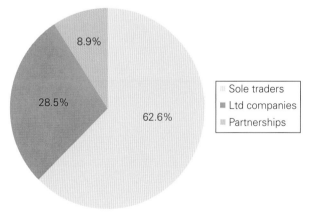

**Figure 2.2** UK business organisations
Source: Office of National Statistics, October 2013

#### Questions (20 marks; 20 minutes)

1. a) Calculate the number of sole traders in the UK; then calculate the number of limited companies. (3)

   b) Explain two possible reasons why there are so many more sole traders than companies. (6)

2. What proportion of British businesses operate with unlimited liability? (1)

3. In September 2014 the Federation of Small Businesses announced record confidence levels among its members. A survey of 2,100 small business owners showed that 61 per cent expected growth in the next twelve months. The biggest improvement was in the North East, with September 2014 showing a confidence score of +44 compared with –7 per cent the year before.

   a) Explain two possible reasons why business confidence is important for small firms. (6)

   b) Explain one possible reason why the North East enjoyed such a boost to business confidence. (4)

## DATA RESPONSE 2

**Starting a new business**

Forming a limited company can be time-consuming compared to a sole trader which can be started straight away. According to the World Bank, the number of actions required to get started varies from 1 in New Zealand to 13 in Brazil and China. As a result of the different processes, the number of days it takes to start up varies from 1 day in New Zealand (the world's quickest) to 144 days in Venezuela (the world's slowest).

Figure 2.3 provides data selected from the World Bank's 2013–14 Global Competitiveness Report.

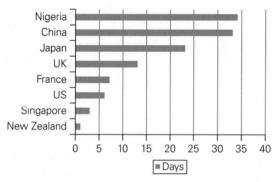

**Figure 2.3** Time required to start a business
Source: Global Competitiveness Report 2013–14

**Questions (20 marks; 25 minutes)**

1. Briefly explain the reasons for it taking longer to set up as a limited company than as a sole trader. (5)

2. To what extent should an entrepreneur be influenced by the length of time to set up when deciding upon the most suitable business structure? (15)

## C. Extend your understanding

1. Non-profit organisations such as charities and mutuals run businesses including shops and banks. To what extent would you expect better value for money from a non-profit business than from a profit-seeking business? (20)

2. Sunil Mittal, Indian software entrepreneur, once said: 'We want to manage and grow our companies ourselves. If we give up 51 per cent we might as well get out of the business.' To what extent would you agree with him? (20)

Linked to: Different business forms, Chapter 2;
Sources of finance, Chapter 43; Decision-making to
improve financial performance, Chapter 44.

### Definition

'Forms of business' includes the factors that affect
and are affected by business owners, especially
shareholders.

## 3.1 The role of shareholders

Shareholders literally own a share of the business,
proportionate to their shareholding. So an individual
who has bought 50,000 shares in a business that has
issued 5 million shares owns a 1 per cent stake in the
company. Therefore he or she has 1 per cent of the
voting rights when it comes to decisions to be made at
the annual general meeting (AGM). For the company,
the role of the shareholder is to provide the capital to
get the business going and to keep it growing; for the
shareholder, the point of share ownership is the degree
of influence it gives, plus the rewards it provides (see
Section 3.2).

In theory, shareholders should be proactive, raising
important issues with the board of directors. In fact,
many have little interest in doing so; they bought shares
in the hope of a price rise or rising dividends, and
may be more likely to sell shares than to spend time
probing what's really happening to the company. Marks
& Spencer, for example, has 188,000 shareholders,
half of whom have fewer than 500 shares (with a
value averaging about £1,000). Even the biggest single
private investor in the company has only 3 per cent of
the shares, and therefore no real say in key business
decisions. Perhaps this is why the directors of Marks
& Spencer have been allowed to get away with huge
salaries but dismal performance. Profits in 2014 were
half the level achieved in 1997/98.

Each year a public limited company must invite all its
shareholders to an annual general meeting. There the
shareholders have the right to question the board of
directors on any aspect of the company's performance
or policies. This is often a low-key affair attended by
a handful of shareholders, but can sometimes burst
into life when there is a controversial issue at stake.
In its 2014 AGM, Barclays directors were criticised
for their own pay and for the size of the bonuses paid
to staff. One shareholder claimed they were 'paying
for Manchester United but getting Colchester United',
while another said the bank was 'a prisoner to its
senior staff'. Despite these criticisms only 24 per cent
of shareholders voted against the pay proposals, so the
directors got their way.

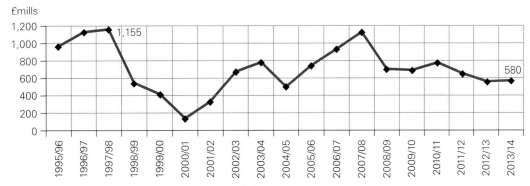

**Figure 3.1** Weak profit performance at Marks & Spencer
Source: Marks & Spencer annual accounts

## 3.2 Shareholder rewards

There are two main financial rewards for company shareholders:

- Annual dividend payments
- A rise in the value of the shares

Annual dividend payments are decided upon by the company directors when they know the final figure for the profit for the year. Most companies have a clearly expressed dividend policy, such as Ted Baker plc's, which is to pay out around half the year's profit to its shareholders. The dividends received are in proportion to shareholdings, that is, they are allocated as a dividend per share figure multiplied by the number of shares each individual owns.

### Real business

Example: the individual with a 3 per cent holding in Marks & Spencer is Bill Adderley. He owned 48.5 million M&S shares in 2014, so his annual dividend payment was:

M&S dividend per share 2014: 17p × 48.5 million shares = £8,245,000

For the average holder of 500 shares, it's 500 × £0.17 = £85 dividend for the year

For most, then, dividends are useful but not hugely significant. What a shareholder wants most of all is a rising share price. Figure 3.2 shows that an investor who had bought £1,000 of Marks & Spencer shares in 1998 would have £1,000 × $\left(\frac{434}{444}\right)$ = £977.50 by August 2014, a loss of £22.50 over a 16 year period! Some investment. By contrast the investor in Ted Baker would have turned £1,000 into £1,000 × $\frac{1805}{98.5}$ = £18,325. Sweet.

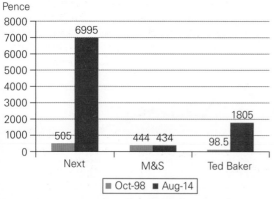

**Figure 3.2** Share price growth between October 1998 and August 2014

Source: www.yahoo.finance.com

'A lot of people love Oreos. So their manufacturer is making money. That means more dividends to shareholders.' Maria Bartiromo, US TV journalist

## 3.3 What influences the price of shares?

What's a share in Apple Inc. worth? In August 2014 the price of one share in Apple rose above $100 in response to investor excitement at the anticipated launch of the iPhone 6 and the iWatch. Does that mean the shares were 'worth' $100? The fact is that nobody knows what a share is going to be worth in future. Nevertheless there are some clear influences on the price of shares.

The value investors place on a share depends on the profit after tax the company makes (known in the UK as its 'earnings') multiplied by the value investors place on those earnings. If investors have a great deal of confidence about the future of the business they'll pay a high multiple (70 times, in the case of Facebook in September 2014). At the same time investors valued Marks & Spencer at just 13 times earnings, i.e. much more lowly.

'With Wrigley chewing gum, it's the lack of change that appeals to me. I don't think it is going to be hurt by the internet. That's the kind of business I like.' Warren Buffett, the world's greatest stock market investor.

## 3.4 The significance of share price changes

In the short term there is no actual impact on a business of a change in its share price. The share capital of the business was invested *permanently* by the shareholders. So if they lose confidence in the business and want to sell their shares, they have to find another buyer – they cannot demand their money back from the company. Just as, when you buy a new car, you'll then need to find a second-hand purchaser if you want to sell it – the same is true of shares. The media love to write scary headlines about 'share price collapse' as if that means 'company collapse' – but that's not true.

**Real business**

In October 2008 shares in Taylor Wimpey plc hit 10p – an amazing fall from 490p eighteen months before. The collapse in UK house prices put the newly-merged Taylor and Wimpey in a difficult financial position. Amidst all the concern and gloom about whether the company could survive, 10p proved an amazing buying opportunity. By August 2014 the shares hit 117p, giving a glorious 1070 per cent profit. Despite the collapse in Taylor Wimpey's share price, no one panicked, and because the share price has no direct impact on the business, recovery was possible.

In the longer term, however, the share price can matter. If the share price is high, it makes it relatively cheap and easy to obtain more share capital. A business can carry out a rights issue which gives existing shareholders the right to buy more shares at a discount to the market value. If the share price is low and remains low, the company is unlikely to be able to raise any extra share capital, which in turn makes it harder to raise loan capital.

## 3.5 Issues with different forms of business

### 1. Unlimited and limited liability

By definition, every 'company' has limited liability. The process of incorporation means that the company is treated as a separate legal entity from those who own the business. So, if the business sells a customer a faulty item, the customer can sue the business but not the owner(s). This becomes important if the business goes into liquidation. Who can then be sued? No one. So consumers have to be wary when dealing with small, limited liability businesses.

The same warning applies to businesses themselves when selling on credit to other businesses. Since 2002 it has been possible for UK firms heading for insolvency to arrange for a 'pre-pack administration'. This allows the business's owners to write off their debts to creditors (including suppliers), yet remain in control of the business. This is how the computer games retailer Game remains in business today even though it, effectively, was bankrupt in 2012. The uncomfortable thing about pre-pack administration

is that suppliers lose everything, yet the bosses who presided over a collapsing business remain in charge! After widespread complaints, the UK government spent 18 months consulting over how to make pre-packs fairer to all parties, but in 2014 it was decided to keep the rules as they are. Today, about a quarter of all businesses falling into administration use the pre-pack device. The ethics of this process remain very murky.

### 2. Ordinary share capital

By definition every company has ordinary share capital that has been issued to at least one shareholder. The company issues the shares in exchange for the investor's capital. The shareholders expect an annual dividend as a reward for their investment, but if the business has a lousy trading year it can choose to drop the dividend. This means that share capital is ideal for a business that naturally has ups and downs, such as one that relies on the British weather (seaside hotels; ice cream parlours, etc.) or one that relies on fashion or new technology.

**Table 3.1** Ordinary share capital vs. (bank) loan capital

|  | Ordinary share capital | (Bank) loan capital |
|---|---|---|
| **Repayment of the capital** | Permanent capital therefore never has to be repaid | Lump-sum repayment at the end of the period (perhaps 3 years) strains the cash flow |
| **Annual payments** | Flexible: dividends are needed in the long term, but can be scrapped in a difficult year | Inflexible: the bank demands its interest payments every month/year, and penalises hugely those that can't pay |
| **Dilution of control** | Selling more shares to raise extra capital might threaten the founder's control of his or her own business | In theory banks have no control (nor do they take a share of future profits) but if interest payments aren't made on time, banks get very heavy-handed |

### 3. Market capitalisation

This is the value the stock market places on the whole business by multiplying the share price by the number of shares issued. Ted Baker has 44 million shares issued and the market values each share at £18, so that's a value of £792 million. That's Ted Baker plc's market capitalisation.

The importance of the figure is that it represents the starting point for any company considering making a takeover bid. After all, if the stock market value is £792 million, any bid has to be above that level in order to persuade existing shareholders to sell. Realistically, any potential buyer of Ted Baker would know that they'd need to find at least £1,000 million to make a successful takeover bid.

## 4. Dividends

These are the annual reward to shareholders for their investment in the business. They represent an income to shareholders. Given that most companies grow over time, the dividends they declare tend to grow as well. So whereas interest rates on bank deposits go up and down over time (with no upward trend), dividends tend to rise over time, giving a rising income as the years go by. Rising income is especially attractive for retired people, who worry about the real value of their pensions. Figure 3.3 shows that annual dividends can be very valuable for investors who hold on to their shares for a number of years.

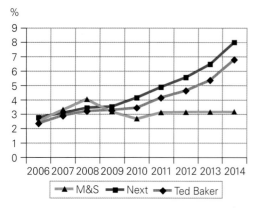

**Figure 3.3** Rising dividend income over time (except for M&S plc)

An important issue with share dividends, though, is that there is a trade-off. The higher the dividend payout agreed by directors, the lower the amount of retained capital available for reinvestment in the business. This can be measured by looking at the dividend cover. If dividend cover is 1, it would mean the business has paid out all its profits to shareholders, leaving zero for reinvestment. At a figure of 2, half is paid out and half is retained. If you see a firm with a low dividend cover you can wonder:

**a)** Why are they paying out such high dividends when they're not making very much profit?

**b)** Will they really be able to go on paying such high dividends?

**c)** Are the directors propping up the share price in a short-termist way? That is, paying high dividends now at the cost of the future growth prospects (or even survival prospects) of the company.

'Investors systematically overvalue short-term payoffs and pass up investment opportunities that could leave them much better off in the longer term.' Sheila Bair, Chair, Federal Deposit Insurance Corporation

## 3.6 Effects of ownership on mission, objectives, decisions and performance

Most large companies are plcs and therefore have a large number of outside shareholders who may care little about the business. They simply want rising dividends and a rising share price. Companies such as Marks & Spencer have to report their latest profits every six months – so this becomes a fixation for the chief executive. Short-term thinking is the curse of a company such as Marks & Spencer, which needs plenty of time to come up with a successful new trading strategy.

This can lead to a fundamental problem: whatever the mission statement says, staff will soon learn the real priorities of senior management. If the chief executive shows clear signs of stress in the lead-up to the 6-monthly profit statement, staff will know what matters most. Ultimately, the staff that rise up the career ladder are the ones that respond best to the *real* mission, not the stated one. If the real mission is to get the 6-monthly profit to rise in order to keep the media off the boss's back – that's where the career possibilities lie. The person with an idea to cut costs by 3 per cent will be welcomed much more than another staffer with a plan for cutting greenhouse gas emissions.

'Short-termism is one of the most disturbing problems affecting modern organisations and produces some of the most common unethical behaviours.' Lorenzo Patelli, accounting academic.

Just as a staff member must uncover the real mission, so they must also understand the real business objectives – and their timescale. Every aspect of the business may be more short-term focused than is said or is written down. Naturally, this also affects decision-making and performance within every business. The long-term successes such as Whitbread plc, Ted Baker plc and Next plc have risen above short-term pressures and managed to implement sound long-term strategies. For struggling businesses such as Tesco, Morrisons' and M&S, long-term strategies can be swept aside as City analysts and the media keep their eyes on short-term performance. This can become a deadweight on the shoulders of the business.

## Key terms

**Annual General Meeting:** a yearly meeting in which company directors invite all shareholders to come to quiz the board and vote on new resolutions. A legal requirement for plcs.

**Dividend cover:** measures how well a firm's dividends are covered by its profits for the year. Accountants recommend a figure of at least 2, i.e., that the company should pay out no more than half its profits to shareholders.

**Market capitalisation:** the value placed on the business by the stock market, calculated as share price × number of shares issued.

## Five Whys and a How

| Question | Answer |
|---|---|
| Why might the shares of a successful company fall in price? | Because their success is less than before, leading to dampened expectations; or because a new competitor makes the future look less encouraging |
| Why might a company hold a rights issue? | Because it wants to raise extra share capital to finance expansion without needing to get into debt to banks |
| Why might a firm's market capitalisation jump up when a rival makes a takeover bid? | The bid pushes up the share price of the company being bid for, which in turn will boost its market capitalisation |
| Why might business ownership affect business objectives? | Ownership might affect whether the objectives are long term or short term |
| Why might short-termism produce unethical behaviours? | Business people may be encouraged to take shortcuts to boost profit, such as painting over cracks that really need to be mended |
| How do directors decide on the 'right' level of dividends to pay out? | They look at the profit for the year, work out how much capital they'll need in the coming year, and then see what dividend level they can afford |

## Evaluation: Issues in understanding forms of business

There is a tendency to exaggerate the role of shareholders and the stock market as a whole. The stock market raises relatively little capital to finance business expansion. The majority (about two thirds) of capital for reinvestment comes from business profits. The stock market provides less than 5 per cent of the new capital businesses need for expansion. Despite this, markets have an extraordinary hold over the decision-making by plc bosses because changes in share prices interest the public and therefore business journalists. If a struggling plc came up with an interesting new strategy that might take some years to bear fruit, few would back it.

Perhaps the incredible speed with which businesses such as Snapchat and Instagram became worth billions has strengthened the tendency to look for quick solutions to company problems. In the UK this is a greater problem than in almost every other country because of the huge influence of the City of London. In Germany in particular, the corporate heart of the country is in family business ownership, not in the stock market. This helps them take a longer-term view of the markets in which they operate.

# Workbook

## A. Revision questions

**(35 marks; 35 minutes)**

1. Comment on whether each of these questions would be suitable for a company's annual general meeting.

   a) What level of sales are we expecting from the new product you've outlined? (2)

   b) What's been the trend in our industrial accident rate lately? (2)

   c) How does our percentage change in profits compare with that of our closest rival? (2)

2. Why might shareholders argue that a company is setting its dividend levels too high? (3)

3. Another war breaks out in the Middle East, pushing oil prices up sharply. What might be the effect on the share price of these companies?

   a) British Aerospace plc, one of the world's Top 5 arms suppliers. (2)

   b) Thomas Cook, travel agency. (2)

   c) BP plc, oil supplier and retailer. (2)

4. Explain why a short-termist approach to running a business might damage a company in the long term. (5)

5. a) Examine Figure 3.3 (above) then outline two reasons why a long-term investor might be better off buying shares than holding savings in cash. (4)

   b) Despite your answer to 5(a), outline one reason why holding savings in cash may still make sense. (3)

6. Outline the advantages and disadvantages of a family-run private limited company compared with a plc. (8)

## B. Revision exercises

### DATA RESPONSE

**Tesco: Dividend under threat?**

Britain's biggest supermarket has had a torrid time in 2014 with its shares falling to a ten-year low. But things could be about to get even worse. Tesco's dividend has been called into question by some analysts, who believe the supermarket giant has no alternative but to cut payments when it next reports to the market on October 1.

Last month Tesco announced the departure of chief executive Phillip Clarke, who will be replaced by Dave Lewis, of Unilever. Mr Lewis is expected to change Tesco's strategy, perhaps to compete with the discounters, such as Aldi and Lidl. To fund the change analysts argue Tesco's only option is to cut the dividend.

The main way investors assess whether a dividend is under threat is the dividend cover. This figure shows the degree to which the dividend payment is exceeded by the company's profits. Those with a low 'cover' score are vulnerable as it means the company is paying out the majority, if not all, of its profits in the form of dividends. The higher the number the safer the dividend, with experts suggesting that a cover of two is reasonably safe. Tesco's dividend cover over the past twelve months has been 1.6, which has come down from 1.8 in 2013.

As the table below shows, Tesco shares looks pretty vulnerable to a cut when looking at the dividend cover compared to its five major competitors. But Morrisons' dividend looks even more insecure. It has been paying out all its profits in the form of dividends. So how can it finance the trading turnaround it needs?

**Table 3.2**

| Supermarket | Dividend cover (last 12 months) | Forecast dividend cover (next 12 months) | Dividend per share |
|---|---|---|---|
| Tesco | 1.6 | 1.8 | £0.15 |
| Sainsbury's | 2.1 | 1.8 | £0.18 |
| Marks & Spencer | 1.9 | 1.9 | £0.17 |
| Morrisons' | −0.8 | 1 | £0.13 |
| Walmart (owns Asda) | 2.5 | 2.7 | $1.9 |

Source: Adapted from *The Telegraph* 20 August 2014

Chris White, who manages the Premier UK Equity Income fund, says: 'We will not know until at least October, if not next year, about the direction Tesco is going to take its businesses, so it is difficult to invest today when there is so much uncertainty. The dividend is at risk, as well as its long-term strategy, so I am not buying,' said Mr White.

**Questions (25 marks; 30 minutes)**

1. Explain why Tesco's chief executive might be reluctant to cut its dividend. (4)

2. Based on the data in the table, explain why Morrisons' dividend 'looks even more insecure'. (5)

3. To what extent may the questions over Tesco's dividend affect the long-term market capitalisation? (16)

## C. Extend your understanding

1. Figures 3.1 and 3.2 show a bleak picture of Marks & Spencer plc over recent years. To what extent may M&S shareholders be able to help the company return to profit growth? (20)

2. Reread the Warren Buffett quote on page 16. To what extent do you think that Warren Buffett is right to have placed a high value on Wrigley's shares because of 'lack of change'? (20)

# Chapter 4

# External factors affecting business

**Linked to:** Understanding the nature and purpose of business, Chapter 1; Understanding the role and importance of stakeholders, Chapter 10; Marketing and competitiveness, Chapter 12.

## Definition

External factors include competition, demographics and environmental issues. Demographic factors involve population composition and trends; environmental factors deal with short- and long-term 'green' issues.

## 4.1 Introduction

Business thrives on confidence. Confident consumers are willing to dip into their savings for a holiday or to borrow to buy a new carpet or car. Confident investors are willing to put more money into businesses in return for shares. And companies themselves will spend to invest in their future: new factory buildings, new machinery and new computer systems. All this spending can create an upsurge in economic activity.

The reverse also applies: gloom can spread doom. Therefore the economic climate is important (but is dealt with more fully in the second year of the A-level). This chapter covers other external factors that help to create a climate of optimism or pessimism. These factors include:

- market conditions
- competition
- changes in household incomes
- changes in interest rates
- demographic factors
- environmental issues

## 4.2 Market conditions

Figure 4.1 shows the tricky period for the UK economy between the start of recession in 2008 and the second quarter of 2014, when the economy finally returned to its pre-recession peak. The straight black line shows the GDP trend excluding the recession and the unprecedentedly slow recovery. The graph also shows the normal progress of the UK economy. For more than 200 years it has grown at just under 2.5 per cent per annum, i.e. growth is normal. Therefore the general expectation is that the underlying market conditions will be positive, with the size of markets expanding on a regular basis.

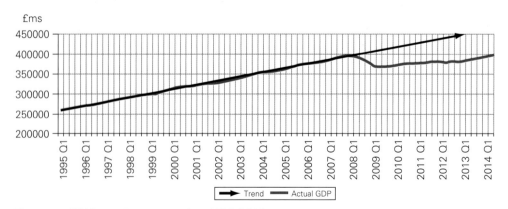

**Figure 4.1** UK Gross domestic product 1995-2014

*Chained volume measure, quarterly figures, seasonally adjusted*

Source: Office for National Statistics

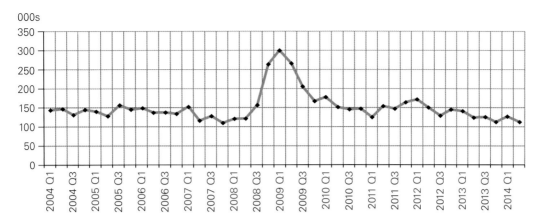

**Figure 4.2** UK redundancies per quarter
Source: ILO, quoted by UK Office for National Statistics

When market conditions are as tough as in 2008/09, there are likely to be failures as businesses run out of cash (Woolworths, La Senza and many others went under). There may also be huge pressures placed on company workforces, as people are forced to choose between redundancy and real wage cuts. In the recessions of 1980 and 1990, huge job losses pushed unemployment up above 3 million. The recent recession saw instead a huge squeeze on people's real incomes, meaning that the pain was shared more fairly across the population. Government statistics show that between July 2008 and March 2014 earnings rose 8.6 per cent while prices rose 16.9 per cent. In addition to this squeeze on incomes, Figure 4.2 shows why consumer confidence was hard hit in 2009, with people worried whether they would be next for a redundancy notice. No wonder that, at times, even products like chocolate and chewing gum saw falls in sales volume as market conditions tightened.

In addition to the economy, other important factors affecting market conditions include:

● Customer taste and fashion. In 2012, for no clear reason, consumers became more sceptical of foods with 'diet' claims. One result was that WeightWatchers' yoghurts suffered a sales decline of 13.7 per cent in 2013.

● Disruptive change, resulting from radical innovation or new technology. This can mean that old-established producers are suddenly struggling to remain competitive in the face of radically new market conditions.

● The competitive structure. 70 per cent of the UK chocolate market, for example, is held by three huge firms: Mondelez (Cadbury), Mars and Nestlé. If the

structure changes (if, for example, Mars bought Ferrero of Italy), market conditions would also change – perhaps making it even harder for a new small firm to enter the chocolate market.

'There's no evidence that the business cycle has been repealed.' Alan Greenspan, former Chairman of the US central bank.

## 4.3 Competition

The tighter the economic and market conditions, the greater the competitive pressures tend to be. In 2009 price cutting was rife within the markets for airline travel, posh hotels, executive cars and more basic things such as furniture and carpets.

Competitive pressures stem from more than price, however. In most modern markets customers are looking for special experiences or product uniqueness to make them part with their cash. Therefore companies need to invest heavily in research and development and in the creativity of their workforce. In April – June 2014 Apple Inc. spent 36 per cent more on R&D than they had in the same period of 2013 ($1.6bn). Analysts concluded that the company was working on new products to be launched in Autumn 2014.

'Competition is the great teacher.' Henry Ford, US auto pioneer.

# 4.4 Changes in household incomes

According to a 2014 report, real household incomes fell by more than 6 per cent between 2007 and 2013/14. As a result of this squeeze, in the first half of 2014 supermarkets faced an unprecedented fall of 3.2 per cent in their sales volumes. A fall in sales volume had not happened since the Second World War. In addition to this decline in sales volumes, shoppers switched to discount stores to try to maintain their lifestyles. Clearly, changes in household incomes are hugely significant.

Household income is affected by three main things:

1. Changes in the real incomes of the main breadwinners. Generally, economies expand and therefore sales of most goods and services follow suit. The only exceptions are 'inferior goods'.

2. The number within the household who work. Partly this is a function of how many people are in the household at all. One reason consumer spending didn't fall *further* in the recession was that fewer young people left home. So instead of two households, each having to face electricity bills and so forth, more were crammed into one house. This helped to offset some of the spending pressure from falling real wages. Another important factor was the rise in the number of people taking part-time jobs.

3. The impact of government decisions on taxation and benefits. The impact of tax changes has been broadly neutral in recent years, but cutbacks in benefits (especially to the disabled) have hit the spending power of many. In 2014 The Trussell Trust reported that the use of food banks rose from 346,992 people in 2012/13 to 913,138 people in 2013/14.

'The last thing you want to do is raise taxes in the middle of the recession.' Barack Obama, US President.

For every business it is invaluable to forecast the rate of change in household incomes. As with every economic forecast, this is easier to say than to do.

## Index numbers and household income

Both economic and business data are often analysed using index numbers. An index means converting a series of data into figures that all relate to a base period where the data is equal to 100. This allows users of the data to see at a glance the percentage changes and trends. In the table below, Column A shows changes in the total price of the average household's shopping basket. As you can see, this rises from £402 in 2005 to £514 in 2014. Column B converts that complex data into an index. This starts by saying 'let £402 = 100', then all the other figures in Column A are related to that base figure of 100 by showing the percentage change from that base figure. For example, the figure for 2014 is $\frac{£514.15}{£402} \times 100 = 127.9$.

The advantage of index numbers is that you can see quickly that, for example, prices rose by 27.9 per cent between 2005 and 2014. So index numbers help you understand trends rather more easily.

**Table 4.1** Changes in the average household shopping basket using the Consumer Prices Index

|  | A. Shopping basket price (£s) | B. Consumer Price Index 2005 = 100 |
|---|---|---|
| 2005 | £402 | 100 |
| 2006 | £411.25 | 102.3 |
| 2007 | £420.90 | 104.7 |
| 2008 | £436.20 | 108.5 |
| 2009 | £445.40 | 110.8 |
| 2010 | £460.30 | 114.5 |
| 2011 | £480.80 | 119.6 |
| 2012 | £494.45 | 123.0 |
| 2013 | £506.90 | 126.1 |
| 2014 | £514.15 | 127.9 |
| 2015 est | £524.60 | 130.5 |

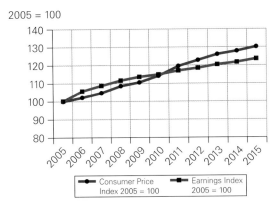

2005 = 100

**Figure 4.3** Price index vs. earning index
Source: Office of National Statistics, October 2014

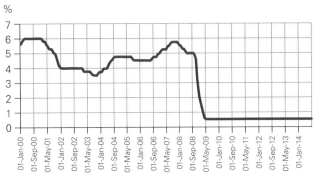

**Figure 4.4** UK bank interest rates, 2000–14
Source: www.bankofengland.co.uk

Their other huge benefit is that they enable direct comparisons to be made between different data series. In the case of price changes (shown by the consumer price index), the interesting recent comparison is with household incomes. This data is shown in Figure 4.3. It shows incomes outstripping prices in 2006 and 2007, but then being dragged back until – from 2011 – the income rises fall behind price rises. That means living standards falling – year after year.

If we had tried to plot the actual figures for price increase or earnings on the same graph, the different scales needed would make a comparison difficult.

## 4.5 Changes in interest rates

The interest rate is the price charged by a bank per year for lending money or for providing credit. Individual banks decide for themselves about the rate they will charge on their credit cards or for the overdrafts they provide. But they are usually influenced by the interest rate that the Central Bank charges high street banks for borrowing money: the bank rate. In Britain, this is set each month by a committee of the Bank of England. As shown in Figure 4.4, the standard rate of interest in the UK has generally been around 4 to 5 per cent. In March 2009, though, the rate was cut to its lowest point in the Bank of England's history: 0.5 per cent. And it remained there as a way of helping to revive an economy hit very hard by the 2009 recession.

'Never has so much money been owed by so few to so many.' Mervyn King, Governor Bank of England, on the £1,000 billion bailout from taxpayers to Britain's banks.

The Bank of England committee is asked to set interest rates at a level that should ensure UK prices rise by around 2 per cent per year. If the committee members decide that the economy is growing so strongly that prices may rise faster than 2 per cent, it will increase interest rates. Then people will feel worried about borrowing more (because of the higher repayment cost) and may cut their spending. This should help to discourage firms from increasing their prices.

For firms, the level of interest rates is very important because:

- It affects consumer demand, especially for goods bought on credit, such as houses and cars. The higher the rate of interest, the lower the sales that can be expected.

- The interest charges affect the total operating costs (that is, the higher the interest rate, the higher the costs of running an overdraft, and therefore the lower the profit).

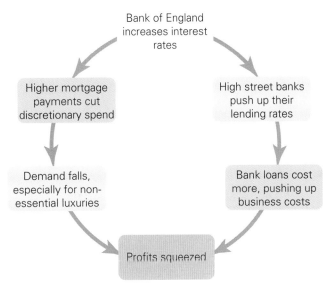

**Figure 4.5** Logic chain: effect on costs and revenues of rising interest rates

- The higher the rate of interest, the less attractive it is for a firm to invest money in the future of the business. Therefore, there is a risk of falling demand for items such as lorries, computers and factory machinery.

If interest rates fall, the opposite effects occur, to the benefit of both companies and the economy as a whole.

## 4.6 Demographic factors

Demographics looks at the make-up of the population. This can usefully start with population size. With a healthy, rising population, the United Nations predicts that the UK will catch up with the population of Germany by 2050. Also interesting is Nigeria's dramatic rise, perhaps to overtake the US, and population decline in Japan, China and Germany. For companies, expanding into Nigeria currently looks more exciting than Japan.

**Table 4.2** Population changes predicted by the United Nations in 2012 (all figures in millions)

|         | 2013  | 2015  | 2050  |
|---------|-------|-------|-------|
| Germany | 83    | 81    | 73    |
| UK      | 63    | 67    | 73    |
|         |       |       |       |
| USA     | 320   | 351   | 401   |
| Nigeria | 174   | 240   | 440   |
| Japan   | 127   | 123   | 108   |
|         |       |       |       |
| China   | 1,386 | 1,449 | 1,385 |
| India   | 1,252 | 1,419 | 1,620 |

For businesses, other key population variables include:
- Age – with the proportion of older people forecast to grow considerably, creating opportunities for the companies that can find the relevant products or services
- Gender – with products such as games consoles tending to be male, while cosmetics remains dominated by female purchasing
- Ethnicity – with opportunities already seized in sectors such as cosmetics, magazines and fast food, there may yet be more opportunities for products targeted at specific ethnicities in the markets for food, soft drinks and confectionery.

## 4.7 Environmental issues and Fairtrade

With changes in the economy, firms can choose how to react but their decision-making powers are limited. With social or moral questions about green issues or Fairtrade supplies, firms have a great deal more scope to choose what to do. They may decide to do the minimum, focusing on profit-maximisation. This would be entirely understandable if the survival of the business was under threat. Other business, though, might choose to do more than the minimum for moral or ethical reasons. Some bosses, though, see something like Fairtrade as a great marketing tool for selling more chocolate, or coffee or whatever. In other words, they view environmental or ethical issues merely as business opportunities.

There are four factors to consider here.

1. The immediate effect on the environment of actions businesses take, especially the impact on the local community. Some of these represent a straight choice between profit and social responsibility, such as fly-tipping. Because the UK has a landfill tax, it costs builders £80 per tonne to dispose of waste materials. Some are tempted to save their money by dumping waste at the side of roads. This fly-tipping disfigures landscapes and is a grimly cynical way to boost a firm's profit.

2. Sustainability, that is making sure that the actions of your business will not rob future generations of the availability of key resources. Toilet roll brand Velvet states on every pack that they plant three trees for every one cut down to make the paper. Other companies may pay less regard for the long-term future.

3. Global warming. The issue here is the impact of the business on greenhouse gases such as $CO_2$. In a year, people and businesses globally generate 31,600 million tonnes of $CO_2$. Some companies make a considerable effort to minimise their own 'carbon footprint'; others do not.

4. Fairtrade supplies, that is whether a business chooses to sign an agreement that all its raw materials will be bought through the Fairtrade organisation. This should guarantee that all supplies will be bought on terms that are more favourable to the farmers/producers than the usual market price. Typically these agreements are for a minimum of five years, thereby helping Fairtrade producers such as Uganda's Gumutindo Coffee Co-operative.

## Five Whys and a How

| Question * | Answer |
|---|---|
| Why might Aldi and Lidl struggle when the UK economy starts to generate higher real incomes? | Because their sales boom in the 2010-2014 period may have been due to 'downtrading', as people switched to lower suppliers, therefore the reverse may happen as the economy recovers |
| Why might a rise in competition mean a fall in standards? | Usually consumers benefit from competition, but with complex products such as pensions, suppliers may compete to see who can exploit ('rip-off') customers the most effectively |
| Why might a rise in interest rates hit profits at a business such as Tesco? | Higher interest rates hit consumers' discretionary income, so spending falls (and so does Tesco revenue); also, higher rates force Tesco to pay more on its bank borrowings/overdrafts |
| Why may a move to Fairtrade supply damage the profits of a chocolate manufacturer? | If the higher supply costs are not outweighed by higher sales volume or higher consumer prices, Fairtrade supply will inevitably dent profits |
| Why may fly-tipping rise in recessions? | If builders are struggling to survive, fly-tipping may be a tempting way to cut costs |
| How are real incomes measured? | By deducting price rises from the changes in people's incomes, for example, 3 per cent more income but prices up 5 per cent - you're 2 per cent worse off in real purchasing power |

## Evaluation: External factors affecting business

When companies publish their annual results commentators groan if the boss blames disappointing results on external factors such as the weather or the weakness of the economy. Business journalists admire chief execs who achieve their targets no matter what. Yet that may not be realistic. If you're running Coca-Cola you have huge control over your pricing and therefore can probably find a way to boost profits to meet analysts' expectations.

Most firms, though, are vulnerable to external factors. Even monopolies (when a single firm dominates a market) are subject to changing consumer habits, as Microsoft and even Apple have found in recent years. If things seem to be going wonderfully well, and every commentator thinks your business is bulletproof, it's probably time to worry. The one-time boss of monopolist microchip supplier Intel, Andy Grove, once said that 'only the paranoid survive'. That remains grimly true.

## Key terms

**Consumer demand:** the levels of spending by consumers in general (not just the demand from one consumer).

**Discretionary income:** a person's income after deducting taxes and fixed payments such as rent and utility bills.

**Disruptive change:** a new initiative that changes the rules within a market or within factory production; its radically different design meant that the iPad did exactly that within the market for tablet computers.

**Economic climate:** the atmosphere surrounding the economy (for example, 'gloom and doom' or 'optimism and boom').

**GDP (Gross Domestic Product)** is the value of all the goods and services sold throughout the economy over a period of time (annually or perhaps per quarter),

**Inferior goods** suffer falling sales when people are better off, and rising sales when people are worse off. (Think Poundland or Iceland frozen foods.)

**Real:** changes in money (for example, wages) excluding the distorting effect of changes in prices. So a fall in real wages might mean that wages are unchanged but prices have risen.

**Recession:** a downturn in sales and production that occurs across most parts of the economy, perhaps leading to six months of continuous economic decline.

# Workbook

## A. Revision questions

(30 marks; 30 minutes)

1. Explain why a fall in spending in London could have a knock-on effect on the economy in Bradford, Plymouth, Norwich or anywhere else in the country. (3)

2. Explain whether the Bank of England should raise or cut interest rates in the following circumstances:

   a) a sharp recession has hit the UK economy. (3)

   b) house prices have risen by 16 per cent in each of the last two years. (3)

   c) household incomes and spending have been rising rapidly. (3)

3. Outline how an economic downturn could affect the level of unemployment. (5)

4. a) Outline a demographic change that could boost sales at Mothercare. (2)

   b) Explain the possible impact on a supermarket chain of an increase in inward migration to the UK. (5)

5. What is meant by the term 'Fairtrade'? (2)

6. Outline two possible reasons why a manufacturer of chemicals might invest more heavily in anti-pollution measures. (4)

## B. Revision exercises
### DATA RESPONSE

**External pressures on the grocery market**

The booming discount supermarket chain Aldi is on the verge of overtaking upmarket Waitrose to become the UK's sixth biggest supermarket as the German-owned grocer continues to open new stores and steal customers from its bigger rivals. Industry data released yesterday shows that while Tesco and Morrisons' continue to decline, Aldi's share of grocery till receipts rose to 4.8 per cent in the 12 weeks to 20 July 2014. A year ago the discounter's market share was 3.7 per cent, according to figures from retail analysts Kantar Worldpanel.

Over the same period, Waitrose's market share edged up to 4.9 per cent from 4.8 per cent last year, while Tesco dropped to 28.9 per cent from 30.3 per cent. The data confirms the trend of shoppers abandoning mid-market players in favour of more upmarket rivals and the discounters, with increasing numbers of shoppers cherry-picking from both ends of the market. 'Waitrose has continued to resist pressure from the competition, testament to its policy of maximum differentiation, and has grown sales by 3.4 per cent. This figure is well above the market average and thereby has lifted its market share', according to Edward Garner, director of Kantar.

Despite this positivity, *The Grocer* magazine has questioned whether Waitrose is now starting to suffer. Its profit margins at 5.4 per cent are well above industry averages, and perhaps shoppers are starting to query its value for money. Partly because of its high prices, Waitrose offers free delivery to online grocery shoppers. With online sales booming it may be that Waitrose profits start to get squeezed by the free delivery, given that picking and delivery is far from free from the shop's point of view.

The numbers come against a backdrop of a challenging market. Kantar says grocery price inflation has fallen for the tenth successive period and now stands at just 0.4 per cent – its lowest level since prices were first measured in 2006. As a result, market growth has fallen to 0.9 per cent.

Tim Vallance, head of retail at property group JLL, said: 'The figures highlight the impact that the big four's response to the rise of the discount retailers is having on the grocery sector, with vicious price cutting leading to shrinking market growth. As shoppers continue to demand a more convenient offer in an increasingly digital world, supermarkets need to think about how and where their customers shop and need to focus on choice, provenance, quality, service and convenience to differentiate from the discounter offering.'

Sources: adapted from *The Guardian*, 30 July 2014 and *The Grocer*, 9 August 2014

**Questions (25 marks; 35 minutes)**

**1.** Analyse the market conditions faced by Waitrose at this time. (9)

**2.** To what extent would Waitrose have been wise, at this time, to have differentiated itself further by switching entirely to Fairtrade supplies? (16)

## C. Extend your understanding

**1.** To what extent may demographic changes influence the future plans of a business that you know? (20)

**2.** In the last recession, the UK steel company Corus closed its Scunthorpe steelworks, making hundreds redundant. Discuss the strategies Corus, or other companies you have researched, could have adopted to prepare for recession. (20)

# Chapter

# 5

# What managers do

---

**Linked to:** Understanding the nature and purpose of business, Chapter 1; Managers, leadership and decision-making, Chapter 6; Motivation and engagement in theory, Chapter 46; Improving organisational design, Chapter 48.

---

### Definition

Managers organise and galvanise staff into implementing the strategies needed to achieve the business objectives.

## 5.1 Introduction

A recent study of jobs across Europe showed that a higher percentage of UK employees defined themselves as 'managers' than in any other country. In the UK 11.6 per cent said they were managers; in Germany the figure was 4.7 per cent and in Denmark just 2 per cent. The report's authors concluded that the British are happier describing themselves as managers than in other countries. Elsewhere, the term 'professional' or 'technician' seems more desirable.

So what is this job that the British seem so keen on? Essentially it's about making things happen. For example, a school might employ a company to design a new website. A manager at the school will be put in charge of the project; that person will make sure that the agreed contract will be delivered on time and within budget. This will require meetings, briefings and contacts to make sure everything is running smoothly. At the end of the project, many of the 'sign-offs' will be straightforward, such as agreeing that yes, the site allows downloads and yes, all the hyperlinks work. Others will require judgement, such as the design of the home page: Professional-looking? Distinctive? Well-branded? And so on.

In effect, the professionals or technicians are doing the time-consuming and tricky things; the manager

is just the overseer. Does that represent a satisfying job? In fact, recent research suggests that managers do enjoy their jobs. Seven of the top 20 places (out of 274 job categories) were taken up by managers. Table 5.1 shows, among other things, the lack of correlation between job satisfaction and income.

---

'Management is getting paid for home runs someone else hits.' Casey Stengel, baseball player and manager

---

**Table 5.1** Cabinet Office Research into Jobs and Life Satisfaction, March 2014

| Top 3 for job satisfaction | Salary (2013) | Score out of 10 |
|---|---|---|
| 1. Clergy | £20,568 | 8.291 |
| 2. Chief executives and senior officials | £117,700 | 7.957 |
| 3. Managers and proprietors in agriculture and horticulture | £31,721 | 7.946 |
| **Bottom 3 for job satisfaction** | | |
| 272. Debt and rent collectors | £17,371 | 6.56 |
| 273. Elementary construction occupations | £20,910 | 6.389 |
| 274. Publicans | £25,222 | 6.38 |

## 5.2 The academic study of what managers do

The first significant study of management was by Henri Fayol, a French business executive. His key book General and Industrial Management (1916) suggested that 'to manage is to forecast and plan, to organise, to command, to co-ordinate and to control'. This list reads perfectly well a hundred years later, though in the modern world there would be an attempt to make it sound less like an Army general giving out orders.

Fayol's list formed the basis of Henry Mintzberg's attempt in the 1970s to identify what, exactly, managers did with their time. Was it all spent planning and controlling? In fact careful research showed that, on average, managers were only able to carry out an activity for 9 minutes before being interrupted. He was able to show that instead of management being a careful, intellectual process of planning, managers were fallible humans being interrupted continuously. To describe the work of a manager, Mintzberg identified six characteristics of the role:

1. Managers process large, open-ended workloads under tight time pressure
2. Managerial activities are short in duration, varied and fragmented and often self-initiated
3. Managers prefer action-driven activities and hate letters, (emails) and paperwork
4. They prefer verbal communications through meetings and phone calls
5. They maintain relationships mainly with subordinates and external parties – least with their superiors.
6. Their involvement in the execution of the work is limited though they initiate many of the decisions.

In truth, Mintzberg's list risks understating the relative chaos he identified. He found that management was largely reactive, fighting short-term fires and often failing to put them out.

'If you ask managers what they do, they will most likely tell you that they plan, organise, co-ordinate and control. Then watch what they do. Don't be surprised if you can't relate what you see to those four words.' Henry Mintzberg, academic and author

If Mintzberg had become the expert on what managers do, Peter Drucker remained the key figure in saying what they *should* do. To Drucker, the key was to keep the manager's eyes on the prize – and that prize was reaching the objectives. It is important to bear in mind that Drucker's key research and writing about business was between 1944 and 1950. In other words, towards the end of – and just after – the Second World War. Although Drucker wanted managers to develop staff and use them humanely, he was even more seized by the need to achieve the mission, be it defeating Hitler or finding a way to survive in a tough competitive environment.

So, what should managers do, according to Drucker?

1. Set clear objectives that all staff believe in
2. Find the right team for meeting the objectives. Drucker believed strongly in teamwork, but knew that many individuals would need to be taught/coached to devote their personal strengths to the group.
3. Help ensure that all staff are motivated. He did not regard 'employee satisfaction' as a relevant measure of this; he thought motivation came from within when people were given responsibility. Therefore delegation was a central management task.
4. Drucker was very conscious of the way that factory automation had eliminated certain job roles; he expected this process to grow in future. Therefore, he thought that managers needed to prepare staff for change in general, and specifically help staff learn to learn –thereby being able to adapt to changing job prospects in the future.

'A manager's job should be based on a task to be performed in order to attain the company's objectives… the manager should be directed and controlled by the objectives of performance rather than by his boss.' Peter Drucker, management guru

From the above analysis of the writings of Fayol, Mintzberg and Drucker it is possible to put together a list of the key roles of managers. This is developed in section 5.3.

## 5.3 The role of managers should include:

**Setting objectives:** managers need a clear idea of what they want to achieve. This, of course, will depend upon the company-wide (or 'corporate') objectives. The objectives need to be set clearly and specifically – and then put into language that all staff can understand. Especially in the modern world where half the staff may be temporary or part-time, it is vital to boil the objectives down into an easily-remembered phrase.

**Analysing:** there are three aspects of this that matter:

- Analysing the underlying conditions the business faces (which may lead to new objectives being set)
- Analysing the performance of different staff; in 2012 Morrisons' supermarkets decided to set its checkout staff the target of scanning items in no more than 3 seconds. The company announced that staff who consistently failed to meet the target would be moved to other jobs in-store.
- Analysing how effectively objectives are being met.

**Leading:** inspiring staff commitment to achieving the goals, in whatever way works for the individual. Some may do this by charisma, that is, by using the power of their personality; others may inspire because of their personal achievements or commitment; finally there may be leadership through effective control and direction – helping staff to see exactly what they must do to be successful. This topic is covered fully in Chapter 6.

**Making decisions:** though perhaps this should say 'getting decisions made' because it may be that the manager will delegate the task to junior staff. With decision-making, the key is to understand that some decisions have to be made by specific deadlines – even though this may be too early to have all the facts available. Successful managers will have confidence that no one will expect them to get every decision right. A success rate above 50 per cent is pretty impressive in most contexts.

**Reviewing:** this is hard to do when the outcome from a decision has been poor, therefore it is excellent business practice to insist that every decision be reviewed – perhaps by a small team that should include someone who was not involved in the original decision.

In the long run the businesses that succeed will be the ones that learn most from their mistakes – and from their successes.

'A manager's task is developing and maintaining a culture that promotes work.' Blake and Mouton, *The Managerial Grid*.

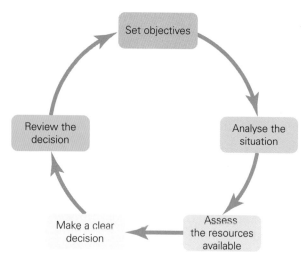

**Figure 5.1** Logic chain: how managers make decisions

## Five Whys and a How

| Question | Answer |
|---|---|
| Why may management represent a satisfying job? | Because it has responsibility and some autonomy (independence), giving it some important motivators |
| Why may the clergy find more satisfaction from their job than anyone else? | Presumably they get satisfaction from helping people (their flock); and there's probably a lot of responsibility involved |
| Why may managers prefer verbal to written communication (according to Mintzberg)? | Perhaps because it makes it easier to get feedback/provoke discussion and also may help in building more team spirit |
| Why might Drucker have emphasized teamwork? | Because a key lesson of the Second World War was that allies can work effectively with each other – as long as they share a common objective |
| Why may it be hard for managers to analyse the underlying conditions they face? | Because the constant interruptions they face (every 9 minutes, says Mintzberg) would make it hard to concentrate on the research |
| How might managers react to Mintzberg's findings about what managers actually do? | They would want to avoid constant interruptions and firefighting; they might demand to work from home one day a week – or close their office door once a week – to create the opportunity to plan |

## Evaluation: What managers do

Mintzberg's research captured the mismatch between management in theory and in practice. One expects managers to be thinking, planning and controlling. Instead they're having to react to a series of short-term pressures. Are things any different today? Recent research suggests that little has changed since 1973. So managers keep themselves busy, but may not achieve much.

One way to change this is to delegate more – and to truly resist the temptation to meddle. Then you can tell your staff to come back when *they* have sorted out the problems. Another way to achieve the same objective is to ban people coming to see you on certain days – but realistically that will just build up a lot of pressure for the 'on' days.

What Mintzberg doesn't quite resolve is whether managers like an over-interrupted existence and therefore encourage it (perhaps unconsciously). Not only would it make the manager feel very important, but it would also save her or him from having to do the hard bit: thinking and planning.

---

'Failing organisations are usually over-managed, but under-led.' Warren Bennis, business academic

---

## Key terms

**Co-ordinate:** the management task of ensuring that staff carrying out different parts of a project are all working to the same time schedule and quality standards.

**Subordinates:** those working for a manager and therefore under his or her command.

# Workbook

## A. Revision questions

(25 marks; 25 minutes)

1. **a)** Within the text covering Fayol, distinguish between 'commanding' and 'controlling'. (4)

   **b)** Explain why each is important to the completion of a project task. (4)

2. Explain in your own words the meaning behind Casey Stengel's quote (see page 30). (4)

3. In relation to Mintzberg, what might be the implications of management activities being 'self-initiated'? (4)

4. Explain in your own words Drucker's view on the implications of rising levels of automation. (4)

5. Other than learning from your mistakes, what else may be the benefit to a business of reviewing activities and decisions? (5)

## B. Revision exercises
### DATA RESPONSE

In the past 18 months Waterstones bookshops have been following a new strategy. Authority has been delegated to each store manager, allowing each to decide on the right range of books for their local area. So whereas a bookstore in one part of town might stock romance and crime, close to the University there might be academic books plus a big section on pop music. In addition, there has been a huge push to train staff to know more and therefore be more helpful to customers. The staff member at the till alongside the crime novels should be knowledgeable and interested in these books.

All this might seem obvious, but for the previous 10 years Waterstones' management had done the reverse. All buying decisions were made at Head Office, and all the stores ended up with the same range of stock (mainly based on the Top 50 sellers), sold on a Buy One Get One Half Price promotional model. Waterstones had ended up with this approach when confronted with twin-pincer competition from supermarkets on the one hand ('New Harry Potter for £9.99!') and Amazon on the other. But trying to beat these rivals on the basis of price was a lost cause. The supermarkets would cherry-pick the Top 20 titles and slash their price, while Amazon not only benefited from much lower overheads (no High Street rents) but also from a tax dodge that saw all sales go through Luxembourg, eliminating UK corporation tax. The latter arrangement still exists, giving wealthy Amazon an unfair competitive advantage.

The decision to allow the store managers to choose their own stock preferences might prove highly successful. It will not only make the stores more interesting for customers to visit, but should also provide the store manager with the motivation that comes from responsibility and from the level of challenge that comes with it.

### Questions (25 marks; 30 minutes)

1. Analyse whether Drucker would agree with the new strategy at Waterstones. (9)

2. To what extent should Waterstones back up its policy of delegation by offering financial incentives to its store managers? (16)

## ASSIGNMENT

Make an appointment to interview a curriculum manager within your school/college (ask your teacher for advice). Then find out:

- Their main areas of responsibility
- How much time they try to devote to each
- How long is it, on average, before they're interrupted from what they're trying to do?

- What they see as the pros and cons of a management role compared with being a classroom teacher.

Write up your findings making comparisons with Mintzberg where helpful. The assignment should be completed in no more than 500 words.

## C. Extend your understanding

1. Henry Mintzberg has written that 'the pressures of the job drive the manager to take on too much work, encourage interruption, respond quickly to every stimulus, seek the tangible and avoid the abstract, make decisions in small increments and do everything abruptly.' To what extent does this description fit in with Drucker's view of what the manager's job should be? (20)

2. Within the UK Civil Service, 53 per cent of employees are female and 9.6 per cent are non-white. Among senior management Civil Service grades, 36 per cent are women and 4.8 per cent are non-white. (2013 figures published by the ONS). Discuss what might be done to address the under-representation of women and non-whites in senior management posts in the UK today. (20)

**Linked to:** Understanding the nature and purpose of business, Chapter 1; What managers do, Chapter 5; Motivation and engagement in theory, Chapter 46; Improving organisational design, Chapter 48.

## Definition

Leadership means taking the initiative to set clear objectives and to motivate or guide staff towards their achievement. Management means organising and galvanising staff to implement the strategies needed to achieve the objectives.

## 6.1. Introduction

In 2013 the UK's best paid boss was Angela Ahrendts, the Chief Executive of Burberry plc. She received £16.9 million in 2013 and was then 'poached' by Apple, who may be about to pay her close to $100 million a year in future. That's a salary that even Christiano Ronaldo can only dream of (he has to 'get by' on £400,000 a week, way short of $2m a week for Angela). She did a wonderful job for Burberry, building it into a serious global luxury brand – with an especially strong position in China. The main criticism of such pay levels, though, is whether it can be morally right for the boss to be paid 1,000 times as much as shop floor staff. Is leadership ever worth that much?

In recent years business leadership has become an industry in itself. It is assumed that dynamic success comes from dynamic, charismatic leaders. By implication, therefore, these fabulous people are worth fabulous sums of money.

Sometimes, this is unarguably true. What was Sir Alex Ferguson 'worth' to Manchester United? And what was Sir Ken Morrison worth, in building his small supermarket business into a national chain between 1967 and 2008? He was worth lots, undeniably lots. Great leaders exist, and they are worth big financial rewards. Unfortunately, there are many examples of ordinary leaders with

ordinary achievements also being paid huge sums. Even though the amount paid may be relatively trivial for a big business, the implications are very significant. The media may over-emphasise the importance of 'the great leader', making it harder for intelligent, but modest, bosses to be given time to succeed.

## Real business

In January 2014 the value of Sainsbury's shares fell by £400 million when boss Justin King announced that he would be standing down after a decade as the chief executive. When he arrived Sainsbury's was struggling after:

- losing its 'No. 1' position to Tesco
- wasting £1 billion on a stock control system that didn't work
- a marketing debacle in which they had to scrap a very expensive TV campaign because sales *fell* when the commercial ran!

In the decade that followed Justin King kept completely focused on rebuilding the Sainsbury's UK business. He didn't allow himself to get distracted by overseas adventures, and managed to keep on top of the three big stories in UK grocery in the past ten years: the growth of online ordering; the growth of smaller convenience stores and the continuing concern over diet and health. During his tenure Sainsbury's profits trebled to £750 million a year. King's remuneration was as high as £2.6 million a year – but it is easy to see that his sensibly focused approach meant that he was worth it.

## 6.2 Introduction to leadership styles

The way in which bosses deal with their employees is known as their leadership style. For example, some managers are quite strict with workers. They always expect deadlines to be met and targets to be hit. Others are more relaxed and understanding. If there is a good reason why a particular task has not been completed by the deadline, they will be willing to accept this and give the employee more time. Although the way in which managers manage will vary slightly from individual to individual, their styles can be categorised under three headings: autocratic, democratic and paternalistic. See Table 6.1.

## Autocratic managers

Autocratic managers are authoritarian: they tell employees what to do and do not listen much to what workers themselves have to say. Autocratic managers tend to use one-way, top-down communication. They give orders to workers and do not want feedback.

'You do not lead by hitting people over the head – that's assault, not leadership.' Dwight Eisenhower, US President

## Democratic leaders

Democratic leaders, by comparison, like to involve their workers in decisions. They tend to listen to employees' ideas and ensure people contribute to the discussion. Communication by democratic managers tends to be two-way. Bosses put forward an idea and employees give their opinion. A democratic leader will regularly delegate decision-making power to junior staff.

The delegation of authority, which is at the heart of democratic leadership, can be approached in one of two main ways: management by objectives and laissez faire.

### Management by objectives

In this situation the leader agrees clear goals with staff, provides the necessary resources, and allows day-to-day decisions to be made by junior staff. These goals will necessarily be SMART, that is Specific, Measurable, Achievable, Relevant and Timebound. As a consequence, junior staff know that their efforts will be monitored against specific targets, such as: 'cut factory wastage costs per unit by 5 per cent within the next 18 months.'

### Laissez-faire

Meaning 'let it be', this occurs when leaders are so busy, or so lazy, that they do not take the time to ensure that junior staff know what to do or how to do it. Some people may respond very well to the freedom to decide how to spend their working lives; others may become frustrated. It is said that Bill Gates, in the early days of Microsoft, hired brilliant students and told them no more than to create brilliant software. Was this a laissez-faire style or management by objectives? Clearly the dividing line can be narrow.

**Figure 6.1** Manager and employee

## Paternalistic leaders

A paternalistic leader thinks and acts like a father. He or she tries to do what is best for their staff/children. There may be consultation to find out the views of the employees, but decisions are made by the head of the 'family'. This type of boss believes employees need direction but thinks it is important that they are supported and cared for properly. Paternalists are interested in the security and social needs of staff.

'As for the best leaders, the people do not notice their existence. The next best, the people honour and praise. The next, the people fear; and the next, the people hate… When the best leader's work is done the people say, "We did it ourselves."' Lao Tzu, quoted in Townsend, R., and Joseph, M., *Further up the Organisation*

**Table 6.1** Assumptions and approaches of the three types of leader

|  | **Democratic** | **Paternalistic** | **Autocratic** |
|---|---|---|---|
| Approach to staff | Delegation of authority | Consultation with staff | Orders must be obeyed |
| Approach to staff remuneration | Salary, perhaps plus employee shareholdings | Salary plus extensive fringe benefits | Payment by results, e.g. piece rate |
| Approach to human resource management | Recruitment and training based on attitudes and teamwork | Emphasis on training and appraisal for personal development | Recruitment and training based on skills; appraisal linked to pay |

## 6.3 Blake's Grid

Following research conducted between 1958 and 1960, Robert Blake and Jane Mouton developed a grid for analysing styles of leadership. The Blake and Mouton Grid looks at two leadership behaviours: 'concern for people' and 'concern for performance'. It then grades people on each of these scales to formulate a judgement on the type of leader they are. If, for example, a leader was obsessed with success at all costs, no matter what the impact on staff, they would be a 9,1 (Highest concern for performance; lowest concern for people). When appointed Fulham manager in the 2013/14 season, Felix Magath was called 'Saddam' and 'The Torturer' by former players. A 9,1 to be sure. By contrast, the best two post-war managers, Brian Clough and Alex Ferguson were both concerned about their people as well as their performance. Both were highly paternalistic; both were 9,9s. That was the combination viewed by Blake and Mouton as the leadership ideal.

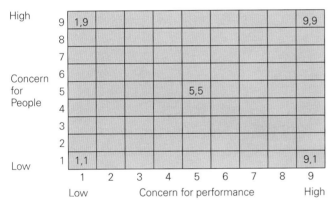

**Figure 6.2** The Managerial Grid, Blake and Mouton 1964
Source: Based on *Gridworks* by Robert Blake, Jane Mouton and Walter Barclay, Scientific Methods Inc. 1993

The labels that Blake and Mouton gave for each of the 5 leadership types were:

9,9 – Team management/Teamwork

9,1 – Authority/Obedience

5,5 – Middle-of-the-road management

1,9 – Country club management

1,1 – Impoverished management

To elaborate further, it can be said that:

- 9,9 (Team management): the boss shows interest and trust in staff, with a full belief in the synergy implied by successful teamwork (the whole is greater than the sum of the parts). Despite this, the steely determination to succeed would make it very tough for any team member who wasn't contributing effectively.

- 9,1 (Authority/Obedience): a fanatical drive to succeed, but on the leader's own terms ('my way or the highway'); staff are truly 'human resources', to be used or cast aside like any other resources; strongly linked to an authoritarian leadership style – and perhaps too likely to succeed in the short term only; in the longer term, good staff will leave.

- 5,5 (Middle of the Road): a decent, honest attempt to get the best of both worlds, but struggling to succeed at either; too willing to trade being nice for being successful; think mid-table obscurity or OK-but-not-great performance; when times are good, investors may not realise that it's all a bit second-rate. A famous Warren Buffet saying comes into effect, though, when times are tough: 'Only when the tide goes out do you discover who's been swimming naked.'

- 1,9 (Country Club): the boss is a really nice person; the staff love her or him but can't stop themselves taking advantage of the situation. There's a lack of urgency about getting things done – and probably quite shockingly poor productivity. This situation can only survive if monopoly power is keeping competition away from the business.

- 1,1 (Impoverished management): the boss has neither concern for the staff nor the performance of the business. Some writers have related this to Laissez faire management, but that may be harsh; some laissez faire managers see advantage in letting staff think and work for themselves. In the case of a 1,1 manager, there is absolutely no interest in the business or the people working for it.

In a later development of their theory, Blake and Mouton accepted that a sixth possibility was an entirely opportunistic approach to leadership in which the leader would adopt any style that would help in achieving a specific objective. This might be for no better reason than to maximise the leader's personal remuneration.

'A leader is like a shepherd. He stays behind the flock, letting the most nimble go out ahead, whereupon the others follow, nor realizing that all along they are being directed from behind.' Nelson Mandela

## 6.4 The Tannenbaum Schmidt Continuum

In 1973 two business academics, Tannenbaum and Schmidt, found a way to present leadership characteristics more dynamically than in the Blake and Mouton Grid. Blake's grid implies that a boss is (and will always be) a 1,9 or a 5,5. By contrast Tannenbaum and Schmidt devised a 'continuum' which suggested that people-centred leadership skills could be learned and developed. This was an attractive idea for Human Resource professionals, who saw an opportunity for devising useful training courses ('learning to lead').

On the continuum (see Figure 6.3) the single issue is a scale relating to the degree to which staff are involved in decision-making. On the left is the purely autocratic process: boss decides. That is steadily softened so that by mid-way, the manager presents the decision but then allows a degree of consultation and discussion in which the decision may change. Further to the right, consultation develops into delegation: getting staff to actually make decisions for themselves.

| Tell | Sell | | Consult | | Delegate | |
|---|---|---|---|---|---|---|
| ⇧ | ⇧ | ⇧ | ⇧ | ⇧ | ⇧ | ⇧ |
| Manager makes & announces decision | Manager sells decision | Manager presents ideas & invites questions | Manager presents decision subject to change | Manager presents problem, gets suggestions then decides | Manager defines limits; then asks group for a decision | Manager permits subordinates to decide within defined limits |

**Figure 6.3** The Tannenbaum and Schmidt Leadership Continuum

Despite the analytic value of the Continuum, Blake's Grid proved to have more of an impact upon managers in general. They found it easier to apply to their own workplaces and to the bosses they knew or had known.

**Table 6.2** Blake's Grid vs. Tannenbaum and Schmidt's Continuum

| Strengths of Blake's Grid | Strengths of Tannenbaum and Schmidt's Continuum |
|---|---|
| Blake's Grid measures two factors: concern for people and concern/drive for performance; Tannenbaum and Schmidt only measures one thing: the leader's use of people | The focus on the boss's use of his or her people gives an interesting amount of detail about the range of approaches between the two extremes (autocratic vs. highly democratic) |
| The understanding that some leaders are driven solely by results/success is perhaps why Blake's Grid is more widely known among managers than the continuum | The continuum gave a basis not only for analysis but also for action, such as persuading new section leaders to get training on how to develop the more democratic aspects of leadership |
| The labels used – such as 'Country Club' and 'Obedience' – made it easy for managers to visualise the type of person implied by a 5,5 or a 9,1 category; that made them talk about the grid and therefore learn to use it | The continuum also gave bosses a measure by which they could judge their own approach, helping them understand that 'tell' (boss decides; boss announces decision) is an extreme approach, not a normal one |

## 6.5. Leaders and managers

It is important to understand that the role of the leader is not the same as that of the manager. Management guru Peter Drucker once said that: 'Managers do things right; leaders do the right thing.'

In other words, an effective manager is someone who can put an idea or policy into action, and get the details right. By contrast, the leader is good at identifying the key issues facing the business, setting new objectives, and then deciding what should be done, by when, and by whom. It is also sometimes argued that a leader needs to inspire staff. This is often confused with charismatic leadership, that is, when the personal charisma of the leader inspires staff to give something extra or work a bit harder. Although some successful leaders such as Ghandi, Churchill and Mandela had charisma, many others had success despite quite dull personalities. The great British Prime Minister Clement Attlee 'had a lot to be modest about', according to Churchill. Liverpool FC's long period as Britain's top club began with the charismatic Bill Shankly, yet the huge haul of trophies came later, under the leadership of the shy, slightly bumbling Bob Paisley.

'All good leaders have the capacity to create a compelling vision and translate it into action and sustain it'. Warren Bennis, author and organisational consultant

## 6.6 Effectiveness of different leadership styles

In a BBC poll, Sir Winston Churchill was voted as the 'Greatest Ever Briton'. This accolade was for his achievement as the country's leader in the Second World War. Few would call him the Prime Minister; he was the leader. Yet before the war Churchill's career had been peppered with poor decision-making and difficulties forming political alliances, let alone leading them. Churchill's charismatic, hands-on and paternalistic style proved to be what the country needed at a time of crisis. Immediately after the war Churchill was voted out of office by a country that revered him. People knew he wasn't the leader for the peace.

The effectiveness of a leadership style, therefore, depends greatly on circumstances. At a time of crisis, autocratic and strong paternalistic approaches can work – bringing speedy decision-making at a time when staff want exactly that. Sometimes leaders who have performed well during a crisis are pushed aside shortly after, as the company needs a more democratic, cohesive leader for the good times.

More controversial is whether different leadership styles are needed in different parts of the world. And, if so, is the explanation cultural or due to differences in standards of living and development. This issue is covered more fully in the second year of the A-level course.

### Key terms

**Autocratic leadership:** when the boss keeps all key decisions to him or herself, and gives orders, rather than power, to subordinates.

**Charismatic leadership:** a leader whose dynamic or magnetic personality makes people willing to follow. The widely held view is that leaders require a dynamic or magnetic personality in order to succeed. Research does not support this.

**Democratic leadership:** this implies empowering people. That is, delegating full power over the design and execution of substantial tasks.

**Laissez-faire leadership:** this means allowing people to get on with things themselves, but without the co-ordination and control implicit within democratic leadership.

**Paternalistic leadership:** this means 'fatherly'. That is, the boss treats staff as part of the family. Typically, this shows through as consultation, but with decision-making remaining at the top ('Dad' decides).

### Five Whys and a How

| Question | Answer |
|---|---|
| Why might an uncharismatic leader be successful? | As long as the leader asks the right questions and makes the right calls on the big decisions, charisma is irrelevant |
| Why might laissez-faire leadership be a problem in a large organisation such as Unilever or Tesco? | Because it would be impossible to co-ordinate a wide range of wholly different approaches by different parts of the business (management by objectives would work far better) |
| Why might a 9,1 leader be more successful than a 5,5? | The 9,1 leader is a fanatic who drives people on to achieve success, quite possibly against their will; the 5,5 is too woolly, too accepting of compromise |
| Why might Blake's Grid be better known among business people than Tannenbaum and Schmidt's Continuum? | It gives more insight into the leaders they work with every day because it looks at their drive for success as well as their attitudes to their staff |
| Why might a leader 'be like a shepherd' (in the words of Nelson Mandela)? | Mandela thought leading from the back was the best approach – that is, letting people show initiative and talent (and only rounding them up if necessary) |
| How might an autocratic leader learn to be more democratic? | By absorbing the lessons of the Continuum, and seeking a training course designed to encourage more consultative, and then more democratic behaviours |

The business writer Robert Townsend suggested that many newly appointed leaders 'disappear behind the mahogany curtain' and are rarely seen again by staff. He thought that 'finally getting to the top' made many leaders focus more on corporate luxuries ('Which jet shall we buy?') than on hard work. Yet he knew that great leaders can make a huge difference to long-term business performance. He advocated a leadership model based on extensive delegation within tight, agreed budgets. Many follow that model today.

Ultimately, judging a leader takes time. The media may find a new 'darling' – perhaps someone who looks and sounds great on TV. That person's achievements may be praised hugely, and they may win 'Business Leader of the Year' awards and a Knighthood. Yet it will be several years before anyone outside the business can appraise the individual's performance. In most businesses it is easy to boost short-term profit: you push prices up here, and make redundancies there. This persuades the media and the shareholders that you are a fine leader. The real question, though, is whether your decisions will push the business forwards or backwards over the coming years. Hold back from rushing to praise (or condemn) a boss on the basis of short-term performance. Big business is a long game. Ninety minutes is a long time in football; a week is a long time in politics; five years is a long time in business.

# Workbook
## A. Revision questions

(40 marks; 40 minutes)

1. Distinguish between autocratic and **paternalistic leadership**. (4)

2. Outline two types of democratic leadership. (4)

3. Outline one advantage and one disadvantage of an **autocratic leadership** style. (4)

4. Explain why autocratic leaders may be of more use in a crisis than democratic ones. (4)

5. Many managers claim to have a democratic style of leadership. Often, their subordinates disagree. Outline two ways of checking the actual leadership style of a particular manager. (4)

6. How may a paternalistic leader set about generating a clear vision for a business? (4)

7. In your own words, explain what Peter Drucker meant by saying: 'Managers do things right; leaders do the right thing'. (4)

8. A consultancy called Stellar Leadership has a questionnaire for managers to test out where they are on the Tannenbaum and Schmidt Continuum.

Read this multiple choice question then answer parts a-d below:

Choose one of the following:

i. As a general rule, I do not delegate

ii. I delegate occasionally, but when I do I follow up carefully

iii. I delegate regularly, to individuals who have demonstrated that they can handle it.

iv. I use delegation as a means of developing new skills in my people.

a) Explain what is meant by the Tannenbaum and Schmidt Continuum. (3)

b) What leadership style would you associate with people who choose answer (i).? (1)

c) Explain which part of the Tannenbaum and Schmidt Continuum you would associate with answer (iii). (4)

d) How effective do you think multiple choice questions might be at assessing managers' leadership styles? Explain your answer. (4)

# B. Revision exercises

## DATA RESPONSE

### Curry Karma

Bangalore Balti (BB) started as a small curry house in Leicester. Word of its fresh, fiery food spread rapidly, creating the opportunity for expansion. By 2011 BB had 12 outlets across the Midlands, each run by a member of the owner's family. With plenty of cash in the bank, owner Safiq bought another chain of 16 Indian restaurants and converted them to the Bangalore Balti concept. This pushed the business into needing bank loans, which became a burden at a time when household spending was being held down by falling real incomes.

While Safiq was focusing on the financial pressures, things were slipping operationally. In particular, the managers of the 16 new restaurants showed less respect for the BB menu and seemed much less able to keep costs down and therefore profit margins up. It was also noticeable that labour turnover was higher in the new restaurants than in the original ones.

As the business came to the end of 2014 its profits were below those of four years earlier (See Table 6.3). It was getting hard to pay the interest bills on the loans. Something had to change.

**Table 6.3** Data for Bangalore Balti 2011–14

|  | 2011 (%) | 2014 (%) |
|---|---|---|
| Labour turnover in the previous 12 months | 8.4 | 19.5 |
| Percentage of staff with cooking skills | 46.5 | 28.5 |
| Operating profit margin in the latest 6 months | 12.8 | 4.7 |
| Head office overheads per £ of sales | 8.4 | 22.3 |

### Questions (25 marks; 35 minutes)

1. Explain one internal pressure and one external pressure for change at Bangalore Balti. (6)

2. a) Analyse how Safiq might set about deciding how to change the business in 2015. (10)

   b) Analyse two problems faced by Safiq. (9)

# C. Extend your understanding

1. To what extent does autocratic leadership have a place in today's business world? (20)

2. 'Great leaders are born, not made.' To what extent do you agree with this view? (20)

3. Discuss whether it can ever be right to pay a business leader 1,000 times more than the lowest paid in the organisation. (20)

# Chapter

# 7

# Decision-making: scientific and intuitive

**Linked to:** What managers do, Chapter 5; Decision trees, Chapter 8; Marketing and decision-making, Chapter 11.

## 7.1 Introduction

Modern managers like to be able to base a decision on numerical evidence. As a consequence, more and more tactical decisions are made by computers. For example, a McDonald's store manager is sent details of how many staff should be employed every hour for next Saturday. The computer makes the 'decision' based on a sales forecast using data from last year and recent weeks. In this way the decision-making can be 'scientific' – in the sense that it is based on objective, numerical data – as opposed to hunch or intuition.

'It is a capital mistake to theorize before one has data. Insensibly one begins to twist facts to suit theories, instead of theories to suit facts.' Arthur Conan Doyle, aka Sherlock Holmes.

When the decision is more strategic, by definition there will be more uncertainty. When Whitbread plc decided to buy Costa Coffee, it couldn't know that it would be able to build the business from 50 outlets to 3,000 (including 350 in China). So computer programmes can't punch out answers. Therefore there is a far greater need for intuition. Whitbread made a brilliant call; Morrisons' made a disastrous one when it bought online site Kiddicare for £70 million in 2011 and sold it for £2 million in 2014!

Scientific decision-making is the goal for most firms because it suggests a method that can be applied in a routine way to measure opportunities or problems. When considering whether to launch a proposed new product, large companies like to have a testing system that they can use for every proposal. Then, over time, enough data is gathered to start to make accurate forecasts.

'Market research will always tell you why you can't do something. It's a substitute for decision-making, for guts.' Laurel Cutler, US business person

## Real business

*The Grocer* magazine regularly features independent research into new product launches using a system called Cambridge Fast Foodfax. It uses various quantitative measures to test the likelihood of sales success. From the answers to those questions a rating score is devised. A look at the data below shows why Marks & Spencer felt optimistic about sales of their new lemonade.

**Table 7.1**

|  | Asda Choc Chip Muffin Cheesecake £1.50 | Cadbury Dairy Milk Banana Caramel Crisp | M&S Still Blackcurrant Lemonade £1.00 |
|---|---|---|---|
| Pre-trial purchase | 49 per cent | 46 per cent | 44 per cent |
| Post-trial purchase | 44 per cent | 39 per cent | 48 per cent |
| Better than what's out there | 30 per cent | 37 per cent | 54 per cent |
| New and different | 59 per cent | 93 per cent | 89 per cent |
| Overall score | 38/50 | 37/50 | 41/50 |

Source: data from *The Grocer*: 2 and 9 August 2014

On these measures experience has shown that a score of 45+ shows a product of huge potential. Between 40 and 44 also shows promise. This approach enables big firms to scrap unpromising new products before taking them to market.

## 7.2 Scientific decision-making

The desire for a scientific approach to management dates back, at least, to F.W. Taylor and the late 19th century. Taylor wanted managers to find the 'one best way' to do things and then instruct and incentivise workers to follow that one best method. Taylor believed in 'time and motion' studies that measured exactly how and when workers completed certain tasks. He also advocated high division of labour, forcing staff to do simple, repetitive tasks in the workplace. With simple tasks came ease of measurement and from there it was only a short step to the business saying 'measurement is management'. In other words, once you start measuring things in the workplace, staff pay more attention and start behaving differently.

Today managers still want to control business variables, from absenteeism to morale. They also want to control external variables as much as possible. So sales are forecast with great precision and computer software is used to model every foreseeable situation, for example an August bank holiday with cloudy but not rainy weather. Scientific management tries to take the art out of business decision-making – replacing intuition with facts and quantitative forecasts.

**Table 7.2** Some good and some awful real business decisions

| Good business decisions | Bad business decisions |
|---|---|
| Coca-Cola buys innocent Drinks – giving it a real competitor to PepsiCo's Tropicana. The £200 million deal was completed in 2013. | Waterstones bookshop decides to stop selling books online, because 'online will never be more than 10 per cent of the market.' |
| In June 2000 Nick Robertson and Quentin Griffiths launch 'As Seen on Screen'; first year sales are £3.6m. By 2014 'ASOS' has sales of £1,000 million. | Malcolm Walker, owner of Iceland Frozen Foods, takes the business upmarket – focusing on organic products. It didn't last. |
| Unloved Mondelez (owner of Cadbury) launched Belvita Breakfast Biscuits in 2010. The Grocery trade laughed at the idea, but by 2013 Belvita sales had grown to £58 million – that's more than Jaffa Cakes. | Rupert Murdoch, media mogul, sells MySpace website for $35m, having bought it for $580m six years before. |
| With recession biting Waitrose launched its 'Essentials' range of lower-priced groceries. By 2013 sales of Essentials are more than £1 billion a year and Waitrose extends the range to 400 more items. | Nestle re-launches its Willie Wonka chocolate bar range in 2013 (sales were poor when it first launched in 2005); time is no healer and the whole range is discontinued in 2014. |

'Whenever decisions are made strictly on the basis of bottom-line arithmetic, human beings get crunched along with the numbers.' Thomas Horton, US business leader

'The best class of scientific mind is the same as the best class of business mind. The great desideratum in either case is to know how much evidence is enough to warrant action.' Samuel Butler, British novelist (1835–1902)

## 7.3 Risk, reward and uncertainty

Uncertainty is the natural state of affairs in businesses where many external factors affect sales and costs. The number of variables makes it impossible to predict what will happen (though some will try, taking their fees prior to the timescale of their predictions). Uncertainty does allow conclusions to be drawn, however. In an uncertain world a business needs a wide-enough range (portfolio) of products to be sure that one flop will not hit the business too hard.

Risk may be quantifiable, at least in some broad ways. If only 1 in 8 Hollywood films brings in more revenue than the cost of making it, it is reasonable to gauge the risk of lossmaking as 7/8 for future films. Then the risk must be set against the potential rewards. With movies, the rewards may be spectacular. *E.T. the Extra-Terrestrial* is believed to have made a 7,000 per cent return; the *Blair Witch Project* a profit of 414,000 per cent!

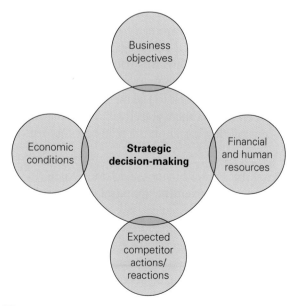

**Figure 7.1** Logic chain: making strategic decisions

For some companies, including those with weak financial positions, low-risk projects are the only ones to consider, even if the returns are quite low too. Other firms are willing to take bigger gambles, figuring that a few failures is not a problem as long as the occasional success proves to be a big one.

## 7.4 Influences on decision-making

1. **Mission.** Good business decisions are those that contribute towards the mission of the organisation. This may mean taking decisions that go against the company objectives, perhaps because ethics come into play. So even if a company's 12-month objective is to boost market share from 26 per cent to 29 per cent, it may be ethically wrong to launch a product that attracts consumer interest but is against the consumer's best interests. So a mission such as Google's ('Don't be evil') should ensure that greed for profit does not take precedence over the interests of customers.

2. **Objectives.** For middle managers intent upon promotion prospects, decision-making is focused on the objectives they have been set. If directors want rising market share, managers will do all they can to deliver. An important factor to consider, though, is the timescale involved. Rising short-term market share can easily be achieved by deciding on price and other sales promotions. Yet this may be at the cost of long-term success. In 2013 Huggies disposable nappies were withdrawn from the UK market, even though sales had been above £100 million a year. The reason was that regular price discounting had undermined the brand. In effect, the company accepted defeat against Procter & Gamble's Pampers. Directors need to be careful to avoid encouraging short-termism. Well-run businesses always look to the medium-long term when setting their objectives. That ensures decision-making based on the true best interests of the company.

3. **Ethics.** Ethics enter business decisions when they form part of the scientific appraisal of risk and reward. If Marks & Spencer saw a sales opportunity for a 'super-indulgent chocolate moussecake' containing 1,000 calories, the risk of bad publicity would be taken into account. But when you scan the shelves of the store, or queue at a checkout alongside many tempting sweet treats you realise that M&S sells masses of spectacularly fattening foods. No one within the business is saying 'no, we really shouldn't be doing this'.

With smaller, family-run businesses the same may not apply. If the family wishes to sell fruitcake but not chocolate cake, it can do so. It can allow a decision to be based purely on ethics. For a large, publicly-owned company, that is not a realistic possibility. Public company shareholders want dividend income and to see a rising share price. Putting ethics before profit would find little favour.

### Real business

In 2012 a prominent sponsor of the London Olympics was Coca-Cola. To create 'social value' from this expenditure, Coca-Cola worked with the charity StreetGames to get 110,000 youngsters participating in sport. Good though that may be, what about the ethics?

In Mexico 70,000 die each year from diabetes. Mexicans are the fattest people in the world and also drink more Coca-Cola per head than anyone else. When a tax was proposed in Mexico on the sugar in soft drinks, Coca-Cola bottlers warned that 20,000 jobs could be lost. This opposition chimed with the Mexican soft drinks' trade association's hostility to the tax.

So, on reflection, how can one view the aid for StreetGames as anything other than a marketing decision? Ethics do not really enter the Coca-Cola corporate mindset.

4. The external environment, including competition. Big strategic decisions must be rooted in the economic, social, competitive and consumer environment of the time and, even more importantly, of the future. When Domino's Pizza began in 1960, it was not clear to everyone that home-delivery was going to become the dominant way of supplying consumers' love of the product. But founder Tom Monaghan saw through the competition from Pizza Hut and from supermarket cook-at-home pizzas, focusing on home delivery. Today Domino's is the world's biggest pizza delivery company, with sales of more than $1,000 million a year.

Of all the economic, social and technological aspects of the external environment, none is more important than trends in consumer taste. In 2014 profits at Gillette fell by 17.5 per cent as its male shaving products struggled because of a fashion towards stubble. Less shaving meant less profit. No amount of clever marketing could make up for that.

Another key factor is competition. The issues are twofold: first, how intense is the competition; and second, is that intensity changing? When Scoop ice cream opened in Covent Garden in 2007 it was the first artisan gelato-maker in Central London. According to Time Out magazine August 2014 there are now 22! Three, it is true, are Scoop outlets, but that still leaves 19 competitors. Naturally that makes it harder to run a comfortably profitable business.

5. Resource constraints. Before making a business decision it is crucial to have considered the resource implications. A restaurant chain can only decide to open 20 more stores in the coming year if it has enough capital and the right amount of management talent. Any attempt to expand with insufficient resources is likely to lead to 'overtrading' – expanding more rapidly than your resource-base allows.

## Five Whys and a How

| Question | Answer |
|---|---|
| Why is the scientific approach to decision-making easier for tactical than for strategic decisions? | Because tactical decisions are more limited in their scope and effect, often stemming from regular, predictable issues such as a shop asking how many kilos of strawberries are needed for next Saturday? |
| Why is uncertainty a bigger worry for firms than risk? | Because risk can often be calculated and therefore brought into the decision-making process. |
| Why might middle managers be inclined to make decisions based on short-term criteria? | Because they are focused more on their next career step than on the long-term best interests of the whole business. |
| Why might a scientific decision prove wrong? | Either incomplete data were gathered or the interpretation of the data must have been faulty. |
| Why might a firm's objectives be out of alignment with its mission? | Mission is often influenced by ethics that are more ambitious than the duller, perhaps profit-focused objectives. |
| How can a firm make sure it takes decisions scientifically? | By gathering as much numerical evidence as possible and weighing it up using a standardized method such as decision trees (see Chapter 8). |

## Evaluation: Decision-making: scientific and intuitive

Good decisions are those that look good (or even obvious) some time later. They are likely to be made in a collaborative way, using the knowledge and wisdom of the more junior staff who are in day-to-day contact with customers. Of course, if the plan is to make a decision scientifically, the views of staff must be used as part of a calculation (in effect, an equation) that carefully sets the risks out against the rewards.

A training director called Donald Bullock once said that 'Most of our executives make very sound decisions. The trouble is many of them have turned out not to be right.' This sums up scientific decision-making in particular. The method for making the decision may be perfect but ultimately all that matters is that the decision is right. As shown in Table 7.1, in business there's scope for making huge, multi-million pound decisions. Good executives manage to get the big decisions right most of the time.

'Participative management is, simply stated, involving the right people at the right time in the decision-making process.' Wayne Barlow, administrator, Federal Aviation Authority

# Workbook

## A. Revision questions

**(30 marks; 30 minutes)**

1. Explain why intuition may be more important for a strategic decision than for a tactical one. (4)

2. For each of the following decisions, outline whether you believe it to be tactical or strategic. If there is some uncertainty, explain why.
   a) Deciding whether to give an order to supplier A or B. (2)
   b) Deciding whether to move head office from London to New York. (2)
   c) Deciding whether to employ full-time only staff, or whether to go for part-timers. (2)
   d) Deciding whether to put the Bolton FC season ticket price up from £600 to £720. (2)

3. Identify three factors that might undermine the accuracy of the data used in a scientific decision. (3)

4. a) What is meant by the term 'business ethics'? (2)
   b) Why may the desire for high ethical standards conflict with the rewards anticipated from a decision? (5)

5. Based on your best understanding of the current economic position, comment on its possible effect on:
   a) the likely revenue and profit trend at Poundland. (4)
   b) the sales prospects for the newly launched Amira Superior Aromatic Rice, which is priced 50 per cent higher than usual brands. (4)

## B. Revision exercises

### DATA RESPONSE

**Big decisions at Tesco**

After his predecessor left in July, new boss Dave Lewis had a few months before starting as Tesco Chief Executive (CEO) in October 2014. This gave him time to think about how to turn the business around. For five years Tesco's market share had been struggling in the UK. But at least it was profitable. Many of its overseas operations were losing money.

Dave Lewis was brought in from outside Tesco, with a strong career at giant Unilever. Lewis was the boss of Unilever's Personal Care division, with annual sales of more than £15 billion (and brands such as Dove and TRESemmé). Before that he had many jobs around the world in a 27-year career with the multinational.

To commentators, Lewis had five main issues to deal with as soon as possible:

- The Tesco brand image, which has been hit hard in the UK
- The perception that Tesco is a relatively expensive store (borne out by *The Grocer's* weekly 'pricecheck')
- Tesco's falling market share in the UK (from 31.2 per cent at its peak to 28.9 per cent by July 2014. NB Each 1 per cent is slightly over £1 billion of sales)
- A series of problems in Tesco's international store portfolio, with sales and profit seeming to struggle post-recession

- More than anything else, should Tesco have all its cost-drivers hacked back to the minimum (scrap Clubcard and so on), in order to take on Lidl and Aldi at the price game?

### Questions (30 marks; 35 minutes)

1. Dave Lewis will have to make some big decisions quite soon. Is it a strength or a weakness that he's an outsider to Tesco? Explain your reasoning. (5)

2. Choose one of the five issues outlined and explain why this should be tackled first. (9)

3. To what extent would a scientific approach to decision-making help Dave Lewis in the early months of his new job? (16)

## C. Extend your understanding

1. To what extent may there be problems when decision-making is based on clear objectives, but unclear resource constraints? (20)

2. To what extent can the decisions made by a multinational oil company such as Shell or BP ever be considered ethical? (20)

**Linked to:** What managers do, Chapter 5; Decision-making: scientific and intuitive, Chapter 7.

### Definition

Decision trees are diagrams that set out all the options available when making a decision, plus an estimate of their likelihood of occurring.

## 8.1 Introduction

Decision trees provide a logical process for decision-making. The decision problem can be set out in the form of a diagram, like a tree on its side. It can take into account the occasions when a decision can be taken and the occasions when chance will determine the outcome. Chance can be estimated by assigning a probability, such as 0.2 (a 1 in 5 chance). While the estimate of the probability may sometimes be a guess, at other times there may be a logical basis. In the past, the chance of a new product launch surviving two years was 1 in 5, therefore it would be fair to give the probability of success for a new launch at 0.2.

'Compromise is usually bad . . . listen to both sides then pick one or the other.' Robert Townsend, author *Up the Organisation* (1920–1998)

## 8.2 Step-by-step approach to decision-tree analysis

### Step 1: the basics

1. The tree is a diagram setting out the key features of a decision-making problem.

2. The tree is shown lying on its side, roots on the left, branches on the right.

3. The decision problem is set out from left to right with events laid out in the sequence in which they occur.

4. The branches consist of:

   **a)** a decision to be made, shown by a square (see Figure 8.1)

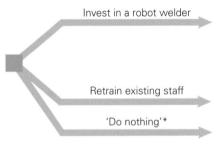

Invest in a robot welder

Retrain existing staff

'Do nothing'*

*Note that 'do nothing' is an option for every business decision

**Figure 8.1** Decision tree

   **b)** chance events or alternatives beyond the decision-maker's control, shown by a circle – a node (see Figure 8.2).

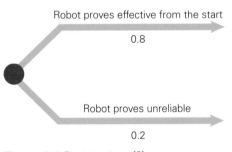

Robot proves effective from the start

0.8

Robot proves unreliable

0.2

**Figure 8.2** Decision tree (2)

Note carefully that a square means a decision and a circle means a chance event, that is, one of two or more events may follow. Therefore:

- there must be a probability attaching to each of the chance events or alternatives
- these probabilities must add up to 1 as one of them must happen.

In Figure 8.2, the decision-maker has allowed for an 80 per cent (0.8) chance that the robot will work well and a 20 per cent (0.2) chance that it will prove unreliable. These figures could be arrived at from experience with robots in the past.

At any square, the decision-maker has the power to choose which branch to take, but at the circles chance takes over. You can choose whether or not to invest in a robot. But there is a chance that the robot may prove unreliable. The full tree so far is shown in Figure 8.3.

The decision-maker will choose which branch provides the better or best value.

If buying costs a net cash outflow of £1,000 per year while hiring costs £800, it is better to hire (see Figure 8.4).

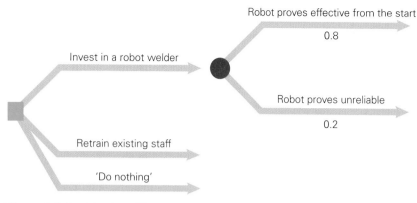

**Figure 8.3** Decision tree (3)

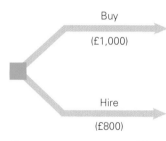

**Figure 8.4** Decision tree (4)

Note that the branch not taken is crossed out, as shown in Figure 8.5.

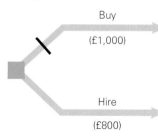

**Figure 8.5** Decision tree (5)

## Step 2: drawing a decision tree

Bantox plc must decide whether to launch a new product (see Figure 8.6).

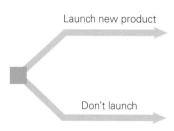

**Figure 8.6** Decision tree (6)

Research suggests there will be a 70 per cent chance of success in a new product launch. This would be shown as a probability of 0.7 (see Figure 8.7).

**Figure 8.7** Decision tree (7)

Note that, because probabilities must add up to 1, the implied chance of failure is 0.3.

To make a decision based on the tree above, estimates are needed of the financial costs and returns. In this case, let's assume:

- the new product launch will cost £10 million
- a new product success will generate £15 million of positive net cash flows
- a new product failure will generate only £3 million
- no launch means no movements in net cash.

The full decision tree now looks like Figure 8.8.

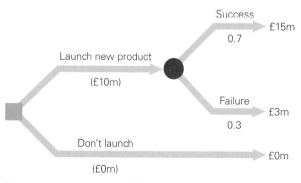

**Figure 8.8** Decision tree (8)

## Step 3: making calculations

At each probability circle, a calculation is required of the average outcome, given the probabilities involved. If a launch costing £10 million will generate either £15 million or £3 million, what will be the average result, if the same circumstances happened several times over? Sometimes the firm would get £15 million and sometimes £3 million. Usually, to work out an average, you would add the numbers and divide by 2; that is:

$$\frac{£15 + £3\,m}{2} = £9\,m$$

That assumes, though, that there is an equal chance of £15 million and £3 million. In fact, the probabilities are not 50/50, they are 70/30. There is a 70 per cent chance of £15 million. So the correct (weighted) average expected value is:

£15 m × 0.7 = £10.5 m
£3 m × 0.3 = £0.9 m
Total £11.4 m

In decision trees, the expected values at probability circles are always calculated by weighted averages.

Calculations on decision trees are carried out from right to left, that is, working backwards through the tree, making calculations at each probability circle.

In the case of Bantox, only one calculation is needed. If there are several circles, it is helpful to number them, and show your weighted average calculations clearly (see Figure 8.9).

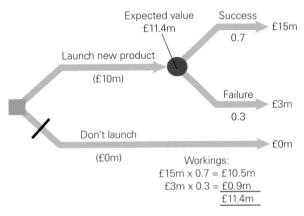

**Figure 8.9** Decision tree (9)

## Step 4: showing your decisions

Having calculated the expected value (weighted average) at each probability circle, a rational decision can be made. As Figure 8.9 shows, launching the new product will, on average, turn £10 million into £11.4

million; that is, generate a net gain of £1.4 million. Therefore it is preferable to launch. The decision to launch is indicated by crossing out the 'don't launch' option.

## 8.3 Summary of key points

A decision tree is a diagrammatic presentation of a problem involving decisions (squares) and chance events (circles).

1. The problem is laid out from left to right. Decisions are shown as squares, chance events as circles.

2. Each chance event has a probability estimated for it. The probabilities must add up to 1 since one of them must happen.

3. Two money values are shown:
   a) the cost of the decision (shown as a negative number, that is, in brackets)
   b) the benefit or cost of a specific outcome occurring. These are shown at the end of each branch of the tree.

4. Working from right to left, the decision-maker calculates the expected value at each circle. These values are calculated by multiplying the money value by the probability, then adding the results.

5. Still working from right to left, the decision-maker decides at each square which branches to cross off, leaving only the better or best alternative open.

## 8.4 Advantages and disadvantages of decision trees

### Advantages of decision trees

1. The most important advantage of the technique is allowing for uncertainty. The most common technique for business decision-making is investment appraisal. This is based upon a single forecast of future cash flows, giving a bogus impression of certainty. In reality, every decision can result in a range of possible outcomes, not just one. The decision tree allows for this. By focusing firms on uncertainty, decision trees can help to ensure that managers make more carefully considered decisions.

2. Decision trees also demand that managers consider all the possible alternative outcomes. Although it is important to be single-minded, too many managers adopt a strategy without fully considering the alternatives. They perhaps choose

the approach that worked the last time, or the one adopted by their competitors. Decision trees not only encourage careful consideration of the options, but also require an estimate of the actual outcome for each. This allows 'best-case' and 'worst-case' scenarios to be costed and considered.

Further advantages of decisions trees are set out below.

1. Decision trees set out problems clearly and encourage a logical approach. The discipline of setting out the problem in a decision tree requires logical thinking and can also generate new ideas and approaches.

2. Decision trees encourage a quantitative approach and force assessments of the chances and implications of success and failure.

3. Decision trees not only show the average expected values for each decision but also set out the probability of a specific outcome occurring.

4. Decision trees are most useful when similar scenarios have occurred before, so that good estimates of probabilities and predicted actual values exist.

5. Decision trees are most useful in tactical or routine decisions, rather than strategic decisions.

## Disadvantages of decision trees

All quantitative methods can be biased, consciously or unconsciously. Optimism is often a virtue in an executive, but it may lead to exaggerated sales figures or excessively high probabilities for success. This does not mean quantitative methods should be rejected. Only that it is sensible to ask who provided the figures and assess whether they had any reason to want a particular outcome. Cynicism about decision trees is out of place; scepticism is wholly valid.

---

'We should never allow ourselves to be bullied by an either-or. There is often the possibility of something better than either of these two alternatives'. Mary Parker Follett, business writer (1868–1933)

---

Further disadvantages of decision trees are set out below.

1. It may be difficult to get meaningful data, especially for estimated probabilities and of success or failure.

2. Decision trees are less useful in the case of completely new problems or one-off strategic problems.

3. It can be relatively easy for a manager seeking to prove a case to manipulate the data. A biased approach to the estimated probabilities or values could 'prove' a pre-desired result rather than a logically determined outcome.

4. Decision trees do not take into account the variability of the business environment.

5. Decision trees may divert managers from the need to take account of qualitative as well as quantitative information when making a decision.

## Evaluation: Decision trees

Small firms run by one person benefit from clear, speedy decision-making. The entrepreneur knows the customers, the competition and the staff. Therefore he or she can make effective decisions quickly, with no need to justify them to others. Some may prove faulty, but the quick responses of a small firm should ensure that damage is limited. The business will stand or fall on the hunches and judgements of the boss.

In large firms, the same rules do not apply. A successful career path at a company such as Mars or Unilever often depends upon avoiding mistakes. Therefore it is important to be able to justify why a decision was made. Even if it proves to be wrong, that should not matter as long as the method for making the decision was thorough and analytic.

After all, if four out of five new products prove to be failures, what would be the reason for firing a manager who has just launched a flop?

It can be a matter for regret that methods such as decision trees are used to 'protect the back' of decision-makers. In other words, they may not be valued for themselves, only for their value as a protector. Often, though, the process of trying to protect themselves encourages managers to think hard about their decision-making methods. Those who use decision trees positively may find an improvement in their record of success, and help the big firms to compete with the faster moving small firms.

## Five Whys and a How

| Question | Answer |
|---|---|
| Why may decision tree analysis be more useful than investment appraisal? | Because it takes into account alternative possible outcomes and the probability of them occurring (investment appraisal is misleadingly 'certain') |
| Why are expected values calculated using a 'weighted' rather than a straight average? | Because it is the only way to gain accuracy when there are different probabilities of your possible outcomes occurring |
| Why may the decision tree technique be useful even if you have no sound basis for estimating the probabilities? | The tree diagram will still indicate the best and worst possible outcomes - a vital part of decision-making (if the worst outcome would threaten the firm's survival, you'd say no) |
| Why may there be dangers in the apparent 'scientific' precision of the decision tree technique? | People may assume that the technique delivers more accuracy than is true given the degree of estimation involved |
| Why may decision trees risk sidelining qualitative factors? | Because people are swayed by a 'definite', numerical 'answer' to a problem – so they subconsciously play down qualitative factors |
| How are calculations done after the decision tree is drawn up? | Working back from right to left, calculating the weighted average at every chance node then cutting off the less profitable decisions |

### Key terms

**Actual values:** although known as 'actual values' or 'payoffs', these are the forecasts of the net cash flows which result from following a sequence of decisions and chance events through a decision tree. They should always be shown at the ends of the branches of the tree.

**Node:** a point in a decision tree where chance takes over. It is denoted by a circle, and at that point it should be possible to calculate the expected value of this pathway.

**Expected values:** these are the forecast actual values adjusted by the probability of their occurrence.

Although called 'expected', they are not the actual cash flows which result. Expected equals actual × probability.

**Net gains** (or losses): subtracting the initial outlay from the expected value to find out whether or not a decision is likely to produce a surplus.

**Probability:** the likelihood of something occurring, usually expressed as a decimal (for example 0.5). The probability of something certain is 1. The probability of something impossible is zero.

# Workbook

## A. Revision questions

(30 marks; 60 minutes)

1. When drawing a decision tree, what symbol is used to show:
   a) when a decision must be made?
   b) when chance takes over? (2)

2. If the probability of the successful launch of a new product is estimated to be 0.72, the probability of a failed launch must be 0.28. Explain why. (3)

3. State whether each of the following is a decision or a chance event:
   a) choosing between three different new product options
   b) a new product succeeding or failing in the marketplace

   c) good weather on the day of the open air concert
   d) whether to advertise or to cut the price. (4)

4. Explain the difference between an expected value and an actual value. (3)

5. State three advantages and three potential pitfalls of using decision trees. (6)

6. Explain the circumstances in which decision trees are least useful. (4)

7. If the chance of achieving £200,000 is 0.2 and the chance of £20,000 is 0.8, what is the expected value of a decision? (4)

8. Explain how decision trees may help managers to assess the best decision by 'what if?' analysis. (4)

## B. Revision exercises

### DATA RESPONSE 1

Look at the tree diagram below and answer the following questions.

Questions (20 marks; 20 minutes)

1. Calculate the expected values at nodes 1–4. (12)

2. State your decisions at decision points A–C. Indicate your decisions on the tree diagram. (8)

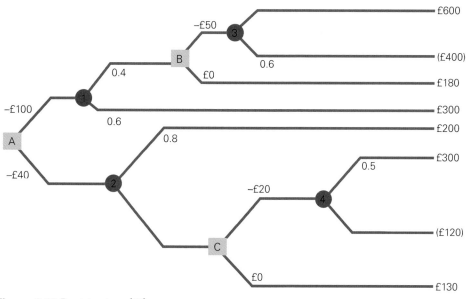

**Figure 8.10** Decision tree (10)

## DATA RESPONSE 2

Denham Potteries has a capital spending budget of £100,000. The production manager has put in a bid for £100,000 for a new tunnel kiln. The marketing manager has countered with a proposal to spend £80,000 on launching a new product. This new product is in line with the firm's objective of diversifying but may be rather risky given the firm's past record of only one success for every five new products.

Ken Coton, the marketing manager, has provided a handy table of figures to summarise the information. This is set out in Table 8.1

**Table 8.1** Denham Potteries

| Outcome | Probability (surplus over next 5 years) | Actual value (£) |
|---|---|---|
| **New product** | | |
| Big success | 0.1 | 900,000 |
| Modest success | 0.1 | 500,000 |
| Failure | 0.8 | 30,000 |
| **Tunnel kiln** | | |
| Success | 0.8 | 200,000 |
| Failure | 0.2 | 60,000 |

### Questions (25 marks; 30 minutes)

1. Draw a fully labelled decision tree to set out the options. (10)

2. What decision should the firm make on purely numerical grounds? (3)

3. Outline the qualitative factors the board should take into account before making the decision. (12)

## DATA RESPONSE 3

Mansfield Town FC is considering buying a South American centre forward player for its team. The club knows statistics show that only one in four overseas forwards succeeds in the lower divisions. But things are desperate. The player's contract will cost £500,000 and, if successful, could increase home attendances sufficiently to be worth £1.2 million over the three-year contract. Even if the player is unsuccessful, income from attendances should rise by £200,000.

### Questions (20 marks; 15 minutes)

1. Draw the decision tree and label it carefully. (12)

2. On the basis of the tree, what decision should the club take? (4)

3. Outline two reasons why the club might decide to proceed. (4)

## C. Extend your understanding

1. Whitbread plc made the brilliant decision in 2000 to move out of the beer market and concentrate on coffee (Costa) and hotels (Holiday Inn). To what extent can decision trees be useful when making long-term strategic decisions such as these? (20)

2. A brilliant fashion designer has been made Chief Executive of Burberry plc. This is a business worth over £1 billion in revenue and in share value. To what extent will the new chief executive's decision-making be improved by using decision trees? (20)

# Chapter 9

# Opportunity cost and trade-offs

Linked to: Understanding the nature and purpose of business, Chapter 1; Decision-making: scientific and intuitive, Chapter 7.

## Definition

Opportunity cost is the cost of missing out on the next best alternative when making a decision. For example, the opportunity cost of not going to university may be to risk missing out on £200,000 of extra lifetime earnings (according to 2013 Government data). Similarly, trade-offs look at what you have to give up in order to get what you want most. They may not easily be expressed as a 'cost' (that is, it may not be possible to quantify them).

## 9.1 Introduction to opportunity cost

This concept will be useful throughout the A-level Business Studies course. It is at the heart of every business decision, from small to multinational companies. Every business faces the same issue: limited resources mean that hiring a marketing manager leaves less money to spend on a marketing campaign. For a start-up business, spending lots of money on a flash opening party means there is less money to pay for staff training.

For a new business the two most important resources are money and time. Both have an opportunity cost. Time spent by an entrepreneur creating a pretty website could mean too little time left for recruiting and training staff, or too little time to sit back and reflect on priorities. The same issue arises with money: it can only be spent once.

It follows that every business decision has an opportunity cost, measured in time, money, and often both. The same is true in other walks of life. A prime minister focused on foreign adventures may lose sight of the key issues affecting people at home. A chancellor who spends an extra £10 billion on education may have to cut back on health care.

For a new business start-up, the most important opportunity cost issues are as follows.

- Do not tie up too much capital in stock (inventory), as this cash could be used more productively elsewhere in the business.
- Do not overstretch yourself: good decisions take time, so make sure you are not doing too much yourself.
- Take care with every decision that uses up cash; at the start of a business it is hard to get more of it, but more is always needed.

## 9.2 Opportunity costs in developing a business idea

### Personal opportunity costs

Starting your first business is likely to be tough. Long hours and highly pressured decisions may cause stress, but the biggest problems go beyond psychology. A difficult cash-flow position is quite normal, yet places a huge strain on the business and its owner(s).

The owner of a first business will probably have come from a background as a salary earner, possibly a very well-paid one. So the first opportunity cost is missing out on the opportunity to earn a regular income. As it could take six months or more to get a business going, this is a long period of financial hardship.

Then comes the investment spending itself, such as the outlay on a lease, on building work, on fixtures and fittings, on machinery and then on the human resources (staff) to make everything work with a human face. All this uses money that could otherwise be used on the proprietor's house, holidays, and so on. The personal opportunity costs add up massively.

Business writers often use the term 'stakeholders', which means all those with a stake in the success or failure of a business. Usually, the key groups are those within the business (internal stakeholders), such as staff, managers and directors; and outside groups (external stakeholders), such as suppliers, customers, bankers and shareholders. In the case of a business start-up, however, there is a whole extra consideration: the wear and tear on the family. Starting a business is a hugely time-consuming and wholly absorbing activity. The restaurant owner might easily spend 80 hours a week on site in the early days, then take further paperwork home. An American business psychologist has said that, 'even when you are home, you're still thinking about the business – it's easy for a spouse to feel neglected, even jealous'.

Despite this, research by a US investment business has shown that, although 32 per cent of new entrepreneurs said that the experience had caused marriage difficulties, 42 per cent of chief executives in fast-growing new firms said that the pressures and exhilarations made their marriages stronger.

'Perpetual devotion to what a man calls his business is only to be sustained by perpetual neglect of many other things.' Robert Louis Stevenson, writer

## 9.3 Deciding between opportunities

Successful business people are those who can make successful decisions. The three founders of innocent Drinks wanted to start a business together, but had no idea what type of business to start. As friends at university they had already run nightclub events together, and two ran an annual music festival in West London. They could have developed a successful festival business, but stumbled upon the idea of a business that made all-fruit smoothies. On finding an investor, in 1999, who could help turn their dream into a reality, they left their salaried jobs, gave up their other business opportunities and concentrated on building the innocent brand. The 2010 sale of a majority of the innocent shares to Coca-Cola for £75 million showed the success of this start-up.

'Alice came to a fork in the road. "Which road do I take?" she asked.

"Where do you want to go?" responded the Cheshire cat.

"I don't know." Alice answered.

"Then" said the cat "it doesn't matter."' Lewis Carroll, *Alice in Wonderland*

When deciding between business start-up opportunities, certain factors are crucial:

## Estimating the potential sales that could be achieved by each idea

This is hugely difficult, both in the short term and – even more – in the longer term. Smoothie maker innocent's first-year sales were £0.4 million. Who could have guessed that, eight years later, its sales would be more than 300 times greater? Yet estimates

### Real business

#### The opportunity costs of developing one business idea as opposed to another

When 30-year-old Mike Clare opened his first Sofa Bed Centre in 1985 he could raise only £16,000 of capital, even though his estimates showed that £20,000 to £25,000 was needed. Fortunately, hard work plus a great first month's sales brought in the cash he needed to get the business going properly. At that time, none of the banks would lend him any money. In the lead-up to Mike Clare's first store opening, he spent time organising public relations events (to get coverage in the local paper), helping with the building work, wrangling with suppliers over credit terms and making decisions about pricing and display. When the store opened, he spent 18 hours a day 'doing everything'. When the first store took £30,000 in month one, he started looking for a second location, which was open within six months. Quite clearly, there was no possibility of starting more than one business at a time.

Later he built up a bedding business called Dreams, which he sold in 2008 for £170 million. Sadly, Dreams collapsed in 2013, in the aftermath of the great recession. Mike Clare, though, had turned £16,000 into £170m. Given how short of money he was at the start, it would have been impossible for him to have chosen to launch two different businesses at the same time. He had to choose one. Fortunately, he chose wisely.

Given the need for focus, the main opportunity cost arises when an entrepreneur has two ideas. One should be chosen and one rejected. This is possible if the entrepreneur is ruthless. After evaluating the two options carefully, the weaker of the two should be stopped completely. The reason is simple: opening one business is tough enough; two would be impossible.

must be made, either by the use of market research, or by using the expertise of the entrepreneur. Mike Clare of Dreams had previously worked as an area manager for a furniture retailer, so he had a reasonable idea about what the sales might be. Inside knowledge is, of course, hard to beat.

## Considering carefully the cash requirements of each idea

The innocent trio were very lucky to find an American investor who put £250,000 into the start of the business in return for a 20 per cent stake. Some new businesses are very hungry for cash (such as setting up a new restaurant in London, which costs over £1 million); other new business ideas (such as a new website) can be started from a back bedroom, keeping initial costs very low.

## Deciding whether the time is right

The innocent brand's launch fitted wonderfully with a time of luxury spending and growing concern about diet. In the same year, a small business started in West London focusing on customising cars: 'souping up' the engines to make the cars go faster and give the engines a 'throaty roar'. As rising fuel prices became a greater concern, the business was squeezed out. Five years before, it might have made a lot of money, but it no longer did so.

## Deciding whether the skills needed fit your own set of skills

Running a restaurant requires a mix of organisational skills, discipline and meticulous attention to detail. Does that describe you? Or are you better suited to running an online business that can be handled in a relaxed way behind the scenes?

## 9.4 Trade-offs

In business there are many occasions when one factor has to be traded off against another. An entrepreneur might get huge help at the start from friends, yet realise that these same friends lack the professionalism to help the business grow. The needs of the business may have to be traded off against the friendships. Can a softie be a real business success? Probably not: some inner toughness is clearly important.

Other trade-offs may include:

- when starting in the first place, trading off the start-up against a year's international travel (perhaps with friends); or trading the start-up against going to university
- trading off the aspects of the business you most enjoy doing against those that prove most profitable for the business. The chef/owner may love cooking yet find the business works far better when she or he has the time to mix with the customers, motivate the waiting staff and negotiate hard with suppliers
- trading off time today and time tomorrow. The entrepreneur's ambition may be to 'retire by the time I'm 40'; that may sound great in the long term but, in the short term, her or his spouse and children may see little of them.

Overall, the key to success will be to be clear about what you and your family want from the business. It may be to become outrageously rich, no matter what, or – more likely – to find a balance between the freedom and independence of running your own business and the need to find time for the family. Books on business success assume that success can be measured only in £1,000,000s. Many people running their own small businesses would tell a different story; the independence alone may be the key to their personal satisfaction.

'Strategy is about making choices, trade-offs; it's about deliberately choosing to be different.' Michael Porter, business author/guru

## Five Whys and a How

| Question | Answer |
|---|---|
| Why is opportunity cost involved in every business decision? | Because every decision commits resources that can then not be used for other things |
| Why might an increase in interest rates be relevant to opportunity cost? | Because spending on assets such as inventories or machinery requires taking cash out of the bank – and the higher the interest rate the higher the opportunity cost of that withdrawal |
| Why might opportunity cost be especially important for a new start-up business? | Because it will almost certainly have little spare capital and even less spare management time – so every wrong decision and every overspend has especially damaging knock-on effects |
| Why is the projected £42.6 billion price of HS2 criticised both for the cost and for the opportunity cost? | The cost is a problem at a time when Britain's fiscal deficit remains huge; the opportunity cost can be measured in potential cutbacks in NHS, education or welfare spending |
| Why is time the ultimate opportunity cost? | Because although it's easy to buy the time of lots of staff, there are usually only a few people in a business who make the important decisions, so their time is very limited and very valuable |
| How might a firm value the opportunity cost of not launching a new product? | Make careful estimates of all the revenues and costs involved in the project, then calculate the potential profit over its lifetime. That's the potential cost of what you're missing out on. |

## Workbook

### A. Revision questions

(20 marks; 20 minutes)

1. Explain in your own words why time is an important aspect of opportunity cost. (3)

2. Give two ways of measuring the opportunity cost to you of doing this homework. (2)

3. Examine one opportunity cost to a restaurant chef/owner of opening a second restaurant. (5)

4. Explain the trade-offs that may exist in the following business situations. Choose the two contexts you feel most comfortable with.

   a) Levi's pushes its workers to produce more pairs of jeans per hour.

   b) A chocolate producer, short of cash, must decide whether to cut its advertising spending or cut back on its research and development into new product ideas.

   c) A football manager decides to double the number of training sessions per week.

   d) A celebrity magazine must decide whether or not to run photos that will generate huge publicity, but probably make the celebrity unwilling to co-operate with the magazine in future. (6)

5. Look at the quote on p. 56. What, according to Robert Louis Stevenson, is the opportunity cost of devotion to business? (4)

# B. Revision exercises

## DATA RESPONSE 1

James Sutton had a job as a marketing manager paying £55,000 a year. His career prospects looked very good, yet he handed in his notice to start up his own online business. He knew that it would take him away from 9-to-5 work and towards the dedication of 8.00 a.m. to 9.00 p.m. If he took on a member of staff, the wage bill would rise by £16,000.

### Questions (15 marks; 15 minutes)

1. Outline three opportunity cost issues within this short passage. (6)

2. Analyse the possible impact on James of the increase in his workload. (9)

## DATA RESPONSE 2

In 2002 a co-operative agreement between coffee farmers in 250 Ugandan villages broke down. It had taken years to put together, but disagreements made it collapse. The prize for a successful co-operative was to produce organic coffee beans grown to Fairtrade standards for partners such as Cafédirect. This would ensure significantly higher prices for the raw coffee beans and also much better credit terms (being paid quickly to help with cash flow).

Over the next two years countless hours of work were put into forming a new co-operative. In early 2004 the new Gumutindo Coffee Co-operative was Fairtrade certified. By 2014 7,000 farmers had joined the Gumutindo Co-operative. They receive a guaranteed price of $1.26 per pound of coffee beans, whereas the world price has been as low as $0.80 over the previous eight years. The extra (and stable) income helps the farmers, of whom only 25 per cent have running water and 79 per cent live in mud huts with iron sheet roofing. The Fairtrade organisation has supported the co-operative in starting up its own production plant, converting the raw coffee into packs of coffee ready for sale. Ongoing investments include motorised pulpers and a major investment in solar panels to create electricity in the home as well as the production plant.

Sources: Adapted from www.fairtrade.org.uk and www.gumutindocoffee.co.uk

### Questions (30 marks; 35 minutes)

1. What would be the opportunity cost of the farmers who put 'countless hours of work into forming a new co-operative'? (4)

2. Explain one risk for the farmers and one risk for the Fairtrade organisation in forming a new co-operative with high guaranteed prices for coffee beans. (6)

3. Some commentators have suggested that Waitrose should make all its coffee 'Fairtrade', therefore getting rid of brands such as Nescafé Gold Blend. Outline the trade-offs Waitrose management would have to consider before making any such decision. (4)

4. To what extent can one be sure that producing coffee ready-for-sale will increase the income levels of the 7,000 members of the co-operative? (16)

# C. Extend your understanding

1. Tesco plc has annual sales of £50 billion and operating profits of over £2 billion a year. To what extent does the leader of such a large business need to consider the concept of opportunity costs? (20)

2. In the 1990s the chairman of Samsung started to send the company's best and brightest young staff to live abroad for a year to learn about American and European lifestyles. Some directors complained that this was a waste of their time and talent. To what extent might the chairman be right to trade off management time against consumer knowledge? (20)

# Chapter 10

# Understanding the role and importance of stakeholders

**Linked to:** Understanding the nature and purpose of business, Chapter 1; External factors affecting business, Chapter 4; Decision-making to improve financial performance, Chapter 44; Decision-making and improved human resources performance, Chapter 52.

## Definition

A stakeholder is an individual or group that has an effect on, and is affected by, the activities of an organisation.

## 10.1 Introduction

All firms come into contact, on a daily basis, with suppliers, customers, the local community and employees. Each of these groups has an impact on the firm's success and at the same time is likely to be affected by any change in its activities. If, for example, the managers decide to expand the business, this may lead to:

- overtime for employees
- more orders for suppliers
- a wider range of products for consumers
- more traffic for the local community.

Groups such as suppliers, employees and the community are known as the firm's stakeholder groups because of their links with the organisation. A stakeholder group both has an effect on and is affected by the decisions of the firm. Each stakeholder group will have its own objectives. The managers of a firm must decide on the extent to which they should change their behaviour to meet these objectives. The belief is that a firm can benefit significantly from co-operating with its stakeholder groups and incorporating their needs into the decision-making process. Examples include:

- giving something back to the community to ensure greater co-operation from local inhabitants whenever the business needs their help; for example, when seeking planning permission for expansion
- treating suppliers with respect and involving them in its plans so that the firm builds up a long-term relationship

'Find the appropriate balance of competing claims by various groups of stakeholders. All claims deserve consideration but some claims are more important than others.' Warren Bennis, business author

Despite the benefits that are evident in a stakeholder approach, many managers believe that an organisation's sole duty is to its investors (that decisions should be made in the best interests of shareholders alone). Generally, this means maximising shareholder value (for example, increasing the share price and the dividends paid to shareholders). Even company directors who instinctively want to serve all the stakeholders often find that day-to-day pressures force them to pay primary concern to shareholders' interests – because shareholders are the only people with the power to get rid of the board of directors.

## 10.2 Stakeholder mapping

In 1991 Professor Mendelow devised a way of analysing the key stakeholders for a specific business. To do this he used the familiar matrix method to measure stakeholder power against stakeholder interest. For instance, if you run a strawberry farm supplying Tesco, your customer may have a huge amount of power over you, but not much interest in you. If you let them down Tesco will walk away and find another supplier. Within this theory there are four stakeholder categories; to help illustrate them, Tesco has been taken as the company whose stakeholders are to be analysed:

- Low power, low interest: such as shareholders with holdings worth less than £750
- Low power, high interest: such as Tesco shopfloor employees
- High power, low interest: such as Tesco's electricity supplier
- High power, high interest: such as the local authorities in Welwyn Garden City (location of Tesco Head Office)

The details of which stakeholders fit which category and what actions the business might take to engage them are given in Figure 10.1:

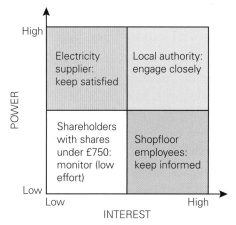

**Figure 10.1** Stakeholder map showing the position of each stakeholder and the action a business might take to engage them

Despite the Tesco examples given above, it may be wrong to generalise at all about stakeholder mapping. The essence of the analysis is to assess the specific circumstances of particular businesses and only then decide which stakeholders fall into which category. So although most small shareholders have little interest in the business they 'own' (beyond the dividend and the share price), external shareholders in a business such as Mulberry might be both fashion-conscious and devoted to the company.

The value of this categorisation is that it helps in setting priorities. As shown in Figure 10.1, the company will work hardest to stay in constant communication with high power, high interest stakeholders.

## 10.3 Overlapping and conflicting stakeholder needs

Certain business circumstances may be to the advantage of all primary stakeholders. If, like Primark, your business concept is working successfully overseas, there are benefits to staff (promotion prospects), the board (bonuses), suppliers, shareholders, financiers and distributors. Even among external shareholders there are potential benefits to Inland Revenue and the wider community. Perhaps the only negative comments might come from environmental pressure groups.

Sadly, this is not often the case. All too often different stakeholders seem unable to stop themselves taking advantage of any weakness in others. In July 2014 Lloyds Bank was fined £105 million by the UK's Financial Conduct Authority and ordered to pay the Bank of England £7.76 million. Lloyds had not only rigged markets but had also deliberately underpaid the British government for help given to keep Lloyds afloat during the tough days in 2009 and 2010. By attempting to benefit its shareholders at the cost of the government and the taxpayer, Lloyds' executives were showing clearly where their stakeholder priorities lay.

'If you look after your customers and you look after your staff then shareholders will do very well . . . If you put shareholder interest – particularly short-term interest – first, you don't create a business.' Ian Gregg, who built Gregg's from one shop to one thousand six hundred.

**Table 10.1** Stakeholder needs in different business circumstances

| Situation | Overlapping stakeholder interests/needs | Conflicting stakeholder interests/needs |
|---|---|---|
| Productivity advance – perhaps coming from new technology | Shareholders, managers and customers | Managers and employees (threats of redundancy) |
| Fashion or weather turns in your favour | Shareholders, managers, suppliers and employees | Perhaps green campaigners |
| Recession: creating a strong reason to cut back capacity | Shareholders and managers | Managers and suppliers, employees and perhaps customers |
| High and rising inflation | Shareholders and managers | Managers and employees; managers and suppliers; managers and retail customers |
| A new proposal is put to shareholders for a huge incentive scheme for directors | The directors of Co A and the directors of other companies (who are Co A's non-executive directors, and like to see high pay) | The directors and the employees; directors and the customers; (possibly) the directors and the shareholders |

## 10.4 Influences on the relationship with stakeholders

One influence is personal conviction; the boss of the business may reject the notion of stakeholders, believing instead that shareholders should be the board's sole focus. If the firm tried to help the local community, for example, this would take funds away from the shareholders. Similarly, more rewards for the owners would mean fewer resources for employees. In the shareholder view, all these different groups are competing for a fixed set of rewards. If one group has a larger slice of the profits it leaves less for others.

Other possible influences on the relationship with stakeholders:

- Financial pressure: if the business is struggling for survival it would be understandable to focus solely on the internal stakeholders – the ones who can help solve the problems.
- The labour market: when jobs are plentiful, staff demand more pay, better working conditions and (sometimes) job redesign to make things more interesting. In these circumstances conflict between managers and workers is easy to conceive.

## 10.5 Managing the relationship with different stakeholders

Over the past ten years a criticism of plcs has been excessive executive pay and the extent to which its growth has outstripped both staff pay rises and dividend payments to shareholders. To manage this situation, directors employ financial public relations experts, i.e. they get the company to pay for a service that only really benefits directors. The ability of the 'PR' to smooth over the problems is an essential test of usefulness.

Arguably, this is quite wrong. A debate between directors and shareholders/owners should take place directly, rather than being mediated through a hired PR. Directors should see the company's money as being different from their own, just as one would hope that a head teacher would treat the school's money as completely separate from personal funds.

Generally, companies will produce websites and will generate publicity that suggests that all stakeholders are treated with equal respect. In the banking sector, the energy sector and in all those *Watchdog* programmes, that view has proven a huge simplification.

'We intend to conduct our business in a way that not only meets but exceeds the expectations of our customers, business partners, shareholders, and creditors, as well as the communities in which we operate and society at large.' Akira Mori, Japanese businessman

## 10.6 Communicating with stakeholders

Today, communicating with stakeholders means electronic communication: a combination of social media, email updates and a website with a 'supplier' section that's as substantial as the customer one. Just as companies talk about employee 'engagement', so they use the same term for 'engagement' of customers when they visit the website. A visit to Unilever's site (www.unilever.co.uk) shows their interest in persuading the outsider to 'follow us on Twitter' and sign up to the Facebook page.

The key issue is whether 'communication' means a two-way process of discussion or whether it's simply a mix of propaganda and public relations. If such communication was open and honest:

- Wouldn't innocent Drinks tell you that it's owned and controlled by Coca-Cola?
- Wouldn't Ben & Jerry's tell you it's owned and controlled by Unilever plc?
- Wouldn't Primark just get on with trying to improve its patchy supply record, instead of making 'Our Ethics' one of four main buttons on its website?

## 10.7 Consulting with stakeholders

Stakeholder mapping is carried out primarily to identify which stakeholders matter most to a company. In most cases, the internal ones are the most important. Yet if a business has allowed things to slip, external groups may become a priority. For example, Primark probably sees external pressure groups as a huge priority, as the business has so often been accused of lacking ethical standards in relation to its supply chain.

Having identified your most important stakeholders, it is then possible to set up regular consultation links and groupings. For Jaguar Land Rover, which buys key drive-chain components from GKN, regular discussions with GKN make sense in relation to future production levels and also new product development plans. Jaguar Land Rover would expect, in turn, to be given early notice of any bright new products GKN is planning, so that they can appear first in a JLR car.

## Five Whys and a How

| Question | Answer |
|---|---|
| Why might it be helpful to a business to use stakeholder mapping? | As part of a process of identifying which of their stakeholders are the most important |
| Why may it be risky for a business to focus solely on shareholder value? | Because the interests of wider stakeholders may be important to the media, as in the example of Primark and its supply chain |
| Why may it be difficult for some firms to communicate effectively with their stakeholders? | Because there's a tension between what a shareholder wants to know about the company and what a pressure group wants to know |
| Why may staff feel that they should be treated as a higher priority than other stakeholders? | Because the staff are actually the heart of the enterprise. It's like football fans and football managers – the latter come and go but the former are there for the long term |
| Why might a new small company treat customers as their only key stakeholder? | Because the business will stand or fall on repeat purchase and word of mouth from those customers |
| How might a large clothing retailer establish effective consultation with its stakeholders? | It would be hard because there are potentially so many of them. Perhaps get two representatives from each stakeholder group – then meet regularly (every two months?) |

## Evaluation: Understanding the role and importance of stakeholders

In recent years, there has been much greater interest in the idea that firms should pay attention to their social responsibilities. Increasingly, firms are being asked to consider, and justify, their actions towards a wide range of groups rather than just their shareholders. Managers are expected to take into account the interests and opinions of numerous internal and external groups before they make a decision. This social responsibility often makes good business sense. If you ignore your stakeholder groups you are vulnerable to pressure group action and may well lose customers and your brightest employees.

It may not be possible to meet the needs of all interest groups, however. Firms must decide on the extent to which they take stakeholders into account. Given their limited resources and other obligations, managers must decide on their priorities. In difficult times it may well be that the need for short-term profit overrides the demands of various stakeholder groups. It would be naive to ignore the fact that TV consumer programmes such as the BBC's *Watchdog* keep exposing business malpractice. Even if progress is being made in general, there are still many firms that persist in seeing short-term profit as the sole business objective.

## Key terms

**Pressure group:** a group of people with a common interest who try to further that interest (for example, Greenpeace).

**Shareholder:** an owner of a company.

**Shareholder value:** a term widely used by company chairmen and chairwomen, which means little more than the attempt to maximise the company's share price.

**Social responsibilities:** duties towards stakeholder groups, which the firm may or may not accept.

**Stakeholder:** an individual or group that affects and is affected by an organisation.

**Supply chain:** all the contractors, sub-contractors and delivery businesses involved in getting supplies/components to your factory/business.

'Companies, to date, have often used the excuse that they are only beholden to their shareholders, but we need shareholders to think of themselves as stakeholders in the well-being of the society.' Simon Mainwaring, businessman

# Workbook

## A. Revision questions

(40 marks; 40 minutes)

1. What is meant by a 'stakeholder'? (2)

2. Distinguish between internal and external stakeholders. (3)

3. Some people believe that an increasing number of firms are now trying to meet their social responsibilities. Explain why this may be the case. (3)

4. Outline two responsibilities a firm may have to:
   a) its employees (4)
   b) its customers (4)
   c) the local community. (4)

5. Explain how a firm could damage its profits in the pursuit of meeting its shareholder responsibilities. (4)

6. Explain why a firm's profit may fall by meeting its stakeholder responsibilities. (4)

7. Some managers reject the idea of stakeholding. They believe that a company's duty is purely to its shareholders. Outline two points in favour and two points against this opinion. (8)

8. What factors are likely to determine whether a firm accepts its responsibilities to a particular stakeholder group? (4)

## B. Revision exercises

### DATA RESPONSE

**Market Basket and stakeholder objectives**

**Figure 10.2** Employees and customers hold a rally in support of Arthur T. DeMoulas and Market Basket, in Tewksbury, Massachusetts, on 25 July 2014.

A protest by thousands of workers at one of New England's largest grocery chains has left store shelves empty and customers scarce as employees demand the return of their fired chief executive. The turmoil is the latest twist in a decades-old feud among members of the DeMoulas family, whose DeMoulas Super Markets Inc. controls 71 Market Basket stores across the North-East of America.

On 23 June, Arthur S. DeMoulas, whose side of the family controls 50.5 percent of shares, fired his cousin, President and Chief Executive Officer Arthur T. DeMoulas, whose side controls 49.5 percent, and replaced him with two co-CEOs (chief executives). Many of the 25,000 employees rose up in support of "Artie T.", who they say is committed to high wages for staff and low prices for customers. Starting wages at Market Basket of $12 an hour are $4 above the minimum wage. Furthermore customers enjoy prices of around 20 per cent below those of rival supermarkets. Kevin Levesque, 53, assistant manager at the Tewksbury store, said his colleagues worry that their compensation won't be nearly as generous in the future. 'They know the changes will come,' he said. 'They have seen it in other companies and businesses in corporate America.'

A groundswell of popular support has followed, with rallies attended by thousands. The protests have been attended by customers as well as staff, especially since eight of the protest leaders were sacked by the new CEOs.

Amid the acrimony within the family, Market Basket has made the various DeMoulas shareholders wealthy. The company has paid out more than $1.1 billion in special dividends since 2001, according to 2013 legal documents. The richest among the family is the ousted Arthur T., who is worth $675 million through his 19 per cent stake and accumulated dividends. Arthur S. is worth about $575 million.

Source: adapted from Bloomberg.com.

### Questions (30 marks; 30 minutes)

**1.** Explain the conflicting objectives among Market Basket's stakeholders. (5)

**2.** For workers to risk their own jobs to protest in favour of a business leader is unprecedented in recent business history in America or Britain. Explain why the situation at Market Basket may be so rare. (9)

**3.** To what extent might the sacking of Arthur T. prove right in the long term from the perspective of the majority shareholders in the company? (16)

## C. Extend your understanding

**1.** 'Meeting the objectives of different stakeholder groups may be desirable but it is rarely profitable.' To what extent do you agree with this view? (20)

**2.** 'A manager's responsibility should be to the shareholders alone.' To what extent do you agree with this view? (20)

# Chapter 11 Marketing and decision-making

**Linked to:** Decision-making: scientific and intuitive, Chapter 7; Setting marketing objectives, Chapter 13; Market research, Chapter 15; Market data and analysis, Chapter 18.

## Definition

Marketing can be seen either as a way of thinking or as a range of activities. For most modern businesses, marketing is focusing the goals and strategies of the business on an identified market opportunity.

**Figure 11.1** Marketing decision-making: the marketing model

## 11.1 Making marketing decisions

In most firms, marketing is at the heart of the decisions taken by the directors. Not marketing in the sense of price cuts and promotions, but marketing in the sense of analysing growth trends and the competitive struggle within the firm's existing markets, and decisions about which markets the firm wishes to develop in future. Effective marketing decisions stem from a process known as the marketing model. It sets out how to tackle a marketing decision methodically.

### Marketing decision-making: the marketing model

Successful marketing is not just about thinking. It is about decisions and action. Marketing decisions are particularly hard to make, because there are so many uncertainties. The procedure shown in Figure 11.1 is one of the most effective ways of ensuring a decision is well thought through.

The intention is to ensure that the strategy decided upon is the most effective at achieving the marketing objectives. In this process, market research is likely to be very important. It is crucial for finding out the background data and again for testing the hypotheses. Test marketing may also be used. This is a way of checking whether the market research results are accurate, before finally committing the firm to an expensive national marketing campaign.

The marketing model is the way to decide how to turn a marketing objective into a strategy.

## 11.2 Developments in technology and marketing decisions

In 2014 a social media consultancy boasted that research among 2500 global marketers showed that 34 per cent believed that marketing through social media delivers a positive return on investment. Logically then, 66 per cent doubted that spending on social media was profitable. Why may this be? Part of the problem is embodied in the idea of Facebook 'Likes' or Twitter 'Followers'. Do Starbucks' 6.38 million followers become more loyal to the brand because they signed up to Twitter? No one is quite sure.

Profitable or not, the wind is blowing strongly in the direction of digital marketing. In 2013 UK business spending on social media advertising rose by 71 per cent to £588 million, with the growth in mobile advertising being the most dynamic. For the market as a whole Figure 11.2 shows that UK spending on mobile digital advertising is forecast to overtake spending on TV advertising airtime by 2016, partly at the cost of newspapers and magazines.

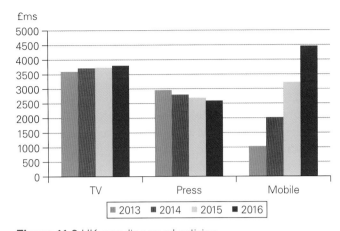

£ms

**Figure 11.2** UK spending on advertising

Source: *eMarketer* magazine, June 2014

---

### Real business

In 2014, with coffee sales stalling in America, Starbucks decided to broaden its appeal from its target of young professional adults. Parents started to notice their teenage and pre-teen kids showing newfound enthusiasm for Starbucks' 13,000 US outlets. The company had started selling a 'secret menu' of drinks that had gone viral via posts on Instagram and other social media. Only those in the know would think to ask for a 'Grasshopper Frap' or a 'Cotton Candy Frap'. One parent reported that when her tweenaged daughter asked for a Cotton Candy Frap, the shocking pink drink was served with a knowing wink. The thrill of posting a pic to her mates seemed to make up for the vile taste. Apparently McDonald's and others are playing with the secret menu concept after Starbucks' success.

---

## 11.3 The use of social media

The use of social media has become a serious alternative to standard press or TV advertising. There are three important benefits to firms from this form of digital marketing:

- The targeting can be especially tightly targeted at the precise tastes and habits of each individual, including noting changes in their behaviour such as when they move from home to University
- Traditional advertising was a one-way process from company to customer. Social media provide the interactivity that may help create some bonding between consumer and brand

- The success of crowdfunding sites such as Kickstarter shows that people are interested in getting involved in businesses, as long as they share the apparent aspirations of the proprietors. This, again, helps create a two-way bond.

From the above come two key benefits. First, social media can provide a way to gain a fuller understanding of what customers really love about the brand and the product range. In other words it can help you gain a fuller understanding of customers and the market you are serving. In the past this was attempted through market research, but the interactions between company and customer now have the potential to be much richer. When innocent Drinks recently introduced their first grass-covered van into Ireland, they asked their social media followers to suggest a name. 'LamborGreeny' was one of many suggestions. The campaign, which also ran in the UK, achieved over 1.4 million impressions for @innocentIreland.

**Figure 11.3** innocent tweets: #NameTheVan

The second benefit is derived from the first. Stronger relationships between consumer and brand can cement brand loyalty and, in the long run, there are few more valuable attributes than that. For innocent, fighting directly in a Coca-Cola (innocent) versus PepsiCo (Tropicana) battle over the relatively undifferentiated UK market in orange juice, customer loyalty is especially valuable.

---

'Profit comes from repeat customers, customers that boast about your product and service, and that bring friends with them.' W. Edwards Deming, quality guru

---

For companies, the ultimate question is whether spending on social media provides a sufficient return on the money spent. Although this question cannot be answered satisfactorily by most companies, they feel that they are better off being 'in' than 'out'. The company that ignores the digital, online world may become the Morrisons' of its own sector.

**Figure 11.4** Logic chain: traditional vs. online advertising

## 11.4 Relationship marketing

Often known as CRM (Customer Relationship Marketing), the idea is to use the storage capacity of modern IT to be able to build an apparent relationship between consumer and producer. In the past the nearest that could be achieved was to use a database to address letters to customers individually ('Dear Ian…'). Today there are many ways to achieve the same result, starting with what you see the next time you access your computer screen. Without you necessarily realising, the advertisement has been tailored to your tastes and habits; so has the junk mail that comes to your inbox.

'Consumers are statistics. Customers are people.' H. Stanley Marcus, businessman

Software provider Sage promotes its CRM software by saying: 'Make every customer interaction count'. This starts by making sure that there is a central record of all customer contacts, so that any manager can know at any time about past problems or successes (and key facts, such as last year's agreed price deals). The database recording all this knowledge about customers can then be interrogated to decide who might be in the market for this or that newly developed product.

Over time, the idea is to build a relationship with your own customers that makes them feel sufficiently special to stay. In effect, each business is trying to raise the barrier to customer exit. Many businesses believe that it costs five times more to get a new customer than to hold onto an existing one. This is the basis for continuous, heavy investment in CRM. Clever companies put their best sales staff onto their top-spending customers, and make sure that the processes involved in giving high customer satisfaction are all working to the highest possible standard.

'Your most unhappy customers are your greatest source of learning.' Bill Gates, founder of Microsoft

## 11.5 Dynamic pricing

In July 2014 the chairman of Center Parcs explained that the company no longer has a price list. The whole business works on 'dynamic pricing', i.e. prices move continually, in line with changes in supply and demand. If a local TV programme features the Sherwood Forest Center Parcs, demand might rise for the forthcoming half-term; Center Parc's computer software will detect the change instantly and push prices up. The computers are programmed to achieve a 97 per cent usage rate – every week of the year. The higher the price they can get for their space the better. That's dynamic pricing.

**Table 11.1** The impact of different supply and demand conditions on price

|  | Supply down | Supply the same | Supply up |
|---|---|---|---|
| **Demand up** | Price up sharply | Price up | Price unchanged |
| **Demand stays the same** | Price up | Price stays the same | Price down |
| **Demand down** | Price stays the same | Price down | Price down sharply |

Table 11.1 shows the impacts of different supply and demand conditions upon the price of Center Parc holidays (or any other commodity).

The strength of dynamic pricing is that it can achieve high capacity utilisation without requiring banks of skilled staff. No wonder that the same method is used by the low-cost airlines, the rail companies and all the major hotel chains.

# 11.6 Ethical influences on marketing decisions

In recent years much has been written and said about marketing ethics, especially by companies. They put forward the idea that modern firms are socially responsible in their dealings with consumers (and suppliers). In many cases this may be true, but not in all. When observing companies it is hard to know which is better, their intentions or their PR (public relations).

Ethical marketing requires an honest, open mindset and the willingness to sacrifice profit where it is incompatible with morality. This is hard even for small businesses, but may simply be asking too much within large corporations.

'It horrifies me that ethics is an optional extra at Harvard Business School.' Sir John Harvey-Jones, former boss, ICI

## Ethical marketing

Companies today know that boxes have to be ticked: recycling, tick; Fairtrade, tick; low in saturated fats, tick. Because there are so many possible positives a company can use in its packaging and marketing, it simply chooses the ones that happen to score most highly with customers. This is all to do with marketing and nothing to do with ethics.

What of the companies with a conscience, though? Perhaps innocent Drinks with its naïf logo and its talk of doing good? But as it's now owned and controlled by Coca-Cola, few would believe that innocent is a haven of goodness within a multinational that struggles to define itself as a good corporate citizen.

What influences marketing decisions is not ethics but social trends. In other words, companies are desperate to present themselves as moral and responsible, as long as the consumer cares. The problem is that consumers are better at saying they care than they are at acting accordingly. Primark has been associated many times with exploitative terms and conditions for workers at its Far Eastern suppliers but its profit and sales growth figures suggest that low prices trump ethics. Needless to say there are small, niche producers who can command premium prices for their ethically sourced goods but this may simply be clever rather than ethical marketing.

## Real business

Feeling unwell? Very unwell? Are you willing to pay $1,000 per pill for a cure? By the way, the cure requires 12 weeks of treatment, so that'll be $84,000, please. That was the price being charged for Sovaldi in August 2014 – a patented new drug that has a 90 per cent success rate at treating hepatitis C. And this condition represents quite a market, with 3.2 million suffers in America. So the potential market size is 3.2m x $84,000 = $268.8bn.

Nobody imagines that the production cost per pill is as high as $1,000 (after all, brand owner Gilead sells the same pills for $11 each in Egypt), so how can Gilead be so greedy as to price the pills at $1,000 each? The answer is that they charge that much because they can. The alternative treatment for hepatitis C is a liver transplant. These usually cost at least $145,000 in American hospitals. So Sovaldi is a cheaper alternative. The US stock market has recognised the strength of Gilead's position, bidding up the value of its shares to total $143bn. This is business; real business, and marketing ethics seem a long way away.

Source: Adapted from *Financial Times* 1 August 2014

'To know what is right and not to do it is the worst cowardice.' Confucius (551-479 BC) Chinese philosopher

## Environmental marketing

The household cleaner Domestos has long announced its purpose through the advertising line: 'Kills germs – dead!' Thoughtfully, though, its website now has a homepage tab on 'Sustainable Cleaning'. No one should doubt that Domestos is the same powerful chemical it always was – and it will be flushed down drains near you – but brand owner Unilever knows it must take into account those interested in the environment.

Far away from that example comes the longstanding but still excellent case of the Toyota Prius. Toyota started developing the Prius when oil/petrol prices were low and persisted with the car for more than ten years before it made any profit. It was an act of faith by the company in a cleaner future and, of course, in Toyota's position at the heart of that future. Overall, it is hard to see the company's actions as anything other than environmentally (and ethically) sound.

When analysing a company that markets itself as environmentally conscious, it is important to consider whether it is 'greenwash' (a green gloss coat over an empty shell) or a genuine attempt to behave responsibly. It would be impressive if the business went ahead with green actions that it felt no need to boast about. And impressive if those actions added to costs (though no one can expect a business to make itself uncompetitive – risking its survival).

## Five Whys and a How

| Question | Answer |
|---|---|
| Why might it be helpful to 'form hypotheses' when making a marketing decision (see Figure 11.1)? | In effect they are the alternative strategy options that can then be tested in research or in a test market |
| What might be the effect on press media of the fall in advertising revenue forecast in Figure 11.2? | It might either force magazines to increase their cover prices or – more probably – force some to cut staffing and others to close down |
| Why might a business decide to double the budget it allocates to relationship marketing? | Perhaps because benchmarked data shows that the business is performing relatively poorly at customer loyalty |
| Why might customers prefer traditional static pricing to dynamic pricing? | Because they can look up prices on a rate card that shows the apparent 'value' of the item; dynamic pricing means today's price is different from yesterdays, which might be unsettling |
| Why does a rise in demand push prices up (in a dynamic market)? | The hike in demand shows that the available supply can be sold more easily; instead of selling everything at low prices, the computer programme pushes prices up (to ration the supply) |
| How might a consumer be taken in by 'greenwash'? | A customer might trust that the product is especially environmentally friendly when it is no better than rival products – just more cleverly advertised or packaged |

## Key terms

**Benchmarked data** is information on how well one company is performing compared with its peers/competitors, e.g. on customer complaints per 100 sales.

**Test market:** trialling a new product in an area of the country to get feedback on real sales in the real world.

## Evaluation: Marketing and decision-making

Good marketing decisions are made by executives who use logical frameworks such as the marketing model. A former boss of Apple Inc. once said, though, that 'no great marketing decisions have ever been made on quantitative data'. In other words, great decisions require intuition and an understanding of consumer psychology (qualitative data). In the case of Apple, the launch of the iPad was a perfect example.

Another feature of a great decision is that it should not work in the short term but come unstuck further on.

This is why it's so foolish to market products in a less-than-honest manner. At present Coca-Cola is being 'clever' in pretending that innocent Drinks is still a small, quirky company. Eventually people will realise that this is pretty dishonest. The company is just a division of Coca-Cola – and there might be quite a backlash when people realise this. As business guru Robert Townsend wrote 50 years ago: 'Try honesty. . . it really works'.

# Workbook

## A. Revision questions

**(35 marks; 35 minutes)**

1. Outline two ways in which a company using the marketing model might 'test the options'. (4)

2. In September 2014 Coca-Cola launched Coke Life in a green can. How might the company judge whether this was the right decision? (5)

3. Explain why digital advertising might be especially cost-effective at reaching target consumers. (5)

4. Why might innocent Drinks want to build a stronger relationship with its customers? (4)

5. In your own words, explain the meaning of the term 'dynamic pricing'. (3)

6. A teacher complained to the chairman of Centre Parcs that 'holidays with you are too expensive in the holidays'. Explain one reason for and one reason against her argument. (6)

7. Is the price of a commodity likely to rise or fall when:

    **a)** supply rises while demand is unchanged? (1)

    **b)** demand falls while supply rises? (1)

    **c)** supply is unchanged but demand rises? (1)

8. Is it ethical to advertise Wall's Funny Feet ice cream on children's TV? (5)

## B. Revision exercises

### DATA RESPONSE

**Figure 11.5** New product launch: Mars Caramel

The Mars Bar was launched over 80 years ago, created in his kitchen by Frank Mars in 1923. Sold in America as Milky Way (and still is), when it came to Britain in 1932 the decision was made to call it the Mars bar. (Astonishingly, when it started in Britain it was covered in Cadbury chocolate as the new Mars factory at Slough was not yet able to make high quality chocolate.)

The Mars bar has been a fabulous financial success, helping to build the still family-run Mars business to a global turnover of $30 billion by 2011. Nevertheless, sales in Britain have been struggling for the last few years. Whereas customers can kid themselves that an Aero or a packet of Maltesers is a 'light' snack, a Mars always seems a piggy option. In 2011 the whole chocolate confectionery market rose by 2.1 per cent, but sales of Mars bars fell by 0.7 per cent. Nevertheless, with annual sales of £92.6 million, Mars bars still represented a huge, profitable brand.

In September 2012 Mars decided on a new way to boost sales. It came from a successful US test of 'Milky Way Caramel', in effect taking the sludgy bit out of the Mars, leaving just the chocolate and the caramel centre. Given that Mars already marketed Galaxy Caramel over here, it was hard to see where the 'room' was in the market for the new Mars product, which was launched in the UK in September 2012. But Mars had investigated that issue using extensive market research.

Mars marketed Mars Caramel by emphasising that it has 20 per cent fewer calories than the Mars bar. This was expected to make it appeal more to women. But wouldn't consumers simply think: why am I paying the same as a Mars bar for a Mars bar with no 'nougat' centre? If so, they would surely see it as bad value, or even as a 'rip-off'. Mars had to handle the promotion of this new product with great care, steering a path between different ethical issues.

In September 2013 Mars announced that they were re-launching Mars Caramel as an 8-week Limited Edition product supported by a £2.8 million marketing budget. They commented on 'the overwhelming popularity of the original launch'.

**Questions (25 marks; 30 minutes)**

**1.** Examine how Mars might have made its decision to go ahead with the launch of Mars Caramel. (8)

**2.** Explain two 'different ethical issues' in the launch of Mars Caramel. (8)

**3.** Analyse the possible determinants of whether Mars Caramel proves a success in the long term. (9)

## C. Extend your understanding

**1.** To what extent do you agree that Arsenal F.C. should abandon their current static pricing model (including season tickets) and switch entirely to dynamic pricing for each home game? (By all means substitute your favourite/local football team.) (20)

**2.** 'It's time for a brand such as Cadbury's Dairy Milk to abandon traditional TV and press media and spend their whole advertising budget on digital and social media.' To what extent do you agree? (20)

# Chapter 12 Marketing and competitiveness

**Linked to:** Understanding markets, Chapter 14; Market research, Chapter 15; Segmentation, targeting and positioning, Chapter 19; Marketing mix: the 7 Ps, Chapter 21.

### Definition

Competitiveness measures a firm's ability to offer a better combination of price and quality than its rivals.

## 12.1 Introduction: What is a competitive market?

In the past, markets were physical places where buyers and sellers met in person to exchange goods. Street markets are still like that. Today, some markets are virtual, such as eBay.

Some markets are more competitive than others. The number of firms operating influences the intensity of competition; the more firms there are, the greater the level of competition. However, the respective size of the firms operating in a market should also be taken into account. A market consisting of 50 firms may not be particularly competitive, if, for instance, one of the firms holds a 60 per cent market share and the remaining 40 per cent is shared between the other 49 firms. Similarly, a market with just four firms could be quite competitive because the firms operating within this market may be of a fairly similar size.

Consumers enjoy competitive markets. However, the reverse is true for firms, as prices and profit margins tend to be squeezed. As a result, firms try hard to minimise competition, perhaps by creating a unique selling point (USP) or using predatory pricing.

It could be argued that marketing is vital no matter what the level of competition is within the market. Firms that fail to produce goods and services that satisfy the needs of the consumers will find it hard to succeed in the long term.

'Competition brings out the best in products and the worst in people.' David Sarnoff, US business leader

## 12.2 Market conditions and competition

### One dominant business

In some markets there is no competition because there is only one business operating. This is called a monopoly. The UK market for chewing gum is close to this position, as Wrigley has a 90 per cent market share. For an example of a total monopoly, look at the situation of Virgin Rail – the sole supplier of rail travel between London and Manchester. Monopolies are bad for consumers because they restrict output, pushing up prices and restricting consumer choice. For this reason governments have legal powers to regulate against monopoly power.

Deciding whether or not a firm has a monopoly is a far from straightforward task. First of all, the market itself has to be accurately defined. Camelot has a monopoly to run the National Lottery, but there are many other forms of gambling, such as horse racing and the football pools. So is Camelot really in a dominant market position? Second, national market share figures should not be used in isolation because some firms enjoy local monopolies.

Firms implement their marketing strategy through the marketing mix. In markets dominated by a single large business, firms do not need to spend heavily on promotion because consumers are, to a degree, captive. Prices can be pushed upwards and the product element of the marketing mix can be focused on creating innovations that make it harder for new entrants to break into the market. Apple spends millions of dollars on research and development in order to produce cutting-edge products such as the iPhone 6 (see Figure 12.1). To ensure that Apple maintains its dominant market position new product launches are patented to prevent me-too imitations from being launched by the competition.

**Figure 12.1** iPhone 6

## Competition amongst a few giants

The UK supermarket industry is a good example of a market that is dominated by a handful of very large companies. Economists call markets like this oligopolistic. The rivalry that exists within such markets can be intense. Firms know that any gains in market share will be at the expense of their rivals. The actions taken by one firm affect the profits made by the other firms that compete within the same market.

In markets made up of a few giants, firms tend to focus on non-price competition when designing the marketing mix. Firms in these markets tend to be reluctant to compete by cutting price. They fear that the other firms in the industry will respond by cutting their prices too, creating a costly price war where no firm wins.

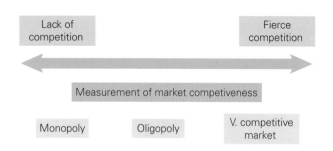

**Figure 12.2** Degree of competition

## The fiercely competitive market

Fiercely competitive markets can also be fragmented, made up of hundreds of relatively small firms, each of which competes actively against the others. In some of these markets competition is amplified by the fact that firms sell near-identical products, called commodities.

Commodities are products, such as flour, sugar or memory sticks, that are hard to differentiate. Rivalry in commodity markets tends to be intense. In markets such as this, firms have to manage their production costs very carefully because the retail price is the most important factor in determining whether the firm's product sells or not. If a firm cannot cut its costs, it will not be able to cut its prices without cutting into profit margins. Without price cuts market share is likely to be lost.

In fiercely competitive markets firms will try, where possible, to create product differentiation. For example, the restaurant market in Croydon, Surrey, is extremely competitive. There are over 70 outlets within a two-mile radius of the town centre. To survive without having to compete solely on price, firms in markets like this must regularly find new innovations because points of differentiation are quickly copied.

'Without competitors there would be no need for strategy.' Kenichi Ohmae, Japanese business guru

## 12.3 How marketing decisions may help improve competitiveness

To be competitive, a brand must have a close fit with consumers' tastes and habits. In the period 2009–2014 Coca-Cola found its sales slipping in America and Europe as people turned away from fizzy soft drinks. So in 2014 it launched Coke Life with the proposition: same Coke, fewer calories. If it succeeds it will be by having understood what modern consumers want – and by finding the right market positioning and image to make people want to try it, then buy it regularly. Every aspect of the proposition was researched with care, from the green pack colour to the careful advertising messages (which never mentioned diet or health).

The most important marketing decision concerns positioning: where exactly does the brand fit into the market? If this is achieved successfully, the brand can acquire a clarity or even a personality that makes it easy for consumers to identify with. If the marketing company can get consumers to want to buy a product because of its image, that's perhaps the ultimate business achievement. Some men want to own a BMW because they think the image (successful, sporty) makes them look good; some women want a Chanel bag because it speaks of their classiness and their success. BMW and Chanel charge premium prices almost as a confirmation of their customers' good taste and deep pockets. The result, of course, is huge profit margins for the companies. Chanel's net profit margins of 32 per cent compare with 6 per cent for Mercedes and less than 5 per cent for Tesco and Sainsbury's.

In addition to market positioning, the following are important ways in which marketing can boost competitiveness.

## Design

Some firms are highly competitive because they sell products that have been differentiated by their design. In countries such as the UK, where wage rates are relatively high, manufacturers cannot compete on price alone. Production costs are too high compared with rivals in countries where wage rates are lower. By using design as a USP, British manufacturers can compete on quality rather than price, making them less vulnerable to competition from China and India. Good-looking design can add value to a product. For example, the BMW Mini relies upon its retro 1960s styling to command its price premium within the small car market.

## Brand image

In many markets brand image is crucial. The results of blind tests indicate that, in many cases, consumers are unable to tell the difference between supermarket own-label products and premium-priced brands. Clever branding and advertising may be the only thing ensuring that Stella Artois carries on outselling Tesco's Premium Lager.

## Marketing mix

To pull the marketing strategy together, businesses look to their marketing mix. This is the combination of marketing variables that turns an idea into a practical reality. That is, setting the right price, for the correctly designed product, promoted correctly and distributed in the right places to reach the target market. When this is done with intelligence and creativity (as with the launch of the Samsung Galaxy and the launch of the Sony PS4) the result can be such a highly competitive proposition that rivals struggle to keep up. Six months after launching its Xbox One, Microsoft had to cut its price by $100 to keep up with the all-conquering PS4.

'Competitive advantage is based, not on doing what others already do well, but on doing what others cannot do as well.' Professor John Kay, economist and writer

## Five Whys and a How

| Question | Answer |
|---|---|
| Why is it hard to compete in a crowded commodity market such as a basic gents' hairdresser? | Because if differentiation is minimal the only way to compete is price, so even though costs are squeezed to the minimum there may be little or no profit |
| Why is market positioning so important? | Because products succeed best when they have a distinct image/'personality' that fits in with customers' psychology and habits |
| Why do customers lose out when a firm has a monopoly position? | The company can push prices up yet cut spending on service and innovation to boost its profit at the expense of customers |
| Why do some firms seem to be able to sustain their competitiveness over many years? | Often, as with Heinz, it's because of a traditional, strong brand and slow-moving markets; with a business such as Sony it's hard to keep coming up with killer innovations |
| Why was Apple able to gain a net profit margin of 22 per cent in 2014? | Because of the hugely competitive nature of its brand image and the clear positioning of its design-led products |
| How might a firm's people affect its competitiveness? | Internally, the key decision-makers are middle-managers who need to work collaboratively; externally, the enthusiasm and efficiency of staff can rub off onto customers |

## Key terms

**Non-price competition:** rivalry based on factors other than price (for example, advertising, sales promotions or 'new improved' products).

**Predatory pricing:** when a large company sets prices low with the deliberate intention of driving a weaker rival out of business.

**USP:** a point of genuine difference that makes one product stand out from the crowd (for example, the Toyota Prius's 'hybrid synergy drive').

## Evaluation: Marketing and competitiveness

Competitiveness is a much wider issue than marketing. It is affected by the quality of the design and build of the products, and by the enthusiasm of the staff. These are clearly operations and personnel issues. Nevertheless, marketing is at the heart of competitiveness for many firms. Mars knows how to produce Galaxy chocolate, so the key to the firm's success next year is how well the brand can be marketed. The managers must understand the customers, and then have the wisdom and the creativity to find a way to make the product stand out.

# Workbook

## A. Revision questions

**(30 marks; 30 minutes)**

1. What is a competitive market? (2)

2. Explain how the marketing mix of Virgin Trains could be affected by a decision by government to allow other train-operating companies to compete on Virgin's routes. (3)

3. Consider the following:
   **a)** what is a price war and … (3)
   **b)** why are they rare? (3)

4. Explain why product differentiation becomes more important as competition within a market increases. (3)

5. Identify four factors that could be used to identify whether or not a business is competitive. (4)

6. How could the size of an organisation affect its efficiency? (3)

7. UK sales of Tropicana fruit juices have struggled in recent years as Coca-Cola's innocent juices have gained market share. Outline two marketing methods Tropicana might adopt to rebuild its competitiveness. (6)

8. Apart from market research, how may a firm achieve its goal of attempting to get closer to the consumer? (3)

## B. Revision exercises
### DATA RESPONSE 1

**Tesco's £9 toaster**

The prices of consumer electronics, including toasters, satellite TV set-top boxes and MP3 players, have tumbled in recent years. So, why have the prices of these goods fallen? In part, the price falls reflect the falling price of the components that go into consumer electronics. Low prices also reflect the fact that there is now more competition in the market. In the past, consumers typically bought items such as TVs and computers from specialist

retailers such as Currys and Dixons. Today, the situation is somewhat different: in addition to these specialist retailers, consumers can now buy electrical goods over the internet and from supermarkets. Industry analysts also believe that some of the supermarket chains are using set-top boxes and DVD players as loss leaders.

In today's ultra-competitive environment, manufacturers of consumer electronics face intense pressure from retailers to cut costs so that retail prices can be cut without any loss of profit margin. To cut prices without compromising product quality, manufacturers such as the Dutch giant Philips have transferred production from the Netherlands to low-cost locations such as China.

## Questions (30 marks; 35 minutes)

1. Describe three characteristics of a highly competitive market. (6)

2. Explain one reason why the market for consumer electronics has become more competitive. (4)

3. How could the degree of competition impact the marketing mix used by a Chinese manufacturer of own-label toasters? (4)

4. In today's increasingly competitive market for consumer electronics, firms must constantly cut costs and prices if they are to survive. To what extent do you agree? (16)

## DATA RESPONSE 2

At the beginning of the 1960s Indian food was a niche market business: there were just 500 Indian restaurants in the whole of the UK. As Table 12.1 illustrates, in the two decades that followed, the UK Indian restaurant market grew at a spectacular rate. In more recent times the market has continued to grow; however, the rate of growth has declined. Today, the Indian restaurant market is firmly established. The industry is one of Britain's largest, employing over 60,000 people.

**Table 12.1** Number of Indian restaurants in the UK

| Year | No. of restaurants | Market growth rate (%) |
|------|--------------------|------------------------|
| 1960 | 500 | – |
| 1970 | 1200 | 140 |
| 1980 | 3000 | 150 |
| 1990 | 5100 | 70 |
| 2000 | 7940 | 56 |
| 2004 | 8750 | 10 |
| 2010 | 8900 | 2 |
| 2014 | 10000 | 12 |

The Indian restaurant market is made up of thousands of small, independent operators. In most British high streets there are several Indian restaurants that compete aggressively against one another. Indian food is very popular: over 23 million portions of Indian food are sold in restaurants each year. Over the years, growing affluence boosted takings and profits at most Indian restaurants. Most owners chose to use some of the profit to upgrade their facilities. Gradually, Indian restaurants became more sophisticated (for example, air conditioning and with dinner-jacketed waiters).

As more Indian restaurants opened up, however, too many looked the same and had very similar menus. As a result, they were forced into competing against

each other on price. Intense price competition led to falling profit margins. Indian restaurateurs began to realise the importance of product differentiation as a competitive weapon. The first real attempt to create differentiation occurred when a handful of forward-looking Indian restaurants, such as the Gaylord in Mortimer Street, London, imported tandoors. A tandoor is a special type of oven made from clay that gives the food cooked inside it a distinctive taste. Restaurants using tandoor ovens found that they could charge slightly higher prices without emptying their restaurants. Today, Indian restaurants use a variety of tactics to compete, including those listed below.

- Décor and design: in recent times several now famous London-based Indian restaurants, such as the Cinnamon Club (opened at a cost of £2.6 million in the Old Westminster Library) ditched the old-style traditional Indian restaurant décor in favour of a more upmarket-looking, modern design. This change inspired many other Indian restaurants up and down the land to upgrade their fixtures and fittings in the hope that they too could charge Cinnamon Club-style premium prices.
- Exotic-sounding premium-priced menu items: for example, Sea Bass Kaylilan prepared with fenugreek and tamarind.

Other restaurants have adopted a different approach. For example, the Khyber in Croydon has tried to win customers by emphasising its authenticity. The restaurant's website informs the reader that 'Our success is based on more traditional recipes.' The slogan 'It's just how mum would cook it back home' also features prominently on its online menu. It also offers:

- balti cooking, including the super-sized big-as-your-table Nan breads!

**Figure 12.3** An Indian restaurant with a contemporary design

- a prestigious imported German lager on draught, or a selection of fine wines

- celebrated curry chefs from the Indian subcontinent flown in for a limited period to cook up special food for a Curry Festival – the equivalent of a nightclub flying in a celebrity DJ.

### Questions (30 marks; 35 minutes)

1. Using the table, explain what has happened to the degree of competition within the UK Indian restaurant market over the last 50 years. (4)

2. Explain how efficiency could affect the competitiveness of an Indian restaurant. (4)

3. Identify and explain three marketing approaches an Indian restaurant could adopt to improve its competitiveness. (6)

4. 'Product differentiation is essential if an Indian restaurant is to survive in the long run.' To what extent do you agree with this statement? (16)

## C. Extend your understanding

1. To what extent could excellent marketing decisions ensure that a business such as Pizza Express stays in a strong competitive position? (20)

2. To what extent might a small company such as Higgidy Pies be affected if its market becomes dominated by one producer? (20)

# Chapter 13 Setting marketing objectives

**Linked to:** Understanding the nature and purpose of business, Chapter 1; Marketing and decision-making, Chapter 11; Market research, Chapter 15; Market data and analysis, Chapter 18.

## Definition

Marketing objectives are the targets set for the marketing department to help meet the goals of the organisation as a whole.

## 13.1 The value of setting marketing objectives

A marketing objective is a marketing target or goal that an organisation hopes to achieve, such as to boost market share from 9 to 12 per cent within 2 years. Marketing objectives steer the direction of the business. Operating a business without knowing your objectives is like driving a car without knowing where you want to go. Some businesses achieve a degree of success without setting marketing objectives; stumbling across a successful business model by accident. But why should anyone rely on chance? If firms set marketing objectives the probability of success increases because decision-making will be more focused.

Marketing objectives must be compatible with the overall objectives of the company; they cannot be set in isolation by the marketing department. Achieving the marketing objective of boosting market share from 9 to 12 per cent will help realise a corporate objective of growth.

To be effective, marketing objectives should be quantifiable and measurable. Targets should also be set within a time frame. An example of a marketing objective that Nestlé might set is: 'To achieve a 9 per cent increase in the sales of Kit Kat by the end of next year.'

'Begin with the end in mind.' Stephen Covey, business writer

## 13.2 Examples of marketing objectives

### Sales volume and sales value

A car manufacturer, such as BMW, could set the following marketing objective: 'To increase the number of BMW 3 Series cars sold in China from 250,000 to 400,000 over the next 12 months'. Setting sales volume targets can be particularly important in industries such as car manufacturing because of the high fixed costs associated with operating in this market. If sales volume can be increased, the high fixed costs of operating will be spread across a greater number of units of output, reducing fixed costs per unit. Lower unit costs will help BMW to widen its profit margins. Higher profit margins will give BMW the opportunity to increase its research and development budgets, raising the likelihood of success for BMW's next generation of new car models.

Nike has benefited from a slightly different way of looking at sales. It set a goal based on sales value rather than volume. In other words, sales measured in money. In 1996 chairman Phil Knight set Nike's sights on being the 'No. 1' supplier of football boots and kit. At the time, Nike was a minor player in the football sector of the sportswear business. Adidas was 'No. 1'. Nike's approach has clearly paid off. In 1996 Nike generated sales of just $40 million from football. In 2014 Nike set, and then subsequently beat, a sales target for its football division of $2,000 million! Nike even outsold Adidas in its German homeland.

### Market size

If a business has a large market share, it may worry that boosting its share further may bring investigations from the Competition and Markets Authority.

Therefore, its best way to achieve further growth is by encouraging growth in the market sector as a whole. In the UK, Wrigley has a 90 per cent share of chewing gum sales. So anything it could do to boost the size of the market would help boost its own sales.

In these circumstances businesses might sponsor research by academics into the health-giving properties of the product. Ocean Spray has a 66 per cent share of the UK market for cranberry juice. So research into the supposed benefits of 'cranberries – the superfruit' could boost sales in the market as a whole, from which Ocean Spray would get 66 per cent of the benefit.

Needless to say, for a company with a 25 per cent market share, boosting the market as a whole would make little sense, as 75 per cent of the benefit would be enjoyed by competitors; whereas for Ocean Spray, as for Wrigley, it can make sense to set marketing objectives based on increasing the size of the market as a whole.

## Market and sales growth

For public limited companies in particular, pressure from outside shareholders forces them to keep pushing for more growth. This presses the company into finding new opportunities and may lead the marketing department to overreach. For example, marketing departments love to boost sales by 'stretching' brands, by developing more and more variants based on a single brand. Nestle tried to stretch sales of Kit Kat in the UK by launching varieties such as Lemon and Yogurt, Christmas Pudding, Tiramisu and Seville Orange. The net effect was a short-term sales boost followed by a significant sales downturn as consumers lost a clear sense of what the Kit Kat brand meant.

Growth, therefore, must be treated with caution. It is a valid objective, but one that can cause its own difficulties. One UK company that has handled it especially well is the clothing business Ted Baker plc. Sales grew every year between 2003 and 2014, including through the severe recession of 2009–10. It achieved this by keeping growth controlled, focusing one-at-a-time upon new market opportunities such as opening Ted Baker shops in Japan, then America, then China. It never overstretched itself, unlike Tesco with its disastrous expansion into America, or Morrisons' with its failed attempt to grow into the baby clothing market (Kiddicare was bought for £70 m in 2011, but in 2014 Morrisons' cut £163 m from the value of its assets to reflect ongoing losses at Kiddicare, and then sold Kiddicare off for £2m!).

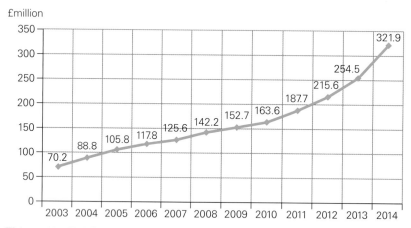

**Figure 13.1** Ted Baker plc annual sales revenue
Source: Ted Baker plc accounts

### Sensations

Launched in 2002 with celeb backing from Victoria Beckham and Gary Neville, Walkers Sensations once had annual sales of over £100 million in the premium crisps market. But by 2009 sales had flagged seriously, hit by newer, more premium brands such as Kettle Chips. Instead of watching sales continue to drift, Walkers responded by relaunching the brand in early 2010, giving it more striking packaging and launching a wider range of flavours. By 2012 and 2013 the success of this relaunch won the brand new distribution outlets in supermarkets and elsewhere. A well-executed marketing strategy brought the brand back to health (see Figure 13.2).

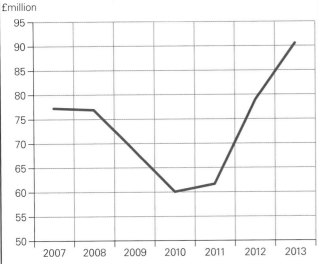

£million

**Figure 13.2** Annual sales of Sensations crisps
Source: *The Grocer* Top Products Survey

## Market share

Nothing is more important to a marketing department than the market share of its key brands. External factors largely control market size, e.g. the weather or the state of the economy. Market share, by contrast, is largely the product of the marketing department's successes or failures. In 2013 UK sales of Galaxy fell by 5.3 per cent while sales of Cadbury's Dairy Milk rose by 14 per cent. Perhaps Mars (Galaxy) focused too much on a slick new TV advertising campaign with the copy line 'Why have cotton when you can have silk'. Cadbury, by contrast, focused on new product development such as the launch of Dairy Milk with Oreo cookies.

In setting a market share objective, a company needs to be cautiously optimistic, for example, aiming to push a brand such as Snickers from its 2.5 per cent share of the £3.6 billion UK chocolate market to 3.0 per cent

within the next two years. This would be ambitious, but conceivable. Note that a 3 per cent market share would generate annual sales of £108 million, making it perfectly possible to afford a marketing budget of perhaps £10 million, allowing for a substantial TV advertising campaign as well as a significant budget for social media advertising.

## Brand loyalty

Brand loyalty exists when consumers repeat-purchase your brand rather than swapping and switching between brands. It is widely agreed that it is far more expensive to have to find a new customer than to keep existing ones happy, so brand loyalty is crucial for achieving high profit margins. For charities, too, it is important to set a marketing objective of improving brand loyalty. If existing donors can be persuaded to set up a direct debit to the charity, its cash flow will improve significantly.

## To enhance, or reposition a brand's image

Although some brands stay fresh for generations (Marmite is over 100 years old) others become jaded due to changes in consumer tastes and lifestyles. At this point the firms need to refresh the brand image to keep the products relevant to the target market. A clear objective must be set. For instance: What brand attributes do we want to create? What do we want the brand to stand for?

## Repositioning

This occurs when a firm aims to a change a brand's image, so that the brand appeals to a new target market. Twelve years into its life cycle, McVitie's decided to reposition its Hobnobs biscuit brand. Hobnobs had been positioned as a homely, quite healthy biscuit for middle-aged consumers. Research pointed McVitie's in a new direction: younger, more male, and less dull. So new packaging was designed and then launched in conjunction with a new, brighter advertising campaign. In 2013 Hobnobs sales were worth £36 million, 9 per cent up on the previous year.

## 13.3 Internal influences on marketing objectives and decisions

From within the business there are several pressures on marketing objectives and decisions. In the online grocery business Ocado, the operations department decided in 2014 to build its third, £200 million distribution depot in Salford, near

Manchester. When opened, perhaps in early 2016, this will create the need for Ocado's marketing department to work hard to boost the number of online Ocado shoppers in the North West. So the pressure for market and sales growth will be due to an internal influence.

Among many other possible internal influences are:

- New corporate objectives set by a new chief executive. The new boss may want to boost sales volume, perhaps in response to a perceived short-term opportunity such as the 2016 Brazil Olympics; or there may be a marketing requirement to strengthen brand loyalty as a way to boost pricing power and therefore profit margins.

- The development of an innovative new product. When Apple Inc. devised the iPod in 2001, it ended up forcing the entire business to refocus from IT to consumer electronics. The marketing department needed to gain an understanding of a new, younger, trendier consumer, and to set objectives based on ambitious market share targets and exceptional brand loyalty.

- New financial objectives. If a new finance director demands higher profit margins, this will have an impact upon the marketing department's objectives and decision-making. As long ago as 1999 the multinational Unilever decided to slash 1,200 brands from its portfolio in order to focus on 400 'power brands'. This was to boost profit margins. Amazingly, even in 2013 and 2014 it is still working on achieving this goal. In 2013 it sold off some minor hair care brands and in 2014 sold its Ragu, Bertolli and Slim-fast food brands.

**Figure 13.3** Logic chain: how to resolve cash flow difficulties

## 13.4 External influences on marketing objectives and decisions

It could never make sense to set a marketing objective that ignores the external context of competitors, changing customer tastes, changing economic circumstances and an ever-changing natural environment, from weather to earthquakes to pollutants.

Among many external influences on marketing objectives and decisions are:

- Changes in fashion or consumer taste/habits. The basis for banks' selling and marketing programmes once rested on their high street branches. These days footfall in UK bank branches is falling at a rate of 10 per cent a year as people use online or mobile methods to pay bills or transfer cash. That forces the banks to find new ways to market to their own customers, never mind potential future customers.

- Changing competitive pressures. Colgate is the world's biggest toothpaste-maker, with a 45 per cent global market share (generating sales of $4.5 billion). Its fiercest brand competitor in recent times has been Procter & Gamble's Oral-B brand, which has grown partly through scare tactics in its digital advertising ('Scary things come to those who don't brush' had 7.5 million YouTube hits). In response Colgate has had to rethink its marketing, deciding to increase substantially its budget for digital advertising.

- Changing economic pressures. In 2013 and 2014 continuing pressure on real incomes gave discounters Aldi and Lidl a huge UK market-share boost compared with the flagging Tesco and Morrisons'. This forced Morrisons' to rethink its marketing objectives, opting for the approach 'We're cheaper' which, in turn, forced the business to chop out a whole management layer in order to cut its operating costs.

- Changing natural environment. With a growing consensus about global warming, more companies are placing environmental greenness on their list of marketing objectives. This leads to actions such as Pret a Manger's decision to only use organic milk, or the creation of Green Tomato Cars – a minicab firm that only uses the eco-friendly Toyota Prius.

'A decision is the action an executive must take when he has information so incomplete that the answer does not suggest itself.' Arthur Radford, US Admiral and business consultant

## Five Whys and a How

| Question | Answer |
| --- | --- |
| Why are marketing objectives important? | Because they determine the strategies that the marketing managers choose to adopt |
| Why may it be better to target sales by value than by volume? | Volume is simply the number bought; value is more important because it includes volume and price, i.e. total revenue |
| Why might market share rise even though brand loyalty has fallen? | Because of an increase in sales to new customers or an increase in demand from customers who feel no loyalty to any brand |
| Why might internal influences lead to the wrong marketing objective being adopted? | Pressure for a short-term boost to profits (perhaps coming from Finance) might lead to a mistakenly short-termist marketing objective |
| Why might external influences clash with internal influences on marketing objectives? | They shouldn't, as insiders should keep an eye on the external context – but internal politics may prevent that from happening |
| How might a company set marketing objectives for an innovative new product? | By deciding on the long-term goal, then considering the internal and external influences on that goal to determine how realistic it really is |

## Key terms

**Competition and Markets Authority:** the renamed Competition Commission, set up in 2014 to intervene where necessary to protect consumers from anti-competitive business practices.

**Corporate objective:** the targets decided for the company as a whole, usually after boardroom discussion.

**Market share:** the percentage of total sales in a market held by one brand or company.

**Repositioning** means tweaking the product, branding and image to shift the proposition to a slightly different place in the market sector, for example, towards younger, more affluent adults.

**Short-termist:** taking decisions on the basis of short-term need rather than long-term benefit.

## Evaluation: Setting marketing objectives

Marketing objectives stem from the corporate goals and from the internal and external circumstances the business faces. The problem for the decision-maker is that there is usually a wide range of contradictory pressures bearing down on the objectives. External forces may point in one direction whereas internal needs suggest a different approach. The expert marketing director will listen to all views and then make a slow, careful decision about what to do. Setting the wrong objectives leads to certain disaster, so it is worth taking time to become as sure as possible about the right step forward.

# Workbook

## A. Revision questions

(30 marks; 30 minutes)

1. In your own words, explain the meaning of the term 'marketing objectives'. (3)

2. What is meant by the phrase 'target market'? (2)

3. a) In Figure 13.1 on Ted Baker plc, calculate the percentage increase in sales between 2003 and 2014. (3)

**b)** Inflation between 2003 and 2014 amounted to 33 per cent. How might this figure be used to assess Ted Baker's sales increase? (4)

**4.** A new chairman sets the Chief Executive of Tesco the corporate objective of restoring Tesco's UK market share to 32 per cent from its current figure of 28.5 per cent. Outline two possible marketing objectives that might help achieve this target. (4)

**5.** Explain how a new financial target of boosting short-term cash flow might affect the marketing objectives at fashion retailer French Connection. (5)

**6. a)** If a company operating in a stable market sees its market share fall from 5 per cent to 4 per cent, what would be the percentage impact on its sales revenue? (3)

**b)** How might the business respond to such slippage in its market share? (6)

## B. Revision exercises
### DATA RESPONSE

**Nākd gains**

**Table 13.1**

| | Price per bar | Weight per bar | Price per 100 g | Calories per bar | Calories per 100 g |
|---|---|---|---|---|---|
| Kellogg's Nutri-grain Strawberry bar | 59 p | 37 g | £1.59 | 130 | 351 |
| Nakd Strawberry Crunch bar | 75 p | 30 g | £2.50 | 109 | 363 |

Source: www.mysupermarket.co.uk. Correct as at 12 July 2014

In 2006 Natural Balance Foods Ltd was founded by Jamie Combs. He saw an opportunity for more honest, natural products in the fast-growing market for cereal bars in the UK (worth £300 million in 2013). The trend towards cereal bars (as a breakfast replacement or as a 'healthy' part of a lunchbox) coincided with one other – a trend towards 'free-from' foods. Although there is little evidence of a widespread need for them, modern consumers like to buy products that are free-from gluten or free-from dairy products. This provided the inspiration behind a very clever brand name: Nākd.

By 2013 sales of Nākd cereal bars put the brand into the top 10 sellers in this sector, with sales of £10 million, up 51 per cent from £6.6 million in 2012. As shown in the table above, these sales stood every chance of being highly profitable given the high value-added in the Nākd brand.

Having created such a successful, growing brand, it was natural to look for new product to launch. So Nākd

Bits was launched in 2013, to offer a 130 g sharing bag in 3 flavours: Cocoa Delight, Berry Delight and Cocoa Orange. The objective was to emulate the success of sharing bags in the chocolate market. Natural Balance Foods Ltd has become a very successful business. Just how far can it grow from here?

### Questions (25 marks; 30 minutes)

**1. a)** Calculate Nākd's cereal bar market share in 2013. (3)

**b)** Comment on that figure. (4)

**2.** The website for Natural Balance Foods suggests that Nākd's customers are brand loyal. Explain one way in which the company might benefit from this. (4)

**3. a)** Based on the above information, suggest a suitable marketing objective for Nākd in 2016. Explain your reasoning. (5)

**b)** Analyse two external factors that might prevent the company from achieving the objective you set in 3a). (9)

## C. Extend your understanding

**1.** With reference to a business of your choice, discuss which single factor seems to be the most important influence on the brand loyalty of its customers. (20)

**2.** Waitrose is a supermarket chain that offers a huge range of well-presented foods, but at distinctly higher prices than its rivals. Discuss the main external influences on the marketing objectives and decisions made by the company and other businesses with which you are familiar. (20)

**Linked to:** Market research, Chapter 15; Market data and analysis, Chapter 18.

> ### Definition
>
> A market is where buyers meet sellers. Examples include eBay (digital market) or Smithfield Market, a meat and poultry market (physical).

## 14.1 Types of market

### Local versus national

Most new small firms know and care little about the size of the national market. If you have just bought an ice cream van that you intend to operate in Chichester, it does not matter whether the size of the UK market for ice cream is £500 million or £600 million per year. Your concern is the level of demand and the level of competition locally. And you will probably be delighted if you achieve annual sales of £0.1 million (£100,000).

In the case of the market for ice cream in Chichester, there are several things to consider:

● How do locals buy ice cream at the moment? (Multipacks from supermarkets? Individual cones from ice cream stalls or vans?)

● How many tourists come to the city? Do they come all year round? What type of ice cream do they buy? Where do they buy it?

● How much competition is there? What do competitors offer and charge at the moment? Are there gaps in the market that you could move into?

Other firms are focused more on the national market. For example, Charlie Bigham is a small food company that started in 1996. It produces high-quality, high-priced, ready-to-eat meals. It started by targeting small grocers, but soon found that the sales volumes were too low to cover their costs. A sales breakthrough in Waitrose supermarkets was followed in 2005 by acceptance by Sainsbury's. This enables the company to deliver to just two warehouses, cutting the business's costs dramatically. Then Waitrose and Sainsbury's distribute to their local shops. So Charlie Bigham Foods has a national presence, even though sales remain well below one per cent of the market for ready meals.

To deal on the national level, Charlie Bigham has to deal professionally with the supermarket buyers, and produce eye-catching packaging that can compete effectively with national and multinational competitors.

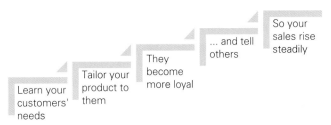

Learn your customers' needs → Tailor your product to them → They become more loyal → ... and tell others → So your sales rise steadily

**Figure 14.1** Logic ladder: understanding customers

'We were filling a need they didn't know they had.'
Howard Schulz, chief executive, Starbucks

### Physical and electronic (virtual)

Markets used all to be physical. The London Stock Exchange was a place where buyers met sellers and face-to-face agreements took place. Similarly, auctions were physical, with bidders having to catch the eye of the auctioneer.

Today an increasing number of markets are digital (or virtual). The stock market exists only on computer screens, and the likes of eBay are transforming auction and other markets worldwide.

From a business point of view the key factors about electronic markets (for example, for finding hotel rooms or flights) are as follows.

**Figure 14.2** Bidding on eBay

- They are fiercely price competitive, so the companies supplying services have huge pressure to keep their costs as low as possible.

- They do not rely on physical location, for example, a business can easily be run from a bedroom, such as selling Wii computer games.

- The market is easy and quite cheap to enter, so new competitors can arrive at any time.

- They provide a 'long tail' of competitive, profitable small businesses, able to carve their own little niche in markets. This is very difficult to achieve in the high street, where rents are so high that only big firms can afford them.

# 14.2 Factors determining demand

Demand is the desire of consumers to buy a product or service, when backed by the ability to pay. It is also known as 'effective demand' (that is, only when the customer has the money is demand effective). Several factors determine the demand for a specific product/service.

## Price

Price affects demand in three ways.

1. You may want an £80,000 Mercedes convertible but you cannot afford it; the price puts it beyond your income level. The higher the price, the more people there are who cannot afford to buy.

2. The higher the price, the less good value the item will seem compared with other ways of spending the money. For example, a Chelsea home ticket costing

£48 is the equivalent of going to the movies 6 times. Is it worth it? The higher the price of an item, the more people there will be who say 'it's not worth it'.

3. It should be remembered that the price tag put on an item gives a message about its 'value'. A ring priced at 99p will inevitably be seen as 'cheap' whether or not it is value for money; so although lower prices should boost sales, firms must beware of ruining their image for quality.

## Incomes

The British economy grows at a rate of about 2.5 per cent a year. This means that average income levels double every 30 years. Broadly, when your children are aged about 16–18, you are likely to be twice as well off as your parents are today. Economic growth means we all get richer over time.

The demand for most products and services grows as the economy grows. Goods like cars and cinema tickets are 'normal goods' for which demand rises broadly in line with incomes. In some cases it grows even faster; for example, if the economy grows by three per cent in a year, the amount spent on foreign holidays can easily rise by 6 per cent. This type of product is known as a luxury good.

Other goods behave differently, with sales falling when people are better off. These products are known as inferior goods. In their case, rising incomes mean falling sales. For example, the richer we get, the more Tropicana we buy and the less Tesco Orange Squash. As Orange Squash is an inferior good, a couple of years of economic struggle (and perhaps more people out of work) would mean sales would increase as people switch from expensive Tropicana to cheap squash.

## Actions of competitors

Demand for British Airways (BA) Heathrow to New York flights does not only depend on their price and the incomes of consumers. It also depends on the actions of their rivals. If Virgin Atlantic is running a brilliant advertising campaign, demand for BA flights may fall as customers switch to Virgin. Or if American Airlines pushes its prices up, people may switch to BA.

## The firm's own marketing activities

Following the same logic, if British Airways is running a new advertising campaign, perhaps based on improved customer service, it may enjoy increased sales. In effect, its sales will rise if it can persuade customers to switch from Virgin and American Airlines to BA. One firm's sales increase usually means reduced sales elsewhere.

## Seasonal factors

Most firms experience significant variations in sales throughout the year. Some markets, such as ice cream, soft drinks, lager and seaside hotels, boom in the summer and slump in the winter. Other markets, such as sales of perfume, liqueurs, greetings cards and toys, boom at Christmas. Other products that have less obvious reasons for seasonal variations in demand include cars, cat food, carpets, furniture, TVs and newspapers. The variations are caused by patterns of customer behaviour and nothing can be done about it. A well-run business makes sure it understands and can predict the seasonal variations in demand; and then has a plan for coping.

'The aim of marketing is to know and understand the customer so well the product or service fits him and sells itself.' Peter Drucker, business guru

## 14.3 Market size and trends

Market size is the measurement of all the sales by all the companies within a marketplace. It can be measured in two ways: by volume and by value. Volume measures the quantity of goods purchased, perhaps in tons, in packs or in units. Market size by value is the amount spent by customers on the volume sold. So the difference between volume and value is the price paid per unit.

Take, for example, the figures shown in Table 14.1 for the UK market for sun care products.

**Table 14.1** UK market for sun care products

| 2013 market by value | £198.2 million |
| 2013 market by volume | 36.1 million litres |
| Average price per litre | £5.49 (£198.2/36.1) |

Source: *The Grocer*, 12 April 2014

Market size matters because it is the basis for calculating market share (the proportion of the total market held by one company or brand). This, in turn, is essential for evaluating the success or failure of a firm's marketing activities. Market size is also the reference point for calculating trends. Is market size growing or declining? A growth market is far more likely to provide opportunities for new products to be launched or for new distribution initiatives to be successful.

Recent figures and forecasts for the car market in China help to show the importance of market trends. In 2001 the UK car market was four times bigger than that of China. In 2005 China accelerated past Britain. And look at the forecasts for the coming years, shown in Table 14.2.

**Table 14.2** Sales of new passenger cars (actual and forecast)

| Year | China | Britain |
|---|---|---|
| 2010 | 13,800,000 | 2,000,000 |
| 2011 | 14,470,000 | 1,940,000 |
| 2012 | 15,500,000 | 2,050,000 |
| 2013 | 17,500,000 | 2,225,000 |
| 2014 (estimated) | 19,100,000 | 2,380,000 |
| 2020 (forecast) | 25,000,000 | 2,400,000 |

Source: Forecasts by industry experts

In 2009 China became the world's biggest car market. Clearly these figures show that success in China will be far more important to car firms than success in Britain.

## 14.4 Market share

Market share is the proportion of the total market held by one company or product. It can be measured by volume, but is more often looked at by value. Market share is taken by most firms as the key test of the success of the year's marketing activities. Total sales are affected by factors such as economic growth, but market share measures a firm's ability to win or lose against its competitors. As shown in Table 14.3, high market share can also lead to the producer's ideal of market leadership or market dominance. Cadbury Dairy Milk has market leadership among confectionery brands, but Pampers and Heinz have dominance of their markets.

**Table 14.3** Brands with high UK market shares

| Leading brand in its market | Sales of leading brand (£ million) | Market size (by value) (£ million) | Market share (%) | Share of nearest competitor (%) |
|---|---|---|---|---|
| Heinz Baked Beans | 216 | 339 | 63.7 | 11.6 |
| Pampers | 299 | 474 | 63.0 | 6.4 |
| Coca-Cola | 1,188 | 2,487 | 47.8 | 14.4 |
| Cadbury Dairy Milk | 506 | 3,600 | 14.1 | 6.0 |

Source: *The Grocer* 21 December 2013, quoting from Nielsen.

There are many advantages to a business of having the top selling brand (the brand leader). Obviously, sales are higher than anyone else's, but also:

- The brand leader gets the highest distribution level, often without needing to make much effort to achieve it. Even a tiny corner shop stocks Pampers, as well as Happy Shopper own-label nappies. Success breeds success.

- Brand leaders are able to offer lower discount terms to retailers than the number two or three brands in a market. This means higher revenues and profit margins per unit sold.

- The strength of a brand-leading name such Walls Magnum makes it much easier to obtain distribution and consumer trial for new products based on that brand name.

## Five Whys and a How

| Question | Answer |
|---|---|
| Why may market share be a better judge of business success than sales? | Sales may rise or fall due to external factors such as recession or new advertising by a rival; market share is a real test of how well the firm has done compared with its rivals |
| Why do firms draw a distinction between market share by volume and by value? | Ultimately, firms need money to cover costs, therefore the *value* of sales is what matters. In the smartphone business, the iPhone gives Apple a huge market share advantage by *value* because of its high price |
| Why may online markets be more profitable than traditional, physical markets? | Physical markets have to be located conveniently for consumers, making them expensive to run. Online markets can be located in cheap premises anywhere |
| Why are seasonal factors important in the market for strawberries? | Because they affect supply and demand, although in different ways (supply in May/June, but demand may jump a little at Christmas) |
| Why does market decline not have to mean sales decline for a particular brand? | The brand's market share could rise sufficiently to outweigh the effects of the decline in market size |
| How is market share measured (by volume)? | $\dfrac{\text{Kilos of beans sold by Heinz}}{\text{Kilos of beans sold in total}} \times 100$ |

### Key terms

**Inferior goods:** products that people turn to when they are 'hard up', and turn away from when they are better off (for example, Tesco Value Beans instead of Heinz Baked Beans).

**Luxury goods:** Products that people buy much more of when they feel better off, (for example, jewellery, sports cars and holidays at posh hotels).

**Normal goods:** Products or services for which sales change broadly in line with the economy. That is, if the economy grows by 3 per cent, sales rise by 3 per cent (for example, travel and sales of fast food).

### Evaluation: Understanding markets

Almost every large business carries out detailed market analysis on a regular basis. They buy 'retail audits' to find out how retail sales are doing. It can be said, though, that some managers suffer from 'paralysis by analysis'. In other words, they gather so much data (some of it conflicting) that they end up unable to make a decision. Contrast this approach with that of Apple. Boss Steve Jobs focused on understanding customers, not analysing the market as it stood. He believed that Apple could always stay one step ahead by thinking about what customers would want in future. Given Apple's success, it is hard to argue with him.

'Don't find customers for your products; find products for your customers.' Seth Godwin, author

# Workbook

## A. Revision questions

(35 marks; 35 minutes)

1. Outline three features of the market for fast food near to where you live. (6)

2. Section 14.2 lists five factors determining the demand for a product: price, incomes, actions of competitors, marketing activities and seasonality. Identify which two of these would most heavily affect sales of:

   a) strawberries

   b) EasyJet tickets to Barcelona

   c) tickets to see Newcastle United

   d) DFS furniture. (8)

3. Explain in your own words the difference between market size by volume and market size by value. (3)

4. a) Look at Table 14.2. Toyota's share of the UK car market is about 6 per cent. If it continues with that share, how many UK car sales would that amount to in 2020? How many Toyota cars would be sold in China in 2020, assuming the same market share? (4)

   b) Outline two ways in which Toyota could respond to that sales difference. (6)

5. Why may a shoe shop focusing on 'Little Feet' be able to charge higher prices per pair than a general shoe shop? (2)

6. Look at Table 14.3. Discuss which business should be happier with its market position: Cadbury or Pampers. (6)

## B. Revision exercises
### DATA RESPONSE 1

**Market size, market growth and market shares: the tablet market**

Since its launch in early 2010 the Apple iPad has scooped up plaudits, sales and profits. Figure 14.3 shows the sales during what Apple hopes will be as long-lived a product life cycle as the iPod (launched 2002 and still going strong).

Figure 14.4, however, shows how hard it can be to keep ahead of the competition. Few would have expected, in early 2012, that Apple's market share would have halved between the third quarter of 2012 and the same quarter of 2013. Samsung's success has been an important part of that, but so too has been the growth of less-known companies such as China's Lenovo.

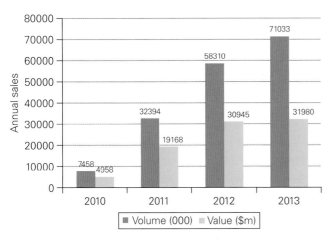

**Figure 14.3** Apple iPad sales since launch

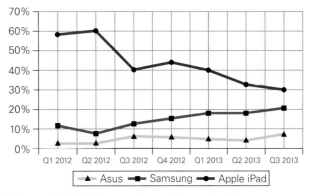

**Figure 14.4** Tablet computers: global market shares

Source of all the data: IDC Analysts, Quarterly Reports

Does it matter about falling market share, though, when sales volumes are as solid as those of the iPad, as graphed in Figure 14.4, and world market size is forging ahead, from 28.3 million tablets in Q2 2012 to 47.6m units in Q3 2013?

**Questions: 30 marks; 35 minutes**

1. Calculate the percentage change in iPad sales between 2012 and 2013:
   **a)** by volume and        **b)** by value.        (3)

2. Explain the implications for Apple of the difference between your answers to Question 1.        (4)

3. Use Figure 14.4 to help explain why the price of iPads was falling in 2013.        (4)

4. **a)** From the text and Figure 14.4, calculate actual sales of iPads in:
   **i.** Q2 2012 and
   **ii.** Q3 2013.        (3)

   **b)** Experts say that the reason Apple's market share is declining is because it has refused to launch a lower-priced tablet computer. To what extent do you agree that now is the time to launch one?        (16)

## DATA RESPONSE 2

### Lidl and Aldi winning grocery wars

Discount grocers are the big winners in 2014, Kantar Worldpanel figures show. The grocery market grew by 1.7 per cent year-on-year in the 12 weeks to 2 February 2014. Waitrose, Sainsbury's and Asda all grew slightly, while sales at Tesco and Morrisons' fell. Lidl and Aldi were the big winners with sales growth of 17 per cent and 32 per cent respectively. Perhaps these discount grocers benefited from the continuing squeeze on household living standards.

The changes leave Tesco as the wounded market leader with its 29.2 per cent down sharply from the 31.5 per cent it enjoyed before the recession. Morrisons' suffered a decline from 11.8 per cent in 2013 to 11.3 per cent in 2014. A decline of 0.5 per cent may seem trivial, but as the value of the UK grocery market is £170 billion per year, 0.5 per cent market share represents sales of £850 million!

**Questions (30 marks; 35 minutes)**

1. **a)** What was the grocery market size and market growth in the 12 weeks to 2 February 2014?        (2)

   **b)** Identify three possible reasons why sales at Morrisons' actually fell in 2014.        (3)

2. **a)** Show the workings to calculate that a 0.5 per cent share of the UK grocery market equals £850 million.        (3)

   **b)** Use the figures and the bar chart to work out the value of Aldi's 2014 sales in the UK.        (2)

   **c)** Analyse two possible reasons why Aldi enjoyed the biggest sales growth within the grocery market in 2014.        (8)

3. Twenty years ago, Sainsbury's was the UK grocery market leader. Discuss whether it could return to that position within the next 20 years.        (12)

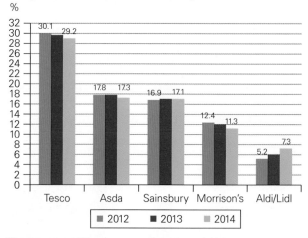

**Figure 14.5** UK grocery market-share 2014
Source: Kantar Worldpanel, 12 weeks to 2 February 2014.

## C. Extend your understanding

1. A recent report by Mintel forecast that the UK market for bicycles is set to grow by 23 per cent to more than £800 million by 2017. To what extent does this guarantee success for a business such as Halfords, a leading bicycle retailer?        (20)

2. The Cadbury brand Crunchie has a 1 per cent share of the UK chocolate market. Discuss the internal and external factors that might determine whether Cadbury could succeed in doubling Crunchie's market share.        (20)

**Linked to:** Different business forms, Chapter 2; Pricing decisions, Chapter 23; Integrating the marketing mix, Chapter 25.

## Definition

Market research gathers information about consumers, competitors and distributors within a firm's target market. It is a way of identifying consumers' buying habits and attitudes to current and future products.

## 15.1 The value of market research

Research shows that the single biggest cause of business failure is failure to understand the market. It is reasonable to suggest that this alone shows why market research has the potential to be valuable to every business.

When opening a first business, the starting point is to discover the marketing fundamentals: how big is the market (market size), what is its future potential and what are the market shares of the existing companies and brands?

Market size means the value of the sales made annually by all the firms within a market. For example, in 2013 the UK market for yoghurts and pot desserts was worth £2,233 million. Market potential can be measured by the annual rate of growth. In the case of yogurt, this has been at a rate of 3 per cent per year, by value. This implies that, by the year 2017, the potential market size will be over £2,500 million.

Market shares are also of crucial importance when investigating a market, as they indicate the relative strength of the firms within the market. In 2013, 25 per cent of the yogurt market was held by Müller, making it the leading brand by far. A benefit it received for its strong market share was a distribution level of almost 100 per cent: nearly every grocery store stocked Müller. If one firm dominates, it may be very difficult to break into the market.

So how can firms find out this type of information? The starting point is secondary research: unearthing data that already exists.

**Figure 15.1** The UK market for yoghurt is worth over £2,000 million.

## 15.2 Methods of secondary research

### Internet

Most people start by 'Googling' the topic. This can provide invaluable information, though online providers of market research information will want to charge for the service. With luck, Google will identify a relevant article that can provide useful information.

### Government-produced data

The government-funded Office for National Statistics produces valuable reports such as the Annual Abstract of Statistics and Labour Market Trends.

These provide data on population trends, and forecasts; for example, someone starting a hair and beauty salon may find out how many 16- to 20-year-old women there will be in the year 2020.

Having obtained background data, further research is likely to be tailored specifically to the company's needs, such as carrying out a survey among 16- to 20-year-old women about their favourite haircare brands. This type of first-hand research gathers primary data. Some of the pros and cons of primary and secondary research are given in Table 15.1.

**Table 15.1** The pros and cons of primary and secondary research

|  | Secondary research | Primary research |
|---|---|---|
| **PROS** | • often obtained without cost<br>• good overview of a market<br>• usually based on actual sales figures, or research on large samples | • can aim questions directly at your research objectives<br>• latest information from the marketplace<br>• can assess the psychology of the customer |
| **CONS** | • data may not be updated regularly<br>• not tailored to your own needs<br>• expensive to buy reports on many different marketplaces | • expensive, £10,000+ per survey<br>• risk of questionnaire and interviewer bias<br>• research findings may only be usable if comparable 'backdata' exists |

'Running a company on market research is like driving while looking in the rear view mirror.' Anita Roddick, founder, Body Shop.

## 15.3 Methods of primary research

The process of gathering information directly from people within your target market is known as primary (or field) research. When carried out by market research companies it is expensive, but there is much that firms can do for themselves.

For a company that is up and running, a regular survey of customer satisfaction is an important way of measuring the quality of customer service. When investigating a new market, there are various measures that can be taken by a small firm with a limited budget.

● Retailer research: the people closest to a market are those who serve customers directly – the retailers. They are likely to know the up-and-coming brands, the degree of brand loyalty and the importance of price and packaging, all of which is crucial information.

● Observation: when starting up a service business in which location is an all-important factor, it

is invaluable to measure the rate of pedestrian (and possibly traffic) flow past your potential site compared with that of your rivals. A sweet shop or dry cleaners near a busy bus stop may generate twice the sales of a rival 50 yards down the road.

For a large company, primary research will be used extensively in new product development. For example, if we consider the possibility of launching Orange Chocolate Buttons, the development stages, plus research, would probably be as shown in Table 15.2.

**Table 15.2** Primary research used in new product development (Orange Chocolate Buttons)

| Development stage | Primary research |
|---|---|
| 1. The product idea (probably one of several) | 1. Group discussions among regular chocolate buyers (some young, some old) |
| 2. Product test (testing different recipes, different sweetness, 'orangeyness', etc.) | 2. A taste test on 200+ chocolate buyers (on street corners, or in a hall) |
| 3. Brand name research (testing several different names and perhaps logos) | 3. Quantitative research using a questionnaire on a sample of 200+ |
| 4. Packaging research | 4. Quantitative research as in item 3 |
| 5. Advertising research | 5. Group discussions run by psychologists to discover which advertisement has the strongest effect on product image and recall |
| 6. Total proposition test: testing the level of purchase interest, to help make sales forecasts | 6. Quantitative research using a questionnaire and product samples on at least 200+ consumers |

### Real business

#### The Toyota MR2

When Toyota launched the MR2 sports car, sales were higher than expected. The only exception was found in France, where sales were very poor. The Japanese head office asked the executives of Toyota France to look into this. Why had it been such a flop? Eventually the executives admitted that they should have carried out market research into the brand name MR2 prior to the launch. Pronounced 'em-er-deux' in France, the car sounded like the French swear word *merdre* (crap).

'The aim of marketing is to know and understand the customer so well the product or service fits him and sells itself.' Peter Drucker, business author/guru

## 15.4 Qualitative research

This is in-depth research into the motivations behind the attitudes and buying habits of consumers. It does not produce statistics such as '52 per cent of chocolate buyers like orange chocolate'; instead it gives clues as to why they like it (is it really because it's orange, or because it's different/a change?). Qualitative research is usually conducted by psychologists, who learn to interpret the way people say things, as well as what they say.

The main form of qualitative research is group discussion (also known as focus groups). These are free-ranging discussions led by psychologists among groups of six to eight consumers. The group leader will have a list of topics that need discussion, but will be free to follow up any point made by a group member. Among the advantages of group discussions is the fact that they:

- may reveal a problem or opportunity the company had not anticipated
- reveal consumer psychology, such as the importance of image and peer pressure.

### Real business

#### Selling luxury in China

A 2013 quantitative study showed that Louis Vuitton, Hermès and Chanel are the luxury brands with the highest reputation in China. But do they share the same image characteristics? To find out, a qualitative study was carried out, depth-interviewing people from three groups: the 'nouveau (super) riche', 'gifters' and 'middle-class luxury'. The study found that the first two groups are price insensitive; indeed, high prices are in some ways attractive. Whereas the third group are very price sensitive within a restricted number of acceptable Western brands. They can be targeted quite differently, for example, online.

**Table 15.3** Typical research questions

| Qualitative research | Quantitative research |
|---|---|
| Why do people *really* buy Nikes? | Which pack design do you prefer? |
| Who in the household *really* decides which brand of shampoo is bought? | Have you heard of any of the following brands? (Ariel, Daz, Persil, etc.) |
| What mood makes you feel like buying Häagen-Dazs ice cream? | How likely are you to buy this product regularly? |
| When you buy your children Frosties, how do you feel? | How many newspapers have you bought in the past 7 days? |

## 15.5 Quantitative research

This asks pre-set questions of a large enough sample of people to provide statistically valid data. Questionnaires can answer factual questions such as 'How many 16 to 20 year olds have heard of Chanel No. 5?' There are three key aspects to quantitative research:

- sampling, ensuring that the research results are typical of the whole population, though only a sample of the population has been interviewed. An important factor is the response rate, that is, what proportion of those approached bothered to respond
- writing a questionnaire that is unbiased and meets the research objectives
- assessing the validity of the results.

### The value of sampling

The two main concerns in sampling are how to choose the right people for interview (sampling method) and deciding how large a number to interview (sample size).

In 1936, an American magazine attempted to forecast the Presidential election by polling 2.4 million potential voters. The magazine announced that the Republican candidate would win with 55 per cent of the poll. When Democrat F. D. Roosevelt won a landslide, commentators laughed at the 'useless' new science of sampling. Yet a sample of just three thousand by Gallup Poll predicted the result correctly. This proved that the size of a sample is no guarantee of accuracy. The magazine had a huge sample, but it had drawn it from telephone directories and car owners – both affluent populations in the 1930s. Dr Gallup had made sure to find a sample that was truly representative of ordinary Americans. Sampling, then, is more about accuracy than size – though size still matters.

### Sample reliability

The key to reliability is to obtain as representative a sample as possible. Dr Gallup's method (still used widely today) was quota sampling. This method involves selecting interviewees in proportion to the consumer profile within the target market. An example of quota sampling is given in Table 15.4.

**Table 15.4** An example of quota sampling

| Adult: | Chocolate buyers (%) | Respondent quota (sample: 200) |
|---|---|---|
| Men | 40 | 80 |
| Women | 60 | 100 |
| | | |
| 16–24 | 38 | 76 |
| 25–34 | 21 | 42 |
| 35–44 | 16 | 32 |
| 45+ | 25 | 50 |

This method allows interviewers to head for busy street corners, interviewing whoever comes along. As long as they achieve the correct quota, they can interview when and where they want to. This ensures a representative sample at relatively low cost. It is the sampling method used most commonly by market research companies.

## Sample size

Having decided which sampling method should be used, the next consideration is to determine how many interviews should be conducted. Should 10, 100, or 1,000 people be interviewed? The most high-profile surveys conducted in Britain are the opinion polls asking adults about their voting intentions in a general election. These quota samples of between 1,000 and 1,500 respondents are considered large enough to reflect the opinions of the electorate of 45 million. How is this possible?

Of course, if you only interviewed 10 people, the chances are slim that the views of this sample will match those of the whole population. Of these 10, 7 may say they would definitely buy Chocolate Orange Buttons. If you asked another 10, however, only three may say the same. A sample of 10 is so small that chance variations make the results meaningless. In other words, a researcher can have no statistical confidence in the findings from a sample of 10.

A sample of 100 is far more meaningful. It is not enough to feel confident about marginal decisions (for example, 53 per cent like the red pack design and 47 per cent like the blue one), but is quite enough if the

result is clear-cut (such as, 65 per cent like the name 'Spark'; 35 per cent prefer 'Valencia'). Many major product launches have proceeded following research on as low a sample as 100.

With a sample of 1,000, a high level of confidence is possible. Even small differences would be statistically significant with such a large sample. So why doesn't everyone use samples of 1,000? The answer is because of the cost of doing so: money. Hiring a market research agency to undertake a survey of 100 people would cost approximately £10,000. A sample of 1,000 people would cost three times that amount, which is good value if you can afford it but not everyone can. As shown in the earlier example of launching Orange Buttons, a company might require six surveys before launching a new product. So the amount spent on research alone might reach £180,000 if samples of 1,000 were used.

## The concept of confidence intervals

When market researchers present their findings from quantitative research they like to state the level of confidence one can have in the sample finding. In particular, they like to show results to a '95 per cent confidence level'. In other words, the data should be correct 95 per cent of the time, or 19 times out of 20. (Because the data is drawn from a small-ish sample of the whole population there can never be 100 per cent confidence in the findings.)

Let us assume that a research company has conducted a survey to find out how many people like a blue pack-colour for a new detergent. As long as over 50 per cent like the blue, they'll proceed. The research result shows that 60 per cent of the sample like the blue pack. But how confident can one be that this result reflects the views of the whole target market?

The key to this would be the confidence interval. That means how wide the possible range might be from the actual result of 60 per cent. If the confidence interval is no more than plus or minus 9, then the company can be assured that the statistical variability of the sample is no wider than 60+9 on the upside and 60–9 on the downside, that is a range from 51–69. In this case, then, there can be 95 per cent confidence that the of the target market lie between 51 and 69. Therefore more than half like the blue pack and the business can proceed.

The net effect of the above is simply to point out that the results of quantitative market research should be treated with care. The smaller the sample size, the wider the confidence intervals and therefore the lower the level of confidence one can have in the accuracy of the findings.

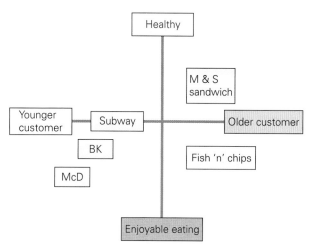

**Figure 15.3** Example of a market map for fast food

Using this approach could help in identifying a product or market niche that has not yet been filled. In the market map shown in Figure 15.3 there appears to be an available niche for healthy eating for younger customers within the fast food sector. The market map points to the possibility of this positioning. Then it would be up to the entrepreneur to investigate further. In particular, the entrepreneur will need to investigate whether there may be a niche, but one that is too small to provide an opportunity for a profitable business.

A great example of positioning is Aldi's position within the UK's price-motivated segment of the grocery market. With Asda, Lidl and Iceland as its direct competitors, Aldi has seen its sales boom as a result of persuading middle-Britain that shopping at Aldi is sensible rather than cheapskate. Its slogan 'Spend a little. Live a lot.' is about having a good time, not about 'low, low prices'. Figure 15.4 shows the value to Aldi of astute positioning.

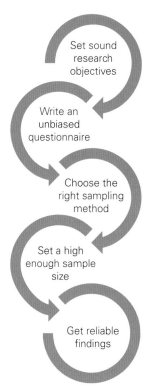

**Figure 15.2** Logic chain: getting research right

## 15.6 Market mapping

Market mapping is carried out in two stages.

1. Identify the key features that characterise consumers within a market; examples in the market for women's clothes would be: young/old and high fashion/conservative

2. Having identified the key characteristics, place every brand on a grid such as that shown in Figure 15.3. This will reveal where the competition is concentrated and may highlight gaps in the market.

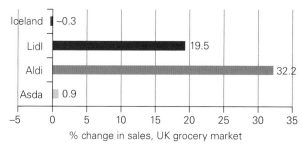

**Figure 15.4** UK grocery market year-on-year percentage change, 12 weeks to July 2014

Source: Kantar Worldpanel

## Five Whys and a How

| Question | Answer |
|---|---|
| Why may start-up companies struggle to get accurate market research data? | They lack a base of existing customers who can be interviewed, e.g. to find out about changing tastes |
| Why is secondary data a first step, but not a sufficient step? | Because it only gives general information. For data tailored to your own needs, you need to commission primary research |
| Why may small samples be dangerous? | Because their findings are subject to high statistical variability, making them unreliable |
| Why may qualitative research sometimes prove especially important? | Whenever the issues involved are psychological, such as whether a logo strays slightly beyond distinctive towards vulgar |
| Will 'Big Data' mean that commissioning primary research becomes a thing of the past? | However much data is captured and analysed, it can only be based on past information (such as sales figures). Primary research can ask important hypothetical questions about the future; so 'no' is the answer |
| How might market mapping help a new company wanting to break into a market? | It places existing brands on a grid based on key consumer variables, to help identify crowded and less-crowded market positions |

## Key terms

**Bias:** a factor that causes research findings to be unrepresentative of the whole population; for example, bubbly interviewers or misleading survey questions.

**Primary research:** finding out information first-hand; for example, Coca-Cola designing a questionnaire to obtain information from people who regularly buy diet products.

**Secondary research:** finding out information that has already been gathered; for example, the government's estimates of the number of 14 to 16 year olds in Wales.

**Sample size:** the number of people interviewed. This should be large enough to give confidence that the findings are representative of the whole population.

**Sampling method:** the approach chosen to select the right people to be part of the research sample; for example, random, quota or stratified.

**Standard deviation:** sample findings tend to form a bell-shaped curve when shown on a graph. Within this curve, the standard deviation of the data reflects how wide or narrow is the likely variation from the mean average of the findings.

'To steal ideas from one person is plagiarism, to steal ideas from many is research.' Anon

## Evaluation: Market research

In large firms, it is rare for any significant marketing decision to be made without market research. Even an apparently minor change to a pack design will only be carried out after testing in research. Is this overkill? Surely marketing executives are employed to make judgements, not merely to do what surveys tell them?

The first issue here is the strong desire to make business decisions as scientifically as possible; in other words, to act on evidence, not on feelings. Quantitative research, especially, fits in with the desire to act on science not hunch. Yet this can be criticised, such as by John Scully, former head of Apple Inc., who once said 'No great marketing decision has ever been made on the basis of quantitative data'. He was pointing out that true innovations, such as the Apple iPad, were the product of creativity and hunch, not science.

The second issue concerns the management culture. In some firms, mistakes lead to inquests, blame and even dismissal. This makes managers keen to find a let-out. When the new product flops, the manager can point an accusing finger at the positive research results: 'It wasn't my fault. We need a new research agency.' In other firms, mistakes are seen as an inevitable part of learning. For every Sinclair C5 (unresearched flop) there may be an iPod (unresearched money-spinner). In firms with a positive, risk-taking approach to business, qualitative insights are likely to be preferred to quantitative data.

# Workbook

## A. Revision questions

**(40 marks, 40 minutes)**

1. State three ways in which a cosmetics firm could use market research. (3)

2. Outline three reasons why market research information may prove inaccurate. (6)

3. Distinguish between primary and secondary research. (3)

4. What advantages are there in using secondary research rather than primary? (3)

5. Which is the most commonly used sampling method? Why may it be the most commonly used? (3)

6. State three key factors to take into account when writing a questionnaire. (3)

7. Explain two aspects of marketing in which consumer psychology is important. (4)

8. Outline the pros and cons of using a large sample size. (4)

9. Identify three possible sources of bias in primary market research. (3)

10. Explain how market mapping could be helpful to **two** of the following.

    a) an entrepreneur looking at opening up a new driving school

    b) the brand manager of Werther's Original sweets, worried about falling market share

    c) a private school thinking of opening its first branch in China (8)

## B. Revision exercises

### DATA RESPONSE

Each year more than £1,500 million is spent on pet food in the UK. All the growth within the market has been for luxury pet foods and for healthier products. Seeing these trends, in early 2014 Town & Country Petfoods launched HiLife Just Desserts, a range of pudding treats for dogs. They contain omega-3 but no added sugar and therefore have no more than 100 calories per tin.

Sales began well, especially of the Apple & Cranberry version. Now sales have flattened out at around £1 million a year and the company thinks it is time to launch some new flavours. Three weeks ago they commissioned some primary research that was carried out using an online survey linked to pet care websites. The sample size was 150.

The main findings were as shown in Table 15.5.

**Table 15.5** Findings of online survey

| 1. Have you ever bought your dog a pet food pudding? | | | |
|---|---|---|---|
| **Ever bought:** | **Never (%)** | **Just once (%)** | **Yes, in the past but no longer (%)** | **Yes, still do (%)** |
| | 61 | 13 | 12 | 14 |

| Which of these flavours may you buy for your dog? | | | |
|---|---|---|---|
| **May try:** | **Never (%)** | **May try** | **May buy monthly (%)** | **May buy once a week (%)** |
| Muesli yoghurt | 61 | 19 | 15 | 5 |
| Rhubarb crumble | 43 | 33 | 22 | 2 |
| Apples and custard | 52 | 34 | 12 | 2 |

The marketing director is slightly disappointed that none of the new product ideas has done brilliantly, but happy that there's one clear winner. She plans a short qualitative research exercise among existing HiLife customers, and hopes to launch two new flavours in time for the annual Crufts dog show in three months' time.

**Questions (30 marks; 35 minutes)**

1. Outline whether the sample size of 150 was appropriate in this case. (4)

2. Analyse the marketing director's conclusion that 'none of the new product ideas has done brilliantly, but happy that there's one clear winner'. (9)

3. a) Explain one method of qualitative research that could be used in this case. (3)

   b) Evaluate two ways in which qualitative research may help the marketing director. Which do you think is the more important, and why? (14)

## C. Extend your understanding

1. 'Market research is like an insurance policy. You pay a premium to reduce your marketing risks.' To what extent do you believe this statement to be true? (20)

2. After ten years of rising sales, demand for Shredded Wheat has started to slip. Discuss how the marketing manager could make use of market research to analyse why this has happened and to help decide the strategy needed to return Shredded Wheat to sales growth. (20)

# Chapter 16 Interpreting marketing data

**Linked to:** Market research, Chapter 15; Market data and analysis, Chapter 18; Segmentation, targeting and positioning, Chapter 19.

## Definition

Today's companies have so much data that the key skill is to identify and draw conclusions from the relatively few nuggets that have yet to be found.

## 16.1 Correlation

Businesses are always keen to learn about the effect on sales of marketing strategies such as TV advertising, sales promotion or direct mailshots. Often researchers will compare sales volume and advertising expenditure. A good way to do this is on a graph. In Figure 16.1 there is clearly a strong relationship, or correlation, between the two. The correlation is positive: as one increases so does the other. It is important to realise that each point correlating the two variables represents one observation covering a period of time.

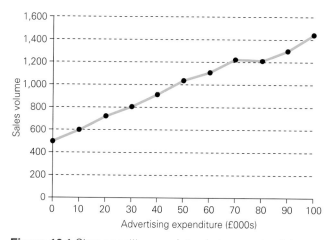

**Figure 16.1** Strong positive correlation between advertising expenditure and sales

In Figure 16.2, however, there is not so much linkage, as the diagram is little more than a collection of randomly dispersed points. In this case there is low correlation between advertising and sales, suggesting that the firm should stop wasting its money until it has found a way to make its advertising work more effectively.

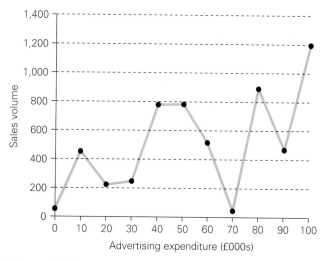

**Figure 16.2** Loose correlation: are other variables important?

What the researcher is looking for is cause and effect, namely evidence that the advertising has caused the increase in sales. Now correlation by itself does not indicate cause and effect. The rising of the sun in the morning may be strongly correlated with the delivery of milk, but it does not cause it to be delivered. Strong correlation is evidence that cause and effect *may* be present. Further evidence is needed to know how the variables affect each other. Clearly, the purpose of advertising is to generate sales, so cause and effect may be the explanation. But the sales of a product could rise because of cheaper credit terms, the disappearance of a competitor, or even unusual weather, and not just because of advertising. Where correlation is weak, as in Figure 16.2, researchers should suspect that advertising is not a significant causal factor.

In addition to positive correlation, it is possible to have negative correlation. The most obvious is between price and sales, as a price increase will surely lead to a fall in sales. Other possible negative correlations include:

- the temperature and sales of cold-weather products such as umbrellas, scarves and chocolate (the higher the temperature, the lower the sales)
- consumer incomes and the sales of 'value' products (Poundland's positioning); the better off people are, the fewer they'll buy of these things

'The most important thing is to forecast where customers are moving and be in front of them.' Philip Kotler, marketing guru

### Real business

#### *Correlation*

In Britain, the Met Office offers businesses a weather-forecasting service, charging a fee for predicting the sales of products ranging from lemonade to cat food. It uses correlation analysis to predict how demand will vary according to the time of year and the prevailing weather. It has found that lemonade sales rise in the summer, but tail away if the weather is very hot (presumably consumers switch to non-fizzy drinks or to ice lollies). More surprisingly, cat food is weather-affected. Rainy days boost demand (the cats don't go out) while if it's hot, cats eat less.

The website www.metoffice.gov.uk recently featured a producer of hot ready-meals that used the Met Office's correlation software to find out that it lost £70,000 of sales for every 1 degree of temperature increase above 20°C. Needless to say, using a weather forecast could enable the business to forecast sales more accurately, and therefore reduce stock losses on its perishable goods.

## 16.2 Understanding extrapolation

Extrapolation means projecting a trend forward in order to make a forecast of what will happen in the future. Often this is done unconsciously, such as the football fan who assumes that the next game will be easy because the last three have been won. In business, extrapolation should be a more formal affair. Figure 16.3 shows the trend sales data for the Apple iPod. It is easy to see how it can be extrapolated forwards to estimate the possible sales volume in the first quarter of 2015.

The simplest way of predicting the future is to assume that it will be just like the past. For the immediate future this may be realistic. It is unlikely that the economy or demand will change dramatically tomorrow. An assumption that the pattern of sales will continue to follow recent trends may therefore be reasonable. If demand for your product has been rising over the past few months, it is fair to assume it will continue in the foreseeable future. The process of predicting based on what has happened before is known as extrapolation. Extrapolation can often be done by drawing a line by eye to extend the trend on a graph (see Figure 16.4).

'Errors using inadequate data are much less than those using no data at all.' Charles Babbage, father of the computer

Here a very steady upward trend over a long period may well continue, and be predicted to continue. However, such stability and predictability are rare. The values of data plotted over time can vary because of seasonal variations or influences and also because of

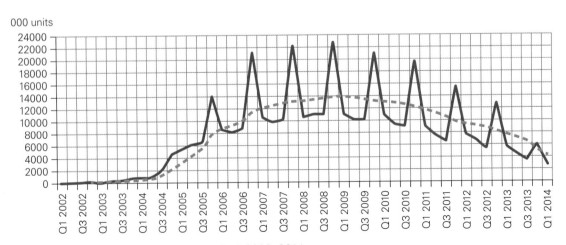

**Figure 16.3** Global quarterly sales Apple iPod, 2002–2014

Source: Apple Inc. accounts

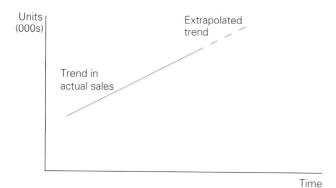

**Figure 16.4** An extrapolated sales trend

random factors that cannot be predicted. Despite the uncertainties, predicting sales based on extrapolated trends is the most widely used method.

# 16.3 How is extrapolation used?

The main use of extrapolation is in sales forecasting. This is crucial because it is at the heart of marketing planning, and key areas such as supply purchasing, production scheduling and staff recruitment and planning.

There are other uses of extrapolation, though. Companies regularly get caught out when believing their own hype. The truly catastrophic purchase by

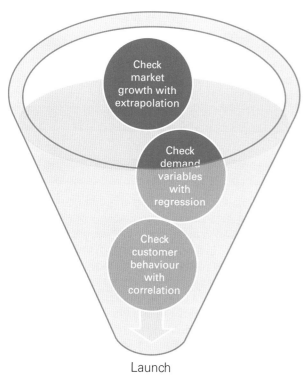

**Figure 16.5** Logic chain: data analysis behind product launches

RBS of ABN AMRO Bank was partly because of the success RBS had had with the purchase of NatWest bank. Management assumed thereafter that 'we're good at takeover bids'.

'Extrapolations are useful, especially in the art of soothsaying called forecasting trends . . . The trend-to-now may be a fact, but the future trend represents no more than an educated guess.' Darrell Huff, author

# 16.4 The value of technology in gathering data

In July 2014 Center Parcs opened its newest location at Woburn Forest, near London. The investment had been spread over a 10-year development period, making it tough to recover the £250 million spent. A key to recovering the capital would be through clever enough pricing to replicate the achievement of a 97 per cent occupancy rate throughout Center Parcs UK. This is done through a detailed computer system that checks constantly on the correlation between customer bookings and factors such as time of year, school holidays, big events (such as the World Cup) and customers' previous experience. The particular process used is called regression analysis. This breaks down all the variables affecting data such as sales figures, and then allocates a numerical importance to each one. For customers, the consequence is annoyingly high prices in school holidays (often three times the price in holidays that would be paid outside of them), but Center Parcs sells 97 per cent of their space, so – from a business point of view — it works.

Of course, there are other marketing decisions for which modern technology helps managers:

- Google Adwords allows a company to bid for a word or phrase, so that, for example, searchers for '5 star beach Ibiza' will instantly see advertisements for relevant hotels. This helps advertisers address one of the most famous problems in advertising: 'Half the money I spend on advertising is wasted; the problem is I don't know which half' (attributed to Lord Leverhulme, founder of Unilever). Adwords ensures that the online advertising you see is (almost always) relevant to you.
- The term 'Big Data' describes the extraordinary amount of information available today about people's purchasing behaviour (through card transactions), their likes and dislikes (via Facebook) and the people or companies they follow (via Twitter).

Huge networks of computers are needed to turn this information into general information about the attitudes of different segments of the market and to identify the habits and desires of individual consumers. Technology not only gathers the data but also analyses it by categories decided upon by business managers. The decision about how to analyse the data may be crucial; one company may spot changing attitudes among older consumers; another may not be looking in that direction.

- If technology such as Google Glass takes off, it may be that data gathering becomes even more widespread, with companies being able to know where and how we window shop, thereby learning more about the products we aspire to.

'Human decision about the future . . . cannot depend on strict mathematical expectation.' J. M. Keynes, British economist and writer

## Five Whys and a How

| Question | Answer |
|---|---|
| Why might a retailer wish to know the correlation between music and mood? | To decide on the type of music to play at the store entrance, perhaps to help relax customers into staying for longer |
| Why is it important for a correlation to be strong rather than weak? | Because a weak correlation may mean there is little or no true cause-and-effect relationship between the variables being looked at |
| Why doesn't correlation prove causation? | Because finding a strong relationship doesn't prove cause and effect; that requires further thought and perhaps analysis |
| Why may extrapolation of sales data sometimes lead to completely wrong estimates? | Extrapolation assumes that past trends will continue into the future; a break in the trend (fruit juice is no longer good becomes juice is too sugary) causes ever-greater inaccuracy |
| Why is it important to know and understand extrapolation? | Because many business (and economic) mistakes have been made by people who don't stop to think about how simplistic an idea extrapolation is |
| How is correlation identified within complex data? | Regression analysis using computer models helps identify the correlation between each variable and the factor being investigated, e.g. sales |

## Key terms

**Regression analysis:** breaking sales data down to assess the relative importance of different determinants of the data.

**Trend:** the general path a series of values (for example, sales) follows along over time, disregarding variations or random fluctuations.

## Evaluation: Interpreting marketing data

Today, no marketing manager can afford to sound ignorant about data-gathering technology or about the maths involved in techniques such as correlation and extrapolation. In many ways, though, the most important skills will remain exactly as they have always been: the ability to specify what aspects of the data are the most important (and therefore point data analysis in the right direction) and the ability to interpret and draw conclusions from the gathered information. Human judgement, therefore, will remain at the heart of whether a marketing company launches an inspired innovation or yet another new product failure.

# Workbook

## A. Revision questions

**(30 marks; 30 minutes)**

1. What is a sales forecast? (2)

2. Explain how you can show the trend in a series of data? (4)

3. Explain how two of the following Heinz managers could be helped by two weeks' warning that sales are forecast to rise by 15 per cent.
   a) the operations manager
   b) the marketing manager, Heinz Beans
   c) the personnel manager
   d) the chief accountant. (8)

4. What do you understand by the term 'extrapolation'? How is it used to make a sales forecast? (5)

5. Explain how Coca-Cola may be helped by checking for correlations between the following factors.
   a) sales and the daily temperature
   b) staff absence levels and the leadership style of individual supervisors. (6)

6. Explain why it is risky to assume cause and effect when looking at factors that are correlated. (5)

## B. Revision exercises

### DATA RESPONSE 1

The US aircraft manufacturer Boeing has predicted that airlines will want more smaller aircraft and fewer large jumbo jets in the next two decades.

Boeing has forecast $2.8 trillion (£1.4 trillion) worth of sales of commercial jets by all manufacturers over the next 20 years, up $200 billion from last year's projections. The company now expects regional, single-aisle and twin-aisle jets for non-stop routes to be the most popular aircraft.

Boeing forecasts a rise of 5 per cent a year in passenger numbers. Cargo traffic will increase by 6.1 per cent, it predicts. The company believes one-third of this demand will come from the Asia-Pacific region, making these developing markets vital for future sales.

The increase in demand for smaller craft is in contrast to an expected fall in demand for jumbos carrying more than 400 people. Boeing says demand for such craft is likely to fall to 960, down from the 990 it forecast a year ago.

The company is banking on its smaller, slimmer 787 plane. It believes this new plane will enable it to triumph over its main rival, Airbus. Twin-engined but with a long range, it will be able to fly direct to more airports in the world, eliminating the need for passengers to make connecting flights to access long-haul flights.

Boeing has forecast the following industry sales over the next 20 years:
- 17,650 single-aisle aeroplanes seating 90–240 passengers
- 6290 twin-aisle jets seating 200–400 passengers
- 3,700 regional jets with no more than 90 seats, up from 3,450 forecast last year
- 960 jumbo jets seating more than 400 passengers.

Adapted from bbc.co.uk

**Questions (25 marks; 30 minutes)**

1. Analyse the ways in which Boeing might have produced its industry sales forecasts. (9)

2. To what extent do Boeing's findings prove that its success is secure? (16)

### DATA RESPONSE 2

#### Bikes from India

In the 1960s the British motorcycle industry was wiped out by competition from Japan: Honda, Yamaha Suzuki and Kawasaki. An important part of Britain's motorcycle heritage was Royal Enfield, which went bust, though the brand ended up in the hands of an Indian company: the Eicher Group. This group built a substantial business in India based on the brand Royal Enfield. In 2013 around 175,000 Royal Enfield bikes are being produced (that's more than double the entire UK motorbike market).

**Figure 16.6** Royal Enfield motorbike

Now, with plans to expand output to 250,000 in 2014, the Eicher Group is eyeing the UK market. It wants to export 5,000 bikes to Britain, which would mean taking a 6 per cent market share. It believes that its market potential is rooted in the fastest growing UK biker demographic: oldie bikers, that is, those aged 55 plus. Today younger people are more likely to ride a bike than a motorbike. Fear of accidents has made motorbikes a tough sell to younger people. Eicher Motor's chief executive, Siddhartha Lal, says that, following secondary research, his group is targeting 'a nostalgic population of older and wealthier leisure riders'. With a price tag set of £5,200 for the October 2013 launch of the Royal Enfield Continental GT, the pitch certainly is at the wealthier end of the market.

In the UK the most obvious direct competitor to the Enfield bike is the rival heritage brand Triumph, the UK's top-selling bike. Although these bikes are made in Thailand, the brand owner has successfully recreated the British image attached to the Triumph brand, which adds value. The Royal Enfield is priced at £1,000 below the equivalent Triumph, but it is yet to be seen whether British bikers will trust the quality standards of bikes from India.

There is another demographic that is not yet being targeted by Eicher. According to a 24-year-old British biker who rented a Royal Enfield during a year-long stay in India, the bikes 'occupy cult status in India. Countless heroes of Bollywood films have been shown riding them . . . The look and feel of the thing, the rawness of the engine, the noise: everyone is obsessed by that'. So perhaps there are also prospects among wealthier Indians living in Britain. Fortunately for Eicher, 56 per cent growth in revenues in 2012 to £120 million has given the group a degree of financial solidity that makes the success of the UK launch desirable but not essential.

One other factor that Eicher will need to face in Britain is the highly seasonal nature of bike sales. In January people think of warm coats, not bikes, so the sales season is limited to the summer months.

All in all, the future of this UK launch seems uncertain. An early review of the Continental GT raises doubts about the 'build compromises', even though it praises the road handling and general modernity of the bike. Siddhartha Lal is hoping that UK success in October 2013 will kickstart a global push by Royal Enfield into export markets. It remains to be seen.

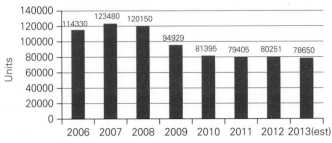

**Figure 16.7** Annual UK motorbike sales, 2006–2013

Source: www.mcia.co.uk

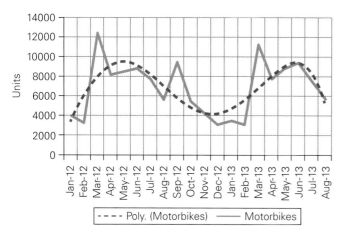

**Figure 16.8** Monthly sales of motorbikes in the UK, Jan 2012–Aug 2013

Source: www.mcia.co.uk

## Questions (25 marks; 30 minutes)

1. Use Figure 16.7 to identify and explain one reason in favour and one reason against launching into the UK market for motorbikes in 2013. (7)

2. Analyse how a British motorcycle producer might use the sales trend information provided in Figures 16.7 and 16.8. (9)

3. Use Figure 16.8 to analyse the possible difficulties created for a motorbike manufacturer from the strongly seasonal sales pattern in the UK market. (9)

## C. Extend your understanding

**(20 marks each)**

1. 'Since we can never know the future, it is pointless trying to forecast it.' To what extent do you agree with this statement? (20)

2. 'Quantitative sales forecasting techniques have only limited use. Qualitative judgements are needed in a constantly changing world.' To what extent do you agree with this statement? (20)

# Chapter 17 Price and income elasticity of demand

**Linked to:** Understanding markets, Chapter 14; Market research, Chapter 15; Segmentation, targeting and positioning, Chapter 19; Niche and mass marketing, Chapter 20; Pricing decisions, Chapter 23.

> **Definition**
>
> Elasticity measures the extent to which demand for a product changes when there is a change in a causal variable, such as price or consumer incomes.

## 17.1 Introduction

When a company increases the price of a product, it expects to lose some sales. Some customers will switch to a rival supplier; others may decide they do not want (or cannot afford) the product at all. Economists use the term 'the law of demand' to suggest that, almost invariably:

Price up $\longrightarrow$ Demand down

Price down $\longrightarrow$ Demand up

Price elasticity looks beyond the law of demand to ask the more subtle question: When the price goes up, by how much do sales fall? Elasticity measures the extent to which price changes affect demand.

## 17.2 Price elasticity of demand

In the short term, the most important factor affecting demand is price. When the price of *The Independent* newspaper increased from £1.20 to £1.40 in 2013, sales fell by 9 per cent between May and October; whereas *The Telegraph's* price rise from £1 to £1.20 (the year before) cut sales by just 4 per cent. Readers of *The Independent* proved more price sensitive than readers of *The Telegraph*. Therefore the owners of *The Telegraph* could feel delighted with their pricing decision. Selling 4 per cent fewer papers but receiving 20 per cent more for each one sold meant a significant boost to revenue and profits.

The crucial business question is: how much will demand change when we change the price? Will demand rise by 1 per cent, 5 per cent or 15 per cent following a 10 per cent price cut? Some products are far more price sensitive than others.

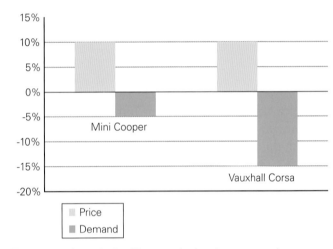

**Figure 17.1** Impact of a 10 per cent price rise on car sales

Price elasticity can be calculated using the formula shown below:

$$\text{Price elasticity (PED)} = \frac{\text{per cent change in quantity demanded}}{\text{per cent change in price}}$$

Price elasticity measures the percentage effect on demand of each 1 per cent change in price. So if a 10 per cent increase in price led demand to fall by 20 per cent, the price elasticity would be 2. Strictly speaking, price elasticities are always negative and therefore the actual figure is –2. This is because a price rise pushes demand down, and a price cut pushes demand up. The figure of –2 indicates that, for every 1 per cent change in price, demand will move by 2 per cent in the opposite direction.

## 17.3 Determinants of price elasticity

Why do some products, services or brands have low price elasticity and some high elasticity? Why is the price elasticity of Branston Baked Beans higher than that of

Heinz Baked Beans? Or the price elasticity of the *Financial Times* as low as –0.05 while the price elasticity of *Look* magazine is as high as –2.0 (that is, 40 times higher)?

The main determinants of price elasticity are as follows.

## The degree of product differentiation

This is the extent to which customers view the product as being distinctive from its rivals. *Look* may be an excellent magazine, but it is offering the same mix of fashion, shopping and 'celebs' as many other magazines aimed at young women. So if the cover price is increased, it is easy for readers to switch to an alternative, whereas readers of the *Financial Times* do not have any other option. Therefore, the higher the product differentiation the lower the price elasticity.

**Figure 17.2**

## The availability of substitutes

Customers may see 7 UP and Sprite as very similar drinks. In a supermarket they may buy the cheaper of the two. At a cinema, though, only Sprite may be available. At a train station vending machine, almost certainly Sprite will be the only lemonade. This is because it is a Coca-Cola brand and the distribution strength of Coke places Sprite in locations where 7 UP never goes. When Sprite has no direct competition its price elasticity is much lower; therefore the brand owner (Coke) can push the price up without losing too many customers.

## Branding and brand loyalty

Products with low price elasticity are those that consumers buy without thinking about the price tag. Some reach for Coca-Cola without checking its price compared with that of Pepsi, or buy a Harley-Davidson motorcycle even though a Honda superbike may be £4,000 cheaper. Strong brand names with strong brand images create customers who buy out of loyalty.

## 17.4 The value of price elasticity to decision-makers

Being able to estimate a product's price elasticity is a hugely valuable aid to marketing decision-making. At West Ham United, ticket prices for Under-16s vary from £70 in top seats for top games such as Manchester United all the way down to £1 when trying to fill the stadium against less attractive opposition on midweek winter evenings. Unusually for a business, the objective is to fill the stadium rather than maximise revenue. Understanding the price elasticity of demand for junior tickets helps West Ham achieve an average capacity utilisation of 95 per cent or more.

Data on a product's price elasticity can be used for two purposes, as outlined below.

### Sales forecasting

A firm considering a price rise will want to know the effect the price change is likely to have on demand. Producing a sales forecast will make possible accurate production, personnel and purchasing decisions. For example, in September 2013 Nintendo cut the price of its Wii U in America by 15 per cent, from $350 to $299. In October–November 2013 sales rose by 150 per cent. At that time, the price elasticity of the Wii U proved to be:

$$\frac{+150 \text{ per cent}}{-15 \text{ per cent}} = -10.$$

Nintendo could then use that knowledge to predict the likely impact of future price changes. Another price cut of 10 per cent could lead to doubling of sales (–10 per cent × –10 = +100 per cent). This information can be passed on to operations and HR, to get the staff in place to produce 100 per cent more stock.

In May 2014 Microsoft cut the US price of its new Xbox One console from $500 to $400. As a result the June sales volumes doubled. So a 20 per cent price cut boosted demand by 100 per cent (five times the amount), suggesting that the short-term price elasticity of the Xbox One was −5.

## Pricing strategy

There are many external factors that determine a product's demand, and therefore its profitability. For example, a soft drinks manufacturer can do nothing about a wet, cold summer that causes sales and profits to fall. However, the price the firm decides to charge is within its control, and it can be a crucial factor in determining demand and profitability. Price elasticity information can be used in conjunction with internal cost data to forecast the impact of a price change on revenue.

## 17.5 Classifying price elasticity

### Price-elastic products

A price-elastic product is one with a price elasticity of above 1. This means that the percentage change in demand is greater than the percentage change in price that created it. For example, if a firm increased prices by 5 per cent and as a result demand fell by 15 per cent, price elasticity would be:

$$\frac{-15 \text{ per cent}}{+5 \text{ per cent}} \times 100 = -3$$

The higher the price elasticity figure, the more price elastic the product. Cutting price on a price-elastic product will boost total revenue. This is because the extra revenue gained from the increased sales volume more than offsets the revenue lost from the price cut. On the other hand, a price increase on a price-elastic product will lead to a fall in total revenue.

**Table 17.1** Summary of price elasticity classification

| | Price-elastic product | Price-inelastic product |
|---|---|---|
| **Characteristic** | • Undifferentiated<br>• Many competitors | • Differentiated<br>• Few competitors |
| **Impact of a price cut** | Sales rise sharply... so revenue rises | Sales rise, but not much... so revenue falls |
| **Numerically** | Between −1 and −5 or more | Between −0.1 and −0.99 |
| **Impact of a price rise** | Sales fall sharply... so revenue falls | Sales fall, but not much... so revenue rises |

## Price-inelastic products

Price-inelastic products have price elasticities below 1. This means the percentage change in demand is less than the percentage change in price. In other words, price changes have hardly any effect on demand, perhaps because consumers feel they *must* have the product or brand in question: the stunning dress, the trendiest designer label or – less interestingly – gas for central heating. Customers feel they must have it, either because it really is a necessity, or because it is fashionable. Firms with price-inelastic products will be tempted to push the prices up. A price increase will boost revenue because the price rise creates a relatively small fall in sales volume. This means the majority of customers will continue to purchase the brand but at a higher, revenue-boosting price.

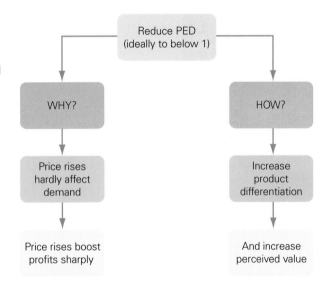

**Figure 17.3** Logic chain: lowering price elasticity

## 17.6 Income elasticity

Another important factor that affects the demand for many products is any change in household incomes. If people are better off they will buy more of most goods, for example, more chocolate, more new cars and more cinema tickets. To measure this effect it is wise to assess the income elasticity (YED) of a product or service. The formula is:

$$\frac{\text{per cent change in demand}}{\text{per cent change in real incomes (incomes after inflation)}}$$

There are three categories a product can be put into:

- a 'normal good', with positive income elasticity, and a YED of between 0.1 and 1.5
- a 'luxury' good, with very positive income elasticity of more than 1.5

- an 'inferior' good, that is, one with negative income elasticity (so, as people get better off, they buy less of it, perhaps including orange squash or Asda Value Milk Chocolate).

Knowing the income elasticity of a product is vital in order to develop a well-balanced product portfolio.

Because inferior goods sell well during recessions, it is helpful for a company to have both inferior goods and luxury goods. Nevertheless, as the UK economy tends to grow at around 2.5 per cent a year in the long term, normal and luxury goods are the most important part of a long-term strategy.

## Five Whys and a How

| Question | Answer |
|----------|--------|
| Why might a company care more about its PED than its sales figures? | Because extra sales do not necessarily boost profit, but control over pricing can transform a firm's profits and prospects |
| Why do products with high price elasticity not necessarily have high income elasticity? | Price elasticity is about competition and differentiation: income elasticity is about luxury. A Bentley has low price elasticity but high income elasticity |
| Why may a product's price elasticity change over time? | Because the degree of competition may change, as may the level of differentiation established by advertising |
| Why are consumers better off buying price elastic products (and services)? | Because the close rivalry between suppliers ensures efficient, value-for-money products |
| Why may a product's price elasticity vary over its life cycle? | If innovative, it would be low at birth, but increase as rivals catch up, then rise more when it falls out of fashion and into decline |
| How might a retail dry cleaner reduce its price elasticity? | By finding a USP or strong point of differentiation, e.g. free local collection and delivery |

## Key terms

**Predatory pricing:** pricing low with the deliberate intention of driving a competitor out of business.

**Price-elastic product:** a product that is highly price sensitive, so price elasticity is above 1.

**Price-inelastic product:** a product that is not very price sensitive, so price elasticity is below 1.

## Evaluation: Price and income elasticity of demand

Elasticity is a convenient concept but how useful is it in the real world? Would the average marketing director know the price elasticities of his or her products?

In many cases the answer is no. Textbooks exaggerate the precision that is possible with such a concept. The fact that the price elasticity of *The Telegraph* proved to be −0.2 in 2012 does not mean it will always be that low. Price elasticities change over time, as competition changes and consumer tastes change.

Even though elasticities can vary over time, certain features tend to remain constant. Strong brands such as BMW and Coca-Cola have relatively low price elasticity. This gives them the power over market pricing that ensures strong profitability year after year. For less established firms, these brands are the role models: everyone wants to be the Coca-Cola of their own market or market niche.

# Workbook

## A. Revision questions

**(40 marks; 40 minutes)**

1.  **a)** If a product's sales have fallen by 21 per cent since a price rise from £2 to £2.07, what is its price elasticity? (4)

    **b)** Is the product price elastic or price inelastic? (1)

2.  Outline two ways in which Nestlé could try to reduce the price elasticity of its Aero chocolate bars. (4)

3.  A firm selling 20,000 units at £8 is considering a 4 per cent price increase. It believes its price elasticity is –0.5.

    **a)** Calculate the effect on revenue. (6)

    **b)** Outline two reasons why the revenue may prove to be different from the firm's expectations. (4)

4.  Explain three ways a firm could make use of information about the price elasticity of its brands. (6)

5.  Identify three external factors that could increase the price elasticity of a brand of chocolate. (3)

6.  A firm has a sales target of 60,000 units per month. Current sales are 50,000 per month at a price of £1.50. If its products have a price elasticity of –2, what price should the firm charge to meet the target sales volume? (4)

7.  Why is price elasticity always negative? (2)

8.  Pol Roger sells 10,000 bottles of champagne a month in the UK at £30 a time. Its PED is -0.4 and its YED is +6.

    **a)** Calculate the value of its UK sales next year if real incomes rise by 2.5 per cent. (3)

    **b)** Briefly explain how it might use the data on its price elasticity of demand. (3)

## B. Revision exercises

### DATA RESPONSE 1

A firm selling Manchester United pillowcases for £10 currently generates an annual turnover of £500,000. Variable costs average at £4 per unit and total annual fixed costs are £100,000. The marketing director is considering a price increase of 10 per cent.

**Questions (20 marks; 25 minutes)**

1.  Given that the price elasticity of the product is believed to be –0.4, calculate:

    **a)** the old and the new sales volume (3)

    **b)** the new revenue (3)

    **c)** the expected change in profit following the price increase. (6)

2.  Analyse the factors that might affect the price elasticity of pillowcases. (8)

### DATA RESPONSE 2

**Sauces and sources**

Heinz Tomato Ketchup is an iconic brand, more than 100 years old. It dominates the market for ketchup with annual sales of £125 million in the UK. It has a share of UK tomato sauce sales believed to be over 75 per cent. It has no effective branded competition, though sales of supermarket own label ketchups can be considerable.

In 2013 it took a risk by increasing its prices by 10 per cent, even though the average price increase for 'table sauces' was only 3.5 per cent. The result was a 5 per cent fall in Heinz sales volumes.

**Figure 17.4** Heinz Tomato Ketchup

Heinz says that the major growth stories in table sauces come from more exotic flavours such as Mexican Chilli and Heinz Sweet Chilli. Perhaps this increased competition explains the collapse in sales of Levi Roots' Reggae Reggae Barbeque sauce, which suffered a 17 per cent fall in 2013 sales volumes following a price rise of 8.5 per cent. The following table sets out the full story.

**Figure 17.5** Reggae Reggae Sauce

### Questions (25 marks; 30 minutes)

1. **a)** Calculate the price elasticity of Heinz Tomato Ketchup in 2013. (4)

   **b)** Explain two reasons why this product may have this degree of price elasticity. (4)

**Table 17.2** Reggae Reggae Sauce sales 2012 and 2013

|  | 2012 | 2013 |
|---|---|---|
| **Selling price** | £1.55 | £1.68 |
| **Sales volume (bottles)** | 3.1 million | 2.56 million |
| **Sales revenue (£ millions)** | £4.8m | £4.3m |

Source: *The Grocer*

Text adapted from *The Grocer* and Mysupermarket.com

2. **a)** Calculate the price elasticity of Reggae Reggae sauce in 2013. (4)

   **b)** It is believed that the price elasticity of Reggae Reggae sauce is higher now than in the past. Explain two possible reasons why this might have occurred. (4)

3. The figures suggest that Heinz Tomato Ketchup has a significantly lower price elasticity than that of Reggae Reggae Sauce. Analyse the implications of that for Heinz. (9)

## C. Extend your understanding

1. WH Smith has found that the price elasticity of its core stationery products (paper, pens, etc.) is quite high. Discuss how it might set about reducing the price elasticity of this part of its business. (20)

2. After its relative failure with Xbox One, Microsoft is preparing to develop and launch Xbox Two. To what extent might it use the concept of price and income elasticity to help it with setting prices and forecasting sales? (20)

**Linked to:** Setting marketing objectives, Chapter 13; Understanding markets, Chapter 14; Market research, Chapter 15; Segmentation, targeting and positioning, Chapter 19.

### Definition

Breaking the market down statistically to assess the types of product, consumer and competitor.

## 18.1 What market are we in?

This sounds like a daft question, but the marketing guru Theodore Levitt considers it vital. Is Liverpool FC in the football business, the sports business or the leisure business? Long ago, Nintendo was Japan's number one producer of playing cards. It decided that its market was the broader games business and experimented with electronic games in the 1970s. Today, despite difficulties in competing with Sony and Xbox, it is a hugely successful producer of games consoles and software. Sales of playing cards represent less than 1 per cent of the modern Nintendo.

**Figure 18.1** Nintendo star: Super Mario

'The railroads collapsed because they thought they were in the railroad business, when really they were in the transport business.' Theodore Levitt, business guru.

## 18.2 The purpose of market analysis

Managers tend to get caught up in the day-to-day needs of the business. A photo of Alexa Chung wearing a silk scarf might make sales leap, forcing clothes store managers to focus 100 per cent on how to find extra stocks of scarves. Market analysis should be a cooler, more thoughtful look at the market's longer-term trends. In 2001 Whitbread decided to sell its pub business to focus on hotels (Premier Inn) and Costa Coffee. It later sold off other businesses such as David Lloyd Health Clubs and TGI Friday's – to focus on where it thought the growth was – in coffee bars especially. Its clever market analysis positioned the business correctly for future growth.

Other clever pieces of market analysis include:

- Danone seeing the opportunity for 'functional foods' (that is, foods bought because they are believed to be good for you), such as Activia yoghurt, then putting more money behind these brands than anyone else. It showed huge confidence in its understanding of the market.
- Harvey Nichols (classic London posh shop) seeing the opportunity for a branch in Leeds, in an era when there was plenty of money in the North. When it made the move, other retailers doubted whether Leeds would be posh enough – it was and it is.

These examples have one thing in common: they are the result of careful analysis of trends within a market, backed by an ability to take bold decisions (and get them right).

'One of the primary objectives of market analysis is to determine the attractiveness of a market.' David Aaker, US writer and businessman

## 18.3 Consumer usage and attitudes

Market analysis is rooted in a deep understanding of customers. Why do they buy Coca-Cola, not Pepsi? Yet they prefer Tropicana (made by Pepsi) to Minute Maid (made by Coke). And who are the key decision-makers? Purchasers (perhaps parents buying a multipack in Tesco) or the users (perhaps young teenage children slumped in front of the television)? Is the brand decision a result of child pester power, or parental belief in the product's superiority? Knowledge of such subtleties is essential. Only then can the firm know whether to focus marketing effort on the parent or the child.

To acquire the necessary knowledge about usage and attitudes, firms adopt several approaches. The starting point is usually qualitative research, such as group discussions. Run by psychologists, these informal discussions help to pinpoint consumers' underlying motives and behaviour. For example, it is important to learn whether Kit Kat buyers enjoy nibbling the chocolate before eating the wafer biscuit; in other words, to discover whether playing with confectionery is an important part of the enjoyment. This type of information can influence future product development.

Multinational Unilever has set up a Knowledge Management Group to ensure that insights such as this can be spread around the business. Its job is to help Unilever achieve its strategic objectives by 'locating, capturing, sharing, transferring and creating knowledge'. The company believes this helps it benefit from:

- improved decision-making
- fewer mistakes
- reduced duplication
- converting new knowledge more quickly into added value to the business.

Among the other ways to gather information on customer usage and attitudes are quantitative research and obtaining feedback from staff who deal directly with customers. An example of the latter would be bank staff whose task is to sell services such as insurance. Customer doubts about a brochure or a product feature, if fed back to head office, may lead to important improvements.

Quantitative research is also used to monitor customer usage and attitudes. Many firms conduct surveys every month, to track changes in brand awareness or image over time. This procedure may reveal that a TV commercial has had an unintended side effect in making the brand image rather too upmarket, or that customers within a market are becoming more concerned about whether the packaging can be recycled.

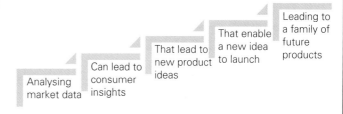

**Figure 18.2** Logic ladder: the value of market analysis

## 18.4 Consumer profiles

Marketing decisions are very hard to make without a clear picture of your customers. Who are they? Young? Outgoing? Affluent? Or not. From product and packaging design, through to pricing, promotion and distribution – all these aspects of marketing hinge on knowing your target market.

A consumer profile is a statistical breakdown of the people who buy a particular product or brand. (For example, what percentage of consumers are women aged 16 to 25?) The main categories analysed within a consumer profile are customers' age, gender, social class, income level and region. Profile information is used mainly for:

- setting quotas for research surveys
- segmenting a market
- deciding in which media to advertise (*Vogue* or *The Sun*?).

A large consumer goods firm will make sure to obtain a profile of consumers throughout the market as well as for its own brand(s). This may be very revealing. It may show that the age profile of its own customers is becoming older than for the market as a whole. This may force a complete rethink of the marketing strategy. The company may have been trying to give the brand a classier image, but may end up attracting older customers.

### Real business

#### *The Jaguar XJ*

Launched in 2010, the new Jaguar XJ was deliberately designed to restore the company's position within the luxury car sector. In the days when Jaguar was owned by Ford, the American car producer had pulled Jaguar's model range down towards the mass market. The XJ, with prices from around £60,000, would emphasise that Jaguar should be seen alongside Mercedes and BMW, not Ford or Volkswagen. In February 2014 Jaguar announced that booming sales of the XJ in China were an important part of its record-breaking £842 million profit in the third quarter of its 2013/2014 financial year.

## Five Whys and a How

| Question | Answer |
|---|---|
| Why is it hard for new firms to break into an established market? | Because the existing firms have rich market understanding that is hard for newcomers to match |
| Why may it be hard to decide on the boundaries of a market? | Because people and technology change, the boundaries can change. Music and gaming were once separate markets; now mobile hardware has brought them into competition |
| Why may consumer attitudes be different from usage? | Many consumers disapprove of fattening products, but buy and eat them; consumer psychology is complex |
| Why does market analysis matter? | Bad day-to-day decisions can waste millions of pounds, but dreadful market analysis (Tesco in America) can waste billions |
| Why might an ice cream producer benefit from careful analysis of sales data in its market? | It might identify a new trend before competitors, such as a trend towards adult iced lollies (vodka and orange, perhaps?) |
| How might Jaguar Land Rover build on its success in China? | Work hard at understanding Chinese car buyers to make sure future models are designed to suit their habits, tastes and pockets |

### Key terms

**Product positioning:** deciding on the image and target market you want for your own product or brand.

**Target market:** the type of customer your product or service is aimed at. For example, the target market for Kit Kat Senses is 15- to 30-year-old women.

### Evaluation: Market data and analysis

Market analysis is at the heart of successful marketing. All the great marketing decisions are rooted in a deep understanding of what customers really want; from the marketing of Lady GaGa through to the sustained success of the (incredibly pricey) Chanel No. 5 perfume. The clever market stall trader acquires this understanding through daily contact with customers. Large companies need the help of market research to provide a comparable feel. Techniques such as market mapping then help clarify the picture.

Having learnt what the customer really wants from a product, perhaps helped by psychological insights from qualitative research, it is relatively easy to put the strategy into practice. If the marketing insight is powerful enough, the practical details of the marketing mix should not matter too much. The Sony PS4 was a brilliant piece of marketing, but few commentators had anything good to say about the brand's advertising or packaging. The genius came earlier in the process.

## Workbook

### A. Revision questions

(30 marks; 30 minutes)

1. Reread Section 18.1 and ask yourself 'What if Nintendo had not decided to define its market more widely? What would the business be like today?' (3)

2. Explain how customer 'usage' may be different from customer 'attitudes'. (4)

3. Explain two reasons why it may be important to distinguish 'purchasers' from 'users'. (4)

4. Explain how qualitative research could be used helpfully when analysing a market. (4)

5. When *Look* magazine was launched it announced that its target market was '24-year-old women'. Explain two ways it could make use of this very precise consumer profile. (4)

6. When Apple launched the Apple Watch it believed that its iPhone customers would spend $350 on an extra gadget. Outline two pieces of market analysis that might have led them to that view. (4)

7. Why does market research need to be carried out regularly, not just related to a new product? (3)

8. Explain the importance of market research in achieving effective market analysis. (4)

## B. Revision exercises
### DATA RESPONSE

What business is Cadbury in? For the first 100 years of the firm's life, the answer would have been chocolate. But in 1989 it bought the Trebor and Bassett's brands to form a large sugar confectionery unit. With Wrigley enjoying uninterrupted growth in chewing gum, Cadbury then bought Adams – a major US gum producer (for £2.7 billion). It followed this up with purchases of other chewing gum producers in countries that included Turkey.

In 2007, Cadbury launched the Trident gum brand in Britain. This was bold because Wrigley enjoyed a market share of more than 90 per cent in the UK. By March 2008 Cadbury was able to announce that 'an astounding £38 million of extra sales value has been added to the gum category, with 75 per cent of this growth delivered by Trident'. Cadbury's management confidently predicted 5 years of growth for Trident of as much as £20 million of sales per year.

By 2009, though, Trident was in sharp retreat, with sales falling to £19 million that year and continuing their slump to reach under £5 million by 2013. By then Cadbury had been submerged into the Kraft food business. So is Cadbury in the food business, the chocolate business, or the confectionery business? It's hard to say.

**Table 18.1** UK confectionery market 2013

| Confectionery | Market value (£ millions) |
|---|---|
| Chocolate | 3,600 |
| Sugar confectionery | 1,147 |
| Chewing gum | 272 |
| **Total market** | 5,019 |

### Questions (23 marks; 30 minutes)

1. Explain why companies such as Cadbury need to ask themselves, 'What market am I in?' (5)

2. a) What is meant by the term 'market share'? (2)

   b) Calculate Trident's share of the chewing gum market in 2013. (2)

   c) Why might Cadbury have been worried about tackling a business with 'a market share of more than 90 per cent'? (5)

3. Analyse what might have gone wrong with Cadbury's understanding of the chewing gum market. (9)

## C. Extend your understanding

1. As a generalisation, your grandparents once loved Marks & Spencer and your parents loved Tesco. Now neither is loved. Discuss the problems a business such as Tesco may have in rebuilding customer usage and attitudes. (20)

2. In the past 5 years the boom in China's car market has only been exceeded by the boom in sales of 4 × 4 cars in China. Having analysed the data, Rolls Royce is now developing the world's most expensive 4 × 4. To what extent would you agree with this strategy? (20)

# Chapter 19 Segmentation, targeting and positioning

**Linked to:** Understanding markets, Chapter 14; Interpreting marketing data, Chapter 16; Market data and analysis, Chapter 18.

---

### Definition

Segmentation means finding ways to divide a market up to identify untapped opportunities, perhaps among older consumers, or among those who believe they are wheat-intolerant. This offers up the possibility of new target markets and a new positioning within the market.

---

## 19.1 Market segmentation

Most markets can be subdivided in several different ways. If you go to WH Smith and look at the magazine racks, you will see the process in action. There are magazines for men and (many more) for women. Within the women's section there are magazines for kids, teens, young adults, those who are middle-aged and some for the elderly. Then there are magazines that target different interests and hobbies, from football to computer consoles to gardening.

Market segmentation is the acknowledgement by companies that customers are not all the same. 'The market' can be broken down into smaller sections in which customers share common characteristics, from the same age group to a shared love of Manchester United. Successful segmentation can increase customer satisfaction (if you love shopping and 'celebs', how wonderful that *Look* magazine is for you!) and provide scope for increasing company profits. After all, customers may be willing to pay a higher price for a magazine focused purely on the subjects they love, instead of buying a general magazine in which most of the articles stay unread.

For new, small companies segmentation is a valuable strategy for breaking into an established market. (Think innocent in fruit juice, first making its mark with smoothies.) For large companies, market segmentation involves two possibilities:

1. Simply to add one niche product to a portfolio otherwise dominated by the mass market

2. Multiple segmentation, in which a wide portfolio of niche brands can add up to a market leading position. This approach would have risked being only marginally profitable in the past, but flexible, high-tech manufacturing systems can make it cost-effective to produce differently targeted products on the same production line. A good example is Ella's Organic – a baby food company which has enjoyed sales growth from £2 million a year in 2009 to £30 million in 2014 by spreading the idea of food good-for-babies across a series of different sectors (and 15 countries overseas).

---

'In multiple segmentation, a company seeks to appeal to two or more well-defined consumer groups by different marketing plans.' J. Evans and B. Berman, academics and authors

---

## 19.2 The process of segmentation

To successfully segment a market, the steps are as follows.

1. Conduct research into the different types of customer within a marketplace; for example, different age groups, gender, region and personality types.

2. See if they have common tastes/habits; for example, younger readers may be more focused on fashion and celebrities than older ones.

3. Identify the segment you wish to focus on, and then conduct some qualitative research into customer motivations and psychology.

4. Devise a product designed not for the whole market, but for a particular segment. This may only achieve a 1 per cent market share, but if the total market is big enough, that could be highly profitable.

In 2003 Camilla Stephens started a pie business that struggled to become profitable. It needed to be refinanced and downscaled in 2004, but from a smaller base it began to grow. Before starting the business, Camilla had been Head of Food at Starbucks UK and also Deputy Editor of Good Housekeeping magazine, so she had a terrific understanding of food trends. Seeing the success of innocent Drinks and Green and Blacks, she focused clearly on hand-made, very high quality, high-priced pies. Think Chicken and Red Pepper rather than Chicken Balti.

In the early years the pie business supplied local cafes and caterers, but in 2006 Camilla (with new partner/husband James Footit) developed the *Higgidy* brand. This proved an incredible turning point. Within 18 months Higgidy was stocked in Sainsbury, Booths and Waitrose supermarkets, giving national distribution and a big boost to sales. By taking their time to understand the market segment for posh pies, Higgidy was put on track to achieve success in the static market for pies and pastries. In the graph below, Higgidy's success is contrasted with the flat sales position of mass-market Pukka Pies.

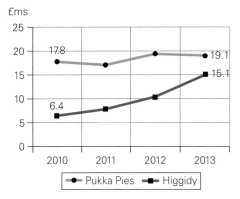

**Figure 19.1** Higgidy's sales growth, 2010-13

Source: *The Grocer* magazine

## 19.3 The value of segmentation

Segmentation offers companies three main benefits.

1. Improved sales volumes. When Xbox 360 and the PS3 were about to be launched, Nintendo surprised the market by bringing out the Wii. Instead of targeting young men, Nintendo had identified market demand for a family console with appeal to young and old. The Wii was a huge success in sales volume terms and in profitability. What Nintendo had expected to be a relatively small segment proved to be a new, differentiated mass-market product. Even for lesser new products, segmentation can build sales volume within a market. In 2013 Cadbury brought out Marvellous Creations – a range of more fun, younger variants on the Dairy Milk theme. Its sales of more than £50 million in 2013 were overwhelming additions to sales of the Dairy Milk brand and of chocolate as a whole. By appealing to a younger segment, more chocolate was sold.

2. Increased prices. When Center Parcs managed to identify a segment in the UK holiday market for a more upmarket version of Butlins and other holiday camps, they effectively became the sole suppliers of this category of holiday. Center Parcs had identified the segment, designed the right product and now enjoy 97 per cent usage, year-round (and made profits of £20 million in 2013/14).

3. Increased diversification and therefore security. It is great to have a blockbuster, mass-market product, but less so if sales start to slip as fashion moves away. Shares in the US shoe brand Crocs fell from $68 in October 2007 to $1.50 in November 2008 as Crocs went from 'hot to what?' Life would have been much more comfortable for the business if it had brands in several segments instead of the one mass-market product.

'In market segmentation a company seeks to appeal to one well-defined consumer group by one marketing plan.' J. Evans and B. Berman, academics and authors

## 19.4 Methods of segmentation

1. Demographic, in other words by population subset: by age, by ethnic origin or by gender. In the UK market for yoghurt, two of the 'Top Ten' brands are focused on children: Petit Filous (sales of £98 million in 2013) and Munch Bunch (£54.4 million in 2013). Both brands were part of a wave of segmentation that transformed the market from a single product with sales of less than £5 million in 1970 (plain, unsweetened yogurt in glass jars) to today's UK market worth more than £2,000 million (figures from *The Grocer*, 21 December 2013). A glance at daytime TV shows all the products that target the older demographic. And a glance at Figure 19.2 shows the growth to come in this age group.

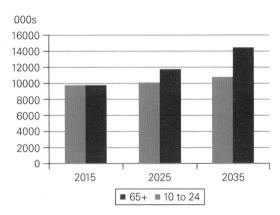

**Figure 19.2** UK population by age category
Source: Office of National Statistics Population Projections

2. Geographic, in other words by region or by country (for a UK exporting business). In the UK, sales of the soft drink Irn Bru have always been concentrated in Scotland. But following three years of a marketing push into England, by 2014 57 per cent of the brand's sales came from England and Wales (with 41 per cent drunk by the 8 per cent of the UK population based in Scotland). To brand owners A.G.Barr, geographic segmentation can be seen as a strength (Irn Bru is a must-stock drink in Scotland) as well as offering interesting sales development opportunities.

3. Income; in other words, segmenting markets in relation to household incomes. This is more relevant than ever, because income and wealth distribution has become significantly more unequal over recent decades. The market for eating out is a good example, with (in London) the price of an evening meal varying between £10 per person and £200. This means that businesses have to think hard about whether they want to be involved in every income segment, or whether they would be better off specialising. For example Tragus operates 300 restaurants in the £10-£20 per head sector, under brands such as Strada, Café Rouge and Bella Italia. Another group, D&D London, runs about 30 outlets in Britain at prices of around £50 per head. By specialising in one income-related segment, these groups can learn about their market and therefore make fewer mistakes when opening new restaurants (one of the highest-risk businesses in Britain).

4. Behavioural, that is dividing up a market into how people behave, for example, taking the market for young fashion and dividing it up into fashion leaders and fashion followers. Or subdividing the games market into 'shoot-em-ups' and strategy games. To do this successfully one has to understand the market exceptionally well.

'In the affluent society no useful distinction can be made between luxuries and necessities.' J. K. Galbraith, economist and (outstanding) author

## 19.5 Targeting

Having analysed a market and identified suitable criteria for segmentation, the business then needs to decide which precise segment it wishes to target. Naturally, it will take into account its own strengths, both real (in terms, say, of design skills) and also based on image, such as the association of Porsche with classy sportiness. So when Porsche decided to develop a 4x4 off-road vehicle, it had to look sporty and exude luxury. It did.

In addition to comparing the segments to your own strengths, it would be important to consider:

- the potential size of each segment, by volume and especially by value
- the potential growth rate within each segment
- whether there is a rival business with a better fit with the segment; for example, Saga for the older audience
- whether an existing producer has already got a foothold in the segment. (It may be hugely valuable to be first into a sector.)
- the accessibility of each possible target audience; for example, reaching young adults is less certain than reaching older people. The latter have more predictable behaviours, for example, watching daytime TV, whereas young people may only be reached effectively if, by luck or skill, a social media viral marketing campaign works well.

Having made the decision about targeting, it's time for the final step: positioning.

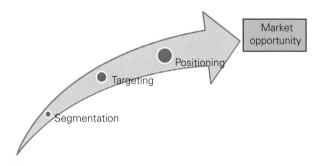

**Figure 19.3** Logic chain: STEP towards market opportunity

## 19.6 Positioning

Having decided which segment to target, there remains the issue of positioning. The decision may be made to aim for the centre of the segment, for example 'for *all* young men'. Or the intention may be to only target the heavily committed shoot-em-up gamers. For Apple consumer electronics, the positioning was clearly 'accessible and easy to use' as opposed to 'for geeks'.

However sure the business is of its segmentation analysis, the decision on positioning will be crucial. A me-too approach works very rarely (though Apple would doubtless argue that Samsung's hugely successful Galaxy model was a me-too of the iPhone). The best approach is to identify a position within the segment that will appeal strongly to a minority, as opposed to appealing a bit to the many.

A great example of positioning is Aldi's position within the UK's price-motivated segment of the grocery market. With Asda, Lidl and Iceland as its direct competitors, Aldi has seen its sales boom as a result of persuading middle-Britain that shopping at Aldi is sensible rather than cheapskate. Its slogan 'Spend a little. Live a lot.' is about having a good time, not about 'low, low prices'. Figure 19.4 shows the value to Aldi of astute positioning.

**Figure 19.4** Aldi year-on-year percentage change in sales, 12 weeks to July 2014
Source: Kantar Worldpanel

## Five Whys and a How

| Question | Answer |
|---|---|
| Why might a company such as Heinz, with a strong mass-market position, choose to segment a market? | Because it's often possible to charge higher prices for segmental products than it is in the mass market |
| Why might multiple segmentation be preferable to having a big-selling mass-market product? | Because prices and profit margins might be higher and there's less risk than there is having 'all the eggs in one basket' |
| Why may segmentation by age become more important in the future? | Because of demographic shifts towards more older people |
| Why might a foreign chocolate company make a targeting mistake if it tried to break into the UK chocolate market? | By not knowing the UK market enough to be able to interpret research findings accurately |
| Why might it be necessary to use qualitative research before deciding finally on the right positioning for a new biscuit brand? | Because you need insight into consumer psychology, which is what qualitative research should be able to provide |
| How might segmentation and positioning help Marks & Spencer? | Instead of aiming at everyone it might help them focus more tightly (and more effectively) on specific groups of people |

## Evaluation: Segmentation, targeting and positioning

In recent years Kellogg's has struggled as breakfast cereal sales have faltered generally in America, Britain and Europe. Its market analysis showed that fewer people eat breakfast, but it struggled to think how to create 'breakfast-on-the-go'. Rice Krispies Cereal Bars do not seem a long-term solution. So the company needs to reposition itself. It made a start in 2012 by buying the Pringles brand for $2.7 billion. But since then it has been unable to see a successful way forward. In the long run, the managements that understand (and are bold enough to implement) a strategy of segmentation, targeting and positioning are the ones that will keep moving from one growth sector to the next.

# Workbook

## A. Revision questions

(35 marks; 35 minutes)

1. Explain how customer satisfaction might increase as a result of more careful market segmentation. (4)

2. **a)** Look at Figure 19.1. Calculate the percentage sales change between 2010 and 2013 for:
   **i.** Higgidy (3)
   **ii.** Pukka (3)

   **b)** Explain what impact this growth might have had on the unit costs of producing Higgidy Pies. (4)

3. Why might diversification be an attraction for a business planning a segmentation instead of a mass-market strategy? (4)

4. Explain in your own words how the market for shoes could be segmented. (4)

5. Figure 19.2 shows how much population growth is expected in the 65-plus age category. Explain how this might affect a supermarket of your choice. (6)

6. Figure 19.4 might suggest that Iceland Foods needs to reposition itself. How might it set about this process? (7)

## B. Revision exercises

### DATA RESPONSE

### Galaxy Chocolate at 15p head for India

Around the globe, the $100 billion chocolate market is a battle between three multinationals: Mars, Nestlé and Mondelez (the Kraft subsidiary that includes Cadbury). An exception is India, where Mars has no significant foothold. Given that India is the world's fastest-growing market for chocolate, it should be no surprise that Mars is determined to tackle this issue. This November it is launching Galaxy Premium chocolate to take on the might of Cadbury Dairy Milk.

Its approach to the launch shows all the signs of desperation. Although the Galaxy launch is supported by a glossy advertising campaign featuring Bollywood actor Arjun Rampal and model Sapna Pabbi, Mars is pricing Galaxy extremely competitively. In the middle of the market, Cadbury Dairy Milk has a 38g 'value' pack priced at 22p and a 60g Dairy Milk 'Silk' pack for 55p. Mars is to price a 40g pack of Galaxy at 15p.

**Figure 19.5** Galaxy's launch in India featured Bollywood actor Arjun Rampal

M.V. Natarajan, general manager of Mars India (Chocolates Division) said: 'India is the world's fastest growing chocolate market and the moulded chocolate segment is the fastest growing sector. India is a very important market for Mars. With this launch we are entering an extremely dynamic segment with our business objective of growing our product range in India.'

The market for chocolate in India has a value of just £555 million at the moment. It is this small because Indians currently eat less than a sixtieth of the amount of chocolate eaten in Britain (0.165kg a year compared with our 10.2 kgs!). But the market is forecast by Cadbury to grow at 23 per cent a year between 2013 and 2018, which will take it towards the UK's market size.

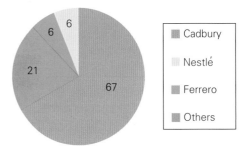

**Figure 19.6** Chocolate market-share percentage, India 2013

Mr Natarajan's marketing strategy has two further elements to it. There is a marketing plan targeting the 0–18 age category, based on free distribution of sweets twice a year, on Independence Day and again on Republic Day. 19–35s will also be targeted using a tie-in with Facebook. One week before, Facebook will send the message 'Do you want to send chocolates on your friend's birthday?' There can be no doubt that Mars is determined to succeed.

### Questions (30 marks; 35 minutes)

1. Explain two possible reasons why Mars wants to build a market share in India. (5)

2. From the text, analyse how well Mars has used 'segmentation, targeting and positioning' in launching Mars Premium chocolate in India? (9)

3. To what extent do you think the pricing strategy for Galaxy is likely to prove successful for Mars? (16)

## C. Extend your understanding

1. Choose one of the following markets (bicycles; shampoos; chicken restaurants or football boots). To what extent would the use of segmentation, targeting and positioning boost the chances of a new company entering the market you've selected? (20)

2. To what extent would companies do better to focus 100 per cent on developing innovative new products than to bog themselves down in segmentation, targeting and positioning? (20)

# Chapter 20

# Niche and mass marketing

**Linked to:** Market research, Chapter 15; Market data and analysis, Chapter 18; Segmentation targeting and positioning, Chapter 19; Pricing decisions, Chapter 23.

## Definition

Mass marketing means devising products with mass appeal and promoting them to all types of customer. Niche marketing is tailoring a product to a particular type of customer.

## 20.1 Mass marketing

Mass marketing is the attempt to create products or services that have universal appeal. Rather than targeting a specific type of customer, mass marketing aims the product at the whole market. The intention is that everyone should be a consumer of the product. Coca-Cola is a good example of a firm that uses mass-marketing techniques. The company aims its product at young and old alike. Its goal has always been to be the market leader and it still is today. The ultimate prize of mass marketing is the creation of generic brands. These are brands that are so totally associated with the product that customers treat the brand name as if it was a product category. Examples include 'Coke' (cola) and 'Bacardi' (white rum).

**Figure 20.1** Mass marketing

As shown in Figure 20.1, when mass marketing is carried out successfully it can be highly profitable. Firms such as Ryanair set out to be high-volume, mass-market operators and achieve handsome profits. However, it is important to note that mass marketing does not have to go hand in hand with low prices. For example, Nintendo, when it launched the DS, decided to become *the* handheld games console. Superb launch advertising and excellent games software development meant that it achieved mass-market sales while keeping its prices high. Even now, with its sales entering the decline phase of its product life cycle (see Figure 20.2), it remains the dominant brand in its market. Mass marketing does not have to aim at the lowest common denominator.

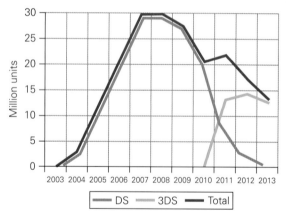

**Figure 20.2** Worldwide annual sales of Nintendo handheld consoles, 2003–13

Source: VGChartz.com

'The mass market has split into ever-multiplying, ever-changing sets of micromarkets.' Alvin Toffler, author and social commentator.

## 20.2 Niche marketing

A niche market is a very small segment of a much larger market. Niche marketing involves identifying the needs of the consumers that make up the niche. A specialised product or service is then designed to meet the distinctive needs of these consumers. Niche-market products tend to sell in relatively low volumes. As a result, the price of a niche-market product is usually higher than the mass-market alternative. Niche market operators often distribute their products through specialist retailers, or directly to the consumer via the internet.

An entrepreneur wanting to set up a niche market business must first identify a group of people who share a taste for a product or service that is currently unsatisfied. A product or a service must then be designed that is capable of meeting this unsatisfied need. To stand a good chance of success, the new niche product will need to be superior to the mass-market equivalent that is currently available. Finally, the niche must be large enough to support a profitable business. Many new niche-market businesses fail because the revenue generated from their niche-market business is not high enough to cover the costs of operating.

A good example is provided by a small neighbourhood restaurant called Bajou that tried, unsuccessfully, to make a business out of selling Cajun food in south Croydon. At the weekend the restaurant was never completely empty, proving that a gap in the market did exist. Unfortunately, this gap in the market was not large enough to cover the overheads of running a restaurant. The restaurant was never full enough to operate above a break-even level. Six months after Bajou opened it was forced to close down. In niche markets entrepreneurs must manage their overhead costs with care if the business is to operate above its break-even point.

Small niche operators lack the economies of scale required to compete on price with larger, established operators. Instead, the small firm could try to find a small, profitable niche. The amount of profit generated by this niche needs to be high enough for the small firm, but too trivial for the big business. Rubicon Exotic has just a 0.6 per cent share of the £2.5 billion UK market for fizzy drinks. Happily, sales of £14 million are profitable enough to satisfy the requirements of Rubicon Drinks, with its low overheads. Small, niche-market businesses survive on the basis that they occupy a relatively unimportant market niche. Larger firms operating in the mass market are happy to ignore the niche businesses because they represent too small an opportunity to be worth their while.

Niche market businesses sell specialised, differentiated products that are designed to appeal to their very specific target market. Firms selling niche-market products can exploit the low price sensitivity created by product differentiation by raising price. Total revenue will rise after the price increase because, in percentage terms, the fall in sales volume will be less than the price increase.

**Figure 20.3** Logic chain

'Most large markets evolve from niche markets.' R. McKenna, businessman

## 20.3 Are niche markets safe havens for small businesses?

In the past many large companies focused on mass markets and ignored small market gaps and the small companies that filled them. To fill lots of small niches would require lots of short production runs (for example, 90 minutes on the printing press producing the Hartlepool FC fanzine, and 60 minutes producing the Darlington one). This has always been expensive, because of the time taken to reset machinery.

This has changed due to technology. As production lines are increasingly set up by computer, they can be reset almost instantly. So large firms can build the sales volumes they need by producing a large variety of low-volume niche-market products. Small-scale producers are coming under threat from larger companies that have begun to target their niches.

Fortunately, small firms are often 'quicker on their feet', so when a large firm 'lumbers' towards the market, the smaller one may still be able to win the competitive war. When the multi-billion dollar PepsiCo bought the smoothie business PJ's, innocent Drinks thought that the market might become very difficult for them. In fact, innocent kept its market share rising within the small smoothie niche within the soft drinks market (but, ironically, sold out to Coca-Cola!).

### Real business

#### Halls Soothers

The £1 billion UK market for sugar confectionery is ferociously competitive. Skittles battle against Jelly Babies, Fruitella against Starburst and so on. In a niche of its own, though, comes Halls Soothers: fruit sweets with a strongly medicinal image, for soothing sore throats. With a recommended retail price of 72p per pack, sales of £17.5 million were achieved in 2013. These sales would have been very profitable as the brand had little direct competition.

Source: Adapted from *The Grocer* Top Products Survey 2013

# 20.4 Influences on choosing a target market and positioning

Let no-one doubt it: every business would love to have the central, mass-market positioning of Wrigley (90 per cent share of UK chewing gum market) or Pampers (63 per cent of UK market for disposable nappies). Better still might be Colgate, with its 45 per cent share of the world market for toothpaste. Unfortunately, for the vast majority of businesses, this glorious position is not an option. Yes, Branston can take on Heinz's mass-market positioning in the baked bean market, but who would expect this to be profitable?

The conclusion is clear: if someone else has already 'captured' the mass market, you would be wiser to find your own, profitable niche. Then, who knows, in the long term you may be able to move from a strong niche positioning to chip away at the mass-market leader. This is what happened to Twinings tea, which – many years ago – was a tiny, upmarket tea brand in a market dominated by PG Tips and Tetley. In 2013 Twinings came close to toppling Tetley to take second place in the sector, and not too far short of market leader PG Tips. See Figure 20.4

When choosing a niche positioning the key issues are authenticity and the ability to gain a true understanding of the niche. In its sector, Alpro has proved masterful at understanding the consumers who believe that dairy products are bad for them. In a completely different sector, the German company Haribo has proved brilliant at carving out a big, profitable business in the UK's sugar confectionery market.

Additional influences on choosing a target market:

- Any evidence of growth in a sub-sector of the market might encourage a company to launch a

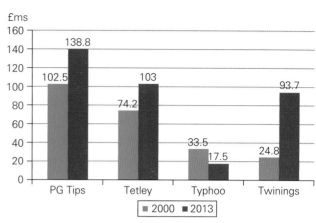

**Figure 20.4** UK tea sales 2000–13
Source: *The Grocer* Top Products Survey

niche product now, even if the sector is small, to establish a sizeable market share in case the sector expands. Once, the juice brand Rubicon's exotic flavours made it a tiny seller. Today its sales exceed £20 million, making it one of the UK's Top 10 juice brands.

- Go where the young go. This is not a bad plan, as it positions a business at the forefront of new tastes and habits. Sometimes it will lead to relatively short-term fads that give little scope for profit, but at other times a company may find itself at the centre of a sales boom, such as Crocs or innocent Drinks.

- Follow the young companies. This is the approach taken by the 'once-young-but-now-cash-loaded' IT companies such as Google, Facebook and Twitter. With piles of cash at their disposal they can easily snap up the next Snapchat or WhatsApp.

## Key terms

**Economies of scale:** factors that cause costs per unit to fall when a firm operates at a higher level of production.

**Generic brands:** brands that are so well known that customers say the brand when they mean the product (for example, 'I'll Hoover the floor.').

**Price elasticity:** the responsiveness of demand to a change in price.

**Product differentiation:** the extent to which consumers perceive your brand as being different from others.

## Evaluation: Niche and mass marketing

Which is better? Is it mass or niche marketing? The answer is that it depends. In the bulk ice cream market, large packs of vanilla ice cream have become so cheap that little profit can be made. It is better by far, then, to be in a separate niche, whether regional (Mackie's Scottish ice cream) or upmarket, such as Rocombe Farm or Häagen Dazs. The latter can cost ten times as much per litre as the mass-market own-label bulk packs.

Yet would a film company prefer to sell a critic's favourite or a blockbuster, smash hit? The answer is the latter, of course. In other words, the mass market is great, if you can succeed there. Businesses such as Heinz, Kellogg's and even Chanel show that mass marketing can be successful and profitable in the long term.

## Five Whys and a How

| Question | Answer |
|---|---|
| Why might a mass-market producer struggle to make a profit? | If the competition is fierce the battle may have to be on the basis of price, making it almost impossible to make satisfactory profits |
| Why might it be beneficial to target an older customer niche? | Demographic trends are boosting the over-60s, so it could be very profitable to get into the Stena/Tena/Saga market |
| Why might a large firm benefit from targeting small niches? | With modern, flexible production it is possible to produce small batches tailored to different customer groups, without forcing costs up |
| Why might a brand new firm benefit from developing a brand new niche? | The first into any market can develop an image of authenticity that can add value in the long term |
| Why do ethnic brands rarely make it to the mainstream? | Probably because few niche brands become mainstream – though the UK's love of Indian and Chinese food point to the possibilities |
| How difficult would it be to switch from a niche-market to a mass-market positioning? | It would require a complete rethink of the marketing mix, perhaps including new pack designs and a lower pricing point. Difficult, yes, but Twinings has shown it's not impossible |

# Workbook

## A. Revision questions

(20 marks; 20 minutes)

1. Identify two advantages of niche marketing over mass marketing. (3)

2. Give three reasons why a large firm may wish to enter a niche market. (3)

3. Why may small firms be better at spotting and then reacting to new niche-market opportunities? (3)

4. Give two reasons why average prices in niche markets tend to be higher than those charged in most mass markets. (2)

5. Outline two reasons why technology has made niche marketing a more viable option for large firms. (4)

6. Explain why it is important for a large firm to be flexible if it is to successfully operate in niche markets. (2)

7. In your own words, explain why niche-market products may generate higher profit margins than mass-market products. (3)

## B. Revision exercises
### DATA RESPONSE 1

**The return of mass marketing to the car industry**

For many years car manufacturers such as Toyota and Nissan have sought out market niches in an attempt to improve profitability. Cars such as the Toyota Prius, a hybrid electric-powered vehicle, are not intended to sell in high volumes. Instead, niche market cars sell for high prices, delivering a higher profit margin per car than more conventional mass-market models.

However, in the last couple of years, there have been signs that car manufacturers have sought a return to conventional mass marketing, particularly in Asia where rapid rates of economic growth have created a growing middle class. At present both the Indian and the Chinese car markets are unsaturated. For example, only 4 per cent of households in India have a car, whereas the corresponding figure in the US is 88 per cent. Income per head, whilst increasing rapidly, is still low by American and European standards, and so far this has limited the demand for new cars in India.

The car market in India is dominated by Suzuki Maruti, a joint venture between a Japanese and an Indian company. In early 2014 its top seller was the Alto 800 model, with prices starting at £2,600 for a new car. This mass-market car has seen off the unsuccessful attempt by Indian rival Tata to introduce a £1,500 car, the Nano. Indian car buyers are willing to accept compromises on Western safety standards, but still want a degree of comfort and – especially, reliability. Suzuki Maruti, with a market share of more than 40 per cent, provides exactly this.

Environmentalists have expressed their concerns that cheap, mass-market cars such as the Alto add to the problem of global warming and climate change. In 2014 Suzuki Maruti should sell nearly one million cars in India.

### Questions (35 marks; 40 minutes)

1. **a)** What is a niche-market product? (2)
   **b)** Explain why the Toyota Prius is a good example of a niche-market product. (4)

2. Explain two reasons why the Indian car market has grown (6)

3. **a)** What is a mass-market product? (2)
   **b)** Explain why the Tata Motor's 'People's car' is a good example of a mass-market product. (4)

4. Analyse the implications for European car manufacturers, such as Renault, of mass marketing £2,000 cars in India. (8)

5. Two thousand pound cars can be profitably made in India. Analyse why UK consumers are unlikely to benefit from similar low prices. (9)

## DATA RESPONSE 2

### Winter melon tea

Mass-market soft drinks like Coca-Cola and Pepsi are very popular in countries such as Hong Kong and Singapore. In an attempt to survive against the imported competition, local producers of soft drinks have managed to establish a flourishing niche market for traditional Asian drinks sold in 33cl cans. Sales of these niche-market products have been rising but from a very low level.

Consumers that make up this niche market are encouraged to believe, through advertising, that traditional drinks such as winter melon tea and grass jelly drink are healthier than their mass-market alternatives. Other firms use economic nationalism to sell their drinks, using slogans such as 'Asian heritage' in their advertising.

However, producers of traditional drinks could now become a victim of their own success. Foreign multinationals have noticed the rapid growth of this market niche, and in response, they have launched their own range of traditional drinks.

**Figure 20.5** Winter melon tea

### Questions (30 marks; 35 minutes)

1. **a)** What is a mass-market product? (2)
   **b)** Identify two reasons why Asian traditional drinks are examples of niche-market products. (2)

2. Explain two ways in which the producers of traditional drinks, such as winter melon tea and grass jelly drink, created product differentiation. (4)

**3.** Niche-market products are normally more expensive than most mass-market products. Using the example of traditional Asian drinks, explain why this is usually so. (6)

**4.** To what extent will the local producers of Asian traditional drinks be able to survive in the long term given that their products now have to compete against me-too brands produced by foreign multinationals such as Coca-Cola and Pepsi? (16)

## C. Extend your understanding

**1.** Choose one of the following markets: women's fashion retailing; computer console software or chocolate bars. For the market of your choice, to what extent are sales dominated by mass-market or niche-market products/brands? (20)

**2.** Some commentators think it's virtually impossible to succeed when trying to turn a niche-market into a mass-market product. To what extent would you agree with that view? (20)

# Chapter 21

# Marketing mix: the 7 Ps

**Linked to:** Setting marketing objectives, Chapter 13; Product decisions: product life cycle and product portfolio, Chapter 22; Pricing decisions, Chapter 23; Place and promotion decisions, Chapter 24.

## Definition

The marketing mix is the balance between seven elements involved in a successful marketing strategy. The traditional '4Ps' – product, price, promotion and place – are joined by people, process and the physical environment.

## 21.1 The elements of the marketing mix

When working out how to market a product successfully, there are seven main variables to consider.

### Product

The business must identify the right product (or service) to make the product both appealing and distinctive. To do this, it needs to understand fully both its customers and its competitors. No product will have long-term success unless this stage is completed successfully.

'Don't try to sell a Rolls Royce when the customer wants a Nissan Micra.' Chartered Institute of Marketing

### Price

Having identified the right product to appeal to its target market, the business must set the right price. The 'right' price for a Versace handbag may be £1,600; it is a great mistake to think that low prices or special discounts are the path to business success.

'Remember that price positions you in the marketplace.' Chartered Institute of Marketing

### Promotion

Marketing managers must identify the right way to create the right image for the product and present it to the right target audience. This may be achieved best by national TV advertising, but specific markets can be reached at far lower cost by more careful targeting (for example, online advertising tailored to the tastes of people who buy from football club websites). 'Promotion' includes both media advertising (TV, press, cinema, radio) and other forms of promotion (including special offers, public relations, direct mail and online promotion).

### Place

For products, 'place' is how to get your product to the place where customers can be persuaded to buy. This may be through a vending machine or on a Tesco shelf, or positioned just by the till at a newsagent (the prime position for purchases bought on impulse). For service businesses, place may be online or in the location of a retail outlet (for example, Tesco Direct and Tesco stores).

## Real business

Both McVitie's Jaffa Cakes and Burton's Jammie Dodgers are well-known biscuit brands, but the former is distributed in 90 per cent of retail outlets, whereas the latter is in only 64 per cent. Both companies have a similar view of what are the right outlets for their products (for example, supermarkets, corner shops, garages, canteens and cafés), so why may Burton's be losing out to McVitie's in this particular race? Possible reasons include the following:

● Jaffa Cakes have higher consumer demand, therefore retail outlets are more willing to stock the product.

● Jammie Dodgers may have more direct competitors; high product differentiation may make Jaffa Cakes more of a 'must stock' line.

● If Jaffa Cakes have more advertising support, retailers know customers will ask for the product by name while the advertising campaign is running

## People

'Anyone who comes into contact with your customers will make an impression, and that can have a profound effect – positive or negative – on customer satisfaction. The reputation of your brand rests in your people's hands. They must, therefore, be appropriately trained, well motivated and have the right attitude,' Chartered Institute of Marketing, www.cim.co.uk.

## Process

Process includes every practical aspect of the customer experience, from phoning or trying to use the website, to how effective the signage is in a store or hotel, to the waiting time at a supermarket checkout. Do customers have to wait? Are they kept informed? Is the service efficient? In other words process is the reality of the customer experience. As this is often the responsibility of operations management rather than marketing, it is possible for there to be a big gap between intention and reality.

**Figure 21.1** Logic chain: how the mix and the factors relate

## Physical environment

However good an advertisement may be, customers pick up clues about a product or service from the physical environment. Arriving to eat at a restaurant, a grubby carpet or dodgy smell might send customers scuttling away. Online, a potential customer may be interested in purchasing, but need a clearer idea of exactly how the holiday cottage looks, or how the dress might look on a person instead of a dummy. Here, too, evidence of the physical environment is needed, perhaps by the ability to take a 360° look at each room in the cottage, or a video clip of the dress being worn in an everyday situation.

Originally the marketing mix focused on 4Ps (product, price, promotion and place). In a world dominated by services and online selling, the further 3Ps have become equally important.

## 21.2 How is the marketing mix used?

The marketing mix can be used by a new business to develop ideas about how and where to market a product or service. If marketing activity is to be effective, each ingredient needs to be considered and co-ordinated. For each market situation, managers are trying to set the ideal combination of the ingredients based on a balance between cost and effectiveness. A good product poorly priced may fail. If the product is not available following an advertising campaign, the expenditure is wasted. A successful mix is the one that succeeds in putting the strategy into practice (Figure 21.2).

'There is no victory at bargain basement prices.' Dwight D. Eisenhower, US General, then President

**Figure 21.2** A balanced marketing mix

## 21.3 Influences on the marketing mix

The focus of the marketing mix will vary according to the market in which the firm is operating. Careful market research should reveal the attitudes and tastes of the target market. An important issue will be whether the goods are:

- regular purchases
- impulse purchases
- emergency purchases.

Impulse purchases (such as chocolate brands) are interesting because they require strong branding, great distribution and display, and eye-catching packaging. In other words, the mix focuses on place and promotion. Price is much less important and the quality of the product may not be hugely important. See Table 21.1.

---

'Don't sell the steak, sell the sizzle.' Advice on advertising from Elmer Wheeler, US business writer

---

**Table 21.1** Different types of purchasing and the marketing mix

| Type of purchasing | Important mix elements when buying a product | Important mix elements when buying a service |
|---|---|---|
| Regular purchases, e.g. a daily Frappucino | Product, promotion and price | Product, price, people and process |
| Impulse purchases, e.g. chocolate or a skirt | Place and promotion (including packaging) | Product, people, process and physical environment |
| Emergency purchases, e.g. bandages | Place and product | Product, place and process |

Other influences on the mix:

● whether the product is sold online or face to face. If it's the former, process and evidence of physical environment will be all-important, along with price. If it's sold face to face, people and the product may be more important.

● whether the product/service is targeted at consumers or other businesses (this point is developed further in Section 21.6)

● which stage of its life cycle the product or service is at (see Chapter 22)

● market research: to understand how the mix may need to be tweaked over time, market research is vital. Medium-sized and large firms need primary research to keep the senior managers in touch with the customers they rarely see. Small firms should constantly listen to what customers say – in praise or in criticism.

## 21.4 Effects of changes in elements of the mix

The traditional view of the marketing mix as being 4Ps had the advantage that all the elements of the mix came largely under the control of the marketing department. So a decision to change the price could be co-ordinated with advertising and promotional campaigns. In the service world of the 7Ps this becomes far harder. The marketing manager does not train the shop floor (customer-facing) staff, and does not get involved in their motivation. Nor does she set up or monitor the processes that try to ensure an efficient customer experience. In the modern world, changes in the marketing mix may be out of the control of the marketing department. So success requires full co-operation from the operations and HR departments.

**Table 21.2** Changes in elements of the mix

| Possible cause of change | Change in mix for an upmarket London hotel | Effects of these changes in elements of the mix |
|---|---|---|
| New visa regulations treble the number of Chinese tourists in Britain | Product tweak: Chinese breakfast option offered; more mix emphasis on Physical Environment; online Process made more China-friendly | Potential Chinese customers will feel more welcome and will enjoy their stay rather more (improving word-of-mouth and online feedback) |
| Severe economic downturn hits demand, especially from UK leisure customers | To switch focus to business travellers, the product is changed by putting free business magazines and papers in each room; promotion switches media from TV to Google AdWords | The media change uses Google to generate pop-up advertisements for business travellers; the product change should increase the rate of repeat purchasing among this target market |
| Unforecast torrential rain closes London's commuter train services in the early evening | The traditional 4Ps are pushed aside by the importance of people and process. Can the hotel cope with a sudden surge in demand? | If staff are so well trained that they impress the influx of new customers (and the processes cope), the result could be a long-term boost to demand |

## 21.5 Marketing mix for goods and services

With many 'goods', that is, products, the mix revolves around the product. For example, the marketing mix for the Audi A4 has the car at its heart. The pricing, promotion, physical environment and so on must all fit with the image and 'attitude' of the product.

For services it may be possible to have a purer, broader marketing mix. If one thinks of Tesco compared with Morrisons', the different elements of the mix all come into play in affecting our feelings and actions. Process, for example, may be as important as price. If a customer keeps finding huge queues in Morrisons', they'll eventually settle on Tesco.

It is important to bear in mind that the marketing mix for every product, brand or service will be different from every other. Goods and services do behave differently, but so too do luxury goods versus everyday ones, and presents compared with self-purchased items.

## 21.6 Marketing mix for B2C and B2B

The key to a successful marketing mix is that every element should be co-ordinated towards delivering a marketing strategy that fits in with the marketing objectives. This is relatively easy to think through in relation to a business that targets the consumer (B2C). Whether it's a product or service, the consumer expects a reality that conforms to the image and therefore delivers value for money. In many cases the image itself may be at the heart of the proposition. If so, keeping that image vibrant and distinctive may be a critical focus of the marketing mix.

Within the category of consumer goods there are three types to be considered:

- Convenience goods are bought out of habit or impulse within a regular process of shopping. Convenience goods are inexpensive, widely available, purchased frequently and with minimal thought or effort. Impulse examples include Coca-Cola, Galaxy chocolate, Wrigley chewing gum and magazines, but the category also includes the regular weekly shop, such as for detergent and shampoo.

- Shopping goods involve a more careful selection process by the buyer, probably because they have a higher unit price than convenience goods and also because they are bought less frequently. Examples include car tyres, mobile phones and clothes.

- Speciality goods are one-off purchases that require a serious purchasing effort, such as a luxury car or an engagement ring. The purchaser will probably shop around a great deal, putting online and shoe-leather time into a research process that should lead to the perfect choice.

By contrast B2B means selling to other businesses, be they retail distributors or businesses that have no direct connection with the public, such as a chemical refinery or a sawmill. A producer of sandwiches for the consumer market might gain a huge order to feed the staff daily at a nearby sawmill employing 800 people. This B2B order carries the financial disadvantage that the customer will want to pay on credit (perhaps 60 days), which hurts the supplier's cash flow. It also means that process will become the critical factor. The sandwiches have to be delivered by a certain time, to a specified quality – and there will be no acceptable excuses for failure.

In some cases companies will be selling homogenous goods to other businesses, for example, 10 litres of white paint or 5,000 light switches. This will make price the most important element in the mix.

### Key terms

**Homogenous goods:** have no points of differentiation and therefore each one is the same as every other (meaning competition is focused on price).

**Marketing budget:** the sum of money provided for marketing a product or service during a period of time (usually a year).

**Marketing mix:** the elements involved in putting a marketing strategy into practice; these are product, price, promotion and place.

**Marketing strategy:** the medium- to long-term plan for meeting the firm's marketing objectives.

### Evaluation: Marketing mix: the 7Ps

A successful marketing mix should be matched to the marketing strategy, and that strategy is rooted in how well the product meets the tastes of the market segment being targeted.

Although the 4Ps are presented as a list, there is no doubt that in almost every case the product is the most important ingredient. No amount of marketing effort will make a poor product succeed. However, a good product with weak promotional support may also fail. The balance will vary.

Within the 7Ps it will be helpful to be able to split them into the traditional 4Ps (with their focus on products) and the newer 3Ps than reflect the modern online, service-focused world. Successful writing is always about rethinking how well theory applies in the real world. Be willing to break a theory down into its component parts.

## Five Whys and a How

| Question | Answer |
|---|---|
| Why may 'people' be especially important when selling speciality goods? | For expensive, one-off purchases customers will want to be fully confident in the helpfulness and expertise of the salesperson |
| Why would it be a problem if 'price' was set by the finance director, with no knowledge of the rest of the mix? | If any one element of the mix is out of alignment it's a problem, but especially when it's price. When Xbox One launched at £100 more than the PS4, sales were laughably slow |
| Why is 'place' still important even in a world of online selling? | Many customers like to look and feel before buying, so 'bricks' are still as important as 'clicks' |
| Why might a business decide that 'price' is the most important element in their mix? | If goods in their market are homogenous, i.e. little or no product differentiation, then price will be the most important factor |
| Why may it be hard to co-ordinate the first 4Ps with the final 3? | Because the 4Ps are in the control of the marketing department; the other 3 are controlled by operations and human resources |
| How does 'place' differ from 'physical environment'? | Place is about getting your products distributed, e.g. in Tesco. Physical environment means giving your potential customers a clue to the quality of a service they want to buy. |

# Workbook

## A. Revision questions

**(35 marks; 40 minutes)**

1. Explain why it was important to stretch the marketing mix from 4Ps to 7. (3)

2. In your own words, outline each of the three 'new Ps' within the marketing mix. (6)

3. Pick the marketing mix factor (the 'P') you think is of most importance in marketing any **two** of the following brands. Give a brief explanation of why you chose that factor.
   a) *The Sun* newspaper
   b) A Costa latte
   c) Cadbury Creme Eggs
   d) Clothes at Primark. (6)

4. Outline how the marketing mix for Mars bars may affect their level of impulse sales in a small corner shop. (4)

5. What is meant by a market segment? (3)

6. Outline two influences on the marketing mix for the Sony PS4. (4)

7. Explain how changes in elements of the mix might affect the price elasticity of a product such as a motor car. (6)

8. Explain why it might be difficult for a new, small firm to get distribution in a supermarket chain such as Sainsbury's. (3)

# B. Revision exercises

## DATA RESPONSE

### The battle for customers

A leading UK supermarket chain is considering expanding into India. It sees this as a relatively untapped market. The home market is saturated, and price wars and loyalty cards have reduced profit margins. In the UK, the supermarkets have been blamed for the disappearance of the corner shop. In India the situation is very different. A recent survey by an Indian market research firm concluded that small grocery shops will continue to dominate the food retailing market for the foreseeable future. Neither of the two main supermarket contenders has managed to break even in India. They are continuing to expand and hoping that, eventually, economies of scale will permit lower prices and hopefully improve their standing and their profitability.

These new supermarkets have faced several problems.

- The local stores do not stock as many brands as the supermarkets, but they will stock an item if a customer wants it. If they do not have what the customer wants they will get it.
- The local stores offer a free delivery service and allow customers credit.
- The supermarkets cannot match the cost base of the local store. The poor infrastructure makes operational costs very expensive.
- Government laws limiting urban development mean that property prices are high. The smaller stores have often been in the family for generations, and so the initial cost of the site has long since been forgotten.

To try to gain customers, one of the supermarket chains has introduced promotions such as coupons, and has advertised in local newspapers. Another has teamed up with local manufacturers. It obtains staples such as lentils and rice locally. These are then packaged and branded by local manufacturers. This has helped to lower prices for customers and improve margins. A recent entrant into the market is trying to stay ahead of the competition. It has invested in air-conditioning and additional telephone lines to ensure that customers do not have to wait when they call.

The UK chain has looked at the existing market in India and feels it can succeed. However, the managers know they will do this only after a struggle to change customer attitudes.

### Questions (30 marks; 35 minutes)

1. What is meant by 'the home market is saturated'? (3)

2. Explain the marketing implications for a business of 'a saturated market'. (4)

3. Why could expansion allow economies of scale? (3)

4. Explain the problems a British retailer could have in marketing its product in India. (4)

5. How important will the marketing mix be in determining the UK chain's chances of success in India? Justify your answer. (16)

# C. Extend your understanding

1. An independent clothes shop has decided to switch from targeting consumers to developing a range of work wear and uniforms aimed at business customers. Evaluate the possible impact of this decision on the company's marketing mix. (20)

2. Choose two rival companies or brands you feel familiar with (PS4 vs. Xbox One? Starbucks vs. Costa? Cadbury vs. Mars?). Which element of the mix do you think is the most important for each company/brand? Justify your answer. (20)

# Chapter 22

# Product decisions: product life cycle and product portfolio

**Linked to:** Setting marketing objectives, Chapter 13; Understanding markets, Chapter 14; Market research, Chapter 15; Interpreting market data, Chapter 16.

### Definition

The product life cycle is the theory that all products follow a similar pattern over time, of development, birth, growth, maturity and decline.

## 22.1 What is the product life cycle?

The product life cycle shows the sales of a product over time. When a new product is first launched sales will usually be slow. This is because the product is not yet known or proven in the market. Retailers may be reluctant to stock the product because it means giving up valuable shelf space to products that may or may not sell. Customers may also be hesitant, waiting until someone else has tried it before they purchase it themselves.

If the product does succeed, then it enters the growth phase of the product life cycle, with new customers buying and existing customers making repeat purchases. However, at some point sales are likely to stabilise; this is known as the maturity phase. This slowing down of the growth of sales might be because competitors have introduced similar products or because the market has now become saturated. Everyone who wants one has bought one, so sales fall back to replacement purchases only.

At some point sales are likely to decline, perhaps because customer tastes have become more sophisticated. So orange squash sales decline as people buy more fresh orange juice. A decline in sales may also be because competitors have launched a more successful model or the original creator has improved

its own product; for example, the iPad drawing sales from the iPhone.

The five key stages of a product's life cycle are known as: development, introduction, growth, maturity and decline. These can be illustrated on a product life cycle diagram. The typical stages in a product's life are shown in Figure 22.1.

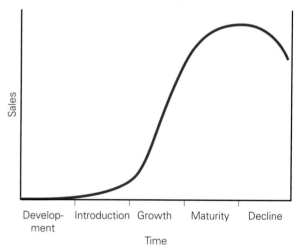

**Figure 22.1** The product life cycle

## 22.2 What is the value of the product life cycle?

The product life cycle model helps managers to plan their marketing activities. Marketing managers will need to adjust their marketing mix at different stages of the product life cycle, as outlined below.

● In the introduction phase the promotion may focus on making customers aware that a new product exists. In the maturity phase it may focus more on highlighting the difference between your product and competitors that have arrived since its introduction.

● At the beginning of the life cycle, a technologically advanced product may be launched with a high price (think of the iPhone). Over time the price may fall

**Table 22.1** Examples of how the marketing mix may vary at different stages of the product life cycle

| | Development | Introduction | Growth | Maturity | Decline |
|---|---|---|---|---|---|
| **Sales** | Zero | Low | Increasing | Growth is slowing | Falling |
| **Costs per unit** | High; there is investment in product development but only a few prototypes and test products being produced | High, because sales are relatively low but launch costs are high and overheads are being spread over a few units | Falling as overheads are spread over more units | Falling as sales are still growing | Still likely to be low as development costs have been covered and reduced promotional costs are needed to raise awareness |
| **Product** | Prototypes | Likely to be basic | May be modified given initial customer feedback; range may be increased | Depends – may focus on core products and remove ones in the range not selling well; may diversify and extend brand to new items | Focus on most profitable items |
| **Promotion** | As development is nearly finished it may be used to alert customers to the launch | Mainly to raise awareness | Building loyalty | May focus on highlighting the differences with competitors' products | Probably no spending at all |
| **Distribution** | Early discussions with retailers will help in finalising the product packaging | May be limited as distributors wait to see customers' reactions | May be increasing as more distributors willing to stock it and product is rolled out to more markets | May focus on key outlets and more profitable channels | Lower budgets to keep costs down |
| **Price** | Not needed | Depends on pricing approach, e.g. high if skimming is adopted; low if penetration is adopted to gain market share | Depends on demand conditions and strategy; e.g. with a skimming strategy the price may now be lowered to target more segments | May have to drop to maintain competitiveness | Likely to discount to maintain sales |

as newer models are being launched. By considering the requirements of each stage of the life cycle, marketing managers may adjust their marketing activities accordingly.

Managers know that the length of the phases of the life cycle cannot easily be predicted. They will vary from one product to another and this means the marketing mix will need to be altered at different times. For example, a product may be a fad and therefore the overall life of the product will be quite short. Many fashions are popular only for one season and some films are popular only for a matter of weeks. Other products have very long life cycles. The first manufactured cigarettes went on sale in Britain in 1873. By chance, sales hit their peak (120,000 million!) exactly 100 years later. Since 1973 sales have gently declined.

It is also important to distinguish between the life cycle of a product category and the life cycle of a particular brand. Sales of wine are growing, but a brand that was once the biggest seller (Hirondelle) has virtually disappeared as wine buyers have become more sophisticated. Similarly, confectionery is a mature market but particular brands are at different stages in their life cycles: Mars bars are in maturity while Maltesers are in the growth stage, even though the brand is 80 years old!

## 22.3 Extension strategies

The aim of an extension strategy is to prevent a decline in the product's sales. There are various means by which this can be achieved, as noted below.

● By targeting a new segment of the market – when sales of Johnson & Johnson's Baby Powder matured, the company repositioned the product towards adults: sales boomed.

● By developing new uses for the product – the basic technology in hot-air paint strippers, for example, is no different from that in a hairdryer.

- By increasing the usage of a product – Actimel's 'challenge' was for consumers to eat one pot a day for a fortnight – a wonderful way to encourage increased consumption.

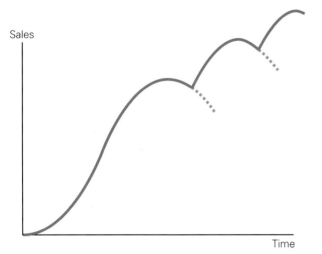

**Figure 22.2** The effect of extension strategies

The continued success of products such as Coca-Cola and Kellogg's Cornflakes is not just due to luck; it is down to sophisticated marketing techniques which have managed to maintain sales over many years despite fierce competition. The Kellogg's logo is regularly updated, new pack sizes are often introduced, and various competitions and offers are used on a regular basis to keep sales high.

Given the fact that developing a product can involve high costs and that there is a high failure rate of new products, it is not surprising that if a product is successful managers will try to prolong its sales for as long as it is profitable. Who would have thought, in the 1880s, that a frothy drink would still be a huge seller more than 125 years later? Clever Coke.

## 22.4 New product development (NPD)

New product development includes the people and processes involved in turning new ideas into products (or services) ready for launch. It is likely to involve research and development (R&D), market research, product engineering and design, plus expertise in packaging, advertising, pricing and branding. It represents all the activities categorised as 'development' in the product life cycle. Some examples of NPD are so excellent (think iPhone, the PS4 or Snapchat) that their life cycles have a remarkably easy start.

Unfortunately even consumer giants such as Cadbury and PepsiCo have poor success rates with new

product launches. The statistics are hard to find, but it seems that fewer than 1 in 5 new products becomes a commercial success. Clearly there must be many reasons why it's hard to create a successful new product, though the single most important is the cautious consumer who would rather buy a trusted product than a new one.

Key influences on successful NPD include:

- a clear understanding of the consumers within a certain market segment, with a special focus on their future needs or wants
- the creativity to be able to see how an everyday problem or issue can be solved innovatively
- enough resources (money and manpower) to be able to develop an idea effectively and market it persuasively.

When a new product succeeds the consequences can be transformational. Nintendo's Wii U was looking down and out before the launch of Mario Kart 8 saw sales of the hardware rise by 600 per cent in June 2014. So the value of NPD cannot be doubted. A successful new product can create its own new life cycle – giving an entire business a morale and profit boost.

### Real business

#### 9 out of 10 fail

In July 2014 the Chief Executive of US marketing consultancy Dine was interviewed about the causes of new product launch failures. He said that, in America, the failure rate among new food products is 9 out of 10. He blamed three main causes:

- undercapitalised launches; that is, good idea, but an underfunded marketing campaign
- 'Customer insight is slightly off', for example, launched too early or too late, or slightly wrong market positioning
- overly innovative idea (he cited bubble-gum flavoured milk) where the producer is pursuing disruptive innovation when incremental innovation would be superior.

## 22.5 The product portfolio

Product portfolio analysis examines the existing position of a firm's products. This allows the firm to consider its existing position and plan what to do next. There are several different methods of portfolio analysis. One of the best known was developed by the

Boston Consulting Group, a management consultancy; it is known as the Boston Matrix.

The Boston Matrix shows the market share of each of the firm's products and the rate of growth of the markets in which they operate. By highlighting the position of each product in terms of market share and market growth, a business can analyse its existing situation and decide what to do next and where to direct its marketing efforts. This model has four categories, as described below.

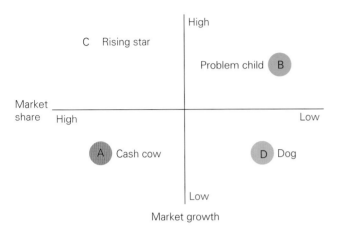

**Figure 22.3** Product portfolio: the Boston Matrix

## Cash cow: a high share of a slow-growing market

In Figure 22.3, product A has a high market share of a low-growth market. The size of the circle depends on the turnover of the product. This type of product is known as a cash cow. An example of a cash cow may be Heinz Baked Beans. The overall market for baked beans is mature and therefore slow growing. Within this market, the Heinz brand has a market share of more than 50 per cent. This type of product generates high profits and cash for the company because sales are relatively high, while the promotional cost per unit is quite low. Heinz can therefore 'milk' cash from baked beans to invest in newer products such as Heinz Organic Ketchup.

## Problem child: a low share of a fast-growing market

Product B, by comparison, is in a high-growth market but has a low market share. This type of product is known as a problem child (also called a 'question mark'). A problem child may well provide high profits in the future; the market itself is attractive because it is growing fast and the product could provide high returns if it manages to gain a greater market share. However, the success of such products is by no means certain and that is why they are like problem children:

they may grow and prosper or things may go wrong. These products usually need a relatively high level of investment to promote them, get them distributed and keep them going.

## Rising star: a high share of a growing market

Rising stars such as product C have a high market share and are selling in a fast-growing market. These products are obviously attractive; they are doing well in a successful market. However, they may well need protecting from competitors' products. Once again, the profits of the cash cows can be used to keep the sales growing. Heinz Organic Soups are in this category. They are very successful, with fast-growing sales, but still need heavy promotion to ensure their success.

## Dogs: a low share of a stable or declining market

The fourth category of products is known as dogs. These products (like product D in Figure 22.3) have a low share of a low growth market. They hold little appeal for a firm unless they can be revived. The product or brand will be killed off once its sales slip below the break-even point.

## The purpose of product portfolio analysis

Product portfolio analysis aims to examine the existing position of the firm's products. Once this has been done the managers can plan what to do next. Typically this will involve four strategies.

1. Building: this involves investment in promotion and distribution to boost sales and is often used with problem children (question marks).

2. Holding: this involves marketing spending to maintain sales and is used with rising star products.

3. Milking: this means taking whatever profits you can without much more new investment and is often used with cash cow products.

4. Divesting: this involves selling off the product and is common with dogs or problem children.

The various strategies chosen will depend on the firm's portfolio of products. If most of the firm's products are cash cows, for example, it needs to develop new products for future growth. If, however, the majority are problem children then it is in quite a high-risk situation; it needs to try to ensure some products do become stars. If it has too many dogs then it needs to invest in product development or acquire new brands.

## Five Whys and a How

| Question | Answer |
|---|---|
| Why does growth slide back towards maturity? | Market saturation is one reason (everyone who wants one has already bought it); the arrival of competition is another |
| Why do many extension strategies fail? | Because the business has failed to find a new market position for a new type of customer |
| Why do new product launches have such a low success rate? | Because many consumers are locked into patterns of repeat behaviour, such as always buying Cadbury Dairy Milk |
| Why may firms struggle to manage their cash flow when their products have short life cycles? | Short life cycles imply a constant need to invest heavily in NPD to develop the next winner to take over from today's fading products |
| Why do firms find it useful to use both product life cycle and portfolio analysis? | Because the product life cycle helps analyse the progress of a single product while portfolio analysis looks at all a firm's products |
| How does R&D differ from market research? | R&D is about scientific research and technical development of products or processes; market research is about consumer habits and tastes |

## Key terms

**Cash cow:** a product that has a high share of a low-growth market.

**Dog:** a product that has a low share of a low-growth market.

**Extension strategy:** marketing activities used to prevent sales from declining.

**Portfolio analysis:** an analysis of the market position of the firm's existing products; it is used as part of the marketing planning process.

**Problem child:** a product that has a small share of a fast-growing market.

**Rising star:** a product that has a high share of a fast-growing market.

## Evaluation: Product decisions: product life cycle and product portfolio

The product life cycle model and portfolio analysis are important in assessing the firm's current position within the market. They make up an important step in the planning process. However, simply gathering data does not in itself guarantee success. A manager has to interpret the information effectively and then make the right decision. The models show where a business is at the moment; the difficult decisions relate to where the business will be in the future.

Product portfolio analysis is especially useful for larger businesses with many products. It helps a manager to look critically at the firm's product range. Then decisions can be made on how the firm's marketing spending should be divided up between different products. By contrast, the product life cycle is of more help to a small firm with one or two products.

# Workbook

## A. Revision questions

**(40 marks; 50 minutes)**

1. Identify the different stages of the product life cycle. Give an example of one product or service you consider to be at each stage of the life cycle. (4)

2. Explain what is meant by an 'extension strategy'. (4)

3. Explain the importance of new product development. (6)

4. How is it possible for products such as Barbie to apparently defy the decline phase of the product cycle? (7)

5. What is meant by 'product portfolio analysis'? (3)

6. Distinguish between a cash cow and a rising star in the Boston Matrix. (4)

7. Explain how the Boston Matrix could be used by a business such as Cadbury? (5)

8. Firms should never take decline (or growth) for granted. Therefore they should never take success (or failure) for granted. Explain why this advice is important if firms are to make the best use of product life cycle theory. (7)

## B. Revision exercises

### DATA RESPONSE

**Monster life cycle**

The market for energy drinks is dominated by Red Bull. First launched in 1987, its UK sales have grown steadily to reach £248 million in 2013. With the market for energy drinks still rising by 10–15 per cent per year, many other companies are determined to take their share of this success.

The attractions are obvious. Not only are sales rising faster than for soft drinks as a whole, but the price per litre is much higher. On 30 December 2013, Tesco charged 49p for a 330ml can of Coca-Cola and £1.58 for 330ml of Red Bull.

As the Coca-Cola Company observed the growth of Red Bull during the 'noughties', it resolved to launch its own rivals. First came Relentless in late 2006, which received its first serious promotional push by being given away at the 2007 Reading and Leeds Music Festivals. Since then it has focused on sponsoring 'extreme' sports. As shown in the graph below, Relentless has achieved significant sales, though sales fell by £5 million between 2011 and 2013.

Perhaps sensing that Relentless was not the answer, in 2010 Coca-Cola took over the distribution of a US energy drink called Monster. The brand holds a 35 per cent share of the $30 billion US market for energy drinks, though there have been questions raised in Congress about the safety of the product.

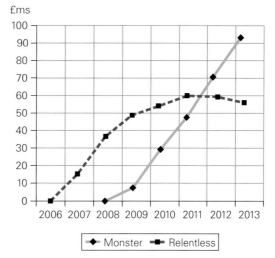

**Figure 22.4** Energy drink life cycles; UK annual sales 2006-13

Source: Data from *The Grocer*

Energy drinks are heavy in three ingredients: caffeine, taurine and sugar. In fact the caffeine level is no higher than in coffee, but the combination of ingredients is thought by some to place it in between alcoholic and soft drinks.

Is Monster a real challenger to Red Bull in the UK? With a sales increase of 30 per cent in 2013 compared with 6 per cent for Red Bull, Coca-Cola can hope. But the risk must remain that the Monster life cycle will end up following that of Relentless. Time will tell.

**Figure 22.5** Monster energy drink

## Questions (30 marks; 35 minutes)

1. Briefly explain the meaning of the term 'product life cycle'. (3)

2. In which stage of its product life cycle was a) Relentless and b) Monster in 2013? (2)

3. Analyse possible extension strategies Coca-Cola might use with Relentless in coming years. (9)

4. To what extent may the future UK life cycle of Monster depend on the marketing of Red Bull? (16)

## C. Extend your understanding

1. After many decades of success in the UK, breakfast cereal manufacturers are suffering from a decline in the market size as consumers want to eat breakfast on the move instead of in the kitchen. Discuss a suitable extension strategy for a cereal producer such as Kellogg's. (20)

2. Cadbury has a wide range of chocolate brands including Dairy Milk, Flake, Crunchie, Twirl and Fudge. It wishes to push its UK market share from 34 per cent to 36 per cent within the next two years. To what extent might the Boston Matrix help achieve this goal? (20)

# Chapter 23 Pricing decisions

**Linked to:** Understanding markets, Chapter 14; Market research, Chapter 15; Price and income elasticity of demand, Chapter 17; Segmentation, targeting and positioning, Chapter 19; Niche and mass marketing, Chapter 20.

> ## Definition
>
> Price is the amount paid by the customer for a good or service.

## 23.1 How important are decisions about price?

Price is one of the main links between the customer (demand) and the producer (supply). It gives messages to consumers about product quality and is fundamental to a firm's revenues and profit margins. As part of the marketing mix it is fundamental to most consumer buying decisions. The importance of price to the customer will depend on several factors, as discussed below.

## Customer sensitivity to price

Consumers have an idea of the correct price for a product (see Figure 23.1). They balance price with other considerations. These include the factors set out below.

### The quality of the product

Products seen as having higher quality can carry a price premium; this may be real or perceived quality.

### How much consumers want the product

All purchases are personal; customers will pay more for goods they need or want.

### Consumers' income

Customers buy products within their income range; consumers with more disposable income are less concerned about price. Uncertainty about future income will have the same effect as lower income. If interest rates are high, hard-pressed homebuyers will be much more sensitive to price; they need to save money and so they check prices more carefully and avoid high-priced items.

**Figure 23.1** The 'right' price

**Table 23.1** Price sensitivity in practice

| Products, services and brands that are highly price sensitive | Products, services and brands that are not very price sensitive |
| --- | --- |
| No-frills air travel | Business-class air travel |
| Fiat and Ford cars | BMW and Mercedes cars |
| Children's white school shirts | Babies' disposable nappies |
| Monday-night cinema tickets | Saturday-night cinema tickets |

## The level of competitive activity

The fiercer the competition in a market, the more important price becomes. Customers have more choice, so they take more care to buy the best-value item. Whereas, a business with a strong monopoly position is able to charge higher prices.

## The availability of the product

If the product is readily available, consumers are more price-conscious. They know they can go elsewhere and find the same product – perhaps cheaper. Scarcity removes some of the barriers to price. This is why perfume companies such as Chanel try to keep their products out of supermarkets and stores like Superdrug.

## 23.2 Price determines business revenue

Pricing is important to the business. Unlike the other ingredients in the marketing mix it is related directly to revenue through the formula:

Revenue = price × units sold

If the price is not right the business could:

- lose customers: if the price is too high, sales may slump and therefore revenue will be lost. It will depend on the price elasticity of the product (see Chapter 17). If goods remain unsold, the costs of production will not be recovered
- lose revenue: if the price is too low, sales may be high, but not high enough to compensate for the low revenue per unit.

Pricing involves a balance between being competitive and being profitable.

## 23.3 How do businesses decide what price to charge?

At certain times during a product's life cycle pricing is especially important. Incorrect pricing when the product is launched could cause the product to fail. At other stages in the product's life, pricing may be used to revive interest in the brand.

There are two basic pricing decisions: pricing a new product and managing prices throughout the product life. Both decisions require a good understanding of the market: consumers and competitors.

Pricing decisions require an understanding of costs. These costs must include purchasing, manufacturing, distribution, administration and marketing. Cost information should be available from the company's management accounting systems.

The lowest price a firm can consider charging is set by costs. Except as a temporary promotional tactic (a loss leader), businesses must charge more for the product than the variable cost. This ensures that every product sold contributes towards the fixed costs of the business.

The market determines the highest price that can be charged. The price that is charged will need to take

account of the company objectives. The right price will be the one that achieves the objectives.

There are several ways that businesses obtain market information. These are set out below.

- Market research can provide consumer reactions to possible price changes.
- Competitive research tells the company about other products and prices.
- Analysis of sales patterns shows how the market reacts to price and economic changes.
- Sales staff can report on customer reactions to prices.

**Figure 23.2** Determining the price

When making changes to product prices the business needs to understand the relationship between price changes and demand. Demand for some products is more sensitive to price changes than for others. Price elasticity of demand measures how sensitive demand is to price changes. If demand for a product is sensitive to price changes an increase in price could cut total revenue.

### Real business

**London's Hoxton Hotel**

If you put '£1 hotel rooms' into Google, London's Hoxton Hotel pops up in front of you. This 200-room hotel sells five rooms per night at £1 and another five at £29. The other 190 are at the 'normal' rate of £229! The Hoxton uses this device to get customers to register as members of the Hoxton Fan Club. They are the only ones to hear when the £1 sale is taking place. The website boasts that in each sale, 1,000 rooms are sold in 20 minutes. So this pricing trick makes sure that Hoxton has a terrific emailing list of people interested in London hotels.

## 23.4 Pricing strategies

A pricing strategy is a company's plan for setting its prices over the medium to long term. In other words it is not about deals such as 'This week's special: 40 per cent off!' Short-term offers are known as tactics. Medium- to long-term plans are called strategies.

For new products, firms must choose between two main pricing strategies:

1. skimming
2. penetration.

Some advantages of price skimming and price penetration are shown in Table 23.2.

### Skimming

This is used when the product is innovative. As the product is new there will be no competition. The price can therefore be set at a high level. Customers interested in the new product will pay this high price. The business recovers some of the development costs, making sure that enthusiasts who really want the product pay the high price they expect to pay. For example, the first DVD players came onto the UK market at a price of around £1,000. Firms use the initial sales period to assess the market reaction. If sales become stagnant the price can be lowered to attract customers who were unwilling to pay the initial price. The price can also be lowered if competitors enter the market.

### Penetration

Penetration pricing is used when launching a product into a market where there are similar products. The price is set lower to gain market share. Once the product is established the price can be increased. It is hoped that high levels of initial sales will recover development costs and lead to lower average costs as the business gains bulk-buying benefits.

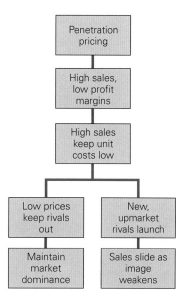

**Figure 23.3** Logic chain: pros and cons of penetration pricing

**Table 23.2** Advantages and disadvantages of price skimming and price penetration

|  | **Price skimming** | **Price penetration** |
|---|---|---|
| **Advantages** | High prices for a new item such as the iPhone help establish the product as a must-have item | Low-priced new products may attract high sales volumes, which make it very hard for a competitor to break into the market |
| | **Early adopters** of a product usually want exclusivity and are willing to pay high prices, so skimming makes sense for them and for the supplier | High sales volumes help to cut production costs per unit, as the producer can buy in bulk and therefore get purchasing costs down |
| | Innovation can be expensive, so it makes sense to charge high prices to recover the investment cost | Achieving high sales volumes ensures that shops will provide high distribution levels and good in-store displays |
| **Disadvantages** | Some customers may be put off totally by 'rip-off pricing' at the start of a product's life | Pricing low may affect the brand image, making the product appear 'cheap' |
| | When the firm decides to cut its prices its image may suffer | It may be hard to gain distribution in more upmarket retail outlets, due to mass-market pricing |
| | Buyers who bought early (at high prices) may be annoyed that prices fell soon afterwards | Pricing on the basis of value for money can cause customers (and therefore competitors) to be very price sensitive |

## Real business

After years of dominance by Nike and Adidas, local sports footwear manufacturers made inroads into the Chinese market in 2010. Local brand Li Ning pulled alongside Adidas as the industry No. 2 (market share by volume). The head of JWT, China (advertising agency) said, 'The moment that a local brand can command the same price as a multinational brand is the day that a breakthrough has been made'.

To push further, Li Ning announced a new, higher-priced product range to sit 15 per cent below its foreign rivals. But by 2013 Li Ning was reporting sales slumping by 25 per cent and more than 1,000 store closures. At the same time Nike sales in China slipped by just 3 per cent. The price breakthrough hasn't happened yet.

**Figure 23.4** Li Ning trainers/sports wear promotion

## Five Whys and a How

| Question | Answer |
|---|---|
| Why should companies be wary of tactical, low pricing, e.g. special offers? | Because of the potential damage to image. Can you imagine a 'special offer' BMW? Or, indeed, buy one BMW, get one free. |
| Why is price cutting a risk to profits even when it helps increase revenue? | If a 10 per cent price cut boosts demand by 15 per cent, revenue rises; but the price cut hits the profit margin, which may mean that profits actually fall. |
| Why may firms set lower prices in the growth phase than in the decline phase of the life cycle? | In the growth phase prices may be kept low to attract a large number of potential loyalists; in decline there are few new customers to attract, so prices may be kept high to exploit customer inertia/loyalty. |
| Why may skimming the market prove the wrong pricing strategy for a new product? | Skimming may generate a good image plus strong profits in the short term, but allow space in the market for new rivals to step in. |
| Why do music acts not price their tickets high enough to make ticket touting irrelevant? | Because the groups worry that their fans will feel they are being 'ripped off'; much better to blame the touts. |
| How should a new, independent pizza business set its prices? | It should find out customer reactions to the brand and the product – and set prices accordingly. |

## Key terms

**Complementary goods:** products bought in conjunction with each other, such as bacon and eggs, or Gillette shavers and Gillette razors.

**Early adopters:** consumers with the wealth and the personality to want to be the first to get a new gadget or piece of equipment. They may be the first to wear new fashions in clothes, and the first to get the new (and expensive) computer game.

**Monopoly:** a market dominated by one supplier.

**Price elasticity:** a measurement of the extent to which a product's demand changes when its price is changed.

**Price sensitive:** when customer demand for a product reacts sharply to a price change (that is, the product is highly price elastic).

## Evaluation: Pricing decisions

Economists think of price as a neutral factor within a marketplace. Many businesses would disagree, especially those selling consumer goods and services. The reason is that consumer psychology can be heavily influenced by price. A '3p off' sticker makes people reach for the Mars bars, but '50 per cent off' might make people wonder whether they are old stock or have suffered in the sun; they are *too* cheap.

When deciding on the price of a brand new product, marketing managers have many options. Pricing high may generate too few sales to keep retailers happy to stock the product. Yet, pricing too low carries even more dangers. Large companies know there are no safe livings to be made selling cheap jeans, cheap cosmetics or cheap perfumes.

If there is a key to successful pricing, it is to keep it in line with the overall marketing strategy. When Häagen-Dazs launched in the UK at prices more than double those of its competitors, many predicted failure. In fact, the pricing was in line with the image of adult, luxury indulgence and Häagen-Dazs soon outsold all other premium ice creams (though today Ben & Jerry's is No. 1). The worst pricing approach would be to develop an attractively packaged, well-made product and then sell it at a discount to the leading brands. In research, people would welcome it, but deep down they would not trust the product quality. Because psychology is so important to successful pricing, many firms use qualitative research, rather than quantitative, to obtain the necessary psychological insights.

# Workbook

## A. Revision questions

**(35 marks; 40 minutes)**

1. Explain why price 'is fundamental to a firm's revenues'. (3)

2. Look at Figure 23.1. Outline two factors that would affect the 'psychologically right price range' for a new Samsung phone. (4)

3. Explain how the actions of Nike could affect the footwear prices set by Adidas. (4)

4. Look at Table 23.1, on the price sensitivity of products, brands and services. Think of two more examples of highly price-sensitive and two examples of not-very-price-sensitive products, services or brands. (4)

5. Explain the difference between pricing strategy and pricing tactics. (2)

6. For each of the following, decide whether the pricing strategy should be skimming or penetration. Briefly explain your reasoning.

   a) Richard Branson's Virgin group launches the world's first space tourism service (you are launched in a rocket, spend time weightless in space, watch the world go round, then come back to earth). (4)

   b) Kellogg's launches a new range of sliced breads for families who are in a hurry. (4)

   c) The first robotic washing machine is launched. It washes, dries and irons the clothes – and places them in neat piles. (4)

7. Is a cash cow likely to be a price maker or a price taker? Explain your reasoning. (3)

8. Identify three circumstances in which a business may decide to use special-offer pricing. (3)

# B. Revision exercises

## DATA RESPONSE 1

On 1 February 2014, Tesco Price Check provided the information given in Table 23.3 on the prices of shampoo brands. Study the table then answer the questions that follow.

**Table 23.3** Prices of shampoo brands in January 2014

| Product description | Tesco price (£) | Asda price (£) |
|---|---|---|
| TRESemmé Instant Refresh Dry Shampoo 200 ml | 4.99 | 5.00 |
| Pantene Volume & Body 250 ml | 2.89 | 2.68 |
| Head & Shoulders Classic 250 ml | 2.99 | 2.79 |
| Vosene Original 250 ml | 1.79 | 2.00 |
| John Frieda Full Repair 250 ml | 5.89 | 5.89 |
| Own-label* Baby 500 ml | 1.00 | 1.00 |
| Own-label* Budget Shampoo 1000 ml | 0.40 | 0.40 |
| Bob Martin Dog Shampoo 250 ml | - | 3.48 |

*Own-label means the supermarket's own brand.*

### Questions (35 marks; 35 minutes)

1. Explain why it may be fair to describe Vosene shampoo as a price taker. (4)

2. John Frieda shampoo is priced at more than 40 times the level of supermarket budget shampoos (per ml). Explain why customers may be willing to pay such a high price. (6)

3. Analyse the position of the long-established brand Head and Shoulders within the UK market for shampoo. What pricing strategy does it seem to be using and why may it be possible to use this approach? (9)

4. To what extent could it ever be right for dogs to have 'better' shampoo than babies? (16)

## DATA RESPONSE 2

### New product pricing strategy

Before the mid-October launch of Maruti Suzuki's new Alto 800, the company set itself a target unprecedented in the history of the Indian automobile industry. Maruti called it the '50/20/10 target'. It meant aiming for 50,000 test drives, 20,000 orders, and 10,000 deliveries - all within the first 10 days.

To make it harder to achieve, the car market was slipping backwards in Autumn 2012 as the Indian economy grappled with 10 per cent inflation and high interest rates. With such high inflation, it would have been understandable if Maruti had priced their new Alto model 10 per cent higher than the previous one. Instead it made headlines by launching at 2 per cent below – even though the specification had been upgraded. Prices for the Alto started at £2,500, with £3,400 for the highest spec.

On the morning of the tenth day, Maruti Suzuki's Managing Executive Officer for Marketing and Sales announced: 'We crossed all three targets. We launched in 821 cities and 1,130 outlets.' That morning, the new Alto had crossed 27,000 bookings and 10,200 deliveries.

Getting the pricing right was critical because Maruti, for so long the dominant force in India with a 45 per cent market share, had lost 3 percentage points in

Introducing the new Alto 800

**Figure 23.5** The new Maruti Alto 800

the previous year. This was partly because the Alto model, which had once sold 35,000 cars a month, had seen its sales slip to 18,000 by early 2012. And with small cars such as this making up 70 per cent of the Indian car market, the Alto launch was vital.

When asked whether this pricing might spark a price war, Maruti suggested that it was simply making use of its competitive advantage. An independent auto analyst confirmed that 'Maruti enjoys huge economies of scale, even at lower margins. No other company can do that.'

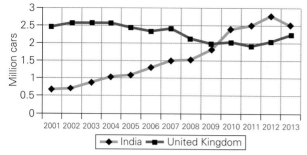

**Figure 23.6** Market for new cars: India vs. UK
Sources: OICA & ICCT

The reduced price is intensifying competition in the market in what Abdul Majeed, Partner at PWC, calls the 'volume game'. He explains that Maruti's pricing may initially spark a price war, but it is important to develop the market three or four years down the line, as it would generate high volumes. 'If you can't sell 200,000 to 300,000 cars, you can't make money,' he says. In the short term, margins will feel the pinch, but in the long run the move will be beneficial, as small cars still make up 70 per cent of the Indian car market. 'Car makers will have to take the risk,' says Majeed.

A year on, in September 2013, the Alto was India's top-selling car and Maruti's market share had recovered from 41 per cent to 43.5 per cent since the same month in 2012.

Source: *Business Today* Copyright © 2014, 2014 Living Media India Limited. All Rights Reserved.

## Questions (30 marks, 35 minutes)

1. Explain one way in which market trends in new car sales in India (see graph) might have influenced the pricing decision for the new Alto 800. (5)

2. Analyse the possible implications for the Indian car market if Maruti's pricing does 'spark a price war'. (9)

3. To what extent was it wise for Maruti to adopt a penetration pricing strategy for its new Alto model? (16)

## C. Extend your understanding

1. At a supermarket, a Mars Bar is priced at 79p and a pack of 3 at £1.00. From the point of view of the consumer and the producer, can both these prices be right? Justify your answer. (20)

2. Research the launch prices and sales of Sony's PS4 and the Microsoft One in 2013/14. To what extent was pricing the key reason for Sony's sales success? (20)

# Chapter 24

# Place and promotion decisions

**Linked to:** Setting marketing objectives, Chapter 13; Market research, Chapter 15; Segmentation, targeting and positioning, Chapter 19; Marketing mix: the 7Ps, Chapter 21.

## Definition

Place is about availability (how to get the product to the right place for customers to make their purchases). It includes physical or online distribution, availability and visibility. Promotion is the part of the marketing mix that focuses on persuading people to buy the product or service.

## 24.1 Introduction to place

The word 'place' can be unhelpful, because it suggests that manufacturers can place their products where they like (for example, at the entrance of a Tesco store). The real world is not like that. Obtaining distribution at Tesco stores is a dream for most small producers, and a very hard dream to turn into reality. For new firms in particular, place is the toughest of the 7Ps.

Persuading retailers to stock a product is never easy. For the retailer, the key issues are opportunity cost and risk. As shelf space is limited, stocking a particular chocolate bar probably means scrapping another. But which one should the retailer choose? What revenue will be lost? The other consideration is risk. A new, low-calorie chocolate bar may be a slimmer's delight, but high initial sales may slip, leaving the shopkeeper with boxes of slow-moving stock.

## 24.2 Choosing appropriate distributors

When a new business wants to launch its first product, a key question to consider is the distribution channel; in other words, how the product passes from producer

to consumer. Should the product be sold directly, as with pick-your-own strawberries? Or via a wholesaler, then a retailer, as with crisps bought from your local shop? This decision will affect every aspect of the business in the future, especially its profit.

Manufacturers must decide on the right outlets for their own product. If Chanel chooses to launch a new perfume, 'Alexa', backed by Alexa Chung, priced at £69.99, controlling distribution will be vital. The company will want it to be sold in a smart location where elegant sales staff can persuade customers of its wonderful scent and gorgeous packaging. If Superdrug or Morrisons' want to stock the brand, Chanel will try hard to find reasons to say no.

Yet the control is often not in the hands of the producer, but of the retailer. If you came up with a wonderful idea for a brand-new ice cream, how would you get distribution for it? The freezers in corner shops are usually owned by Walls and Mars, so they frown upon independent products being stocked in 'their' space. To the retailer, every foot of shop floor space has an actual cost (the rental value) and an opportunity cost (the cost of missing out on the profits that could be generated by selling other goods). In effect, then, your brand-new ice cream is likely to stay on the drawing board, because obtaining distribution will be too large a barrier to entry to this market.

## 24.3 Multi-channel distribution

There are three main channels of distribution. These are described below.

### Traditional physical channel

Small producers find it hard to achieve distribution in big chains such as B&Q or Sainsbury's, so they usually sell to wholesalers who, in turn, sell to small independent shops. The profit mark-up applied by the 'middleman' adds to the final retail price, but a small producer cannot afford to deliver individually to lots of small shops.

Larger producers cut out the middleman (the wholesaler) and sell directly to retail chains, from Boots to Tesco. This is more cost effective, but exposes the seller to tough negotiation from the retail chains on prices and credit terms.

## Direct online

Using this channel of distribution the producer sells directly to the consumer. Manufacturers can do this through mail order or – far more likely today – through a website. This ensures that the producer keeps 100 per cent of the product's selling price. So the benefit of the direct distribution channel is that the producer's higher profits can finance more spending on advertising, on website development or on new product development.

## Online retail

Small firms often lack the ability and/or the finance to build a successful e-commerce sales platform. So it can make sense to piggyback on an established platform such as eBay in the West or the amazingly successful TaoBao in China. TaoBao has more than 2 million businesses using the site to sell to China's hundreds of millions of online shoppers. TaoBao is one part of Jack Ma's Alibaba business that had sales, in 2014, of $420 billion – dwarfing Amazon and eBay combined.

'Establish channels for different target markets and aim for efficiency, control and adaptability.' Philip Kotler, marketing guru

### Real business

In 2013 internet sales of groceries rose by 19 per cent according to market research agency Kantar. By comparison, sales from grocery shops only rose by 2 per cent. This trend towards online shopping has been developing for ten years and may be accelerating. In the four days leading up to Christmas 2013, 15 per cent of all grocery sales were online. No wonder that Morrisons', the only UK grocery chain with no online presence, was rapidly losing market share. In (belated) response Morrisons' started its first online deliveries in a test market in Warwickshire in January 2014. The same company proved extraordinarily slow to spot the success of smaller, urban grocery outlets such as Tesco Metro.

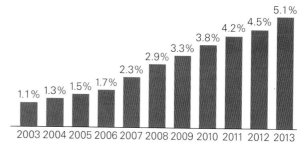

**Figure 24.1** E-commerce share of UK grocery spending 2003–13

Source: Kantar Worldpanel, 'Shopping for Groceries,' 6 Aug 2013

## 24.4 What is promotion?

Promotion is a general term that covers all the marketing activity that informs customers about a product and persuades them to buy it. The different elements of promotion can be grouped into two broad categories: those that stimulate short-term sales and those that build sales for the long term. This distinction provides the basis for analysis of most business situations and questions.

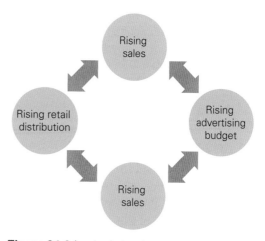

**Figure 24.2** Logic chain: place, promotion and sales

## 24.5 Types of promotion for building long-term sales

These include those described below.

### The value of branding

One of the best forms of promotion is branding. Branding is the process of creating a distinctive and lasting identity in the minds of consumers. Establishing a brand can take considerable time and marketing effort, but once a product brand is established it becomes its own means of promotion. The brand name is recognised and this makes it more likely that the customer will buy the product for the first time. If the experience is satisfactory the customer is very likely to continue to choose the brand. Once established, branding has many advantages, such as the following.

- It enables the business to reduce the amount spent on promotion.
- Customers are more likely to purchase the product again (repeat purchases).
- It is easier to persuade retailers to put the products in their stores.
- Other products can be promoted using the same brand name.

'The best advertising is done by satisfied customers.'
Philip Kotler, marketing guru

## Persuasive advertising

Persuasive advertising is designed to create a distinctive image. A good example is BMW, which has spent decades persuading us that it produces not a car but a 'Driving Machine'. Advertising of this kind has also helped to create clear consumer images for firms such as McDonald's and L'Oréal (see Table 24.1).

**Table 24.1** Examples of persuasive advertising

| Company | Slogan | Meaning |
| --- | --- | --- |
| innocent Drinks | 'Chain of good: tastes good, does good' | 'Our smoothies are good for you (whatever the anti-fruit juice folk say) and we give 10 per cent of our profits to charity (please forget we're now owned by Coca-Cola) |
| L'Oréal | 'Because you're worth it' | Go on, spoil yourself; you can afford that bit extra, so buy our products, not our competitors' |
| McDonald's | 'I'm Lovin' it' | Our food may be unhealthy, but it tastes great |

**Figure 24.3** Corporate sponsorship may be used as a form of promotion

## Public relations

This is the attempt to affect consumers' image of a product without spending on media advertising. It includes making contacts with journalists to try to get favourable mentions or articles about your product. It would also include activities such as sponsorship of sport or the arts. (See Figure 24.3) In 2014 Waitrose decided to sponsor the England cricket team. The upmarket image of cricket is the perfect match for the posh image of Waitrose stores.

## 24.6 Promotional activity needs to fit in with marketing strategy

The type of promotion used and the level of promotional activity will vary not only from company to company and product to product but also in terms of the marketing strategy being

**Table 24.2** Marketing strategies and types of promotion

| Marketing strategy | Promotion needs to: |
|---|---|
| Launching a new product | • be informative<br>• reach the target customers |
| Differentiating the product | • identify the special features of the product<br>• persuade customers that it is different/better than rival products |
| Extending the life of an existing product | • reinforce the reasons for customers choosing it<br>• highlight any new features<br>• attract new customers |
| Increasing market share | • attract new customers<br>• reinforce buying in existing customers |
| Building brand identity | • increase awareness of the company/product name<br>• create customer recognition and loyalty |

followed. Different forms of promotion will serve different purposes. Much will depend on what the business is trying to achieve (see Table 24.2).

The correct promotional mix will be achieved only if the business has clear marketing objectives. Once the objectives and strategy are determined it is much easier for the business to develop an effective promotional campaign.

## Five Whys and a How

| Question | Answer |
|---|---|
| Why is it hard for a new company to achieve retail distribution for its products? | No retailers have gaps on their shelves, so accepting a new product means dropping an existing one, risking lost revenue |
| Why might it be a mistake for a company to seek 100 per cent distribution for its products? | Long-term sales success relies on having a clear, positive image. Nike doesn't want its latest sportswear sold cheaply at Sports Direct; the short-term sales would be at a long-term cost |
| Why do most modern firms pursue multi-channel distribution strategies? | Because today's consumers sometimes want traditional, browsing shopping and sometimes want speedy online purchasing from home |
| Why may it be a profitable strategy for a producer to offer extra-high profit margins to retailers? | The bigger the slice of a sale taken by the retailer, the less there is for the producer, but high margins attract higher distribution levels and better display at the point-of-sale (e.g. right by the cash till) so sales volumes are boosted |
| Why may short-term promotions be a mistake in the long term? | No serious business sees short-term sales maximisation as a proper objective; to build for the long term, image has to be built, not exploited |
| How important is branding for a business-to-business company? | Even business customers like the promise of quality and consistency that are the appeal at the heart of many brands |

## Evaluation: Place and promotion decisions

Competitiveness is a much wider issue than marketing. It is affected by the quality of the design and build of the products, and by the enthusiasm of the staff. These are clearly operations and personnel issues. Nevertheless, marketing is at the heart of competitiveness for many firms. Mars knows how to produce Galaxy chocolate, so the key to the firm's success next year is how well the brand can be marketed. The managers must understand the customers, and then have the wisdom and the creativity to find a way to make the product stand out.

Place is of particular importance in Business Studies because it can represent a major barrier to entry, especially for new, small firms. The practical constraint on the amount of shop-floor space makes it hard for new products to gain acceptance unless they are genuinely innovative. Therefore, existing producers of branded goods can become quite complacent, with little serious threat from new competition.

Famously, in the nineteenth century Ralph Waldo Emerson said: 'If a man can make a better mousetrap, though he builds his house in the woods the world will make a beaten path to his door.' In other words, if the product is good enough, customers will come and find you. In a modern competitive world, though, the vast majority of products are not that exciting or different from others. So it is crucial to provide customers with convenient access to your products and/or shelf space in an eye-catching location. Getting products into the right place should not be taken for granted.

Successful branding is one way to ensure good distribution and good in-store display. Shopkeepers want to show off the latest and the classiest brands. In this way, promotion and place come together.

# Workbook

## A. Revision questions

(45 marks; 45 minutes)

1. Outline the meaning of the term 'place'. (2)

2. Explain in your own words why it may be that 'place is the toughest of the 4Ps'. (3)

3. Outline what you think are appropriate distribution channels for:

   **a)** a new F1 racing game for mobiles and tablets

   **b)** a new adventure holiday company focusing on wealthy 19 to 32 year olds. (3)

4. Retailers such as WH Smith charge manufacturers a rent on prime store space such as the shelving near to the cash tills.

   **a)** How may a firm work out whether it is worthwhile to pay the extra? (3)

   **b)** Why may new, small firms find it hard to pay rents such as these? (4)

5. Explain in your own words what is meant by the phrase 'a better mousetrap'. (3)

6. Outline three reasons for the success of direct online distribution in recent years. (5)

7. Explain what form of promotion you think would work best for marketing:

   **a)** a new football game for the PS4 (3)

   **b)** a small, family-focused seaside hotel (3)

   **c)** organic cosmetics for women. (3)

8. Why is it important for businesses to monitor the effect of their promotional activity? (4)

9. What is meant by the phrase 'promotion needs to be effective'? (4)

10. Explain why promotion is essential for new businesses. (5)

# B. Revision exercises
## DATA RESPONSE 1

### Getting distribution right

Secondary data can be hugely helpful to new companies looking for distribution of their first products. A company launching the first 'Kitten Milk' product has to decide where to focus its efforts. Where does cat food sell? Is it in pet shops, in corner shops or in supermarkets? Desk research company BMRB reports that, whereas 65 per cent of dog owners shop for pet food at supermarkets, 81 per cent of cat owners do the same. A different source (TNS) puts the cat food market size at £829 million. TNS also shows that the market is rising in value by around 2.5 per cent a year.

Further secondary data shows that pet food shoppers spend only 80 per cent of the amount they intend to when they go to a shop. This is because poor distribution stops them finding what they want. And 50 per cent of shoppers will not return to the same store after being let down twice by poor availability.

### Questions (25 marks; 25 minutes)

1. State the meaning of the term 'market size'. (2)

2. Consider the following:
   a) The Year 1 sales target for Kitten Milk is £5 million. What share of the total market for cat food would that represent? (3)
   b) Explain why it might be hard to persuade retailers to stock a product with that level of market share. (4)

3. The marketing manager for Kitten Milk is planning to focus distribution efforts on getting the brand placed in pet shops. To what extent do you agree with this approach? (16)

## DATA RESPONSE 2

### An arm's length from desire

From its origins in America in 1886, Coca-Cola has been a marketing phenomenon. It was the world's first truly global brand; it virtually invented the red, jolly Christmas Santa, and its bottle design (1919) was the first great piece of packaging design.

Yet a 1950 *Time* magazine article quoted another piece of marketing genius: 'Always within an arm's length of desire.' The marketing experts at Atlanta (home of Coca-Cola) realised nearly 60 years ago that sales of Coca-Cola were limited mainly by availability. Especially on a hot day, a cold Coke would be desired by almost anyone who had it an arm's length away. This led the company to develop a distribution strategy based on maximum availability, maximum in-store visibility and therefore maximum impulse purchase.

From then on, Coca-Cola targeted four main types of distribution:

1. in supermarkets and grocers

2. in any kiosk in a location based on entertainment (for example, a bowling alley or a cinema)

3. in any canteen, bar or restaurant

4. in a vending machine near you. Automatic vending proved one of the most valuable ways of building the market until worries about healthy eating saw them banned in schools. A vending machine is the ultimate barrier to entry.

Overall, though, the Coca-Cola approach to distribution set out in 1950 is what most companies still try to do today.

**Questions (25 marks; 30 minutes)**

1. Explain how a vending machine can be a 'barrier to entry' to new competitors. (4)

2. Explain what the text means by the difference between 'maximum availability' and 'maximum visibility'. (4)

3. Explain two reasons why 'an arm's length from desire' may be less important for a business that does not rely upon impulse purchase. (8)

4. From all that you know about today's Coke, Diet Coke and Coke Zero, analyse whether Coca-Cola's distribution strategy was at the core of the firm's marketing success. (9)

## C. Extend your understanding

1. Heinz has found that its famous brand limits it from expanding its product portfolio, as people won't accept Heinz chilled ready meals or Heinz pizzas. Discuss how it might try to overcome this consumer resistance. (20)

2. You have just developed a new console game that combines the appeal of Candy Crush with the force of Call of Duty. To what extent would obtaining high levels of distribution guarantee the product's success in the UK? (20)

# Chapter 25 Integrating the marketing mix

**Linked to:** Marketing and decision-making, Chapter 11; Market research, Chapter 15; Market data and analysis, Chapter 18; Segmentation, targeting and positioning, Chapter 19; Motivation and engagement in theory, Chapter 46; Motivation and engagement in practice, Chapter 47.

## Definition

Success comes from a co-ordinated campaign that directs every marketing variable towards the right market positioning for the product or brand.

## 25.1 The importance of an integrated marketing mix

How do some brands thrive over generations while others arrive, look promising, but then fade away? Do you remember Nokia phones, Strollers (chocolate flop), the McHotel and Virgin Cola (it would wipe out Coke, according to Richard Branson)? In the meantime, some brands keep on going, such as Heinz Tomato Ketchup (born 1888), Marmite (born 1902), Maltesers (born 1932) and the Ford Fiesta (born 1976).

Part of the difference between the successes and the flops is the understanding shown of the mix. Maltesers and Marmite have in common an exceptional level of product differentiation. Therefore the key has been to make the product the central element of the mix, and simply ensure that the other mix factors fit in. Pricing, for example, has generally been quite high, to confirm psychologically the quality of the product. For Heinz Ketchup the degree of differentiation is not as high, but fortunately the image of authenticity has put the brand at the centre of many a table. Only in the case of the Ford Fiesta has the toughly competitive market made it necessary to have a succession of top-notch brand managers making the right decisions about all aspects of the mix.

The reason the mix must be integrated is simple: we the consumers are committing our hard-earned cash in exchange for an uncertain return. Will the dress really look good after a couple of wears? Will the restaurant meal be quite what your fiancé wanted? Therefore we are looking at all the clues surrounding the product or service and weighing them up together. Good-looking menu but prices seem oddly low? No thanks. Good-looking dress but the salesperson can't answer a question about washing? No thanks.

**Figure 25.1** Logic chain: links to an effective mix

## 25.2 Influences on an integrated marketing mix

The brand manager at Mercedes knows that the key is to create an integrated, enveloping image of the car as an aspirational luxury. Customers arriving at a showroom should have an experience in keeping with the brand image: efficient, classy and pampering.

Marketing influences on an integrated mix:

● Position in the product life cycle. In the development stage the central focus is on the product/service and the extent to which it meets existing or new customer needs or wants. Only when market research gives a green light to the product does it make sense to test the appropriate price, packaging and perhaps advertising/promotion. Once those factors have been settled it is time to set out the process that is to be followed by the people who will interact with the customers – and to decide on any physical environment needed to back up the promotional platform. Once the product is launched, the price may change (perhaps increase after penetration pricing at launch).

- The Boston Matrix. When a business has a wide product portfolio (400 'superbrands' in the case of Unilever) it has to prioritise. Cadbury will have sales staff focused on the chocolate market who are to sell perhaps 40 different product lines. Shopkeepers cannot possibly find the time for a hard sell on 40 products, so Cadbury will select two or three to focus on each month. Dairy Milk is such a cash cow (UK 2014 sales of over £500 million) that it will get regular support. In addition, rising stars and the occasional problem child will be selected. A rising star has the twin benefits of a high market share in a growth sector; the problem child is also in the growth sector, but lacks the market share to be strong – yet.

- The type of product. The most important distinction is between goods and services. For the most part the marketing mix for goods is based on the 4Ps, especially if the goods are marketed through traditional retail channels. Services, though, need the extra 3Ps to ensure that there are high-quality people working to highly efficient systems making intelligent use of physical environment where necessary. Other categories to consider are B2B versus B2C, and convenience vs. shopping vs. speciality goods.

- Marketing objectives. If the target for the marketing managers is to boost market share significantly, perhaps as in the case of Müllerlight, from 7.4 to 9 per cent of the £2,200 million market for yoghurts and potted desserts, there will be a need for a big rethink. Going from 7.4 to 9 requires a sales increase of $1.6/7.4 \times 100 = 21.6$ per cent, assuming a static market. Therefore there may be a need for significant new product innovation, or a distribution innovation that competitors cannot easily copy. Either way there may be a significant realignment of the marketing mix in order to achieve the new objectives

- The target market. A posh brand must have all seven mix variables pointing in the same direction, towards aspiration and quality. As mentioned before, the fact that only four of the seven Ps are the direct responsibility of the marketing department can make this a serious challenge. Each week *The Grocer* magazine rates the quality of customer service across all the leading grocers. Given its high prices and posh image, you would expect Waitrose to win this regularly. In fact it wins it less often than Tesco or Morrisons' – far, far behind the 2014 winner Sainsbury. Surely Waitrose customers will notice this at some point.

---

'You can duplicate the airplanes. You can duplicate the gate facilities. You can duplicate all the hard things, the tangible things you can put your hands on. But it's the intangibles that determine success.' Herb Kelleher, airline chief executive

---

- Competition. Pukka Pies has long been an important brand at football grounds, but it also was developing a useful retail sideline. By 2012 it was selling £3.1 million pies a year in supermarkets. Then Greggs decided to produce its own pies to be sold in supermarkets. Sales of £11 million in 2012 jumped 91 per cent to £21.1 million in 2013. This hit other pie-makers but especially Pukka, which suffered a 12 per cent sales decline in 2013. To survive in this tougher retail environment Pukka will have to think how best to react: reposition the pies, perhaps, to distinguish Pukka more clearly from Greggs, or bring out new, better recipes to beat Greggs on taste.

---

'Give them quality. That's the best kind of advertising.' Milton Hershey, US chocolate-maker

---

- Market positioning. Today's consumers want something that is targeted tightly at them. This is why Marks & Spencer's clothing is in no man's land; even middle-aged people struggle to think the ranges are targeted at them, because it's all too mass-market. In the clothing sector, this is where Next succeeds (office wear for young adults) and where Zara triumphs worldwide (targeting the under 30s). Clever companies are clear about where their market position is – and focus every aspect of their marketing mix at that positioning. This leads to a co-ordinated, integrated mix.

## Real business

The all-time biggest-selling games console was Sony's PS2, which sold 158 million units. So when Microsoft chose to launch its second generation Xbox 360 a year before the PS2, there was no doubting its target – young, male game-players: the Sony heartland. Nintendo had been doing some thinking, however. They saw Xbox and Sony hammering the same demographic and decided on an innovative new positioning. Their Wii would target children, girls, families and older adults – in other words, position themselves firmly away from the crowd. The result was a triumph for Nintendo. The Wii sold 101 million consoles compared with PS3's 83 million and Xbox 360's 82 million. Clever market positioning gave Wii the marketing edge.

Among other influences on an integrated marketing mix are:

- Budgets: has the business enough finance to achieve a co-ordinated approach to all seven aspects of the mix? If competitive pressures have forced the business to cut out a whole layer of supervisory management (as happened recently at Asda and at Morrisons') it may be very difficult to deliver People and Processes to the right standard.

- Staff turnover: at McDonalds UK 35 per cent of staff leave each year, having to be replaced. This might make it hard to build consistency into the marketing mix, as new staff will constantly be arriving, each with a lot to learn about service levels. To McDonalds' credit, the business seems well enough managed to be able to overcome this problem.

- External factors, such as changes in the market structure, perhaps introducing fiercer competition; or a switch from good times to recession, causing a rethink in marketing objectives and strategy – and therefore in the marketing mix.

## 25.3 Digital marketing, e-commerce and the marketing mix

Traditionally, location has been a key factor for retailers. For online retailers it is irrelevant. Yet there are many other potential pitfalls.

In the case of Glasses Direct (see below) outstanding prices combined with a good product, good service and a small investment in advertising to create a highly successful mix. In effect, it was the original idea (high-street glasses at non-rip-off prices) that was the key. In other cases this will not work, because the offer has to be similar to the competition. If you are selling skateboards online, your prices will not be much different to those of other suppliers. This will make it much more important to identify a winning marketing strategy.

Here are some that work well.

- The saturation approach: as used by Moneysupermarket.com to make sure that everyone thinks of you first. The downside, of course, is the huge cost of the TV advertising.

- Google search optimisation: that is, design your website so that it comes very high on the list when people are Googling for something you want to sell. This takes time and a small amount of money, but is much, much cheaper than a multi-million-pound advertising campaign.

- Build a website people will talk about: some good examples are those of BMW (won 2013 'Website of the Year' award) and Ocado. A fun website can provide strong support to a brand image, and get the brand written about in the media, which provides extra, free promotion.

## Real business

### The £100 million glasses

James Murray-Wells started Glasses Direct at the age of 21, just after completing a degree. He offered pairs of glasses online for £15 instead of the £150 paid in the high street.

James designed the website himself, but – with no money and no publicity – sales in the first month averaged just one or two pairs a day. The only expense he could afford was to get some leaflets printed. This is often a weak form of advertising, but with his incredibly competitive price proposition his leaflets proved highly effective. He took a train from Bristol, handing out flyers to people who would be stuck on a train with nothing else to do but read them. Within days sales started coming through from people living in Bristol. Shortly afterwards came emails of thanks, with people clearly surprised that the glasses were every bit as good as those available on the high street. By the end of the summer, word of mouth had spread and the first articles started appearing in papers. Orders were received for up to 100 pairs a day and the business was booming. Within two years turnover hit £3 million and was rising. By 2013 sales were heading for £40 million a year and there was City talk of floating the business for £100 million. In fact, after selling the business to a German private equity house, Murray-Wells stood down. Having made unknown millions, he is now looking for other business opportunities.

## Five Whys and a How

| Question | Answer |
|---|---|
| Why is it important for the marketing mix to be co-ordinated? | So that the consumer gets a single, clear idea and image of the product/service |
| Why might some brands live forever? | Because the managers might have the ability to keep reinventing the brand to suit new generations |
| Why might a manager start focusing upon higher and higher prices for a product in its decline phase? | Because the manager believes there's no potential for future growth, making it sensible to maximise revenue from the few remaining loyal customers |
| Why might a change in target market make it hard to maintain an integrated marketing mix? | It is perhaps easier to change the 4Ps than it is to change the ones that are to do with the efficiency and understanding shown by customer-facing staff |
| Why might a switch from retailing to online selling lead to a better-integrated marketing mix? | Online selling keeps everything within head office control and may therefore help achieve consistency in dealing with customers |
| How might a football club learn from the three extra Ps within the marketing mix? | They could learn that the People they employ are supposed to be polite and helpful to fans and that the Process should be efficient enough to minimise queuing and delay |

## Key terms

**Penetration pricing:** pricing low enough to attract high sales in order to establish a satisfactory market share

**Product differentiation:** is the extent to which consumers perceive your product to be distinct from rival products.

## Evaluation: Integrating the marketing mix

In an era where the most dramatic business stories are about new technology companies and online businesses, it might seem that the marketing mix is an old-fashioned concept. It is hard to believe that Sergey Brin or Mark Zuckerberg have ever heard of it. Yet it remains an important touchstone – almost a checklist – for middle managers. These days the biggest challenge is to co-ordinate the 7Ps across the three relevant departments: marketing, operations and human resources. Successfully achieving this requires company-wide training and understanding that can only be expected in a very well-run company. If, furthermore, a company has to achieve this across countries worldwide, the challenge is massive indeed.

# Workbook

## A. Revision questions

(35 marks; 35 minutes)

1. Outline two possible reasons why Maltesers is still selling successfully over 75 years after the brand's birth. (4)

2. Explain why it is important to distinguish between a trend and a fad. Look at the quote by Milton Hershey on page 156. Explain how quality can be the best kind of advertising. (4)

3. Why might new competition in the soft drinks business force Pepsi to rethink its marketing mix? (4)

4. Reread the Real business feature 'The £100m glasses'. Outline two aspects of the marketing mix that were especially important to this business's success. (4)

5. Consider the following:
   a) In February 2008, Cadbury announced the launch of a range of Easter eggs that would not have any outer packaging (they would just be sold in a foil wrapper). Outline one advantage and one disadvantage of this. (4)
   b) In 2012 they admitted that they had returned to full, traditional packaging for Cadbury Easter Eggs. Why might this be? (5)

6. Should a company switching from retail to online distribution consider it a moral duty to cut prices to the consumers? (5)

7. What might be the most important element of the marketing mix for a business such as British Airways? Explain your answer. (5)

## B. Revision exercises

### DATA RESPONSE

**The software triumph**

Federico and Cara formed their business (Fedaria Ltd) just two weeks before *Angry Birds* launched in December 2009. The company would develop app games that would be free to download and play, with income to be generated by players choosing to buy extra lives or extra playing time.

By late 2010 Cara developed a brand new game based on a classic game of pirates looking for treasure. Federico knew various journalists who reported on games software, so *Dubloon* received reviews in several paper and digital media. Reviewers loved the game, but sales proved disappointing. Soon after, they produced a successful series of games for the 2012 Olympics: *Shotput*, *Rowing* and – most successful of all: *Javelin*.

By this time – mid 2011 – Fedaria's revenue was hitting £400,000 a month, making it necessary to hire a series of new managers and developers. This made it hard to keep every aspect of the marketing mix co-ordinated, but Federico worked hard to achieve this.

As Britain focused on the Olympics in Spring 2012 downloads went crazy – and so did income. Fedaria *Javelin* became the top Apple app for the UK, and sales were also strong in America and Japan. But in the April 2012 board meeting things went less well.

Cara was unhappy that customer feedback was not as strong as it might be. Customers loved the games but found online ordering difficult and deliveries erratic.

Luckily for the business, Cara's frustration was deflected over the coming weeks as one of her developers came with a near-completed game that she loved. The idea was so simple: stocks. You could download a photo or choose a face to be put in the stocks and then take aim. Tomatoes splattered convincingly; eggs producing dripping yellow yolk and many other options gave lots of idle pleasure. Within three days Cara had a test version on the Fedaria website, where devotees were keen to test out new ideas. Two days after that she knew that – with a few tweaks – this would be a smash.

Now it was time to chat about the game to Federico. He had just finished a meeting with the newly-appointed marketing director (MD). The MD had insisted on a £400,000 advertising budget to 'consolidate the Fedaria brand values in the mind of the target market'. Federico knew that current revenues made this affordable, but his experience made him want to preserve plenty of profit for possible tough times in the future. And now Cara wanted £200,000 to launch *Stocks*. He said no.

Furious, Cara threatened to leave and set up on her own. Federico found a compromise by offering a £50,000 budget to create an online viral PR campaign. Cara accepted and the launch was scheduled for June 2013. By September, *Stocks* was the UK's No. 2 download for mobiles (behind *Candy Crush*), and broke through the £500,000-a-day revenue level.

**Questions (30 marks; 35 minutes)**

1. Briefly explain how Fedaria handled two aspects of the 7Ps. (5)

2. Analyse the importance of a fully integrated marketing mix in the case of Fedaria Ltd. (9)

3. To what extent does a digital business such as Fedaria hinge on the effectiveness of its marketing mix? (16)

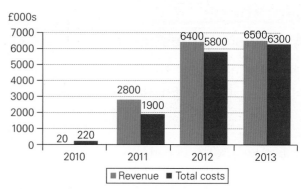

**Figure 25.2** Fedaria Ltd: revenues and costs
Figures for 2013 are Jan-Jun only

## C. Extend your understanding

1. For a brand you are familiar with, analyse each of the 7Ps then decide which is the most important element of its mix. Justify your answer. (20)

2. No matter how big the brand, there is a limit to its marketing budget. How important is it, therefore to decide which elements of the mix to prioritise? Justify your answer. (20)

# Chapter
# 26
# Setting operational objectives

**Linked with:** Efficiency and labour productivity, Chapter 27; Technology and operational efficiency, Chapter 30; Analysing operational performance, Chapter 31; Decision-making to improve operational performance, Chapter 35.

## Definition

Operational objectives are the specific, detailed production targets set by an organisation to ensure that its overall company goals are achieved.

## 26.1 Introduction

All organisations share common operational objectives regardless of their size and the sector in which they operate. All firms will attempt to produce goods and services that are 'fit for purpose', delivered quickly and on time. They will also aim to produce the right number of goods as cheaply as possible, bearing in mind the overall strategy.

If, like Ryanair, your target is to be the lowest-cost airline in Europe, every cost will be shaved to the minimum. If your business strategy is to be the highest-rated airline in the world (such as Singapore Airlines), you may accept costs that will seem high to other airlines. The crucial thing is that a firm's operational objectives must be fully in line with its objectives regarding marketing and management of its people.

Finally, there needs to be enough flexibility within operations to allow activities to be varied or adapted quickly, in order to accommodate changes in demand.

## 26.2 Key operational objectives

The key operational objectives are shown in Figure 26.1 and described below.

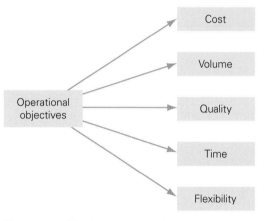

**Figure 26.1** The key operational objectives

## Cost

All firms are concerned with keeping costs down, particularly those that compete directly on price. Costs affect what is charged to the customer and therefore the profits that can be generated. During a period of economic downturn, a firm's ability to make further cost reductions can mean the difference between survival and failure. Costs are determined by the efficiency of a business. This can be measured in a number of ways; for example, wastage rates or the productivity of the workforce.

## Real business

### Will Asda's cost-cutting prove costly?

Faced with ferocious price competition from Aldi and Lidl, in May 2014 Asda announced a plan to cut 4,100 department manager positions at its stores. The result was fury on the part of middle managers who felt their career progression was being blunted. From Asda's point of view, the delayering of its stores was a major part of a £1 billion cost-cutting exercise called 'We Operate for Less'. The company could also defend itself by pointing to a 6-month trial of ⇨

⇨

the flatter organisational structure at two of its stores, which started the previous November. Underlying the decision was the customer shift to online purchasing, putting pressure on the cost structure at large stores such as supermarkets. As one retail analyst explained, the long-term success of the new approach would depend on the difference between cost-cutting and efficiency gains: 'If you can reduce the cost of servicing customers without impacting upon quality, that's efficiency. If you can't, that's cost-cutting'.

## Quality

The exact meaning of quality for any individual organisation will depend to some extent on the nature of its operations. Put simply, quality is about getting things 'right' by meeting or beating customer expectations over and over again. Quality has a crucial role to play in guaranteeing customer satisfaction. Not only should firms aim to produce goods or services that are 'fit for purpose', they also need to create a sense of dependability by ensuring that products are ready when customers expect them. Failure to do so is likely to create customer dissatisfaction and encourage customers to switch to rival products. A high degree of quality and dependability is also required within the organisation. Managers need to ensure that quality standards are being met. They also need to synchronize production so that products pass smoothly from one stage to the next. This will help to reduce production time and costs, meaning that goods are ready for dispatch to customers sooner.

## Speed of response

This factor is important in many ways, both to the consumer and the producer. Many consumers are 'money-rich, time-poor' as they rush from a well-paid job to pick up the kids, eat, then go out. So operations that save time for the customer can be very successful (for example, Next Directory shopping or pizza delivery). Time-based management is also important to firms in product development. The firm that is first to market is able to charge higher prices than its slower rivals. Speed is also important within the business. The faster items pass through the production process, the lower the costs of warehousing materials and work-in-progress.

'The goal as a company is to have customer service that is not just the best, but legendary.' Sam Walton, founder WalMart.

## Flexibility

Firms need to be able to vary the volume of production relatively easily, in order to respond effectively to unexpected increases or decreases in demand. The ability to adapt or modify a standard product range allows a firm to appear to be offering customised products that meet customer needs more precisely, but still benefit from high-volume production, keeping costs down. This flexible approach to production is a form of lean production that has been used successfully by a number of companies, including retail clothing giant Zara.

### Real business

#### Lean production reaches sportswear

Nike became the first sportswear manufacturer to embrace the concept of lean production when it established a new online design facility. Nike iD allows customers to create their own versions of a range of footwear and clothing. Customers follow a step-by-step customisation process, picking from a choice of colours and materials, and adding logos, names and personalised messages in order to create a 'unique' product. The customised goods are manufactured and delivered within four weeks of an order being placed. A 'team locker' version of the service also exists, offering the facility to sports teams and groups. The success of the concept has been followed up with the opening of a number of Nike iD Studios around the world, including London's Oxford Street. Each studio has a team of qualified design consultants on hand to help customers make their choices.

Source: Adapted from www.nike.com

## Dependability

These days most large retailers place deliveries straight onto the shelf. They have no stockroom because they have in mind the just-in-time (JIT) goal of zero buffer stock. If a delivery is late, shelves empty and customers are irritated. Therefore dependability is a valuable quality in a supplier. It would be worth paying slightly higher prices to buy from a wholly reliable supplier: one who supplies the correct number of the correct items, on time and to the right quality standard.

## Environmental objectives

Most consumer-facing plcs produce annual reports to cover social and environmental aspects of their business. These may include environmental objectives – though they seem more likely to list environmental achievements. The problem with the latter is that they can be self-selected, that is, picking out only the good bits and publicising these.

Next plc is an example of a business that has had clear environmental objectives, set in 2007 and with a target achievement date of the 2015–16 financial year. In its 2013 Corporate Responsibility Report it provided information on one target: cutting waste sent to landfill. As shown in Table 26.1, setting a clear objective has helped Next achieve a remarkable improvement, with the level of waste going to landfill falling from 55 per cent to 15 per cent. But they have some way to go to achieve their objective of 5 per cent.

**Table 26.1** Next plc Environmental objectives: waste to landfill

|  | Target for 2015–16 | Actual in 2007–08 | Actual in 2011–12 | Actual in 2012–13 |
|---|---|---|---|---|
| **General waste to landfill** | 5 per cent | 55 per cent | 15 per cent | 15 per cent |
| **General waste recycled** | 95 per cent | 45 per cent | 85 per cent | 85 per cent |

The adoption of environmental objectives by a firm will have a number of implications for its operations. For instance, it may mean that the business will need to change its supplies of materials to those that come from replenishable or recycled sources. It may need to adopt new processes that are more energy efficient, and produce less waste and pollution. Even the methods of transportation used to bring in materials and deliver goods to customers may need to be investigated in an attempt to reduce congestion. Furthermore, staff will need appropriate training in order to ensure that these policies achieve their objectives.

## Added value

To be sustainable in the long term, every business needs added value. That is, the process of turning materials or ideas into a finished product or service must make the selling price higher than all the costs. From that comes the profit the business needs to reinvest in new technologies or higher capacity. Therefore, whether a firm states it or not, it must have added value as a key underlying objective.

### Real business

In 2014 the campaign group Make Chocolate Fair estimated that the value added chain on a £1 bar of chocolate was as follows:

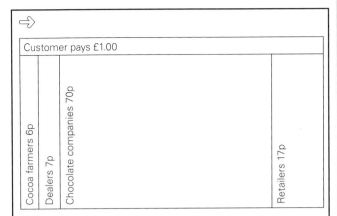

**Figure 26.2** Value added chain on a £1.00 bar of chocolate

The charity Oxfam disagreed, saying that the true income to the cocoa farmer was 3 per cent of the value of the bar, not 6 per cent. Both organisations agreed, however, that in 1980 West African cocoa farmers received 16 per cent of the final shop value of the bar. So the value added has steadily been absorbed by the western chocolate companies at the expense of the growers.

'Crisps cost 4 cents more per ounce for every additional 'no' on the packet.' Professor Jurafsky, Stanford University

## 26.3 The importance of innovation

Innovation means more than merely inventing a new product or process; it involves turning a new idea into a commercial success. Innovation within operations is crucial to the long-term survival and growth of a firm, allowing it to keep ahead of the competition. New products will often require new production methods and machinery. New processes for producing existing goods or delivering services can help to reduce costs and improve the quality and speed of production.

In mid-2014 analysts Research and Markets published a forecast of the future progress of 3D printing (also known as 'additive manufacture'). This technology had grown dramatically as it developed from producing prototype, one-off items to becoming a full-scale way to manufacture economically. According to Research and Markets, continuing innovation in 3D printing will see global sales spiral from $2,200 million in 2013 to $5,600 million by 2019 (see the bar chart).

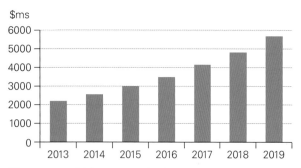

**Figure 26.3** Global market for 3D printing, 2013–19

Source: *Research and Markets*

## 26.4 Internal influences on operational objectives

### The nature of the product

The product is at the heart of any firm's operations, so its nature will affect operational objectives. For example, car manufacturers such as BMW and Mercedes have a long-established reputation for high standards of quality, which must be taken into account when developing new models.

### The personal characteristics of the operations director

People matter in business, so objectives will differ depending upon the preferences of the boss. In the case of Dyson Ltd, the views of overall founder/owner James Dyson will ensure that any operations director knows that innovation is a primary goal within the business. In plcs such as Unilever, with a less dominant chief executive, it will be the preferences of the operations director that matter. One might feel passionately about the environment, whereas another might be much more focused on profit-related targets connected to speed of response or dependability.

## 26.5 External influences on operational objectives

### Demand

The level and nature of demand will act as a major influence on operational objectives. A business must attempt to predict sales volumes and any likely fluctuations, in order to ensure that customer expectations are met in a cost-effective manner.

### Availability of resources

A lack of availability of the right level and quality of resources, including human resources, can act as a major constraint in attempting to achieve operational objectives. For example, skills shortages in a number of industries in the UK, including health care, have led to a reliance on workers from abroad. Similarly, a shortage of financial resources will act as a constraint on the achievement of operational objectives.

### Competitors' behaviour

Few firms have the luxury of operating alone in a market and no firm, however successful, can afford to become complacent. Rival firms will strive to increase their market share, and their activities are likely to have a major influence on operational objectives.

**Evaluation: Setting operational objectives**

The effective management of operations is central to the success of any business, regardless of its size or sector. The key is for all staff to have a clear understanding of what the business is attempting to achieve. The establishment of appropriate operational objectives is only a starting point. At least as important is that they be communicated effectively to everyone: to the part-time and shift workers; to the delivery drivers; to the staff in distribution depots across Europe and so on. In many businesses, the people at the top spend their time setting clear objectives, but the people at the bottom have no idea of what they are or why they matter. Successful operations management hinges on good people management.

## Five Whys and a How

| Question | Answer |
|---|---|
| Why is it valuable for a business to set clear operational objectives? | So that all operations staff understand the company's real priorities |
| Why might a company set the objective of quite low quality standards? | If 'low, low prices' are the marketing approach, low, low costs will be more important than quality, e.g. for a hotel targeting 'hen nights' (low prices are crucial; all the customers seek is a mirror, a bed and a toilet) |
| Why might operational objectives change if the economy slips into a sharp recession? | Cost minimisation may become a greater priority, perhaps at the cost of quality, speed or innovation |
| Why might flexibility be an especially important objective for a small business? | Because it's hard to compete with big firms on cost, quality and environmental programmes, so small firms must focus on where they can add value |
| Why may external influences on operational objectives be more important than internal ones? | Because a factor such as tough competitive pressure can force a business to follow a single approach, as Lidl/Aldi have forced UK supermarkets to cut prices and therefore costs |
| How might a business such as Gillette increase the added value on its shaving products? | Launching an innovative new shaving system might allow them to charge more for a similar amount of plastic, steel and packaging |

### Key terms

**Buffer stock:** is spare stock held just-in-case there's an unexpected demand upturn or an unwanted delay in supplies arriving.

**Efficiency:** refers to how effectively a firm uses its resources. It can be measured in a number of ways, including labour productivity and wastage rates.

**Innovation:** this means taking an idea for a new product or process and turning it into a commercial success.

**Just-in-time:** production is based on zero buffer stocks, that is, new supplies arrive just when they are needed.

**Lean production:** instead of mass producing, the firm produces goods to order and therefore satisfies the customer while helping to avoid stockpiles of unsold stock.

**Productivity:** measures how efficiently a firm turns inputs into the production process into output. The most commonly used measure is labour productivity, which looks at output per worker.

# Workbook

## A. Revision questions

(50 marks; 50 minutes)

1. Explain what is meant by the term 'operational objectives'. (3)

2. Outline two reasons why it is important for a business to keep its costs as low as possible. (4)

**3.** Analyse the main consequences for a firm of failing to accurately forecast the volume of production required to meet demand. (6)

**4.** Briefly explain what is meant by quality for a car manufacturer such as Mercedes. (4)

**5.** Choose one of the following businesses. Outline two possible ways in which it delivers quality to its customers.

  **a)** electronics manufacturer, Sony

  **b)** luxury hotel chain, Ritz-Carlton

  **c)** discount retailer, Aldi. (6)

**6.** Examine two key benefits for a firm that develops a reputation for quality. (6)

**7.** Give two reasons why a firm may aim to achieve a high degree of flexibility in its operations. (2)

**8.** Look at Table 26.1 and explain the value of setting an ambitious environmental objective such as going from 55 per cent to 5 per cent of waste going to landfill. (5)

**9.** Explain, using examples, what is meant by the term 'lean production'. (4)

**10.** Analyse two ways in which a business can benefit from a commitment to innovation. (6)

**11.** Outline one advantage and one disadvantage for a business of establishing environmental objectives. (4)

## B. Revision exercises
### DATA RESPONSE

### Renault targets the cheap mass market

In the first half of 2014 French car maker Renault enjoyed a 25 per cent profit increase, largely thanks to a 35 per cent rise in sales of its low-cost Dacia brand. When Renault bought Dacia in 1999, many commentators thought the French company had made a big mistake. Dacia's productivity was low and profits were non-existent. Now Renault is enjoying a payback on its investment. Dacia's no-frills Logan saloon has a price tag of the equivalent of around £6,000, while the Logan estate sells for the equivalent of £7,500. Both models are targeted at customers who would normally opt to buy a second-hand, rather than a brand-new car.

Until recently, all the cars were made at Renault's Dacia plant in Romania. The Logan was originally intended to be sold in Romania only, but proved to be a huge success in both France and Germany, with waiting lists of customers eager to get hold of the car. Annual output at the plant was increased by the company from 200,000 to 350,000 in 2008. By 2013 the factory was close to its maximum capacity level,

with 342,620 cars rolling off the line. In 2014 Renault expanded its Dacia factory in Morocco from 200,000 to 340,000 cars, to absorb the rising demand for the Dacia. Workers at the Romanian plant are highly skilled, but low paid compared with France. In 2014 a French car worker typically earns £18 an hour, while in Romania it's £6 and in Morocco £3. The low-cost production is matched by low-tech factories, with a much lower investment in robots than in the west.

The Dacia car models are practical and cheap to produce, but with far less production flexibility than achieved today on sophisticated production lines for producers such as Mercedes.

### Questions (25 marks; 30 minutes)

**1.** Analyse Renault's operational objectives in launching its Logan car range. (9)

**2.** To what extent is it likely that the other major car manufacturers will be forced to follow Renault and target the low-cost segment of the market? (16)

## C. Extend your understanding

**1.** To what extent is the long-term success of an online grocery business dependent on setting the right operational objectives? (20)

**2.** For a business you know well, how important are the main internal and external influences on their operational objectives and decisions? (20)

# Chapter 27

# Efficiency and labour productivity

**Linked with:** Technology and operational efficiency, Chapter 30; Analysing operational performance, Chapter 31; Motivation and engagement in theory, Chapter 46; Motivation and engagement in practice, Chapter 47.

## Definition

Labour productivity is a measure of efficiency; it measures the output of a firm in relation to the labour inputs.

## 27.1 Are efficiency and productivity the same thing?

Directly, the answer is no. Productivity is output per worker per time period (hour, month or year). That ignores some other key features of efficiency, notably waste. One super-fast worker may produce a lot of output, but in a wasteful manner. A decorator may paint speedily but messily, wasting 20 per cent of the paint. So productivity may be high but overall efficiency no better than average. And a company may produce chemicals with high productivity, but create pollution locally (waste products leaking out of the chimney, perhaps). Again this would not be efficient.

Overall, though, labour productivity is regarded by businesses as one of the most important tests of management efficiency. Therefore most of this chapter focuses on labour productivity.

## 27.2 Productivity: what is it?

Labour productivity measures the amount a worker produces over a given time. For example, an employee might make ten pairs of jeans in an hour. Measuring productivity is relatively easy in manufacturing, where the number of goods can be counted. In the service sector it is not always possible to be sure what to measure. Productivity in services can be measured in some cases: the number of customers served, number of patients seen, and the sales per employee. But how can the productivity of a receptionist be measured?

It is important to distinguish between productivity and total output. By hiring more employees a firm may increase the total output, but this does not mean that the output per employee has gone up. Similarly it is possible to have lower production with higher productivity because of a fall in the number of employees. Imagine, for example, 20 employees producing 40 tables a week at a furniture company. Their productivity on average is 2 tables per week. If new machinery enables 10 employees to make 30 tables the overall output has fallen, but the output per worker has risen to 3. This rise in productivity would lower the labour cost per table.

## 27.3 The importance of productivity

The output per employee is a very important measure of a firm's performance. It has a direct impact on the cost of producing a unit. If productivity increases then, assuming wages are unchanged, the labour cost per unit will fall. Imagine that in one factory employees make five pairs of shoes per day, but in another they make ten pairs per day; assuming the wage rate is the same, this means the labour cost of a pair of shoes will be halved in the second factory (see Table 27.1). With lower labour costs this firm is likely to be in a better competitive position.

**Table 27.1** Shoe factory productivity and wage costs

|  | Daily wage rate (£) | Productivity rate (per day) | Wage cost per pair (£) |
|---|---|---|---|
| Factory | 50 | 5 | 10 |
| Factory 2 | 50 | 10 | 5 |

By increasing productivity a firm can improve its competitiveness (ability to equal or beat its rivals). It can either sell its products at a lower price or keep the price as it is and enjoy a higher profit margin. This is why firms continually monitor their productivity relative to their competitors and, where possible, try to increase it. However, they need to make sure that quality does not suffer in the rush to produce more. It may be necessary to set both productivity and quality targets.

'Engineering is the ability to do for $1 what any damn fool can do for $5.' Arthur Wellington, nineteenth century US engineer

## 27.4 How to increase labour productivity

### Increase investment in modern equipment

By investing in modern, sophisticated machines and better production processes, it shouldn't be hard to improve output per worker. That, in turn, would improve individual companies' competitiveness and help to boost the country's economic growth. Yet Figure 27.1 is a reminder that Britain consistently invests less than other countries as a share of GDP – despite repeated cuts to corporation tax that are said to encourage greater business investment.

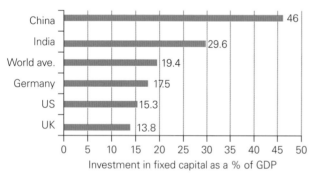

**Figure 27.1** Investment spending: too low in UK

Investment in fixed capital as a percentage of GDP

Source: CIA *World Factbook* 2014

'Not everything that can be counted counts, and not everything that counts can be counted.' Albert Einstein, the ultimate boffin.

### Improve the ability level of those at work

To increase productivity a firm may need to introduce more or better training for its employees. A skilled and well-trained workforce is likely to produce more and make fewer mistakes. Employees should be able to complete tasks more quickly and will not need as much supervision or advice. They will be able to solve their own work-related problems and may be in a better position to contribute ideas on how to increase productivity further.

However, firms are often reluctant to invest in training because employees may leave and work for another firm once they have gained more skills. There is a danger that the training will not provide sufficient gains to justify the initial investment and so any spending in this area needs to be properly researched and costed. Simply training people for the sake of it is obviously of limited value. However, in general UK firms do not have a particularly good record in training and more investment here could have a significant effect on the UK's productivity levels.

It should also be remembered that elaborate training may not be necessary for a firm that recruits the right people. Great care must be taken in the selection process to find staff with the right skills and attitudes. A firm with a good reputation locally will find it much easier to pick the best people. This is why many firms take great care over their relations with the local community.

### Improve employee motivation

Professor Frederick Herzberg, the American psychologist and business management theorist, once said that most people's idea of a fair day's work is less than half what they can give.

The key to success, he felt, was to design jobs that contained motivators to help employees give much, much more. His suggestions on how to provide job enrichment are detailed in the Chapter 46.

There is no doubt that motivation matters. A motivated sales force may achieve twice the sales level of an unmotivated one. A motivated computer technician may correct twice the computer faults of an unmotivated one. And, in both cases, overall business performance will be boosted.

### Motivation on the pitch

When Fulham Football Club appointed a new groundsman, few people even noticed. The fans had always been proud of the pitch, but newly appointed Frank Boahene was not impressed. He thought it needed a dramatic improvement before the start of the new season in August. With no time to reseed the pitch, he decided the best way to strengthen the grass was to cut it three times a day. Doing so first thing in the morning and last thing in the afternoon was not a problem. But he also chose to 'pop back' from his home in Reading (an hour's drive) to do the third cut at 11.00 at night. Every day! That's motivation.

**Figure 27.2**

'Looking for differences between the more productive and less productive organisations, we found that the most striking difference is the number of people who are involved and feel responsibility for solving problems.' Michael McTague, management consultant.

## 27.5 Difficulties increasing productivity

### The role of management

A serious problem for UK management is that productivity has never been a central focus for directors. In the UK directors focus on profits; elsewhere they look for efficiency first, trusting that profits will follow.

Perhaps the key management role is to identify increasing productivity as a permanent objective. The Japanese bulldozer company Komatsu set a target of a 10-per-cent productivity increase every year, until they caught up with the world-leading American producer, Caterpillar. Today Komatsu is the world No. 2 producer, with annual sales of £11.5 billion.

In many firms, productivity is not a direct target. The focus, day by day, is on production, not productivity. After all, it is production which ensures that customer orders are fulfilled. An operations manager, faced with a 10-per-cent increase in orders, may simply ask the workforce to do overtime. The work gets done; the workforce is happy to earn extra money; and it's all rather easy to do. It is harder by far to reorganise the workplace to make production more effective. Managers whose main focus is on the short term, therefore, think of production not productivity.

As shown in Figure 27.3, productivity has been very weak in Britain since 2007. If this continues the economic recovery will stall.

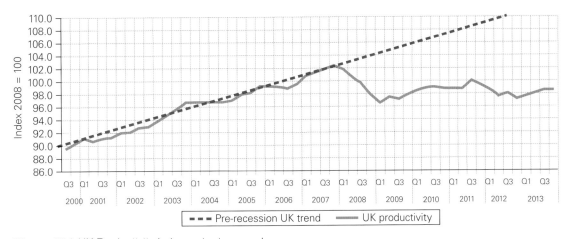

**Figure 27.3** UK Productivity Index, output per worker

Source: Office for National Statistics, June 2014

## Boosting productivity when markets are static

Everyone in a business is happy when higher sales lead to higher production. Bonuses look more secure and so do the jobs themselves. But productivity is a measure of efficiency, so it is more controversial. If a productivity-boosting production method is introduced to a business in a static market, there is only one possible outcome: job losses. In other words, if production next month is to be 1,000 units, just like last month, better productivity means fewer people will be needed to produce those units. As staff are perfectly aware of this, those working in static markets are very wary of changes to production methods. They resist change because they fear the outcome. In the long term everyone in the business needs to help improve productivity, or else the business will become uncompetitive. But in the short term people worry about their income, their families and so on. So it can be difficult to introduce productivity-boosting measures.

## Five Whys and a How

| Question | Answer |
|---|---|
| Why might employees be concerned about moves to increase productivity? | Because if the business operates in a static market, higher productivity probably means fewer jobs |
| Why might it be hard to measure the productivity of a doctor? | Although you could measure patients seen per month, you couldn't measure the quality of diagnosis and care |
| Why might it be useful for a manufacturing company to set targets for annual productivity improvement? | Because this would help the business gain competitiveness in relation to UK and overseas rivals |
| Why may it matter (Fig 27.1) that capital spending in the UK is relatively low? | As capital spending is an important way to boost productivity, low spending is a concern for long-term UK competitiveness |
| Why (see Fig 27.3) is it a concern that UK productivity growth flattened out between 2007 and 2013? | Because rising efficiency is what creates economic growth. If productivity stays flat Britain's economic growth will be flat as well |
| How might a service business try to increase productivity? | By getting staff to care more, work smarter and contribute ideas on how the business could work more effectively |

## Key terms

**GDP:** Gross Domestic Product is the value of all the goods and services produced in a country in a year.

**Job enrichment:** giving people the opportunity to use their ability (Professor Herzberg's definition).

## Evaluation: Efficiency and labour productivity

Greater labour productivity can lead to greater efficiency and higher profitability. This is because, other things being equal, it lowers the labour cost per unit. However, productivity is only one factor that contributes to a firm's success. A firm must also ensure it produces a good quality product that it is marketed effectively and that costs are controlled. There is little point increasing productivity by 20 per cent if at the same time you pay your staff 30 per cent more. Similarly, there is no point producing more if there is no actual demand. Higher productivity, therefore, contributes to better performance but needs to be accompanied by effective decision-making throughout the firm.

The importance of productivity to a firm depends primarily on the level of value added involved. Top price perfumes such as Chanel have huge profit margins. Production costs are a tiny proportion of the selling price, therefore a 10 per cent productivity increase might have only a marginal effect on profit and virtually none on the competitiveness of the brand. For mass-market products in competitive markets, high productivity is likely to be essential for survival. A 5-per-cent cost advantage might make all the difference. Therefore, when considering an appropriate recommendation for solving a business problem, a judgement is required as to whether boosting productivity is a top priority for the business concerned.

# Workbook

## A. Revision questions

**(40 marks; 45 minutes)**

1. What is meant by the term 'unit costs'? (2)

2. What's the difference between 'unit costs' and 'costs per unit'? (1)

3. What would usually happen to unit costs if extra demand led to higher output? (4)

4. Outline three factors that might cause a fall in a firm's productivity. (6)

5. Calculate the change in productivity at AB Co. (see Table 27.2) since last year. (4)

**Table 27.2** Productivity at AB Co.

|  | Output | Number of staff |
|---|---|---|
| **Last year** | 6,000 | 80 |
| **This year** | 7,200 | 90 |

6. Analyse how a large supermarket chain might benefit from improving its labour productivity. (6)

7. Explain why fixed costs per unit vary as output varies. (4)

8. Calculate the change in productivity at BDQ Co. (see Table 27.3) since last year. (4)

**Table 27.3** Productivity at BDQ Co.

|  | Output | Number of staff |
|---|---|---|
| **Last year** | 32,000 | 50 |
| **This year** | 30,000 | 40 |

9. Explain how motivation and productivity may be linked. (4)

10. Explain how productivity might be *too* high. (5)

## B. Revision exercises
### DATA RESPONSE 1

In developing countries labour is often wasted by employers because it is relatively cheap. The result is workers being profitably employed in low productivity activities such as shoe cleaning, street vending and sandwich boards (a human, walking advertising poster).

Real wages in the UK have fallen sharply over the last decade. This has encouraged some British firms to adopt some of the same methods used by employers in developing countries. Cheap British labour is now being employed in activities that are profitable, but where productivity is very low.

A good example is Domino's pizza. In recent years the takeaway chain has used some of its employees to act as human advertisements. Workers are asked to wave and dance at passing motorists on busy street corners whilst wearing giant pizza boxes featuring the company's brand and details of special promotional prices. The company has defended their use of 'wobble boarding' by claiming that 'it is a key part of our marketing activity'. The use of wobble boards to boost sales of pizza has attracted criticism. In Cambridge local residents wrote letters of complaint arguing that it was demeaning and degrading for young people, including graduates, to be paid minimum wages to act as little more than walking advertisements. Other criticized the adverts on the grounds that they could distract motorists, causing accidents. Presumably, Domino's uses wobble boards because the extra revenue generated from this form of advertising exceeds the wages paid to wobble boarders.

**Figure 27.4** Domino's advertising using 'wobble boards'

1. How might the manager of a Domino's pizza outlet measure the productivity of their wobble boarders? (4)

2. The manager of a Pizza Express estimates that a team of five wobble boarders working for eight hours daily will boost the restaurant's gross profit by £500 per day. According to the local job centre there will be plenty of people willing to undertake this work at the national minimum wage of £6.50 per hour. Calculate whether it would be profitable for Pizza Express to employ the wobble boarders. (6)

3. Analyse the factors that might cause profitability to be high when productivity is low. (9)

4. To what extent is it ethical to employ graduates to act as human advertisements. (16)

## DATA RESPONSE 2

### Going potty

Farah Stewart was trying to explain the need to boost productivity to the employees at her ceramics factory, FS Ltd. Relations between Farah and her staff had not been good in recent years. The company was not doing well and she blamed the workers. 'On average you work 8 hours a day at £8 an hour and produce around 160 pots each. Meanwhile at Frandon, I am told, they produce 280 pots a day. Can't you see that this makes it cheaper for them and if things go on like this we'll be out of business? You need to work much harder to get our unit costs down! I know you are expecting to get a pay rise this year, but I cannot afford it until you produce more; then we'll think about it.'

Jeff Battersby, the spokesperson for the employees, was clearly annoyed by Farah's tone. 'Firstly Ms Stewart have you ever considered that if you paid us more we might produce more for you? I'm not surprised productivity is higher at Frandon – they get about £80 a day. There's no point demanding more work from us if you are not willing to pay for it – we're not slaves you know. If you paid us £10 an hour, like Frandon, I reckon we could increase productivity by 50 per cent. However that's not the only issue: they've got better equipment. It's not our fault if the kilns don't work half the time and take an age to heat up. Sort out the equipment and our pay and you'll soon see productivity improve. Why not ask us next time instead of jumping to conclusions?'

### Questions (30 marks; 35 minutes)

1. **a)** FS Ltd employs 50 pot makers whilst Frandon Ltd employs 30 people in production. Calculate the total output for each of the two companies. (3)

   **b)** With reference to FS Ltd and Frandon Ltd explain the difference between 'total output' and 'productivity'. (4)

2. **a)** Calculate the average labour cost per pot at FS Ltd if employees are paid £8 an hour and their daily output is 160 pots each. (4)

   **b)** What is the wage cost per pot at Frandon? (Assume an 8-hour day.) (3)

3. To what extent might the business benefit from involving employees in discussions about how to improve productivity? (16)

## C. Extend your understanding

1. Faced with falling sales and sharply falling market share, the boss at Morrisons' Supermarkets decides to implement a 12-month Productivity Improvement Programme (PIP). Discuss how the boss should set about this task. (20)

2. New competition from Chinese-made cars is undercutting the prices of British-made cars by 35 per cent. To what extent can this problem be overcome by a sustained management programme to boost labour productivity at a British car factory? (20)

# Chapter
# 28 Lean production

**Linked with:** Niche and mass marketing, Chapter 20; Efficiency and labour productivity, Chapter 27; Managing inventory, Chapter 34; Decision-making to improve operational performance, Chapter 35.

## Definition

Lean production is a philosophy that aims to produce more using less, by eliminating all forms of waste ('waste' being defined as anything that does not add value to the final product).

## 28.1 Introduction

The rise of this Japanese approach to production has been unstoppable. The whole approach has been termed 'lean production', though its ideas have been spread more generally to include service businesses as well. It is based upon a combined focus by management and workers on minimising the use of the key business resources: materials, manpower, capital, floor space and time. The main components of lean management are:

- just-in-time (JIT)
- total quality management (TQM)
- time-based management.

### Toyota and the origins of lean production

In most industries, new ideas and methods tend to emerge during a period of crisis, when old ideas no longer seem to work. The motor industry is no different. The inspiration came from Eiji Toyoda's three-month visit to Ford's Rouge plant in Detroit in 1950. Eiji's family had set up the Toyota Motor Company in 1937. Now, in Japan's situation of desperate shortages after the Second World War, he hoped to learn from Ford. On his return, Eiji reported that the mass production system at the Rouge plant was riddled with

*muda* (the Japanese term for wasted effort, materials and time). By analysing the weaknesses of mass production, Toyota was the first company to develop lean production.

Toyota realised that mass production could only be fully economic if identical products could be produced continuously. Yet Henry Ford's statement that 'they can have any colour they want ... as long as it's black' was no longer acceptable to customers. Mass production was also very wasteful, as poor-quality production led to a high reject rate at the end of the production line.

Toyota's solution was to design machines that could be used for many different operations – flexible production. Mass producers took a whole day to change a stamping machine from producing one part to making another. Toyota eventually reduced this time to just three minutes, and so simplified the process that factory line workers could do it without any help from engineers! This carried with it the advantage of flexibility. If buying habits changed in the USA, Ford could not react quickly, because each production line was dedicated to producing a particular product in a particular way. Toyota's multi-purpose machines could adapt quickly to a surge of demand for, for example, open-top cars or right-hand-drive models.

By a process of continuous refinement, Toyota developed the approach to:

- maximise the input from staff
- focus attention upon the quality of supplies and production
- minimise wasted resources in stock through just-in-time.

Above all else, the company was able to turn the spotlight onto product development – to shorten the time between product conception and product launch. With its ability to be 'first-to-market' and its terrific reputation for quality, in 2013 Toyota was the world's No. 1 car producer.

There is nothing so useless as doing efficiently that which shouldn't be done at all.' Peter Drucker, business guru

## 28.2 The benefits of lean production

Lean production:

- creates higher levels of labour productivity, therefore it uses less labour
- requires less stock, less factory space and less capital equipment than a mass producer of comparable size; the lean producer therefore has substantial cost advantages over the mass producer
- creates substantial marketing advantages: first, it results in far fewer defects, improving quality and reliability for the customer; second, lean production requires half the engineering hours to develop a new product, which means that the lean producer can develop a vast range of products that a mass producer cannot afford to match.

### Real business

Pioneered decades ago by carmakers determined to cut waste, those same ideas are now starting to influence modern biotech companies. Innovative R&D is no longer enough, for success there needs to be manufacturing efficiency. So biotech companies are applying 'just-in-time' principles to the equipment and labour aspects of their business.

One example is at the US producer of proteins, Aldevron, which has hired researchers from the University of Wisconsin to study the company's manufacturing processes and outline a strategy for improving efficiency. The company hopes that the university will help shrink the facility's product delivery timeline by at least 25 per cent - shaving a week or two off of a typical four - to five-week process. 'Because our labour force is more expensive, we've got to figure out how to do things faster,' said Aldevron's vice president. The productivity gains from lean manufacturing could help Aldevron fend off overseas manufacturers that provide the same services at cheaper rates.

## 28.3 The components of lean production

### Lean people management

Lean producers reject the waste of human talent involved in narrow, repetitive jobs. They believe in empowerment, team working and job enrichment. Problem solving is not just left to specialist engineers. Employees are trained in preventative maintenance, to spot when a fault is developing and correct it before the production line has to stop. If a problem does emerge on the line, they are trained to solve it without needing an engineer or a supervisor. Teams meet regularly to discuss ways in which their sections could be run more smoothly.

### Lean approach to quality

In a mass production system, quality control is a specialised job that takes place at the end of the line. In a lean system, each team is responsible for checking the quality of its own work. If a fault is spotted, every worker has the power to stop the assembly line. This policy prevents errors being passed on, to be corrected only after the fault has been found at the end of the line. The lean approach, therefore, is self-checking at every production stage so that quality failures at the end (or with customers) become extremely rare.

One way to achieve lean quality is total quality management (TQM). This attempts to achieve a culture of quality throughout the organisation, so that the primary objective of all employees is to achieve quality the first time around without the need for any reworking. To achieve total quality, managers must 'make quality the number one, non-negotiable priority, and actively seek and listen to the views of employees on how to improve quality,' (Roger Trapp, in The Independent).

### Lean design

As consumers become more demanding and technology advances, car design has become highly complex. This threatens to increase costs and development times. Lean producers combat this by simultaneous engineering. This means integrating the development functions so that separate design and engineering stages are tackled at the same time. This speeds up development times, which cuts costs and reduces the risk of early obsolescence.

## Lean component supply

The approach to component supply varies greatly from company to company. Mass producers tend to have rather distant relationships with suppliers, often based on minimising the delivery cost per unit. They may buy from several sources to keep up the competitive pressure. The supplier, in turn, may be secretive about costs and profit margins to prevent the buyer from pressing for still lower prices. Lean producers work in partnership with their suppliers or, more often, with a single supplier. They keep the supplier fully informed of new product developments, encouraging ideas and technical advice. This means that by the time the assembly line starts running, errors have been ironed out so there are very few running changes or failures. Both parties are also likely to share financial and sales information electronically. This encourages an atmosphere of trust and common purpose, and aids planning.

'To be competitive, we have to look for every opportunity to improve efficiencies and productivity while increasing quality. Lean manufacturing principles have improved every aspect of our processes.' Cynthia Fanning, general manager, General Electric

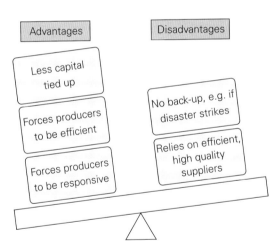

**Figure 28.1** Advantages and disadvantages of 'lean' production

## 28.4 Just-in-time

Lean producers run with minimal buffer stocks, relying on daily or hourly deliveries from trusted suppliers. As there is no safety net, a faulty shipment of components could bring an entire factory to a halt. Mass producers rely on stockpiles, 'just-in-case'.

The just-in-time (JIT) system of manufacturing is perhaps the best-known element of lean production. JIT aims to minimise the costs of holding unnecessary stocks of raw materials, components, work in progress and finished products. The principle that underpins JIT is that production should be 'pulled through' rather than 'pushed through'. This means that production should be for specific customer orders, so that the production cycle starts only once a customer has placed an order with the producer.

## Summary of the just-in-time approach

- No buffer stocks of any type are held.
- Production is to order.
- Stock is ordered only when it is needed, just in time.
- Zero defects are essential as no stock safety net exists.
- No 'spare' workers are employed.
- Staff are multi-skilled and capable of filling in for absent colleagues.
- It is used by lean producers.

'Great companies will have strong lean vision in place... and are working daily at getting on with doing a small number of important things consistently – day in, day out.' TXM, Total Excellence Manufacturing

The advantages and disadvantages of a JIT system are listed in Table 28.1.

**Table 28.1** The advantages and disadvantages of using a JIT system

| Advantages of using JIT | Disadvantages of using JIT |
|---|---|
| • Improves the firm's liquidity<br>• The costs of holding stocks are reduced<br>• Storage space can be converted to a more productive use<br>• Stock wastage and stock rotation become lesser issues for management<br>• Response times to changing demands are speeded up as new components can be ordered instantly | • Any break in supply causes immediate problems for the purchaser<br>• The costs of processing orders may be increased<br>• The purchaser's reputation is placed in the hands of the external supplier |

## 28.5 Time-based management

Time-based management involves managing time in the same way most companies manage costs, quality or stock. Time-based manufacturers try to shorten rather than lengthen production runs in order to reduce costs and to increase levels of customer satisfaction. To do this, manufacturers invest in flexible capital; that is, machines that can make more than one model. Training must also be seen as a priority because staff have to be multi-skilled.

Time-based management creates five benefits:

1. By reducing lead and set-up times, productivity improves, creating a cost advantage.

2. Shortening lead times cuts customer response times, increasing consumer satisfaction as customers receive their orders sooner.

3. Lower stock holding costs: short lead and set-up times make firms more responsive to changes in the market. Consequently there should be less need for long production runs and stockpiles of finished products. If demand does suddenly increase, production can simply be quickly restarted.

4. An ability to offer the consumer a more varied product range without losing cost-reducing economies of scale. Time-based management therefore makes market segmentation a much cheaper strategy to operate.

5. Keeping time under tight control can help achieve first mover advantage if you can get your new product out before rivals get theirs to market.

### Real business

#### Time-based management

Zara is a fashion retailing phenomenon built on an understanding of the importance of time. When Christian Dior featured a glamorous embroidered Afghan coat on the catwalk, Zara had its own version in its shops within a fortnight. It was able to design, manufacture and distribute the coat to its shops throughout Europe within 14 days – and sell it for just £95. If a style doesn't succeed within a week, it is withdrawn. No style stays on the shop floor for more than four weeks. The immediate result is obvious. Fashion- and price-conscious women flock to Zara.

Less obviously, Zara benefits from a vital secondary factor. In Spain, Zara's home country, an average high-street clothes store expects its regular customers to visit three times a year. Yet the average is 17 times for Zara! As the stock is constantly changing, the store is constantly worth visiting. Zara's owner started the business with €25 in 1963; today he is one of the world's three richest men, with wealth of over $60 billion. Time well spent.

Figure 28.2 Zara

### Key terms

First mover advantage: the benefits to distribution and brand credibility from beating rivals to the market with an innovative new product.

Just-in-time: producing with minimum stock levels so every process must be completed just in time for the process that follows.

Kaizen: continuous improvement (that is, encouraging all staff to regularly come up with ideas to improve efficiency and quality).

Total quality management: a passion for quality that starts at the top, then spreads throughout the organisation.

## Five Whys and a How

| Question | Answer |
|---|---|
| Why isn't mass production more efficient than lean production? | Because it relies on everyone wanting the same. In fact, people love products to be tailor-made to their own requirements |
| Why do mass producers hold stocks of finished goods, 'just-in-case'? | Because they aren't sure what future demand will be, so they keep stocks just in case they're needed |
| Why are lean producers likely to have higher-than-average profit margins? | Their production methods save costs by cutting out waste, while adding value by customising products to match exact tastes |
| Why is just-in-time so popular with grocery chains such as Tesco? | Because stock forms a huge part of their total costs, so it's vital to minimise it |
| Why are lean producers particularly reliant on keen, well-trained staff? | Eliminating waste requires staff involvement, as it's the staff who know best where the production process has weaknesses |
| How might a business set about moving from mass production to lean production? | It needs to establish a new culture based on trusting and giving authority to staff; it's a mistake to assume it's to do with mechanisation or robots. |

## Evaluation: Lean production

Some of the arguments put forward above could be criticised for being too black and white (mass production = terrible; lean production = wonderful). The reality of business is often to do with shades of grey, with some lean producers having their own weaknesses. Some trends are unarguable, however. When people first started writing about the Toyota production system, Toyota was a failure compared with the giant US car producers Ford and General Motors. Today Toyota is the world's No. 1 car maker.

However, there is a downside. By definition, lean thinking involves the elimination of waste. This waste could be over-manning. So by switching to a leaner system the consequence could be redundancies. In this context, lean management becomes little more than a 'fig leaf' that a ruthless manager may wish to hide behind when seeking to justify controversial staffing decisions.

# Workbook

## A. Revision questions

(35 marks; 35 minutes)

1. State the three components of lean production. (3)

2. State three problems of mass production. (3)

3. Distinguish between just-in-time and just-in-case. (4)

4. What advantages are there in using time-based management? (4)

5. Why is it important to reduce machine set-up times? (3)

6. What are the opportunity costs of holding too much stock? (4)

7. Outline possible sources of waste in any organisation with which you are familiar. (Your school? Your part-time employer?) (4)

8. What is reworking and why does it add to costs? (5)

9. Why could it be important to be first to the market with a new product idea? (5)

# B. Revision exercises

## DATA RESPONSE

### Operations management and the Airbus A350

The baker round the corner from my house often grumbles about the impossibility of predicting daily customer demand. He hates being left with unsold bread, but also hates selling out at midday then spending his afternoon apologising to disappointed customers. But compared with the aircraft manufacturing business, baking is a doddle. The bar chart shows the crazily unpredictable sales of the Airbus A350 plane – each one listed at a price of around $275 million. Orders in 2013 alone, therefore, were worth around $63 billion. As Britain receives 40 per cent of the value of each plane (we make the wings and Rolls Royce makes the aero engines) these orders mean huge amounts in terms of orders and exports.

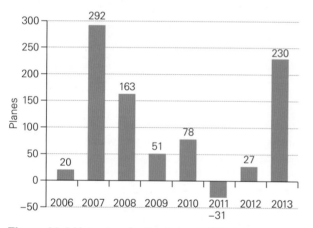

**Figure 28.3** Net orders for the Airbus A350 plane

But how does Airbus manage its production in the light of such erratic demand? Well, although Airbus launched the A350 in 2006, it was still in development until the maiden flight in mid-2013. In the meantime it accumulated over 800 firm orders for the plane. Production started in late 2013 at a rate of just 1 plane a month. Although it had only just started, time was taken expanding the assembly line in Toulouse, France, to allow for growth in the future. By the end of 2014 they will be producing 3 per month and by the end of 2015 maximum capacity will have risen to 10 A350s a month. Airbus is very optimistic about this plane, expecting to deliver its first planes early to its first customers. This has surprised many observers because more than 50 per cent of the plane is made from new, light, composite materials – and high technology in aircraft has traditionally been a cause of late rather than early deliveries.

The world's duopoly plane manufacturers have such huge order books that Kuwait's 10 A 350s will not be delivered until 2018 – that is part of the purchase agreement. So even though demand is highly erratic, production works steadily through a huge order book, one plane at a time.

### Questions (25 marks; 30 minutes)

1. Given the erratic demand, analyse the significance of the statement: 'by the end of 2015 maximum capacity will have risen to 10 A350s a month'?   (9)

2. Based on the bar chart and the text, to what extent would Airbus benefit from a move to JIT plane manufacture for the A350?   (16)

## C. Extend your understanding

1. To what extent should managers ignore the short-term difficulties faced when switching to lean methods of production?   (20)

2. Evaluate why some firms seem far better than others in terms of their ability to successfully implement lean production techniques.   (20)

# Chapter 29 Capacity utilisation

Linked with: Efficiency and labour productivity, Chapter 27; Technology and operational efficiency, Chapter 30; Analysing operational performance, Chapter 31.

## Definition

Capacity utilisation measures a firm's output level as a percentage of the firm's maximum output level. A football stadium is at full capacity when all the seats are filled.

## 29.1 The importance of capacity

Few products have completely predictable sales (baked beans? Marmite?) and therefore there is a fine balance to be struck between using your factory capacity fully and therefore efficiently, and yet having the wiggle room to meet unexpectedly high orders.

So it is vital to have sufficient spare capacity to cope with higher demand, while keeping maximum capacity low enough to keep costs down: a fine balance.

## 29.2 How is capacity utilisation measured?

Capacity utilisation is measured using the formula:

$$\frac{\text{current output}}{\text{maximum possible output}} \times 100$$

What does capacity depend upon? A firm's maximum output level is determined by the quantity of buildings, machinery and labour it has available. Maximum capacity is achieved when the firm is making full use of all the buildings, machinery and labour available, that is, 100 per cent capacity utilisation.

For a service business the same logic applies, though it is much harder to identify a precise figure. This

is because it may take a different time to serve each customer. Many service businesses cope with fluctuating demand by employing temporary or part-time staff. These employees provide a far greater degree of flexibility to employers. Part-time hours can be increased, or extra temporary staff can be employed to increase capacity easily. If demand falls, temporary staff can be laid off without redundancy payments, or part-time staff can have their hours reduced, thus reducing capacity easily and cheaply.

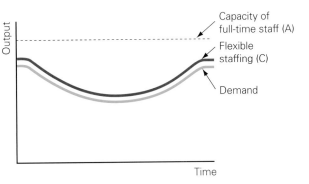

**Figure 29.1** How flexible staffing can reduce wastage implied by having under-used full-time staff

## 29.3 How to utilise capacity efficiently

Fixed costs are fixed in relation to output. This means that whether capacity utilisation is 50 per cent or 100 per cent, fixed costs will not change. So if a football club invests in an expensive playing staff (whose salaries are a fixed cost) but matches are played to a half-empty stadium, the fixed costs will become a huge burden. This is because the very fact that fixed costs do not change *in total* as output changes means that they do change *per unit* of output/demand. A half-empty stadium means that the fixed costs per unit are double the level at maximum capacity (see Table 29.1).

**Table 29.1** Fixed costs and capacity

|  | Full stadium | Half-empty stadium |
|---|---|---|
|  | 50,000 fans | 25,000 fans |
| Weekly salary bill (fixed costs) | £750,000 | £750,000 |
| Salary fixed cost per fan | £15 | £30 |
|  | (£750,000/50,000) | (£750,000/25,000) |

When the capacity utilisation of the stadium is at 50 per cent, then £30 of the ticket price is needed for the players' wages alone. The many other fixed and variable costs of running a football club would be on top of this, of course.

The reason why capacity utilisation is so important is that it has an inverse (opposite) effect upon fixed costs per unit. In other words, when utilisation is high, fixed costs are spread over many units. This cuts the cost per unit, which enables the producer either to cut prices to boost demand further, or to enjoy larger profit margins. If utilisation is low, fixed costs per unit become punishingly high. In June 2014 a newspaper in Zimbabwe reported that manufacturing capacity utilisation had fallen in the last year by 10 per cent to 30 per cent. According to the report, firms had reduced output in response to falling demand. This would make fixed costs per unit three times higher than necessary, which is an almost impossible situation.

The ideal level of capacity utilisation, therefore, is at or near 100 per cent. This spreads fixed costs as thinly as possible, boosting profit margins. There are two key concerns about operating at maximum capacity for long, however. These are the risks that:

1. if demand rises further, you will have to turn it away, enabling your competitors to benefit, and

2. you will struggle to service the machinery and train/retrain staff. This may prove costly in the long term and will increase the chances of production breakdowns in the short term.

The production ideal, therefore, is a capacity utilisation of around 90 per cent.

---

'On a hot summer's day we're churning out ice cream at our absolute maximum. And it hurts.' Matteo Pantani, founder of Scoop, Covent Garden

---

**Real business**

In 2014, suffering from a sharp downturn in sales at its biggest stores, Tesco re-evaluated the size of its car parks. Their average utilisation rate had fallen to an all-time low. In response it invited Avis car hire to take over sections of the big store car parks. For Avis, it could be a winner: 'We think this will work really well for customers who want a convenient place to pick up their hire car and do a quick shop before heading off on their travels.' For Tesco it reduces the waste involved in empty car spaces. It increases Tesco's capacity utilisation and therefore (slightly) reduces costs per customer.

## 29.4 How to get towards full capacity utilisation

If a firm's capacity utilisation is an unsatisfactory 45 per cent, how could it be increased to a more acceptable level of around 90 per cent? There are two possible approaches, as discussed below.

### Increase demand (in this case, double it!)

Demand for existing products could be boosted by extra promotional spending, price-cutting or – more fundamentally – devising a new strategy to reposition the products into growth sectors. If supermarket own-label products are flourishing, perhaps offer to produce under the Tesco or Sainsbury's banner. If doubling of sales is needed, it is unlikely that existing products will provide the whole answer. The other approach is to launch new products. This could be highly effective, but implies long-term planning and investment.

### Cut capacity

If your current factory and labour force is capable of producing 10,000 units a week, but there is demand for only 4,500, there will be a great temptation to cut capacity to 5,000. This may be done by cutting out the night shift (that is, making those workers redundant). This would avoid the disruption and inflexibility caused by the alternative, which is to move to smaller premises. Moving will enable all fixed costs to be cut (rent, rates, salaries, and so on) but may look silly if, six months later, demand has recovered to 6,000 units when your new factory capacity is only 5,000.

### How to select the best option

A key factor in deciding whether to cut capacity or boost demand is the underlying cause of the low utilisation. It may be the result of a known temporary demand shortfall, such as a seasonal low point in the toy business. Or it may be due to an economic recession, which (on past experience) may hit demand for around 18 to 24 months. Either way, it could prove to be a mistake in the long run to cut capacity. Nevertheless, if a firm faces huge short-term losses from its excess fixed costs, it may have to forget the future and concentrate on short-term survival.

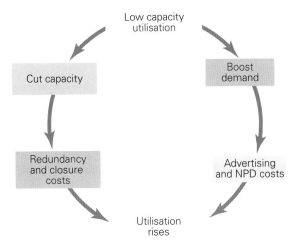

**Figure 29.2** Logic chain: improving capacity utilisation

## 29.5 Capital and labour intensity

A further factor affecting production efficiency concerns the balance struck between capital- and labour-intensive production. Measuring up a bride-to-be and then making a wedding dress by hand is the ultimate in labour-intensive production. However hard the dressmaker works, his or her productivity will be very low. This is because so little can be mechanised or automated. By contrast, a dress designer for Topshop may be able to order 5,000 identical size 10 dresses to be distributed across the Topshop stores. This batch of 5,000 can be produced largely by machine (that is, through capital- rather than labour-intensive production).

The importance of this topic is that it points to a huge opportunity for small firms. In almost every industry there is scope for some labour-intensive production. This is because there are always some people who want – and can afford – an entirely individual product. In addition, there are businesses where labour-intensive production is inevitable, such as plumbing, advertising (creating and producing commercials), legal advice and running a school. Starting a new car-manufacturing firm will be massively expensive and make you compete head-on with huge firms. Starting a new advertising agency has neither problem.

### Labour-intensive production

Labour-intensive production:

- means that labour costs form a high percentage of total costs

- has low financial barriers to entry, because it is cheap to start up production
- makes it necessary for management to focus on the cost of labour (making it especially attractive to switch production to a low-cost country such as Cambodia)
- has the advantage of being highly flexible, making it possible for a small firm to operate successfully without direct competition from a large one.

'When a man tells you that he got rich through hard work, ask him whose.' Don Marquis, author and playwright

## Capital-intensive production

Capital-intensive production:

- has a large percentage of its total costs tied up in the fixed costs of purchasing and operating machinery
- has high financial barriers to entry
- may be able to keep producing in a high-cost country because labour costs are such a small proportion of the total costs (for example, mass production of Coca-Cola or Heinz Beans)
- can be inflexible, both in terms of switching from one product to another, and in the ability to tailor a product to an individual customer.

'Capital intensive production is great on the way up, but trouble on the way down.' Anon

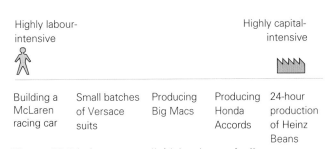

**Figure 29.3** Labour- vs. capital-intensive production

## 29.6 How to choose the optimum mix of resources

There are three main targets focused on by operations managers:

1. quality targets (for example, to have no more than 1 in 100 customers demand a refund)
2. capacity utilisation targets (such as, that the factory should be working at 85 to 95 per cent of its maximum possible capacity)

3. unit costs (for instance, keeping the average cost per unit at below £1.99 in order to keep the selling price below £2.99).

The optimum mix between these is the best compromise that can be found – which may mean that none of the three targets is met at its ideal point. Companies have to start by choosing the degree of automation they think they require, that is, where on the spectrum between absolute labour-intensive and absolute capital-intensive production, then the actual level of capacity utilisation will kick in. Ideally, the production mix should mean a compromise between cost efficiency and the ability to respond flexibly to changing customer requirements.

## Five Whys and a How

| Question | Answer |
|---|---|
| Why is a company's capacity utilisation an important non-accounting ratio? | Because it gives insight into unit costs, the effectiveness of its marketing strategy and the job security of its staff |
| Why might a company's capacity utilisation vary during the year? | For a seasonal business such as hotels, it will be much harder to sell rooms in the winter than the summer |
| Why might a struggling business choose not to cut its maximum capacity level during a recession? | It may be confident that the end of the recession will see a recovery in sales, i.e. that it would be short-sighted to cut capacity today, then run out of capacity tomorrow |
| Why may companies move from labour-intensive to capital-intensive production as they get bigger? | Increased scale of production provides scope for increasing specialisation and then automation of the relatively simple, repetitive tasks |
| Why are labour-intensive products likely to be made in developing countries? | Labour-intensive means that labour costs will be a relatively high proportion of total costs; so it makes sense to look for production locations where labour is cheap |
| How might a business boost its capacity utilisation? | Either find a way to increase demand/usage or cut the maximum capacity at the existing premises |

## Key terms

**Downtime:** any period when machinery is not being used in production. Some downtime is necessary for maintenance, but too much may suggest incompetence.

**Excess capacity:** when there is more capacity than justified by current demand (that is, utilisation is low).

**Rationalisation:** reorganising in order to increase efficiency. This often implies cutting capacity to increase the percentage of utilisation.

## Evaluation: Capacity utilisation

Most firms aim to operate close to full capacity but probably not at 100 per cent. A small amount of spare capacity is accepted as necessary, bringing a certain degree of flexibility. In this way, sudden surges of demand can be coped with in the short run by increasing output, or downtime can be used for maintenance.

Firms operating close to full capacity are those that may be considering investing in new premises or machinery. Building new factories takes time, as well as huge quantities of money. Can the firm afford to wait 18 months for its capacity to be expanded? Perhaps the firm would be better served subcontracting certain areas of its work to other companies, thus freeing capacity.

Capacity utilisation also raises the difficult issue of cutting capacity by rationalisation and, often, redundancy. This incorporates many issues of human resource management, motivation and social responsibility. There are fewer more important tests of the skills and far-sightedness of senior managers.

# Workbook

## A. Revision questions

**(40 marks; 40 minutes)**

1. What is meant by the phrase '100 per cent capacity utilisation'? (3)

2. At what level of capacity utilisation will fixed costs per unit be lowest for any firm? Briefly explain your answer. (4)

3. What formula is used to calculate the capacity utilisation of a firm? (2)

4. How can a firm increase its capacity utilisation without increasing output? (3)

5. If a firm is currently selling 11,000 units per month and this represents a capacity utilisation of 55 per cent, what is its maximum capacity? (4)

6. Use the information given in Table 29.2 to calculate profit per week at 50 per cent, 75 per cent and 100 per cent capacity utilisation. (8)

**Table 29.2** A firm's data

| Maximum capacity | 80 units per week |
|---|---|
| Variable cost per unit | £1,800 |
| Total fixed cost per week | £150,000 |
| Selling price | £4,300 |

7. Briefly explain the risks of operating at 100 per cent capacity utilisation for any extended period of time. (5)

8. Outline two benefits to a business of using labour-intensive production methods. (4)

9. Explain why a business might want to achieve the optimum rather than the maximum when setting operational objectives. (4)

10. Explain why the manufacture of the Mini car might benefit from capital-intensive production. (3)

## B. Revision exercises

### DATA RESPONSE

**Ryanair load factors**

The Irish low-cost airline, Ryanair carried over 81 million passengers in 2013, making it the world's most popular airline. The company's success is based on highly efficient operations management. The low fares charged by Ryanair will only generate profit if the company can minimise its costs. To that end the airline only operates with one type of plane, the Boeing 737. This decision enables the company to benefit from a range of economies of scale. Some airlines operate with leased planes, others like Ryanair buy outright. In July 2014 a Boeing 737 could be leased for $463 000 per month or bought outright for $81 million; either way the fixed costs are significant. In these circumstances load factors (the phrase used in the aviation business for capacity utilisation) must be kept very high in order to dilute the punishing fixed costs. The tactics used by Ryanair to achieve high load factors include:

- charging low prices
- reducing seat pitch – by removing some leg room extra rows of seats can be crammed into each plane

- fast turnarounds in-between flights, ensuring the each plane spends as much time in the air as possible earning revenue.

According to the Centre for Aviation in March 2014, the number of passengers carried by Ryanair grew by over 7 per cent compared to the previous year and their load factor averaged 78 per cent.

**Questions (30 marks; 35 minutes)**

1. **a)** A Boeing 737 can accommodate 213 passengers when full. Calculate the load factor of a flight carrying 150 passengers. (2)

   **b)** The operating cost of flying a 737 is approximately £7,000 per hour. What would be the average cost per passenger of a two-hour flight to Ibiza assuming a load factor of 70 per cent. (3)

   **c)** What would the new average cost per passenger be for the same flight if the load factor can be increased to 95 per cent? (3)

**2.** Other than price, explain two tactics Ryanair could employ in order to increase its load factors. (6)

## C. Extend your understanding

**1.** Discuss the implications of a decision by Arsenal FC to increase its stadium capacity from 60,000 to 80,000. (By all means substitute for Arsenal any other sports club with which you are familiar.) (20)

**3.** In recent years Ryanair has been on the receiving end of bad publicity regarding the quality of its customer service. To what extent could this be due to the airline's high load factors/capacity utilisation. (16)

**2.** Due to a significant change in shopping habits Tesco finds that its huge Tesco Extra shops are 40 per cent under-utilised. Evaluate the strategies Tesco might adopt to overcome this problem. (20)

# Chapter

# 30

# Technology and operational efficiency

**Linked to:** Setting operational objectives, Chapter 26; Efficiency and labour productivity, Chapter 27; Analysing operational performance, Chapter 31; Decision-making to improve operational performance, Chapter 35.

> **Definition**
>
> Technology means the computer hardware and software used to automate systems, and to handle, analyse and communicate business data.

## 30.1 Introduction

Information technology (IT) applications in business are various and rapidly changing. Often, the changes that occur are to processing speed and business jargon; the essential tasks remain the same. Many commentators have pointed out how minor have been the changes brought about by the internet compared with the coming of railways and then the motor car. It may be, though, that the biggest changes are still to come. Certainly an idea such as Google's self-drive car paints a possible future that could be hugely different. Van driving may be automated, leaving drivers unemployed; dramatic cost-reductions in robotics may mean the end of McJobs; and online teaching platforms may cut into that profession. The big changes to operational efficiency may be to come.

Key technology applications that can boost efficiency:

- automated stock control systems
- computer-aided design (CAD)
- 3D printing
- robotics
- communicating with suppliers, including electronic data interchange (EDI).

## 30.2 Automated stock control systems

Modern stock control systems are based on laser scanning of bar-coded information. This ensures the computer knows the exact quantity of each product/size/colour that has come into the stockroom. In retail outlets, a laser-scanning till is then used to record exactly what has been sold. This allows the store's computer to keep up-to-date records of current stocks of every item. This data can enable a buyer to decide how much extra to order, or an electronic link with the supplier can re-order automatically (see Section 30.6).

All this information will be held in the form of a database. This makes it easy for the firm to carry out an aged stock analysis: the computer provides a printout showing the stock in order of age. Table 30.1 shows a list of stock in a clothes shop, with the oldest first. It enables the manager to make informed decisions about what to do now and in the future. In this case:

- Big price reductions seem to be called for on the first five items; they have been around too long.
- There should be fewer orders in future for size 8 dresses.

---

'Computers are useless. They can only give you answers.' Pablo Picasso, artist

---

**Table 30.1** An example of aged stock analysis

| Garment | Received (days ago) | Number received | In stock today |
|---|---|---|---|
| Green *Fabrice* dress, size 8 | 285 | 2 | 1 |
| Blue *Channelle* dress, size 14 | 241 | 1 | 1 |
| Red *Channelle* dress, size 8 | 241 | 2 | 2 |
| Red *Grigio* jacket, size 10 | 249 | 4 | 3 |
| Black *Grigio* dress, size 8 | 205 | 3 | 2 |
| Black *Fabrice* dress, size 12 | 192 | 2 | 1 |
| Blue *Florentine* suit, size 8 | 179 | 1 | 1 |

## 30.3 Design technology

Computer-aided design (CAD) has been around for more than 20 years, but is now affordable and hugely powerful. Before CAD, product designers, engineers and architects drew their designs by hand. A CAD system works digitally, allowing designs to be saved, changed and reworked without starting from scratch. Even better, CAD can show a 3D version of a drawing and rotate to show the back and sides.

For multinationals such as Sony, a product designed in Tokyo can be sent electronically to Sony offices in America and Europe, for local designers to tweak the work to make it better suited to local tastes. And when work is behind schedule, designers in Tokyo can pass a design on to London at the end of the Japanese working day; then the design can be sent on to America. The time differences mean that 24-hour working can be kept up.

The benefits of CAD systems to successful design are that:

- The data generated by a CAD system can be linked to computer-aided manufacturing (CAM) to provide integrated, highly accurate production.
- They are hugely beneficial for businesses that are constantly required to provide designs that are unique, yet based on common principles (for example, designing a new bridge, car or office block).
- CAD improves the productivity of designers and also helps them to be more ambitious; the extraordinary buildings of Frank Gehry could not have been produced without CAD (because only computers could calculate whether the unusual structures would fall down in a high wind).

**Real business**

### A Triumph

The Triumph motorbike business collapsed in 1983 and people said Britain could no longer make bikes. But entrepreneur John Bloor bought the name and rebuilt the company. The first new Triumph hit the streets in 1991 and by 2013 the business had grown to 2,100 employees, a turnover of £368 million and a 6 per cent share of the world market for 500cc motorbikes.

The success has been built on design. Triumph has the biggest motorcycle design department outside Japan. The designers work on up-to-date CAD systems to ensure that the bikes have the key combination of looks and performance. Although some of the production takes place in the Far East, all the research, design and engineering jobs are in Britain.

**Figure 30.1** A Triumph motorbike
Source: Adapted from news reports and the Triumph website

**Figure 30.2** A Frank Gehry building which might not have been possible without CAD

## 30.4 3D printing

3D printers can make three-dimensional solid objects of almost any shape from a digital design/model. The printer works by adding layer after layer of material (such as plastic resin) to build up the shape. This enables businesses to print a prototype of a new car part, or false tooth or high-heeled shoe. In turn, this makes prototyping hugely cheaper than the traditional method of designing and building machines simply to produce a single item. A modern 3D printer costs around £3,000 and would provide the scope to make hundreds of different prototype designs.

In 2014 there was a great deal of discussion about whether 3D printing could become a new method of cost-effective, flexible manufacturing. In particular there was a hope that it would work for small-scale batch production, for example, of 10 pairs of size 7 shoes. If this could be done to the right quality standard it might make it possible for individuals to design and manufacture products at home, then perhaps sell them online.

'The most impressive part (of 3D printing): economies of scale cease to be an issue' Brad Hart, Forbes magazine

### Real business

In April 2014 it was reported that a Chinese business called Winsun had produced ten detached houses using 3D-printers and a superfast-drying concrete mixture made of waste materials. Each had been created at a cost of less than £3,000 according to Winsun's chief executive, Ma Yihe, who went on to say: 'We can print buildings to any digital design our customers bring us. It's fast and cheap.' The house may not look great, but in a world where millions need a home, this technology will surely find a market.

## 30.5 Robotics

Industrial robots are fundamental to the car industry worldwide and are becoming increasingly important in the production of electrical goods such as TVs and computers. Nevertheless, it remains a bit of a surprise that robots have not become a more powerful force in industry. Thirty years ago, people assumed that few workers would be left in factories – the robots were coming. In Britain today there are fewer than 50 robots per 10,000 workers. Even in Japan (with more than

40 per cent of the world's robots) the figure is only 500 robots per 10,000 manufacturing workers.

Figure 30.3 shows that despite the dip in worldwide sales of industrial robots during the 2009 recession, sales have boomed since. The single biggest growth market since 2009 has been China.

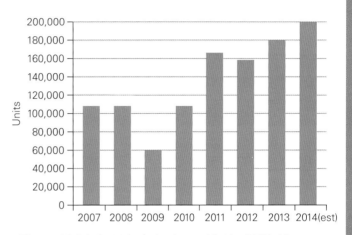

**Figure 30.3** Industrial robot sales worldwide, 2007–14

Source: World Robotics Report, IFR Statistical Department

### Real business

#### Toshiba robots

Three Toshiba robots are used at a pet food factory in Bremen, northern Germany. The company has made substantial investment in factory automation in order to improve productivity. Toshiba Machine robots now package birdseed sticks at a rate of 90 per minute. Where once there were seven people working on the application across three shifts, now three Toshiba Machine TH490 robots achieve the same results. The people have been redeployed across the plant.

The robots are part of a production line that manufactures birdseed sticks that are like a fat-based lollypop, embedded with nuts and seeds. The sticks are fed down three conveyors, each with a ceiling-mounted robot at its end. As this happens, the boxes are fed down another conveyor. A robot gripper then picks up the seed sticks and transfers them into boxes on a moving conveyor. Ceiling-mounted SCARA robots make the best use of the available work area.

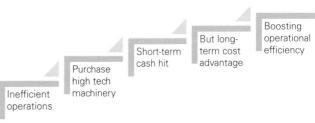

**Figure 30.4** Logic ladder: boosting operational efficiency

## 30.6 Communication with suppliers

### Electronic data interchange (EDI)

EDI is a permanent link between computers on different sites, enabling specified types of data to be exchanged. By establishing an EDI link, firms can ensure that the latest information is available instantly to other branches of their business, or even to other businesses. For example, Heinz's link with Tesco enables it to see how sales of soups are going this week. If chicken soup sales have pushed ahead by 20 per cent (perhaps because of being featured on a TV programme), production increases can be planned, even before the Tesco head office phones through with a large order. This makes a just-in-time operation far more feasible.

### Five Whys and a How

| Question | Answer |
|---|---|
| Why do workers fear the growth of lower-cost new technologies? | Because they *are* a threat to jobs, especially in the short term |
| Why may automated stock control systems help with firms' cash flow? | Because accurate stock records and ordering should allow lower buffer stocks and therefore less cash tied up in stock |
| Why might 3D printing 'democratise' manufacturing? | One day, from their own homes, people may be able to design and 'print' shoes, vacuum flasks or whatever – and sell them online (cutting into the power of big business) |
| Why might physical shops survive, despite the rise of online shopping? | Because shopping remains an important social/leisure/fun activity for many |
| Why might it seem surprising that the big growth in industrial robots is in China? | Because Chinese wages have always been very low compared with the West, making it surprising that robots would be cost-effective in China |
| How might new technology affect schools in coming years? | It is now possible to have one 'super-teacher' leading a class that is taken online by every school in the country. It's hard to imagine that this won't be tried in future. |

### Evaluation: Technology and operational efficiency

Years ago managers at Guinness thought change management was a technical question. When a change was needed, such as a new distribution system, they hired consultants whose main focus was to establish effective information technology links. Time after time they were disappointed by the results. Improvements began only when they realised that the key variable was not the technology but the people. Not only were results better if staff were consulted fully but, also, the new systems were successful only if staff applied them with enthusiasm and confidence.

Technology is only a set of tools. It can form the basis of a major competitive advantage, as with easyJet's early move into online booking. More often, though, the successful application of IT relies on good understanding of customer and staff needs and wants. This suggests that good management of information technology is no different from good management generally.

'One machine can do the work of fifty ordinary men. No machine can do the work of one extraordinary man.'
Elbert Hubbard, nineteenth century writer

# Workbook

## A. Revision questions

(35 marks; 35 minutes)

1. A database could be used by an aircraft manufacturer such as Boeing to record the supplier and batch number of every part used on every aircraft. How could this information be used? (3)

2. State two benefits of good database management in achieving efficient stock control. (2)

3. Read the Real business on Triumph. Identify one benefit and one drawback of keeping all design work in the UK. (2)

4. Look at Figure 30.3. Explain one possible implication for:
   a) a UK factory owner feeling under pressure from competition from China (3)
   b) a UK worker, with few qualifications or skills, who is thinking of taking a job in a factory. (3)

5. Explain one benefit and one drawback of computer-aided manufacture (CAM). (4)

6. From your reading of the whole unit, outline three ways in which technology can lead to improved quality. (6)

7. How significant could online shopping become for each of the following types of business?
   a) a music shop specialising in 1980s classic pop and rock (2)
   b) a builders' merchant (selling bricks, cement, etc.) (2)
   c) a firm specialising in made-to-measure 3D-printed hats. (2)

8. From your reading of the whole unit, explain two ways in which technology can reduce waste within a business. (6)

## B. Revision exercises

### DATA RESPONSE

**Printed fashion**

Operations management has long required the co-ordination of a complex series of processes: R&D and product development; production engineering; the production process itself, part-internal and part-outsourced; ordering materials and components; storing finished stock; and on-time delivery. Part of the complexity comes from tension between designers who want to create magical new products and engineers who want products that can be manufactured with ease, efficiency and reliability.

All that may be about to change. Suddenly the process of manufacturing may come under the control of the designer. Welcome to the world of 3D printing (also known as 'additive manufacture'). The 3D printer simply adds layer after layer of material that is moulded into a seamless, strong product. In future, young designers will be able to produce finished goods from their own bedrooms, without needing skilled craftsmen to do the work.

Figure 30.5 shows a 3D printed shoe made from woven nylon. The heel is (virtually) unbreakable

**Figure 30.5** A 3D printed shoe

and the delicate, thin 'straps' are very strong nylon. Shoes like this are designed using 3D Computer-Aided Design (CAD) software, allowing prototypes to be 3D printed then trialled.

Today, if you want to buy a pair, they will be made to fit your foot size exactly, that is, made-to-measure and printed-to-order. So producers hold no finished goods stock and the designer controls the whole process – from idea to design to finished product.

The *Financial Times* reported on 27 January 2013 that a trends think-tank believed: 'Brands could use it (3D printing) to enhance the in-store experience.

Burberry could invite customers to print their own personalised sunglasses designs and have them ready to go in minutes. The process would still be branded but would invite the customer in'.

3D printing hit Paris Fashion Week in January 2013 with garments such as the dress shown in Figure 30.6. In the past, 3D printing only worked in hard materials such as plastic, but now it's possible with softer polyurethanes.

**Figure 30.6** 3D-printed clothes at Paris Fashion Week

'The ability to vary softness and elasticity inspired us to design a "second skin" for the body, acting as armour-in-motion,' said co-designer, Neri Oxman. 'In this way we were able to design not only the garment's form but also its motion.'

### Questions (30 marks; 35 minutes)

1. Explain how 3D printing might make a business more able to meet customer expectations.　(4)

2. Small fashion businesses can find it hard to match production and demand. Examine two ways in which 3D printing might help such businesses. (10)

3. To what extent might 3D printing help a fashion business develop and manage its operations effectively?　(16)

## C. Extend your understanding

1. Information technology is reducing the need to meet people face to face. To what extent might this change the best way to run a successful business?　(20)

2. 'Internet retailing will mean the death of the high street.' To what extent do you agree with this?　(20)

# Chapter

# 31 Analysing operational performance

Linked with: Efficiency and labour productivity, Chapter 27; Capacity utilisation, Chapter 29; Technology and operational efficiency, Chapter 30.

### Definition

Operational performance is monitored regularly by businesses in order to ensure that the business remains competitive.

## 31.1 What is operational performance?

Ultimately, operational performance can be measured in three ways:

- What's the total unit cost to get the right product to meet the consumer's requirement? And how does that compare with rivals?

- Does the quality of the product and service create customer delight? Or satisfaction? Or mild disappointment? Or 'I'm going to fill social media with my disgust'?

- Does the price charged create enough of a premium over the unit cost to make the business sustainable and profitable in the long term?

To understand competitiveness and unit costs, it is helpful to look at three factors: labour productivity, capacity utilisation and issues surrounding a company's total available capacity.

## 31.2 Labour productivity

Labour productivity measures the amount produced per worker over a given time. For example, the Nissan factory in Sunderland has a productivity rate of 100 cars per worker per year. Interestingly, though, Nissan first achieved this productivity level in 1998!

By 2014 its productivity level had hardly changed. Fortunately this didn't matter too much to the business, because Nissan in 2014 was making car models such as Qashqai and the all-electric Leaf. These are cars that are so distinctive that customers are thinking about the brand-tag not the price-tag. When the Nissan factory opened in 1990 it employed just 450 people. By 2014 this figure had risen to more than 7,000. Successful operational performance is about profitable sales, not an obsession with productivity (or any other performance measure). For more detail on productivity and how it can be improved, go to Chapter 27.

$$\text{Productivity formula:} \quad \frac{\text{Output per unit of time}}{\text{Number of workers}}$$

Example: 24 staff produce 720 vacuum cleaners a day, so

$$\text{productivity} = \frac{720}{24} = 30 \text{ units per worker per day.}$$

## 31.3 Difficulties measuring productivity

Productivity is said to be output per worker, per time period. A few moments' thought, though, makes that seem unsatisfactory. Nissan's Sunderland car factory makes 100 cars per worker per year. But what if it's doing little more than assembling sections of cars made at other factories? It may be that a car factory operating at 50 cars per worker per year is really more productive. They may be making some of the parts on-site and doing a great deal more assembly and paint work. Comparing the productivity of different factories is actually very difficult.

The ideal measure for comparison would be added value per worker, such as the value of all the finished cars minus the cost of all the bought-in components and services, divided by the number of workers. Even then there would be problems. As a Range Rover has a higher price tag than a comparable Ford, the value added would be higher – so the marketing achievement of a higher price tag would artificially affect the productivity measure. Oh for a simple life.

The situation can be even harder in service businesses where there is no concrete way to measure output. This is one reason why working at telephone call centres can be so frustrating. 'Metrics' such as calls answered per hour can obstruct an employee who wants to help a caller, but needs time to be able to do so. A really caring approach equates to low productivity and

perhaps a stern word from the boss. And then there's the attempt to apply productivity metrics to the NHS – heart operations per hour, perhaps?

## 31.4 Unit costs

Unit costs (also known as costs per unit and as average costs) are important in business, but quite tricky to deal with. The problem comes from the nature of fixed costs.

---

**Worked example**

### Fixed costs per unit

Your sister is in her 'leaving year' at school and is excited about the prom. She wants to go by limo and enquires about the price. The limo will cost £240 for an hour. If she goes by herself that's a lot of money. If she could get three others to come it'll just be £60 each. Actually, there's room for five others. The fixed costs per unit work out as follows.

**Table 31.1** Hiring a limo

| Number of passengers paying | Total fixed cost | Fixed cost per unit (per person) |
|---|---|---|
| 1 | £240 | £240 |
| 2 | £240 | £120 |
| 3 | £240 | £80 |
| 4 | £240 | £60 |
| 5 | £240 | £48 |
| 6 | £240 | £40 |

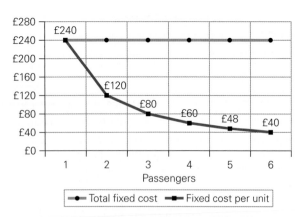

**Figure 31.1** Converting Table 31.1 into a line graph

After booking the limo the supplier phones up and offers a special catering option: food and unlimited soft drinks for an extra £20 per person. That would add £20 to the total if your sister goes alone, but £120 if she invites five friends.

**Table 31.2** Hiring a limo (2)

| Number of passengers paying | Total fixed cost | Fixed cost per unit (per person) | Total cost | Total cost per unit (unit cost) |
|---|---|---|---|---|
| 1 | £240 | £240 | £260 | £260 |
| 2 | £240 | £120 | £280 | £140 |
| 3 | £240 | £80 | £300 | £100 |
| 4 | £240 | £60 | £320 | £80 |
| 5 | £240 | £48 | £340 | £68 |
| 6 | £240 | £40 | £360 | £60 |

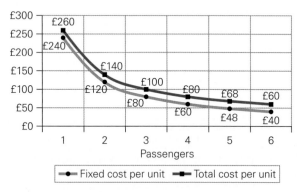

**Figure 31.2** Converting Table 31.2 into a line graph

The important things to remember about the above are:

- Fixed costs per unit fall as output increases (the fixed costs get spread more thinly)
- … so fixed costs per unit rise as output decreases
- … which, in turn, means that total unit costs increase as demand/output falls.
- Unit costs and average costs are exactly the same thing.

Fixed costs per unit formula: $\dfrac{\text{Total fixed costs}}{\text{Number of units}}$

Unit costs formula: $\dfrac{\text{Total costs}}{\text{Number of units}}$

---

Total fixed costs don't change when output changes, but they do change per unit.

## 31.5 Capacity utilisation

This has been covered in detail in Chapter 29, so just a few points need to be added:

- Capacity utilisation relates directly to fixed and total costs per unit. If poor sales push capacity utilisation rates down to 50 per cent then fixed costs per unit will be twice as high as they need be; that, in turn, will push unit (average) costs higher than they should be. This is why football teams relegated from the Premier League can hit such massive financial buffers: they still have high wage bills and the same large grounds – but now have lower capacity utilisation as supporters stay away.

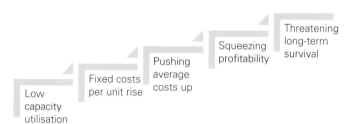

**Figure 31.3** Logic ladder: danger of low capacity utilisation

- When capacity utilisation starts to move above 90 per cent, it may be time to increase capacity. In 2014 Renault added 60 per cent to the capacity of its car factory in Morocco to cope with booming demand for its low-cost Dacia car model.

## 31.6 The use of data in operational decision-making and planning

Right up until the end of 2013 executives at Apple believed that iPad sales would keep growing for several years to come. This was especially the case because Apple had made some important sales breakthroughs in China. Rising sales would spread the fixed costs of running the brand (Apple spends more than $1 billion a year on advertising, for example). Figure 31.4 shows that operational decision-making has to be based on accurate sales forecasts. These rely on a combination of good analysis of actual sales figures plus effective use of market research to anticipate when shifts are going to take place. In this case research into customers' future purchasing plans should have shown that the cult of the iPad was wearing thin.

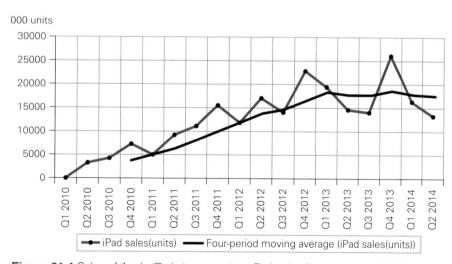

**Figure 31.4** Sales of Apple iPad stops growing; iPad sales from launch to Q2 2014

## Five Whys and a How

| Question | Answer |
|---|---|
| Why might productivity and quality of service be inversely related in the service sector? | Because rapid, cold-hearted service may be efficient but not pleasant for the customer |
| Why do average costs rise when demand falls? | Because there are fewer customers, so the total fixed costs rise per unit, pushing up the unit (average) total costs |
| Why are average costs important? | Because they have to be below the selling price if the company is to make a profit |
| Why might a seaside hotel decide to close in November and reopen in April? | Because it wants to limit its annual capacity and thereby increase its capacity utilisation |
| Why is capacity utilisation a most-favoured metric in the airline business? | Because flying has huge fixed costs but not many variable ones, so fixed costs per passenger matter and that is affected by capacity utilisation |
| How does capacity utilisation have an impact on average costs? | High utilisation spreads the fixed costs per unit thinly, bringing the average (total) costs down |

> **Key term**
>
> **Metrics:** are numerical measures used to determine the performance of an employee or a department.

## Evaluation: Analysing operational performance

Greater labour productivity can lead to greater efficiency and higher profitability. This is because, other things being equal, it lowers the labour cost per unit. However, productivity is only one factor that contributes to a firm's success. A firm must also ensure it produces a good quality product, that it is marketed effectively and that costs are controlled. There is little point increasing productivity by 20 per cent if at the same time you pay your staff 30 per cent more. Similarly, there is no point producing more if there is no actual demand. Higher productivity, therefore, contributes to better performance but needs to be accompanied by effective decision-making throughout the firm.

The importance of productivity to a firm depends primarily on the level of value added involved. Top price perfumes such as Chanel have huge profit margins. Production costs are a tiny proportion of the selling price. Therefore a 10 per cent productivity increase might have only a marginal effect on profit and virtually none on the competitiveness of the brand. For mass-market products in competitive markets, high productivity is likely to be essential for survival. A 5 per cent cost advantage might make all the difference. Therefore, when judging an appropriate recommendation for solving a business problem, a judgement is required as to whether boosting productivity is a top priority for the business concerned.

# Workbook

## A. Revision questions

**(40 marks; 45 minutes)**

1. What is meant by the term 'productivity'? (3)

2. Why may it be hard to measure the productivity of staff who work in service industries? (4)

3. How does productivity relate to labour costs per unit? (4)

4. Explain how a firm may be able to increase its employees' productivity. (4)

5. How can increased investment in machinery help to boost productivity? (3)

6. Identify two factors which help and two factors which limit your productivity as a student. (4)

7. Outline the likely effect of increased motivation on the productivity of a teacher. (5)

8. Calculate the change in productivity at BDQ Co. (see Table 31.3) since last year. (4)

**Table 31.3** Productivity at BDQ Co.

| | Output | Number of staff |
|---|---|---|
| Last year | 32,000 | 50 |
| This year | 30,000 | 40 |

9. Explain how motivation and productivity may be linked. (4)

10. Explain how productivity can be linked to unit labour costs. (5)

## B. Revision exercises
### DATA RESPONSE

**Operations management at JCB**

Midway through 2014 JCB looked set to break the £3 billion turnover mark for the first time in its history. One of the country's biggest and most important engineering companies, JCB's yellow and black construction vehicles are among the top three bestsellers globally. In its UK heartland of Staffordshire and Derbyshire, JCB employs over 5,000 people in highly skilled, secure jobs.

One of JCB's secrets has been its willingness to invest. Its 1979 decision to start up in India has led to the achievement of a 50 per cent market share in this huge, fast-developing country. India's new government is embarking on a huge programme of investment in roads and other infrastructure which should be great for JCB. Just in 2014 the company has announced:

- a £25 million programme to double production in Germany
- a £45 million investment in a six-cylinder engine to slot into its fuel-efficient Dieselmax range
- and a £150 million plan to expand production in the UK, with the expectation of creating 2,500 more jobs by 2018.

As the bar chart shows, not long ago – in the 2009 recession – the company's plans were thrown into turmoil by a collapse in sales. That year the company was saved by sales growth in India and China. Even so, with an estimated total capacity of 62,000 units in 2009, the rate of utilisation was very poor. To their credit, senior managers kept their heads and kept investing in the firm's future. From a struggle to break even in 2009 the company bounced back to make £365 million in profit in 2012.

In late 2014 JCB was holding to its long-term plan for significant increases in its global capacity. Its factories in India and Brazil are getting greater investment and new factories are being built in Uttoxeter and Cheadle in Britain. JCB believes that developing countries will continue to plough funds into construction investment and that JCB should be at the heart of this business. It shows no fear of its two huge global rivals: Caterpillar of America and Komatsu of Japan.

Another plan for the future is to improve the productivity of the JCB factories worldwide. In 2014 the 12,000-strong workforce were on course to produce 72,000 units. By 2018 the hope is to get annual productivity up to 8 units per worker.

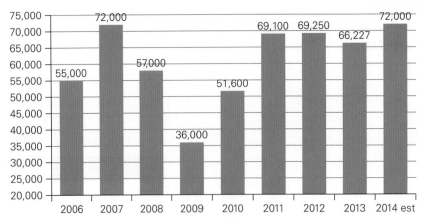

**Figure 31.5** JCB annual global sales (in units)

Source: JCB press reports

### Questions (25 marks; 30 minutes)

1. **a)** Calculate JCB's capacity utilisation in 2009. (3)

   **b)** Explain how JCB might have set about rebuilding this figure? (5)

2. Analyse the problems JCB might have faced in matching output to the order levels shown in the bar chart. (9)

3. **a)** Calculate JCB's labour productivity in 2014. (3)

   **b)** Explain the problems there may be in getting productivity up to 8 units per worker by 2018. (5)

## C. Extend your understanding

1. After years of profitable growth Aldi's operational performance is starting to deteriorate. To what extent is this inevitable at a time of rapid growth? (20)

2. British Airways' costs per passenger are five times those of Ryanair. How important is it for British Airways to close that gap? Justify your answer. (20)

**Linked with:** Setting operational objectives, Chapter 26; Managing supply chains, Chapter 33.

## Definition

Quality means providing what the customer wants, at the right time, to the right standard of product and service, and therefore yielding high customer satisfaction.

## 32.1 The importance of quality

W. Edwards Deming, the American quality guru, said that 'quality is defined by the customer'. The customer may insist on certain specifications, or demand exceptional levels of customer comfort. Another definition of quality is 'fit for use'. Although hard to define, there is no doubt that customers are very aware of quality. Their perception of quality is an important part of the buying decision.

Customers will accept some trade-off between price and quality. There is, however, a minimum level of quality that is acceptable. The customer wants the product to work (be fit for use), regardless of the price. If the customers think that the quality is below a minimum level they will not buy. Above the minimum level of acceptable quality, customers will expect to get more as they pay more.

The importance of quality is related to the level of competitiveness in the market. When competition is fierce, the quality of the product can tip the balance in the customer's decision-making. Yet the consumers' perception of quality can change. For many years computer manufacturer Dell was hugely successful selling directly to customers through the internet or newspaper advertising. Yet when the stunningly successful launch of the iPad turned people back towards Apple computers, Dell's famously high quality manufacture became irrelevant in the face of Apple's high quality design.

For all customers, quality is about satisfying their expectations. The customer will take into account the total buying experience. Customer service and after-sales service may be as important as the product itself. The way the product is sold, even *where* it is sold, all contribute to the customer's feelings about the quality of the product.

Quality is a moving target. A quality standard that is acceptable today may not be in the future. Customer expectations of quality are constantly changing. As quality improves, customer demands also increase.

Quality:

- is satisfying (preferably beating) customer expectations
- applies to services as well as products
- involves the whole business process, not just the manufacturing of the product
- is an ever-rising target.

'Quality has to be caused, not controlled.' Philip Crosby, American quality guru

## Real business

### Ryanair

Between 1991 and 2013 Ryanair boss Michael O'Leary built up the airline from almost nothing to become Europe's largest carrier. In all that time O'Leary focused on three things: low costs to make low prices possible, plus two aspects of quality: on-time arrivals and fewest bags lost. By 2005 Ryanair was the best in Europe on both these measures of customer quality. Yet in 2013 O'Leary announced that in future Ryanair would be more sensitive to other aspects of customer quality – above all else being friendlier, smilier and keener to give customers a more pleasant flying experience. Customers' quality needs had changed, and quality had become more important in customers' purchasing decisions.

'Reducing the cost of quality is in fact an opportunity to increase profits without raising sales, buying new equipment, or hiring new people.' Philip Crosby, American quality guru

## 32.2 The consequences of poor quality

Where the consumer has choice, quality is vital. A reputation for good quality brings marketing advantages. A good quality product will:

- generate a high level of repeat purchase, and therefore a longer product life cycle
- allow brand building and cross marketing
- allow a price premium (this is often greater than any added costs of quality improvements; in other words, quality adds value and additional profit)
- make products easier to place (retailers are more likely to stock products with a good reputation).

The consequences of a poor product or poor service for the business are shown in Table 32.1.

Table 32.1 Implications of poor product or service quality

| Marketing costs | Business costs |
|---|---|
| Loss of sales | Scrapping of unsuitable goods |
| Loss of reputation | Reworking of unsatisfactory goods – costs of labour and materials |
| May have to price-discount | Lower prices for 'seconds' |
| May impact on other products in range | Handling complaints/warranty claims |
| Retailers may be unwilling to stock goods | Loss of consumer goodwill and repeat purchase |

'Quality is remembered long after the price is forgotten.' Gucci slogan

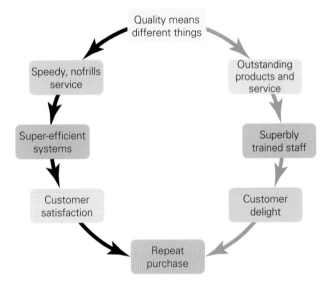

**Figure 32.1** Logic chain: quality is different things to different people

## 32.3 Methods of improving quality

As the importance of quality for both marketing and cost control has been recognised, there has been a growth in initiatives to control and improve quality. Techniques for quality control, such as inspection and statistical control, continue. They have been supplemented by other policies aimed at controlling and improving quality. These include total quality management, quality control and quality assurance. The pros and cons of each of these policies are set out in Table 32.2.

### Total quality management

Total quality management (TQM) was introduced by American business guru W. Edwards Deming. He worked with Japanese firms, and his techniques are said to be one of the reasons for the success of businesses such as Honda and Toyota. TQM is not a management tool: it is a philosophy. It is a way of looking at quality issues. It requires commitment from the whole organisation, not just the quality control department. The business considers quality in every part of the business process – from design right through to sales. TQM is about building-in rather than inspecting-out. For it to be successful, it should be woven into the organisational culture.

### Quality control

Quality control (QC) is the traditional way to manage quality, and is based on inspection. Workers get on with producing as many units as possible, and quality control inspectors check that the output meets minimum acceptable standards. This might be done by checking every product; for example, starting up every newly built car and driving it from the factory to a storage area. Or it might be done by checking every two hundredth Kit Kat coming off the end of the factory's production line. If one Kit Kat is faulty, inspectors will check others from the same batch and – if concerned – may scrap the whole batch. The problem with this system is that faulty products can slip through, and it stops staff from producing the best quality: they just focus on products 'good enough' to pass the checks. TQM is therefore a superior approach.

### Quality assurance

Quality assurance (QA) is a system that assures customers that detailed systems are in place to govern quality at every stage in production. It will start with the quality-checking process for newly arrived raw

**Table 32.2** Pros and cons of TQM, QC and QA

| | TQM | QC | QA |
|---|---|---|---|
| **Pros** | Should become deeply rooted in the company culture (e.g. product safety at a producer of baby car seats) | Can be used to guarantee that no defective item will leave the factory | Makes sure the company has a quality system for every stage in the production process |
| | Once all staff think about quality, it should show through from design to manufacture and after-sales service (e.g. at Lexus or BMW) | Requires little staff training, therefore suits a business with unskilled or temporary staff (as ordinary workers needn't worry about quality) | Some customers like the reassurance provided by keeping records about quality checks at every stage in production; they believe they will get a higher-quality service and may therefore be willing to pay more |
| **Cons** | Especially at first, staff sceptical of management initiatives may treat TQM as 'hot air'; it lacks the clear, concrete programme of QC or QA | Leaving quality for the inspectors to sort out may mean poor quality is built into the product (e.g. clothes with seams that soon unpick) | QA does not promise a high-quality product, only a high-quality, reliable process; this process may churn out 'OK' products reliably |
| | To get TQM into the culture of a business may be expensive, as it will require extensive training among all staff (e.g. all British Airways staff flying economy from Heathrow to New York) | QC can be trusted when 100 per cent of output is tested, but not when it is based on sampling; Ford used to test just 1 in 7 of its new cars; that led to quality problems | QA may encourage complacency; it suggests quality has been sorted, whereas rising customer requirements mean quality should keep moving ahead |

materials and components. Companies have to put in place a documented quality assurance system. This should operate throughout the company, involving suppliers and subcontractors. The main criticism of QA is that it is a paper-based system and therefore encourages staff to tick boxes rather than care about the customer experience.

## Improvement

Customer expectations of quality are always changing. It is important that businesses seek to improve quality. Therefore, staff need to be encouraged to put forward ways in which their jobs can be done better. The Japanese term *kaizen* (meaning 'continuous improvement') has become common in British manufacturing.

## 32.4 Other quality initiatives

### Six Sigma

A programme developed by America's General Electric Company, which aims to have fewer defective products than 1 per 300,000. To achieve this, staff are trained to become 'Green Belt' or 'Black Belt' quality experts. Although gimmicky, this has been followed widely by other companies.

'Quality is our best assurance of customer allegiance, our strongest defence against foreign competition, and the only path to sustained growth and earnings.' Jack Welch, General Electric chief

## Quality circles

A quality circle is a group of employees who meet together regularly for the purpose of identifying problems and recommending adjustments to the working processes. This is done to improve the product or process. It is used to address known quality issues such as defective products. It can also be useful for identifying better practices that may improve quality. In addition, it has the advantage of improving staff morale through employee involvement. It takes advantage of the knowledge of operators.

## Zero defects

The aim is to produce goods and services with no faults or problems. This is vital in industries such as passenger aircraft production or the manufacture of surgical equipment.

### Real business

#### *Boeing Dreamliner*

In January 2013 all of Boeing's new 787 Dreamliner aircraft were grounded. With each plane having a list price of over $200 million this was a huge and costly embarrassment for the American plane maker and its global airline customers.

The specific problem was a battery on the plane that overheated and sometimes caught fire. In fact, though, the Dreamliner had already suffered far more teething problems than would usually be expected from Boeing.

⇨

⇨

The reason proved to be the way Boeing had organised the huge operation of developing and engineering the production process. Due to lack of production capacity, 60 per cent of the design and production of key components had been outsourced to suppliers from around the world. Because Boeing's own quality standards had not been applied uniformly, the company's quality assurance and quality control systems struggled to cope.

## 32.5 Benefits and difficulties of improving quality

The traditional belief was that high quality was costly: in terms of materials, labour, training and checking systems. Therefore, managements should beware of building too much quality into a product (the term given to this was 'over-engineered'). The alternative approach, put forward by the American writer Philip Crosby, is that 'quality is free'. The latter view suggests that getting things right first time can save a huge amount of time and money.

Benefits when improving quality:

- A great deal of research shows that staff like to take pride in their work, and that working to high quality standards is important. Management focus on quality, therefore, can boost morale and motivation.
- Really high quality standards can boost price levels remarkably. At the time of writing, Waitrose supermarkets has champagne at prices from £20 to £255 for a bottle; so customers are willing to pay £255 for a product they only need to pay £20 for.

Difficulties when improving quality:

- If quality control is to be effective it must balance the costs against the advantages; 100 per cent quality is possible, but it may make the product so expensive that sales suffer.
- Companies that rely on outsourced or temporary staff may struggle to achieve the high levels of quality implied by a TQM culture. True quality is about service as well as the product – which relies on the wholehearted commitment of staff

### Five Whys and a How

| Question | Answer |
|---|---|
| Why are some companies able to get away with the appalling quality revealed on TV programmes such as *Cowboy Builders* or *Watchdog*? | Some companies can make high, long-term profits without needing customer loyalty. They rely on finding a steady stream of naïve customers; consumer protection laws try – but often fail – to stop these things happening |
| Why may companies find it hard to correct an image of poor quality? | Images tend to build up over time, so they can be hard to shift. Change may require consistent quality programmes over several years |
| Why is quality assurance more popular these days than quality control? | Quality assurance can be used to check the whole supply chain, rather than just the final product. That fits with the needs of Tesco or Waitrose, who want to be sure of provenance |
| Why does quality matter if you're buying a £10 skirt from Primark? | It still matters, even if the customer may not mind about queues or scruffy displays. The skirt must be cut well enough to fit properly and made of fabrics that look good |
| Why do new firms sometimes struggle with quality? | They may have a very positive culture, but not yet have the processes in place to ensure quality |
| How would you set about improving quality at a struggling handbag maker? | First, give each worker a complete unit of work, i.e. producing the whole bag without division of labour, which would be hugely motivating; and drop any piecework payments |

## Evaluation: Improving quality

In recent years, there has been a change in the emphasis on quality. The quality business has itself grown. The management section of any bookshop will reveal several titles dedicated to quality management. The growth of initiatives such as TQM and continuous improvement goes on. The number of worldwide registrations for ISO 9000 increases by more than 25 per cent each year. Not all of these are from British businesses; there has been a rapid rise in overseas registrations. With an increase in the international awareness of quality, British businesses will have to ensure that they continue to be competitive.

This growth in emphasis on quality has undoubtedly brought benefits to business. Increased quality brings rewards in the marketplace. Companies have also found that the initiatives, especially where they are people-based, have brought other advantages: changes in working practices have improved motivation and efficiency, and have reduced waste and costs.

This change in emphasis has not been without problems. The shift to a focus on the customer and the role of the employee could result in additional costs. Unless this results in increased profits, shareholders may feel that they are losing out. Some businesses have found that changing cultures is not easy. Resistance from workers and management has often caused problems.

# Workbook

## A. Revision questions

(30 marks; 30 minutes)

1. State two reasons why quality management is important. (2)
2. How important is quality to the consumer? (3)
3. Suggest two criteria customers may use to judge quality at:
   a) a budget-priced hotel chain (2)
   b) a Tesco supermarket (2)
   c) a McDonald's. (2)
4. Why has there been an increase in awareness of the importance of improving the quality of products? (3)
5. Give two marketing advantages that come from a quality reputation. (2)
6. What costs are involved if the firm has quality problems? (3)
7. What is Total Quality Management? (3)
8. Outline two benefits of adopting quality circles to a clothing chain such as Topshop. (4)
9. Outline two additional costs that may be incurred in order to improve quality. (4)

## B. Revision exercises
### DATA RESPONSE

**Horsemeat and food quality in 2013**

In January 2013 supermarkets were hit by an extraordinary scandal as it emerged that foods made of processed 'beef' actually contained horsemeat. Tesco was quickly forced to admit that one of its products contained 30 per cent horsemeat. Discounter Aldi also had to endure some tough headlines. Broadly, higher-priced retailers such as Waitrose, Sainsbury and Marks

& Spencer came out of the saga pretty well; Tesco, Asda and Morrisons' fared worse. In the 12 weeks to 17 February Tesco's market share slipped below 30 per cent for the first time in several years.

So how could it happen?

Amazingly, most supermarkets do not check the meat when it arrives at their depots. This task is outsourced ('farmed out') to companies approved by the British Retail Consortium. Inspectors go once to the source of supply, acting on behalf of all retailers. But in evidence to a government committee in February 2013, Paul Smith, a recently retired food inspector told the committee: 'The suppliers can select which "approved inspection body" they use. They also pay for the audit. Yes, they can pick which audit company, the alleged policeman, they wish. In practice they also pick the individual auditor by heaping praise and requesting the same individual for the next visit.'

> **Throughout the world, our customers want safe, affordable products. Many also want to know that what they buy is sourced to robust ethical and environmental standards.**
>
> **We believe it is possible to provide for all our customers, whatever their needs, whilst upholding strong standards across our business and in our supply chains.**
>
> Source: Tesco Social Responsibility Report

So despite the claims it makes in its Social Responsibility Report, Tesco does nothing to check on its food supplies. Other companies such as Waitrose may well do so, as they had no problem with horsemeat contamination.

The consequence of this slack approach to quality is clear in the impact of the scandal on food sales. In the four weeks after the scandal first hit, sales of frozen burgers were down (nationally) by over 40 per cent and sales of all ready meals were down by 12 per cent.

So what should Tesco have done? First, it should have switched its focus from public relations to quality management. Tesco shoppers probably believed that tough Tesco buyers went to suppliers, checked the quality standards, then negotiated toughly on price. Clearly the checking part may have been a bit of a myth. To clear the air, the company should have brought in a new policy of checking at the producer, and then checked as products arrived at Tesco. In effect this would have been a full Quality Assurance regime. Having set the new policy up, it would then have been time to tell the consumer.

> **The meat inspection workforce managed by the Food Standards Agency has shrunk from a high point of 1700 - during the BSE and E. coli crises in the 1990s - to around 800 today. This has been a direct consequence of the deregulatory policies of both the European Commission and UK Government to hand over more and more meat inspection duties to the meat industry and dispense with proper independent inspection.**
>
> Source: Unison (trade union)

Tesco knew perfectly well that government inspection of food had been run down in recent years (see box). So it should have been making greater efforts to protect its customers (and its own reputation). It seems to have been very short-sighted in its approach to quality. It is likely to keep feeling the impact on its market share.

### Questions (25 marks; 30 minutes)

1. Explain Tesco's performance at choosing effective suppliers. (9)

2. To what extent is quality of importance to a business such as Tesco? (16)

## C. Extend your understanding

1. To what extent should quality management be solely a matter for the production department? (20)

2. To what extent is quality a major competitive issue in service businesses? (20)

# Chapter 33 Managing supply chains

Linked with: Analysing operational performance, Chapter 31; Improving quality, Chapter 32; Managing inventory, Chapter 34.

## Definition

The supply chain is the complete sequence of stages involved in transforming raw materials into finished goods and getting them into the hands of customers.

## 33.1 Influences on the choice of suppliers

### Cost

Cheaper supplies mean higher profit margins. The incentive to find a cheap supplier is huge for any firm; therefore, the price charged will be a key factor in the relationship between a firm and its suppliers. Large purchasers may almost be able to dictate prices to their suppliers. This is because the quantities they purchase may account for most of the supplier's output, giving a huge amount of power to the buyer. However, for small businesses with limited purchasing power, the supplier may have the upper hand. The lower the purchase price, the lower the buyer's variable costs and therefore the higher its gross profits.

### Quality

There is likely to be a trade-off between the price charged by suppliers and the quality of their offering. The cheapest supplier may be one with a poor reputation for the quality of its products or service. Choosing to use a supplier with quality problems is likely to lead to operational problems. Poor-quality supplies can lead to machinery breakdowns, along with poor-quality output. This can lead to worsening customer complaints, guarantee claims or reputation. Choosing the cheapest supplier may sow the seeds of long-term problems for a business.

### Reliability

Supplies at the right price and of a high quality may be of little use if they arrive late. It is important that a supplier can offer reliability to the purchaser. Failure to deliver on time can stop a manufacturing process or leave shop shelves empty. Suppliers' reliability will be easy to assess once a business has started working with them. However, a new business or a business sourcing new supplies may need to rely on word-of-mouth reputation to inform its choice.

### Frequency

Depending on the type of business and the production system it uses, frequent deliveries may be needed from suppliers. Firms selling fresh produce will need to ensure that they are using suppliers that can supply and deliver frequently – probably as often as a new batch each day. Similarly, a firm that uses a just-in-time (JIT) production system will need very frequent deliveries to feed its production system without it having to hold stock (Honda, for example, requires hourly deliveries of parts to its Japanese car factories). For firms such as these, it makes sense to look for a local supplier; they are far more likely to be willing to deliver with a greater level of frequency.

### Flexibility

In a similar way to ensuring the right frequency of supplies, many firms will need to find a supplier with the capacity to cope with widely varying orders. Businesses selling products with erratic demand patterns, caused by changes in the weather or fashion, will need to find suppliers that can meet their ever-changing needs. Probably the most common scenario is to ensure that suppliers have the spare capacity available to cope with sudden rush orders. A key to supplier flexibility is a short lead time (that is, there should not be too long a period between placing an order and receiving a delivery).

## Payment terms

Most business transactions are on credit, not for cash. If Tesco wants to order 2,000 cases of Heinz Beans, the bill is unlikely to be paid for 30 or more days after the goods have been delivered. This gives time for the goods to be sold, providing the cash to make it easy to pay the bill. Small business start-ups will struggle to get the same terms. A newly opened corner shop will not be given credit by Heinz. The supplier will want to be paid in cash until the new business has shown that it can survive and pay its bills. So a new small firm has to pay up front, placing extra strain on its cash flow. This should not be a problem as long as it has been built into its start-up cash-flow forecast).

'All we are doing is looking at the timeline from the moment the customer gives us an order to the point when we collect the cash. And we reduce that timeline by removing non-value-added wastes.'
Taiichi Ohno, father of the Toyota Production System

## 33.2 Managing the supply chain efficiently

Some businesses enjoy telling their shareholders how tough they are with their suppliers: after all, the lower the supply cost, the higher the profit. Many firms encourage competition between rival suppliers by threatening to go elsewhere if the terms are not what they want. This approach has been important in building the hugely profitable business of many high-street stores, which find cheap goods by negotiating toughly in Cambodia, China or the Philippines.

An alternative approach was followed in the past by Marks & Spencer, and today by car firms such as Toyota and Honda. These companies build long-term relationships with their suppliers, in order to have a more efficient supply chain. There are many potential benefits from this approach, as discussed below.

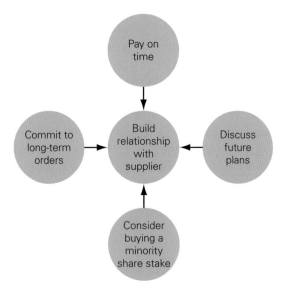

**Figure 33.1** Logic chain: how to build strong relationships with suppliers

## Working together on new product development

Developing new products involves many considerations. One of these will be how the product is to be manufactured, what materials will be used and what properties will be needed. Meanwhile, launching a new product will require careful production planning to ensure that consumers can get hold of the new product that the marketing department has told them about. The result is that suppliers have a major part to play in developing and launching new products. Many firms have recognised the importance of this and work hand in hand with their suppliers from the very earliest stages of developing a new product.

## Flexibility

A strong relationship with a supplier should mean it is willing to make special deliveries if a business is running low on stock. A strong relationship may also allow some flexibility on payment. A toyshop may struggle to find cash in the months leading up to Christmas, so a trusting supplier may accept a delay in payment. This could be the lifeline required for the small firm. However, no supplier is likely to be able to sustain this generosity for a long period.

## Sharing information to improve the efficiency of the supply chain

Large businesses with sophisticated IT systems have direct links between their cash tills and their suppliers. Cadbury knows at any hour of the day how many Twirls are selling in supermarkets. This enables Cadbury to plan its production levels (for example, pushing up output if sales are proving brighter than expected). The supermarket can even allow Cadbury to make the decisions about how much stock to produce and deliver on the basis of the information it is receiving.

---

'When you went into a Boston Chicken and ordered quarter-chicken, white, with mash and corn, when that was rung up it would signal all the way along the supply chain the need for more potatoes to be put on a truck a thousand miles away.' Stephen Elop, Microsoft vice-president

---

## 33.3 Matching supply to demand

Many factors can cause sales levels to fluctuate, including:

- fashion
- temperature and weather
- marketing activity
- competitors' actions.

Some of these are predictable; others less so. Sales forecasting can help in production planning, especially for predictable changes in demand (such as higher swimwear sales in early summer than early winter). However, the fundamental issue is the same for most businesses: how to organise their operations to cope with demand variations.

Matching supply to demand is relatively easy when demand is highly predictable, as with sales of Heinz Tomato Ketchup. Seasonal sales variations are minor and the strength of the (£125 million) brand means that competitors' actions matter little. By contrast, think of sales of lawnmowers. These are extremely seasonal, with almost no one buying one in the winter (the grass doesn't grow!), but a burst of demand occurring when spring warms up to the point that the grass needs cutting.

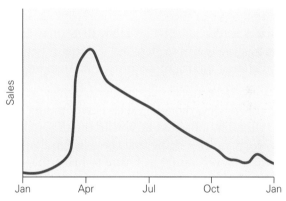

**Figure 33.2** Lawnmower sales

Figure 33.2 shows a possible sales graph for lawnmowers – but imagine trying to match those monthly figures with production/supply: idle factories for half the year and then an incredible burst of activity when the weather improves. Surely it might be better to produce in the way shown in Figure 33.3. Line A shows steady production year-round. This would entail building up stocks throughout the winter, then selling them when demand arrives in the spring.

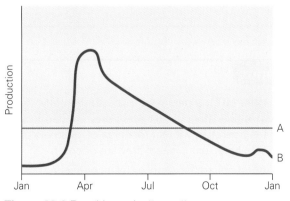

**Figure 33.3** Possible production options

| Advantages of Figure 33.2 (Match production to sales) | Advantages of Figure 33.3 (Constant production level) |
|---|---|
| • Minimal inventory (stock) levels so very little cash tied up | • Stable production so factory usage high (lower fixed costs per unit) |
| • No risk of overproduction (unsold stock if sales proved disappointing) | • Workers fully utilised year-round so labour costs per unit kept low |
| • Products are freshly made so quality is high (not an issue in this case!) | • Entering spring with high buffer stock, so customers will be supplied |

## Other ways to match supply to demand

**1.** Outsourcing (or subcontracting) means getting an outside company to produce for you.

This is valuable when there are predictable peaks in the workload or when there are 'non-core' operations that outsiders could do better. Top law firms may be great at managing their practice, but feel that others would be better at managing security, catering and cleaning.

There are downsides, though. When outsourcing is carried through, jobs are lost within the original company, with the risk being that the expertise is lost – making it ever harder in future to bring the work back in-house. Alternatively the outsourcing may be in part, that is, being used as a top-up for when demand exceeds the original factory's ability to supply.

When outsourcing there is a risk that the contractor cares little for 'your' customers and your reputation. Therefore it is important to get the contractor to sign up to a service agreement that sets out exactly what quality standards are required.

'If I start outsourcing all my navigation to a little talking box in my car, I'm sort of screwed. I'm going to lose my car in the parking lot every single time.' Ken Jennings, US celebrity nerd

**2.** Hiring temporary and part-time staff

Temporary and part-time staff give extra flexibility to an employer. Temporary staff can be hired on fixed term contracts designed to last no longer than the expected busy period. Most tourist attractions keep very few full-time staff, relying instead on an army of summer temps to run their attractions. Part-time staff can be hired with contracts that include flexible working hours, offering employers the chance to call them in during busy periods. In recent years there has been a growing use of 'zero-hours contracts'. These promise staff no hours of work at all (and therefore no income); employers might contact zero-hours employees on a Thursday to let them know their work schedule for the following week. This gives huge benefits to the employer but no obvious advantages to the employee, who has no stability of income and therefore no chance of taking out a mortgage and little chance of saving.

Through the use of temporary and part-time staff, a company can reduce its fixed salary costs thus reducing the break-even point to a level that is sustainable during quiet periods. However, motivation, quality and customer service issues may arise with a workforce that may feel only loosely engaged with the company.

**3.** Producing to order

An important feature of modern operations management is recognising that customers will go to the producer that offers as close to a tailor-made product as possible. The term 'mass customisation' sums this up: production lines that combine the cost efficiency of mass production with the flexibility of tailor-making to each customer's specific requirements. On the Mercedes UK website the Car Configurator button allows customers to specify their precise requirements, to be built into the car at the factory. The uniquely specified Merc rolls off the line a couple of weeks later and is delivered to the customer.

> **Key terms**
>
> **Just-in-time (JIT):** ordering supplies so that they arrive 'just in time' (that is, just when they are needed). This means operating without reserves of materials or components held 'just in case' they are needed.
>
> **Lead time:** the time the supplier takes between receiving an order and delivering the goods.
>
> **Mass customisation:** producing flexibly on a mass production assembly line, giving the twin benefits of customer satisfaction and cost effectiveness.
>
> **Service agreement:** a contract between a company and its supplier that sets out exactly what is required by when and at what quality standards.

## Five Whys and a How

| Question | Answer |
|---|---|
| Why might it be a mistake to use short-term, low-cost contracts for supplies? | Because building a long-term relationship with the supplier can yield benefits in terms of quality and innovation |
| Why might outsourcing raise difficult ethical questions? | Because products are being made for you, but with terms and conditions that may be out of your sight and out of your control |
| Why do new, small firms find it hard to get trade credit from their suppliers? | New firms have a high failure rate, so it would be very risky for a supplier to give you goods on credit, perhaps later to find you in liquidation and unable to pay |
| Why might it be a mistake for a NHS hospital to outsource its cleaning services? | If the outside business was disconnected from the ethos of the hospital, quality standards might be low and disease might spread |
| Why may a business such as Cadbury choose to pay higher prices to buy Fairtrade supplies? | Perhaps for ethical reasons, but more probably because they think the image advantages outweigh the costs |
| How might mass customisation help a producer of racing bikes? | It would enable individual customer needs to be met while keeping production costs reasonably low |

## Evaluation: Managing supply chains

Evaluative themes relating to suppliers will centre on judgements that firms make as to which supplier to choose. This unit has covered a range of factors that need to be considered, but effective evaluation will come from a willingness to appreciate which factors are most important for the specific business. A retailer that sells high volumes of cheap products at low prices may be right to compromise on quality to use the cheapest suppliers. The reverse would be the case for a firm with a luxury image or targeting socially conscious consumers. Take care to work out which factors will be most important for the firm mentioned in the question.

Another judgement that should improve your answers is to determine who has the most power in the relationship between company and supplier. Larger firms tend to have more power; indeed there are concerns over the way Britain's huge supermarket chains treat small farmers. However, size may not be the only factor to consider. A supplier with a patent on a crucial component will need to be dealt with even if it fails to prove 100 per cent reliable.

# Workbook

## A. Revision questions

(30 marks; 30 minutes)

1. Explain why the cheapest supplier may not be the best choice. (4)

2. Identify two businesses for which daily deliveries may be absolutely crucial. (2)

3. Briefly explain two problems that may arise when a firm uses a supplier with poor levels of quality. (4)

4. Describe why attractive credit terms from a supplier will be particularly useful for a new business. (4)

5. Outline two reasons why a firm may choose to change its supplier of an existing component. (4)

6. Explain one benefit a mobile phone shop may receive by encouraging several suppliers to continually compete with each other for every month's order of components. (4)

7. What benefits could the mobile phone shop miss out on by not building a long-term relationship with its suppliers? (4)

8. Describe how a car manufacturer such as Volkswagen may benefit from including its component suppliers in the development process when designing a new car. (4)

# B. Revision exercises
## DATA RESPONSE

### Operations management in a heatwave

**Figure 33.4**

The July 2013 British heatwave caused a delighted chaos in the ice cream business. In the first week, sales of single lollies and ice creams soared by 195 per cent year-on-year. And Yorkshire-based R&R ice cream (previously called Frederick's Dairies) reported a 300 per cent hike in sales. The managing director said: 'We are doing everything we can to fulfil the unprecedented demand... this hot weather has seen an uplift of 120 per cent on the forecast sales.' In fact customers of R&R's reported stock shortages as too little was delivered.

Needless to say, ice cream manufacturers know that sales in the summer months will be higher than in the winter. Typically, sales in June, July and August are four times higher than in the winter months. So production is ramped up in April, May and June to build up stock levels.

In addition to this predictable sales pattern comes the weather. To help match production to demand, Unilever (Wall's) buys 10-day weather forecasts and plans accordingly. R&R, though, says: 'We think that weather forecast data is too expensive so we've

stopped buying it. We have all our production facilities on one site in Skelmersdale. We can build stock up and react very quickly if the weather gets warm. We can make changes to our production schedule in a day.' Despite its forecasting, Unilever could not keep up with demand for its Ben & Jerry's brand, forcing it to source stock from its factories outside the UK.

Over the longer term, ice cream sales have been in decline. This accentuated the supply shock for the manufacturers. In July, Unilever's brand building director told *The Grocer* magazine: 'In the spring the sales team were pulling their hair out while the supply chain team were looking calm because stock levels were optimal. Now it's the other way round.' The worry for manufacturers is that consumer demand reacts quickly to worsening weather as well. Most supply chains struggle to keep up with this, so may be pushing out too much stock for a few days after the heatwave has subsided.

### Questions (30 marks; 35 minutes)

1. Explain the approaches taken by Wall's and R&R's to match ice cream supply to demand. (4)

2. Outline two operational objectives that would be suitable for an ice cream producer such as Wall's. (4)

3. Explain one benefit and one drawback of a capital-intensive production strategy in the ice cream business. (6)

4. To what extent do you agree that lean production is the best operational strategy for ice cream manufacturers? (16)

# C. Extend your understanding

1. To what extent is it unethical for a profitable retailer such as Sports Direct to hire part-time sales staff only on the basis of zero-hours contracts? (20)

2. To what extent should cost be the main influences on the choice of suppliers for a major retailer of your choice? (20)

# Chapter 34 Managing inventory

**Linked with:** Lean production, Chapter 28; Technology and operational efficiency, Chapter 30; Analysing operational performance, Chapter 31; Decision-making to improve operational performance, Chapter 35.

## Definition

Inventory is the American term for stock, and its management is to ensure that supplies are ordered, delivered and handled to balance customer demand against the cost of holding stocks.

## 34.1 Types of inventory

Manufacturing firms hold three types of inventory. These are:

- raw materials and components: these are the stocks the business has purchased from outside suppliers; they will be held by the firm until it is ready to process them into its finished output

- work in progress: at any given moment, a manufacturing firm will have some items it has started to process, but that are incomplete; this may be because they are presently moving through the production process; it may be because the firm stores unfinished goods to give it some flexibility to meet consumer demand

- finished goods: once a product is complete, the firm may keep possession of it for some time; this could be because it sells goods in large batches or no buyer has yet come in for the product. For producers of seasonal goods such as toys, most of the year's production may be building stock in preparation for the pre-Christmas sales rush, a process known as producing for stock, or stockpiling.

The firm's costs increase if it holds more stock. However, this needs to be set against the opportunity cost of keeping too little stock, such as not being able to meet customer demand. One theory is that a firm should try to keep as little stock as possible at all times. This system, known as just-in-time, is covered in Section 34.6. The firm must keep control of all the different types of stock to ensure that it runs at peak efficiency.

'Substitute information for inventory' Anon

## 34.2 Influences on the amount of inventory held

A firm can hold too much or too little inventory. Both cases will add to the costs of the firm. Too much inventory can lead to:

- opportunity costs: holding the firm's wealth in the form of stock prevents it using its capital in other ways, such as investing in new machinery, or research and development on a new product; this may dent its competitiveness

- cash flow problems: holding the firm's wealth as stock may cause problems if it proves slow moving; there may be insufficient cash to pay suppliers

- increased storage costs: as well as the rental cost of the space needed to hold the inventories, the higher the stock value, the higher the cost of insurance against fire and theft

- increased finance costs: if the capital needs to be borrowed, the cost of that capital (the interest rate) will be a significant added annual overhead

- increased stock wastage: the more stock is held, the greater the risk of it going out of date.

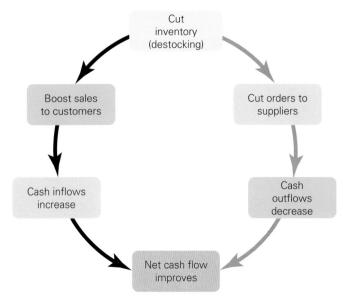

Figure 34.1 Logic chain: how destocking boosts cash

This does not, however, mean that the business is free to carry very low stocks. There are potential costs from holding too little inventory, including the following.

- Lost orders, if urgent customer orders cannot be met because there is too little finished goods stock
- Worker downtime if essential components have been delayed in arriving from suppliers (and the very low buffer has been used up already)
- The loss of the firm's reputation and any goodwill it has been able to build up with its customers.

The total cost of inventory to the firm will therefore be a combination of these factors. As the level of inventory grows, the costs of holding that stock will increase, but the costs of being out of stock decrease. The cost of holding stock will therefore look like Figure 34.2.

For a firm, the optimum level of stock to hold will be where the total costs of holding stock are the lowest.

## 34.3 Inventory control charts

One way in which a firm analyses its stock situation is by using an inventory control chart. This line graph looks at the level of stock in the firm over time. Managers can see how stock levels are changing, and act quickly if slow sales have led to excessive stock levels.

A typical inventory control chart will look like that shown in Figure 34.3. On this chart there are four lines, which represent the levels described below.

- Stock levels: This line shows how stock levels have changed over the time period. As the stock is used up, the level of stock gradually falls from left to right. When a delivery is made, however, the stock level leaps upwards in a vertical line. The greater the rise in the vertical line, the more stock has been delivered.
- Maximum stock level: This shows the largest amount that the firm is either willing or able to hold in stock.
- Reorder level: This is a 'trigger' quantity. When stocks fall to this level a new order will be sent in to the supplier. The reorder level is reached some time before the delivery (shown by the vertical part of the stock level line). This is because the supplier will need some 'lead time' to process the order and make the delivery.
- Minimum stock level: This is also known as the buffer stock. The firm will want to keep a certain minimum level of stock so that it will have something to fall back on if supplies fail to arrive on time or if there's a sudden increase in demand.

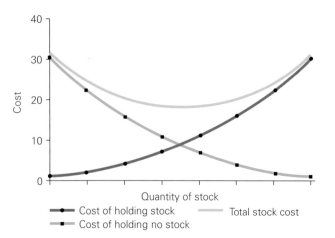

Figure 34.2 The cost of stockholding

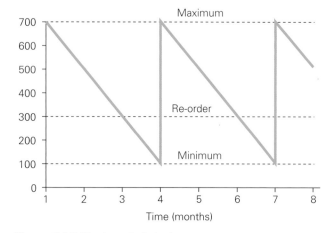

Figure 34.3 Stock control chart

Diagrams such as this, showing a neat and regular pattern to stockholding, will not happen in reality. Orders may arrive late and may not always be of the correct quantity. The rate of usage is unlikely to be constant. The slope of the stock level line may be steeper, showing more stock being used than normal, or shallower, showing a slower use of stock.

However, inventory control charts such as these give managers a clear picture of how things have changed, and show them what questions need to be asked. For example, perhaps suppliers are regularly delivering late. Managers will then know to ask if suppliers were taking longer than the agreed lead time, or if orders were being placed too late.

Figure 34.4 shows a more realistic stock control graph. It is based on actual sales of Nestlé Lion Bars at a newsagent in South West London.

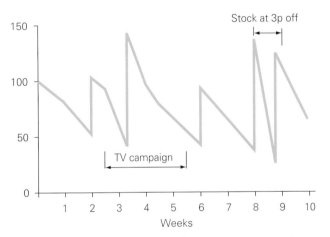

**Figure 34.4** Weekly sales of Lion Bars at one newsagent

## 34.4 Buffer level of inventory

Buffer stocks are needed just-in-case something goes wrong. If warm weather sends customers rushing to buy ice creams, there's a serious chance of running out. So grocers try to keep a minimum number of ice creams in stock throughout the summer, just in case the sun bursts through.

Companies today love the idea of holding zero buffer stocks, but that is only possible if customers place orders and are willing to wait for delivery (as would be true of ordering a Mercedes with factory-fitted optional extras). Most companies need to set a buffer stock level and make sure to reorder early enough so that there's little or no chance of running out of stock.

> 'Inventory in work-in-progress hides inefficiencies. It's better to expose them by removing buffer stock.'
> J.K. Liker, business author

## 34.5 Lead time and reorder levels

### Lead time

This is the time between an order being placed and the supplies being delivered. This might be months, if the supplier company is based in China and the stock is too heavy to be flown to Britain. If so, the British company may have to hold quite a few of this part in stock, because it takes so long to get hold of another.

Alternatively the component may be made locally, available within hours, and available from more than one supplier. If so, it may only be necessary to have one day's worth of supplies in stock.

### Reorder levels

When the level of inventory falls due to the sale or usage of stock, it may start to approach the buffer stock level. That, remember, is the minimum desired stock level and therefore the business wants the stock reordered early enough for it to arrive before the inventory sinks below that buffer stock level. The reorder level must be set, therefore, taking into account the rate of usage, the lead time for the stock item, and the level of the buffer stock.

### Worked example

Reorder levels for a shop selling 6 items a week, with a buffer stock of 8, a reorder quantity of 18 and a supplier lead time of 1 week. Assumed starting point is 14 units of stock at the start of week 1.

**Table 34.1** Inventory control at a shop selling sofas

| Week | Inventory at start of week | Delivery from supplier | Usage of stock | Inventory at end of week |
|------|------|------|------|------|
| 1 | 14 | - | 6 | 8 |
| 2 | 8 | 18 | 6 | 20 |
| 3 | 20 | - | 6 | 14 |
| 4 | 14 | - | 6 | 8 |
| 5 | 8 | 18 | 6 | 20 |
| 6 | 20 | - | 6 | 14 |

In the above example, the reorder level is 14, because when the stock level falls to 14 you need to phone the supplier asking for your next delivery of sofas in a week's time.

## Reorder quantities

A further consideration is how much stock to order at any one time, that is, the reorder level. Large orders need only be made occasionally to keep sufficient stock levels, while smaller orders would have to be placed more regularly. The arguments for both of these are shown in Table 34.2.

**Table 34.2** Large versus smaller orders

| Advantages of many small orders | Advantages of few large orders |
|---|---|
| Less storage space needed | Lower cost per unit due to economies from buying in bulk |
| More flexible to changing needs | Avoids chance of running out of stock |
| Less stock wastage | Prevents machines and workers standing idle |

### Real business

#### RFID (Radio Frequency Identification) at Carlsberg

Brewers such as Carlsberg sell most of their beer and cider to pubs in 36-gallon aluminium kegs. The kegs are supposed to be sent back to the brewery by the pubs when they are empty. Unfortunately, in many cases they are not returned promptly, or they go missing.

In the past Carlsberg overcame this problem by purchasing extra kegs from their supplier. The problem with this cautious, just-in-case approach is cost. Each empty beer keg costs Carlsberg nearly £75. In early 2013 Carlsberg began fitting RFID tags to its latest product – Somersby Cider. The tags send digital information back to Carlsberg HQ. The tags have helped Carlsberg in two ways. First, fewer barrels are now going missing because Carlsberg now knows the precise locations of all its barrels. Second, the tags also tell Carlsberg how much cider is left in each barrel. This enables Carlsberg to better match supply with demand, ensuring that pubs don't run out of stock.

## 34.6 Just-in-time

Just-in-time (JIT) is a Japanese system of production; it is the attempt to operate with a zero buffer stock. At the same time, a system must be developed so that the costs and risks of running out of stock are avoided by the firm.

Establishing a JIT system is not something that can or should be achieved overnight. The risks of running out of stock are too great. Figure 34.5 shows how a firm might set out to achieve a JIT system in a carefully planned way. The diagram shows five phases, after which the firm would intend to continue with phases six, seven and thereafter, until it could get as close as possible to zero buffer stock. The five phases are as follows.

1. The firm orders 20,000 units of stock to arrive every third week.

2. Suppliers are asked to move to weekly deliveries, therefore only one-third of the quantity is ordered.

3. As Phase 2 has proved successful, there is no longer any need for such a high buffer stock. Stock levels are allowed to fall to a new, lower level.

4. With Phase 3 complete, the firm now moves to receiving deliveries twice a week. Therefore the order level is halved.

5. The suppliers have proved reliable enough to allow the buffer to be cut again…

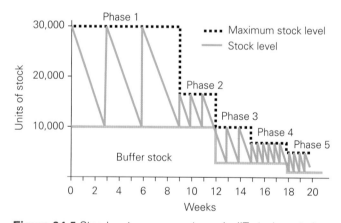

**Figure 34.5** Step-by-step progress towards JIT stock control

## Five Whys and a How

| Question | Answer |
|---|---|
| Why is stock control especially important for some firms, such as greengrocers? | Too much stock would mean tired displays and high wastage levels; too little would mean frustrated customers |
| Why might an umbrella-seller want relatively high buffer stocks? | Because rain arrives erratically and high customer demand arrives instantly |
| Why is there a high opportunity cost to holding a large buffer stock? | Because all the money tied up in the stock could be used – profitably – elsewhere in the business |
| Why may JIT be the wrong approach for managing inventory at a hospital? | Because running out of stock may be a life-and-death matter – so buffer stocks are essential |
| Why should companies wanting to minimise their inventory look for suppliers with short lead times? | The faster the supplier can deliver, the less stock you need to hold as a buffer |
| How might the rise of online shopping affect decisions by retailers about inventory? | It gives suppliers a slight buffer between the customer order and the delivery time, making it easier to operate with minimal buffer stock |

### Key terms

**Buffer stock:** the desired minimum stock level held by a firm just in case something goes wrong.

**Competitiveness:** the extent to which a firm can stand up to – or beat – its rivals.

**Opportunity cost:** the cost of missing out on the next best alternative when making a decision (or when committing resources).

**Stockholding costs:** the overheads resulting from the stock levels held by a firm.

### Evaluation: Managing inventory

Stock control is at the heart of many business operations. For retailers such as Zara, Topshop and Primark, the desire for a constant flow of new, fashion-orientated stock means huge pressure to clear away old inventory. Therefore, a JIT approach is ideal, with little or no buffer stock. In some cases it is quite helpful commercially to run out of stock, if it means that, next Saturday, shoppers come earlier to make sure they can get the must-have item. The thing that will not work is when customers go to a clothes shop and see tired, over-fingered stock that's outdated.

Yet there are still firms that believe mass production plus high inventories is the only way to be efficient. If that's what Cadbury says about making chocolate – even the highly seasonal Creme Egg – it would be arrogant to argue. So it is always important to keep an open mind about what is right for a specific company.

# Workbook

## A. Revision questions

(35 marks; 35 minutes)

1. Why may it be important to maintain good relationships with suppliers? (3)

2. State the three main categories of stock. (3)

3. Outline two factors that might lead to a fall in stockholding costs. (4)

4. Explain the difference between inventory reorder level and inventory reorder quantity. (4)

5. Sketch a typical stock control chart. (6)

6. State three costs associated with holding too much stock. (3)

7. Give three costs associated with running out of stock. (3)

8. What is meant by just-in-time stock control? (3)

9. Explain the meaning of the sentence in the text 'The purchaser's reputation is placed in the hands of the external supplier.' (3)

10. Why is inventory control of particular importance to an ice cream seller? (3)

## B. Revision exercises

### DATA RESPONSE 1

Ann Brennan established a bakery in Wigan twenty years ago. Although the firm is profitable, Ann is considering the introduction of modern techniques to help the company develop. In particular, she wishes to introduce information technology to improve communications between her five shops and the central bakery, and to help her manage her stock of raw materials more effectively.

Stocks of raw materials at the business are currently purchased in response to usage. For example, the bakery uses on average of 500 kg of flour per week. The most Ann wishes to hold at any time is 2,000 kg. She would be worried if the stock fell below 500 kg. An order takes one week to arrive, so Ann always reorders when her stock falls to 1,000 kg.

Questions (25 marks; 30 minutes)

1. What is meant by the following terms?
   a) reorder level (2)
   b) buffer stock (2)
   c) lead time. (2)

2. a) Draw a stock control graph for flour at Brennan's Bakery over a six-week period. (6)
   b) Draw a second graph showing the situation if twice the normal amount of flour were used in the fourth week. (6)

3. How might information technology be used to improve communication between Ann's shops and between the bakery and its suppliers? (7)

### DATA RESPONSE 2

**Is JIT always the best option?**

In March 2011 a devastating earthquake and tsunami hit Japan. The effects of this natural disaster were arguably amplified by the widespread use of just-in-time production in Japan, whereby firms operate with very little, if any, buffer stock. This means that a whole production line will grind to a halt if just one component or raw material fails to be delivered by a supplier. The globalised nature of modern supply chains also meant that firms as far away as Britain and America suffered from the natural disaster in Japan. For example, Honda's factory in Britain quickly ran out of imported components from Japan, causing car production to halt in Swindon.

Fujitsu is one of the leading suppliers of semi-conductors in Japan. One of its Japanese factories was badly damaged by the 2011 earthquake, which reduced output. Despite this, Fujitsu was able to bounce back quickly. In less than three months production was back up to the pre-earthquake level. The key to Fujitsu's success was planning. Three years earlier, in response to another earthquake, the company developed an emergency response strategy. The strategy was based on creating additional capacity in other Fujitsu factories located in areas less susceptible to earthquakes. In 2011 Fujitsu wasted no time in implementing its plan, which worked.

Aside from acts of nature and war, manufacturers who want to be successful with JIT need to prepare for demand spikes (A demand spike is a sudden, unexpected upsurge in demand). Both Nintendo and Sony Corp. have had out-of-stock issues with their console systems, notably the PS4 in 2014. 'Just-in-time is OK, but if all of a sudden there is a surge in demand, you may not have the flexibility available to meet the demand,' says one noted business analyst.

## C. Extend your understanding

1. 'The use of information technology makes stock control an automatic function, requiring little input from human beings.' To what extent do you agree with this statement? (20)

### Questions (30 marks; 35 minutes)

1. Explain the one weakness of JIT that was revealed by the 2011 earthquake and tsunami in Japan. (5)

2. A noted business analyst has said that 'JIT is about meticulous planning'. How well did Fujitsu stand up to that test? Explain your answer. (5)

3. Explain one benefit to a business from operating JIT with a zero buffer stock level. (4)

4. To what extent might a JIT approach to stock management be appropriate to a business with demand 'spikes', such as Sony? (16)

2. Evaluate how important it might be for a retailer such as Next to move to a just-in-time system of inventory control. (20)

# Chapter

# 35

# Decision-making to improve operational performance

**Linked to:** Technology and operational efficiency, Chapter 30; Analysing operational performance, Chapter 31; Improving quality, Chapter 32; Managing supply chains, Chapter 33; Managing inventory, Chapter 34.

## Definition

Operational performance implies an evaluation of the effectiveness of the policies that relate capacity utilisation, stock and quality management to the corporate business objectives.

## 35.1 Introduction

Management guru Peter Drucker once wrote that there are only two real business functions: marketing and innovation. Oddly he failed to see that nothing in business matters unless there is sound operational performance. Nobody pays for the promise of a product; they pay for a finished, manufactured, delivered product of the right quality. Operations management matters and therefore the quality of operational decision-making has an important impact on competitiveness.

## 35.2 Operational decisions and competitiveness

In the 50/50 global duopoly market for aeroplanes, Boeing had gained a significant lead in the 250–300 passenger sector thanks to its innovative B787 plane. At the 2014 Farnborough Airshow, Airbus announced the decision to launch a new variation on its A330 aircraft called A330NEO. The wings would be redesigned and new, more fuel-efficient engines attached. And – crucially – the A330NEO would be priced 25 per cent below the $257 million list price for a B787. In this business battle for a sector worth $1 trillion over the next twenty years, operational excellence is a key factor.

In the market for aircraft, there are a series of key factors to consider when choosing between Airbus (Europe) and Boeing (US).

● Function: this is a combination of size (and therefore passenger capacity) and range; long-haul customers want to fly without a refuelling stop.

● Design: some planes are attractive to travellers, making them willing to pay a higher ticket price – which, in turn, helps the manufacturers charge higher prices.

● Economy: the most important element is fuel economy, as fuel accounts for about 30 per cent of all operating costs. Aircraft maintenance is also a big item, accounting for a further 12 per cent of costs

● Reliability: though when the competition is Airbus vs Boeing, no one really takes time over this – both have equally high quality standards

● Availability: if an airline places an order for a Boeing 787 in 2015, it cannot hope for delivery before 2022. This is largely because of supply constraints. In 2014 Boeing produced 787s at a rate of 10 per month. It will increase this capacity to 12 per month in 2016 and 14 by 2019. In the meantime there's a huge queue. So a Chinese airline needing more planes in the next year or so would struggle to get hold of 787s.

To boost its competitiveness the European manufacturer needs to tackle one or more of these issues. If it was able to boost the fuel economy of its aircraft, for instance, that operational step forward should help boost market share.

## 35.3 Operational decisions and the other business functions

In August 2014 the boss of the giant multinational Procter & Gamble (P&G) announced that the company planned to cut in half its huge brand portfolio. Culling perhaps 100 brands would enable the business to focus on the brands making perhaps 95 per cent of the company's profits. This is fundamentally an operational decision designed to help cut costs and therefore boost profit margins.

The knock-on effects, though, will impact the other business functions. If P&G sells higher volumes on fewer product lines, there will be more automation, perhaps leading to a round of redundancies. That will not only affect the human resources function, but also finance. The marketing department will also be affected by the halving of the product portfolio. Marketing staff will have to devise bold strategies to boost sales of the brands being retained.

In business, every decision by one department has a knock-on effect upon the other functions. This is why the job of co-ordination is such an important aspect of management. The table below shows the impact of other operational decisions.

Table 35.1 The impact of operational decisions

| Operational decision | Impact on other functions |
|---|---|
| Build a factory extension to increase production capacity | Marketing must provide the confirmation from a forecast of future sales; finance must provide the capital and HR must plan the workforce flow |
| Outsource a component of production to an outside supplier | HR will need to consult with staff on whether to make redundancies or redeploy; finance will have to fund the exercise – possibly high short-term cash outflows on redundancy payments |
| To move to a just-in-time production strategy | Finance will benefit from improved cash flow; HR will have to plan for more frequent deliveries and more erratic production schedules |

'There's nothing so useless as doing efficiently that which shouldn't be done at all.' Peter Drucker, business academic and writer

## 35.4 Impact on operations of market conditions and competition

In the period 1995–2007, the extremely low labour costs in China made it easy for UK companies to see the attractions of outsourcing to Chinese suppliers, or even building factories in the Far East. Since then the dramatic rise in industrial wages in China (up nearly twenty times in real terms since 1995), plus a strengthening of the Chinese currency, have altered the cost equation. Wages in China today are still much lower than in the West (around a fifth of UK levels), but

they now represent a significant cost. When transport costs and different productivity levels are factored in, the Chinese advantage is less clear-cut.

For one western company, Zara, this change in market conditions is pleasing because they have always kept supply close to their native Spain. This used to be a punishing strain on the company's competitiveness. Today it is far less so. In any case Zara always believed that there was a greater marketing advantage in being able to react quickly to changing fashions – by producing in Europe it could get new designs into UK shops more quickly than waiting for the boat from China.

'China is a great manufacturing centre, but it's actually mostly an assembly plant.' Noam Chomsky, philosopher.

Other market and competition factors affecting operations:

- In August 2014 Sony announced that PS4 sales had passed the 10 million mark, while Xbox One had sold half that figure. Although the higher demand for the Sony product was obvious, both consoles were still being held back by supply problems, nine months after launch. Competition for the highest quality suppliers and supplies is important in high technology markets

- Market demand and variability is another important factor. Some products have highly unpredictable demand, be it ice cream and the weather, clothing sales and changing fashions, toy sales and different fads or the randomising element that comes from a social media craze for a particular item. Operations managers have got to understand their product well enough to choose the right balance between capital-intensive (but inflexible) production and labour-intensive flexibility.

### Real business

In Spring 2014 New Look suddenly found sales booming for one specific beachwear product: a kimono. Between April and August sales ran at 40,000 units a week (an amazing sales level). The company struggled but managed to keep supply levels up to capitalise on this unexpected demand. Clearly it's vital in the fashion business to keep supply lines very flexible. As a result, the company was able to sell £800,000-worth of kimonos a week, helping to boost New Look's April–June sales by 9 per cent and profits by 38 per cent. ⇨

**Figure 35.1** The appeal of kimonos helped to boost New Look's profits in 2014

## 35.5 Ethical and environmental influences on operational decisions

In many companies Corporate Social Responsibility (CSR) lies within the public relations function of the business. Therefore it is understandable that many operations departments see ethical and environmental factors as 'outsourced'. When the Rana Plaza building collapse in Bangladesh killed 1,129 and injured 2,515 textile workers, the UK clothing chain Matalan was caught in the lights of media publicity (along with Primark, Asda and Debenhams). Matalan worsened its own position by dragging its feet about contributing to the victims' compensation fund. It seemed as if the company had neither taken its supply chain responsibilities very seriously, nor had it been quick to accept moral liability in the aftermath of the disaster.

Although there is little evidence that Matalan or Primark's sales are affected significantly by consumer concerns over the supply sources being used, it still could be hoped that some operations managers will push internally to get their companies to do more than is strictly necessary. For example, they could push to set up their own factory inspection teams to monitor what goes on at low-cost suppliers in countries that lack a government-financed inspection regime as exists in the UK.

Other ethical and environmental influences:

● Operations managers who have adopted the philosophy of lean production will see that not only can the approach aid long-term competitiveness and profitability but it will also lead to significant environmental benefits. After all, lean production is about the elimination of waste; lean producers want production to be right first time so that no materials need to be scrapped. Therefore a lean producer should be able to produce the same output as a mass producer, but using fewer materials.

● For ethics to mean anything, they must be given priority over profit rather than seen as a way to generate more business or to differentiate a brand. Therefore one should respect a business that opts into a Fairtrade agreement with suppliers purely because it sees it as morally correct. Is this always the case, though? How is it that Nestlé use the Fairtrade badge on its Kit Kats, yet ignores Fairtrade for other brands such as Yorkie and Quality Street?

## 35.6 Technological influences on operational decisions

It is important at the outset to be clear that however 'obvious' it is that new technology will have boosted labour productivity, the data shows something different. And not just for the UK, as America shows the same pattern: productivity over the past ten years has grown more slowly than in previous decades. See Figure 35.2.

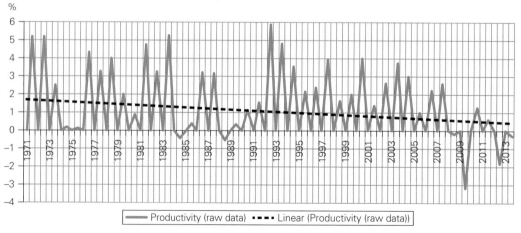

**Figure 35.2** UK labour productivity 1971–2013

*Annual percentage change in output per hour, in constant prices*

Source: Organisation for Economic Co-operation and Development (OECD) 2014

The reality is that modern operations managers have to steer a tricky course between maximum efficiency and customer satisfaction. This is clear to see at any supermarket. At some you'll see half the checkouts open and a queue at every one. In this case labour productivity is being maximised – but at the cost of customers' time (and patience). At another supermarket more checkouts may be open, there may be less queuing, and the occasional 'idle' operator – sitting waiting for the next customer. Result? Happier customers but lower labour productivity figures (and maybe a smacked wrist from head office). So all the new technology in the world cannot prevent operations managers having to think hard about the proper balance between efficiency and customer satisfaction.

Other IT developments and their effect on operational decisions:

- The growth of online businesses creates a greater separation between the company and the production/operational process; for example ASOS doesn't need to ever touch a product. The order for a summer dress comes into the ASOS website together with the customer payment and feeds straight through to the supplier, who packs the item and posts it. In effect almost every aspect of operations is outsourced (except IT and purchasing)

- Better links with customers may be a consequence of new technology, though it could be argued that online relationships are weaker than face-to-face. Online gives opportunities (as on TripAdvisor) for suppliers to gain feedback from customers, and then reply to that feedback. That sounds good until you see that the company feedback looks evermore like a cut-and-paste exercise.

- Better links with suppliers can come about through a permanent EDI (Electronic Data Interchange) connection. This can be used to feed retail customer orders directly through to a factory, enabling the supplier to anticipate orders to come. This makes lean production much more viable.

- Better inventory control is made possible by more accurate data, for which RFID (Radio Frequency Identification) is the ideal technology. A study by Walmart showed that RFID reduced out-of-stocks by 30 per cent on low-selling items. In general, though, the big step forward came with barcodes and laser-barcode readers. Further improvements in inventory management will be relatively marginal.

'The first rule of any technology used in a business is that automation applied to an efficient operation will magnify the efficiency. The second is that automation applied to an inefficient operation will magnify the inefficiency.' Bill Gates, Microsoft founder

## Key terms

**Right first time:** producing with 100 per cent accuracy so that there is no need for re-work (and, ultimately, no need for a quality control/inspection system).

**Workforce flow:** planning for the right combination of recruitment, training and productivity levels to meet future production requirements efficiently.

## Evaluation: Decision-making to improve operational performance

In the 1990s the move by western companies to follow the Japanese towards lean production was hugely significant. It meant that, for a while, changes in operations were often of real importance in company competitiveness. In 2009 this culminated in America's auto giants General Motors and Chrysler both going under and needing to be bailed out by the US government. Only then were significant changes achieved.

Today, most of the big wins have already happened – until dramatic new technologies emerge, or until radical new ways of working come about. Therefore, if you consider any of the big global business battles: VW vs Toyota; Pepsi vs Coke; Unilever vs Procter & Gamble, the factors that sway market share are more to do with marketing or big strategic choices (Kellogg's buying Pringles for example) than to do with operations. James Dyson rightly points out that scientific and engineering expertise is needed to achieve innovation, but the more day-to-day aspects of operations management provide little scope for huge breakthroughs in competitiveness.

## Five Whys and a How

| Question | Answer |
|---|---|
| Why is this function called operations rather than 'production'? | Because 'production' sounds strange for the 80 per cent of UK business that is within the service sector |
| Why may the trend towards online retailing help the move to just-in-time stock management? | Whereas the customer *must* have the precise size and colour available when buying in-store, online ordering gives a day or two to obtain supplies |
| Why might an economic downturn make an operations manager's job easier? | Because it will be easier to negotiate deals with suppliers and there will be less pressure to get huge orders out to retail customers |
| Why might it be short sighted for a clothing retailer to ignore the working conditions of those within its supply chain? | Because the media likes to tell a story about business greed in ignoring the plight of those who create the products that generate the profits |
| Why might outsourcing to overseas suppliers prove a long-term mistake? | Even if unit costs are cut in the short term, future wage levels may rise as in China, reducing the cost advantages; and having suppliers close by gives the advantage of short lead times |
| How might a company measure the performance of a new operations manager? | By monitoring quantifiable data such as reject levels, customer satisfaction levels and stock value per £ of sales. But it's also important to consider qualitative factors such as morale in the factory and the distribution depots |

# Workbook

## A. Revision questions

(35 marks; 35 minutes)

1. Explain how operational decisions might affect the competiveness of **one** of these companies:
   a) Urban Outfitters
   b) British Airways
   c) United Biscuits (McVities) (4)

2. Identify three aspects of operations management that might affect the reliability of a complex durable such as a car. (3)

3. Explain the possible impact on other business functions of an operational decision to 'reshore' production, that is, cancel an outsourced contract and bring production back to the UK. (6)

4. How might a retailer's operational decisions be affected if a new US competitor started offering a virtually identical product range to your own? (6)

5. Figure 35.2 shows that labour productivity has been falling in many of the recent years in the UK. How is this possible? (5)

6. Analyse the benefits of RFID that might explain Walmart's 30 per cent fall in out-of-stocks. (6)

7. In your own words, explain Peter Drucker's statement quoted on page 217. (5)

# B. Revision exercises

## DATA RESPONSE

### Tesco and its suppliers

Tesco has had several years of difficult trading; that is, weak customer demand leading to falling market share and profitability. But buried within the company's website is some more data that could give senior management pause for thought. The graph below shows Tesco's own figures on the views of their own suppliers. And because the response rate from suppliers averages 50 per cent, it is possible that these figures overstate suppliers' attitude to the company.

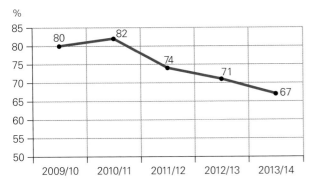

**Figure 35.3** Tesco suppliers: 'I am treated with respect'

Source: *Tesco and Society* reports, from www.tescoplc.com

Perhaps the decline in the suppliers' relationship with Tesco can be related to the February 2013 public relations disaster in which a series of its own-label meat products proved to contain horsemeat. Ultimately, every business needs to manage its relationship with suppliers with as much care as it deals with customers.

### Questions (35 marks; 40 minutes)

1. Describe the information given in the graph shown above. (5)

2. Explain why conclusions from the graph need to bear in mind the suppliers' response rate. (5)

3. Either Tesco knew that its products contained horsemeat, or it chose not to test the products. Analyse the ethics of this situation. (9)

4. To what extent might an increase in the use of technology solve the problem of Tesco's relationship with its suppliers? (16)

# C. Extend your understanding

1. When I buy a chocolate bar I do not consider the working conditions of the West African cocoa farmers. Is it fair, therefore, to expect companies such as Primark to know every detail of the workers within the supply chain from raw cotton through to delivered clothing? Justify your answer. (20)

2. To what extent should the other business functions get involved in key operational decisions such as cutting capacity or moving away from a just-in-time system of inventory control? (20)

**Linked to:** Break-even analysis, Chapter 38; Profit and how to increase it, Chapter 41; Sources of finance, Chapter 43; Decision-making to improve financial performance, Chapter 44.

## Definition

Financial objectives outline what the business wishes to achieve in financial terms during a certain period of time. Constraints are the internal and external factors that affect the firm's ability to achieve these objectives.

## 36.1 How are financial objectives set?

Financial objectives are determined by taking into account the overall company aims. They express the financial aspects of the overall company plan. They will be decided like any other business objective, by taking into account the internal position of the business and the external business environment. The internal aspects of the business, such as what the business is currently doing and what resources it has available, will determine what the business can achieve. This has to be put into the perspective of the external environment. The external environment will affect how easy it is to carry out the plans. An increase in sales is unlikely to be achieved in an economy that is going into recession.

## What makes a good financial objective?

As with any other business objective, financial objectives should be SMART:

- Specific: they should be clearly defined so that all staff know and understand the aims

- Measurable: if the objective can be measured then it is possible to see if the target has been achieved
- Achievable: a good objective is challenging but it must be achievable. To set a target that is impossible is demoralising for staff and it could also create poor shareholder and public confidence if objectives are not met
- Realistic: any objective should make good business sense
- Timebound: financial targets usually relate to the company's financial year. They can also look further into the future.

'You read a book from beginning to end. You run a business the opposite way. You start with the end, and then you do everything you must to reach it.' Harold Geneen, fabled US businessman

## 36.2 Types of financial objective

It is generally assumed that all businesses operate in order to maximise profit. This is of course true to a certain extent. Why would people invest in a business if not to make profit? However, there are other considerations, as outlined below.

### Return on investment

Companies (and people) put their capital at risk whenever they take it out of the bank and invest it in an asset or an activity. Sometimes the investment proves a success, such as Whitbread plc's brilliant purchase of Costa Coffee for £23 million in 1995. Today it's the second biggest coffee shop chain in China, quite apart from being Britain's No. 1. But sometimes the investment proves unwise, either producing disappointing profits or, like Morrisons' purchase of Kiddicare, significant losses.

**Table 36.1** Return on investment: Sublime Costa to Ridiculous Morrisons'.

| | Morrisons' buys Kiddicare | Whitbread buys Costa |
|---|---|---|
| Sum invested | £70 million | £23 million |
| Date of investment | Morrisons' paid this in 2011 for a fast-growing online retailer of kid's clothes | Bought in 1995 from the Costa brothers Bruno and Sergio, who founded Costa in London in 1971 |
| Since then | In March 2014 Morrisons' writes the value of its assets down by £163 million to allow for the horror-show losses made by Kiddicare | |
| Latest information | Kiddicare is sold for £2 million in 2014<br><br>Morrisons' is glad to get rid of the business without further losses | In 2014 Costa's latest profit figure is £110 million |
| Implicit 2014 return on investment (ROI) | In 3 years £163m is lost, i.e. £54.3m a year.<br><br>That's a ROI of -£54.3/£70 x 100 = *minus* 77.6 per cent a year | £110m/£23m x 100 = 478 per cent ROI |

## Financial safety

A key to long-term financial safety is to keep debt levels under control. A good rule of thumb is to say that no more than half a firm's financing should come from debt. Financial analysts are especially likely to check the long-term finances of a business, to see if long-term bank loans are more than half the total sum invested in the business in the long term. It would be a good financial target to say that 50 per cent should be the maximum allowable debt level for the business. This would help to avoid business collapses such as the RBS Bank in 2009 or La Senza retail outlets in 2014.

## Capital structure objectives

To maximise the chance of long-term financial safety, directors need to think of the right capital structure for their business. This should be based on an assessment of the level of operational risks they face. Between 1997 and 2005 French Connection was the coolest young fashion brand in Britain, with its clever logo FCUK. Then the fashion-conscious moved on, leaving French Connection with eight years in the wilderness. Even in 2014 the business was still making operating losses. Fortunately for the company, founder and chief executive Stephen Marks had – during the

good times – made sure that the capital structure was super-safe. He reasoned that fashion businesses are inherently risky; therefore the long-term capital structure was based on zero debt. At the time it hit the rocks operationally, French Connection plc was debt-free and therefore could survive its operational difficulties. If its capital structure has been based on debt, the company would probably have collapsed during the 2009/10 recession.

**Figure 36.1** Logic chain: capital structure

## Capital spending objectives

For businesses in fiercely competitive technological markets, a key to long-term success is to generate high enough profit margins to fund high levels of investment spending on capital equipment and on research and development (R&D). The spending on capital equipment enables the quality and efficiency of production to rise (think industrial robots), while spending on R&D can lead to product innovation. This is the world of Microsoft vs Sony vs Nintendo (games consoles) or Apple vs Samsung (phones, etc.).

To achieve the long-term market share desired by the directors, generous objectives may be needed for capital spending and spending on R&D.

## Cost minimisation

A business may concentrate on minimising costs. Lowering costs will increase profitability. This may be a general overall aim, such as reducing fixed costs by 5 per cent, or it may be more specific, such as reducing wastage in the factory and therefore reducing material costs by 4 per cent. A strategy of cost minimisation may be necessary when times are hard (see Table 36.1).

**Table 36.2** Cost-cutting strategies

| To cut fixed costs | To cut variable costs |
|---|---|
| • Consider closing loss-making branches or factories<br>• Consider moving the head office or main factory to a lower-cost location<br>• Consider carefully whether a layer of management could be removed to reduce staffing costs | • Renegotiate with existing suppliers to try to agree lower prices<br>• Look for new suppliers, perhaps from a low-cost country such as China<br>• Redesign the goods to make them simpler and therefore quicker and cheaper to produce |

## 36.3 Internal and external influences on financial objectives

There are many factors that will influence the way a firm sets its financial objectives. These can be categorised as internal and external constraints.

### Internal influences

#### The ambitions of the leader

In 2014, the appointment of outsider Dave Lewis as Tesco chief executive came with a great deal of decision-making power. In the months leading up to his predecessor's sacking, many senior Tesco executives had left the company. So Dave Lewis could set the agenda and choose his own objectives. In fact he chose to take his time before deciding what the targets should be. As he was an outside appointment (from Unilever) City analysts were willing to give him that time.

#### Financial

Although it may seem strange to talk about internal finance as a constraint on financial objectives, it can play an important part. The pursuit of higher profit might be constrained by lack of cash flow, especially at times when demand is rising sharply.

#### Operational

A firm that is close to full capacity may find that it has fewer opportunities for improving the profitability of the business, unless it has the confidence and the resources to increase capacity, perhaps by moving to bigger premises.

'We want to become the fastest-growing company with the highest profit margins in the business of renting and leasing vehicles without drivers.' Robert Townsend, former Chairman of Avis car rentals

### Real business

**Table 36.3** Financial objectives of major businesses

| Company | Financial objectives |
|---|---|
| Thornton's Chocolate plc | (2012) 'To boost operating margins to match the industry average within three years'; by 2013 margins had risen from 1.3 per cent to 3.3 per cent. |
| ASOS plc | 'To achieve a £1 billion annual sales turnover.' In the 2014 financial year sales were over £955 million, so the target was in sight. |
| Marks & Spencer plc | 'An online push to target the 19 million customers who shop at our stores, but shop elsewhere online' (May 2014) |

### External influences

#### Competitive environment

The plans of almost every business can be affected by the behaviour and reaction of competitors. A plan to increase profit margins by increasing prices may be wrecked if competitors react by reducing theirs.

#### Economic environment

The state of the economy plays a vital part in the ability of a business to meet its financial objectives. Higher taxes might reduce customers' disposable income and therefore spending, so financial objectives may not be met. The effect will depend on the business. Supermarket own-brand producers (of 'inferior goods') may do better, whereas branded goods may suffer.

#### Government

A firm may find its financial objectives limited by regulatory or legislative activity. Consumer watchdogs such as the Office of Fair Trading (OFT) have powers to fine businesses that they believe are not acting in the best interests of consumers. Legislation may also be introduced that increases business costs.

### Building the outside in

Good business planning involves being aware of the possible external influences that may act as constraints. External constraints will always be subject to more uncertainty as they are outside the control of the business. It is therefore important when setting financial objectives that the business includes a series of 'what if' scenarios. This will prepare them for outside factors that may impede their progress.

## 36.4 The use of data for financial decisions

In new product development it can be argued that pure judgement may prove more successful than carefully researched 'facts'. Certainly that is what Apple says. If you look at Apple's accounts, however, you are left in no doubt that their finance director is as serious-minded as every other. In finance, decisions are made on the basis of data.

Apple's capital structure, therefore, will be decided upon after careful analysis of the company's accounts and those of rivals. Apple wants to stand out because of its products, not because its finances seem curious.

Every finance director will have daily information available to show the latest trends in profits, profitability, balance sheet health, cash flow and much more. All financial decisions are driven by data.

## 36.5 Ethical and environmental influences on financial decisions

In some businesses the pursuit of profit may cause conflict between the different groups with an interest in the business (the stakeholders), as in the following examples.

- The rise of interest in the environment has meant that costs have increased for many firms and therefore profit has been reduced. However, many firms have also discovered that they can make huge savings, such as by limiting waste.

- Some firms, most notably supermarket chains, are accused of driving the prices of their suppliers to the lowest possible level. Low supply costs increase profits. Businesses need to ensure that there is a balance between keeping costs low and maintaining the quality of the supplies. In the food chain, tough bargaining by supermarkets may cause unacceptable welfare conditions for animals such as chickens and piglets. This, in turn, may backfire, affecting the retailer's reputation.

- Taxation may be a consideration. Large multinational companies may deliberately reduce profit figures in one country in order to pay less tax, increasing profit figures in another where profits are taxed at a lower level.

  They are able to do this by charging differential prices between subsidiaries in different countries. Such tax avoidance is legal, but arguably not ethical.

- Public image: a firm may choose to spend money on charitable concerns or sponsorship. This, as a cost, will reduce profit. However, it may well get a return on its investment through creating a better brand image or good public relations.

### Key terms

**Cash flow:** the flow of cash into and out of the business.

**External constraint:** Something outside the firm's control that can prevent it achieving its objectives.

**Full capacity:** when the business is fully utilising all its assets.

**Public limited company (plc):** a company with limited liability and shares that are available to the public. Its shares are usually quoted on the stock exchange.

**Stakeholders:** groups with an interest in the success or failure of a firm's decisions and actions.

### Evaluation: Financial objectives

There are advantages and disadvantages to setting tight financial objectives. Some people consider that objectives are vital to give direction to the business. A good set of objectives will enable plans for each sector of the business to be developed. Each individual within the organisation will then know the role that they are to play. Without objectives, the business may drift aimlessly.

Other people consider that objectives can stifle entrepreneurship and initiative. They feel that managers operate to satisfy the objectives but do not go beyond them. They also feel that they dampen risk-taking, which may prevent a business from taking the kind of leaps forward shown by Apple (iPhone, iPad) and Nintendo (Wii).

'Rapid growth is not necessarily the best measure of success. Indeed it is probably detrimental to most businesses.' Mark Spohr, US company president

## Five Whys and a How

| Question | Answer |
|---|---|
| Why might a small, fast-growing company focus its financial objectives on cash-flow objectives? | Because cash-flow difficulties are common among fast-growing firms |
| Why might a firm focus on financing higher R&D spending? | To stay competitive with other, perhaps overseas, high-technology companies |
| Why might employees think that senior management sees business ethics as subordinate to profit? | Because financial objectives that only mention profit or profitability implicitly suggest that ethics come second |
| Why may a firm's financial objectives seem impossible to achieve when a recession kicks in? | If the company mainly produces luxury goods it may be impossible, in the short term, to overcome falling sales and profits |
| Why might a plc keep its financial objectives secret? | Because it doesn't want competitors to plan accordingly: 'if they're focusing on cost minimisation we can increase our advertising spending and they won't follow us.' |
| How might a private school be affected by a capital structure based largely on debt? | Like any other business, a period of poor trading may cause the debts to accumulate, threatening the school's future |

# Workbook

## A. Revision questions

(30 marks; 30 minutes)

1. What is meant by 'financial objectives'? (2)

2. Why is improving or maintaining profit likely to be the most important financial objective? (4)

3. Outline two examples of how stakeholder interests could affect the setting of business objectives. (4)

4. Outline two likely results for shareholders if profits fall. (4)

5. List and explain two possible internal constraints on achieving the financial objectives for a multinational chocolate producer. (6)

6. Discuss two external constraints that should be taken into account when financial objectives are set by *one* of the following businesses.
   a) Spotify (rapidly growing subscription service for streamed music)
   b) ASOS (rapidly growing online clothes retailer)
   c) Versace clothing. (8)

7. What government activity could act as a constraint on businesses achieving their financial objectives? Give an example. (2)

## B. Revision exercises

### DATA RESPONSE

#### Ethics and financial decisions at Glaxo

In July 2013 Gao Feng, the head of China's fraud unit, accused Glaxo Smith Kline (GSK) of bribing Chinese doctors to get them to buy GSK vaccines. GSK is one of Britain's largest pharmaceutical companies, so the London-based media were sceptical of these claims. Gao Feng, though, said: 'We found that bribery is a core part of the activities of the company. To boost their share price and sales, the company performed illegal actions.'

Later in the year, GSK implicitly accepted that up to £300 million in bribes had been paid in China. Later, further accusations of bribery by GSK staff emerged in Poland, Iraq, Jordan and Lebanon.

In July 2014 chief executive Sir Andrew Witty made it clear that the allegations were 'contrary to the values' he believed in. The company's 2013 Corporate Responsibility report spoke of 'our four core values: transparency, respect for people, integrity and patient-focus.' Unfortunately, as reported by the authoritative *Forbes* magazine: 'investors are still uneasy about the criminal probe by Chinese officials into allegations that GSK executives engaged in widespread bribery. GSK executives have been accused of illegally paying doctors, hospitals and other medical organisations in an effort to increase sales of Glaxo products.'

Sir Christopher Gent, GSK Chairman, said in the 2012 annual accounts (the report immediately before the bribery crisis emerged): 'Ultimately the aim of our strategy is to deliver sustainable earnings per share growth (EPS) and improved returns to shareholders.' His objective of improved profits and higher dividends to shareholders could help explain the pressures on staff that might lead to fraudulent behaviour.

### Questions (25 marks; 30 minutes)

1. Analyse the factors GSK might take into account when setting financial objectives for its next financial year. (9)

2. To what extent is it inevitable that profit comes into conflict with ethics in business today? (16)

## C. Extend your understanding

1. Evaluate the importance of external influences on the financial objectives of a business such as easyJet. (20)

2. For a business such as BP, to what extent should environmental factors influence financial decisions? (20)

**Linked to:** Break-even analysis, Chapter 38; Profit and how to increase it, Chapter 41.

### Definition

Revenue is the value of total sales made by a business within a period, usually one year.

Costs are the expenses incurred by a firm in producing and selling its products, such as wages and raw materials.

Profit is made when a firm's sales revenue exceeds its total costs.

## 37.1 The measurement and importance of profit

Profit is measured by deducting all business costs from the revenues generated within a trading period – say six months. Business people sometimes say that 'revenue is vanity; profit is sanity'. In other words, making lots of sales feels great, but there is no business purpose in selling things unless profits are generated. Full details on measuring profit are covered in Section 37.4.

Profits are important for the following reasons:

- They provide a measure of the success of the organisation
- Profits are the best source of capital for investment in the growth of the business, for example, to finance new store openings or to pay for new product development
- They act as a magnet to attract further funds from investors enticed by the possibility of high returns on their investment.

'One of our most important management tasks is maintaining the proper balance between short-term profit performance and investment for future strength and growth.' David Packard, computer pioneer

However, it is not uncommon for a new business to fail to make profits in the first months – or even years – of trading. The need to generate profits becomes more important as time passes. A business ultimately needs to make profits to reward its owners for putting money into the enterprise.

Perhaps oddly, profit is also important to not-for-profit organisations such as charities. In the 2009 recession charitable giving in the UK fell by 11 per cent. A charity with important long-term programmes such as Oxfam would have needed to dip into their reserves to tide themselves over the fall in their income. Accumulated profits can insulate organisations from erratic factors, allowing them to keep achieving their stated objectives.

To understand profit fully, it is first necessary to look at revenues and costs.

## 37.2 Business revenues

The revenue received by a firm as a result of trading activities is a critical factor in its success. Entrepreneurs start their financial planning by assessing the revenue that they are likely to receive during the coming financial year. This can be calculated using this formula:

$$\text{Sales revenue} = \text{volume of goods sold} \times \text{average selling price}$$

A firm seeking to increase its revenue can plan to sell more or aim to sell at a higher price. Some firms may maintain high prices even though this policy depresses sales. Such companies, perhaps selling fashion or high-technology products, believe that in the long run this approach will lead to higher revenue and higher profits.

The term revenue is also sometimes referred to as 'turnover' or 'sales'.

### Real business

**Blackberry's falling revenue**

In the three months ending 30 November Blackberry saw its revenue plunge from £1,660 million in 2012 'to £730 million in 2013. The reason for the 56 per cent fall in revenue was a collapse in phone sales from 3.7 to 1.9 million, plus a fall in the average price charged per Blackberry. The company had pinned everything on a new range of phones based on a new operating system, but it proved unable to dent sales of the iPhone and the Samsung Galaxy. As a consequence of the revenue decline, Blackberry made losses of £2.7 billion in its third quarter of 2013.

The other way to boost revenue is to charge a low price in an attempt to sell as many products as possible. In some markets this may lead to high revenues and profits. Firms following this approach are likely to be operating in markets in which the goods are fairly similar and consumers do not exhibit strong preferences for any brand. This is true of the market for young holidaymakers going to Spain or Thailand. Price competition is fierce as businesses seek to maximise their revenue.

Traditionally, companies printed price lists that might run for 12 months. These days online purchasing makes dynamic pricing more common; that is, allowing prices to rise and fall depending on demand and supply conditions. This is a way to maximise revenue, by charging high prices when demand is at its highest, but much more modest prices during periods of low demand. Football teams such as West Ham do something similar, offering 'Kids for a Quid' when their home game is against an unfashionable opponent such as Stoke City.

## Real business

### *Price manipulation for maximised revenue*

In a world increasingly dominated by online purchasing, businesses have the ability to vary prices to maximise revenue. This is quite open with airline prices where, for example, the easyJet Sunday 11.40 a.m. flight to Barcelona was priced at £98.99 for 28 December, £41.99 for 25 January, and £65.99 for 1 March 2015 (prices as at 16 December 2014). But it's less clear-cut with online purchasing of insurance, where the same car might cost £475 to insure on a Monday and £650 on a Tuesday, as the sellers try to reward those who can be bothered to shop around while simultaneously catching out the lazier shoppers. As the saying goes: let the buyer beware!

## 37.3 The costs of production

Costs are a critical element of the information necessary to manage a business successfully. Managers need to be aware of the costs of all aspects of their business for a number of reasons.

- They need to know the cost of production to assess whether it is profitable to supply the market at the current price.
- They need to know actual costs to allow comparisons with their forecasted (or budgeted) figures. This will allow them to make judgements concerning the cost-efficiency of different parts of the business.

## Fixed and variable costs

This is an important classification of the costs encountered by businesses. This classification has a number of uses. For example, it is the basis for calculating break even, which is covered in Chapter 38.

### Fixed costs

Fixed costs are any costs that do not vary directly with the level of output. These costs are linked to time rather than to level of business activity. Fixed costs exist even if a business is not producing any goods or services. An example of a fixed cost is rent, which is usually calculated monthly, but will remain the same whether business is great or awful that month. The landlord doesn't care; she or he just wants to be paid!

If a manufacturer can double output from within the same factory, the amount of rent will not alter, thus it is a fixed cost. In the same way, a seaside hotel has mortgage and salary costs during the winter, even though there may be very few guests. Given that fixed costs are inevitable, it is vital that managers work hard at bringing in customers to keep the fixed costs covered.

In Figure 37.1, you can see that the firm faces fixed costs of £50,000 irrespective of the level of output.

Other examples of fixed costs include the uniform business rate (local taxes), management salaries, interest charges and depreciation.

In the long term, fixed costs can alter. The manufacturer referred to earlier may decide to increase output significantly. This may require renting additional factory space and negotiating loans for additional capital equipment. Thus rent will rise as may interest payments. We can see that in the long term fixed costs may alter, but that in the short term they are — as their name suggests — fixed.

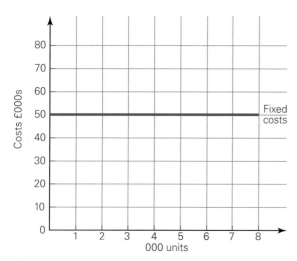

**Figure 37.1** Fixed costs of £50,000 per year

## Variable costs

Variable costs are those costs which vary directly with the level of output. They represent payments made for the use of inputs such as labour, fuel and raw materials. If our manufacturer doubled output then these costs would double. A doubling of the sales of innocent Strawberry Smoothies would require twice the purchasing of strawberries and bananas. There would also be extra costs for the packaging, the wage bill and the energy required to fuel the production line.

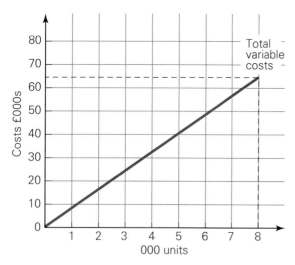

**Figure 37.2** Variable costs of £8 per unit

The graph in Figure 37.2 shows a firm with variable costs of £8 per unit of production. This means that variable costs rise steadily with, and proportionately to, the level of output. Thus a 10 per cent rise in output will increase total variable costs by the same percentage.

However, it is not always the case that variable costs rise in proportion to output. Many small businesses discover that as they expand, variable costs do not rise as quickly as output. A key reason for this is that as the business becomes larger it is able to negotiate better prices with suppliers. Its suppliers are likely to agree to sell at lower unit prices when the business places larger orders.

Examples of some variable, fixed and hard-to-classify costs are given in Table 37.1.

**Table 37.1** Some costs are easy to classify, some are hard

| Variable costs | Fixed costs | Hard to classify |
|---|---|---|
| Raw materials | Rent | Delivery costs |
| Packaging | Heating and Lighting | Electricity |
| Piece-rate labour | Salaries | Machine maintenance costs |
| Commission (percentage on sales) | Interest charges | Energy |

## Total costs

When added together, fixed and variable costs give the total costs for a business. This is, of course, a very important element in the calculation of the profits earned by a business.

The relationship between fixed, variable and total costs is straightforward to calculate but has some important implications for a business. If a business has relatively high fixed costs as a proportion of total costs, then it is likely to seek to maximise its sales to ensure that the fixed costs are spread across as many units of output as possible. In this way, the impact of high fixed costs is lessened.

### Real business

#### Paying the costs

In 2012 Scoop opened its third London ice cream parlour. The company intended to continue making all the ice cream at the original Covent Garden store, but deliver ice cream daily to the new branch at Gloucester Road (two miles away). This meant that all the fixed production costs would remain unchanged (rent on the floor space, the machinery and the professional ice cream maker's salary). Variable costs would increase by around 50 per cent, as long as the new parlour's sales matched the first two. These costs would be the ingredients, especially milk, cream and sugar; plus the cost of the electricity to run the ice cream-making machines. There would also be some brand new fixed costs: an extra refrigerated van plus the rent and the staff at the new premises. Overall, owner Matteo Pantani knew that he could increase his revenue by 50 per cent while total costs should increase by no more than 30 per cent. This should boost profit considerably.

## 37.4 Profits

Profit occurs when revenues are greater than costs. The key formula is:

Profit = total revenue − total costs

### Calculating profits

Although the profit formula is simple (revenue − costs), it is easy to make mistakes when calculating the figures. The problems rarely come from calculating revenue; the hard part is getting total costs right. The following example may help:

> **Worked example**
>
> Gwen and John's pasta restaurant charges £10 for three courses and has an average of 800 customers per week. The variable costs are £4 per customer and the restaurant has fixed costs of £3,400 per week. To calculate profit:
> 1. Calculate revenue:
>    Price × no. of customers
>    £10 × 800 = £8,000
> 2. Calculate total costs:
>    Fixed costs + total variable costs (No. of customers × variable costs per meal)
>    £3,400 + (800 × £4 = £3,200)
> 3. Calculate profit:
>    Total revenue − Total costs
>    £8,000 − (£3,400 + £3,200) = £1,400 per week
>
> See the Workbook section for exercises to practise this very important skill.

'If you're not in business for fun or profit, what are you doing here?' Robert Townsend, the original business guru

## 37.5 Revenue, cost and profit objectives

In 2014 Italian café chain Carluccio's, with £120 million of sales from its 81 outlets, set itself the objective of doubling revenue within the next four years. This could be achieved by increasing its £1.5 million revenue per outlet or – more probably – by doubling the number of cafés it has. Having set that objective it can calculate how much capital will be required; work out how much it can generate from within the business; and then see how much might be needed from outside.

Carluccio's revenue objectives also make it possible (necessary, even) to set cost objectives. In other words, set maximum cost levels for the start-up cost of each new outlet plus cost objectives for the food costs, staff costs and overheads costs per outlet. From the revenue and cost objectives will come the calculation of likely profit (though the profit figure will depend a great deal on how successful the new outlets prove to be).

The purpose behind setting these objectives is to ensure that every manager in the business understands how they fit together. For a business such as Carluccio's there can be a serious gap between what head office thinks and knows, and what is known by the 81 operating stores. It can make it easier to delegate authority to the store managers if they are clear about the revenue, cost and profit objectives.

**Figure 37.3** Logic chain: setting profit objectives

## Five Whys and a How

| Question | Answer |
|---|---|
| Why is it important for businesses to make a profit? | Because that provides the long-term capital for reinvestment and for business expansion |
| Why might a business want to separate its variable from its fixed costs? | Because it helps it to analyse the impact on profit of a change in demand or change in price |
| Why would a firm be worried if its revenue had slipped below its total costs? | Because it would be making operating losses; in the short-term that might be okay, but continual operating losses would force the company to close |
| Why might a business choose to lower its prices? | Because it feels that the increase in sales volume will outweigh the loss in revenue caused by the price cut, pushing total revenue up |
| Why might companies such as Aldi be willing to operate with low prices that provide low profits per item sold? | It's okay to have low profits per sale as long as you can sell masses of units. Aldi makes strong operating profits because its rate of sale is high |
| How does revenue differ from profit? | Revenue is just the value of sales, without taking costs into account. Profit includes the deduction of costs |

## Key terms

**Dynamic pricing:** using software that allows changing demand and supply levels to set ever-changing prices, as used by airlines and hotel chains.

**Fixed costs:** these costs do not vary as output (or sales) vary.

**Piece-rate labour:** paying workers per item they make; that is, without regular pay.

**Profit margin:** profit as a percentage of sales revenue.

**Total costs:** all the costs of producing a specific output level; that is, fixed costs plus total variable costs.

**Total variable costs:** all the variable costs of producing a specific output level; that is, variable costs per unit multiplied by the number of units sold.

**Variable costs:** the costs of producing one unit (can be known as unit variable costs).

## Evaluation: Calculating revenue, costs and profits

When evaluating costs, revenues and profits for a new enterprise it is necessary to judge the likely accuracy of the forecast figures. It is also worth thinking about whether profits are the best measure of success for a new business. A successful first year of trading may see an enterprise gain a customer base and repeat orders by supplying at competitive prices. This may result in small profits initially while the business builds a reputation. Profits may become a more important measure of success in the longer term.

An assessment of the true worth of a business's performance as measured by its profits would also take account of the general state of the economy. Are businesses in general prospering, or is it a time of recession? They would also take into account any unusual circumstances such as, for example, the business being subject to the emergence of a new competitor.

# Workbook

## A. Revision questions

(30 marks; 30 minutes)

1. Why may a business initially receive relatively low revenues from a product newly introduced to the market? (3)

2. State two circumstances in which a company may be able to charge high prices for a new product? (2)

3. For what reasons may a firm seek to maximise its sales revenue? (4)

4. If a business sells 4,000 units of brand X at £4 each and 2,000 units of brand Y at £3 each, what is its total revenue? (4)

5. Outline two reasons why firms need to know the costs they incur in production. (4)

6. Distinguish, with the aid of examples, between fixed and variable costs. (4)

7. Explain why fixed costs can only alter in the long term. (3)

8. Give two reasons why profits are important to businesses. (2)

9. State one advantage and one disadvantage that may result from a business deciding to lower the proportion of profits it distributes to its owners. (2)

10. State two purposes for which a business's profits could be used. (2)

## B. Revision exercises

### DATA RESPONSE 1

(30 marks; 30 minutes)

1. During the summer weeks Devon Ice Cream has average sales of 4,000 units a week. Each ice cream sells for £1 and has variable costs of 25p. Fixed costs are £800.

   a) Calculate the weekly total costs for the business in the summer. (3)

   b) Calculate Devon Ice Cream's weekly profit in the summer. (3)

2. a) If a firm sells 200 Widgets at £3.20 and 40 Squidgets at £4, what is its total revenue? (3)

   b) Each Widget costs £1.20 to make, while each Squidget costs £1.50. What are the total variable costs? (3)

   c) If fixed costs are £300, what profit is the business making? (3)

3. 'Last week our sales revenue was £12,000, which was great. Our price is £2 a unit, which I think is a bit too cheap.'

   a) How many unit sales were made last week? (2)

   b) If a price rise to £2.25 cuts sales to 5,600 units, calculate the change in the firm's revenue. (4)

4. BYQ Co. has sales of 4,000 units a month, a unit price of £4, fixed costs of £9,000 and unit variable costs of £1. Calculate its profit. (4)

5. At full capacity output of 24,000 units, a firm's costs are as follows:

   | | |
   |---|---|
   | managers' salaries | £48,000 |
   | materials | £12,000 |
   | rent and rates | £24,000 |
   | piece-rate labour | £36,000 |

   a) What are the firm's total costs at 20,000 units? (4)

   b) What profit will be made at 20,000 units if the selling price is £6? (1)

### DATA RESPONSE 2

#### Chalfont Computer Services Ltd

Robert has decided to give up his job with BT and to work for himself offering computer services to local people. He has paid off his mortgage and owns his house outright, so feels this is the time to take a risk. Robert has no experience of running a business, but is skilled in repairing computers and solving software problems. In the past Robert has repaired computers belonging to friends and family and is aware of the costs involved in providing this service. He believes that with the increase in internet usage there will be plenty of demand for his services. Robert has spoken to a few people in his local pub and this has confirmed his opinion. Robert needs to raise £10,000 to purchase equipment for his business and to pay for a new vehicle and intends to ask his bank for a loan.

The work Robert has already done allows him to forecast that the average revenue from each customer will be £40, while the variable costs will be £15. His monthly fixed costs will be £1,000. Table 37.2 gives Robert's estimates of the number of customers he expects to have.

**Table 37.2** Estimates of number of customers

| Month | Number of customers |
|-------|---------------------|
| January | 40 |
| February | 50 |
| March | 60 |
| April | 82 |

**Questions (20 marks, 25 minutes)**

1. What is meant by the term 'variable costs'? (2)

2. Calculate Robert's forecast profits for his first three months' trading. (3)

3. Robert estimates that if he cut his prices by 10 per cent he would have 20 per cent more customers each month. Calculate the outcome of these changes and whether this would benefit Robert. (6)

4. Analyse the case for a bank lending Robert £10,000 on the basis of his forecast profits. (9)

## C. Extend your understanding

1. In 2014 Tesco plc suffered a slide in its sales, with weekly data showing a 4 per cent decline compared with 2013. To what extent is it possible for a supermarket chain to rebuild its revenue without damaging its profit? (20)

2. When a rival surfing school opened next door, Jo's Surf School started to make weekly losses. To what extent would cutting variable costs restore Jo's Surf School's profitability? (20)

# Chapter 38 Break-even analysis

Linked to: Calculating revenue, costs and profit, Chapter 37; Profit and how to increase it, Chapter 41.

## Definition

Break-even analysis compares a firm's revenue with its fixed and variable costs to identify the minimum level of sales needed to cover costs. This can be shown on a graph known as a break-even chart.

## 38.1 Introduction

Businesses need to know how many products they have to produce and sell in order to cover all of their costs. This is particularly important for new businesses with limited experience of their markets.

Look at Table 38.1, which shows forecast revenue and cost figures for a new business.

Table 38.1 Forecast revenue and cost figures for a new business

| Output of ties (per week) | Sales income (£ per week) | Total costs (£ per week) |
|---|---|---|
| 0 | 0 | 10000 |
| 100 | 4000 | 11500 |
| 200 | 8000 | 13000 |
| 300 | 12000 | 14500 |
| **400** | **16000** | **16000** |
| 500 | 20000 | 17500 |
| 600 | 24000 | 19000 |

You can easily identify that 400 is the number of sales that must be achieved each week to break even. If sales are only 200 units the business will be making losses of a punishing £5,000 a week, so the break-even analysis is providing vital data.

To calculate the break-even point we need information on both costs and prices. Break-even can be shown on a graph or, more quickly, calculated in the following way.

## 38.2 Calculating break even

Calculating the break-even point for a product requires knowledge of:

● the selling price of the product
● its fixed costs
● its variable costs per unit.

Fixed costs are expenses which do not change in response to changing demand or output, such as rent and salaries. Variable costs will alter in relation to changes in demand and therefore output. A doubling of demand will double variable costs, but leave fixed costs the same.

The break-even output level can be calculated by the following formula:

$$\text{Break-even output} = \frac{\text{fixed costs}}{(\text{selling price per unit} - \text{variable cost per unit})}$$

## Real business

Igloo ice cream costs 50p per unit to make and is sold for £2.50. The fixed costs of running the production process and the shop amount to £2,000 per week. Therefore the break-even output level is:

$$\frac{\text{Fixed costs}}{(\text{selling price per unit} - \text{variable cost per unit})} = \frac{£2,000}{£2.50 - 50p}$$

$$= 1,000 \text{ ice creams per week}$$

So although a £2 surplus per ice cream seems a lot of profit, it's only the 1001st ice cream that really makes £2. Before getting to the break-even point each ice cream sold is simply reducing the losses.

⇨

'(HMV) is now in danger of failing to break even in the full-year.' Nick Bubb, retail analyst (in December 2011, not long before the company collapsed into administration)

## 38.3 Contribution

In the above formula for break even, price *minus* variable costs is known as contribution. It is the surplus of £2 between the £2.50 selling price and the variable costs of 50p per unit.

Contribution per unit = selling price *minus* variable costs per unit

Total contribution = contribution per unit × quantity sold

So, in the above example, if 1,200 ice creams were sold, the total contribution would be: £2 × 1,200 ice creams = £2,400

Total contribution is a useful short-cut way to calculate profit, as:

Total contribution – fixed costs = profit

So,       £2,400 – £2,000 = £400 profit

## 38.4 Break-even charts

A break-even chart is a graph showing the revenue and costs for a business at all possible levels of demand or output. The break-even chart uses the horizontal axis to represent the output per time period for the business, for example, between 0 and 1,000 units a month. The vertical axis represents costs and sales in pounds.

### Real business

#### Berry & Hall Ltd

Berry & Hall Ltd manufactures confectionery. The company is planning to launch a new sweet called Aromatics at a price of £5 per kg. The variable cost of production per kg is forecast at £3 and the fixed costs associated with this product are estimated to be £50, 000 a year. The company's maximum output of Aromatics will be 50,000 kg per year.

First, put scales on the axes. The horizontal output scale has a range from zero to the company's maximum output of 50,000 kg. The vertical axis records values of costs and revenues. For the maximum vertical value, multiply the maximum output by the selling price and then place values on the axis up to this figure. In this case it will have a maximum value on the axis of £250,000 (£5 × 50,000 kg). ⇨

Having drawn the axes and placed scales upon them, the first line we enter is fixed costs. Since this value does not change with output it is simply a horizontal line drawn at £50,000.

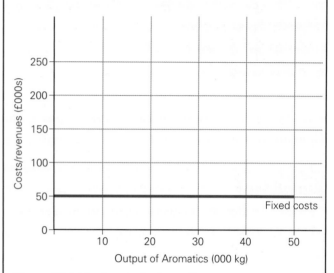

Figure 38.1 Fixed costs for Aromatics

Next, add on variable costs to arrive at total costs. Total costs start from the left hand of the fixed costs line and rise diagonally. To see where they rise to, calculate the total cost at the maximum output level. In the case of Aromatics this is 50,000 kg per year. The total cost is fixed costs (£50,000) plus variable costs of producing 50,000 kg (£3 × 50,000 = £150,000). The total cost at this level of output is £50,000 + £150,000 = £200,000.

This point can now be marked on the chart; that is, £200,000 at an output level of 50,000 kg. This can be joined by a straight line to total costs at zero output: £50,000. This is illustrated in Figure 38.2.

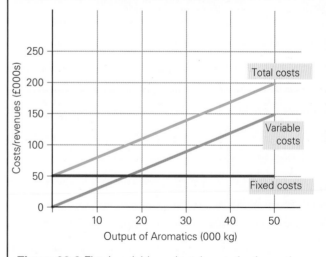

Figure 38.2 Fixed, variable and total costs for Aromatics

Finally, sales revenue must be added. For the maximum level of output, calculate the sales revenue ⇨

⇨ and mark this on the chart. In the case of Aromatics the maximum output per year is 50,000 kg; multiplied by the selling price this gives £250,000 each year. If Berry & Hall does not produce and sell any Aromatics it will not have any sales revenue. Thus zero output results in zero income. A straight diagonal line from zero to £250,000 represents the sales revenue (see Figure 38.3).

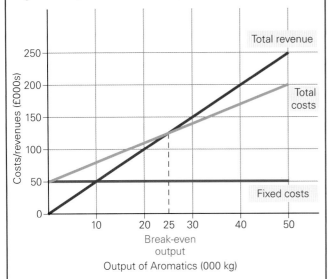

**Figure 38.3** Break-even output for Aromatics

This brings together costs and revenues for Aromatics. A line drawn down from the point at which total costs and sales revenue cross shows the break-even output. For Aromatics, it is 25,000 kg per year. This can be checked using the formula method explained earlier.

## 38.5 Using break-even charts

Various pieces of information can be taken from break-even charts such as that shown in Figure 38.3. As well as the level of break-even output, it also shows the level of profits or losses at every possible level of output. Many conclusions can be reached, such as:

● Any level of output lower than 25,000 kg per year will mean the product is making a loss. The amount of the loss is indicated by the vertical distance between the total cost and the total revenue line

● Sales in excess of 25,000 kg of Aromatics per year will earn the company a profit. If the company produces and sells 30,000 kg of Aromatics annually, it will earn a profit of £10,000

● **The margin of safety**. This is the amount by which demand can fall before the firm starts making losses. It is the difference between current sales and the break-even point. If annual sales of Aromatics were 40,000 kg, with a break-even output of 25,000 kg, then the margin of safety would be 15,000 kg.

Margin of safety = sales *minus* break-even point

Margin of safety = 40,000 – 25,000

= 15,000 kg

The higher the margin of safety the less likely it is that a loss-making situation will develop. The margin of safety is illustrated in Figure 38.4.

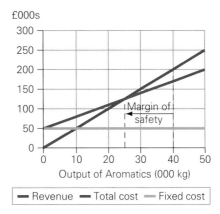

**Figure 38.4** Margin of safety

Figure 38.4 shows how changes in business circumstances affect the break-even chart.

**Table 38.2** How changes in business circumstances affect the break-even chart

| | Cause | Effect |
|---|---|---|
| **Internal factors** | Extra launch advertising | Fixed costs rise, so total costs rise and the break-even point rises |
| | Planned price increase | Revenue rises more steeply; break-even point falls |
| | Using more machinery (and less labour) in production | Fixed costs rise while variable costs fall; uncertain effect on break-even point |
| **External factors** | Fall in demand | Break-even point is not affected, though margin of safety is reduced |
| | Competitors' actions force price cut | Revenue rises less steeply; break-even point rises |
| | Fuel costs rise | Variable and total cost lines rise more steeply; break-even point rises |

## 38.6 The effects of changes in price, output and cost

On its own, a limitation of the break-even chart is that it's a static model. It doesn't show sales trends over time. Fortunately it can be a useful method for showing when changes are planned, for example, when the business is considering a price increase.

The main changes to consider are:

1. The impact on revenue, profits and break even of a change in price
2. The impact on revenue and profits of a change in demand, perhaps because the product has become more or less fashionable
3. The effect of a rise or fall in variable costs such as raw materials
4. The effect of a rise or fall in fixed costs, perhaps when a business chooses to 'downsize' to smaller, cheaper head office premises.

### 1. Price rise:

If a company increases its prices, its revenue line will rise more steeply than before. The line will start at the same point as before (0 sales = 0 revenue) but will rise to a higher revenue point at maximum output. This steepening of the revenue line will increase the profit potential at each level of output and lower the break-even point. So if you charge more, you don't need to sell as many to break even. This is shown in Figure 38.5.

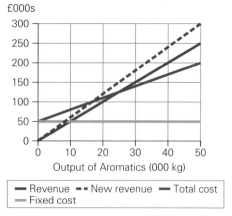

£000s

Figure 38.5 A rise in price; price increase to £6

### 2. A rise or fall in demand:

A change in demand has no effect on the lines of the break-even chart. It is simply that you have to read the change off the chart by drawing a line vertically up from the new sales quantity.

### 3. Rise in variable costs:

Between March and November the price of cocoa beans rose from $2,150 per tonne to $2,700. This 25 per cent increase would make the variable costs line rise more steeply, though it would start from the same point (zero). Naturally, if the variable costs rise, the total costs must also be affected. So if you are asked to show the effect on a break-even chart of a rise in variable costs, you must also adjust the total cost line. This is shown in Figure 38.6 – though in relation to Aromatics, not cocoa beans.

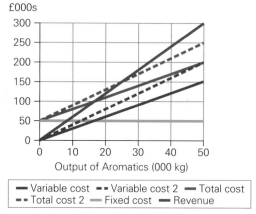

£000s

Figure 38.6 A rise in variable costs

### 4. Fall in fixed costs:

If a company's sales are falling it may be necessary to cut fixed costs in order to lower the break-even point. The fall in fixed costs will cut the total costs. All these things are indicated in Figure 38.7.

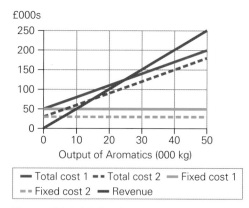

£000s

Figure 38.7 A fall in fixed costs

**Summary of possible changes to the break-even chart to look out for:**

1. Prices can go up or down. If a price is increased, the revenue line starts in the same place but rises more steeply.
2. Fixed costs can rise or fall, so you may have to draw a new horizontal line. But ⇨

remember that a change to fixed costs will also affect the total cost line.

3. Variable costs can rise or fall. An increase will make the variable cost line rise more steeply, though it will still start at the same point – at the fixed cost line. A change in variable costs will change the total costs line as well.

Note that each of these three changes will alter the break-even point.

'Because break-even points shift as conditions change, break-even analyses should be performed regularly, preferably on a quarterly basis.'

www.lplbatavia.com

## 38.7 The value of break-even analysis

### Strengths

Break-even analysis is simple to understand. It is particularly useful for small and newly established businesses, where the managers may not be able to employ more sophisticated techniques. Businesses can use break-even to:

- estimate the future level of output they will need to produce and sell in order to meet given profit objectives
- assess the impact of planned price changes upon profit and the level of output needed to break-even
- take decisions about whether to produce their own products or components or whether to purchase from external sources.

### Weaknesses

The weaknesses of break-even analysis are set out below.

- The model is a simplification. It assumes that variable costs increase constantly, which ignores the benefits of bulk buying. If a firm negotiates lower prices for purchasing larger quantities of raw materials then its total cost line will no longer be straight.
- Similarly, break-even analysis assumes the firm sells all its output at a single price. In reality, firms frequently offer discounts for bulk purchases.
- A major flaw in the technique is that it assumes that all output is sold. In times of low demand, a firm may have difficulty in selling all that it produces.

## Five Whys and a How

| Question | Answer |
|---|---|
| Why might a business want to calculate its margin of safety? | To know how much of a cushion it has between current (profitable) sales and the break-even point |
| Why might a sales revenue line pivot more steeply (to the left), even though it will start at £0 = 0 units? | Because there's been a price increase |
| Why might a cut in variable costs affect the total costs line? | Total costs consists of fixed costs plus variable costs, so of course a change in variable costs will change the total costs line |
| Why might it be useful to calculate profit using contribution instead of revenue minus total costs? | It's significantly quicker, and time has a substantial opportunity cost in exam conditions |
| Why might it be hard for a brand new business to use break-even analysis effectively? | Because the entrepreneurs cannot yet be sure of running costs or revenues – making the exercise a bit of a guess |
| How is the margin of safety calculated? | Sales volume *minus* break-even output |

## Evaluation: Break-even analysis

There is a risk of assuming that break-even charts tell you 'facts'. Break-even analysis seems simple to conduct and understand. That assumes the business knows all its costs and can break them down into variable and fixed. Tesco certainly can, but not every business is as well managed. Football clubs such as Sheffield Wednesday, Portsmouth and Darlington have hit financial problems partly because of ignorance of their financial circumstances. Similarly, few NHS hospitals could say with confidence how much it costs to provide a heart transplant.

Break-even analysis is of particular value when a business is first established. Having to work out the fixed and variable costs will help the managers to make better decisions, for example on pricing. As long as the figures are accurate, break-even becomes especially useful when changes occur, such as rising raw material costs. The technique can allow for changing revenues and costs and gives a valuable guide to potential profitability.

## Key formulae

**Break-even output:** $\dfrac{\text{fixed costs}}{\text{contribution per unit}}$

**Contribution per unit:** selling price − variable costs per unit

**Margin of safety:** sales volume − break-even output

**Total contribution:** contribution per unit × unit sales

# Workbook

## A. Revision questions

(25 marks; 25 minutes)

1. What is meant by the term 'break-even point'? (2)

2. State three reasons why a business may conduct a break-even analysis. (3)

3. List the information necessary to construct a break-even chart. (4)

4. How would you calculate the contribution made by each unit of production that is sold? (2)

5. A business sells its products for £10 each and the variable cost of producing a single unit is £6. If its monthly fixed costs are £18,000, how many units must it sell to break even each month? (3)

6. Explain why the variable cost and total revenue lines commence at the origin of a break-even chart. (3)

7. What point on a break-even chart actually illustrates break-even output? (2)

**8.** Explain how, using a break-even chart, you would illustrate the amount of profit or loss made at any given level of output. (2)

**9.** Why might a business wish to calculate its margin of safety? (2)

**10.** A business is currently producing 200,000 units of output annually, and its break-even output is 120,000 units. What is its margin of safety? (2)

# B. Revision exercises
## DATA RESPONSE 1

### An entrepreneur's first hotel

Paul Jarvis is an entrepreneur and about to open his first hotel. He has forecast the following costs and revenues:

- maximum number of customers per month: 800
- monthly fixed costs: £10,000
- average revenue per customer: £110
- typical variable costs per customer: £90

Some secondary market research has suggested that Paul's prices may be too low. He is considering charging higher prices, though he is nervous about the impact this might have on his forecast sales. Paul has found his break-even chart useful during the planning of his new business, but is concerned that it might be misleading too.

### Questions (45 marks, 50 minutes)

**1. a)** Construct the break-even chart for Paul's planned business. (9)

    **b)** State, and show on the graph, the profit or loss made at a monthly sales level of 600 customers. (4)

    **c)** State, and show on the graph, the margin of safety at that level of output. (4)

**2.** Paul's market research shows that in his first month of trading he can expect 450 customers at his hotel.

    **a)** If Paul's research is correct, calculate the level of profit or loss he will make. (5)

    **b)** Illustrate this level of output on your graph and show the profit or loss. (3)

**3.** Paul has decided to increase his prices to give an average revenue per customer of £120.

    **a)** Draw the new total revenue line on your break-even chart to show the effect of this change. (3)

    **b)** Mark on your diagram the new break-even point. (1)

    **c)** Calculate Paul's new break-even number of customers to confirm the result shown on your chart. (6)

**4.** Paul is worried that his break-even chart may be 'misleading'. Do you agree with him? Justify your view. (10)

## DATA RESPONSE 2

### The Successful T-shirt Company

Shelley has recently launched the Successful T-shirt Company. It sells a small range of fashion T-shirts. The shirts are available in a range of colours and contain the company's logo, which is becoming increasingly desirable for young fashion-conscious people.

The shirts are sold to retailers for £35 each. They cost £16.50 to manufacture and the salesperson receives £2.50 commission for each item sold to retailers. The distribution cost for each shirt is £1.00 and current sales are 1,000 per month. The fixed costs of production are £11,250 per month.

The company is considering expanding its range of T-shirts and has approached its bank for a loan. The bank has requested that the company draw up a business plan including a cash-flow forecast and break-even chart.

### Questions (25 marks, 30 minutes)

**1.** What is a break-even chart? (4)

**2.** Calculate the following:

    **a)** the variable cost of producing 1,000 T-shirts

    **b)** the contribution earned through the sale of one T-shirt. (4)

**3.** Shelley has decided to manufacture the shirts in Poland. As a result, the variable cost per T-shirt (including commission and distribution costs) will fall to £15 per T-shirt. However, fixed costs will rise to £12,000.

   **a)** Calculate the new level of break-even for Shelly's T-shirts.

   **b)** Calculate the margin of safety if sales are 1,000 T-shirts per month. (8)

**4.** Should Shelley rely on break-even analysis when taking business decisions? Justify your view. (9)

## DATA RESPONSE 3

### Start-up break-even analysis

On 27 September 2013 Mary's Garden opened in Raynes Park, South London. Oddly, Mary's Garden is a Japanese restaurant. It opened without any fanfare; without even putting a menu outside for passers-by. This was because, as at 1.30 that afternoon, 'we haven't decided on the prices yet'. Amazingly, at 7.30 that evening every table was taken.

The premises had been unused for more than a year, since an Indian restaurant closed down. Accordingly Mary's had been able to negotiate a stunningly low rent: £1,000 per month; business rates of £500 a month must be added, however. By Monday 30th, Mary had been able to estimate a probable average spend of £40 per customer, of which £15 goes on food costs and another £5 on other variable costs. With staffing costs of £5,000 a month and other monthly fixed costs amounting to £1,500, Mary's Garden has most of the information required for a break-even chart.

There remains one difficult issue, though; what is the maximum capacity level of the restaurant? Amazingly the current opening times are from 9.00 a.m. to 11.00 p.m.; it surely is the only Japanese restaurant in suburbia offering a breakfast menu. The restaurant itself is small, with just 25 seats. Theoretically it could fill them lots of times in 14 hours, but it seems wise to bet on a maximum of just 50 customers per day, 6 days a week, that is, 1,200 a month.

For break-even analysis the above is sufficient, but for real business insight there is one more critical variable: the actual level of customer demand. In conversation with Mary's son it emerged that no research has been done into this. My own local knowledge suggests that it should be full on Friday and Saturday evenings, a third full on Monday-Thursday and gain a smattering of breakfast and lunchtime customers (until this loss-making approach is stopped). Overall, my estimate is for 500 customers a month.

### Questions (20 marks; 25 minutes)

**1.** Calculate the total:

   **a)** monthly fixed costs (1)

   **b)** variable costs per customer (1)

   **c)** contribution per customer (1)

**2.** Calculate the monthly:

   **a)** break-even number of customers (3)

   **b)** safety margin based on estimated customer numbers (2)

**3.** Outline three ways in which Mary's Garden's safety margin could be expanded. (6)

**4. a)** Calculate the monthly profit based on the estimated number of customers. (3)

   **b)** Calculate the monthly profit if customer numbers prove to be 50 per cent higher. (3)

## C. Extend your understanding

**1.** To what extent might break-even analysis benefit a new small business offering Thai food for takeaway and delivery. (20)

**2.** To what extent would break-even analysis be of value when running a business such as Tesco or Primark or any other business you have researched? (20)

# Chapter 39

# Cash flow management and forecasting

Linked to: Cash flow versus profit, Chapter 42; Sources of finance, Chapter 43.

> **Definition**
>
> Cash flow is the flow of money into and out of a business in a given time period. Cash flow forecasting is estimating the flow of cash in the future.

## 39.1 The importance of cash flow management

Managing cash flow is one of the most important aspects of financial management. Without adequate availability of cash from day to day, even a company with high sales could fail. As bills become due there has to be the cash available to pay them. If a company cannot pay its bills, suppliers will refuse to deliver and staff will start looking for other jobs. Cash flow problems are the most common reason for business failure. This is particularly true for new businesses. It is estimated that 80 per cent of businesses that collapse in their first year fail because of cash flow problems.

Businesses need to continually review their current and future cash position. In order to be prepared and to understand future cash needs, businesses construct a cash flow forecast. This sets out the expected flows of cash into and out of the business for each month. In textbooks cash flows are normally shown for six months, but they can be done for any period of time. Most firms want to look 12 months ahead, so the cash flow forecast is constantly updated.

## 39.2 Constructing a cash flow forecast

To prepare a cash flow forecast businesses need to estimate all the money coming into and out of the business, month by month. These flows of money are then set onto a grid showing the cash movements in each month.

## Cash in

In the example shown in Table 39.1 the business is a new start-up. The business will receive an injection of capital of £30,000 in March. The business will start production in April and will only receive cash when sales start in May. Cash inflows are expected to increase each month until reaching a maximum of £15,000 in August.

It is important that the income from sales is shown when the cash is received not when the sale is made.

**Table 39.1** Example of cash inflow (March to August)

| Month £s | March | April | May | June | July | August |
|---|---|---|---|---|---|---|
| Cash inflow | | | | | | |
| Capital | 30,000 | | | | | |
| Sales | | | 7,000 | 10,000 | 13,000 | 15,000 |
| Total inflow | 30,000 | 0 | 7,000 | 10,000 | 13,000 | 15,000 |

## Outflow

In the example shown in Table 39.2:

- in March the firm will buy machinery for £23,000
- materials cost 50 per cent of the value of sales, but have to be paid in cash in the month before the sales take place, for example, £3,500 in April. In the early stages of a firm's life, suppliers are rarely willing to offer credit, so they have to be paid up front
- rent for the building costs £2,000 per month but the owner requires two months' rent in advance
- wages are estimated to be £2,000 per month and there are other expenses of £1,000 per month.

When these figures have been entered onto the grid the total expenditure can be calculated.

**Table 39.2** Example of cash outflow (March to August)

| Cash outflow £ | March | April | May | June | July | August |
|---|---|---|---|---|---|---|
| Equipment | 23,000 | | | | | |
| Materials | 0 | 3,500 | 5,000 | 6,500 | 7,500 | 7,500* |
| Rent | 4,000 | 2,000 | 2,000 | 2,000 | 2,000 | 2,000 |
| Wages | | 2,000 | 2,000 | 2,000 | 2,000 | 2,000 |
| Other expenses | | 1,000 | 1,000 | 1,000 | 1,000 | 1,000 |
| Total outflow | 27,000 | 8,500 | 10,000 | 11,500 | 12,500 | 12,500 |

*assuming September sales of £15,000

## Cash flow

The cash flow forecast can now be completed by calculating the following:

### Monthly balance

This is cash inflow for the month minus cash outflow. It shows each month if there is a positive or a negative movement of cash. When outflow is greater than inflow the monthly balance will be negative. This is shown in brackets to indicate that it is a minus figure.

'A wise business owner once said: "Happiness is positive cash flow".' Quoted at www.freetaxquotes.com

### Opening and closing balance

This is like a bank statement. It shows what cash the business has at the beginning of the month (opening balance) and what the cash position is at the end of the month (closing balance). The closing balance is the opening balance plus the monthly balance. For example, the business starts with £3,000 in the bank in April; a net £8,500 flows out during the month, so the closing bank balance is (£5,500).

The closing balance shows the overall state of the bank account at the end of the month.

The completed cash flow forecast is shown in Table 39.3

This shows that there is a negative cash balance from April onwards, though the accumulated position (the closing balance) is improving from the end of June.

As there is no such thing as negative money the cash flow forecast shows that action is needed to avoid problems in the early months. The easiest remedy would be to negotiate a bank overdraft.

## 39.3 Analysing cash flow forecasts

There are three main ways to analyse a cash flow forecast:

1. Calculate the difference between the closing balance at the end of the period and the opening balance at the start. This gives a sense of what is happening over time. If the overall cash balances are building up, then cash inflows are greater than cash outflows and the situation is comfortable. If the balance is declining, urgent action may be necessary.

2. Use the monthly closing balance to assess trends in the data. If the closing balance from Table 39.3 is

**Table 39.3** Example of a cash flow forecast

| Month £'s | March | April | May | June | July | August |
|---|---|---|---|---|---|---|
| Cash inflow | | | | | | |
| Capital | 30,000 | | | | | |
| Sales | | | 7,000 | 10,000 | 13,000 | 15,000 |
| Total inflow | 30,000 | 0 | 7,000 | 10,000 | 13,000 | 15,000 |
| Total outflow | 27,000 | 8,500 | 10,000 | 11,500 | 12,500 | 12,500 |
| Monthly balance | 3,000 | (8,500) | (3,000) | (1,500) | 500 | 2,500 |
| Opening balance | 0 | 3,000 | (5,500) | (8,500) | (10,000) | (9,500) |
| Closing balance | 3,000 | (5,500) | (8,500) | (10,000) | (9,500) | (7,000) |

turned into a graph (see Figure 39.1) it helps highlight that the short-term plunge into the red seems, by July, to be stabilising into a steady recovery in the cash position of the business.

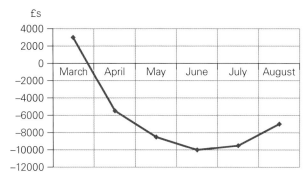

**Figure 39.1** Closing balance from Table 39.3

3. Analyse the timings of cash inflows and outflows. Although some firms sell goods for cash, most provide customers with interest-free credit, for example, Cadbury selling to Tesco. The longer the customers take to pay, the longer the seller is without their cash. So any method of speeding up customer payments can boost a firm's cash flow. The sum of money outstanding from customers is known as 'receivables'. Logically, firms should want this figure to be as low as possible.

Firms not only have customers, they also have suppliers. When buying goods on credit, the longer the credit period you can negotiate from suppliers, the longer your cash will be sitting in your bank account. As it sits in your bank account, this money owed is known as 'payables'.

If a company has customers who pay in 30 days and suppliers who are paid in 30 days, businesses call this a 'cash-to-cash' figure of zero (which is fantastic). If customers take 60 days to pay but suppliers have to be paid in cash on delivery, that is a cash-to-cash figure of 60, which would put a strain on any business's cash flow position.

## 39.4 Cash flow objectives

For established, large businesses with many different products and numerous customers, cash flow is rarely an important issue. Many senior managers may never have heard the term mentioned in the workplace. The focus is much more on profits and profit margins.

For smaller firms, cash flow may be a daily concern, for example, will we have enough in the bank to pay this Friday's wage bill? This illustrates the first cash flow target for a small business: enough cash to meet all the expected bills in the coming months – with a bit to spare.

When small firms are growing, though, the objectives may become far more ambitious. Having opened a very successful tapas (Spanish snack) restaurant, it took brothers Eddie and Sam Hart five years to identify the right premises for their second outlet. Barrafina (2) opened in July 2014 in London's Covent Garden, and probably required close to a £1 million investment. Targeting the cash balance for that investment would be part of the reason it took them 5 years to complete their plan.

### Real business

#### Late payments woes

A survey from the bank settlement organisation BACS showed that in April 2013 small businesses were owed £30.2 billion. This figure was up from £16 billion in 2007, before the recent recession. The same research showed that close to one million businesses said they were suffering from late payments. The Confederation of British Industry (CBI) followed this up by saying that 'Late payment is a serious issue for all businesses but particularly for smaller firms, as cash flow is their life blood. The reality is that few choose to act on late payment for fear of fall out with their customers'.

Source: several, including *The Guardian* 18 September 2013

'An important thing in business is to look after your suppliers. They must look after you, but you need them, so I always pay my bills on time.' Duncan Bannatyne, Dragon investor

## 39.5 Methods of improving cash flow

A business can improve its cash flow in several ways.

- Getting goods to the market in the shortest possible time; the sooner goods reach the customer, the sooner payment is received. Production and distribution should be as efficient as possible.

- Getting paid as quickly as possible; the ideal arrangement is to get paid cash on delivery. Most business, though, works on credit. Even worse, it is interest-free credit, so the customer has little incentive to pay up quickly. Early payment should be encouraged by offering incentives such as discounts for early payment.
- Debt factoring (see Chapter 43) It may be possible to speed up payments by factoring money owed to the business. The seller receives 80 per cent of the amount due within 24 hours of an invoice being presented. The factor then collects the money from the customer when the credit period is over and pays the seller the remaining 20 per cent less the factoring fees.
- Keeping stocks of raw materials to a minimum. Good stock management such as a just-in-time system means that the business is not paying for stocks before it needs them for production.

---

'There's nothing more important than cash flow. I lost my computer business when I was 29 because I gave credit to firms I didn't investigate (credit check).' Peter Jones, Dragon investor (worth £475 million, Sunday Times Rich List 2014)

---

Cash flow can also be improved by keeping cash in the business. Minimising short-term spending on new equipment keeps cash in the business. Things that the business can do include:

- Lease rather than buy equipment. This increases expenses but conserves capital.
- Renting rather than buying buildings. This also allows capital to remain in the business.
- Postponing expenditure, for example on new company cars.

Only as a last resort should a business ask its bank to increase its overdraft facility. A higher overdraft will not improve the cash flow – it just makes sure that negative cash flow can be managed temporarily.

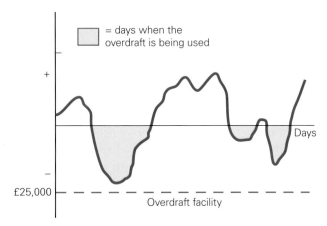

**Figure 39.2** Daily cash balances for a firm with a £25,000 overdraft

Some methods that may be used to improve cash flow are set out in Table 39.4

**Table 39.4** Ways to improve cash flow

| Measure | Result | Drawbacks |
|---|---|---|
| Discounting prices | Increases sales | May undermine pricing structure |
| | Reduces stock | May leave low stocks for future activity |
| | Generates cash | |
| Reduce purchases | Cuts down expenditure | May leave business without means to continue |
| Negotiate more credit | Allows time to pay | May tarnish credit reputation |
| Delay payment of bills | Retains cash | Will tarnish credit reputation |
| Credit control – chase debtors | Gets payments in, and sooner | May upset customers |
| Negotiate additional finance | Provides cash | Interest payments add to expenditure |
| | | Has to be repaid |
| Factor debts | Generates cash | Reduces income from sales |
| | A proportion of the income is guaranteed | Costs can be high |
| Selling assets | Releases cash | Assets are no longer available |
| Sale and leaseback | Releases cash | Increases costs – lease has to be paid |
| | Asset is still available | Company no longer owns asset |

## Five Whys and a How

| Question | Answer |
|---|---|
| Why is it important to ask who constructed the cash flow forecast? | Because unconscious bias may have slipped in, e.g. an entrepreneur's optimism may make the cash inflow projections unrealistic |
| Why may it be a concern if a company's sales are dominated by one large customer | Because any disagreements about the invoice may lead to payment delays – which may be crippling if the bulk of cash inflow is due from that one customer |
| Why is cash flow often referred to as 'the lifeblood' of the business? | Partly because it's *that* important to business survival and partly because, like blood, you only think about it when something's gone wrong |
| Why is it important to distinguish between slow payment and slow sales as causes of cash flow problems? | Slow payment is a purely cash-related issue that can be sorted out between accounts departments; slow sales may be a far more long-term problem – and will involve the marketing department. |
| Why should a business analyse the causes of a cash problem before opting to increase its overdraft limits | Because overdrafts are expensive and all they do is cover over the cash flow problems, they don't solve them |
| How should a business make its estimates for future cash inflows and outflows? | By being pessimistic with the cash inflows (keep them low) and also with the cash outflows (be pessimistic; suspect they'll be quite high) |

### Key terms

**Best case:** an optimistic estimate of the best possible outcome, for example if sales prove much higher than expected.

**Cash flow forecast:** estimating future monthly cash inflows and outflows, to find out the net cash flow.

**Debt factoring:** obtaining part-payment of the amount owed from a factoring company. The factoring company will then collect the debt and pass over the balance of the payment.

**Overdraft:** short-term borrowing from a bank. The business only borrows as much as it needs to cover its daily cash shortfall.

**Worst case:** a pessimistic estimate assuming the worst possible outcome, for example sales are very disappointing.

'The fact is that one of the first lessons I learned in business was that balance sheets and income statements are fiction; cash flow is reality.' Chris Chocola, businessman

### Evaluation: Cash flow management and forecasting

There is no doubt that cash flow management is a vital ingredient in the success of any small business. For a new business, cash flow forecasting helps to answer key questions:

- Is the venture viable?
- How much capital is needed?
- Which are the most dangerous months?

For an existing business the cash flow forecast identifies the amount and timing of any cash flow problems in the future. It is also useful for evaluating new orders or ventures.

Nevertheless, completing a cash flow forecast does not ensure survival. Consideration needs to be given to its usefulness and limitations. It must be remembered that cash flow forecasts are based on estimates of amounts and timing. When preparing cash flow forecasts, managers need to ask themselves 'what if?' A huge mistake is to only look at one forecast. It is far better to look at best case and worst case possibilities. The firm needs to be continually aware of the economic and market climate and its current cash position.

**247**

# Workbook

## A. Revision questions

(30 marks; 30 minutes)

1. What is meant by 'cash flow'? (2)
2. Why is it important to manage cash flow? (4)
3. What is a cash flow forecast? (3)
4. Explain two limitations of cash flow forecasts. (4)
5. Give two reasons why a bank manager may want to see a cash flow forecast before giving a loan to a new business. (2)
6. How could a firm benefit from delaying its cash outflows? (3)
7. What problems could a firm face if its cash flow forecast proved unreliable? (3)
8. Outline three ways in which a business can improve its cash flow situation. (6)
9. What internal factors could affect a firm's cash flow? (3)

## B. Revision exercises

### DATA RESPONSE 1

(18 marks; 20 minutes)

A business is to be started up on 1 January next year with £40,000 of share capital. It will be opening a designer clothes shop. During January it plans to spend £45,000 on start-up costs (buying a lease, buying equipment, decorating, and so on). On 1 February it will open its doors and gain sales over the next five months of: £12,000, £16,000, £20,000, £25,000 and £24,000 respectively. Each month it must pay £10,000 in fixed overheads (salaries, heat, light, telephone, and so on) and its variable costs will amount to half the revenue.

Complete the cash flow table below (Table 39.5) to find out:

1. the company's forecast cash position at the end of June
2. the maximum level of overdraft the owners will need to negotiate with the bank before starting up.

**Table 39.5** Cash flow table

|  | Jan | Feb | Mar | Apr | May | June |
|---|---|---|---|---|---|---|
| Cash at start |  |  |  |  |  |  |
| Cash in |  |  |  |  |  |  |
| Cash out |  |  |  |  |  |  |
| Net cash flow |  |  |  |  |  |  |
| Opening balance |  |  |  |  |  |  |
| Closing balance |  |  |  |  |  |  |

### DATA RESPONSE 2

#### Cash problems at a pound store

PoundLandline was quickly a media success after opening day publicity, due to a row between the online start-up and the long-established Poundland retail chain. As the row spread over social media, opening day sales through PoundLandline were eight times higher than the budget. At 3 p.m. the site crashed – incapable of dealing with all the hits to its website. Founders Sonia and Colin had set the site up with an expectation of selling 8,000 items a day at £1 each, leading to annual revenue of £2.8m but with slim gross margins and therefore gross profit of £420,000. With fixed overheads of £200,000 (covering the warehouse rental and other costs), they anticipated a very satisfactory net profit.

The problem now was the cost of fixing the website crash. They needed extra bandwidth and a more robust site. Although Colin was a very good programmer, he needed to hire in extra expertise. Their budget had 'been too tight for contingency allowances' according to Sonia, so this was a strain on cash flow. A second issue was that high sales would mean speedy purchasing of extra stock – and paying for it. There was much to be done.

An underlying problem faced by the two entrepreneurs had been the unhelpful attitude of the banks. Despite TV advertisements boasting how much they help small firms, Sonia and Colin had found them unwilling to commit to the slightest risk. Therefore they refused to give bank loans and would

only provide an overdraft when guaranteed by the security of Sonia's flat. If things went wrong, even though the business was PoundLandline Ltd, Sonia could end up homeless. As shown in the cash flow forecast, the pair had needed to invest £54,000 to get the business up and running. That was the limit of their financial resources.

So now, with customers desperate to shop at the first online pound store, the entrepreneurs had a cash flow problem – on Day 1 of Month 1! The carefully constructed cash flow forecast was already being disrupted.

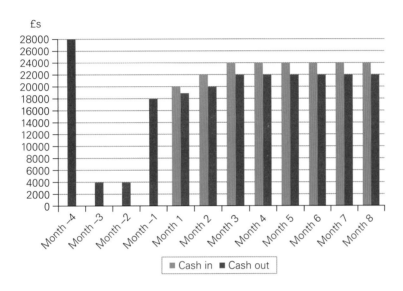

**Figure 39.3** Cash flow forecast for PoundLandline Ltd

## Questions (25 marks; 25 minutes)

**1. a)** Explain two reasons for the Day 1 cash flow problems at PoundLandline Ltd. (8)

**b)** Explain whether Sonia and Colin could be blamed for these causes of the cash flow difficulties. (5)

**2.** Given the situation the business was in by the end of Day 1, discuss what the entrepreneurs could do to overcome their cash flow problems. (12)

## C. Extend your understanding

**1.** Evaluate the importance of cash flow forecasting for a new retail business. (20)

**2.** 'Cash flow management is important for small companies but not for large companies.' To what extent do you agree with this statement? (20)

# Chapter

# 40 Budgets and budgeting

**Linked to:** Financial objectives, Chapter 36; Cash flow management and forecasting, Chapter 39; Sources of finance, Chapter 43.

## Definition

A budget is a target for costs or revenue that a firm or department must aim to reach over a given period of time. An income budget sets a floor, that is, a minimum target, while an expenditure budget sets a ceiling, for example, a maximum target for costs.

## 40.1 How to construct a budget

Budgeting is the process of setting targets, covering all aspects of costs and revenues. It is a method for turning a firm's strategy into reality. Nothing can be done in business without money; budgets tell individual managers how much they can spend to achieve their objectives. For instance, a football manager may be given a transfer expenditure budget of £20 million to buy players. With the budget in place, the transfer dealing can get under way.

A budgeting system shows how much can be spent per time period, and gives managers a way to check whether they are on track. Most firms use a system of budgetary control as a means of supervision. The process is as follows:

1. Make a judgement of the likely sales revenues for the coming year.

2. Set a cost ceiling that allows for an acceptable level of profit.

3. The budget for the whole company's costs is then broken down by division, department or by cost centre.

4. The budget may then be broken down further so that each manager has a budget and therefore some spending power.

In a business start-up, the budget should provide enough spending power to finance vital needs such as building work, decoration, recruiting and paying staff, and marketing. If a manager overspends in one area, she or he knows that it is essential to cut back elsewhere. A good manager gets the best possible value from the budgeted sum.

'The budget is our guide. It tells us what we're supposed to do for the year. We couldn't get along without it.' Jim Bell, US factory manager

## Real business

### The BP disaster

On 23 March 2005 a huge explosion at BP's Texas oil refinery killed 15 people and injured more than 180. Most were the company's own staff. After an enquiry, the chairwoman of the US Chemical Safety Board reported that 'BP implemented a 25 per cent cut on fixed costs from 1998 to 2000 that adversely impacted maintenance expenditures at the refinery'. The report stated that 'BP's global management' (the British Head Office) 'was aware of problems with maintenance spending and infrastructure well before March 2005'. Yet they did nothing about it. The chairwoman delivered the final critique:

'Every successful corporation must contain its costs. But at an ageing facility like Texas City, it is not responsible to cut budgets related to safety and maintenance without thoroughly examining the impact on the risk of a catastrophic accident.' BP confirmed that its own internal investigation had findings 'generally consistent with those of the CSB'.

In 2010, there was an echo of this disaster when an explosion on a BP well in the Gulf of Mexico killed 11 people and caused the biggest oil spill in American history. By 2014 the costs associated with this had forced BP to sell off more than $42 billion of assets, wiping out a fifth of the value of the company. Cost cutting can be costly.

Source: Adapted from *Topical Cases*, www.a-zbusinesstraining.com

## 40.2 Setting budgets

Setting budgets is not an easy job. How do you decide exactly what level of sales are likely next year, especially for new businesses with no previous trading to rely on? Furthermore, how can you plan for costs if the cost of your raw materials tends to fluctuate? Most firms treat last year's budget figures as the main determinant of this year's budget. Minor adjustments will be made for inflation and other foreseeable changes. Given the firm's past experience, budget setting should be quite quick and quite accurate.

'Any jackass can draw up a balanced budget on paper.' Lane Kirkland, former US trade union president

For start-ups, setting budgets will be a much tougher job. They are fundamental to the business plan, but as heavyweight boxing champ Mike Tyson once said: "Everyone has a plan until they get punched in the mouth". To succeed, the entrepreneur will need to rely on:

- a 'guesstimate' of likely sales in the early months of the start-up
- the entrepreneur's expertise and experience, which will be better if the entrepreneur has worked in the industry before
- the entrepreneur's instinct, based on market understanding
- a significant level of market research.

### Real business

#### Budgeting helps but is not easy for start-ups

Stanford University research into 78 business start-ups showed that firms with budgeting systems were more likely to survive and experience significant growth rates. They reported that budgeting systems allowed senior staff access to the information needed when making decisions. However, they acknowledged the difficulties in setting budgets for new start-ups. They point out that, for a new company, predicting the future is hugely unpredictable and setting 12-month budgets is likely to be unrealistic.

The best criteria for setting budgets are:

- to relate the budget directly to the business objective; if a company wants to increase sales and market share, the best method may be to increase the advertising budget and thereby boost demand
- to involve as many people as possible in the process; people will be more committed to reaching the targets if they have had a say in how the budget was set.

'(Budgets) must not be prepared on high and cast as pearls before swine. They must be prepared by the operating divisions.' Robert Townsend, the original business guru

## Simple budget statements

An example of a simple budget statement may look like that shown in Table 40.1.

**Table 40.1** Example of a budget statement

|  | January | February | March |
|---|---|---|---|
| Income | 25,000 | 28,000 | 30,000 |
| Variable costs | 10,000 | 12,000 | 13,000 |
| Fixed costs | 10,000 | 10,000 | 11,000 |
| Total expenditure | 20,000 | 22,000 | 24,000 |
| Profit | 5,000 | 6,000 | 6,000 |

This information is only of value if it proves possible for a manager to believe that these figures are achievable. Only then will she or he be motivated to try to turn the budget into reality.

## 40.3 Budgetary variances

Variance is the amount by which the actual result differs from the budgeted figure. It is usually measured each month, by comparing the actual outcome with the budgeted one. It is important to note that variances are referred to as adverse or favourable – not positive or negative. A favourable variance is one that leads to higher than expected profit (revenue up or costs down). An adverse variance is one that reduces profit, such as costs being higher than the budgeted level. Table 40.2 shows when variances are adverse or favourable.

**Table 40.2** Adverse or favourable variance?

| Variable | Budget | Actual | Variance | Fav/Adv |
|---|---|---|---|---|
| Sales of X | 150 | 160 | 10 | Favourable |
| Sales of Y | 150 | 145 | 5 | Adverse |
| Material costs | 100 | 90 | 10 | Favourable |
| Labour costs | 100 | 105 | 5 | Adverse |

The value of regular variance statements is that they provide an early warning. If a product's sales are slipping below budget, managers can respond by increasing marketing support or by cutting back on production plans. In an ideal world, slippage could be noted in March, a new strategy put into place by May and a recovery in sales achieved by September. Clearly, no firm wishes to wait until the end-of-year to find out that things went badly. An early warning can lead to an early solution.

## 40.4 Analysing budgets and variances

When significant variances occur, management should first consider whether the fault was in the budget or in the actual achievement. In January 2014 Nintendo announced to shareholders that it was cutting the sales budget for its Wii U from 9 million units to 2.8 million in the period to the end of March 2014. That's a cut of about 70 per cent! Nintendo's management decided that its budget was at fault and it would not therefore blame its marketing managers. The launch of the PS4 had been known about, but Nintendo never expected it to be as successful as it was.

When adverse variances occur, senior managers are likely to want to hear an explanation from the responsible 'line manager'. He or she will need to have a clear explanation of what has gone wrong. Clearly, if recession has hit sales throughout a market, it will be easy to explain adverse income variances. Far tougher is when the blame lies with falling market share rather than market size.

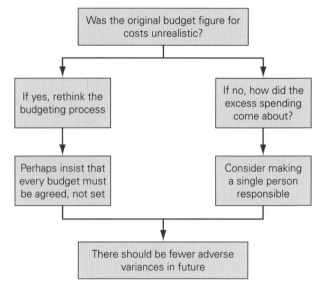

**Figure 40.1** Logic chain: making variance analysis more effective

### Five Whys and a How

| Question | Answers |
|---|---|
| Why are budgets used in most organisations? | To keep costs under control while allowing some degree of delegation of power |
| Why may over-optimistic revenue budgets be demoralising? | Because managers feel they're being set up to fail |
| Why might an adverse cost variance be forgivable? | If it's a new product or a new technique, there's a learning curve for staff to climb |
| Why might it be wise to reset budgets during the middle of a financial year? | If variances have been high, perhaps the original budgets were wrongly set – so now's the time to try to get them right |
| Why should positive variances be investigated? | Because you need to understand why things have gone well in order to achieve the same again. |
| How are variances calculated? | By comparing the actual to the forecast data |

## Key terms

**Adverse variance:** a difference between budgeted and actual figures that is damaging to the firm's profit (for example costs up or revenue down).

**Criteria:** yardsticks against which success (or the lack of it) can be measured.

**Delegated:** passing authority down the hierarchy.

**Expenditure budget:** setting a maximum figure for what a department or manager can spend over a period of time. This is to control costs.

**Favourable variance:** a difference between budgeted and actual figures that boosts a firm's profit (for example, revenue up or costs down).

**Income budget:** setting a minimum figure for the revenue to be generated by a product, a department or a manager.

**Profit budget:** setting a minimum figure for the profit to be achieved over a period of time.

**Zero budgeting:** setting all future budgets at £0, to force managers to have to justify the spending levels they say they need in future.

## Evaluation: Budgets and budgeting

The sophistication of budgeting systems is usually directly linked to the size of a business. Huge multinationals have incredibly complex budgeting systems. For a small business start-up, any budgeting system will be quite simple. Most will rely on a rough breakdown of how the start-up budget is to be divided between the competing demands. There is, however, no doubt that budgeting provides a more effective system of controlling a business's finances than no system at all.

Budgets are a management tool. The way in which they are used can tell you a lot about a firm's culture. Firms with a culture of bossy management will tend to use a tightly controlled budgetary system. Managers will

have budgets imposed upon them and variances will be watched closely by supervisors. Organisations with a more open culture will use budgeting as an aid to discussion and empowerment.

Whatever the culture, if a manager is to be held accountable for meeting a budget, she or he must be given influence over setting it, and control over reaching it. Budgets are set for future time periods and analysis of actual against budgeted performance can take place only after the event. This is true of all financial monitoring and leads to doubts as to its effectiveness as a planning tool. Measures such as market research may be far more reliable in predicting future performance.

# Workbook

## A. Revision questions

**(40 marks; 40 minutes)**

1. Explain the meaning of the term 'budgeting'. (2)

2. List three advantages that a budgeting system brings to a company. (3)

3. Why is it valuable to have a yardstick against which performance can be measured? (3)

4. Briefly explain how most companies actually set next year's budgets. (3)

5. Why should budget holders have a say in the setting of their budgets? (3)

6. Complete the budget statement shown in Table 40.3 by filling in the gaps: (8)

**Table 40.3** A budget statement

|  | January | February | March | April |
|---|---|---|---|---|
| Income | 4200 | 4500 | 4000 | |
| Variable costs | 1800 | | 2000 | 1800 |
| Fixed costs | 1200 | 1600 | | 1600 |
| Total costs | | 3600 | 4100 | |
| Profit | | | | 600 |

8. How could a firm respond to an increasingly adverse variance in labour costs? (4)

9. Explain what is meant by a 'favourable cost variance'. (3)

10. Look at Table 40.4, then answer the following questions.

**Table 40.4** Budgeted and actual figures for May and June

| | May | | June | |
| | Budgeted | Actual | Budgeted | Actual |
|---|---|---|---|---|
| Revenue | 3500 | 3200 | 4000 | 4200 |
| Variable costs | 1000 | 900 | 1200 | 1500 |
| Fixed costs | 1200 | 1200 | 1300 | 1100 |
| Total costs | 2200 | 2100 | 2500 | 2600 |
| Profit | | | | |

a) Calculate the budgeted and actual profit figures for both months. (2)

b) Identify a month with:
   i) a favourable revenue variance
   ii) an adverse fixed cost variance
   iii) an adverse variable cost variance
   iv) a favourable fixed cost variance
   v) an adverse total cost variance
   vi) an adverse revenue variance
   vii) a favourable total cost variance
   viii) an adverse profit variance
   ix) a favourable profit variance. (9)

# B. Revision exercises
## DATA RESPONSE 1

**Table 40.5** Variance analysis

| | January | | | February | | |
| | B | A | V | B | A | V |
|---|---|---|---|---|---|---|
| Sales revenue | 140* | 150 | 10 | 180 | 175 | ? |
| Materials | 70 | 80 | (10) | 90 | 95 | ? |
| Other direct costs | 30 | 35 | (5) | 40 | 40 | 0 |
| Overheads | 20 | 20 | 0 | 25 | 22 | ? |
| Profit | 20 | 15 | (5) | ? | 18 | ? |

*All figures in £000s

### Questions (20 marks; 20 minutes)

1. What are the five numbers missing from the variance analysis shown in Table 40.5? (5)

2. Examine the financial strength or weakness in this data, from the company's viewpoint. (9)

3. Explain the ways a manager might set about improving the accuracy of a sales budget. (6)

## DATA RESPONSE 2

**Table 40.6** Budget data for Clinton & Collins Ltd (£000s)

| | January | | February | | March | | April | |
| | B | A | B | A | B | A | B | A |
|---|---|---|---|---|---|---|---|---|
| Sales revenue | 160 | 144 | 180 | 156 | 208 | 168 | 240 | 188 |
| Materials | 40 | 38 | 48 | 44 | 52 | 48 | 58 | 54 |
| Labour | 52 | 48 | 60 | 54 | 66 | 62 | 72 | 68 |
| Overheads | 76 | 76 | 76 | 78 | 76 | 80 | 76 | 80 |
| Profit | (8) | (18) | (4) | (20) | 14 | (22) | 34 | (14) |

**Questions (30 marks; 30 minutes)**

**1.** Use the data given in Table 40.6 to explain why February's profits were worse than expected. (5)

**2.** Why may Clinton & Collins Ltd have chosen to set monthly budgets? (5)

**3.** Explain how the firm could have set these budgets. (4)

**4.** The directors of Clinton & Collins Ltd knew that the recession was causing problems for the firm but were unsure as to whether things were improving or worsening. To what extent does the data suggest an improvement? (16)

## DATA RESPONSE 3

### Chessington World of Adventures

In April 2014 Chessington World of Adventures opened up for its summer season. The newly appointed merchandise manager (in charge of all non-food sales) was given his sales budget for the year. It had been set 4 per cent higher than for 2013. He thought the budget was quite ambitious, especially when a wet April and May meant that there were fewer visitors in the early part of the season. Then the period July to August saw hot, dry weather and the turnstiles were 'buzzing' again. As a hot day at Chessington can boost crowds by 50 per cent, the merchandise manager did not need to make any effort to meet his budget.

**Questions (25 marks, 25 minutes)**

**1.** Outline two other ways in which management might have constructed the sales budget for 2014. (4)

**2.** Explain one problem that might arise if the merchandise manager's pay was linked to sales figures. (5)

**3.** To what extent are budgets worthwhile in a business such as Chessington? (16)

## C. Extend your understanding

**1.** 'Budgeting systems can often be demotivating for middle managers.' To what extent do you agree with this statement? (20)

**2.** To what extent is it true to suggest that budgets are the most important financial documents for most managers? (20)

# Chapter 41

# Profit and how to increase it

Linked to: Calculating revenue, costs and profit, Chapter 37; Break-even analysis, Chapter 38; Sources of finance, Chapter 43.

> **Definition**
>
> Gross profit is the difference between selling price and the direct costs generated by the goods sold. Operating profit is the profit left after all fixed and variable operating costs have been deducted from revenue.

## 41.1 Gross profit, operating profit and profit for the year

Profit can be calculated in many different ways. For most business purposes, though, it is enough to know gross profit, operating profit and profit for the year. Table 41.1 shows a simplified version of Ted Baker plc's 2014 accounts, to help show how these three levels of profit are calculated.

## 41.2 Gross profit and gross profit margin

The gross profit of a business is an absolute number, for example, £10,000. The number is calculated by deducting direct costs from sales revenue. Is £10,000 a good level of profit or not? To find out, it is helpful to measure the profit in relation to the sales revenue. This is the gross profit margin:

$$\text{Gross profit margin} = \frac{\text{gross profit}}{\text{sales revenue}} \times 100$$

For example, if the gross profit is £10,000 and the sales are £40,000 the gross profit margin is:

$$\frac{£10,000}{£40,000} \times 100 = 25 \text{ per cent}$$

Having turned the profit figure into a percentage, a comparison can be made with the profitability achieved by other companies. Comparing fashion retailers Ted Baker plc and SuperGroup plc, for example: the former made a 2014 gross margin of 61.5 per cent while SuperGroup's margins were 59.7 per cent. Both figures are remarkably high, confirming the strength of the Ted Baker and SuperDry brand names. Needless to say, Ted Baker's is a little more impressive than SuperGroup's – and both are hugely better than the original calculation of 25 per cent.

## 41.3 Operating profit and operating profit margin

When City and media analysts are evaluating companies, the number they focus on is operating profit, and then take that as a percentage of revenue to

**Table 41.1** Ted Baker plc's 2014 accounts

| Accounting item | Figure (£ millions) | Method of calculation | Comment |
|---|---|---|---|
| Revenue | 322.0 | | The value of all the sales made in the financial year |
| Cost of sales | (123.5) | | The cost of the clothes Ted buys in |
| **Gross profit** | **198.5** | Revenue – Cost of sales | |
| Fixed overheads | (159.0) | | Cost of running the stores + head office |
| **Operating profit** | **39.5** | Gross profit – Fixed overheads | |
| Net financing cost | (0.6) | | |
| Corporation tax | (10.0) | | Unlike some, Ted pays his taxes |
| **Profit for the year** | **28.9** | Operating profit – Financing and tax | |

calculate the operating profit margin:

$$\text{Operating profit margin} = \frac{\text{operating profit}}{\text{sales revenue}} \times 100$$

For example, if the operating profit is £3,000 and the sales are £40,000 the operating margin is:

$$\frac{£3,000}{£40,000} \times 100 = 7.5 \text{ per cent}$$

Having turned the profit figure into a percentage, a comparison can be made with the profitability achieved by other companies, or looking at one company over time. In 2014 Ted Baker plc had an operating margin of 12.3 per cent. Sainsbury's, by contrast, had a 2014 operating margin of just 3.3 per cent. As the businesses operate in different types of retailing, it would be unfair to conclude that Ted Baker is better run than Sainsbury's.

### Real business

If a business cannot make a reasonable operating profit it has no chance of long-term survival. A good example is Blockbuster UK. In its 2010 financial year it made an operating profit that was less than 1 per cent of its sales. Then, with sales falling as the DVD market declined, operating profits of £1.7m slipped to losses of £8.5m in 2011 and £11.2m in 2012 before collapse in 2013. The final Blockbuster stores were closed by early 2014.

## 41.4 Ratio analysis

The calculations of profit margins undertaken above can come under the heading 'ratio analysis'. This is a technique used by accountants to analyse business in comparison with a close rival, or to investigate the performance of a business over time. A ratio is simply a comparison of one piece of numerical data with another. In the case of profit margins, these comparisons are shown in percentage terms.

Table 41.2 shows how ratio analysis allows questions to be asked, and sometimes answered. It provides data on Tesco plc over time, and then shows Tesco versus Sainsbury and Morrisons'. Over time, it is clear that Tesco's profitability has fallen steadily. Nevertheless, in 2014, despite Sainsbury's steady improvement in its operating profit margin, Tesco remained significantly more profitable. As for Morrisons', in 2014 it made operating losses rather than profits. So, at that time, there were positives in Tesco's ratio analysis as well as negatives.

**Table 41.2** Trading profit margins in the UK grocery market

|  | Tesco (UK only) | Sainsbury's | Morrisons' |
|---|---|---|---|
| 2009 | 6.65 per cent | 3.0 per cent | 4.6 per cent |
| 2010 | 6.2 per cent | 3.1 per cent | 5.3 per cent |
| 2011 | 6.15 per cent | 3.2 per cent | 5.5 per cent |
| 2012 | 5.8 per cent | 3.2 per cent | 5.5 per cent |
| 2013 | 5.2 per cent | 3.25 per cent | 5.2 per cent |
| 2014 | 5.0 per cent | 3.3 per cent | (0.55 per cent) |

## 41.5 Profit for the year

After every possible cost has been deducted, including interest charges and tax bills, the resulting figure is the profit for the year (also known as 'earnings'). The profit for the year is important because it leads to a huge boardroom decision: the directors must decide how much of that profit to pay out in dividends to shareholders and how much to leave in the business for reinvestment. In the case of Next plc, about one third of the profit for the year is paid out as dividends, leaving two thirds to finance the growth of the business. By contrast, in 2013 Tesco paid out nearly all its profit in dividends. So, at a time when it needed capital to invest in repositioning its shops, it gave nearly all its capital away to its shareholders. Short-termism in the extreme.

Ted Baker in 2014 kept about half of its profit for the year (after paying the other half out as dividends). At first that £15 million would sit in the bank account, boosting the firm's cash position. Then, if management chose to do it, the capital could be taken from the current account to buy new shop leaseholds, or a new distribution centre or to pay for a new advertising campaign. However the money is spent, it's reasonable to see it as an investment in Ted Baker's future growth prospects.

## 41.6 What is a good net profit margin?

The typical net profit margin in an industry will vary from one sector to another. Net profit margins from selected 2013 company accounts are shown in Table 41.3. The food retail market, for example, is very competitive and the profit per sale (the profit margin) is likely to be quite low (for example, 5 per cent). However, provided you can sell a high volume of items your overall net profits can still be high. You may make relatively little profit per can of beans, but provided you sell a lot of beans your overall profits may still be high.

In the case of luxury items such as SuperDry clothes or Rolex watches the profit margin is likely to be much higher. However, although the profit per sale is relatively high, this does not automatically mean the profits are high –that depends on how many items you sell.

**Table 41.3** Net profit margins from selected 2013 plc accounts (half-year figures)

| | Sales (£ million) | Underlying net profit (£ million) | Profit margin (%) |
|---|---|---|---|
| Tesco | 31,914 | 1,466 | 4.6 |
| Sainsbury's | 12,684 | 400 | 3.2 |
| SuperGroup | 192 | 18 | 9.4 |

'I generally disagree with most of the very high margin opportunities. Why? Because it's a business strategy trade-off: the lower the margin you take, the faster you grow.' Vinod Khosla, Indian billionaire entrepreneur

'Market leadership can translate directly to higher revenue, higher profitability, greater capital velocity, and correspondingly stronger returns on invested capital.' Jeff Bezos, founder of Amazon.com

## 41.7 Methods of improving profits

To increase profits a business must:

1. increase revenue
2. decrease costs
3. do a combination of 1 and 2.

To increase revenue a business may want to consider its marketing mix. Changes to the product may mean that it becomes more appealing to customers. Better distribution may make it more available. Changes to promotion may make customers more aware of its benefits. However, the business needs to be careful that rising costs do not swallow up the rise in sales revenues.

To reduce costs a business may examine many of the functional areas (such as marketing, operations, people and finance):

- Could the firm continue with fewer staff?
- Could money be saved by switching suppliers?
- Do the firm's sales really benefit from sponsoring the opera?
- Are there ways of reducing wastage?

Essentially, a business should look for ways of making the product more efficiently (for example, with better technology) by using fewer inputs or paying less for the inputs being used. However, a business must be careful that when it reduces costs, the quality of service is not reduced. After all, this might lead to a fall in sales and revenue. Cutting staff in your coffee shop may cut costs, but if long queues form it may also reduce the number of customers and your income. Managers must weigh up the consequences of any decision to reduce costs.

### Real business

#### Vietnam as a production base

Average wages in Vietnam are lower than those of two of its neighbours: Thailand and China. Vietnamese factory workers earn just two thirds of what their colleagues in China take home (about 65p an hour compared with £1 in China).

Companies such as Foxconn, which assembles consumer electronics and phones for big-brand companies like Apple and Sony, operate on very low profit margins and so try to find the lowest cost location they can. This makes Vietnam very attractive as a production base. Even high profit margin businesses such as Nike are shifting production to Vietnam, simply to keep costs down and therefore margins up.

## 41.8 Methods of increasing profitability

Profitability (as opposed to 'profits') is a relative term. It is mainly measured using the operating profit margin. To increase operating profits in relation to sales a business could do the following.

### Increase the price

Increasing the price would boost the profit per sale, but the danger is that the sales overall may fall so much that the overall profits of the business are reduced. (Notice the important difference again between the operating profit margin and the overall level of profits; you could make a high level of profit on one can of beans relative to its price, but if you only sell one can your total profits are not that impressive!). The impact of any price increase will depend on the price elasticity of demand; the more price elastic demand is, the greater the fall in demand will be, and the less likely it is that a firm will want to put up its prices.

## Cut costs

If cutting costs can be done without damaging the quality in any significant way then this clearly makes sense. Better bargaining to get the supply prices down or better ways of producing may lead to higher profits per sale. However, as we saw above, the business needs to be careful to ensure that reducing costs does not lead to a deterioration of the service or quality of the product.

### Five Whys and a How

| Question | Answer |
|---|---|
| Why might Sainsbury's want to compare its gross profit margin to that of Tesco? | To see which is creating a wider gap between costs paid to suppliers and prices charged to customers |
| What's the difference between gross profit and operating profit? | Fixed overheads |
| Why is 'profitability' looked at separately from 'profit'? | Because profit is an absolute (number) whereas profitability is a relative figure (e.g. as a percentage of revenue) |
| Why is 'profit for the year' so important to companies? | Because it pays for dividends and reinvestment; both are crucial for financing long-term growth |
| Why is it important to fair, long-term competition that every company should pay the same percentage rate of corporation tax? | If Ted Baker pays up but rivals find ways to avoid tax, in the long run the competitors will keep more profit for the year, be able to invest more, and therefore have an unfair advantage |
| How might a struggling firm attempt to increase its operating profitability? | By squeezing supply costs a bit more or by acting on fixed overhead costs, e.g. moving its head office to somewhere smaller and cheaper |

### Key terms

**Corporation tax** is a levy on the incomes of companies, that is, you pay a percentage of your pre-tax profit.

**Fixed overheads** are the indirect costs that have to be paid however the business is performing, for example, rent and salaries.

### Evaluation: Profit and how to increase it

A difficulty with questions about poor profits is that it's easy to provide responses that are too obvious. Sainsbury's has a significantly lower profit margin than Tesco. But is it worth pointing out that Sainsbury's could look for bulk-buying discounts on its supplies? Surely it will be doing that already.

A good answer needs to look beyond the obvious to consider, perhaps, that Sainsbury's may have to address its head office (fixed overhead) costs in order to boost its margins to match those of Tesco.

# Workbook

## A. Revision questions

**(30 marks; 30 minutes)**

1. What is meant by 'revenue'? (2)

2. What is meant by 'operating profit'? (2)

3. Does an increase in price necessarily increase revenue? Explain your answer. (5)

4. How could a company jeopardise its future by paying out generous dividends to shareholders? (4)

5. Is profitability measured in pounds or percentages? (1)

6. What is the formula for the operating profit margin? (2)

7. Explain two ways of increasing profits. (4)

8. Why may cutting costs end up reducing profits? (4)

9. Outline one way in which operating profit might be affected by a decision within:
   a) the marketing function (3)
   b) the operations function. (3)

## B. Revision exercises

### DATA RESPONSE 1

SOFA-SOGOOD Ltd is a retailer of sofas. It had been experiencing a 'very slow' summer. Revenues had been falling and costs had been pushed up by pay increases, higher rent costs and higher interest payments on debts. As a result, net profits had fallen by 20 per cent on last year. Renis, the managing director, was very disappointed that revenue had fallen because he had cut prices by 5 per cent and had expected customer numbers to increase sharply. Once it became clear that this discounting policy was not working, he imposed a pay freeze on everyone in the company and a policy of non-recruitment. If any staff member left, she or he would not be replaced.

**Questions (25 marks; 30 minutes)**

1. Distinguish between revenue, costs and net profit. (3)

2. Explain why a fall in price might not have led to an increase in revenue. (4)

3. Apart from the methods mentioned in the text, analyse two other actions SOFA-SOGOOD could take to improve its profitability. (9)

4. Analyse the implications for the business of the staffing cost-saving actions taken by Renis. (9)

### DATA RESPONSE 2

**Measuring and increasing profits: Padrone Pizza**

The news that the economy recovered in 2013 just made Pat more depressed. For the last 5 years his business (Padrone Pizza) had been sinking and sinking, caught up in a whirlwind of local competition driven by promotional discounting. 85 per cent of all his takings were now through some kind of promotion: 2-for-1; £5 Mondays; Häagen Dazs Wednesdays and so on. Five years ago he made £6 gross profit for every £10 of sales; now, in early 2014, he made just £2.50 on every £10 – and that's before counting all the fixed overheads: rent, rates, energy bills and advertising.

Over Christmas he'd talked it over with his dad and his 15-year-old daughter. She'd been full of ideas,

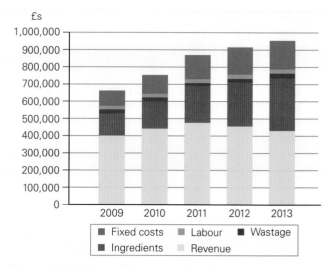

**Figure 41.1** Padrone Pizza: revenue and costs

some from her GCSE Business course, but most from her knowledge of the local area and people. One phrase of hers kept coming back into Pat's mind: "Kids in class love boasting about the big pizza deals they've had last night; you need them talking about the pizza, not the deal." But how, given that every type of pizza was offered by his six local competitors? And what about other ways of improving profits?

**Questions (25 marks; 25 minutes)**

1. Calculate the profits made by Padrone Pizza in 2009 and in 2013. (4)

2. **a)** Outline three ways you can see to increase Pat's profit. (6)

   **b)** Discuss which one would be the best approach. Construct strong arguments in favour of your recommendation. (15)

## C. Extend your understanding

1. In 2014 Next plc's retail business enjoyed operating profit margins of 15.6 per cent. Marks & Spencer plc had operating margins of 6.7 per cent. To what extent might price increases be the right way to boost M&S profits to match those of Next? (20)

2. In 2014 Snapchat boosted user numbers to more than 200 million people, but had not found a way to generate revenue, let alone profit. Discuss the difficulties for a new app in turning usage into profit. (20)

# Chapter 42 Cash flow versus profit

**Linked to:** Cash flow management and forecasting, Chapter 39; Profit and how to increase it, Chapter 41; Sources of finance, Chapter 43.

> **Definition**
>
> Cash flow is the movement of cash into and out of a firm's bank account. Profit is when revenue is greater than total costs.

## 42.1 Introduction

A year ago a busy bar in Wimbledon closed down. Regulars were surprised, shocked even, that such a successful business had failed. The business was operating profitably, but the owners had become too excited by their success. Their investment in two new bars elsewhere in London had drained too much cash from the business, and the bank had panicked over the mounting debts. It forced the business to close. A profitable business had run out of cash.

To understand how cash differs from profit, the key is to master profit. On the face of it, profit is easy: total revenue *minus* total costs. Common sense tells you that revenue = money in and costs = money out. Unfortunately that's far too much of a simplification.

## 42.2 Distinction between cash flow and profit

To understand the difference, it is helpful to break it down into its two components.

### 1. Distinguishing revenue from cash inflows

Revenue is *not* the same as money in. Revenue is the value of sales made over a specified period: a day, a

month or a year. For example, the takings at a Topshop outlet last Saturday: £450 of cash sales, £2,450 on credit cards and £600 on the Topshop store card (£3,500 in total). Note that the cash inflow for the day is just £450, so revenue is not the same as 'cash in'.

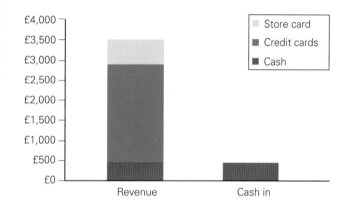

**Figure 42.1** Saturday takings at a clothing outlet

Whereas revenue comes from just one source (customers), cash inflows can come from many sources. It is not limited to trading. Selling an old warehouse for £600,000 does not generate revenue, but it does bring in cash. Similarly, taking out a bank loan could not be classed as revenue, but it does put cash into your bank current account.

So cash inflows *can* be part of the revenue, but they do not have to be. Therefore cash and revenue are not the same. Examples of differences between cash inflows and revenue are given in Table 42.1.

**Table 42.1** Differences between cash inflows and revenue

| Financial item | Cash inflow | Revenue |
|---|---|---|
| Cash sales made to customers | ✔ | ✔ |
| Credit sales made to customers | ✘ | ✔ |
| Capital raised from share sales | ✔ | ✘ |
| Charge rent on flat upstairs | ✔ | ✔ |
| Take out a £20,000 bank loan | ✔ | ✘ |
| Carry out a sale and leaseback | ✔ | ✘ |

'Revenue is vanity; profit is sanity; cash is King.' Anon

## 2. Distinguishing costs from cash outflows

The same distinction applies to costs and cash outflows. There are many reasons why a firm might pay out cash. Paying for the business's costs is only one of them. For example, the firm may pay out dividends to its shareholders, or it may repay a bank loan, or it may buy a piece of land as an investment.

In the case of the Wimbledon bar, the £200,000 annual profit gave the owners the confidence to buy leases on two new premises. They put together a business plan for expansion and received a £90,000 bank loan plus an £80,000 overdraft facility from a high street bank. They then hired architects and builders to turn the premises into attractive bars. Unfortunately, building hitches added to costs while delaying the opening times. The first of the new bars opened without any marketing support (there was no spare cash) and with the second of the bars still draining the business of cash, the bank demanded to have its overdraft repaid. As there was no way to repay the overdraft, the business went into liquidation.

So, a profitable business may run out of cash, simply because it expands too ambitiously, perhaps unluckily. There are other reasons why a profitable business might run into negative cash flow. These are set out below.

### Seasonal factors

A firm that is generating sufficient revenue to cover its costs over a 12-month period might still hit short-term cash flow problems. This is a particularly difficult problem for new small firms. A new bicycle shop opens in the spring and may enjoy an excellent first 6 months' trading. The owners may get excited at the good profit level, buy a new van and have a much-needed holiday. They would have expected the winter half-year to be fairly poor for bike sales, but may be shocked by the level of decline. By February they may run out of cash and be unable to pay their staff. If only they had known the pattern of demand, the owners could have saved money in the first half of the year; but a fundamentally profitable business may close down due to a cash flow crisis.

### Problems with credit periods

If a firm gives credit periods to its customers, there is risk from a long delay to a credit payment. For example, a builder who has put a great deal of money into renovating a large house finds that the client keeps delaying the final payment. The more serious the builder's cash flow problems become, the stronger the position of the client. So a profitable business may be thrown into a cash crisis that could threaten its survival. Examples of differences between cash outflows and costs are given in Table 42.2.

**Table 42.2** Differences between cash outflows and costs

| Financial item | Cash outflow | Costs |
|---|---|---|
| Cash payments to suppliers | ✔ | ✔ |
| Purchases from suppliers on credit | ✘ | ✔ |
| Paying out wages | ✔ | ✔ |
| Repayment of bank loans | ✔ | ✘ |
| Tax bill received but not yet paid | ✘ | ✔ |
| Buying freehold property* | ✔ | ✘ |
| Paying the electricity bill | ✔ | ✔ |

*Because a £500,000 property is worth £500,000, an accountant would not treat it as a cost.

## 42.3 Analysing the difference between cash flow and profit

The key is to appreciate that cash flow and profit are different aspects of the same thing. Cash flow and profit are linked, but they are not the same. Good financial planning requires an estimate of the likely profitability of a course of action. It then requires a careful forecast of the flows of cash in and out of the business. Profitability shows the long-term value of a financial decision; cash flow shows the short-term impact of that decision on the firm's bank balance.

### Real business

Trish decides to open a beauty salon. She estimates that annual fixed overheads will be £160,000 and annual revenues £300,000 offset by variable costs at 20 per cent of revenue (£60,000).

In other words annual profit should be: £300,000 − (£160,000 + £60,000) = £80,000

The start-up costs of opening the salon are expected to be £60,000, so the business will be profitable from year 1.

However, there are some important cash flow issues to consider: first, how long will it take before the salon opens its doors (and cash starts flowing in)? Second, will the business *really* start at a revenue level equivalent to £300,000 per year (£25,000 per month), or will it take many months before sales rise to a satisfactory level?

⇨

**Figure 42.2**

Table 42.3 shows the cash flow position of the business, assuming that it takes three months to prepare the beauty salon (building work, decoration, and so on) and that it will take four months before regular custom has built up fully. The forecast is for the first eight months.

**Table 42.3** Cash flow forecast for new beauty salon

| All figures in £000s | 1 | 2 | 3 | 4 | 5 | 6 | 7 | 8 |
|---|---|---|---|---|---|---|---|---|
| Cash at start | 0 | (20) | (40) | (60) | (64) | (64) | (59) | (51) |
| Cash in | 0 | 0 | 0 | 10 | 15 | 20 | 25 | 25 |
| Cash out | 20 | 20 | 20 | 14 | 15 | 15 | 17 | 17 |
| Net cash | (20) | (20) | (20) | (4) | (0) | 5 | 8 | 8 |
| Cumulative cash* | (20) | (40) | (60) | (64) | (64) | (59) | (51) | (43) |

*This is the firm's bank balance at the end of each month.

As you can see, even after eight months the business still has a serious cash flow problem. If the figures remain the same, it will be another six months before cumulative cash flow (the bank account) becomes positive. So the 'profitable' first year (and any accountant would confirm that the year is profitable) ends in the red.

The reason is simple. The cash investment to set up the business all takes place at the start, before the salon can generate a penny of cash inflow. The cash flow problem is because the cash outflow occurs before the cash inflows arrive. Therefore, the bank must be kept informed, so that it is willing to keep the business afloat. Unless the overdraft requirements are clear, and predicted, the bank manager may lose faith and demand all loans to be repaid.

'Every calculation of net profit reflects choices from competing theories of accounting… Profit is an opinion, cash is a fact.' Alex Pollock, American Enterprise Institute

## 42.4 Difficulties improving cash flow

Company cash flow is dominated by credit. Few companies pay cash: they buy on credit; and few sell for cash: they sell on credit. Therefore the biggest difficulty is if a company loses its financial credibility. If other businesses fear that a business will close it will surely do so. Suppliers will no longer give credit, so more cash is needed simply to keep in business; and if customers are increasingly worried about your survival, they'd prefer to go elsewhere.

It's critical, therefore, to avoid any suggestion that you are struggling financially. So if you need to improve cash flow you need to do it with subtlety. Beware of demanding shorter credit periods from your customers – or longer ones from suppliers. This is a reason why companies try to improve their cash flow position by cutting inventories or by speeding up their production programme.

**Table 42.4** Difficulties improving cash flow

| Business factor | How to boost cash flow | Difficulty in practice |
|---|---|---|
| **1.** Credit from suppliers | Delay payment to them | They may lose confidence in your solvency – and demand cash on delivery |
| **2.** Credit to customers | Cut credit period | Risk that they will go off and find a more generous supplier |
| **3.** Short of working capital | Use debt factoring | Fees take quite a slice of the profit, so it's hard to carry on for long |
| **4.** Use your assets | Sell underperforming assets for cash | There's a risk the business will end up with few assets for the future |

## 42.5 Difficulties improving profit

Profit can be improved in one of three ways: raise prices (if price elasticity isn't too high), raise sales volumes or cut costs. In reality each will be difficult because the business will already have done what is necessary to optimise revenues and profits. Therefore, prices will already be set at the 'right' level and costs will already have been driven down as low as

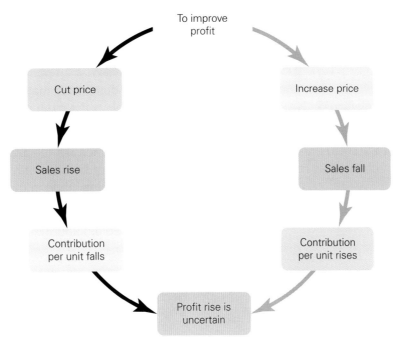

To improve profit

Cut price

Increase price

Sales rise

Sales fall

Contribution per unit falls

Contribution per unit rises

Profit rise is uncertain

**Figure 42.3** Logic chain: difficult to increase profit

makes sense. It's unwise, therefore, to make it sound easy to improve profit.

In practice the main difficulties are:

1. Raising prices: for price elastic products this inevitably cuts revenue, as the percentage fall in sales outweighs the percentage price rise. But even for price inelastic products there can be concerns. If other companies can see that one high-priced brand is making big profit margins, they will be attracted to compete. So pushing the price up provides a nice short-term boost to profit but perhaps at the cost of a future decline in market share.

2. Boosting sales volumes: the problem here is that either it is done by cutting prices (which will make it very

hard to boost profits) or the strategy will require some addition to costs, for example, extra advertising spending, the launch of a new flavour, or a flashy competition with prizes in Hawaii. Careful analysis is required to demonstrate that boosting sales volumes will end up improving profit

3. Cutting costs: it may seem obvious that you should look for a cheaper supplier, but every business is always on the look-out for that; so there's a risk that a cheaper supplier will have negatives such as: poorer quality, worse delivery reliability or perhaps – in some months' time – a scandal about child labour. Similarly, cutting fixed overhead costs by moving to a cheaper location may mean losing key staff – or stirring some hostile press coverage.

## Evaluation: Cash flow versus profit

Especially for small firms, every significant decision needs to be assessed in terms of cash flow as well as profit. The cash flow forecast predicts the impact on the bank balance and may show the need for extra overdraft facilities to be negotiated. Or, if the firm's cash position is already weak, it may be safer to postpone the proposal.

Yet cash flow is no substitute for calculating profit. A cash-rich business idea (such as insurance) may

inevitably lead to **insolvency** if the business is not profitable. Getting cash inflows at the start seems great, but will turn into a nightmare if the cash outflows eventually start flooding in.

Remember, then, that cash flow and profit are not the same. Cash flow measures the short-term and profit shows the longer-term financial result of a decision. Clever managers look at both before they proceed.

## Five Whys and a How

| Question | Answer |
|---|---|
| Why may a shoe shop's Saturday sales be different from its cash inflows? | Because some customers may use credit cards, which delays the cash inflows by several working days |
| Why is taking out a £20,000 bank loan a cash inflow, but not counted as revenue? | It's a cash inflow because the £20,000 is credited to the bank account but it's not revenue; revenue is just the value of sales made in the trading period |
| Why might a profitable business face a cash flow crisis? | Because it's inefficient at collecting sums owed by customers (payables) and therefore runs out of cash |
| Why should an overdraft be a last resort if a company faces a cash flow problem? | Because the interest charges will eat away part of the company's profit; far better to solve the cash flow problem, e.g. cut inventory (stock) levels |
| Why do small firms have to focus upon cash flow rather than profit? | Their cash-to-cash position is usually poor because customers want plenty of credit while suppliers give little or no credit |
| How may seasonal factors disrupt the cash flow of a profitable business? | Acutely seasonal sales create highly seasonal cash inflows, making it hard to manage financially during the slack part of the year |

## Key terms

**Dividends:** annual payments to shareholders from the profits made by the company. It is the equivalent of the interest paid to those who lend money.

**Insolvency:** inability to pay the bills, forcing closure.

**Negative cash flow:** when cash outflows outweigh cash inflows.

**Sale and leaseback:** selling the freehold to a piece of property then simultaneously leasing it back, perhaps for a period of 20 years. The owner gives up tomorrow's valuable asset in exchange for cash today.

'Banks only deal with those that don't need them.' Robert Townsend, Avis boss and business author

# Workbook

## A. Revision questions

(20 marks; 25 minutes)

1. Explain in your own words why cash inflow is not the same thing as revenue. (3)

2. Look at Table 42.1. Explain why taking out a £20,000 bank loan generates a cash inflow but not revenue. (3)

3. Give two reasons why a profitable business could run out of cash when it expands too rapidly. (2)

4. Look at Table 42.2. Explain why 'purchases from suppliers on credit' is treated as a cost, yet not as a cash outflow. (3)

5. Identify whether each of the following business start-ups would be cash-rich or cash-poor in the early years of the business.

   a) A pension fund, in which people save money in return for later pay outs. (1)

   b) Building a hotel. (1)

   c) Starting a vineyard (grapes can only be picked after 3 to 5 years). (1)

6. Look at Table 42.3. Use it and the accompanying text to explain why the cash flow of the beauty salon is different from its profit. (4)

7. Why is it important for a small business to look both at profit and cash flow? (2)

## B. Data response

**Investment Dragon Peter Jones on cash and profit**

**Managing your cash** in a focused manner is fundamental to survival, let alone success. Businesses are more likely to fail because they run out of cash – not because they're unable to generate a profit. You can have a lorry load of orders with the promise of untold profits in the pipeline, but if you don't have the cash to make and sell your products in the first place, and you are unable to pay your immediate bills, your business will fold.

Cash flow is a common hurdle for small and start-up enterprises. For that reason, it is important to **strengthen cash flow** from the outset.

**Monitor profit** and **avoid over-commitment**. One common mistake entrepreneurs make is that they see a run-rate of business and immediately start to incur costs. They'll rent an office, take on new lease commitments, buy a new car. These monthly payments can result in losing sight of the real cash that's generated through the business.

**Grow the business organically** and **keep costs down**, especially if you can't access bank finance. Focus on keeping costs to a bare minimum. Forget the office; work from home. Forget the car; use public transport. Grow the business, grow a pot of cash and then invest in the business. Using that money to reinvest is vital.

**Reinvest profits wisely. It is important to:**
- Understand what your start-up and on-going costs are. Be realistic. It is better to overestimate expenditure and time and underestimate revenue than fall short of revenue and overspend.

- Evaluate and monitor profit continually.
- Reinvest your profit. That way, you'll scale the business far quicker than if you use the profit to rent another office building or buy a car. It's how you spend the profit that's important. Entrepreneurs always spend profit on the business. Successful entrepreneurs invest that profit on the right areas to maximise growth and enhance existing offerings.

Source: www.peterjones.com

### Questions (25 marks; 30 minutes)

1. Explain why, in the first paragraph, Peter Jones seems to be suggesting that cash flow is more important than profit for a small business. (5)

2. By 'run-rate' Peter Jones means the revenue generated by the business once it is up and running. Why does he think an entrepreneur should wait before spending at this rate? (6)

3. Growing 'organically' means from within; that is, not rushing to buy up other businesses. Organic growth is usually at a slow enough pace to cope with cash flow pressures. Analyse why rapid growth can cause big cash flow problems. (9)

4. Explain why it is 'better to overestimate expenditure and time and underestimate revenue'. (5)

## C. Extend your understanding

1. When recession hits, wise financial managers focus more on cash flow and less on profit. Discuss why that might be the case. (20)

2. 'In the long run net cash flow and profit must be related. But in the short term they can differ wildly.' To what extent do you agree or disagree with this statement? (20)

# Chapter

# 43 Sources of finance

Linked to: Different business forms, Chapter 2; Issues in understanding forms of business, Chapter 3; Financial objectives, Chapter 36; Decision-making to improve financial performance, Chapter 44.

## Definition

All businesses need money. Where the money comes from is known as the 'sources of finance'.

## 43.1 The need for finance

### Starting up

New businesses starting up need money to invest in long-term assets such as buildings and equipment. They also need cash to purchase materials, pay wages and to pay the day-to-day bills such as water and electricity. Inexperienced entrepreneurs often underestimate the capital needed for the day-to-day running of the business. Generally, for every £1,000 required to establish the business, another £1,000 is needed for the day-to-day needs.

### Growing

Once the business is established there will be income from sales. If this is greater than the operating costs, the business will be making a profit. This should be kept in the business and used to help finance growth. Later on, the owners can draw money out, but at this stage as much as possible should be left in. Even so, there may not be enough to allow the business to grow as fast as it would like to. It may need to find additional finance and this will probably be from external sources such as bank loans.

### Other situations

Businesses may also need finance in other circumstances, such as a cash flow problem. A major customer may refuse to pay for the goods, causing a huge gap in cash inflows. Or there may be a large order, requiring the purchase of additional raw materials. In all these cases businesses will need to find additional funding.

## 43.2 Internal sources of finance

Internal finance comes from within the business and its resources. The most important is profit, that is a surplus of revenue over costs. That surplus will start by accumulating in the company bank account, and then will typically be spent, perhaps on buying new machinery, new vehicles or on a launch advertising campaign in a new country. Nothing soothes a difficult cash situation better than profit. It is also the best (and most common) way to finance investment into a firm's future. Research shows that over 60 per cent of business investment comes from reinvested profit.

Another internal source of finance is from within the company's working capital, that is the cash spent on building inventory and in credit provided to customers. If that investment can be cut, cash will be generated. In the case of Ted Baker plc in 2014, it had £80 million tied up in stocks (inventory) and £35 million owed to it by customers. If it was able to halve its stock levels it could boost its cash holdings by £40 million; and halving the figure for customer receivables would generate £17.5 million of cash. That's a lot of potential finance generated from within the business.

## 43.3 External sources of finance

If the business is unable to generate sufficient funds from internal sources then it may need to look to external sources. There are two sources of external capital: loan capital and share capital.

### Loan capital

The most usual way is through borrowing from a bank. This may be in the form of a bank loan or an overdraft. A loan is usually for a set period of time. It may be short term – one or two years; medium term – three to five years; or long term – more than five years. The loan can either be repaid in instalments over time or at the end of the loan period. The bank will charge interest on the loan. This can be fixed or variable. The bank will demand collateral to provide security in case the loan cannot be repaid.

An overdraft is a very short-term loan. It is a facility that allows the business to be 'overdrawn'. This means that the account is allowed to go 'into the red'. The length of time that this runs for will have to be negotiated. The interest charges on overdrafts are usually much higher than on loans. Fortunately the interest charges only apply to actual debts instead of the facility itself. For firms that use the overdraft as a way of smoothing short-term cash variations, the interest payments can be quite small.

## Share capital

As an alternative to debt, if the business is a limited company it may look for additional share capital. This could come from private investors or venture capital funds. Venture capital providers are interested in investing in businesses with dynamic growth prospects. They are willing to take a risk on a business that may fail, or may do spectacularly well. They believe that if they make ten investments, five can flop, and four do 'OK' as long as one does fantastically. Peter Thiel, the original investor in Facebook, turned his $0.5 million investment into just over $1,000 million, making a profit of 199,900 per cent between 2004 and 2012!

Once it has become a public limited company (plc), the firm may consider floating on the stock exchange. For smaller UK businesses this will usually be on the Alternative Investment Market (AIM).

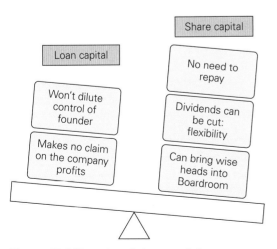

**Figure 43.1** The value of share capital

### Real business

#### *Financing growth*

How do rapidly growing small firms finance their growth? To find an answer to this question, Hamish Stevenson from Templeton College, Oxford, looks each year at 100 of the fastest growing UK firms. One of these is The Gym Group, which offers low-cost memberships for 24-hour gyms. Its sales grew from £1 million in 2008/9 to £22.6 million in 2012/13. The business started in 2007 with venture capital backing. Founder John Treharne had already built and sold a profitable chain of health clubs. Therefore, he was able to persuade venture capital company Bridges Ventures to provide £20 million of start-up equity in exchange for a substantial share stake. When the business required more capital to fulfil a plan of growing from 38 to 74 gyms by the end of 2015, another venture capital group invested a further £50 million in June 2013.

The Gym Group's easy access to capital contrasts with many others. As many as 54 of the 100 fastest growing firms financed all their early growth from a combination of personal savings and reinvested profits, that is, with no external funding at all.

## 43.4 Advantages and disadvantages of sources of finance

### Internal sources

The advantages and disadvantages of internal sources of finance are set out below.

### Retained (reinvested) profit

From any profits generated by the business most companies pay out about half as an annual dividend to the shareholders, ploughing the other half back into the business to help it grow. The advantage of reinvested profit is that it does not have an associated cost. Unlike loans it does not have to be repaid and there are no interest charges. The disadvantage is that there may be too little profit to allow the business to grow to its full capability.

### Cash squeezed out of day-to-day finances

By cutting stocks, chasing up customers or delaying payments to suppliers, cash can be generated. This has the advantage of reducing the amount that needs to be borrowed. However this is a very short-term solution and if the cash is taken from day-to-day capital for a purpose such as buying long-term assets, the firm may find itself short of cash flow.

## Debt factoring

One way to squeeze capital from day-to-day finances is by the use of debt factoring. A company that sells goods on credit can arrange that its bank take over the invoicing, giving the seller 80 per cent of the value of the sale immediately, then collecting the payment from the customer. Having taken its own commission, the bank then hands over the remaining sum to the seller (probably around 16 per cent). So the seller has most of the cash immediately, to help build the business, and does not have to chase the payment from the customer. It receives about 96 per cent of the value of the sale. The bank does the legwork but keeps a cut of about 4 per cent for itself.

## External sources

The advantages and disadvantages of external sources of finance are set out below.

### Bank overdrafts

This is the commonest form of borrowing for small businesses. The bank allows the firm to overdraw up to an agreed level. This has the advantages that the firm only has to borrow when and as much as it needs. It is, however, an expensive way of borrowing, and the bank can insist on being repaid within 24 hours.

The old saying holds: 'Owe your banker £1,000 and you are at his mercy; owe him £1 million and the position is reversed.' – John Maynard Keynes, British economist and author.

### Trade credit

This is the simplest form of external financing. The business obtains goods or services from another business but does not pay for these immediately. The average credit period is two months. It is a good way of boosting day-to-day finance. A disadvantage could be that other businesses may be reluctant to trade with the business if they do not get paid in good time.

### Bank loan

A bank loan is usually for a period of 2–5 years and is therefore classified as medium-term finance. It is an excellent form of finance for a new, growing business because there is no need to repay any capital until the contract says so – usually at the end of the period.

### Venture capital

This is a way of getting outside investment for businesses that are unable to raise finance through the stock markets or loans. Venture capitalists invest in smaller, riskier companies. To compensate for the risks, venture capital providers usually require a substantial part of the ownership of the company. They are also likely to want to contribute to the running of the business. This dilutes the owner's control but brings in new experience and knowledge. The term 'dragon' became a well-known term for a venture capital provider, thanks to the BBC TV series *Dragon's Den*.

---

'One thing I'm so grateful for is sidestepping the usual venture capital, private equity route. My friends who have gone that way are many times beholden to their boards of directors, to 'sell' ideas to a team.' Blake Mycoskie, founder TOMS Shoes

---

A modern version of venture capital is 'crowdfunding'; it's a way of getting small investors to put money into a new business – often with an incentive such as to get a sample product or service in return for their investment. It works via the internet and works most effectively when the sponsors use social media to promote their business. In the UK, Seedrs and Kickstarter are two of the best-known sponsors of crowdfunding.

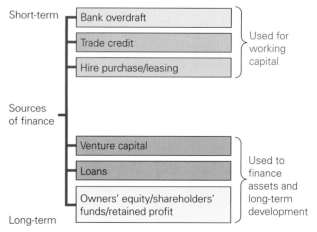

**Figure 43.2** Short- and long-term sources of finance

---

'62.4 per cent of venture capital investments were completely lost while 3.1 per cent of the investments accounted for 53 per cent of the profits for roughly 600 investments.' Mahendra Ramsinghani, business author

---

## 43.5 Finance for short- and long-term uses

Businesses need sufficient access to finance to meet current and future needs. This is a major issue for new firms and for those that are expanding rapidly. When a business expands without sufficient finance it is known as 'overtrading'.

The key is to match the type of finance to its use. A distinction is made in company financing between short- and long-term finance (see Figure 43.2). Short-term finance is usually considered to be for less than one year. Medium-term is one to five years. Long-term finance is longer than five years.

Short-term finance should not be used to finance long-term projects. Using short-term finance such as overdrafts puts continual pressure on the company's cash position. An overdraft should only be used to cope with ups and downs in cash flow. By its very nature,

growth is a long-term activity, so appropriate long-term finance should be sought to fund it.

Another key aspect of appropriate finance is that businesses should find the right balance between 'equity' and debt. Equity means share capital, which is safe and stable, as shareholders need not be paid a dividend if times are tough. Debt-based finance such as an overdraft or loan is more risky. Even when business is poor the bank still expects to be paid interest on the loan, plus – with an overdraft – the bank may demand that the overdraft is repaid immediately.

## Five Whys and a How

| Question | Answer |
|---|---|
| Why might a business finance expansion using debt rather than equity? | Issuing more equity dilutes the value of shares, putting the founders' control of the business at risk |
| Why might debt factoring be a mistake for some types of business? | Banks take a cut of about 4 per cent of the value of the sale; if the business has low profit margins (say, 8 per cent) this would halve the sellers' profit |
| Why might a bank refuse to lend to a business? | It may doubt the firm's ability to repay, i.e. see it as too risky; or the bank may think it can make more profit elsewhere, e.g. property speculation |
| Why might a business collapse from overtrading (growing too fast)? | If sales increases outstrip the firm's capital base, it can run out of cash and slide into administration |
| Why do venture capital companies invest in some businesses but not others? | Venture capitalists seek huge potential gains, therefore they love 'scalability': a high potential for the business to grow massively |
| How might crowdfunding prove harmful to a new small business? | Getting a bank loan for £250,000 is simple to administer; 50,000 crowdfunders investing £5 each could become an administrative nightmare |

## Key terms

**Angel investors:** investors who back a business before it's opened its doors, taking a full equity risk, that is, if it fails the angel investor will lose everything.

**Collateral:** an asset used as security for a loan. It can be sold by a lender if the borrower fails to pay back a loan.

**Crowdfunding:** instead of getting one angel investor to finance a £50,000 start-up, crowdfunding looks for many small investors, perhaps each investing an average of £100 (so 500 such investors will be needed).

**Overtrading:** when a firm expands without adequate and appropriate funding.

**Public limited company (plc):** a company with limited liability and shares which are available to the public. Its shares can be quoted on the stock market.

**Share capital:** business finance that has no guarantee of repayment or of annual income but gains a share of the control of the business and its potential profits.

**Stock market:** a market for buying and selling company shares. It supervises the issuing of shares by companies. It is also a second-hand market for stocks and shares.

**Venture capital:** high-risk capital invested in a combination of loans and shares, usually in a small, dynamic business.

# Workbook

## A. Revision questions

**(30 marks; 40 minutes)**

1. Describe the problem caused to a company if a major customer refuses to pay a big bill. (3)

2. Why do banks demand collateral before they agree to provide a bank loan? (2)

3. Outline two ways in which businesses can raise money from internal sources. (4)

4. What information may a bank manager want when considering a loan to a business? (4)

5. Explain briefly the benefits to a manufacturing business of using debt factoring instead of an overdraft. (4)

6. Outline two sources of finance that can be used for long-term business development. (4)

7. Explain why a new business could find it difficult to get external funding for its development? (5)

8. Outline one advantage and one disadvantage of using an overdraft. (4)

## B. Revision exercises
### DATA RESPONSE 1

**Indian in China?**

Posting to www.chinasuccessstories.com:

Hi everyone, I am from India and wish to open a quick takeaway and a small restaurant or café but with Indian snacks and food in Nanjing, near the International University. I would like to know about:

1. the rules and regulations

2. the approximate budget

3. the minimum area requirement

4. the real estate prices in an area like Shanghai Lu, Nanjing.

Please contact me by leaving a comment here.

Thank you,

Karishma

Hi Karishma,

You have to know that the life expectancy of a new foreign restaurant on Nanjing Road is between three and six months, in 50 per cent of cases. Many foreigners open restaurants without complying with all the rules… Be ready to have enough funds to survive for one year minimum without any revenues. If you want I could give you contacts with very good companies that could help you for all legal aspects. Good luck, and I will come to your restaurant!

Paul Martin

**Questions (30 marks; 30 minutes)**

1. Explain to Karishma the implications for start-up financing of Paul Martin's reply. (5)

**2.** Analyse the circumstances in which Karishma should proceed with her idea, if she were able to obtain the start-up finance. (9)

**3.** To what extent should Karishma be looking for share rather than loan capital to finance her start-up? (16)

## DATA RESPONSE 2

### Kickstarter

In recent years crowdfunding has become an alternative to traditional market research and also a different way to finance a start-up. The Kickstarter website helps a creative business idea to be put to the public, asking for start-up capital in exchange for a free 'taste' of the product.

**Figure 43.3** The Boombox bag

One successful 2014 start-up was Chivote, a producer of leather bags and accessories. It raised £20,000 through Kickstarter by offering products in exchange

for investment. A £7 investment received a leather nametag in return, while £240 yielded a Boombox bag.

Crowdfunding uses online technology and social media to replace the traditional role of banks.

Chivote has another unusual aspect to its business. It sources its leather goods from a small partnership of craftsmen which works as a partner instead of a supplier to Chivote. This is another way to help minimise the capital needed to start up the business. Usually a new business would have to pay cash up front for supplies; the partnership ensures that normal credit terms can smooth the cash flow requirements.

### Questions (30 marks; 35 minutes)

**1.** Explain the benefit to cash flow of having a supplier who offers credit terms instead of cash-only. (5)

**2.** Analyse the benefits of crowdfunding compared with traditional venture capital funding when starting a business such as Chivote. (9)

**3.** A weakness of crowdfunding might be that it's effective only with consumer-friendly, attractive products or services. To what extent is that a problem? (16)

## C. Extend your understanding

**1.** While at University you develop a game for mobiles based on tractors, farms, rabbits and foxes – and everyone loves it. Your parents lend you £4,000 and you have £2,000 but you estimate that it'll cost about £20,000 simply to get the game ready for use and to get it some publicity. To what

extent might venture capital be the best way to finance the start-up of your business? (20)

**2.** For the founder of a rapidly growing small business, how important is it to keep 51-plus per cent of the share capital? Justify your answer. (20)

# Chapter 44 Decision-making to improve financial performance

Linked to: Financial objectives, Chapter 36; Cash flow management and forecasting, Chapter 39; Profit and how to increase it, Chapter 41; Sources of finance, Chapter 43.

### Definition

Financial performance means measuring the achievements of the business in relation to the financial objectives set.

## 44.1 Introduction

Financial performance can be measured in many ways. Entrepreneurs in the Dragon's Den are trying to obtain finance; later they'll be hoping for break even and in the longer term profit will become the key form of measurement. This chapter looks at the constraints that can prevent companies from finding it easy to meet their financial objectives.

## 44.2 Financial decisions and competitiveness

Whenever possible, finance directors like to compare their own firm's financial performance with that of a direct competitor. A good case in point is the competition between two fashion clothing businesses: Ted Baker plc and SuperGroup plc (aka SuperDry). As shown in Table 44.1 both companies could learn from this comparison. SuperGroup is doing brilliantly to convert a lower gross margin into a higher operating margin (implying tighter control of fixed overhead costs). Ted Baker can take huge pride in its recent growth rate, especially for e-commerce.

In terms of financial decisions, SuperGroup might consider heavier investments into its website – perhaps it needs to catch up with Ted. For Ted Baker, perhaps serious thought is needed about the overhead costs; for example, should Ted move its headquarters to somewhere cheaper?

Table 44.1 Financial performance at Ted Baker plc and SuperGroup plc

|  | Ted Baker plc | SuperGroup plc |
|---|---|---|
| Revenue 2014 | £322 m | £431 m |
| Revenue growth re: 2013 | +26.7 per cent | +19.6 per cent |
| E-commerce growth 2014 | +55.7 per cent | +26.7 per cent |
| Gross profit margin | 61.7 per cent | 59.7 per cent |
| Operating profit margin | 12.3 per cent | 14.3 per cent |

Among other financial decisions that might affect business competitiveness are:

- Borrowing more: this is a quick and easy way to add capital to a business that is growing, or one that needs a dramatic change in strategy. Unfortunately it runs the medium- to long-term risk that the indebted capital structure will create significant operational risks. Growth can evaporate if customer taste turns sour and dramatic changes in strategy are – by definition – risky. A severely weakened balance sheet can undermine a company's competitiveness.

- Cutting costs: removing a whole layer of store management, as Asda and Morrisons' did in Spring 2014, may cause short-term disruption to both operations and HR, but all in the cause of stronger long-term competitiveness. Where price competition is as fierce as in grocery retailing, keeping costs down (especially fixed overheads) will always be a critical success factor.

- Boosting cash flow: recently ASOS stretched its time to pay suppliers from 43 days in 2012 to 59 in 2013; taking an extra half a month to pay enables the company to keep nearly £20 million extra in its bank account. That helps finance growth, though competitiveness may be worsened if suppliers start to show preference for other retailers (for example, with stock of newly launched product lines).

'Competitive prices may result in profits which force you to accept a rate of return less than you hoped for.' Alfred Sloan, CEO, General Motors

## Real business

A massive restructuring by the supermarket chain Asda has put 4,100 management jobs in consultation. It is thought thousands of middle managers will leave the company rather than accept alternative lower-paid jobs. The restructuring comes as the grocer realigns itself to deal with the growing popularity of online shopping and home delivery.

'We haven't updated our structure for five to six years,' said Asda's chief operating officer, Mark Ibbotson. 'We believe we are about 18 months ahead of our competitors. They're all going to have to do this at some point.'

Ibbotson is tasked with finding £1 billion of cost savings over the next five years as a fierce battle on price continues among the nation's largest supermarkets.

As part of the restructuring Asda has created in-store e-commerce manager roles and will devote more staff to services such as click-and-collect and grocery home delivery.

Source: Several, including *The Grocer*, *The Guardian* and *RetailWeek*

## 44.3 Financial decisions and the other business functions

No department is as central as finance. Its decisions affect and are affected by every other function. If marketing decides to run a '20 per cent off' price promotion that unexpectedly doubles demand, finance will need to find the cash for buying the extra supplies and to pay the overtime bill. Figure 44.1 shows this.

What most finance directors hate most is unexpected surprises. This is why they are so keen on budgeting, which requires staff to plan ahead and then record any variations from the planned income or expenditure.

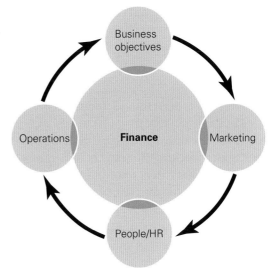

**Figure 44.1** Logic chain: finance at the core

## 44.4 Impact on finance of market condition and competition

Following its scandal-ridden era from 2007–2013 Barclays Bank announced in 2014 that 15,000 jobs would go that year, and that the medium-term plan was to cut staff from 140,000 worldwide to 100,000. These huge job cuts reflected the bank's worsening revenue position and its withdrawal from some of its highest-risk banking sectors. In this case, then, worsening market conditions dictated the finance department's demand for cost cuts. Perhaps sadly, in the case of Barclays, there was no additional competitive pressure facing it or other high street banks. Despite all the banks' failings and the low esteem in which they were held, most people remained reluctant to switch their current account.

Perhaps it's fair to say that bad times place finance at the heart of every business decision. A bigger test comes in good times. If sales and profits are rising, marketing and R&D people may push harder for bigger budgets – and it may be difficult to stop this happening. Those finance departments that 'succeed' in good times are probably managing to persuade directors that it's time for shareholders to get some significant rewards. In 2014 Apple Inc. spent $30 billion in cash to buy shares back from its stockholders. This boosts the share price (which, handily, can boost bonus payments for directors) but at the cost of the firm's cash flow position.

Overall, the finance function tends to want to keep on-going costs as low as possible, so that profit margins are as high as possible. They tend not to mind share buy-backs because they are a one-off expenditure rather than an on-going one.

And competition? The typical finance manager wants as little of it as possible. So any proposal to buy up direct competitors will always get a good hearing – and probably enthusiastic backing from the company's bankers. Competition is a threat to profit margins and a threat to a secure, easy life for the company. The last thing finance staff want to see is a price war.

---

'Cost accounting is the number one enemy of productivity'. Johnson and Kaplan, business writers

---

## 44.5 Ethical and environmental influences on financial decisions

Those working in finance tend to have a pragmatic view of ethical or environmental issues. In other words they want to see them pay their way. So an environmental programme based on recycling and waste minimisation can get the support of the finance function if its advocates can prove that cost reductions will make the proposal profitable. Similarly, a move to Fairtrade supplies (such as Nestlé/Kit Kat in 2010) needs to justify itself in terms of the value it adds to consumers' perception of the brand. In other words, it's okay to add half a penny to the costs if the price can be pushed up a full penny. For a business to make a genuine move towards ethical practices it would be essential that the finance department got instructions from on high (the chief executive or the board). Then co-operation will happen.

Another important aspect of modern finance is tax 'planning', that is, the deliberate act of tax avoidance. In the UK there has been a successful effort to point the finger of blame at US companies, especially those in the technology sector. Starbucks, Amazon, Apple, Google and many others have been picked out. In fact there are many British firms or organisations that deserve huge criticism, including Vodafone, the Virgin group and perhaps the whole of the private equity sector (owners of Boots, Pret A Manger, many energy companies and

much, much more). Ultimately, the tax-dodging deals are done by senior finance executives. And if you think that tax avoidance is ethically neutral, how can it be fair that a tax-paying company such as Ted Baker should have to compete with a rival fashion retailer that rigs things to pay little or no tax. A level playing field is an important underpinning to an effective market.

---

## 44.6 Technological influences on financial decisions

Currently crowdfunding is a fashionable approach to capital raising, especially for businesses with a consumer-friendly business proposition. From Seedrs in the UK to M-Changa in Kenya, this is seen as a valuable application of online technology to financial needs. In fact the approach can be dated at least as far back as Mozart in the 1700s, raising money to fund three concerts in Vienna. But the crowdfunding of today is unquestionably an online process.

More fundamental, perhaps, are the financial implications of key strategic decisions about whether to function via 'bricks' or 'clicks'. Setting up a network of shops or physical outlets implies huge fixed operating costs and therefore a high break-even point. Having only a digital/online presence cuts those costs dramatically and therefore brings the break-even down. Much though this would please finance managers, the downside is that it may be much harder to build sales virtually than physically.

---

**Real business**

Future Ad Labs is a UK business focused on intelligent targeting of advertising to users of hand-held devices. Having achieved funding from Seedrs in 2012, it obtained an extra $1 million from venture capital and angel investors in 2013 and then returned to Seedrs in 2014 to raise more finance via convertible shares. A sceptic would worry about all this capital-raising (How about making some profit, guys?), but because Future Ad Labs specialises in high technology online and social media advertising, investors have been happy to support its cash-hungry growth.

## Five Whys and a How

| Question | Answer |
|---|---|
| Why might new, low-cost Chinese competition help boost a UK firm's competitiveness in the long term? | It would force the UK firm to rethink its costs and perhaps encourage operations to become more efficient |
| Why might finance professionals believe finance is the most important business function? | Success in business is measured by profit and loss, so it's understandable to see finance as all-important |
| Why might finance professionals care less about ethical standards than managers in HR or marketing? | Because the finance executives feel only distantly involved in decisions that might include price fixing or tax avoidance |
| Why don't finance professionals take into account the external costs and benefits of the company's actions? | Because only the government can calculate based on social benefits and costs; business organisations just look at their internal costs and benefits |
| Why may high debts represent a risky capital structure? | Because, if things go wrong, high debts mean high interest payments and therefore a threat to cash flow |
| How might operations management be affected by big cutbacks in the budgets allocated by finance? | A short-term cutback in investment spending might be followed by a longer-term need to cut capacity so as to boost capacity utilisation |

## Evaluation: Decision-making to improve financial performance

Day by day, staff working within finance will rarely see those from other functions. Finance staff are busy gathering data on what has happened to revenue and costs, and projecting forward to try to anticipate what's going to happen over the coming months. The single most important period of time for working with other departments is when budgets are to be agreed. Then finance staff will try to identify budget claims that are unwarranted. In addition, there will occasionally be major changes to strategy (perhaps marketing or operations) which require a very different financial approach. The best finance director will be the one that knows when to stop saying no. Bold strategies need bold financial decisions.

'Business is a good game – lots of competition and a minimum of rules. You keep score with money.'
Nolan Bushnell, computer game pioneer

# Workbook

## A. Revision questions

(25 marks; 25 minutes)

1. Look at the data in Table 44.1. Give two possible reasons why Ted Baker's gross profit margin is greater than SuperGroup's. (2)

2. If a company is enjoying rising profits at a time when the economy is booming, what might it do to check on the strength of its performance? (5)

**3.** Briefly explain why Barclays had to cut its staff numbers so dramatically in 2014. (3)

**4.** Explain how a firm's competitiveness might be affected if it ends up adopting too risky a capital structure. (4)

**5.** Briefly explain the inter-relationship between finance and the other functional areas. (4)

**6.** What might be the implications of a business deciding to outsource its finance department? (4)

**7.** Why might crowdfunding be a good alternative to bank borrowing when a company wishes to raise more capital? (3)

# B. Revision exercises
## DATA RESPONSE

### Change of strategy at Hovis

**Figure 44.2** Hovis white loaf

In 2006 UK food giant Premier Foods plc paid £2 billion to take over Hovis bakeries. The stock market was impressed, boosting the Premier share price by 10 per cent in a day. Yet when Michael Clarke took over as chief executive at Premier Foods in August 2011, he described the business as 'virtually broken'. Huge debts plus poor trading had cut the value of Premier shares by 98 per cent. The prime cause was Hovis.

In March 2012 Premier announced a £259 million pre-tax loss after writing down the value of its bread division (Hovis). Fierce price competition meant that trading profits for the bread division fell by 90 per cent in 2011/12 to £3.4 million. With Premier weighed down by more than £1 billion of debt, Clarke decided it was time to tackle the Hovis problem.

In 2011 the Hovis strategy had been to build market share by boosting advertising spending using cycling star Victoria Pendleton as the face of the brand. This increased sales by a higher percentage than the bread market as a whole, yet did not prevent the 90 per cent profit slide mentioned above. When the profit figures came through, the marketing plan was deemed to have failed. So, for 2012, Clarke decided that cost minimisation was required.

The first signal came in October 2012 when Premier announced that it was withdrawing from a £75 million contract to supply bread to the Co-op retail chain. This supply contract (two-thirds Hovis branded, one third Co-op own brand) was described by Premier as a 'high-cost, low-margin retail partnership'. The purpose behind the cancellation became clear a month later when Premier announced the closure of two bakeries and the removal of 130 distribution routes, leading to 900 job losses (10 per cent of bread division staffing).

The company announced that: 'The bread contract loss takes volume out and that is a catalyst for us to be able to make changes and manage the bread business in a different way... The move forms part of a long-term strategy to drive efficiency.'

Later, in November 2012, the managing director of Premier's bakery arm resigned. He had only been in the job for a year, but perhaps he was unwilling to be part of a switch from market-share growth to severe cost cutting. The cutbacks associated with the Co-op contract are unlikely to be the last.

**Figure 44.3** Hovis Best of Both loaf

Meanwhile, Premier's big rival Allied Bakeries says it is delighted to pick up the Co-op contract on the same terms as those rejected by Hovis. In other words Allied thinks it can make money from the deal. A City analyst commented that 'Allied anticipates the benefits of marginal economies from the Co-op deal... It is fair to say that Allied is more efficient than Hovis and so has more ammunition at hand.' Can Premier really strengthen itself by strengthening the market-share position of its rivals? Time will tell.

## C. Extend your understanding

1. It is sometimes said that in Germany businesses revolve around engineers, but in Britain they revolve around accountants. To what extent might this be a disadvantage to Britain? (20)

### Questions (25 marks; 30 minutes)

1. For a business such as Premier Foods plc, analyse the factors that might lead to a decision to focus on cost minimisation. (9)

2. Examine one alternative financial strategy that Premier Foods might adopt. (7)

3. Analyse how the finance department might have judged that the 2011 Hovis marketing plan was unprofitable. (9)

2. 'Many financial measurements which are useful and valid in static situations are strategic traps in growth situations.' Bruce Henderson, Boston Consulting Group. To what extent do you agree with this statement? (20)

# Chapter 45 Setting human resource (HR) objectives

**Linked to:** Motivation and engagement in theory, Chapter 46; Managing the human resource flow, Chapter 49; Analysing human resource performance, Chapter 51; Decision-making and improved human resource performance, Chapter 52.

## Definition

Human resource management is a common term for the personnel function. HR professionals think of their role as central to the overall goals of the business, and set their HR objectives accordingly.

## 45.1 Human resource objectives

The management of people (otherwise known as human resource management) involves a wide range of activities. The overall aim is to maximise the contribution of employees on an individual and group level to the organisation's overall objectives. To do this, specific goals need to be met. These HR objectives will be derived from the targets of the business as a whole.

'Management by objectives works if you know the objectives. Ninety per cent of the time you don't.' Peter Drucker, business writer/guru

### Employee engagement and involvement

As shown in Figure 45.1, companies simply cannot assume that hiring and training staff is enough. According to Gallup Poll, only 13 per cent of staff worldwide are fully engaged in their job. If they aren't engaged and interested, they will never give 100 per cent.

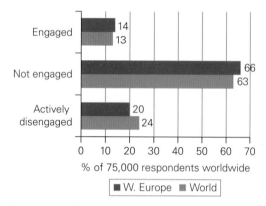

**Figure 45.1** Employee engagement study, October 2013
*Percentage of 75,000 respondents worldwide*
Source: Gallup Poll Worldwide

The problem is that there is no reason to suppose that HR professionals have any real solution to this problem. 'Employee engagement' is little different from 'motivation', but even though it has been known for fifty years that motivation can best be addressed through job enrichment, the HR approach is quite different. Nor is this a surprise. Job enrichment requires jobs to be redesigned, with high division of labour replaced by giving people a complete unit of work. Yet this is outside the scope of HR professionals, who couldn't possibly advise an operations manager about how to lay out a factory or a supermarket checkout. So the HR approach is to pretend that employee engagement can be achieved through financial devices and bureaucratic devices such as staff appraisal. Professor Herzberg, whose theories are discussed in Chapter 46, would see little value in any of this. Given the prevalence of HR departments today, the 'engaged' figure of 13 per cent is a clear pointer to the need for a different approach.

'British management doesn't seem to understand the importance of the human factor.' Charles, Prince of Wales

## Talent development

For many businesses, the key to long-term success is training and motivation of the staff as a whole. In some circumstances, though, it is understandable that the focus may be on the talented few rather than the entire staff. Southampton FC has been a leading light in football talent development, having consistently devoted a large chunk of budget to developing youth players. The result, from Gareth Bale and Theo Walcott through to Luke Shaw, has generated enough transfer cash to justify the policy.

For other businesses, graduate 'fast-track' schemes have long existed, with the view that those with extra talent should be given every opportunity for career progression as rapid as their talents allow. There is a risk, though, that the focus on the talented few could seem to come at the expense of the majority. This is unlikely to help morale.

In 2014 the Chartered Institute of Personnel Development (CIPD) published research showing that the median annual training budget per employee in Britain is £286 (down from £303 in 2013). With such a tiny figure, the idea of switching it away from the majority towards the 'talented' could negatively affect the teamwork and culture of an organisation.

## Training

Professor Herzberg once said that 'the more a person can do, the more you can motivate them.' Therefore training people to be able to do more, and do it with confidence, represents a big potential step forward for a business. Yet there is scant evidence that UK firms understand this fully. They like to blame schools and universities for failing to prepare students for the world of work, but their own reluctance to train is quite odd. Figure 45.2 shows data from America and Britain that

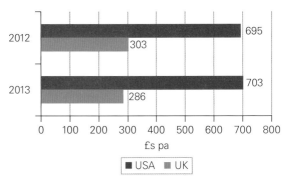

**Figure 45.2** Employer annual spend on training UK vs USA
Source: CIPD and ASTD

paints British employers in a poor light. British government data in 2014 suggested a UK productivity gap of about 30 per cent compared with America. Perhaps it is time to address this – starting by spending more on training.

### Real business

On 13 December 2013 the American Society for Training and Development published their latest annual survey. It showed that the average US employee had $1,195 (£703) spent per year on their training, which amounted to an average of 30.3 hours. Sixty-one per cent of the spending was done internally (on-the-job) and the top areas of training content were managerial and supervisory followed by mandatory and compliance (that is, legal requirements). The total spent on training by US organisations amounted to $164.2 billion in a year.

## Diversity

The Greggs website (http://corporate.greggs.co.uk/greggs-at-a-glance/main-board) includes photographs of the executive directors of Greggs plc. The non-executive directors include three women, but decisions in business are driven through by executive directors, so these are the ones who count. Excellent a company though Greggs has long been, it is striking to see the lack of diversity by age, gender and race. Surely, given that Greggs' customers are a cross-section of British consumers, the boardroom would benefit from some voices other than those of middle-aged, white blokes.

This is why some companies have set themselves the objective of diversifying their middle and senior management teams. They have been encouraged by statements such as this, by David Tyler, Sainsbury's chairman: 'Shareholders benefit when boards have a diversity of skills, background and experience. That's the way the most effective boards tend to be composed – with both men and women playing a full part.' The UK organisation '30 Per Cent Club' wants to see women making up at least 30 per cent women of board directors. This focus on female representation risks sidelining race as an issue. In 2014 two-thirds of Britain's Top 100 companies had no non-white full-time executive board members. The case for diversity is clear; the drive to achieve it is less so.

**Figure 45.3** In 2014 two-thirds of Britain's Top 100 companies had no non-white full-time executive board members.

## Alignment of values

Business author Jim Collins has said that businesses spend too long worrying about their new mission or vision. They would be stronger if they spent more time aligning staff to the organisation's core values. He cites the US company 3M (famous for Post-it Notes), which has long had at its centre: sponsoring innovation, protecting the creative individual and solving problems in a way that makes people's lives better.

Collins suggests that firms should work at identifying their core values, then make sure that every employee sees these values as central to decision-making throughout the business. Accordingly, recruitment and induction training should focus on making sure that there is a true fit between staff and the values. This should not only ensure that ethical issues are tackled in a consistently moral way, but should also help build a sense of purpose throughout the staff – which may help with motivation and retention levels.

---

### Real business

US giant 3M is proud of its first patent from its operation in India. India's massive textile industry had long sent discarded cotton threads to landfill. Now 3M's technology allows handloom weavers to transform the threads into floor-cleaning cloths, creating jobs for local residents – and providing a commercial incentive for recycling.

---

## The number, skills and location of employees

Organisations are continually changing in terms of the work being done and the way it is done. This reshaping requires changes in the human resource input. For example, it may require more people, greater flexibility or different skills. The human resource function is responsible for making sure the business has the right number of people at the right time, with the right skills and attitudes. A lack of appropriate staff can lead to delays for customers, rushed and poor-quality work, and an inability to accept some contracts. By comparison, if the human resource requirements are met, a business is more likely to be able to provide a high-quality service and fulfil the expectations of customers. Achieving the right number of staff may be relatively easy if you can simply recruit more people when you need them. However, it can also be a very long-term process that involves enormous planning. In the case of the health service, for example, there is a very long training period for doctors and surgeons. The NHS has to plan years in advance for the number of doctors it will need.

A further factor is the location of staff. HR departments like staff to be willing to work in Portsmouth for six months, then move to Manchester. For many staff this flexibility is impossible, so careful planning is required to make sure that Manchester has the right manager at the right time.

---

## 45.2 Internal and external influences on HR objectives and decisions

### Internal influences

The recent history of a business often provides insight into its corporate and HR objectives. The German industrial giant Siemens was involved in a series of bribery scandals in 2005. Its response was to appoint a new boss from outside the company (Peter Loescher). He encouraged the company to develop a bureaucratic style of 'ethical tick boxes' which made staff reluctant to take responsibility for decisions. This undermined the efficiency of the business, leading to poor engineering project management, contract losses and the dismissal of Loescher in 2013.

In addition to recent history, other internal influences are:

- the past experiences, character and ambitions of any newly appointed chief executive
- any financial pressures felt by the business, for example, cash flow problems requiring a quick fix
- changing marketing objectives, such as the decision by Aldi to move upmarket in the UK in 2011. This would have forced a change in recruitment and training from an HR perspective.

### External influences

Few external influences are more important in HR than the economy. When economic growth is sustained for a few years and unemployment is falling, HR departments have to work hard to attract the best recruits, especially graduates. If a recession takes hold, HR objectives revert to efficiency maximisation, involving redundancies, a switch to temporary and part-time working, and outsourcing (which usually means lower wage rates).

In addition to economic factors, other external influences are:

- whether the business is a stock market-quoted plc or a large family-run business. This affects the timescales for HR and other objectives; for example, the bosses of under-pressure businesses such as Marks & Spencer have to fulfil shareholders' half-yearly expectations regarding sales and profit performance. This is not helpful for long-term HR planning.

- The social and ethical climate: sometimes the media and the public seem to develop huge concern for specific issues such as Fairtrade supplies; HR objectives must take these things into account (though it would be a lot more impressive if ethical concerns were a consistent business feature).

- Legal factors may have an effect. In 2014 the Labour opposition warned that it might feel the need to legislate to enforce greater ethnic diversity in Britain's boardrooms. In Norway, legally enforceable quotas have taken female board representation from 9 per cent in 2003 to over 40 per cent by 2014. British businesses always warn of terrible consequences from employment legislation; Norway's experience suggests it would be relatively painless.

## 45.3 HR strategies: soft and hard HRM

### Hard HRM

While all organisations undertake the various activities involved in managing human resources (such as recruitment, selection and training) the attitude and approach of managers towards employees can differ significantly. At one extreme is hard HRM. This regards employees as a necessary if unwelcome cost; people are an input required to get the job done, but add little to the overall value created by the business. With this approach managers see themselves as the 'thinkers'; they develop the best way of doing things and employees are expected to get on with it. This fits with the 'scientific management' approach of F. W. Taylor (see Chapter 46).

Hard HRM usually adopts a top-down management style in which employees are directed and controlled. Employees are expected to fit in with the design of the organisation. Managers and supervisors instruct

them and then monitor their actions. Jobs tend to be broken down into relatively small units so that one person does not have much control over the process and a replacement can easily be recruited, selected and trained. This type of approach can often be seen in call centres, where the work of operatives is very closely monitored, or in highly controlled outlets such as McDonald's.

The hard approach to HRM has many benefits, such as:
- the outcomes should be predictable because employees do as they are told
- employees should be easily replaceable
- managers retain control for decision-making and this reduces the risk of major errors being made.

However, the disadvantages of this approach include:
- a possible failure to build on the skills, experience and insights of the employees; this can lead to dissatisfied employees and low morale
- a danger that the organisation as a whole is at risk because it relies so heavily on the senior managers; if they make mistakes the business as a whole could fail because there is no input from lower levels.

'"Top" management is supposed to be a tree full of owls hooting when management heads into the wrong part of the forest. I'm still unpersuaded they even know where the forest is.' Robert Townsend, author of *Up the Organisation*

### Soft HRM

By comparison, the soft HRM approach takes the view that employees can add a great deal of value to an organisation, and the business should develop, enhance and build on their interests, skills and abilities. Under a soft approach managers see themselves more as facilitators. They are there to coach and help employees to do their job properly, perhaps by ensuring sufficient training is provided and that the employee can develop in his or her career.

The advantages of a soft approach to HRM are that:
- the organisation is building on the skills and experience of their employees; this may enable the business to be more creative, more innovative and differentiated from the competition
- the organisation may be able to keep and develop highly skilled employees with expectations of a career within the business
- individuals throughout the business are encouraged to contribute, which may make the organisation more flexible and adaptable to changing market conditions.

The disadvantages of a soft HRM approach may be that:

- time is taken in discussion and consultation rather than 'getting the job' done

- employees may not have the ability or inclination to get involved; they may just want to be told what to do and be rewarded for it. In this case a soft approach to HRM may be inappropriate and ineffective.

## Five Whys and a How

| Question | Answer |
|---|---|
| Why might a business set out clear HR objectives? | To make sure they match the corporate objectives and to make sure that the HR plans/strategies match the HR objectives |
| Why might the HR objectives be affected by the recent history of the business? | Recent trading or public image difficulties will affect the objectives and decisions made within HR |
| Why might a company talk about diversity but do little more than appoint diverse non-executive directors? | Because companies care about public relations (PR) and therefore want to avoid embarrassment, yet they perhaps fail to see the operational benefits that might result from true diversity |
| Why might Marks & Spencer benefit if it had younger, more ethnically diverse executive directors? | They might help the business realise how much it has to do to break free from its current image as a shop for middle-aged, middle class, white Britain |
| Why might a business need to switch from a soft to a hard approach to human resources? | In a situation of crisis, tough decisions have to be made, and made quickly. Even if these decisions are regretted later on, they may be needed for survival |
| How would a manager interested in talent development set about solving a long-term problem of staff engagement? | By delegating to a talented young manager the task of looking at the problem and possible solutions |

## Key terms

**Hard HRM:** when managers treat the human resource in the same way they would treat any other resource (for example, ordering more one week, and less the next). In such a climate, employee relations are likely to be strained and staff may see the need for trades union involvement.

**Line managers:** staff with responsibility for achieving specific business objectives, and with the resources to get things done.

**Soft HRM:** when managers treat the workforce as a special strength of the business and therefore make sure that staff welfare and motivation are always top priorities.

**Staff appraisal:** a regular (perhaps annual) meeting between employee and line manager to discuss past performance and future business and career objectives.

## Evaluation: Setting human resource (HR) objectives

Human resource management is one of the functions of a business. The overall approach to HRM (for example, soft versus hard) and specific HRM decisions (for example, to recruit or train) will be linked to the objectives and strategy of the business as a whole. A decision by a business to downsize or to expand abroad, for example, will have major implications for the HRM function. At the same time, the HRM resources of a business will influence the strategies a business adopts.

'Once people feel challenged, invigorated and productive, their efforts translate into profits.'
Ricardo Semler, maverick businessman

# Workbook

## A. Revision questions

(30 marks; 30 minutes)

1. What may be the effects of managing human resources in the same way as all the other resources used by a business? (4)

2. Identify three important features of the job of a human resource manager. (3)

3. Some people think that schools should stop teaching French and instead teach Mandarin (Chinese). If a school decided to do this, outline two implications for its training programme. (4)

4. A fast-growing small business might not have a human resources manager. The tasks may be left up to the line managers. Examine two reasons in favour of creating a human resources management post within such a business. (6)

5. Outline two ways in which a human resources manager may be able to help increase productivity at a clothes shop. (4)

6. Analyse the circumstances in which it might be appropriate for a manager to adopt a 'hard HRM' approach. (9)

## B. Revision exercises
### DATA RESPONSE

### Hard and soft HRM

While Google is famous for its 'soft HRM' approach based on wonderful working conditions and time off to pursue personal projects, IT giant Yahoo has adopted a different tack with its 12,000 staff. In early 2014, tech blog *AllThingsD* reported that Yahoo staff were reeling from 600 recent firings as a result of a 'stack-ranking' system adopted by new chief executive Marissa Mayer. Stack-ranking is known more commonly as 'rank and yank'.

Of all the possible 'hard HRM' strategies, none was more famous than 'rank and yank,' as practised at General Electric USA (GE) during the 20-year rule of chief executive Jack Welch. It required managers to create an annual ranking of staff performance in each division of a business; the bottom 5 per cent would automatically be fired and the next 5 per cent would have to fight for their jobs. The top 20 per cent would get generous bonuses. Welch claimed that this was one of his most successful schemes, at the heart of GE's growth between 1981 and 2001. The case in favour was simple: it ensured that all staff felt at all times that they had to perform to their best – coasting was not an option. The case against was that it encouraged cronyism, that is, staff 'sucking up' to their bosses, to try to avoid a low ranking.

Yahoo's move is all the more surprising because IT giant Microsoft was abandoning stack ranking at exactly the same time. Soon after Microsoft fired boss Steve Balmer in Autumn 2013, the new chief executive announced the ending of this long-standing HR approach. A US magazine article on Balmer in 2012 (called 'Microsoft's lost decade') highlighted stack ranking as a major contributor to the company's difficulties in competing with Apple, Google and Samsung. The journalist wrote that 'Every current and former Microsoft employee I interviewed – every one – cited stack ranking as the most destructive process inside Microsoft'. The typical comment by staff was that the program pitted staff against each other, hampering collaboration and focusing staff on internal instead of external competition.

For Yahoo, the adoption of stack ranking might go down as one of the classic business mistakes. The company has been responsible for quite a few. As one of the earliest internet companies it was valued at $128 billion in early 2000. Fourteen years on it has a value of less than a third of that figure. Its greatest mistake was in 2006. It had agreed to buy a young software business for $1 billion from Mark Zuckerberg. When Yahoo tried to cut the price to $850 million Zuckerberg walked away. Today Facebook is worth $140 billion. It could have been Yahoo's.

**Questions (25 marks; 30 minutes)**

1. Explain how the HR strategy known as 'stack ranking' might help achieve the HR objectives at a large business such as Yahoo. (5)

2. Explain one possible reason why new boss Marissa Meyer may have decided to harden Yahoo's approach to human resources management. (4)

3. To what extent might the adoption of stack ranking damage the effectiveness of employer/employee relations at Yahoo? (16)

## C. Extend your understanding

1. To what extent would you agree that a 'hard HRM' approach is the right way to run a supermarket branch where 50 per cent of the staff are part-time students? (20)

2. In 2014 Tesco announced that it planned to open a supermarket chain in India, one of the world's fastest growing economies. To what extent will Tesco's success or failure in India depend upon a successful HR strategy? (20)

# Chapter 46

# Motivation and engagement in theory

Linked to: Motivation and engagement in practice, Chapter 47; Analysing human resource performance, Chapter 51; Decision-making and improved human resource performance, Chapter 52.

## Definition

To Professor Herzberg, motivation occurs when people do something because they *want* to do it; others think of motivation as the desire to achieve a result.

## 46.1 Introduction

A study by the Hay Group found that just 15 per cent of UK workers consider themselves 'highly motivated'. As many as 25 per cent say they're 'coasting' and 8 per cent admit to being 'completely demotivated'. In the same survey, employees felt they could be 45 per cent more productive if they were doing a job they loved. Poor management is part of the problem, as 28 per cent say they would be more productive with a better boss.

The Hay Group calculates that if the under-performance was tackled successfully, the value of UK output would rise by more than £350 billion a year. So motivation matters.

## 46.2 F.W. Taylor and scientific management

Although there were earlier pioneers, a good starting point for the study of motivation is F.W. Taylor (1856–1917). As with most of the other influential writers on this subject, Taylor was American. Much business practice in America, Europe, Japan and the former Communist countries is still rooted in his writing and work.

A recent biography of Taylor is titled *The One Best Way*; this sums up neatly Taylor's approach to management. He saw it as management's task to decide exactly how

every task should be completed, then to devise the tools needed to enable the worker to achieve the task as efficiently as possible. This method is evident in every McDonald's. Fries are cooked at 175 degrees for exactly three minutes; then a buzzer tells employees to take them out and salt them. In every McDonald's there is a series of dedicated, purpose-built machines for producing milkshakes, toasting buns, squirting chocolate sauce, and much else. Today, 120 years after his most active period working in industry, F.W. Taylor would feel very much at home ordering a Big Mac.

So, what was Taylor's view of the underlying motivations of people at work? How did he make sure that the employees worked effectively at following 'the one best way' laid down by managers?

Taylor believed that people work for only one reason: money. He saw it as the task of the manager to devise a system that would maximise efficiency. This would generate the profit to enable the worker to be paid a higher wage. Taylor's view of human nature was that of 'economic man'. In other words, people were motivated only by the economic motive of self-interest. Therefore, a manager could best motivate a worker by offering an incentive (the 'carrot') or a threat (the 'stick'). Taylor can be seen as a manipulator, or even a bully, but he believed his methods were in the best interests of the employees themselves.

Taylor's influence stemmed less from his theories than his activities. He was a trained engineer who acted as a very early management consultant. His methods were as follows.

- Observe workers at work, recording and timing what they do, when they do it and how long they take over it (this became known as time and motion study).
- Identify the most efficient workers and see how they achieve greater efficiency.
- Break the task down into small component parts that can be done quickly and repeatedly (high division of labour)
- Devise equipment specifically to speed up tasks.

- Set out exactly how the work should be done in future. 'Each employee,' Taylor wrote, 'should receive every day clear-cut, definite instructions as to what he is to do and how he is to do it, and these instructions should be exactly carried out, whether they are right or wrong.'
- Devise a pay scheme to reward those who complete or beat tough output targets, but that penalises those who cannot or will not achieve the productivity Taylor believed was possible; this pay scheme was called piece rate – no work, no pay.

As an engineer, Taylor was interested in practical outcomes, not in psychology. There is no reason to suppose he thought greatly about the issue of motivation. The effect of his ideas was profound, though. Long before the publication of his 1911 book *The Principles of Scientific Management*, Taylor had spread his managerial practices of careful measurement, monitoring and – above all else – control. Before Taylor, skilled workers chose their own ways of working and had varied, demanding jobs. After Taylor, workers were far more likely to have limited, repetitive tasks; and to be forced to work at the pace set by a manager or consultant engineer.

Eventually workers rebelled against being treated like machines. Trades union membership thrived in factories run on Taylorite lines, as workers wanted to organise against the suffocating lives they were leading at work. Fortunately, in many Western countries further developments in motivation theory pointed to new, more people-friendly approaches.

'In our scheme, we do not ask the initiative of our men. We do not want any initiative. All we want of them is to obey the orders we give them, do what we say, and do it quick.' F.W. Taylor, *The Principles of Scientific Management*, 1911

### Real business

More than 100 years after F.W. Taylor's book was published, 2013 saw a wave of criticism of the working conditions at Amazon.com's distribution depots in Britain and Germany.

Many staff work under zero-hours contracts that provide no guaranteed income but can still have to walk up to 15 miles during a shift, while toilet breaks are monitored and timed. It is also claimed they can be sacked and re-hired.

⇨

⇨ Former staff at Amazon's warehouse in Rugeley, Staffordshire, told newspaper reporters that they were hired for 12 weeks before being sacked and re-employed so that the company did not have to give them the same rights as full-time employees.

An investigation by Channel 4 News found that employees are tracked using GPS tags while inside the warehouse. A BBC Panorama reporter concluded that the work was much harder physically than seemed reasonable. If staff are found to breach any of the company's rules, such as talking to colleagues or leaving work early, they can be dismissed on a 'three strikes and you are out' basis.

F.W. Taylor would have agreed with Amazon's desire for full control of workers' actions, but would have made more effort to make sure that the job requirement represented a 'fair day's work'.

'Direction and control are of limited value in motivating people whose important needs are social and egotistic.' Douglas McGregor, author of *The Human Side of Enterprise*.

## 46.3 Maslow and the hierarchy of needs

Abraham Maslow (1908–70) was an American psychologist whose great contribution to motivation theory was the 'hierarchy of needs'. Maslow believed that everyone has the same needs, all of which can be organised as a hierarchy. At the base of the hierarchy are physical needs such as food, shelter and warmth. When unsatisfied, these are the individual's primary motivations. When employees earn enough to satisfy these needs, however, their motivating power withers away. Maslow said: 'It is quite true that humans live by bread alone – when there is no bread. But what happens to their desires when there is bread?' Instead of physical needs, people become motivated to achieve needs such as security and stability, which Maslow called the safety needs. In full, Maslow's hierarchy consisted of the elements listed in Table 46.1.

'What a man can be, he must be. This need we call self-actualisation.' Abraham Maslow, psychologist

**Table 46.1** Maslow's hierarchy of needs: implications for business

| Maslow's levels of human need | Business implications |
|---|---|
| Physical needs, e.g. food, shelter and warmth | Pay levels and working conditions |
| Safety needs, e.g. security, a safe structured environment, stability, freedom from anxiety | Job security, a clear job role/description, clear lines of accountability (only one boss) |
| Social needs, e.g. belonging, friendship, contact | Team working, communications, social facilities |
| Esteem needs, e.g. strength, self-respect, confidence, status and recognition | Status, recognition for achievement, power, trust |
| Self-actualisation, e.g. self-fulfilment; 'to become everything that one is capable of becoming,' wrote Maslow | Scope to develop new skills and meet new challenges, and to develop one's full potential |

Ever since Maslow first put his theory forward (in 1940) writers have argued about its implications. Among the key issues raised by Maslow are the following.

- Do all humans have the same set of needs? Or are there some people who need no more from a job than money?

- Do different people have different degrees of need? For example, are some highly motivated by the need for power, while others are satisfied by social factors? If so, the successful manager would be one who can understand and attempt to meet the differing needs of her/his staff.

- Can anyone's needs ever be said to be fully satisfied? The reason the hierarchy diagram (see Figure 46.1) has an open top is to suggest that the human desire for achievement is limitless.

**Figure 46.1** Maslow's hierarchy of needs

Maslow's work had a huge influence on the writers who followed him, including Fred Herzberg. The hierarchy of needs is also used by academics in many subjects beyond Business Studies, notably Psychology and Sociology.

## 46.4 Herzberg's 'two factor' theory

The key test of a theory is its analytic usefulness. On this criterion, the work of Professor Fred Herzberg (1923–2000) is the strongest by far.

The theory stems from research conducted in the 1950s into factors affecting workers' job satisfaction and dissatisfaction. It was carried out on 200 accountants and engineers in Pennsylvania, USA. Despite the limited nature of this sample, Herzberg's conclusions remain influential to this day.

Herzberg asked employees to describe recent events that had given rise to exceptionally good feelings about their jobs, then probed them for the reasons why. 'Five factors stand out as strong determiners of job satisfaction,' Herzberg wrote in 1966, 'achievement, recognition for achievement, the work itself, responsibility and advancement – the last three being of greater importance for a lasting change of attitudes.' He pointed out that each of these factors concerned the job itself, rather than issues such as pay or status. Herzberg called these five factors 'the motivators'.

The researchers went on to ask about events giving rise to exceptionally bad feelings about their jobs. This revealed a separate set of five causes. Herzberg stated that 'the major dissatisfiers were company policy and administration, supervision, salary, interpersonal relations and working conditions.' He concluded that the common theme was factors that 'surround the job', rather than the job itself. The name he gave these dissatisfiers was 'hygiene factors'. This was because fulfilling them would prevent dissatisfaction, rather than causing positive motivation. Careful hygiene prevents disease; care to fulfil hygiene factors prevents job dissatisfaction.

To summarise: motivators have the power to create positive job satisfaction, but little downward potential. Hygiene factors will cause job dissatisfaction unless they are provided for, but do not motivate. Importantly, Herzberg saw pay as a hygiene factor, not a motivator. So a feeling of being underpaid could lead to a grievance; but high pay would soon be taken for

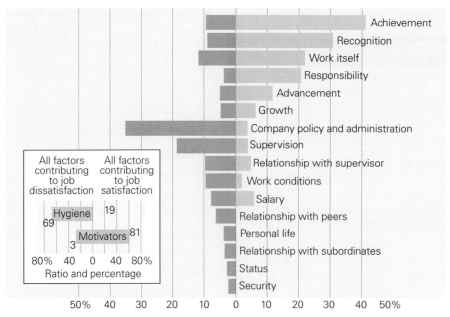

**Figure 46.2** Comparison of satisfiers and dissatisfiers

granted. This motivator/hygiene factor theory is known as the 'two factor theory' (see Table 46.2).

**Table 46.2** Herzberg's two factor theory

| Motivators (can create positive satisfaction) | Hygiene factors (can create job dissatisfaction) |
|---|---|
| Achievement | Company policy and administration (the rules, paperwork and red tape) |
| Recognition for achievement | Supervision (especially being over-supervised) |
| Meaningful, interesting work | Pay |
| Responsibility | Interpersonal relations (with supervisor, peers, or even customers) |
| Advancement (psychological, not just a promotion) | Working conditions |

## Movement and motivation

Herzberg was keen to distinguish between movement and motivation. Movement occurs when somebody does something; motivation is when they *want* to do something. This distinction is essential to a full understanding of Herzberg's theory. He did not doubt that financial incentives could be used to boost productivity: 'If you bully or bribe people, they'll give you better than average performance.' His worries about 'bribes' (carrots) were that they would never stimulate people to give of their best; people would do just enough to achieve the bonus. Furthermore, bribing

people to work harder at a task they found unsatisfying would build up resentments, which might backfire on the employer.

Herzberg advised against payment methods such as piece rate. They would achieve movement, but by reinforcing worker behaviour, would make them inflexible and resistant to change. The salaried, motivated employee would work hard, care about quality and think about – even welcome – improved working methods.

'Our goal should be minimum standardisation of human behaviour.' Douglas McGregor, author *The Human Side of Enterprise*, 1960

## 46.5 The use of non-financial methods of motivating employees

Although the UK's banking sector seems convinced of the need for financial incentives to achieve high performance, few in key industries such as advertising or aircraft design and manufacture would agree. Most people believe that motivation is as much about psychology as money. One of the reasons why Herzberg's work had such an impact on business is because he not only analysed motivation, he also had a method for improving it. The method is job enrichment, which he defined as 'giving people the opportunity to use their ability'. He suggested that, for a job to be considered enriched, it would have to contain the following.

## A complete unit of work

People need to work not on just a small repetitive fragment of a job, but on a full challenging task. Herzberg heaped scorn upon the 'idiot jobs' that resulted from Taylor's views on high division of labour.

## Direct feedback

Wherever possible, a job should enable the worker to judge immediately the quality of what she or he has done; direct feedback gives the painter or the actor (or the teacher) the satisfaction of knowing exactly how well they have performed. Herzberg disliked systems that pass quality inspection off onto a supervisor: 'A man must always be held responsible for his own quality.' Worst of all, he felt, was annual appraisal, in which feedback is too long delayed.

## Direct communication

For people to feel committed, in control and to gain direct feedback, they should communicate directly – avoiding the delays of communicating via a supervisor or a 'contact person'. This leads to an important conclusion: that communications and motivation are interrelated.

'Blue collar and white collar call upon the identical phrase: "I'm a robot."' Studs Terkel, much-missed US journalist (from his book *Working*, 1974)

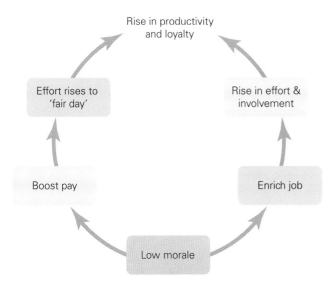

**Figure 46.3** Herzberg logic chain: take care of hygiene factors and motivators

# 46.6 The value of theories of motivation

Herzberg's original research has been followed up in many different countries, including Japan, Africa and Russia. His main insight was to show that unless the job itself was interesting, there was no way to make working life satisfying. This led companies such as Volvo in Sweden and Toyota in Japan to rethink their factory layouts. Instead of individual workers doing simple, repetitive tasks, the drive was to provide more complete units of work. Workers were grouped into teams, focusing on significant parts of the manufacturing process, such as assembling and fitting the gearbox, and then checking the quality of their work. Job enrichment indeed. Some key quotes from Professor Herzberg are given in Table 46.3.

**Table 46.3** Key quotes from Professor Herzberg

| On the two factor theory: | 'Motivators and hygiene factors are equally important, but for different reasons.' |
|---|---|
| On movement: | 'If you do something because you want a house or a Jaguar, that's movement. It's not motivation.' |
| The risks of giving bonuses: | 'A reward once given becomes a right.' |
| The importance of training: | 'The more a person can do, the more you can motivate them.' |
| The importance of always treating staff fairly: | 'A remembered pain can lead to revenge psychology... They'll get back at you some day when you need them.' |
| On communication: | 'In industry, there's too much communication. And of course its passive... But if people are doing idiot jobs they really don't give a damn.' |
| On participation: | 'When participation is suggested in terms of control over overall goals, it is usually a sham.' |

As with all theories, though, both Maslow and Herzberg have their critics. With Maslow, the questions concern the existence of any hierarchy – certainly no research has been able to prove this idea. Yes his five sets of needs are well chosen, but don't different people perhaps have different hierarchies of those needs? In Herzberg's case the most common criticism is that his original research was conducted on a small sample size (200) and just on middle-class employees: accountants and engineers.

As mentioned above, the ultimate test is how well a theory performs in the real world. Herzberg's remains a marvellous way to predict disasters (the misuse of financial bonuses in the banking sector) and a successful way to run a business.

## Five Whys and a How

| Question | Answer |
|---|---|
| Why did trade unions dislike F.W. Taylor with his financial incentives and 'one best way'? | They disliked the shift in power towards management and hated being 'deskilled'; doing the same repetitive task every day |
| Why do theorists such as Herzberg distinguish motivation from morale? | Morale can be high if the future looks bright and job security is strong – that doesn't mean that motivation will be high; motivation is doing a good job because you want to |
| Why might 'esteem needs' be hard to provide in some workplaces? | It might be hard in some jobs that society rates lowly, such as bin collecting or road sweeping |
| Why does Herzberg think financial incentives aren't motivating? | He accepts that they incentivise and therefore can generate some 'movement' – but to him, motivation comes from within |
| Why may companies find it difficult to provide a 'complete unit of work'? | Some tasks can be completed far more efficiently with high division of labour, so a complete unit of work can seem an indulgence |
| How could you increase the motivation of England's national football team? | Recruit players who love playing, give them plenty of responsibility – perhaps to discuss and plan tactics – and let them do the pre- and post-match interviews |

## Key terms

**Division of labour:** subdividing a task into a number of activities, enabling workers to specialise and therefore become very efficient at completing what may be a small, repetitive task.

**Hygiene factors:** 'everything that surrounds what you do in the job', such as pay, working conditions and social status; all are potential causes of dissatisfaction, according to Herzberg.

**Job satisfaction:** the sense of well-being and achievement that stems from a satisfying job.

**Piece rate:** paying workers per piece they produce (for example, £2 per pair of jeans made).

**Productivity:** output per person (that is, a measure of efficiency).

**Trades union:** an organisation that represents the interests of staff at the workplace.

## Evaluation: Motivation and engagement in theory

Most managers assume they understand human motivation, but they have never studied it. As a result they may underestimate the potential within their own staff, or unthinkingly cause resentments that fester.

The process of managing people takes place in every part of every organisation. So every manager should be aware of motivation theory. In some cases, ignorance leads managers to ignore motivation altogether; they tell themselves that control and organisation are their only concerns. Other managers may see motivation as important, but fail to understand its subtleties.

For these reasons, there is a case for saying that the concepts within this unit are the most important in the whole subject. Certainly it is true to say that Taylor, Maslow and Herzberg are studied from Russia to Japan and Angola to Zimbabwe.

## Further reading

Herzberg, F. (1959) *The Motivation to Work*. Wiley International.

Maslow, A.H. (1987) *Motivation and Personality*. HarperCollins (1st Edition, 1954).

# Workbook

## A. Revision questions

**(30 marks; 30 minutes)**

1. Which features of the organisation of a McDonald's could be described as Taylorite? (3)

2. Explain the meaning of the term 'economic man'. (3)

3. Explain how workers in a bakery may be affected by a change from salary to piece rate. (3)

4. Which two levels of Maslow's hierarchy could be called 'the lower-order needs'? (2)

5. Describe in your own words why Maslow organised the needs into a hierarchy. (3)

6. State three business implications of Maslow's work on human needs. (3)

7. Herzberg believes pay does not motivate, but it is important. Why? (4)

8. How do motivators differ from hygiene factors? (3)

9. What is job enrichment? How is it achieved? (3)

Choose one answer from the four choices in each of the following questions:

10. If staff absenteeism is increasing, is it likely to be because: (1)

| a) Hygiene factors are over-rewarded | b) Wage increases are outstripping inflation | c) There's too much self-actualisation | d) Division of labour is too high |
|---|---|---|---|

11. Herzberg's 'hygiene factors' relate best to: (1)

| a) Taylor's focus on the 'one best way' | b) Maslow's concept of self-actualisation | c) Taylor's idea of self-actualisation | d) Maslow's physiological needs |
|---|---|---|---|

12. Maslow's idea of 'self-actualisation' means: (1)

| a) Striving to get a promotion | b) Finding just what you're capable of | c) Getting the money rewards you deserve | d) Finally enjoying true self-esteem |
|---|---|---|---|

## B. Revision exercises
### DATA RESPONSE

Tania was delighted to get the bakery job and looked forward to her first shift. It would be tiring after a day at college, but £52 for eight hours on a Friday would guarantee good Saturday nights in future.

On arrival, she was surprised to be put straight to work, with no more than a mumbled: 'You'll be working packing machine B.' Fortunately, she was able to watch the previous shift worker before clocking-off time, and could get the hang of what was clearly a very simple task. As the 18.00 bell rang, the workers streamed out, but not many had yet turned up from Tania's shift. The conveyor belt started to roll again at 18.16.

As the evening wore on, machinery breakdowns provided the only, welcome, relief from the tedium and discomfort of Tania's job. Each time a breakdown occurred, a ringing alarm bell was drowned out by a huge cheer from the staff. A few joyful moments followed, with dough fights breaking out. Tania started to feel quite old as she looked at some of her workmates.

At the 22.00 meal break, Tania was made to feel welcome. She enjoyed hearing the sharp, funny comments made about the shift managers. One was dubbed 'Noman' because he was fat, wore a white coat and never agreed to anything. Another was called 'Turkey' because he strutted around, but if anything went wrong, got into a flap. It was clear that both saw themselves as bosses. They were not there to help or to encourage, only to blame.

Was the bakery always like this, Tania wondered? Or was it simply that these two managers were poor?

**Questions (30 marks; 35 minutes)**

1. Analyse the working lives of the shift workers at the bakery, using Herzberg's two factor theory. (9)

293

**2.** If a managerial follower of Taylor's methods came into the factory, how might she or he try to improve the productivity level? (5)

## C. Extend your understanding

**1.** Followers of F.W. Taylor and Professor Herzberg each set about increasing the motivation of teachers. To what extent do you think that followers of Taylor would be the more successful? (20)

**3.** Later on in this (true) story, Tania read in the local paper that the factory was closing. The reason given was 'lower labour productivity than at our other bakeries'. The newspaper grumbled about the poor attitudes of local workers. To what extent is there justification in this view? (16)

**2.** To what extent might it be successful if Tesco's new boss applied Maslow's hierarchy of needs to the whole workforce? (20)

# Motivation and engagement in practice

Linked to: Motivation and engagement in theory, Chapter 46; Analysing human resource performance, Chapter 51; Decision-making and improved human resource performance, Chapter 52.

## Definition

Assessing how firms try to motivate their staff and how successful these actions are. In this context, companies take 'motivation' to mean enthusiastic pursuit of the objectives or tasks set out by the firm.

## 47.1 Introduction

There are two main variables that influence the motivation of staff in practice:

1. the financial reward systems

2. job design and enrichment.

These will be analysed with reference to the theories outlined in Chapter 46.

The chapter will then look at how businesses choose and assess the effectiveness of reward systems.

'My best friend is the one who brings out the best in me.' Henry Ford, founder of Ford Motors

## 47.2 Financial methods of motivation

### Piece rate

Piece rate means working in return for a payment per unit produced. Pieceworkers receive no basic or shift pay, so there is no sick pay, holiday pay or company pension.

Piecework is used extensively in small-scale manufacturing, for example, of jeans or jewellery. Its attraction for managers is that it makes supervision virtually unnecessary. All the manager needs to do is

operate a quality control system that ensures the finished product is worth paying for. Day by day, the workers can be relied upon to work fast enough to earn a living wage.

### Disadvantages of piece rate

Piecework has several disadvantages to firms, however, including the following.

● Scrap levels may be high, if workers are focused entirely on speed of output.

● There is an incentive to provide acceptable quality, but not the best possible quality.

● Workers will work hardest when they want higher earnings (probably before Christmas and before their summer holiday). This may not coincide at all with seasonal patterns of customer demand.

● Worst of all is the problem of change; Herzberg pointed out that 'the worst way to motivate people is piece rate…it reinforces behaviour.' Focusing people on maximising their earnings by repeating a task makes them very reluctant to produce something different or in a different way (they worry that they will lose out financially).

'I have never found anybody yet who went to work happily on a Monday that had not been paid on a Friday.' Tom Farmer, Kwik-Fit founder

## Real business

Most football clubs have signed expensive new players who subsequently fail to perform on the pitch. In 2013 Liverpool decided to overcome this problem by offering new signings lower basic salaries offset by lucrative performance-related bonuses. According to Managing Director Ian Ayre, 'From the football club's perspective, our view has to be that people are rewarded for contributing towards what we achieve. As long as contracts are structured in that way then everyone wins.' That year Liverpool went on to enjoy one of their highest finishes in the Premier League.

## Performance-related pay

Performance-related pay (PRP) is a financial reward to staff whose work is considered above average. It is used for employees whose work achievements cannot be assessed simply through numerical measures (such as units produced or sold). PRP awards are usually made after an appraisal process has evaluated the performance of staff during the year.

The usual method is outlined below.

1. Establish targets for each member of staff/management at an appraisal interview.

2. At the end of the year, discuss the individual's achievements against those targets.

3. Those with outstanding achievements are given a Merit 1 pay rise or bonus worth perhaps six per cent of salary; others receive between zero per cent and six per cent.

---

'Motivating people over a short period is not very difficult. A crisis will often do just that, or a carefully planned special event. Motivating people over a longer period of time, however, is far more difficult. It is also far more important in today's business environment.' John Kotter, management thinker

---

### Lack of evidence for benefits of PRP

Despite the enthusiasm they have shown for it, employers have rarely been able to provide evidence of the benefits of PRP. Indeed the Institute of Personnel Management concluded in a recent report that: 'It was not unusual to find that organisations which had introduced merit pay some years ago were less certain now of its continued value… it was time to move on to something more closely reflecting team achievement and how the organisation as a whole was faring.'

This pointed to a fundamental problem with PRP: rewarding individuals does nothing to promote teamwork. Furthermore, it could create unhealthy rivalry between managers, with each going for the same Merit 1 spot.

### Why do firms continue with PRP?

So why do firms continue to pursue PRP systems? There are two possible reasons:

1. to make it easier for managers to manage/control their staff (using a carrot instead of a stick)

2. to reduce the influence of collective bargaining and therefore trades unions.

## Commission

Commission is a bonus earned on top of a basic salary, usually in line with a specific achievement such as meeting a sales target. It might be that a member of staff is expected to generate £80,000 of sales a year, and for every £1,000 above that total a commission will be paid of £50. That five per cent rate of commission might enable the individual to boost income considerably by the end of the year.

Commission is used widely to incentivise staff in clothes shops, furniture shops and other outlets where it can take effort and skill to clinch a sale. Note that it would be incorrect to write about commission as a 'motivator'. In Professor Herzberg's terms, commission is simply a hygiene factor.

## Salary schemes

According to Professor Herzberg, 'the best way to pay people is a salary.' He considered every attempt to 'motivate' people through financial incentives doomed to fail – simply because people would be incentivised to do the wrong thing – again and again. This proved true in the 2008/09 financial crisis, when the mayhem in the financial sector was often the result of faulty financial incentives (such as encouraging excessive risk-taking in the short-term).

To Herzberg, then, paying the 'right' salary is the goal. He warned against underpaying people every bit as much as overpaying. And was also a fan of non-incentivised benefits such as company pensions and holiday and sick-pay schemes – to apply to all staff within the organisation.

## 47.3 Job design and enrichment

Professor Herzberg defines job enrichment as 'giving people the opportunity to use their ability'. A full explanation of his theory is outlined in Chapter 46.

How can job enrichment be put into practice? The key thing is to realise the enormity of the task. It is not cheap, quick or easy to enrich the job of the production line worker or the supermarket checkout operator. Herzberg's definition of job enrichment implies giving people 'a range of responsibilities and activities'. To provide job enrichment, workers must have a complete unit of work (not a repetitive fragment), responsibility for quality and for self-checking, and be given the opportunity to show their abilities.

Full job enrichment requires a radical approach. Take a conventional car assembly line, for example. As shown in Figure 47.1, workers each have a single task they carry out on their own. One fits the left-hand front door to a car shell that is slowly moving past on a conveyor belt – every 22 seconds. Another worker fits right-hand front doors, and so on. Job enrichment can be achieved only by rethinking the production line completely; coming up with a new job design.

**Figure 47.1** A traditional production line

Figure 47.2 shows how a car assembly line could be reorganised to provide a more enriched job. Instead of working in isolation, people work in groups on a significant part of the assembly process. An empty car shell comes along the conveyor belt and turns into the Interior Group Area. Six workers fit carpets, glove boxes, the dashboard and much else. They check the quality of their own work; then put a rather impressive-looking vehicle back on the conveyor belt. Not only does the teamwork element help meet the social needs of the workforce, but there are also knock-on effects. The workers can be given a time slot to discuss their work and how to improve it. When new equipment is needed, they can be given a budget and told to go out to meet potential suppliers. In other words, they can become managers of their own work area.

**Figure 47.2** An enriched 'team-working' line

Such a major step would be expensive. Rebuilding a production line may cost millions of pounds and be highly disruptive in the short term. There would also be the worry that team-working could make the job

more satisfying, yet still be less productive than the boring but practical system of high division of labour.

'Motivation is everything. You can do the work of two people, but you can't be two people. Instead, you have to inspire the next guy down the line and get him to inspire his people.' Lee Iacocca, successful boss of Chrysler Motors

## 47.4 Choice and assessment of financial and non-financial reward systems

Research regularly shows that financial reward systems are extremely difficult to get right. Think of it in relation to your class. If the teacher had £1,000 to hand out as financial rewards to the students 'that deserved it most', what would be the result? Possibly a well-motivated class if the teacher manages to satisfy everyone, but probably a bit of a disaster as various students feel the rewards are unfairly distributed.

This points to an important influence on financial reward systems: can the rewards be clearly related to the quantity and quality of work done? In a clothes factory making jeans, it may be that paying piecework (such as £2 per pair) works effectively at incentivising staff to work hard. If I produced 40 pairs earning £80, while you produced 70 pairs earning £140, I might be disappointed, but I wouldn't call it unfair.

Other important influences on the choice of whether to use financial or non-financial reward systems include:

- The results of careful measurement of past reward systems – what was the impact of financial incentives the last time they were used?

- The timescale being considered; if there are urgent requirements for production over the next six months, financial incentives might be effective, but in the long run you want people to want to give of their best, all the time

- The level of change the business faces; financial incentives are very difficult to change, because some staff will already do well out of them and fear lower earnings if there is change.

Ultimately, assessing financial and non-financial reward systems is extremely difficult when the job is complex. Surgeons, for example, do far more than just operate on patients. So if a measurement system looks solely at operations per day, it will fail to capture the real job, from training new doctors to talking to patients. Systems that claim to do so should be treated with scepticism. Human resource professionals are keen to find measurable solutions to complex problems, but research suggests that this is near impossible.

In well-run businesses, a clear sense of purpose and the freedom to act responsibly and collaboratively is usually the best way to have motivation in practice.

## Five Whys and a How

| Question | Answer |
|---|---|
| Why might bonus payments fail to motivate? | They provide incentives, but Herzberg says motivation comes from within, i.e. doing something because you want to. If there's a financial incentive, that only achieves movement* |
| Why may the payment of piece rate make it hard to achieve change in the workplace? | Those with high earnings on the old system will fear change – and all staff will have been conditioned to do one thing repeatedly |
| Why is empowerment more powerful than delegation? | Delegation passes down the hierarchy the power to do things; empowerment gives the power to decide what to do |
| Why do you think that HR departments love performance-related pay? | Because it gives them a role and a degree of control. Pay everyone a salary, and who needs an HR department? |
| Why would F.W. Taylor be thrilled to see that performance-related pay is still a powerful force in the 21st century? | Taylor believed that workers should be under the tight control of management; PRP can achieve this by forcing staff to do what they're told in order to maximise their pay |
| How might performance-related pay for teachers affect lessons in future? | It may make them more formulaic, with all teachers focused solely on maximising grades |

*For the difference between movement and motivation, remember the English football team at the 2014 World Cup.

## Key terms

**Division of labour:** subdividing a job into small, repetitive fragments of work.

**Job design:** having designed a new product, it is time to design the jobs needed to make the product. Merely subdividing it into repetitive work fragments will be unmotivating, so design the job with people in mind.

**Motivation:** to Professor Herzberg, it means doing something because you want to do it. Most business leaders think of it as prompting people to work hard.

## Evaluation: Motivation and engagement in practice

When writing about financial incentives, there is a serious risk of over-simplification. The reality is that using money to try to motivate people often proves a dreadful mistake (as Herzberg always made clear). Exaggerated commissions or performance-related pay can lead sales staff to oversell goods or services which may cause customers huge difficulties later on, such as cosmetic surgery or questionable investments. Also, within the workplace, serious problems can arise: bullying to 'motivate' staff into working harder, or creating a culture of overwork which leads to stress.

Fortunately, there are many businesses in which the management of motivation is treated with respect: companies which know that quick fixes are not the answer. Successful motivation in the long term is a result of careful job design, employee training and development, honesty and trust. It may be possible to supplement this with an attractive financial reward scheme, but money will never be a substitute for motivation.

'There is no room for criticism on the training field. For a player – and for any human being – there is nothing better than hearing "well done". Those are the two best words ever invented in sports.' Sir Alex Ferguson, former manager of Manchester United

# Workbook

## A. Revision questions

(40 marks; 45 minutes)

1. 'Job design is the key to motivation.' Outline one reason why this may be true, and one reason why it may not. (4)

2. Look at the famous saying by Lee Iacocca on page 297. Explain in your own words what he meant by this. (3)

3. How *should* a manager deal with a mistake made by a junior employee? (4)

4. State three reasons why job enrichment should improve staff motivation. (3)

5. Distinguish between job rotation and job enrichment. (4)

6. How does 'empowerment' differ from 'delegation'? (4)

7. Identify three advantages to an employee of working in a team. (3)

8. State two advantages and two disadvantages of offering staff performance-related pay. (4)

9. What could be the implications of providing a profit share to senior managers but not to the workforce generally? (5)

10. What problems may result from a manager bullying staff to 'motivate' them? (6)

## B. Revision exercises
### DATA RESPONSE 1

Fifty per cent of primary teachers and 52 per cent of secondary teachers believe that incremental pay rises should depend at least in part on performance. This was the finding of a survey of over 1000 teachers on behalf of The Sutton Trust. But the survey conducted by The National Foundation for Educational Research found that a large minority favoured the old system of linking pay to length of service. Schools are required to link pay progression to classroom performance for teachers in the first five years of their career, under a government initiative introduced in September 2014. Teachers have previously had yearly incremental rises.

In the US teachers receive bonuses depending on their pupils' progress, but evidence that the approach can improve learning outcomes is inconclusive. Professor Steven Higgins of Durham University's School of Education said the evidence was not convincing. 'Attracting the best teachers and retaining them, for which pay may be a significant component, is more important than rewarding teachers on the basis of their pupils' recent test scores or their observed lesson performance.' Research has suggested that observing

lessons is 'not a reliable way of identifying teacher effectiveness, so any system which relies only on observation or test scores or even a combination is likely to be flawed,' according to Professor Higgins.

Christine Blower, general secretary of the National Union of Teachers, opposes performance-related pay for teachers on the grounds that it is less transparent and open to biased judgments.

Source: Adapted from bbc.co.uk

### Questions (30 marks; 35 minutes)

1. Why does the government appear to believe that teachers are motivated by money? (3)

2. Apart from money, identify and explain two other factors which might motivate teachers. (6)

3. Explain one method the government might use to measure the individual performance of teachers. (5)

4. To what extent might teacher performance be affected by a switch to performance-related pay? (16)

## DATA RESPONSE 2

**An October 2013 study finds 'emotional factors' are strongest motivators in the workplace.**

Bonuses are not the top motivator for employees, according to a study into what makes workers most productive by the Institute of Leadership and Management (ILM).

The survey of more than 1,000 workers found that only 13 per cent of people agreed that a bonus would have an effect on their motivation, however having a good basic salary and pension was viewed as an important incentive by almost half of the respondents.

In fact, the top motivator was 'job enjoyment' according to 59 per cent of respondents, while other emotional factors such as good working relationships and fair treatment also rated highly in the survey. More than two-fifths of the respondents cited 'getting on with colleagues' as a key motivator, while just over a fifth agreed that 'how well they are treated by their managers' affected motivation, with a further fifth saying that higher levels of autonomy motivated them.

The ILM said the findings suggested that the £36.9 billion spent on performance bonuses in the UK last year had 'no impact on the motivation and commitment levels of the vast majority of recipients'.

The survey highlights how important good managers are to ensuring happy and motivated staff. When asked to identify one thing that would motivate them to do more, 31 per cent of employees said 'better treatment from their employer', 'more praise' and 'a greater sense of being valued'. However, while the majority of managers (69 per cent) said they 'always give feedback' to their staff, just 23 per cent of employees agreed.

'Understanding your employees and what makes them tick is vital in having a happy and motivated workforce,' said Charles Elvin, chief executive of the ILM. 'In the past year UK companies have collectively spent an astronomical amount on financial incentives for their staff. But this report is telling us there are far more effective, and cost-effective, ways to motivate people. These include giving regular feedback, allowing people to have autonomy in a role, the opportunity to innovate and improved office environments.'

Source: www.cipd.co.uk

### Questions (25 marks; 30 minutes)

1. From the passage:
   a) Outline two points that fit into the category called 'motivators' by Herzberg. (4)
   b) Outline two points that fit into the category called 'hygiene factors' by Herzberg. (4)

2. The ILM implies that 'the £36.9 billion spent on performance bonuses' was a waste of money. Explain two possible reasons why businesses might persist with staff bonuses despite the evidence provided here. (8)

3. Use the evidence provided in the text to examine how a manager might improve the workplace performance of one of the following: a school cleaner; a full-time employee at Tesco; or a bus driver. (9)

## C. Extend your understanding

1. To what extent do you agree with the view that there is no one ideal method to motivate staff, because everyone is different? (20)

2. To what extent are financial reward systems important in the motivation of young, part-time staff at a business such as Nando's chain of chicken restaurants? (20)

# Chapter 48 Improving organisational design

**Linked to:** Analysing human resource performance, Chapter 51; Decision-making and improved human resource performance, Chapter 52.

## Definition

Organisational design means creating the formal hierarchy that establishes who is answerable to whom throughout the organisation. When presented as a diagram, it shows the departmental functions plus the vertical and horizontal links that represent the formal communications system.

**Table 48.1** Examples of management layers

| Military | Business |
|----------|----------|
| Captain | Senior Manager |
| Lieutenant | Manager |
| Sergeant | Team Leader |
| Corporal | Supervisor |
| Foot soldier | Shop-floor worker |

'If a sufficient number of management layers are superimposed on top of each other, it can be assured that disaster is not left to chance.' Norman Augustine, US chief executive

## 48.1 Introduction

As organisations became larger and more complex, early management thinkers such as F.W. Taylor and H. Fayol considered how to structure an organisation. Both saw the function of organisations as converting inputs, such as money, materials, machines and people, into output. Therefore, designing an organisation was like designing a machine, the objective being to maximise efficiency.

Taylor and Fayol based their thoughts largely on the way an army is organised. The key features of the hierarchy would be:

- To break the organisation up into divisions with a common purpose. In business, this was usually the business functions: marketing, finance and so on.

- Every individual would answer to one person: their line manager

- No manager would be overloaded with too many subordinates, so the span of control was kept low.

- To achieve low spans of control, it was necessary to have many management layers. Examples of management layers are shown in Table 48.1.

## 48.2 The growing business

In the early stages of a new business, there are often only one or two people involved. When the business is so small the day-to-day tasks are carried out by the owner/s. No formal organisation is needed as communication and co-ordination will be carried out on an informal, face-to-face basis. However, as the business grows and more people become involved, the firm will need to develop a more formal organisational structure. This will show the roles, responsibilities and relationships of each member of the firm. This is often illustrated through an organisational chart. This is a diagram that shows the links between people and departments within the firm. They also show communication flows/channels, lines of authority and layers of hierarchy. Each of these terms will be explained later in the chapter.

When Matteo Pantani founded Scoop ice cream in Covent Garden in 2007, he only employed part-time staff at the counter to serve the ice cream and take the money. Matteo made the ice cream and ran the business. He did not need to think about a 'hierarchy' or a 'structure'. But the organisational structure that existed in 2007 is shown in Figure 48.1.

As the business grew, he opened a second outlet in 2010, in Brewer Street, Soho, and a third in South Kensington in 2012. This meant he needed managers to run the other outlets, while Matteo was largely at Covent Garden. By mid-2014, the organisational hierarchy looked like the one shown in Figure 48.2.

The point, of course, is to appreciate how much more complex a hierarchy becomes as the business grows.

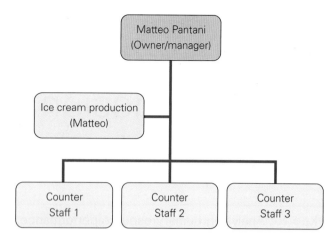

**Figure 48.1** Scoop: old organisational structure

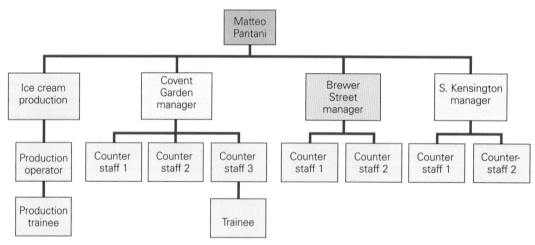

**Figure 48.2** Scoop: new organisational structure

## 48.3 Influences on organisational design

This section will examine the main areas of theory associated with organisational structure and how it is designed. To help clarify, references will be made to the above chart (Figure 48.2).

### Levels of hierarchy

These show the number of different supervisory and management levels between the bottom of the chart and the top of the hierarchy. Figure 48.2 shows that at Scoop there are now four levels of hierarchy. In an organisation such as Tesco plc, which employs more than 500,000 staff, it is easy to see how there might be 25 levels of hierarchy. The problem that will cause is extremely slow (and unreliable) communications between the top and bottom of the organisation. TV programmes such as *Undercover Boss* consistently show how hard it is for the chief executive to understand the problems faced by those on the shop floor.

### Span of control

This describes the number of people directly under the supervision of a manager. Matteo has the widest span of control, as he has four staff under him directly. If managers have very wide spans of control, they are directly responsible for many staff. In this case they may find that there are communication problems, or the workers may feel that they are not being given enough guidance. The ideal span of control will depend upon the nature of the tasks and the skills and attitude of the workforce and manager. (See Table 48.2)

'Every company has two organisational structures: the formal one is written on the charts; the other is the living relationship of the men and women in the organisation.' Harold Geneen, US management guru

### Chain of command

This shows the reporting system from the top of the hierarchy to the bottom; that is the route through which information travels throughout the organisation. In an

**Table 48.2** Advantages and disadvantages of a narrow span of control

| Advantages | Disadvantages |
|---|---|
| Allows close management supervision; this is vital if staff are inexperienced, labour turnover is high or if the task is critical, e.g. manufacturing aircraft engines | Workers may feel over-supervised and therefore not trusted; this may cause better staff to leave, in search of more personal responsibility |
| Communications may be excellent within the small, immediate team, e.g. the boss and three staff | Communications may suffer within the business as a whole, as a narrow span means more layers of hierarchy, which makes vertical communications harder |
| Many layers of hierarchy means many rungs on the career ladder, i.e. promotion chances arise regularly (though each promotion may mean only a slightly different job) | The narrow span usually leads to restricted scope for initiative and experiment; the boss is always looking over your shoulder; this will alienate enterprising staff |

organisation with several levels of hierarchy the chain of command will be longer and this could create a gap between workers at the bottom of the organisation and managers at the top. If information has to travel via several people there is also a chance that it may become distorted.

'Every management layer you can strip away makes you more responsive.' John Whitney, US academic

## Delegation

This means passing authority (power) down the hierarchy, to give greater responsibility to junior managers or staff. It should therefore be seen as a democratic process. Sadly, some bosses simply pass down the tasks they do not want to tackle. Passing on the dull or difficult stuff should not be confused with delegation.

Influences on delegation include the attitude of management towards its workforce. If there is mistrust, then delegation will never be genuine. Assuming trust exists, it may still be important that the junior staff are highly trained. No one wants to be delegated power without the knowledge and therefore confidence that they are able to get the job done.

## Centralisation and decentralisation

This describes the extent to which decision-making power and authority is delegated within an organisation. A centralised structure is one in which decision-making power and control remains in the hands of the top management levels. A decentralised structure delegates decision-making power to workers lower down the organisation. Many organisations will use a combination of these approaches, depending upon the nature of the decision involved. For example, in many schools and colleges, the decisions concerning which resources to use will be decentralised; that is, taken by teachers as opposed to the senior management team. Other decisions, concerning future changes in subjects being offered, may be centralised; that is, taken by senior managers.

Influences on centralisation versus decentralisation are primarily internal; that is, within the business. Often they represent alternatives that look rosier if the opposite approach has proved disappointing. Therefore there is a risk that a company in difficulties will lurch from one approach to the other – and perhaps back again. The Waterstones bookshop chain has suffered from this. It was set up by founder Tim Waterstone as a decentralised, locally-oriented chain of stores. When bought by W.H. Smith, book buying and store layouts were centralised. Today they are back with a more localised, decentralised approach.

'It's a paradox that the greater the decentralisation, the greater the need for both leadership and explicit policies from the top management.' Bruce Henderson, chief executive, Boston Consulting Group

## 48.4 Influences on job design

Professor Herzberg believed that worker motivation would improve only when some vertical barriers were broken down within hierarchies. His idea of job enrichment was that jobs should be redesigned to give people a range of activities and responsibilities at work. Explicitly he wanted 'self-checking', effectively meaning scrapping supervisory roles and therefore cutting a tall hierarchy down to size.

This work was developed further by US academics Richard Hackman and Greg Oldham. Writing in the 1970s they described Herzberg's two factor theory as 'by far the most influential behavioural approach to work redesign' and set out to build on it. They developed a model that looked beyond the analysis of job-related factors to consider three aspects of what they termed 'the job characteristics model'. These were:

1. Core job characteristics, that is, the factors involved at the heart of the job.

   These included skill variety, task variety, task significance, autonomy (personal independence) and feedback. All five characteristics could be

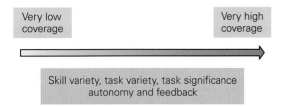

Very low coverage          Very high coverage

Skill variety, task variety, task significance autonomy and feedback

**Figure 48.3** Core job characteristics

measured against a scale from very low coverage to very high (see Figure 48.3)

2. Psychological states

This aspect of the theory focuses on people rather than the job. In effect it asks: what are the core factors affecting an individual worker's psychological state? Hackman and Oldham suggest three:

● meaningfulness in the job itself

● responsibility for work outcomes

● knowledge of the results of the work.

The greater the level of one or (preferably) all these three, the more positive and more relaxed will be the individual's psychological state.

3. Outcomes

Unlike Herzberg, Hackman and Oldham build the consequences into the theory. The core job characteristics and the psychological states both impact upon the workplace outcomes. These outcomes can and should be measured. They consist of:

● employee motivation

● employee performance, for instance productivity

● employee job satisfaction

● plus the practical measurements: absenteeism and labour turnover.

The whole of the job characteristics model can be illustrated as:

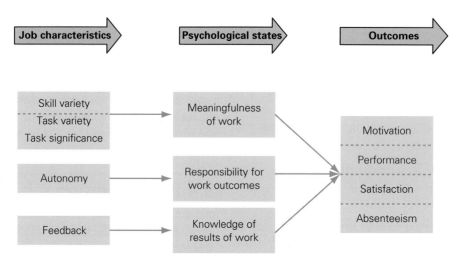

**Figure 48.4** Job characteristics model
Source: Adapted from Hackman and Oldham, 1975

'Lots of jobs are not so well designed. They demotivate people rather than turn them on.' Hackman and Oldham, US academics

## 48.5 The value of changing job and organisational design

Following the publication of Herzberg's theory the US giant AT&T experimented with job redesign, focusing especially on job enrichment. 'These studies appear to demonstrate, for a diversity of jobs, that job enrichment can lead to beneficial outcomes both for the individuals involved and for the employing organisation.' (Hackman and Oldham, 1980)

An important result of improved job design is that stress levels are reduced. Stress is associated with lack of control of the employee's environment; so improved job control is an important target. With lower stress levels, absenteeism and labour turnover figures tend to improve.

Changing organisational design is a much more difficult problem. To an extent, job design can be tackled one person at a time. By definition a change in organisational design affects everyone. That might involve 500,000 staff (Tesco) or over 1.3 million staff (the NHS). Some companies lurch from decentralisation to centralisation and then back again (Waterstones); others such as Unilever change vertical structure from functional (marketing, finance, etc.) to divisional

(Foods division; Cosmetics division, etc.) and then back again. No criticism is implied; it is simply that company bosses desire a perfect organisational structure, but none exists. Every large business suffers severe problems of communication, co-ordination and motivation. The occasional change to the organisational design may improve things temporarily, but there is no magical solution to the problems of size.

## Real business

Up until the 1990s Marks & Spencer was Britain's most successful and admired retailer. Since then it has had more than twenty years of struggle. Following the decline of M&S Tesco took over the mantle as Britain's top retailer. It grew in size and scale and profits until a series of management errors began with its failed attempt to create a Tesco USA business from scratch in 2007. For Tesco, which hit a series of trading and financial disasters in 2014, the underlying problem was that of growth. In 1999 Tesco employed 200,000 people; by 2014 it was more than 500,000. So however clever the organisational design, the people at the top get ever more removed from the shop floor workers and the customers.

## Five Whys and a How

| Question | Answer |
|---|---|
| Why is organisational structure so important? | Because, however keen and competent the staff, large organisations can operate slowly, frustratingly and bureaucratically if the organisational structure is wrong |
| Why might there be benefits from widening an organisation's span of control? | A wider span means fewer layers of hierarchy are needed. This would allow delayering to take place – which saves money and can improve vertical communication |
| Why might Asda and Morrisons' both have decided (in 2014) to remove a layer of supervisory management from all their stores? | Perhaps both felt the need to cut fixed overhead costs given the market share gains achieved by the discounters Aldi and Lidl. |
| Why do firms such as Google usually start with an informal management hierarchy, but firm it up when the business has grown? | Because a formal structure is unnecessary when everyone knows/can talk to the boss or bosses. Once Google had 20,000 staff that was no longer possible. |
| Why are businesses so scared of the word 'bureaucracy'? | Because it suggests slowness and complacency that firms believe only happens in government departments |
| How might a large plc improve its performance by improving its organisational structure? | Usually, the flatter the structure the better the business. This also serves as a warning against growing too big (through takeovers) |

## Key terms

**Delayering:** removing a management layer from the organisational structure.

**Line manager:** a manager responsible for meeting specific business targets, and responsible for specific staff.

**Matrix management:** where staff work in project teams in addition to their responsibilities within their own department. Therefore, staff can be answerable to more than one boss.

**Span of control:** the number of staff who are answerable directly to a manager.

There is no 'ideal' organisational structure or span of control. What works for one business may fail in another, even if both are the same size. In case studies there will usually be hints about whether the structure is working. A flat hierarchy may be at the heart of an innovative business, or there may be signs that staff lack direction and have low morale. A tall hierarchy may be at the centre of a focused, career-orientated workforce, or it may be bureaucratic and incapable of a quick decision. The judgement is yours.

# Workbook

## A. Revision questions

**(30 marks 30 minutes)**

1. What is meant by the chain of command? (2)

2. Define 'span of control'. (2)

3. Some theorists believe that the ideal span of control is between three and six. To what extent do you agree with this? (5)

4. Explain two implications of a firm having too wide a span of control. (4)

5. Explain what an organisational chart shows. (4)

6. Why is it important for a growing firm to think carefully about its organisational structure? (4)

7. State three possible problems for a business with many levels of hierarchy. (3)

8. What is meant by the term 'accountable'? (2)

9. What do you think would be the right organisational structure for a hospital? Explain your answer. (4)

## B. Revision exercises

### DATA RESPONSE 1

These questions are based on the Scoop organisation charts (Figure 48.1 and Figure 48.2).

**Questions (20 marks; 25 minutes)**

1. Explain why communication might be harder in the larger Scoop of 2010. (6)

2. Should the Brewer Street counter staff be allowed to contact ice-cream production directly; for example, if they see they are running out of vanilla ice cream? Explain your reasoning. (6)

3. Explain two ways in which Matteo may find his management responsibilities more difficult when he opens his third Scoop outlet. (8)

### DATA RESPONSE 2

**Management changes at ailing Morrisons' could see 2,000 jobs axed**

UK supermarket chain Morrisons' has revealed plans to cut over 2,000 jobs in an overhaul of its management structure. The move, which will reduce layers of management across the firm's 500 UK stores, is expected to primarily affect middle managers.

The move follows similar cost-cutting measures by Morrisons' main rivals Tesco, Sainsbury's and Asda, which are all facing competitive pressure from low-cost supermarkets Aldo and Lidl, as well as from upmarket chains such as Waitrose.

Morrisons', which has run trials of the new leaner management structure, said it had led to better performance. Currently each store has a manager, deputy manager and multiple assistant deputy managers covering broad product categories (such as fresh food). Individual departments (such as green groceries, meat or fish) are led by supervisors reporting to them.

Many of these old posts will now be eliminated to make way for team leaders who will spend most of their time on the shop floor and be responsible for the management of a smaller number of merged departments.

Adapted from *The Guardian* and bbc.co.uk

## DATA RESPONSE 3

### Chicken Little

Peter (known as 'Paxo') Little set up his free-range chicken farm in the early 1990s. At the time it was an unusual move, especially on the grand scale envisaged by Paxo. His farm had the capacity to produce 250,000 chickens every 45 days; that is, 4 million birds a year. Since then the business has grown enormously, to a turnover of £25 million today.

But Paxo is getting concerned that his business is not as efficient as it used to be. As managing director, he finds that he rarely hears from junior staff; not even the quality manager's five staff, who used to see him regularly. As he said recently to the operations director, 'The communication flows seem like treacle today, whereas they used to be like wildfire.'

Fortunately, the boom in demand for free range and organic produce has helped the business. So even though the team spirit seems to have slipped away, profits have never been higher. Unfortunately, the marketing director repeatedly talks about rumours

### Questions (25 marks; 30 minutes)

1. Describe how Morrisons' organisational chart will change following the restructuring. (4)

2. Explain the probable thinking behind Morrisons' decision to change its management structure. (5)

3. To what extent do you think the changes are guaranteed to improve Morrisons' profitability. (16)

that a huge Dutch farming business is about to set up poultry farms in Britain. That could 'set the cat among the chickens'; in other word, provoke quarrelling and dissension.

### Questions (25 marks; 30 minutes)

1. **a)** What is the managing director's span of control? (1)

   **b)** Comment on the strengths and weaknesses of this organisational structure. (4)

   **c)** How important do human resources seem within this business? (2)

2. Examine why vertical communications may not be as effective today as they were in the past at Chicken Little. (9)

3. Examine the ways in which the factory manager may benefit or suffer from the organisational structure shown in Figure 48.5. (9)

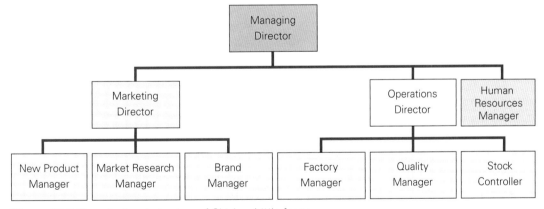

**Figure 48.5** Organisational structure of Chicken Little farms

## C. Extend your understanding

1. To what extent is a business of your choice moving towards – or moving away from – a centralised management approach? (20)

2. Organisational hierarchies were originally modelled on the army, with many ranks and clarity about who was the boss of whom. To what extent is this approach out-of-date in a business world dominated by online sales and online businesses? (20)

# Chapter 49

# Managing the human resource flow

Linked to: Analysing human resource performance, Chapter 51; Decision-making and improved human resource performance, Chapter 52.

## Definition

The flow of labour and skills into, within and out from an organisation. Assessing these flows is the first step towards devising an effective human resource (workforce) plan.

## 49.1 The human resource (workforce) plan

Human resource planning is about thinking ahead so that staff have the right balance of the right skills in each year into the future. In 2013 Fulham FC started the season with the oldest squad in the Premier League (by far). At the season end the club was relegated. A succession of managers had failed to develop an effective workforce plan. The key components of human resource planning are set out below.

- Audit what you have at the moment; how many staff and what their skills are. Ideally, this audit would include aspirations (for example, staff who say 'I'd love to travel' or 'I've always wanted to learn a foreign language').

- Analyse the corporate plan to turn plans into people. For example, if Sainsbury's corporate plan says '20 new stores to be opened in Britain in the next two years', the workforce plan can be set: 20 new stores, each staffed by 200 people = 8,000 new staff needed.

- Take into account the changes on the way from here to there. How many will leave to retire, have kids or just to have a career change? Some football teams age together; eleven 29 year olds may be great, but four years later there will be a problem.

- Calculate the gaps that need to be filled between now and two years' time. This can be done through the following sum:

  Staff needed in 2 years *minus* staff now *plus* staff leaving between now and then = extra staff required

An example of a human resource plan by UK grocery chain Tesco is given in Table 49.1

Table 49.1 Components of a human resource plan for Tesco

| UK grocery chain Tesco, investigating opening stores in India | |
|---|---|
| 1. Audit current staff, to find out their skills | How many current staff speak Hindi, and how many have significant, recent local knowledge? |
| 2. Identify the workforce needs in 2 years' time, based on the corporate plan | How many staff will be needed in the UK in 2 years' time, broken down by skill and seniority; and how many will be needed in India? |
| 3. Estimate employee loss through natural wastage | Research into HR records to find how many of the 500,000 staff will be retiring; if the labour turnover is 10 per cent, 50,000 people need to be recruited just to maintain the present situation. |
| 4. Calculate the gaps between what exists now and what will be needed in 2 years – then plan to fill them | If Tesco plans 10 new store openings in the UK plus 10 in India, it may need 8,000 new staff in addition to the 50,000 needed to replace leavers. These 58,000 must be divided up to plan for how many Hindi speakers, how many butchers, bakers, accountants, etc. are needed |

Having completed this process (which should be done carefully, with full consultation with every senior manager), it is time to put it into practice. The process of human resource planning includes recruitment and selection, training and development, and planned redundancies.

## 49.2 Recruitment

A human resource plan emphasises quantity (the right number of people with the right skills) plus quality (the soft skills shown by staff, such as the ability to collaborate and communicate). The plan provides a structure within which effective recruitment can take place. Within this, the character and personalities of the new staff should be treated as of equal importance as their skills and aptitudes.

'If each of us hires people smaller than we are, we shall become a company of dwarfs.' David Ogilvy, advertising guru

The recruitment process may be triggered by a number of events, including retirement or finding employment elsewhere. At this point, it would be worth analysing the vacant job role. Do all of the responsibilities associated with the vacant job still need to be carried out or are some redundant? Could the remaining duties be reorganised amongst the existing employees? Alternatively, additional workers may need to be recruited in order to support a firm's expansion strategies, or employees with new skills may be required to help develop new products or new markets.

Once the firm has established its human resources requirements, the next step is to consider the nature of the work and workers required in order to draw up a job description and a person specification. Both documents have an important influence on both recruitment and selection; not only can they be used to draw up job advertisements, but also to assess the suitability of the candidates' applications.

'Mediocrity knows nothing higher than itself; but talent instantly recognises genius.' Sherlock Holmes (Arthur Conan Doyle), *The Valley of Fear*

## 49.3 Training and development

Training is the process of instructing an individual about how to carry out tasks directly related to his or her current job. Development involves helping an individual to realise his or her full potential. This concerns general growth in personal skills, for example in public speaking or in assertiveness, and is not related specifically to the employee's existing job.

Even before training kicks in, new recruits will have been put through an induction programme. That should provide insights into working methods within the business, plus a clear understanding of the firm's aims, objectives and key strategies.

The four key objectives of training and development are as follows.

1. To help a new employee reach the level of performance expected from an experienced worker. This initial preparation upon first taking up a post is known as 'induction' training. It often contains information dealing with the precise nature of the job, layout of the firm's operating facility, health and safety measures, and security systems. An attempt may also be made to introduce the individual to key employees and give an impression of the culture of the organisation. The firm's induction training should aim to drive each employee along their own personal learning curve as quickly as possible (see Figure 49.1).

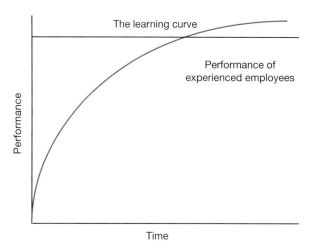

**Figure 49.1** Objective of induction training

2. To provide a wide pool of skills available to the organisation, both at present and in the future (see Figure 49.2).

3. To develop a knowledgeable and committed workforce.

4. To deliver high-quality products or services.

**Figure 49.2** The training gap

'You can't make a crab walk straight.' Aristophanes, 448-380 BC

## Two types of training

### 1. On-the-job training

For this method of training employees are not required to leave their workplace but actually receive instruction while still carrying out their job. This means that workers can receive training while remaining productive to some extent. Common methods include mentoring, coaching and job rotation.

### 2. Off-the-job training

For off-the-job training employees leave their workplace in order to receive instruction. This may involve using training facilities within the firm, for example seminar rooms, or those provided by another organisation, such as a university, college or private training agency. Although this will inevitably involve a temporary loss of production, it should allow the trainee to concentrate fully on learning and perhaps allow access to more experienced instructors than those available within the workplace.

**Table 49.2** Training: benefits and costs

| Training | |
|---|---|
| **Benefits** | **Costs** |
| It increases the level and range of skills available to the business, leading to improvements in productivity and quality. | It can be expensive, both in terms of providing the training itself and also the cost of evaluating its effectiveness. |
| It increases the degree of flexibility within a business, allowing it to respond quickly to changes in technology or demand. | Production may be disrupted while training is taking place, leading to lost output. |
| It can lead to a more motivated workforce by creating opportunities for development and promotion. | Newly-trained workers may be persuaded to leave and take up new jobs elsewhere (known as poaching), meaning that the benefits of training are enjoyed by other businesses. |

'Train everyone – lavishly… You can't overspend on training.' Tom Peters, business writer

## 49.4 Redeployment

Even in the most successful businesses, changes in market demand or in technology can make certain tasks or responsibilities redundant. For example,

since 2007 there has been a 40 per cent cut in university modern foreign language courses. In such circumstances, many specialist languages teachers will lose their jobs. Some, however, may have general skills (or other teaching specialisms) that enable them to be redeployed. In other words, switched from their redundant job to another post for which there are future prospects.

Redeployment has several benefits for the organisation:

- saves the cost of redundancy payments
- helps internal morale, as staff see the organisation trying its best to avoid redundancy
- avoids recruiting from outside, when existing employees already understand the culture and procedures within the business – thereby avoiding the induction learning curve shown in Figure 49.1.

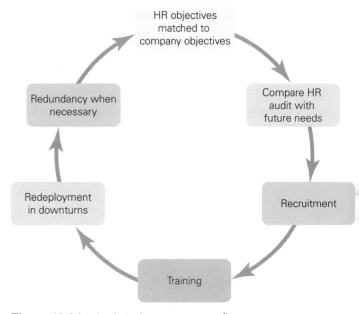

**Figure 49.3** Logic chain: human resource flow

## 49.5 Redundancy and dismissal

Human resource plans are as important in downturns as in the good times. Whereas it may be necessary to dismiss an incompetent employee at any time, redundancies only occur when there is a reduced need for staff – usually because sales are declining or technology is changing labour requirements. Human resource managers are the ones who have to cope with the difficult task of selecting those to be made redundant – and then informing them.

### Lloyds Bank

In January 2014 Lloyds announced that it would be shedding 1,400 jobs in Britain. Over 1,000 job roles would be axed, including more than 600 staff who provide face-to-face support to small businesses. In their place would be more work for Lloyds' call centres. In addition, more than 300 staff would be transferred to work for a service supplier to the banking group.

Within the workforce plan Lloyds expected that up to two-thirds of the job reductions would come from voluntary redundancies. This might mean that the HR department would have to make fewer than 400 compulsory redundancies.

## Five Whys and a How

| Question | Answer |
| --- | --- |
| Why may it be hard to ensure that the human resource flow fits with a new business strategy? | Because company employees develop ways of thinking and working that can be hard to change. Can Marks & Spencer staff change to become more like Pret A Manger? Hum. |
| Why should companies take plenty of time deciding on their staff recruitment – even for shop floor workers? | Because customers are more likely to come into contact with 'ordinary' staff than with managers, so the attitude and competence of shop floor staff is vital to competitiveness |
| Why might management with a Taylorite approach to staff only be interested in skills rather than attitudes? | Because F.W. Taylor emphasised that financial incentives dictate behaviour; therefore all you need is competent people incentivised by well-structured bonus payments (Herzberg disagrees) |
| Why may staff redeployment prove more expensive than redundancy plus fresh recruitment? | Redeployment from teaching German to teaching Economics may cost more in training than the cost of redundancy plus recruiting a new, young economist |
| Why is poaching thought damaging to the economy? | The more companies poach staff, the lower the incentive for any company to induct and train new people – so the productive potential of the economy is weakened |
| How might Tesco improve its human resource flow? | By clarifying exactly what its corporate plans are, making it easier for HR to decide exactly what skills and attitudes are needed from staff in future |

## Key terms

**Job description:** a statement of what the job tasks and duties are, that is, the job itself (rather than describing the right person for the job).

**Induction training:** familiarises newly appointed workers with key aspects of their job and their employer, such as health and safety policies, holiday entitlement and payment arrangements. The aim is to make employees fully productive as soon as possible.

**Person specification:** an account of the qualifications, attributes and experience required from a successful candidate for the post.

**Poaching:** persuading staff to leave the company that trained them, thereby getting fully trained staff without paying the training cost (Premier League clubs are often accused of this by lower league teams).

**Soft skills:** personal qualities such as warmth, openness, willingness to act on criticism and empathy.

Human resource flow emphasises that business organisations are on a continuous journey of change and development but also disappointment. The key thing is that HR decisions must fit in with the aims, ethos and strategy laid down for the business as a whole. Pret A Manger is a great example, because its recruitment and training practices are all focused on its company-wide plan: good, safe food but outstanding service. Other organisations continue to view training as an avoidable expense, choosing to cut training budgets when under pressure to cut costs, or to poach employees already equipped with the necessary skills from other firms. New employees can bring a number of benefits, including fresh ideas and approaches to work. Yet however excellent the staff, there can still be a need for redeployment or even redundancy if market trends move against the business.

# Workbook

## A. Revision questions

**(30 marks; 30 minutes)**

1. Explain the idea of human resource flow. (3)

2. Outline two reasons why a business may need to recruit new employees. (4)

3. Briefly explain the difference between a job description and a person specification. (4)

4. Outline two factors that would influence the method of recruitment used by a business. (4)

5. Outline two reasons why a firm should provide induction training for newly recruited employees. (4)

6. Briefly explain why poaching may lead to a skills gap in the UK labour market. (3)

7. Outline two possible disadvantages of redeploying staff instead of making them redundant. (4)

8. Explain the difference between redundancy and dismissal. (4)

## B. Data response

### Recruiting people with a passion at Pret A Manger

According to Pret A Manger, talent management is one of the biggest challenges for firms operating in the fiercely competitive UK hospitality industry. The company has grown steadily since its set up in 1986 but still retains a strong entrepreneurial character, despite employing over 5,000 people. Its workers are chosen from a wide pool of recruitment, in order to reflect its customer base. In 2014, around 70 per cent of vacancies at the company were filled within four days.

Job candidates undergo an initial screening interview and are selected on the basis of their personal qualities and passion for customer service, rather than their hospitality skills. Personal qualities include a genuine smile and an eagerness to learn and to progress. Those candidates that pass successfully through the interview stage complete a 'joiner experience day', where they are paid to work in a Pret A Manger store close to where they live. At the end of this, the store team vote on whether or not the candidates should be appointed.

Source: Adapted from multiple sources including Pret A Manger

### Questions (25 marks; 30 minutes)

1. Analyse two benefits of Pret A Manger's approach to recruitment. (9)

2. Evaluate the importance of effective recruitment and selection for a company like Pret A Manger. (16)

## C. Extend your understanding

1. Stamford Software Solutions, a medium-sized IT company based in the south-east of England, needs to recruit a new sales manager. Evaluate how the company should do this. (20)

2. According to a recent report, UK employers spend an estimated £33 billion in total each year on training, yet one third of employers provide no training at all. To what extent are damaging consequences inevitable for firms who choose not to train their staff? (20)

# Chapter 50 Improving employer–employee relations

**Linked to:** Managing the human resource flow, Chapter 49; Analysing human resource performance, Chapter 51; Decision-making and improved human resource performance, Chapter 52.

## Definition

The relationship between staff and management is on a spectrum that has complete trust at one end and 'them and us' mistrust at the other.

## 50.1 Introduction

The relations between bosses and workers will be effective if communications are good and there is a sensible amount of give-and-take between them. They will be bad if there is a lack of trust, leading to restricted communication and the tendency to make demands rather than conduct conversations. In a perfect world, adults would behave in an adult manner towards each other. But just as no family is perfect, neither is any individual business organisation. The key is not to be perfect, but to be better than most.

Research into staff engagement in 2014 found a close correlation between 'trusting your boss' and employee commitment. The 8 per cent who trusted bosses 'to a very great extent' were the happiest of all at work. The 67 per cent who trusted 'to a great or moderate' extent were the second most engaged group.

There are three main areas to consider within the heading 'effective employer–employee relations':

1. good communications
2. methods of employee involvement
3. the causes and solutions to industrial disputes.

## Real business

### ACAS

ACAS (the Advisory Conciliation and Arbitration Service) is Britain's most important, independent voice on the workplace. Over forty years it has developed a view of what it thinks is the 'model workplace'. The ACAS model includes the following six themes:

1. ambitions, goals and plans that employees know about and understand
2. managers who genuinely listen to and consider their employees' views, so everyone is actively involved in making important decisions
3. people to feel valued so they can talk confidently about their work, and learn from both successes and mistakes
4. work organised so that it encourages initiative, innovation and working together
5. a good working relationship between management and employee representatives that in turn helps to build trust throughout the business
6. formal procedures for dealing with disciplinary matters, grievances and disputes that managers and employees know about and use fairly.

Source: www.acas.org.uk

## 50.2 Good communications

### The importance of effective communication

Effective communication is essential for organisations. Without it, employees may not know what to do, why they are supposed to do it, how to do it or when to do it by. Similarly, managers have little idea of how the business is performing, what people are actually doing or what its customers think. Communication links the activities of all the various parts of the organisation. When it's effective it ensures everyone is working towards a common goal and enables feedback on performance. This could help staff feel they have a real input into key business decisions.

> 'We provide our Partners with the knowledge they need to carry out their responsibilities effectively as co-owners of the Partnership.' John Lewis constitution, 2014

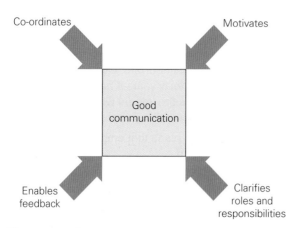

**Figure 50.1** Good communication

Effective communication is also vital for successful decision-making. To make good decisions, managers need high-quality information. If they do not know what their shop floor staff know about customers and competitors, their decision-making will be faulty. Good communication provides managers with the information they need, in a form they can use, when they need it.

Good-quality information should be:

- easily accessible
- up to date
- cost effective.

### How to manage and improve employer–employee communications and relations

In a well-run organisation with effective delegation and consultation, good communication will flow from the top and to the top. If vertical communications are weak, frustrated staff may look for a trades union to represent their views to management. The overall business leader can do many things to help, as outlined below.

- Have a chat with every new member of staff; this may be impossible for the boss of Tesco's 510,000 employees, but is perfectly possible in most cases.

- Take regular initiatives to meet with staff; some retail bosses go out every Friday to two or three different stores to discuss problems with shop-floor staff
- If staff know that their complaints or suggestions are being addressed, they will be happy to keep contributing their thoughts. Most staff want their workplace to be efficient, to allow them to do as good a job as possible; inefficiency is frustrating for all.

## 50.3 Influences on employer–employee relations

In addition to the importance of effective engagement and good communications, employer–employee relations are influenced by:

- The underlying demand conditions faced by the business. If revenue is growing strongly it's easy for the whole staff to feel optimistic about job security and promotion prospects. Staff will know that the employers (represented by senior managers) will have a shared view of the optimistic prospects for the business and therefore its staff
- The level of skill required by the producers of the product or service being sold. There can be a risk of a 'them and us' divide opening up if the management see the workforce as low-skilled. A 'them and us' divide implies a serious rift in communication and trust, with a likelihood of solidarity building up among shopfloor staff in opposition to management. It is important to appreciate that one or both sides can be at fault in these circumstances
- Conditions in the broader labour market. If the economy is booming, demand for labour can be high enough to make staff push hard for perhaps overly-ambitious improvements to their pay and conditions of service. At such times faultlines can appear between employers and employees.

## 50.4 Value of good employer–employee relations

In 2014, in a very difficult grocery market, Asda decided to cut overhead costs by stripping out a layer of middle-management in the stores. This meant thousands of jobs were lost, with most individuals being offered an alternative, lower-paid and lower-status job instead. Naturally this was hugely unpopular, but because of an underlying pattern of good employer–employee relations in the business, staff quite quickly got on with working within the new structure. There was no apparent impact of these changes on Asda's market share.

Good relations are valuable because staff and management have to get along in the long term for the business to do well. As changing external market conditions can force change (including redundancies) on a business, a degree of trust is hugely valuable. Staff will accept a difficult short-term if they believe that staff and management are headed in the right direction. That is why it can be so disruptive to have senior executives paying themselves huge salaries and bonuses. Good employer–employee relations needs to be based on the belief that 'we're all in it together'.

## 50.5 Methods of employee involvement

Intelligent bosses realise that success depends on the full participation of as many staff as possible. Football managers typically use the club captain as the representative of the players. Small firms may have an informal group consisting of one person from each department; monthly meetings are used as a way to raise issues and problems, and discuss future plans. In larger firms, more formal methods are used to ensure that there is a structure to allow an element of workplace democracy. Alternatively the organisation's staff may be represented by a trades union.

## 50.6 Trades unions

### What is a trades union?

A trades union is an organisation that employees pay to join in order to gain greater power and security at work. The phrase 'unity is strength' is part of the trades union tradition. One individual worker has little or no power when discussing pay or pensions with a large employer. Union membership provides greater influence collectively in relations with employers than workers have as separate individuals.

Some people assume that union membership is only for people in low-status jobs. In fact, although trades unions are in decline in Britain, some powerful groups of 'workers' remain committed to membership. For example, the PFA (Professional Footballers' Association) includes almost all Premiership players, and more than 75 per cent of airline pilots belong to their union BALPA.

Traditionally, unions concerned themselves solely with obtaining satisfactory rates of pay for a fair amount of work in reasonable and safe working conditions. Today the most important aspect of the work of a trades union is protecting workers' rights under the law. Far more time is spent on health and safety, on discrimination and bullying, on unfair dismissal and other legal matters than on pay negotiations. One other important matter today is negotiations over pension rights. Recently, many companies have cut back on the pension benefits available to staff; the unions fight these cutbacks as hard as they can.

'Collective bargaining' remains an important aspect of union activity. This means that the union bargains with the employers on behalf of all the workers. In April 2014 a one-year wrangle between the Post Office and the Communication Workers' Union resulted in agreement to pay rises of up to 7.3 per cent.

'Let's deliver fair pay for all with a living wage, new wages councils, and action to tackle greed at the top.' Frances O'Grady, TUC General Secretary, 2014

### Union recognition

'Recognition' is fundamental to the legal position of a trades union. In other words, management must recognise a union's right to bargain on behalf of its members. Without management recognition, any actions taken by a union are illegal. This would leave the union open to being sued. Until recently, even if all staff joined a union, the management did not have to recognise it. Why, then, would any company bother to recognise a union?

- It is helpful for managers to have a small representative group to consult and negotiate with. Collective bargaining removes the need to bargain with every employee individually.

- In situations of potential difficulty, such as relocation, union officials can be consulted at an early stage about causes, procedure and objectives. This may give the workforce the confidence that management are acting properly and thoughtfully. It promotes consultation rather than conflict.

- Trades unions provide a channel of upward communication that has not been filtered by middle managers. Senior managers can expect straight talking about worker opinions or grievances.

Today, UK employers with 21-plus staff members must give union recognition if more than 50 per cent of the workforce vote for it in a secret ballot (and at least 40 per cent of the workforce takes part in the vote).

'Strong, responsible unions are essential to industrial fair play. Without them the labour bargain is wholly one-sided.' Louis Brandeis, lawyer, 1856-1941

### Unite

In March 2013 workers at Green Core's cake factory in Hull voted overwhelmingly to accept management's offer to restore pay and conditions to their original levels. This was the culmination of an 18-month dispute. In October 2011 Green Core (supplier of cakes to supermarkets) gained agreement from its staff and trade union to a temporary cut in payments for overtime and bank holiday working. A year later, though, when the 'temporary' period was over, the company refused to reinstate the original terms. Staff, who were mainly paid minimum wage levels, stood to lose £40 a week (according to Unite, their trade union). Legal appeals and a one-day strike followed – eventually leading to the company's climb down.

## 50.7 Other methods of employee involvement

### Works council

A works council is a committee of employer and employee representatives that meets to discuss company-wide issues. Although works councils have worked well in Germany they have not been so popular in the UK. However, under European Union legislation larger companies that operate in two or more EU countries must now set up a Europe-wide works council. Works councils will usually discuss issues such as training, investment and working practices. They will not cover issues such as pay, which are generally dealt with in discussions with trades union representatives.

### Employee groups

Employee groups are organised by the business but with representatives elected by the staff. These are little different from a works council, but because they are the invention of the business (that is, the management) they lack real credibility. Staff may suspect that management frown upon those who raise critical issues. In a similar way, some school councils are vibrant and meaningful, while others are largely ignored by the school management.

## Employee co-operatives

These range from huge organisations such as the John Lewis Partnership to the 150 staff at Suma. Because all staff are part-owners of the business, all have a right to have their voices heard at every stage in the decision-making process. Inevitably, the board of directors includes representatives from ordinary shop-floor workers, ensuring that everyone's voice is heard.

### Suma

Suma was born when Reg Taylor started a wholefoods wholesaling co-operative in Leeds. Its purpose was to allow small independent health food shops to be able to buy together in bulk. Suma was one of the pioneers of organic foods, and has benefited greatly from the growing consumer interest in chemical-free food. This has caused its own pressures, as the co-operative has had to cope with employee growth from seven members in 1980 to over 150 today. All staff receive the same pay, no matter what their responsibilities may be, and all have an equal say in how the business should be run. The high level of staff motivation and participation has allowed Suma to become the number one organic foods wholesaler in the north of England, with yearly sales turnover of over £26 million.

For further information on Suma, go to www.suma.co.uk.

**Figure 50.2**

## Five Whys and a How

| Question | Answer |
|---|---|
| Why might a company turn to ACAS? | To benefit from its credibility as an independent body that helps resolve industrial disputes |
| Why might employees become disengaged in the workplace? | Their jobs may be too repetitive or too pressurised, or they may no longer trust in the word/s of management |
| Why might customer service be worse at an employee co-operative than at an ordinary company? | Staff may be too focused on themselves and care too little about customers |
| Why might a company voluntarily offer recognition to a trade union? | As a mechanism for gaining good communication from every part of the business |
| Why might a trade union ask for arbitration to resolve a dispute with management? | They presumably feel confident in their case and therefore happy to see an independent 'judge' decide on the right resolution to the dispute |
| How might a conciliation process be conducted? | By inviting both sides to a meeting, but allowing the conciliator to act as a go-between – helping to get people talking |

## Key terms

**Arbitration:** when an independent person listens to the case put by both sides, then makes a judgement about the correct outcome.

**Conciliation:** an independent person encourages both sides in a dispute to get together to talk through their differences. The conciliator helps the process but makes no judgements about the right outcome.

**Feedback:** obtaining a response to a communication, perhaps including an element of judgement (for example, praise for a job well done).

**Vertical communications:** messages passing freely from the bottom to the top of the organisation, and from the top to the bottom.

## Evaluation: Improving employer–employee relations

Good relations are built on shared goals, on trust and on good communications. Yet they are always fragile. One instance of hypocrisy can ruin years of relationship building. A boss may claim to be acting for the good of all the staff, yet switch production from Britain to Asia (James Dyson), or cut pension benefits to staff while keeping them intact for directors. In the long term, some firms really stick by the view that 'our people are our greatest asset', while others just pretend. Staff will learn which is which. Where they find they cannot trust their bosses, joining a trades union becomes a sensible way to get greater protection and greater negotiating power. Union representation will make the employer–employee relationship more formal, and occasionally more fractious. Yet trades union representation can help to move a business forward. It is wrong to jump to the conclusion that unions are 'trouble'. Real trouble comes when employers and employees have no relationship at all.

# Workbook

## A. Revision questions

**(30 marks; 30 minutes)**

1. Explain why good communications within a firm are important. (3)

2. Explain why feedback is important for successful communications. (3)

3. State three actions a firm could take in order to improve the effectiveness of communication. (3)

4. Explain why good communication is an important part of motivating employees. (4)

5. Why might a company choose to accept strike action in preference to settling a dispute? (3)

6. How could a business benefit from a successful works council? (4)

7. Why may an employee co-operative have better employer–employee relations than a public company? (5)

8. Why is it so important to a union to gain recognition from employers? (5)

## B. Revision exercises
### DATA RESPONSE

There have been over 100 arrests at McDonald's corporate headquarters in Illinois, as a national debate on pay inequality gains momentum. Protesters converged on the Oak Brook corporate campus outside Chicago to demand a minimum wage of $15 (£9.60) per hour and the right to unionise. Organisers said 2000 people had attended the rally, which occurred the day before a vote by shareholders at the giant fast-food chain on executive pay. Don Thompson, the chief executive of McDonald's earned close to $10 million in total compensation in 2013.

The US Bureau of Labor Statistics says median hourly wages for fast-food workers is $8.83 (£5.65). Research by a NY think tank has suggested that in 2013 CEOs in the fast-food industry earned 1000 times what their workers did. Jessica Davis is one of 3.5 million fast-food and counter workers in the US. The 25-year-old McDonald's crew trainer has two children and earns $8.98 per hour (£5.75) at a Chicago McDonald's. She said Don Thompson was earning his millions on the backs of working mothers and fathers. 'We need to show McDonald's that we're serious and that we're not backing down.'

'Fifteen dollars is unrealistic, but we know that the minimum wage will increase over time,' a McDonald's spokeswoman was quoted as saying. She said the company and its franchisees were monitoring the minimum wage debate.

Mary Kay Henry, president of the Service Employees International Union (SEIU) said it was time for the McDonald's Corporation 'to stop pretending that it can't boost pay for the people who make and serve their food.' She was among those arrested at the McDonald's protest.

Source: Adapted from Reuters.com

### Questions (30 marks; 35 minutes)

1. Outline one reason why McDonald's customers might care about the pay levels of the company's staff. (2)

2. The famous banker J.P. Morgan once said that the highest earner in a company should earn no more than twenty times that of the lowest earner. At McDonald's today the differential is 1,000 times. Explain one reason in favour and one against McDonald's approach. (8)

3. Evaluate the implications for McDonald's of the successful unionisation of its workers. (16)

## C. Extend your understanding

1. To what extent do you agree that effective communications are at the heart of successful business management? (20)

2. 'Good managers welcome trades unions as a way of improving workplace performance.' To what extent do you agree with this statement? (20)

# Chapter 51 Analysing human resource performance

Linked to: Setting human resource (HR) objectives, Chapter 45; Motivation and engagement in practice, Chapter 47; Managing the human resource flow, Chapter 49; Decision-making and improved human resource performance, Chapter 52.

## Definition

Staff costs are usually between 25 and 50 per cent of a firm's total costs. So firms try to measure the performance of their people objectively (that is, in an unbiased way). Calculations such as staff productivity can be used to measure the success of initiatives such as new working methods.

## 51.1 The need to measure performance

Managers require an objective, unbiased way to measure the performance of personnel. The firm needs to be able to see several things:

- Is the workforce fully motivated?
- Is the workforce as productive as it could be?
- Are the personnel policies of the business helping the business to meet its goals?

It is not possible to measure these things directly. How, for example, can the level of motivation of workers be measured accurately? Instead, a series of indicators are used which, when analysed, can show the firm if its personnel policies are contributing as much to the firm as they should.

There are two main performance indicators used to measure the effectiveness of a personnel department. They are:

1. labour productivity
2. labour turnover.

## 51.2 Labour productivity

### Calculating labour productivity

Labour productivity is often seen as the single most important measure of how well a firm's workers are doing. It compares the number of workers with the output that they are making. It is expressed through the formula:

$$\frac{\text{Output per period}}{\text{Number of employees per period}}$$

For example, if a window cleaner employs ten people and in a day will normally clean the windows of 150 houses, then the productivity is:

$$\frac{150}{10} = 15 \text{ houses per worker per day}$$

Any increase in the productivity figure suggests an improvement in efficiency. The importance of productivity lies in its impact on labour costs per unit. For example, the productivity of AES Cleaning is 15 houses per worker per day; MS Cleaning achieves only 10. Assuming a daily rate of pay of £45, the labour cost per house is £3 for AES but £4.50 for MS Cleaning. Higher productivity leads to lower labour costs per unit. And therefore leads to greater competitiveness both here and against international rivals.

**Figure 51.1**

'There was a time when people were "factors of production" managed little differently from machines or capital. No more. The best people will not tolerate it.' Robert Waterman, business writer

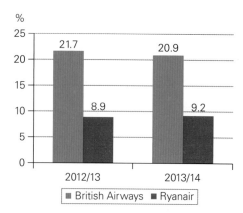

**Figure 51.2** Employee costs as a percentage of turnover
Source: Company accounts

---

**Real business**

The UK's largest recruitment firm is 'on the front foot for the first time in years' says its boss. Perhaps white-collar recruitment group Hays can teach Britain's economic policymakers a thing or two. While they fret about the country's low productivity, the UK's biggest recruitment firm has been investing heavily to ensure it becomes more productive.

That effort is now paying off, according to chief executive Alistair Cox, and helped Hays post a forecast-beating pre-tax profit, up 10 per cent at £62.5 million, as it delivered first-half results yesterday. 'We've had a diligent focus on productivity,' said Mr Cox. 'As a recruiter, we're the ultimate people business. We've brought in quality people, we've trained them, managed them, equipped them to do the job as best as is possible. We're the only recruiter to bother investing in technology.'

Cynics might argue that he's taking the credit for an improving global economy that's actually driving the performance. However, credit where credit's due: net income rose by just 1 per cent to £363.4 million, so the 10 per cent profit increase was impressive. During the half-year in question, total operating costs fell by just over 1 per cent.

Source: adapted from *The Telegraph*, 27 February 2014

---

'We have always found that people are most productive in small teams with tight budgets, time lines and the freedom to solve their own problems.' John Rollwagen, chief executive, Cray Research

## Employee costs as a percentage of turnover

Another way to look at the impact of productivity on the finances of a business is to calculate staff costs as a percentage of sales revenue, that is, turnover. This would help show how serious might be the impact of inefficiency. Figure 51.2 shows that labour costs are twice as high in relative terms at British Airways as they are for Ryanair. This might be a serious problem if Ryanair and BA were in head-to-head competition. In fact, customers are willing to pay a slightly higher price for a BA ticket than for a Ryanair one, so it's not too serious an issue.

## 51.3 Labour turnover

### Measuring labour turnover

This is a measure of the rate of change of a firm's workforce. It is measured by the ratio:

$$\frac{\text{number of staff leaving the firm per year}}{\text{average number of staff}} \times 100$$

So a firm which has seen 5 people leave out of its staff of 50 has a labour turnover of:

$$\frac{5}{50} \times 100 = 10 \text{ per cent}$$

As with all business data, it is best to find comparative data, either from a rival business or how the figure has changed over recent years, and then to look for the reasons behind the data.

### Factors affecting labour turnover

If the rate of labour turnover is increasing, it may be a sign of dissatisfaction within the workforce. If so, the possible causes could be either internal to the firm or external.

#### Internal causes

Internal causes of an increasing rate of labour turnover could be:

- A poor recruitment and selection procedure, which may appoint the wrong person to the wrong post. If this happens, then eventually the misplaced workers will wish to leave to find a post more suited to their particular interests or talents.

- Ineffective motivation or leadership, leading to workers lacking commitment to this particular firm.

- Wage levels that are lower than those being earned by similar workers in other local firms. If wage rates are not competitive, workers are likely to look elsewhere to find a better reward for doing a similar job.

### External causes

External causes of an increasing rate of labour turnover could be:

- More local vacancies arising, perhaps due to the setting up or expansion of other firms in the area.
- Better transport links, making a wider geographical area accessible for workers. New public transport systems enable workers to take employment that was previously out of their reach.

## Consequences of high labour turnover

### Negative effects

A high rate of labour turnover can have both negative and positive effects on a firm. The negative aspects would be:

- the cost of recruiting replacements
- the cost of training replacements
- the time taken for new recruits to settle into the business and adopt the firm's culture
- the loss of productivity while the new workers learn the new ways of working (reach the peak on their learning curve).

### Positive effects

On the positive side, labour turnover can benefit the business in several ways:

- new workers can bring new ideas and enthusiasm to the firm
- workers with specific skills can be employed rather than having to train up existing workers from scratch
- new ways of solving problems may be identified by workers with a different perspective, whereas existing workers may rely on tried and trusted techniques that have worked in the past.

On balance, then, there is a need for firms to achieve the right level of labour turnover, rather than aiming for the lowest possible level.

Another way of measuring the loyalty and commitment of staff is to look at labour retention rates. This calculation is based on exactly the same raw data as labour turnover, but uses the information differently.

Formula for labour retention:

$$\frac{\text{staff not leaving in the past year}}{\text{average number of staff employed in the year}} \times 100$$

## 51.4 Using data for human resource decision-making and planning

Productivity and labour turnover data provide the firm with a commentary on its performance. Poor productivity and high labour turnover might suggest poor management in the workplace. For the most effective comparisons, good managers analyse the figures to identify:

- changes over time (this year versus last)
- how the firm is performing compared with other similar firms (or perhaps benchmarking against the best performers in the sector)
- performance against targets, such as a 20 per cent improvement on last year.

Each of these comparisons will tell the firm how it is performing in relation to a yardstick. This will indicate to the firm where it is performing well and where it may have a problem. The firm must then investigate carefully the reasons for its performance before it can judge how well its personnel function is operating.

For example, labour productivity may have fallen during the previous 12 months. Closer investigation may show that the fall was due to the time taken to train staff on new machinery installed at the start of the year. Figures may show that productivity in the last six months has been climbing satisfactorily. An apparent problem was actually masking an improvement for the firm.

---

### Key terms

**Benchmarking:** measuring yourself against the best, or sometimes against the average of businesses within your industry.

**Culture:** the accepted attitudes and behaviours of people within a workplace.

**Labour productivity:** output per person.

**Labour turnover:** the rate at which people leave their jobs and need to be replaced.

## Five Whys and a How

| Question | Answer |
|---|---|
| Why might productivity fall during a period when sales are rising? | Management might get complacent, recruiting more staff than the revenue increase warrants |
| Why does rising productivity tend to push labour costs per unit down? | Because employees' wages are being spread over more units of output |
| Why might staff retention figures improve during a recession? | Staff are scared to risk unemployment, so they stay put even if they get little satisfaction from their jobs |
| Why might a company's labour turnover figures have worsened steadily over the past four years? | There may be a new management approach that puts more pressure on staff, encouraging increasing numbers of them to look for work elsewhere |
| Why might the Chancellor of the Exchequer be concerned if UK productivity figures failed to rise? | The Chancellor would worry, because without productivity gains our economy has no prospects for sustained economic growth; rising efficiency makes it easier to export, and easier to fight off imported goods |
| How might a head teacher view a big rise in labour turnover since his or her arrival? | It depends on how highly he or she rates the staff; if she's not keen then she should be delighted they're going |

## Evaluation: Analysing human resource performance

Performance ratios such as labour turnover raise questions. They do not supply answers. Follow-up staff surveys or chats may be needed to discover the underlying problems. Figures such as these give the firm an indication of what issues need addressing if the firm is to improve its position in the future, but this must be taken within the context of the business as a whole. A high labour turnover figure may have been the result of a deliberate policy to bring in younger members of staff who may be more adaptable to a changing situation in the workplace.

It must be remembered that these figures are all looking to the past. They tell the firm what has happened to its workforce. Although this has a strong element of objectivity, it is not as valuable as an indication of how the indicators may look in the future.

# Workbook

## A. Revision questions

(20 marks; 20 minutes)

1. Define the following terms:
   a) labour productivity    b) labour turnover.  (4)

2. Why could an increase in labour productivity help a firm to reduce its costs per unit?  (3)

3. In what ways could a hotel business benefit if labour turnover rose from 2 to 15 per cent per year?  (4)

4. Some fast food outlets have labour turnover as high as 100 per cent per year. What could be the effects of this on the firm?  (4)

5. How might a firm know if its human resource strategy was working effectively?  (5)

# B. Revision exercises

## DATA RESPONSE 1

A firm has the data shown in Table 51.1 on its human resource function.

Table 51.1 Data held by a firm on its human resource function

|  | Year 1 | Year 2 |
|---|---|---|
| Output | 50,000 | 55,000 |
| Average no. of workers | 250 | 220 |
| No. of staff leaving the firm | 12 | 8 |
| Working days per worker – possible | 230 | 230 |
| Average no. of staff absent | 4 | 3 |

### Questions (15 marks; 15 minutes)

1. Calculate the following ratios for both years:
   a) labour productivity
   b) labour turnover (6)

2. Analyse the questions these figures could raise in the minds of the firm's management. (9)

## DATA RESPONSE 2

Turner's Butchers is a chain of three shops in a large town in the North of England. The shops are all supplied with prepared and packaged produce from Turner's Farm, owned by the same family.

The management is particularly concerned at present by the differing performance of the three shops. In particular, they feel there may be a problem with the personnel management in the chain. The concerns were highlighted recently in a report looking at various indicators of personnel effectiveness.

The key section of the report is shown in Table 51.2.

### Questions (28 marks; 30 minutes)

1. Briefly outline your observations on each of the three shops in terms of their personnel management. (6)

Table 51.2 Key section of a report on indicators of personnel effectiveness

| Workforce performance data per shop | | | |
|---|---|---|---|
|  | Grayton Road | St. John's Precinct | Lark Hill |
| Staff (full-time) | 8 | 6 | 7 |
| Labour turnover (per cent) | 25 | 150 | 0 |
| Absence rate (per cent) | 5 | 12 | 1 |
| Sales per employee (£000s) | 14 | 15 | 18 |

2. Analyse the factors that may have contributed to the problems. (7)

3. Taking the business as a whole, make justified recommendations as to how any problems could be tackled by the management. (15)

## DATA RESPONSE 3

### Employers face high staff turnover in 2014

A fifth of employees plan to quit their job this year, according to a survey from the Institute of Leadership and Management (ILM). The study, of 1,001 workers, found that of the staff who are preparing to change job, 16 per cent want to leave because they do not feel valued. Of this group, the vast majority would like a similar job (40 per cent) or a different post (39 per cent) at a new company, while one in 10 would like to start their own business.

However, in addition to the fifth of workers planning to leave, a further 31 per cent are unsure about whether they will stay in their current role,

suggesting employers face high staff turnover in the coming months.

Charles Elvin, ILM's chief executive, said: 'The New Year is always a popular time for workers to look ahead and think about how they can progress. Our findings show that UK employees are beginning to reassess the job market and look into a range of new opportunities, from starting a new job to developing a new business.

'The survey illustrates just how crucial it is that workers feel valued in the workplace. As many workers like to make a change at this time of year, it is important that organisations adapt to this phase by offering the chance to learn new skills and opportunities to progress wherever possible.'

The survey also asked employees about their workplace resolutions for the New Year. Most respondents (31 per cent) said improving their work/life balance was a top priority for 2014. This was closely followed by a desire to receive more training or attain a new qualification (28 per cent), to become a better manager (13 per cent), and be more productive at work (11 per cent). The ILM said that the findings revealed a desire to improve the standards of leadership in organisations, with 19 per cent hoping to improve their own leadership skills this year and 17 per cent hoping for more transparent leadership from their boss.

'The survey reinforces the importance of leadership to workers in the UK, and in particular the desire for greater transparency in the workplace,' Elvin added. 'This should be an important consideration for both current managers and those looking to improve their leadership skills.'

Source: http://www.cipd.co.uk/pm/peoplemanagement/b/weblog/archive/2014/01/07/employers-face-high-staff-turnover-in-2014-survey-suggests.aspx

### Questions (25 marks; 30 minutes)

1. Explain the fall in labour turnover during the recent recession. (4)

2. Explain the reasons for the expected rise in labour turnover in 2014. (5)

3. To what extent should high labour turnover always be a cause for concern for managers? (16)

## C. Extend your understanding

1. 'Human resource ratios raise questions. Good managers make sure they answer them.' To what extent do you agree with this statement? (20)

2. Evaluate the ways in which a firm may respond to an increasing rate of labour turnover. In your answer, refer to one retail business and one other organisation you have researched. (20)

# 52

# Decision-making and improved human resource performance

**Linked to:** Setting human resource (HR) objectives, Chapter 45; Motivation and engagement in theory, Chapter 46; Managing the human resource flow, Chapter 49; Analysing human resource performance, Chapter 51.

## Definition

Human resource performance implies an evaluation of the effectiveness of the policies that relate labour productivity, turnover and engagement to the corporate business objectives.

## 52.1 Introduction

People are a resource of the business. Like any other resource they have to be managed. Many organisations claim their people are 'our most important asset' and that HR management makes a significant difference to business success. All too often, though, staff are treated like a cost, not an asset.

'You have got to have an atmosphere where people can make mistakes. If we're not making mistakes we're not going anywhere'. Gordon Forward, President, Chaparral Steel

## 52.2 Human resource decisions and competitiveness

A huge number of decisions and circumstances affect competitiveness. Among the great British business successes of recent times (Jaguar Land Rover, especially the Evoque; Costa Coffee; aircraft and aero-engine manufacture, especially Rolls Royce; ASOS; Primark) it is hard to see human resources at their heart. The most important factors have been strategic decisions, for instance Costa taking on Starbucks in China, and ASOS having the courage to develop internationally while still growing in Britain.

Despite this, these companies could not have enjoyed success if their people had been alienated or misdirected from the organisations' objectives. Therefore it is valid to see human resources as a key factor. In the case of Jaguar Land Rover (JLR) the most important HR decisions have related to flow. In other words, having identified the remarkable sales boom it has been vital to recruit, train and retrain staff quickly enough to keep up with demand. As a result of that HR success, the business can enjoy the fruits of the boom in demand for its products (see Table 52.1).

**Table 52.1** Sales of Jaguar Land Rover cars (almost all UK made, then exported)

| Sales in units | 2005 | 2009 | 2010 | 2011 | 2012 | 2013 | 2014 (est) |
|---|---|---|---|---|---|---|---|
| China JLR sales* | n/a | 15,000 | 26,126 | 42,063 | 73,347 | 95,200 | 118,000** |
| Total JLR sales | n/a | 195,663 | 232,839 | 274,280 | 357,773 | 425,000 | 476,000 |
| China per cent share of JLR sales | 1 per cent | 7.60 per cent | 11.20 per cent | 15.30 per cent | 20.50 per cent | 22.40 per cent | 24.80 per cent |
| China ranking (out of JLR sales) | 12th | 6th | 4th | 3rd | 1st | 1st | 1st |
| Total JLR employee numbers | n/a | 17,529 | 16,384 | 17,255 | 20,887 | 24,913 | 28,000 |

*At an average price of £70,000.

**This sales level represents £8.3 billion of retail sales in China

Source: All data from JLR accounts and press releases

Of course, successful HR decisions can affect competitiveness. In 2003 James Dyson decided to separate the engineering and design part of his business from the manufacturing. Production headed east while R&D stayed in Wiltshire. Perhaps, by focusing HR efforts on the highly skilled part of the business it made it easier for Dyson Appliances to become one of the most profitable consumer goods companies in the world.

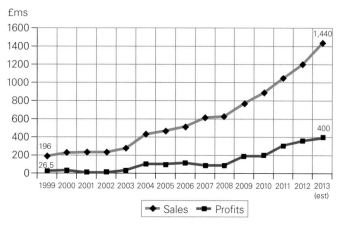

**Figure 52.1** UK's most competitive private limited company: Dyson sales and profits

Source: various newspaper reports

## 52.3 Human resource decisions and the other business functions

Whereas there are plenty of marketing directors and finance directors in Britain's boardrooms, it is difficult to find many human resource directors. Unilever was one of the first to boast having an HR director, but today the 'Chief HR Officer' is one of fifteen members of the Unilever Leadership Executive, but not on the Board. Among other UK businesses (HSBC Bank; Associated British Foods – owners of Primark; BP and Sainsbury's) the same is true. Chief finance officers are at the top table; the HR people are rarely so.

The implication is that it is naïve to think that HR departments make decisions that the other business functions have to follow. The reality is more likely to be that the board decides on general aims and objectives; that these are firmed up into an overall corporate strategy by the chief executive and his or her team – then the functional areas have to play their part in making things happen.

The relationship between HR and operations or marketing, therefore, has to be collaborative not dominating. If the plan is to reposition Ryanair as a customer-friendly airline, HR will play an important part in organising the retraining and perhaps changing

the recruitment criteria. But it will all be in conjunction with what the operations managers want and what the finance function says can be afforded.

## 52.4 Impact on HR of market conditions and competition

The key impact on HR decisions comes from the labour market. If jobs are plentiful, HR departments have to focus hugely on staff recruitment and retention. This ensures that issues such as flexible working are tackled with people in mind instead of the company.

When times are tough, HR managers focus on flexibility from the company's viewpoint. There is no better example than the zero hours contract. This is an employment contract promising nothing, in which staff may be contacted with short notice to be told when and for how long they are working the following week. For the company, this effectively turns a fixed cost into a variable one; but the very thing that makes this great for the boss makes it lousy for the worker, especially if she or he has obligations such as a mortgage.

There is a tendency to assume that it's the personality of the HR boss that determines whether a 'hard HR' or 'soft HR' approach is taken. In fact it's often a function of market and competitive conditions. During times of recession, many more firms will adopt a 'hard' HR approach – simply because they can get away with it. A surprise in the 2009 recession was that exactly the same tendency affected the public sector. Given fairly tough public spending cuts, the problem shifted from the private to the state sector. Figures for 2014 showed zero-hours contracts were used by 17 per cent of private sector firms but in 25 per cent of public sector contracts.

Ultimately, competition is the key factor affecting HR performance. The great Japanese business writer Kenichi Ohmae once said that: 'Without competitors there is no need for strategy'. Here, the competition in question is the battle to hire and keep the best people. When the labour market is buoyant, the brightest graduates can expect lavish inducements from prime employers such as management consultants and investment banks. In late 2008, Aldi was offering newly graduated recruits a starting salary of £40,000 plus a company car, to try to compete for the best. With the benefit of hindsight it may well have been a very shrewd move.

In another famous quote from a famous man, Karl Marx once described 'the unemployed as the reserve army of capitalism'. He meant that unemployment made it easier for companies to get their way in the labour market, because the competition from that 'reserve army' meant that HR departments did not have to try so hard.

'Our goal should be to minimise standardisation of human behaviour.' Douglas McGregor, author, *The Human Side of Enterprise*

## 52.5 Ethical and environmental influences on HR decisions

People like to think that the ethical environment for business is improving, perhaps because companies make more of an effort to sound concerned. Sadly in many areas of business there is little evidence of improvement. A good example is the banking sector. Every one of Britain's high street banks has been found guilty of a series of mis-selling and market-rigging scandals. When individual employees have tried to stem the tide, they have been swept aside. At Lloyds Bank a whistleblower HR manager (Ian Taplin) tried between 2005 and 2010 to get senior managers at the bank to take seriously his evidence that bank employees were persuading its poorer customers to pay more for life insurance than richer ones. Instead of taking an interest in their customers, Lloyds made three offers to pay Taplin off (with gagging clauses) and then fired him anyway. This is in no way exceptional; many other corporate whistleblowers have suffered the same fate (even more shockingly, the same is true in the public sector, notably the NHS).

If you are working in an organisational culture where truth and fairness come second to getting things done (maximising your personal bonus or achieving your NHS targets), the logical thing is to lie low – and perhaps start looking for another job. Regrettably often, whistleblowers have found it impossible to get another job in their chosen profession.

Environmental influences on HR perhaps focus mainly on transport factors. In London the number of people cycling to work rose by 144 per cent between 2001 and 2011 (these are census figures that won't be updated until 2021!). Much of the reason for this increase was a government scheme offering tax incentives to firms to encourage cycling. The reality, though, is that such schemes were pushed by HR departments that could see fitness benefits for staff together with environmental benefits for the City. Outside London, cycling numbers also rose between 2001 and 2011, as follows: Bristol +94 per cent, Manchester +83 per cent and Newcastle +81 per cent.

(Source: Office for National Statistics, March 2014)

(Referring to homeworking): 'It's against corporate culture not to have people on site. Executives want to own their employees.' Margrethe Olsen, company director

## 52.6 Technological influences on HR decisions

There is a tendency to assume that information technology will grow ever greater in importance in every aspect of business. In fact the CIPD's 2014 report on Learning and Development in the UK says that: 'E-learning may have reached its peak, as fewer predict growth of e-learning (2014: 23 per cent, 2013: 29 per cent, 2012: 24 per cent, 2011: 30 per cent). Respondents found e-learning to have a bigger gap between use and effectiveness than any other L&D (learning and development) practice.' So whereas there had been a move towards online training courses, HR professionals believe that boom is now over.

Other important technological influences on HR decisions include:

● the ever developing improvements in international communications, which makes it more possible to interview overseas recruits online, and to discuss common problems with HR departments in different parts of the world

● the impact of real technological change, for instance if a high street seller decides to switch to online selling. There would probably be redundancies, retraining and new recruitment needed to carry out such a strategy.

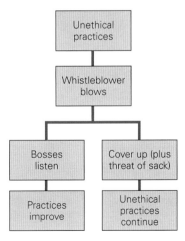

**Figure 52.2** Logic chain: risks of whistleblowing

## Five Whys and a How

| Question | Answer |
| --- | --- |
| Why might competitiveness falter if HR is mismanaged? | HR has to plan ahead however long is necessary to make sure that the right staff, with the right motivation are available at the right time |
| Why might senior HR managers find it hard to affect overall business strategy? | HR is seen in firms as a service department – getting the right staff at the right time – HR staff rarely have board-level input into strategy |
| Why is HR not regarded more highly in business? | It has rarely been possible to show the effect of great HR on sales/profits (though Pret A Manger is an example of a business that's got it right) |
| Why might a moral individual put up with unethical practices at work? | For simple reasons of need: mortgage to be paid; kids to be fed; and lack of self-confidence to look for another job |
| Why may new technology start to threaten HR jobs in the future? | If unmanned computer-controlled delivery vans are the future, why would HR jobs be required? |
| How much does an HR director earn? | According to Reed 2014, £80,003 a year, compared with £91,000 a year for finance directors |

### Key terms

**Whistleblower:** an employee who reveals unethical or risky practices that line managers have been trying to keep quiet. The secrets may be passed up the hierarchy or (if that has no effect) be revealed to the media/outside world.

**Zero-hours contract:** an employment contract that promises nothing more than a last minute offer of work for the following week. This is flexibility for employers at the cost of uncertainty for employees.

### Evaluation: Decision-making and improved human resource performance

Human resource management it easy to put on a pedestal, because motivation theory is such a compelling part of a business course. Sadly for HR professionals, their tasks are less exciting, though no less important than that. Getting things right is a management art – far removed from clever decision-making. HR professionals make sure that the directors' wishes can be achieved, cost-effectively and competently. In modern business, people who get things right are not necessarily given the opportunities they deserve.

# Workbook

## A. Revision questions

(31 marks; 30 minutes)

1. A new pizza place opens two doors from yours and some of your staff switch to the new employer. Outline two ways an HR manager should react to this situation. (4)

2. Identify three aspects of HR management that get easier when there's a recession. (3)

3. If an HR manager suspects that one of the staff has won a large contract using bribery, what might she or he do? (4)

4. Explain the reasons for a multinational business operating in 35 countries around the world holding all HR management meetings in English. (6)

5. Analyse why online training courses may be less successful than face-to-face ones. (6)

6. Explain two reasons why an HR director would make a good future managing director of the whole company. (8)

## B. Revision exercises
### DATA RESPONSE

#### Barclays Bank – Ethics and HR

Over a period of perhaps 10 years, Barclays Bank developed a culture that damaged the interests of an extraordinary range of its stakeholders, including retail customers, business customers and the wider community. The bank has been at the centre of extreme tax avoidance plans, the Libor rate-fixing scandal, the PPI mis-selling scandal and much else. What was once a straightforward high street bank became dominated by the casino culture of investment banking. In 2013 its staff were the next stakeholders to suffer – with a wave of job losses.

> # Our culture
>
> **Our culture evolves as the world in which we live and work changes. Sitting still is simply not an option so we are always looking at ways to improve ourselves and better serve all our customers.**
>
> **The result is a culture where everyone is encouraged to stretch themselves, take responsibility for their actions and challenge the status quo by coming up with fresh ideas.**
>
> Source: Barclays website 24/2/13

Following a parliamentary inquiry into banking standards in July 2012, Lord McFall, a member of the committee, said there is 'no hint' Barclays are thinking of changing their culture following the Libor rate-fixing scandal. Lord McFall said the bank's apology was 'nothing more than a futile gesture'. Eventually, in July 2012 the Bank of England leaned on Barclays to get rid of its highly-paid boss Bob Diamond.

At first, Bob Diamond's successor, Antony Jenkins, kept a low profile. Only in February 2013 did he emerge with a round of press conferences and media interviews to announce his new vision for Barclays. Above all else, he claimed to be 'shredding' the Barclays culture of the past, and would instead build the new culture around 'the bank's new values – respect, integrity, service, excellence and stewardship.'

On 12 February *The Guardian* reported that: 'The new boss of Barclays has attempted to break from the bank's scandal-ridden recent past by announcing plans to pull out of controversial businesses that speculate on food prices, specialise in "industrial scale" tax avoidance schemes and use the bank's money to bet on markets.'

Antony Jenkins, promoted to the top job last year when Bob Diamond was forced out in the wake of the Libor-rigging scandal, had vowed to shut down businesses that were unethical, regardless of the profits they generate for the bank. However, he stepped back from the most radical reform by insisting the investment bank – which generates 60 per cent of the bank's total profits – would remain a 'very large part and an important part of the group.' He said changing the bank's culture and rebuilding its reputation would take five to 10 years.

Some 3,700 jobs are to be axed as the bank retrenches from troubled businesses in continental Europe to focus on the UK, US and Asia after a six-month review of 75 individual business lines. Some 1,600 investment banking jobs have gone in the last six weeks alone. The bank's shares jumped 9 per cent to 327p on the measures to cut costs and avoid the most radical options for reform.

In a room emblazoned with the bank's new values – respect, integrity, service, excellence and stewardship – Jenkins insisted: 'This is not window dressing or PR. They define the work we will do and the work we won't do.'

'There will be no going back to the old ways of doing things,' said Jenkins. He is linking the pay and bonuses of the bank's 125 top staff to his new 'values' this year. All employees will have their pay linked to them next year.

Independent analyst Louise Cooper was asked by *The Guardian* just what Barclays would have to do to achieve culture change: 'I believe strongly that corporate culture is set by executives and management – their behaviour and attitudes implicitly tell employees what is acceptable and important and how to behave. Standards and morality trickle down an organisation. If a firm has been proven to be highly toxic then bosses must leave. That is the first rule. It is very difficult to reprimand an employee for bad or illegal behaviour when it's been previously sanctioned, even encouraged or copied from bosses. Nothing can change without executives leaving.

'Secondly, the new team must publicise there has been a change from the old world order. This is what the new boss at Barclays has done. He has sent a clear message to staff that if they don't like the new morality then they should leave. This is also important for clearing out the middle managers who refuse to adapt.

'Thirdly, follow the advice of the [former] New York mayor Rudy Giuliani and adopt a "zero tolerance policy". The new standards of behaviour must be rigorously enforced. Fourthly, reward those who embrace the new rules and penalise those who don't – the carrot and the stick.

'And finally, for those seeking to make the changes, it is important to realise it is a long process. It is a sad comment on human nature that bad behaviour spreads like wildfire through an organisation and yet good behaviour takes forever to develop. Leaders get the organisations they deserve.'

Source: Adapted from guardian.co.uk

### Questions (30 marks; 35 minutes)

1. Explain the importance of 'the carrot and the stick' in the theories of either F.W. Taylor or Professor Herzberg. (5)

2. Analyse the implications for HR managers of '3,700 jobs' being axed in the near future. (9)

3. To what extent may a 'zero-tolerance policy' make it possible for the HR department to eliminate unethical behaviour throughout the bank? (16)

## C. Extend your understanding

1. Mr Mao Chinese takeaway has grown to 30 outlets in the North West and plans to go national. At present it has no HR department. How important is it to establish a human resource function within the business? Justify your answer. (20)

2. In the hotel business fierce price competition can encourage a company to cut costs, cut back on employee benefits and outsource important business functions. An alternative is to offer a differentiated product and encourage staff to give great service. To what extent is a hotel likely to succeed by using the second approach? (20)

# Chapter 53
## Influences on the mission of a business

**Linked to:** Understanding the nature and purpose of business, Chapter 1; Corporate objectives, strategy and tactics, Chapter 54.

### Definition

Aims are a generalised statement of where you are heading, from which objectives can be set. A mission is a more fervent, passionate way of expressing an aim.

## 53.1 Introduction

Some children, as young as 10 or 11 years old, are clear about what they want from life. They are determined to become a doctor or vet. The clarity of their aim makes them work hard at school, choose science subjects and overcome any setbacks (a weak teacher, perhaps). So whereas most GCSE and A-level students drift from one day to the next, these individuals are focused: they have their eyes on their prize. This is the potentially huge benefit that can stem from clear aims.

Indeed, you could say that some of these focused students are driven by a sense of mission. Their aim is not just to get the label of 'doctor' but also to help make the world a better place. The drive shown by these students will be the most impressive of all.

For new small businesses there can also be a powerful sense of mission. A chef may open his or her own restaurant, driven largely by the desire to win a Michelin star (the *Michelin Guide* to restaurants is the world's most prestigious). In Gordon Ramsay style, the approach to achieving this may prove to be ruthless or even fanatical. Such a person is far more likely to achieve this aim than one who opens a restaurant thinking, 'It would be nice to get a star; let's see if it happens.

'It takes a person with a mission to succeed.'
Clarence Thomas, US Supreme Court judge

**Figure 53.1** Gordon Ramsay

In marketplaces where competition is fierce, businesses that are passionate and determined are always more likely to succeed than those that are drifting. This has always been one of the secrets to the success of Apple. Its boss and senior managers have always believed in the superiority of Apple design and technology, but were also fanatically hostile to 'the evil empire': Microsoft. This shared view kept Apple going through the dark days before the success of the iPod transformed the business.

From the clear sense of mission at Apple has come its objectives and the strategies that flow from the objectives – but also its perceived moral laxity. Apple has avoided paying tax on its profits despite having $150 billion in cash in its balance sheet. It has also been accused of allowing its Chinese production workers to work in very poor conditions. So there is a risk that a strong sense of mission can create a sense of entitlement which may sow the seeds for future difficulties.

## 53.2 Aims

Possible examples of aims include:

- 'To become a profitable business with a long-term future' (Zayka Indian restaurant, started in January 2011)
- 'To become a Premier League club' (Nottingham Forest FC, currently in football's second tier)
- 'To diversify away from dependence on Britain' (the implicit aim of Tesco between 2003 and 2013).

One of the stated aims of the McDonald's fast food chain is to provide 'friendly service in a relaxed, safe and consistent restaurant environment'. The success of the organisation depends upon turning this aim into practice. In order for this to be achieved, employees must understand and share the aim. When a customer enters a McDonald's restaurant anywhere in the world they know what to expect. The organisation has the ability to reproduce the same 'relaxed, safe and consistent' atmosphere with different staff, in different locations. This has built the company's reputation. This corporate aim is effective because it recognises what lies at the heart of the organisation's success.

The Tesco example above shows that aims can be mistaken. In Tesco's case not only did this aim lead to specific disasters such as the £2 billion wasted on trying and failing in America, but more importantly it meant that successive Tesco bosses took their eye off changing customer requirements in Britain. The British shopper's image of Tesco lurched from believing 'Every Little Helps' to 'Every Little Helps Tesco' – and they switched to Aldi, Lidl or Waitrose.

Whether right or wrong, corporate aims act as the basis for setting the organisation's objectives. These are the targets that must be achieved if the aims are to be realised. The success or failure of each individual decision within the firm can be judged by the extent to which it meets the business objectives. This allows the delegation of authority within the organisation, while at the same time maintaining co-ordination.

## 53.3 Mission statements

A mission statement is an attempt to put corporate aims into words that inspire. The mission statement of WalMart, the world's biggest retailer, is 'to give ordinary folk the chance to buy the same thing as rich people'. Shop floor staff are more likely to be motivated by a mission statement of this kind than by the desire to maximise profit.

It is hoped that by summarising clearly the long-term direction of the organisation, a focus is provided that helps to inspire employees to greater effort and ensure the departments work together. Without this common purpose each area of a firm may have different aims and choose to move in conflicting directions.

### Real business

**Examples of mission statements**

- *Google:* 'organise the world's information and make it universally available'.
- *Coca-Cola:* 'To refresh the world – in mind, body and spirit'.
- *Pret A Manger (sandwich chain):* 'Pret creates handmade natural food avoiding the obscure chemical additives and preservatives common to so much of the prepared and "fast" food on the market today'.
- *Nike:* 'To bring inspiration and innovation to every athlete\* in the world (\*If you have a body you are an athlete).'

It is also important to note that not every company has a written mission statement. Some companies are clear that they and their staff 'live the mission' and therefore do not need to write it down. Marks & Spencer plc has stopped publicising a mission statement, perhaps because it has learnt that one statement cannot sum up the driving forces behind a whole, complex business.

## 53.4 Influences on business mission

The model shown in Figure 53.2 shows the main influences on mission. It is necessary to link each of the four elements of the model so that they reinforce one another.

'Facebook was not originally created to be a company. It was built to accomplish a social mission - to make the world more open and connected.' Mark Zuckerberg, founder of Facebook

PURPOSE
Why the company exists

STRATEGY
The competitive position
of the company

VALUES
What the company
believes in

STANDARDS
AND
BEHAVIOURS
The policies and behaviour
patterns expected of
company employees

**Figure 53.2** The mission model

In turn, each element suggests the following.

## Purpose (reason why the company exists)

This is clearly shown by the Nike mission, which emphasises the desire to provide innovative products for athletes. In fact a sceptic could point out that Nike builds much of its branding around advertising, imagery and visual design rather than product innovation. Nike's brilliance has been to keep customers and staff confident that the company wants to support athletes rather than exploit them.

## Values (what the company believes in)

In the case of Pret A Manger, it is not just that it believes in natural, fresh food, but also that the business has always:

- used packaging that is made from recycled materials and can be recycled in future

- taken care to source its products from suppliers that treat staff fairly

- wanted to push customers to try new things, especially from sustainable sources

- The values of the business are a key part of its culture, and should also include the way staff are treated and other ethical considerations.

'A lot of economists feel you do incentives and nothing else. I disagree. You have to motivate people around a central mission, a set of values, and then the incentives become the frosting on the cake; they become the payoff.' Bill George, professor, Harvard Business School

## Standards and behaviours

This refers to the standards set by managers and the behaviour expected from staff. Cambridge graduate

Polly Courtney has told the *Observer* newspaper about her experiences as a highly paid banker in the City of London. The work culture meant that people would send emails at two o'clock in the morning to show how late they worked, and Polly found sexism rooted in a 'lads' culture in which nights out ended at the strip club. As the only woman in an office of 21, she was treated like a secretary and bypassed for promotion. Polly wrote a book about her experiences, whereas others have successfully sued merchant banks on grounds of sex discrimination. Clearly the managements are wholly at fault in allowing such a situation to develop.

## Strategy

Strategy means the medium- to long-term plans adopted by the business to make the aims and mission achievable. This is dealt with in chapter 54.

**Aims/Mission**

Company/corporate
objectives

Corporate strategy

Plans, e.g.
marketing plans

**Figure 53.3** Logic chain: from mission to strategy

## 53.5 The links between mission, corporate objectives and strategy

Corporate objectives are the medium-long term targets for the whole enterprise. Some companies break these down into time periods, perhaps targeting a rise in operating profit margins from 6.5 per cent to 7.5 per cent within two years – and then to 10 per cent within five years. Objectives such as these take the company's mission and turn it into something measurable. This helps the different business functions work together towards a clear target.

**Table 53.1** Companies and their possible missions and objectives

| Company | Possible mission | Possible objectives |
|---|---|---|
| Rolls Royce plc (Aerospace) | Become the world's leading producer of aero engines | Maintain 50% global market share in wide-body planes; grow share of single aisle planes to 30% by the end of 2019 |
| ASOS plc | To become the world's No 1 online fashion destination for 20-somethings* *ASOS call this their 'ambition' but it means the same as mission | To be profitable in China by 2017, with a fashion online market share of at least 15% |
| Booths Grocers | To become the nation's most admired supplier of groceries | To open at least 12 profitable shops in the south within three years |

After the objectives are set – probably by a senior executive committee and then 'signed off' (given formal, written approval) by the board – the business can decide on the corporate strategy. This will be the plan for meeting the objectives. The risk here is that the strategy may stray away from the mission. This could happen if the objectives are not aligned fully with the mission. For example in the 2009 financial crisis the Co-op Bank, despite its mission to be the UK's ethical bank, set objectives based on sales revenue and profit. The resulting strategy included selling financial services that were later deemed by the regulator to have been mis-sold. In other words the 'ethical' bank lost its ethical compass when selling products to its own customers.

Clearly it's very important to make sure that the objectives line up with the mission and the strategy lines up with the objectives. But it isn't easy.

'A small body of determined spirits fired by an unquenchable faith in their mission can alter the course of history.' Mahatma Ghandi, founder of modern India

## Five Whys and a How

| Question | Answer |
|---|---|
| Why may a clear sense of mission help a business to succeed? | A believable, but inspiring mission can unite staff and customers behind the business |
| Why may mission be especially important in a new business? | It's invaluable to have customers who 'buy-in' to the business; they'll not only be loyal but will also spread the word |
| Why may companies with aims outperform those with mission? | The weakness of mission is that it can blind the company to its weaknesses; aims are less powerful, so they can be appraised more coolly |
| Why might the mission be lost from a company's strategy? | Because there's a stage in between: the objectives; if the objectives don't quite fit the mission, there may be a mismatch between mission and strategy |
| Why might a new, clear mission help a giant but struggling company such as Marks & Spencer? | Marks & Spencer needs something inspirational that will help customers and staff believe in the company again |
| How might a company set about devising a new mission? | Aims and mission come from the top, so the directors need to spend time discussing and agreeing a suitable new mission |

## Evaluation: Influences on the mission of a business

Good evaluation is based upon a questioning approach to the subject matter. This should apply to the case material being looked at, and to the underlying theory. This section of the course provides huge scope for careful questioning; this should not be in the form of blanket cynicism ('all mission statements are rubbish'), but by carefully considering the evidence. Is a new boss genuinely trying to improve the motivation and behaviour of staff for the benefit of customers and the business as

a whole? If so, perhaps a mission statement is a valuable centrepiece to a whole process of culture change.

At other times, though, the case material may present a new mission statement as no more than a sticking plaster on a diseased wound. Genuine problems need genuine solutions, not slogans. You need to make judgements about which situation is which, then justify your views with evidence from the case and drawn from the theory set out in this unit.

## Key terms

**Aims:** a generalised statement of where the business is heading.

**Mission:** an aim expressed in a particularly inspiring way.

**Mission statement:** a short passage of text that sums up the organisation's mission. This may get displayed on walls throughout the business and placed prominently on the website.

# Workbook

## A. Revision questions

(25 marks; 30 minutes)

1. Why do clear aims help people or businesses to achieve their goals? (3)

2. What is the difference between mission and a mission statement? (3)

3. Outline one weakness of Nike's mission statement (see 53.3). (3)

4. Explain briefly what is shown by the 'mission model'. (4)

5. Outline two possible aims for one of the national supermarket chains. (4)

6. Briefly explain who is responsible for setting a firm's objectives. (2)

7. Is it possible to have a SMART mission? Outline your answer. (3)

8. Look at the ASOS objective shown in Table 53.1. Suggest one strategy that might help achieve this. (3)

## B. Revision exercises
### DATA RESPONSE

In early 2007 Tesco confirmed rumours that it was to launch into the US grocery market: the world's biggest and most competitive. This would bring it face-to-face with WalMart in a market worth $500 billion. Huge though Tesco had become, with 500,000 employees worldwide, it remained a minnow compared with WalMart. Despite scepticism by some analysts, most assumed that the magic touch of Tesco's long-time boss Terry Leahy would ensure success. Leahy had switched his best executives from China to America and allowed them to carry out a year's research and investigation into the US grocery market. Leahy never quite said it, but analysts were

starting to wonder whether his real mission was to make Tesco the world's number 1 retailer.

In its 2007 annual report, Tesco confirmed its plan to invest £250m a year for five years to develop a new grocery concept called Fresh & Easy. Its stores would be one third of the size of a typical US supermarket, but double the size of the average convenience store. Tesco believed it had found a market gap. By Spring 2008 Tesco had 60 Fresh & Easy stores in operation, and was trumpeting that sales were 'ahead of budget'. It said 150 more would be opened in the 2008/2009 financial year. Break-even would be achieved, it said, within two years.

By 2009 it was clear that the original launch plan had been a flop. Not enough cash was coming through the tills to generate a profit. Tesco claimed that all it needed was 'scale', i.e. enough stores to deliver sufficient economies of scale to push the business beyond its break-even point. It announced a series of changes that would be made to store design and layout, and to the range of goods on offer. Effectively it was admitting 'we got it wrong' – but without acknowledging that if the concept was wrong, it was time to cut the losses and withdraw.

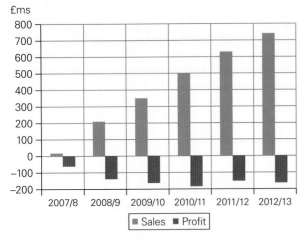

**Figure 53.4** Tesco Fresh & Easy annual sales and profits

Only after the retirement of Terry Leahy in 2011 did serious questions start to be asked within Tesco about the future of its US lossmaker. In February 2013 the new CEO Phillip Clarke made it clear that Fresh & Easy had to go. Embarrassingly, Tesco couldn't even give the stores away – they had to pay an American company to take some of the stores and the rest of the business was liquidated. In 2013 Tesco said they would have to write-down their balance sheet by more than £1 billion to account for the failure of Fresh & Easy, but as nearly £900 million of operating losses had been made (see the table below), the total loss for Tesco was probably around £2 billion.

Important though £2 billion is, the long-term consequences of the Fresh & Easy fiasco may be much greater. In 2007/8, Tesco was making a serious commitment to Asia, especially China. This commitment seemed to slip away as the American disaster required ever-more management time. In 2013 Tesco effectively sold out of its long-term operational commitment to China. Worse still, perhaps, has been the impact on Tesco's UK performance, with sales, market share, profits and credibility being eroded away in 2013 and 2014. Not long ago Tesco was Britain's most admired company; no longer.

**Table 53.2** Tesco's sales and profit in the USA and Asia

|  | Tesco USA (£ms) | | Tesco Asia (£ms) | |
|---|---|---|---|---|
|  | Sales | Profit | Sales | Profit |
| 2007/8 | 16 | −62 | 5,988 | 304 |
| 2008/9 | 208 | −142 | 7,578 | 355 |
| 2009/10 | 349 | −165 | 8,465 | 440 |
| 2010/11 | 495 | −186 | 10,278 | 570 |
| 2011/12 | 630 | −153 | 10,828 | 737 |
| 2012/13 | 740 | −165 | 11,479 | 661 |

### Questions (40 marks; 50 minutes)

1. Analyse the factors Terry Leahy might have considered before pursuing his Fresh & Easy strategy. (12)

2. By switching their best executives from China to America Tesco appeared to be prioritising developed economies over developing ones. Analyse why Tesco might have decided to do this. (12)

3. Such was Terry Leahy's status within Tesco that he was able to push ahead with a quite personal ambition to succeed in the US market. To what extent can any business leader be the dominant force in setting the objectives and strategies of a business? Justify your answer. (16)

## C. Extend your understanding

1. In Jose Mourinho's first period as Chelsea manager the club won many trophies but failed to meet owner Abramovic's desire for exciting, beautiful football. To what extent is there an inevitable trade-off between a mission for beautiful football and winning trophies? (25)

2. 'In a small firm the mission can be absorbed by the staff. In a big business it's hard for it to get through to all staff, so it's written down as a mission statement.' To what extent is this likely to prove effective within a big business? (25)

**Linked to:** Understanding the nature and purpose of business, Chapter 1; Influences on the mission of a business, Chapter 53.

## Definition

Corporate objectives are the company-wide goals that need to be achieved to keep the business on track to achieve its aims. Ideally they should be SMART (that is, Specific, Measurable, Ambitious, Realistic and Timebound). Corporate strategy provides a medium- to long-term plan for meeting the objectives.

'A man without a goal is like a ship without a rudder.'
Thomas Carlyle, nineteenth-century writer

## 54.1 Introduction

The key to success in understanding business is to see that every business is different. Even among public limited companies, the personality of the boss and the circumstances of the business separates firms that seem to be in similar positions. In consumer electronics, the objectives of Apple are completely different from the objectives of Microsoft. Similarly, the objectives of fast-growing, low-cost AirAsia are wholly different from those of long-established airlines such as Cathay Pacific or British Airways. Then there are the other types of business, from sole traders and private limited companies through to social enterprises and employee co-operatives.

A distinction needs to be drawn between public companies (plcs) and every other type of business organisation. Only plcs have shareholders who have no connection with the business other than that they own its shares. A 30-year-old who decides to buy £2,000 worth of easyJet shares cares about only two things: the share price and the level of annual payments (dividends) paid out by the business. The share price depends upon current profits and investors'

expectations of the business's future. If people think the growth prospects are terrific, the shares will be highly rated and therefore highly priced. Some shareholders may care about the social or environmental record of the business, but most are in it for the money.

For organisations other than plcs, there are many possible alternative objectives. There will be fishing shops that open up because individuals with a love of the sport have it as a lifetime ambition. The profits may not be great, but the satisfaction may be terrific. There will also be companies that start up with the intention of running a social enterprise. One well-known example is Duncan Goose, who founded Global Ethics Ltd in order to channel profit from selling bottled water into digging water wells in Africa.

## 54.2 Corporate objectives for plcs

### Maximising shareholder value

Maximising shareholder value (see Figure 54.1) is increasingly presented by the board of directors of large companies as the modern equivalent of profit maximisation. Share prices reflect the present value of the dividends the company is expected to pay out in the future. As a result, this objective means taking actions that maximise the price of the organisation's shares on the stock market.

### Growth in the size of the firm

The managers of a business may choose to take decisions with the objective of making the organisation larger. The motivation behind this goal could be the natural desire to see the business achieve its full potential; it may also help to defend the firm from hostile takeover bids. If your firm is the biggest, who could be big enough to take you over? Being number one in a marketplace is a version of the growth objective. It has been at the centre of the long-running battle between Nike and Adidas – both want to be the world's top provider of sportswear.

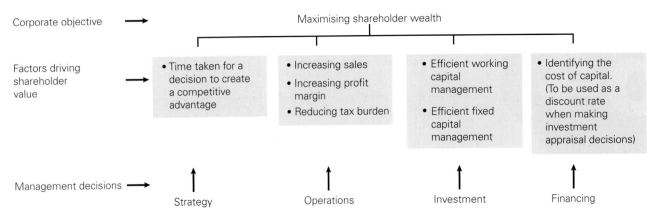

**Figure 54.1** Maximising shareholder value

### Adidas

In 2006 Adidas completed a £2 billion takeover of American sportswear rival Reebok. Herbert Hainer, boss of the German giant Adidas, said that the deal 'represents a major strategic milestone for our group'. The real purpose was to bring Adidas closer to its long-term goal of overtaking Nike as the world's biggest sportswear business. Mr Hainer went on to say, 'This is a once-in-a-lifetime opportunity to combine two of the most respected and well-known companies in the worldwide sporting goods industry.'

Sadly for Adidas, by the time of the 2014 World Cup Nike was on the front foot and it looked harder than ever for Adidas to catch it. Takeover bids are a tempting way to grow quickly – but often prove disappointing.

## Diversification in order to spread risk

In other words, diversify to reduce dependence on one product or market. This is what Tesco plc did between 2000 and 2013 (then abandoned); in a similar vein Rentokil Initial plc attempted various diversifications including a disastrous foray into parcel delivery with City Link. For both of these companies, diversification proved an extremely risky way to spread risk. Of course if, like PepsiCo, you can succeed at producing fruit juice (Tropicana) and water as well as soft drinks, you become much less vulnerable to consumer mistrust of fizzy, sugary drinks.

## Conclusions on objectives for plcs

Some academics argue that plc bosses act quite cunningly in relation to profit objectives: they 'satisfice' rather than 'maximise'. A chief executive may be able to see how to get profit up by 30 per cent in the coming year, but worry that short-term profit gains will hit the longer-term security of the business. Therefore the boss makes decisions that can boost profit by 15 per cent (enough to keep the shareholders happy) leaving scope for more profit growth in the coming years. Having found a way to keep the shareholders quiet, the directors can then decide on other objectives, such as to diversify.

## 54.3 Internal influences on corporate objectives and decisions

Companies act in their own long-term interests, influenced primarily by the views and goals of those at the top, plus the practical constraints caused by limited financial and human resources. So the main internal influences are:

● The ambitions of those leading the company. In 2013 BT appointed Gavin Patterson as chief executive; unusually, he reached that position after a background in marketing and was known for his bold, flamboyant style. Within a few months BT's successful bid for football TV rights gave an indication that he was far more ambitious than his predecessor about a growth path for BT.

● Financial influences. In BT's case, if the Financial Director had been worried that the business could not afford £900 million on football screening rights, the deal would have been called off. Accountants can't know what a company *should* buy, but they do know when a company must walk away from a deal.

● Human Resource influences. In setting objectives and in making decisions, senior managers have to take into account the qualities and abilities of senior staff. In 2014 fashion retailer New Look made a bold move into China, opening fourteen stores. The decision to do this was made hugely easier because the company's new chief executive had experience running fashion businesses across China. Of course local expertise can be hired in, but companies want to be sure that they are in full control – local managers have different ways of working.

## 54.4 External influences on corporate objectives and decisions

New Look's 2014 international strategy had not just focused on China. Its Chairman also boasted at the start of the year of building a 'very substantive' business in Russia. In fact with continuing unrest between Russia and Ukraine plus the economic effects of a collapsing oil price and rouble (the Russian currency), New Look decided in November to shut down their Russian shops and withdraw completely. This was an interestingly rapid decision based entirely on external influences. New Look's ability to decide in weeks that withdrawal would be the best option contrasts with Tesco's six-year, £2 billion US nightmare with Fresh & Easy. No business can prevent disruption due to external influences, but the ability to change course quickly is a function of the degree of internal bureaucracy – and the extent to which senior managers feel free to express themselves. It seems that no one dared tell Tesco boss Terry Leahy that his Tesco USA idea was a turkey.

Other external influences on corporate objectives and decision-making include:

● Taste, fads and fashion: in 2013/14 commentator after commentator attacked the consumption of fruit juice; before, it had been viewed as healthy – now it was condemned as sugary. For Tropicana (Pepsi) and innocent (Coca Cola) this meant an unexpected downturn in sales. Sales of Tropicana fell 6.8 per cent in 2014 and those of innocent by 11.2 per cent; this would have to affect both companies' ambitions and therefore objectives for the future.

● Changing legislation: on 1 September 2014, new energy-saving European Union (EU) rules on vacuum cleaners came into force. Shoppers, worried that they would no longer be able to buy vacuums with big engines, cleared the shops in the weeks leading up to the change. Next on the EU's list are products such as hair dryers and toasters – these must be more energy-efficient by 2017. Manufacturers will build this external influence into their objective-setting and decision-making during 2015 and 2016.

## 54.5 Influences on corporate objectives

Any business has certain objectives that may become fundamental to the operation. For new businesses, and for any that are struggling in the marketplace, the key

one is survival. If things are going reasonably well, so that survival is not in doubt, a business could aim to increase its growth rate or its profitability. If these are also going well, the directors may look beyond the immediate financial needs to the 'market standing' of the business (see Figure 54.2).

**Figure 54.2** Pyramid of business objectives

There is the possibility of a business organisation that has no commercial drivers, other than to generate the funds to achieve a social objective. Such an approach is rare, because many of the firms proclaiming their social or 'green' credentials are simply cashing in on a consumer concern. Even though non-profit motives are unusual, good answers show an understanding that different businesses have different objectives.

### Market standing

For firms that already have a profitable, growing business and reasonable insulation from operational risks, the final piece in the corporate jigsaw is to establish an image that helps to add value to the product range, and gives the consumer the confidence to assume the best of the company, not the worst.

To have high market standing, the public needs to believe that the business operates as a force for good, whether through its products, its employment practices or its positive approach to its social responsibilities. All these things can be managed, as long as the commitment and the resources are available. For instance, the voluntary use of social and environmental audits can be the basis for building a reputation for ethical trading.

To have really high market standing, though, more is needed than just clever management of public relations. The John Lewis Partnership has become a national treasure – with customers 'believing in' Waitrose and in John Lewis department stores. Partly this is because customers feel positive towards the fact that John Lewis is a worker co-operative rather than a profit-seeking company.

## Short-termism

Whereas market standing is a classic long-term objective, some companies can only focus on the short term. This is usually because trading difficulties have made business reporters critical of the management, and are therefore scrutinising each six-monthly profit statement, line by line. The expectation of this scrutiny may make the leader of a business such as Tesco or Marks & Spencer take a 'short-termist' view of corporate objectives and decision-making. In 2014, both companies announced a sharp reduction in their capital investment programmes. For Marks & Spencer capital spending would fall from £830 million in 2013 to £530 million in 2015. Such cutbacks help short-term cash flow and (to a lesser extent) profit, but perhaps at the cost of the company's long-term prospects.

## Business ownership

These days there are three main types of ownership of big businesses:

- a publicly quoted plc, with shares available on the stock market

- a family-run business such as JCB, Dyson Holdings or the Virgin Group – all huge, multi-billion pound businesses, but with no shares available publicly

- a private equity-owned business, which will trade as a separate private limited company (and can therefore be liquidated as easily as happened to City Link couriers on Christmas Eve, 2014 – quite a Christmas surprise to its 2,500 staff).

Private equity companies buy businesses either with the intention of 'asset stripping', that is selling off any assets of value, taking management fees for so doing and then discarding the rest – or to rebuild the business in order to sell it. Either way, the focus is pretty short-term. The focus for plc shareholders can also be fairly short-term. Only the family structure of a private limited company is likely to be consistent in thinking about the decades to come. In the Virgin Group, Richard Branson's children Sam and Holly are likely to take over; naturally Sir Richard will have been planning for this for years.

## 54.6 Corporate strategy

The managers of a business should develop a medium-to long-term plan about how to achieve the objectives they have established. This is the organisation's corporate strategy (see Figure 54.3). It sets out the actions that will be taken in order to achieve the goals, and the implications for the firm's human, financial and production resources. The key to success when forming

**Figure 54.3** Corporate strategy

a strategy of this kind is relating the firm's strengths to the opportunities that exist in the marketplace.

This analysis can take place at each level of the business, allowing a series of strategies to be formed in order to achieve the goals already established. A hierarchy of strategies can be produced for the whole organisation in a similar manner to the approach adopted when setting objectives.

- Corporate strategy deals with the major issues such as what industry, or industries, the business should compete in, in order to achieve corporate objectives. Managers must identify industries where the long-term profit prospects are likely to be favourable

- Business unit (or divisional) strategy should address the issue of how the organisation will compete in the industry selected by corporate strategy. This will involve selecting a position in the marketplace to distinguish the firm from its competitors; in the case of Costa Coffee in China, the question is how to differentiate the business from Starbucks.

- Functional (or department) strategy is developed in order to identify how best to achieve the objectives or targets set by the senior managers.

If a strategy is to achieve the objectives set, it must match the firm's strengths to its competitive environment (see Figure 54.4). Whitbread decided that the market for health clubs in the UK was saturated, so it would be better to sell off its David Lloyd health clubs and put its money behind the rapidly growing Costa chain. It proved one of the cleverest strategic moves of the past 25 years.

'If your train's on the wrong track every station you come to is the wrong station.' Bernard Malamud, writer

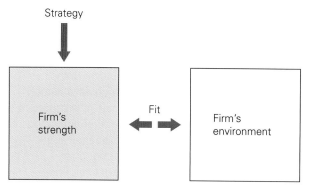

**Figure 54.4** If a strategy is to achieve the objectives set, it must match the firm's strengths to its competitive environment

## 54.7 The distinction between strategy and tactics

'Setting a goal is not the main thing. It is deciding how you will go about achieving it and staying with that plan.' Tom Landry, American football coach

Strategy can be regarded as the route map to get a business from here to there (from where it is to where it wants to be) over the medium to long term. Tactics are responses to short-term opportunities or threats. Sometimes tactical opportunities may be irrelevant to or even a diversion from the route map. For instance, a night club may decide to reposition itself as classier and older than before – yet still not be able to resist running a 'School's Out' session in mid-July.

**Table 54.1** Strategy and tactics

|  | **Strategy** | **Tactics** |
|---|---|---|
| **The football manager** | Recruit more flair players to give fans more enjoyment (and sell more season tickets) | With the league leader visiting this Saturday, pack midfield with hard-tackling defenders |
| **The clothing brand** | Exclusive clothes sold through exclusive, independent outlets | Accept a special deal with Miss Selfridge in which two product lines will be sold at a discount |
| **A chain of coffee bars** | Have no more than two outlets in any high street | Buy a lease on a third outlet because it's incredibly cheap |

There can also be times when the business has to focus on the threats it faces. If Cadbury brought out a new chocolate bar with four fingers of chocolate-coated wafer, rival Nestlé (KitKat) might run a short-term 'Now with Five!' promotion with the first ever five-finger KitKat. Once the Cadbury product had flopped, KitKat would soon revert to its four-finger format.

## Five Whys and a How

| **Question** | **Answer** |
|---|---|
| Why are corporate objectives important? | Because they help departmental managers work together towards the same goal |
| Why may some objectives prove impossible to achieve? | Changing external factors may make a sales or profit target too high for the foreseeable future |
| Why might businesses owned by private equity tend to have short-term objectives? | Because private equity is about maximising short-term returns, so quick sell-offs would be regarded as a triumph |
| Why might a firm want to diversify? | To reduce its dependence on one product or market |
| Why do tactics not always fit in with the overall strategy? | Because they're responses to opportunities or threats, which may call for a different approach from the long-term plan |
| How might short-termism damage the long-term interests of a business? | Focusing on the next profit statement can lead to underspending on items such as training, R&D and capital expenditure |

## Evaluation: Corporate objectives, strategy and tactics

Among the judgements that can be made is whether the strategy fits the objectives and the key issue of the external context. In other words, the corporate objectives and strategy must not only be right for the business, but also right for the year in question. If the economy is in recession, as in 2009, cautious corporate objectives may be very wise. The exact same objectives in 2015 may be more questionable, given the economic recovery that has taken place and the opportunities that exist in China and India.

Judgements must always be subtle, so it is important to read with care about the external situation of the business. If the text includes phrases such as 'a fiercely competitive market' or 'a saturated market', it is important to try to pick up the messages. It is worth remembering that very few businesses can risk complacency about their market and their competition. A former chief executive of the giant computer business Intel, Andy Grove, once said 'only the paranoid survive'. Many business leaders love to quote that to their own staff.

## Key terms

**Five forces:** the five pressures on the business that Michael Porter says affect its success in the marketplace: near competitors; market accessibility to new entrants; possibility of substitutes; power of suppliers; power of customers.

**Satisfice:** to make a decision that achieves a compromise between different objectives.

# Workbook

## A. Revision questions

(30 marks; 30 minutes)

1. **a)** List four possible corporate objectives. (4)

   **b)** Explain the extent to which each is focused on the short or long run. (8)

2. Explain why every leader of a public limited company must think hard about maximising the company's share price. (4)

3. Increasingly, chief executives gain huge rewards from bonus payments linked to the price of their company's shares. Outline how this could affect their approach to running the business. (4)

4. Explain the benefits Tesco is receiving from its corporate objective of diversification. (4)

5. What is meant by the term 'satisficing'? (2)

6. Explain why it may be true to say that 'diversification is a risky way to reduce risk'. (4)

## B. Revision exercises

### DATA RESPONSE

**Corporate strategy at Morrisons**

When Morrisons bought southern supermarket chain Safeway for £3 billion in 2004, it was expected that the combined business would hold a 16 per cent share of the UK grocery business. This would have created a business with a UK presence comparable with Sainsbury and Asda. In fact, by 2010, Morrisons held just a 12.3 per cent share of the market, but after several years' struggling to amalgamate the two businesses, things had stabilised.

Then, at about the time new boss Dalton Philips arrived in 2010, one or two question marks began to be raised about strategy at Morrisons. With the business steeped in the culture left by Sir Ken Morrison, who had run the business for 50 years, it naturally focused on grocery basics such as fresh food, low prices and special offers. But by 2010 Sainsbury's and others had found new ways to boost sales, largely through two strategies: i) online grocery selling (and delivery) and ii) convenience stores, especially in towns. Morrisons was the only major grocer with neither approach in its portfolio. Instead, it developed a strategy followed by none of its rivals: vertical integration. In 2011 and 2012 the company bought a series of supplier organisations such as meat-packing businesses. This gave it more control over its supply chain, and could be justified to shareholders on the grounds that it enabled the company to seize a higher proportion of the value added.

In 2011 the business was ready to trial three M local convenience stores. Their unique selling point was to be a greater focus on fresh food than rivals Tesco and Sainsbury, plus a promise to keep fresh food

**Figure 54.5** A Morrisons M local store

prices the same as at their supermarket outlets. By the end of 2012 Morrisons had grown the chain to 14 outlets (compared with over 1,500 for Tesco!), but then looked to accelerate in 2013 by buying sites from collapsed retailers Blockbuster, Jessops and HMV (49 sites, 7 sites and 5 sites respectively).

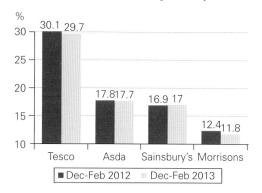

**Figure 54.6** UK Grocery market share, 12 weeks to Feb 28
Source: Kantar Worldpanel

On 1 March 2013 Dalton Philips was interviewed by the London Evening Standard. He suggested that there were three strategy options: to make a big move into grocery online (growing at 20 per cent a year), to boost substantially the investment into M local stores and/or to 'scale up in London'. At present Morrisons has a 6 per cent share of grocery within the M25 compared with 12 per cent outside it. Oddly, he made little of another strategic option. For some years it has been possible to see the company as in the classic squeezed middle of Porter's strategic matrix. The recent horsemeat scandal offered a possible escape to a more differentiated position: 'At Morrisons we control our supply lines and employ our own butchers. You know where you are with Morrisons fresh produce'. Dalton Philips has plenty of options. The company's latest balance sheet, below, gives an idea of his financial resources.

**Table 54.2** Morrisons plc balance sheet

| Morrisons plc Balance sheet as at: | 4 August 2013 | 29 July 2012 | 31 July 2011 |
|---|---|---|---|
| Fixed (non-current) assets | 9,570 | 8,700 | 8,300 |
| Inventories | 760 | 700 | 700 |
| Receivables | 330 | 300 | 300 |
| Cash and cash equivalents | 260 | 300 | 200 |
| Current liabilities | (2,540) | (2,300) | (2,300) |
| Non-current liabilities | (3,120) | (2,500) | (1,850) |
| **Net assets** | **5,260** | **5,200** | **5,350** |
| Share capital | 355 | 350 | 350 |
| Reserves | 4,905 | 4,850 | 5,000 |
| **Total equity** | **5,260** | **5,200** | **5,350** |

**Questions (30 marks; 35 minutes)**

1. Analyse the possible problems a business such as Morrisons might face in trying to expand its retail operation rapidly. (10)

2. Morrisons is a UK grocery business with more than £17 billion annual sales and a market share that is slightly declining. To what extent should Morrisons focus on short-term profit when deciding on a new corporate strategy? (20)

## C. Extend your understanding

1. To what extent can 'corporate' objectives shape the whole of a business as big and as complex as Tesco plc. (25)

2. The management expert Peter Drucker believes that it is a mistake for a business to focus upon a single objective. To what extent do you support him in this view? (25)

# Chapter

# 55

# The impact of strategic decision-making on functional decision-making

**Linked to:** Decision-making: scientific and intuitive, Chapter 7; Decision trees, Chapter 8; Investment appraisal, Chapter 73; Strategic positioning, Chapter 77 and Methods and types of growth, Chapter 80.

## Definition

A strategic decision is so fundamental that it cannot easily be reversed.

## 55.1 Introduction

In 2013 the UK multinational Glaxo Smith Kline (GSK) sold Ribena and Lucozade to the Japanese drinks company Suntory for £1.35 billion. GSK had decided to focus solely on its pharmaceuticals business, so although Ribena and Lucozade were highly profitable brands, they were sold off. That's a strategic decision and – as you can see – cannot really be reversed.

Strategic decision-making is not limited to buying and selling businesses. It can also come from within. In 2000 a computer business called Apple took a strategic decision to try to break in to the consumer electronics business; its 2001 launch of iPod proved a multi-billion dollar success.

'Strategic management is not a box of tricks or a bundle of techniques. It is analytical thinking and commitment of resources to action. But quantification alone is not planning. Some of the most important issues in strategic management cannot be quantified at all.' Peter Drucker, the business guru's guru.

## 55.2 How are strategic decisions made?

Most business decisions involve middle-ranking executives preparing recommendations based on a combination of decision trees (see Chapter 8) and investment appraisal (see Chapter 73). The recommendations will be backed by careful research and careful numerical analysis. Part of the reason this can work is that such decisions can be relatively routine, such as Topshop deciding whether or not to open its 302$^{nd}$ store in the UK. The company has already opened 301 stores, so it's quite easy for it to know the key variables affecting the likely profit to be made from the 302$^{nd}$.

By contrast, even though strategic decisions can be worth £billions instead of £millions, there may be relatively little for the senior managers to go on. Just as Apple's Steve Jobs couldn't possibly have known the fortune that would be made from the iPod/iPhone/iPad, so many business leaders don't know the downside risk if their strategic vision goes wrong. Making decisions such as these is likely to be make-or-break in terms of the reputation of the business leader – and may also be make-or-break for the company itself.

So these decisions are usually made by a combination of boardroom discussion backed by independent management consultancy advice. Ultimately, having taken soundings from the most trusted advisors, the chairman and chief executive simply have to go with their intuition.

'There is no perfect strategic decision. One always has to pay a price. One always has to balance conflicting objectives, conflicting opinions, and conflicting priorities. The best strategic decision is only an approximation – and a risk.' Peter Drucker, business academic and author

For every strategic lemon (Tesco USA) there are a number of strategic marvels, including:

- Apple
- Whitbread (betting everything on Costa Coffee and Premier Inn)
- JCB (starting in India in 1979, now taking a 55 per cent share of the Indian construction vehicle market)
- Tata Motors of India, buying Jaguar Land Rover from Ford.

## 55.3 The impact of strategic decisions on functional decision-making

When a major strategic decision has been made, new objectives need to be set which in turn will affect functional objectives, strategies and decision-making. Each of the four functions within a business (marketing, finance, operations and people) has its own objectives. Together, the four sets of objectives must match the organisation's own corporate objectives. Each of the four must knit together a strategy that makes the overall targets reachable.

A good example would be New Look's decision to open 14 stores in China in 2014, with a view to establishing a major presence in what it described as a 'real gap' for an 'affordable, fashion-forward retailer'. Naturally, this strategic decision required action by each of the four functions.

1. The marketing department had to decide where exactly to set the 'affordable' prices and how best to promote the new Chinese stores.

2. The finance function had to decide what budget could be afforded each year for the Chinese strategy.

3. The operations department needed to decide how much warehousing was needed for stock and for efficient deliveries to the stores (and New Look's online presence in China).

4. The HR function needed to start hiring and training regional managers to supervise the work of local Chinese store managers.

## 55.4 Functional objectives

Functional objectives are the targets of the individual business departments (functions). They will stem from the corporate objectives and are either set by the chief executive or may be the result of discussion between directors.

Having set the company's objectives, the key is to take care over each department's objectives. They must work separately and together, so that the overall goal can be achieved.

Success requires that the leaders within each department/function do the following.

- *Co-ordinate what they are doing:* what, when and how. Timing will be crucial, such as a new product having the right amount of stock to cope with the demand expected on the launch day. So marketing, operations and HR must act together, perhaps using enterprise resource planning (ERP) software to make sure that the whole project is kept on track.

- *Make sure that all within their own department know the overall objective* as well as the functional one, and that all are motivated towards achieving it. In 2010 British Airways cabin crew staff went on strike repeatedly in the face of the company's attempt to cut costs and restructure the business; the staff refused to believe management's suggestion that BA's survival was at stake.

- *Work together to achieve a common goal:* this may seem obvious, but in many organisations managers and even directors jostle for promotions or positions without really working together. So the marketing director might be happy to see the operations director humiliated. Well-run organisations want to succeed together, not just succeed as individuals.

'The formulation of strategy can develop competitive advantage only to the extent that the process can give meaning to workers in the trenches.' David Hurst, management consultant

## 55.5 Functional strategies

A strategy is a medium- to long-term plan for meeting objectives. This should be the result of a careful process of thought and discussion throughout the business, though key decisions will almost always be made at the top. To make the right decision about strategy, a useful approach is known as the 'scientific decision-making model' (Figure 55.2). It shows that strategy decisions must:

1. be based on clear objectives

2. be based on firm evidence of the market and the problem/opportunity, including as much factual,

quantitative evidence as possible (for example, trends in market size, data on costs, sales forecasts)

3. look for options (that is, alternative theories – hypotheses – as to which would be the best approach); for example, to meet an objective of higher market share we could either launch a new product or put all our energies and cash behind our Rising Star existing product

4. be based on as scientific a test of the alternatives as possible (for example, a test market of the new product in the Bristol area, while doubling advertising spending on the Rising Star in the north-east – then comparing which approach provided the bigger market share gains)

5. control the approach decided upon – the final stage (for example, if it's a new product launch, to manage the quality and timing of every aspect of production, sales, advertising and delivery) – then review, to learn from any mistakes or unexpected successes before (the dotted line on the diagram) starting again with a new objective and a new strategy.

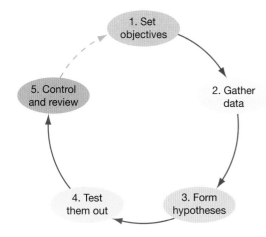

**Figure 55.1** Scientific decision-making model

Within this process, the single most important thing is that the business should make sure that the functional strategies are all part of one overall strategy (and match the strategic objective). In 2014, Morrisons responded to many months of sharply falling market share by making a strategic shift – based on lower operating profit margins. Prices were cut and a loyalty card was introduced based on matching prices to the discount kings Lidl and Aldi. Table 55.1 shows what this meant for each functional area.

**Table 55.1** Morrisons' strategic shift

| Functional areas | Impact of the new strategy |
| --- | --- |
| Marketing strategy | Promoting Morrisons as a viable alternative to discount grocers based on the 'Match & More' loyalty card |
| Operations strategy | Putting suppliers under even greater pressure to cut their prices |
| Human Resource strategy | Train staff to be better salespeople; pushing customers into taking on a Match & More card |
| Financial strategy | Morrisons had long enjoyed higher operating margins than Sainsbury's, now the profit premium would disappear; with profit squeezed, efficient management of working capital would be even more important |

### Key term

**Enterprise Resource Planning:** software that models the whole business operation, allowing a customer order to trigger a series of activities, from ordering more materials, to scheduling overtime and sequencing production.

'Weak leadership can wreck the soundest strategy.' Sun Tzu, Chinese general and author of *The Art of War*, around 500BC

## Five Whys and a How

| Question | Answer |
|---|---|
| Why might a strategic decision 'make or break' a business leader's reputation? | Because if it goes wrong it's impossible to reverse it – so it must stand out as a failure |
| Why might a strategic decision lead to a sharp fall in a plc's share price? | Because stock market analysts perceive the decision to be too risky |
| Why may it be hard for all functions to work effectively towards the new strategic decision? | Some staff may feel threatened by the new direction and therefore be reluctant to commit themselves |
| Why might human resources be the most important function in making the strategic decision successful? | Because even the best companies tend to be short of staff capable of implementing a change in strategic direction |
| Why might strategic change be easier for a business operating in a high tech sector? | Those working in high tech businesses expect innovation and change to be part of everyday life |
| How might a business make sure that all staff are working towards the new strategic decision? | By communicating the new approach to all staff |

## Evaluation: The impact of strategic decision-making on functional decision-making

Having analysed the business situation, judgements have to be made and perhaps a new strategic direction chosen. Then it's vital to allow time for the new strategy to take hold. In the first year or two the strategy may actually lead to falling sales or profits. An example would be if The Telegraph newspaper decided to reposition itself towards a younger market; in the short term it might alienate its elderly readership and lose market share.

It's also important to acknowledge the importance of external factors. It is sometimes the case that no one deserves blame (or praise for success). In 2013 Chanel and Gucci had booming years for sales and profit. But both struggled in 2009 as the severity of the world recession took both firms (and economists) by surprise. External factors were in control; for sales to fall by 7 per cent in a recession is no disgrace.

If a business hits problems, is one department (function) to blame? For example, has the marketing department let the side down because of a poor advertising campaign? Are there specific staff who lack ability or motivation? Or was the problem more collective, due to poor communications within a department or (much more likely) between the functional areas?

The key judgement, then, is whether a firm's success is entirely down to its own good management. A better explanation might be that external factors were largely

the reason, in which case managers deserve credit for taking advantage of favourable circumstances; but they should beware of jumping to the conclusion that they have the magic touch.

**Figure 55.2** External factors will impact firms like Chanel and Gucci

# Workbook

## A. Revision questions

**(30 marks; 30 minutes)**

1. What is meant by the term 'functional areas'? (2)

2. Why is it important that objectives should be:
   a) measurable? (2)
   b) timebound? (2)

3. Are the following good or bad corporate objectives? Briefly explain your reasoning.
   a) To boost our share of the fruit juice market from the current level of 22.3 per cent. (4)
   b) To become the best pizza restaurant business in Britain. (4)

4. What would be a successful overall objective for each of the following?
   a) The charity Oxfam, which focuses on preventing and relieving famine. (2)

   b) A political party. (2)

5. Explain in your own words why it is important that the different business functions should work together to achieve the corporate (overall) objective. (3)

6. Explain the difference between an objective and a strategy. (3)

7. What is the difference between the terms 'strategic' and 'strategy'? (3)

8. In your own words, explain the implications of the quote by David Hurst (see page 346). (3)

## B. Revision exercises
### DATA RESPONSE

**L'Oréal: Thinking ahead to 2019**

L'Oréal is the world's No 1 cosmetics company. Not many French companies are leaders in their field, so this is remarkable. To stay No 1, L'Oréal set the objective of doubling its customer base. As almost every woman in the West uses L'Oréal products (whether they know it or not, as brands such as Garnier, Maybelline, Giorgio Armani and Body Shop are actually L'Oréal) growth has to come from developing countries. In 2010 more than 33 per cent of L'Oréal's €16.5 billion of sales came from developing countries. Ten years before, the figure was 16 per cent; ten years before that it had been 8 per cent.

The strategy for achieving this change is partly based on a refocusing of the marketing efforts. In 2009, for instance, the cover of L'Oreal's annual report did not feature Cheryl Cole, but Freida Pinto: the beautiful young (Indian) star of the hit film *Slumdog Millionaire*. More importantly, though, the decision had been made to invest in research and development facilities in China and Brazil. In 2010 the Shanghai R&D centre turned three years of work into a new haircare range. A careful study of Chinese hair, plus market research into local customs and tastes, led to the launch of a range of shampoos and haircare products suited to local hair types and cultural traditions, focusing on fragrance and gloss.

The value of L'Oréal's longstanding focus on developing countries was shown in the 2009 recession (see Figure 55.3).

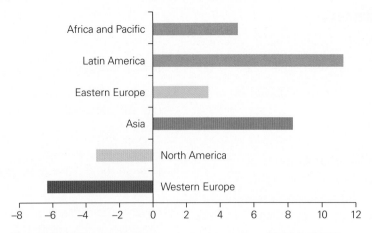

**Figure 55.3** L'Oreal sales: percentage change from 2008 to 2009

## Questions (30 marks; 35 minutes)

1. Explain L'Oréal's corporate objective and its strategy for achieving it. (6)

2. Explain why L'Oréal might have chosen this objective and strategy. (8)

3. To what extent does L'Oréal's strategy in relation to its marketing and operations functions seem likely to help it to achieve its corporate objective? (16)

## C. Extend your understanding

1. 'It's time to close down Marks & Spencer's clothing and homewear business and just focus on food.' To what extent would a strategic decision such as that rely on judgement and to what extent would it rely on evidence? (25)

2. Is the essence of a strategic decision that it cannot be reversed (for example building HS2) or that it can only be made by the board of directors? Justify your answer? (25)

# 56 The value of SWOT analysis

**Linked to:** Influences on the mission of a business, Chapter 53; Corporate objectives, strategy and tactics, Chapter 54; The impact of strategic decision-making on functional decision-making, Chapter 55; Problems with strategy, Chapter 96.

### Definition

SWOT analysis investigates a company's current strengths and weaknesses and uses them to help foresee future opportunities and threats.

## 56.1 The purpose of SWOT analysis

When the appointment of new Tesco boss Dave Lewis was announced in July 2014 it was said that Lewis would conduct a 'root and branch' objective review of the whole Tesco operation. In effect Lewis was conducting a SWOT analysis – to try to gain insight as quickly as possible into the business he was now in charge of.

Dave Lewis's three predecessors had been Tesco career men, with decades of experience from the shop floor to the boardroom. Lewis had been appointed from outside – and with no retail experience. But he had to make sure that he knew enough about the business to not only make the right strategic decisions, but also to have full credibility when discussing Tesco issues with other staff who had decades of experience with the business.

By January 2015 Lewis was ready to announce his new corporate strategy for Tesco. This would emerge logically from the SWOT process. After all, once you've uncovered the firm's strengths and weaknesses, you can start to think about what should come next for a business. And that's the purpose of SWOT analysis: to

provide sufficient insight into the current and potential position of the business to enable senior executives to make sound decisions based on good evidence.

## 56.2 How to conduct a SWOT analysis

There are two main ways to undertake a SWOT. The first is a top-down process, controlled by the boss and probably carried out by management consultants, answerable only to the boss. This has the advantage of being dispassionate, that is, unaffected by emotion or tradition or 'the way we do things round here' – the culture. In a business such as Tesco, with half a million staff, it may be possible for an outsider to see opportunities for cutting one hundred thousand jobs. Unfortunately, long-established staff will know the threat posed by the outside consultants, and therefore try to hide weaknesses that might lead to job losses. So there is a risk that a top-down process will lack the insight required for a really helpful SWOT analysis.

The ideal SWOT would be conducted in a consultative manner, with the boss spending time in every key department, chatting to staff in an informal manner. There might also be elements of democratic delegation, in which middle managers are invited to conduct their own SWOTs – and then discuss the findings with the boss. This scenario highlights the benefit of appointing an outsider to the top job. No staff member need feel worried about what they say when the blame for any blatant weaknesses can be pinned on the previous leadership team. A SWOT conducted by a long-established leader would be a very different beast.

TV programmes such as 'Undercover boss' (Channel 4) make a big thing of a boss being disguised to get an authentic flavour of working lives at the bottom of an organization. A new outsider leader needs no disguise; staff will love to say what's been wrong in the past and how to improve things.

## 56.3 The theory behind SWOT analysis

SWOT must be broken down into two parts. Strengths and Weaknesses represent the current situation for the business. In effect it's 'What are we good at? What are we bad at?' Opportunities and Threats are external to the business and therefore largely outside management's control.

Naturally the current business situation has to be considered in relation to competitors, so it's useful to analyse strengths and weaknesses with the help of a benchmarking exercise. This shows how the business performs on key variables compared with the best in the industry. Nissan UK may be pleased that its labour turnover has fallen from 12 per cent to 10 per cent, but if it sees that Jaguar Land Rover's achievement is 2 per cent it will see there's more to be done.

Among the external factors that can give rise to opportunities or threats are:

- Economic changes such as the sharp fall in the price of oil at the beginning of 2015; this would threaten the future of alternative energy provision such as wind power – but provide an opportunity to a specialist producer of acrylic clothes – as acrylic is made from oil, and will now be much cheaper than cotton or wool.

- Technological change such as the development of graphene, a form of carbon that's one atom thick yet – gram for gram – is one hundred times stronger than steel. In a market where weight matters hugely, such as aerospace, companies that fail to master the potential for graphene may find their futures under threat.

## 56.4 Strengths and Weaknesses

'Strengths are not activities you're good at, they're activities that strengthen you.' Marcus Buckingham, business consultant

A key starting point in analysing strengths and weaknesses is to distinguish between those that *are* and those that *matter*. Inditex (owner of Zara) publishes a huge amount of environmental and human resource data that is presented as a strength, but perhaps doesn't matter much in relation to overall business performance. Eighty per cent of staff are permanent and only 20 per cent temporary (out of

nearly 120,000 staff). In an era of outsourcing and contract labour, this is admirable. But does it actually matter?

To address this issue companies use the concept of KPIs: Key Performance Indicators. These are the numbers that a business acknowledges to be proper measures of strength or weakness. Typically these might include sales per employee, absenteeism, image ranking within the market sector and so on. These are measures that matter. Figure 56.1 shows how Tesco has prioritised returning the company's reputation to one that has empathy for customers as well as impressive size. This can be measured by regular quantitative research studies among Tesco users and non-users.

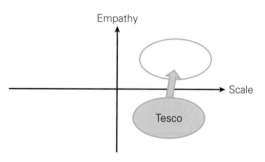

**Figure 56.1** Empathy towards the customer makes an important contribution to Tesco's reputation

Source: From Tesco presentation by Dave Lewis, 23 October 2014

When Googling KPIs, one site offered '75 KPIs for business success'. Actually that sounds like a recipe for disaster! What businesses need is relatively few KPIs that will – between them – add up to the achievement of the overall business goals. Among the most common KPIs are:

- Like-for-like sales, which show sales revenues this year compared with last, but eliminating any differences in shop floor space; so if a business has opened ten new stores in the past year, their sales will be excluded from the like-for-like comparison. On 6 January 2015 House of Fraser announced an 8 per cent improvement in Christmas 2014 like-for-like sales; the previous day John Lewis had boasted of its 4.8 per cent increase in like-for-like sales; in this case House of Fraser was the one showing strength.

- Market share: this is a number that every business cares hugely about; it is, after all, the ultimate test of you compared with your competitors. Even if your sales are rising rapidly you should worry if market share is falling. After all, when the market matures, continuing falls in market share would then mean falling sales. Rising market share is a strength; falling market share is a weakness.

- Capacity utilisation: even a business that's enjoying rising sales may have a fall in utilisation if it has expanded its capacity too greatly. Ryanair suffered exactly this problem in 2012 and early 2013. Sales were rising, but not fast enough to fill all the planes they had bought. An aircraft order can take as long as five years to fulfil, so it's very hard to keep supply and demand in balance. The falling capacity utilisation forced Ryanair to mothball some of its planes and then forced boss Michael O'Leary into an unexpected backtrack – switching the sales strategy to be far more positive about customer care – to attract more customers.

---

'Build your weaknesses until they become your strengths.' Knute Rockne, U.S. football player and coach

---

So how should a business use its KPIs to address its strengths and weaknesses? The answer is simply to break them down as much as possible into their component parts. Capacity utilisation can first be broken down into size of capacity and the level of customer demand. In Ryanair's case there was a recognition that – for the first time – stories about bad customer experiences was denting demand. So the cause of the weakness was identified and tackled. On 5 January 2015 Ryanair reported a 20 per cent rise in passenger numbers for December, with their load factor (capacity utilisation) up from 81 per cent to 88 per cent. In effect they had managed to turn a weakness into a strength, in less than eighteen months.

## 56.5 Opportunities and Threats

These relate to the external context of the business. They are therefore outside the direct control of managers – though in some cases (governmental and political, for example) companies will do everything they can to influence the decisions made by others.

### Demography

An important factor to bear in mind is demography, that is, population change. In the UK the population is rising by just over 0.5 per cent a year, but more important changes are occurring in the age distribution of that population. Not long ago, economists despaired at how a shrinking working

population would cope with the huge rise in the elderly. Now immigration has gone some way to solving that problem – though it hasn't altered the business opportunities in the sharp rise in the number of elderly consumers. See Figure 56.2.

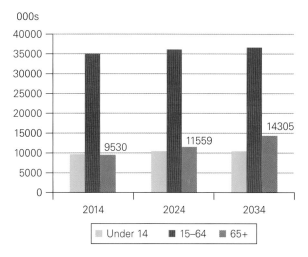

**Figure 56.2** Changing age distribution 2014 to 2034

### New laws and regulations

Changes in the law can have a dramatic effect on a business. A good example came from the regulation changes made to child car seats, which came into effect in September 2006. They forced all motorists to provide 'seat restraints' for children sitting in the back of a car. Children under the age of 12 must sit on a 'booster seat' and babies must have their own special car seat.

Overnight, this regulation created a huge boost for businesses like Britax (car seat manufacturer) and Halfords, the biggest motoring retailer. Because the government gave eighteen months' notice of the change, the companies had plenty of time to build production capacity and stock levels.

### Technological factors

Technological change can also create opportunities and threats for firms. Before the advent of digital technology, ITV only had two competitors: the BBC and Channel 4. Today the situation is dizzying. Technological advances mean that ITV has to compete against the hundreds of channels provided by Sky and cable TV plus subscription providers such as Netflix. In addition, the opening up of social media has provided indirect competition with conventional TV. These technological advances threaten ITV's ability to generate revenue from selling advertising slots. On the other hand, these same technological advances have created opportunities for the entrepreneurs behind Twitter, Facetime, Instagram and so many more.

> 'So it is said that if you do not know others and do not know yourself, you will be imperilled in every single battle; if you do not know others but do know yourself, you win one and lose one; if you know others and know yourself, you will not be imperilled in a hundred battles.' Sun Tzu: *The Art of War* (written about 500 BC)

## Commodity prices

Commodities are internationally-traded goods that include oil, copper, wheat and cocoa. Commodities are normally bought by firms as a raw material. As Figure 56.3 shows, the price of oil has fluctuated dramatically between 2006 and 2015. The price of oil is an important external influence for most firms. It not only affects transport costs directly, but also affects the costs of road building, as oil forms a key part of road construction materials.

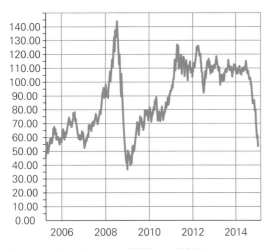

**Figure 56.3** Oil prices 2006-Jan 2015

Source: MoneyAM

Oil is also a very important raw material. Even companies such as Apple will be affected by rising oil prices because it will cost Apple more to buy in the plastic pellets needed to produce the casings for its laptop computers, iPads and iPhones. The price of oil is determined by the relative strength of the world supply and the world demand for oil. The world oil price is beyond the control of any single firm; making it an excellent example of an external influence.

## Economic factors

Individual firms have no influence over economy-wide factors such as the rate of economic growth, the level of unemployment and the rate of inflation. However, these factors will definitely affect firms. Firms will also be affected by government fiscal and monetary policy responses. For more details see Chapter 66.

## 56.6 What can firms do to influence opportunities and threats?

Organisations seem to spend an increasing amount of time and senior manpower on attempting to influence – even control – their environment. In some ways this is logical. Why would you wait for a train to hit you if you could a) stop it setting off or b) find out it was coming and then get out of the way? So businesses began – many years ago – to 'lobby' their MPs. **Lobbying** usually meant local businesses coming to London to put their case to their MP, who would then ask questions in parliament. Today lobbying is an industry which allows unelected, professional lobbyists access to Ministers or even the Prime Minister.

The point remains a simple one, though. Companies want to encourage favourable legislation, discourage unfavourable legislation (both from the perspective of the companies) and switch the balance of taxation away from companies and towards households. In many ways this is perfectly sensible. The only problem comes when legitimate influence goes too far. Young mothers, skilled workers and those with disabilities are categories with as much right to lobby the government as business. They just don't have as much money or as much access to those with power.

> 'Strength does not come from winning. Your struggles develop your strengths.' Arnold Schwarzenegger, film star and politician

## Five Whys and a How

| Question | Answer |
|---|---|
| Why may it be hard for some senior managements to get to know their company's strengths and weaknesses? | Because they aren't asking the right questions of the right people; they're operating in their own boardroom bubble, like Tesco in the period 2007-2013/4 |
| Why don't all strengths matter? | Because some have little bearing on the company's success or failure; consistent use of the colour orange may be a strength of easyJet, but does it make a difference to sales? |
| Why do some companies focus on their strengths while others tackle their weaknesses? | Most strategists would say build on your strengths, but Ryanair showed in 2014/15 the value of tackling their (service) weakness; so there's no single 'right' way |
| Why do some firms seem blind to their opportunities? | Up until early 2015 neither Primark nor Topshop had opened a single store in China; this lack of ambition is hard to fathom; a risk-averse board perhaps? |
| Why do threats so often seem to hit companies by surprise? | If they'd been anticipated they may never have emerged as a real threat; it's unexpected events such as the severity of the 2009 crash that threaten a firm's stability |
| How often should a business conduct a SWOT analysis? | Many keep an ongoing one, updated each year. There's a case for starting from scratch every year, so that the material is up to date |

### Evaluation: The value of SWOT analysis

Regarding strengths and weaknesses the most important factor is to distinguish fact from hearsay or even delusion. One of the key characteristics of bosses who turn out to be failures is that they insulate themselves from real news. They effectively lock themselves away, listening only to 'yes-men' (usually men) and visiting the real world only as the Queen does – with plenty of warning and lots of security. Fred Goodwin, boss of RBS bank (which had to be bailed out by £46 billion from UK taxpayers in 2009) knew little about the real strengths and nothing of the weaknesses of his own business. If the person at the top is blind, it's very hard for others to see.

An important aspect of any evaluation of external factors is to distinguish between external change that is predictable and change that is not. For example, tourist businesses had five years to plan for the opportunities opened up by the 2012 London Olympics. By contrast no one would have expected that the Brazilians would have staged huge protests against their government immediately before the 2014 World Cup. Managers that fail to deal with predictable events are exceptionally weak. Those that succeed in unexpected situations are especially impressive.

### Key terms

**Demographic:** factors relating to the population, such as changes in the number of older people or in the level of immigration.

**Lobbying:** the term originated in the 'lobby' between the House of Commons and House of Lords; it was where electors came to talk to their local MP.

**'What if' questions:** these are hypothetical (that is, they are used to test out different possibilities or theories).

# Workbook

## A. Revision questions

(30 marks; 30 minutes)

1.  **a)** State two possible strengths and two weaknesses of McDonalds. (4)

    **b)** Explain how McDonalds might tackle **one** of those weaknesses. (4)

2.  Explain how a company such as Cadbury might be affected by a decision by Britain to withdraw from the European Union. (4)

3.  Explain two possible reasons why a company might reject an opportunity. (6)

4.  Explain how the quote from Sun Tzu (see page 347) relates to SWOT analysis. (4)

5.  Several parts of Britain have suffered from floods in recent years. Explain how a retail business might prepare for that. (4)

6.  Outline one UK business opportunity and one business threat that may emerge from global warming. (4)

## B. Revision exercises

### DATA RESPONSE

**Rolls-Royce to shed 2,600 jobs - Financial Times, 4 November 2014**

John Rishton, chief executive of Rolls-Royce, sought to show he had a firm grip on the struggling FTSE 100 engineer as he unveiled the company's biggest job reduction programme in six years. Analysts welcomed initiatives that would reduce the group's 55,000 workforce by 2,600 and bring down annual costs by £80m when fully implemented. However some raised concerns about the ability of the UK's flagship industrial company to innovate in future if the cuts hit its engineering capability.

'This implies they are firing engineers. That is surprising to me,' said Christian Laughlin of Bernstein Research. Mr Rishton insisted the reduction would not hit the group's ability to compete against its bigger rivals, such as General Electric. 'The measures announced today will…contribute towards Rolls-Royce becoming a stronger and more profitable company,' he said. 'We will work…to achieve the necessary reductions on a voluntary basis where possible, while making sure we retain the skills needed for the future.'

A large engineering team had been required for the development phase of the Trent 1000 and Trent XWB engines, the group said, but with the development phase complete, the need for engineers was reduced. These two engines are the main engines for the hugely successful Boeing Dreamliner and Airbus A350 wide-bodied jets. Orders for the Trent 1000 and Trent XWB run into tens of £billions.

**Figure 56.4** Engineers at Rolls Royce faced job cuts once the development phase of the Trent 1000 and Trent XWB engines was over

The news of the job cuts sent shares in Rolls Royce 1.4 per cent higher to close at 846p. The market took heart from signals that another cost-cutting programme was being planned for the power systems and marine business. The current job cuts would come over the next 18 months and largely be made across its aerospace division. The majority of the job cuts would be achieved in 2015. Two-thirds of the 2,600 job cuts would come in the UK. The company employs 24,800 people in Britain out of 55,200 worldwide. The job cuts would include engineers as well as managerial, operational and administrative positions.

Rolls Royce is the world's second largest aero-engine maker, with a market share of 34 per cent.

### Questions (20 marks; 25 minutes)

1.  Based on the information provided, carry out a SWOT analysis on Rolls Royce Aero Engines. (20)

# C. Extend your understanding

1. Tesco is a complex organisation employing half a million staff in more than twenty countries. To what extent could the boss of Tesco be expected to know fully the company's Strengths, Weaknesses, Opportunities and Threats? (25)

2. Consider an online or social media business that you use regularly and know well. Briefly research its company history and financial background. Then conduct a full analysis of its Strengths, Weaknesses, Opportunities and Threats. (25)

# Chapter 57 Financial objectives and constraints

**Linked with:** Financial objectives, Chapter 36; Balance sheets and income statements, Chapter 58; Financial ratio analysis, Chapter 59; Value and limitations of financial ratios, Chapter 60; Assessing short- and long-term performance, Chapter 62

## Definition

Financial objectives outline what the business wishes to achieve in financial terms during a certain period of time.

## 57.1 Types of financial objective

**Table 57.1** Financial objectives of major businesses

| Company | Financial objectives |
|---|---|
| Ford Motor Corp (USA) | 'By 2020, Ford projects annual global sales to increase 45 to 55 per cent to approximately 9.4 million a year. Our automotive operating margin is projected to improve to about 8 per cent during the same period' |
| Unilever plc (Multinational producer of foods and household brands) | 'Double the business by achieving volume growth ahead of our markets … with steady and sustainable core operating margin improvement' |
| Amazon.com (seller of books and more) | 'Our primary goal remains maximising long-term free cash flow and doing so with high rates of return on invested capital' |
| Gap Inc (One of the world's biggest clothing retailers) | 'Our goal is to strike a good balance between growing the top and bottom line, as well as returning excess cash to shareholders' |

'Crystallize your goals. Make a plan for achieving them and set yourself a deadline. Then, with supreme confidence, determination and disregard for obstacles and other people's criticisms, carry out your plan.' Paul J Meyer, US businessman

## Profit is a major objective

Whether it is long or short term it is safe to say that, for most businesses, high and rising profits are a major objective. However, just stating that the firm wants to increase profit is a very general objective. Most companies will be more specific in defining their financial objectives. They may look to increase gross or net profit. They may also use other measures, such as return on capital employed (ROCE). The measurements of profitability are interlinked. Firms that have a high gross profit margin will find it easier to finance high spending on research and development, marketing or investing in assets. Firms that have better control of costs are going to be more profitable than other firms in their sector. Businesses that generate high profits are going to have contented shareholders.

## Revenue targets

The directors may set an overall aim, such as to increase revenue by 10 per cent or more. This approach will be especially important for a business in the early stages of a growth market. For example, in the early days of Snapchat, the key thing for the business was to grow rapidly before rivals could get established with a comparable product.

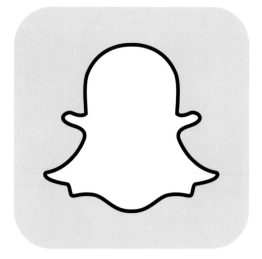

**Figure 57.1** Snapchat cornered the market before rivals could get established

## Cash flow targets

All businesses need to keep a healthy cash flow. The level of cash flow should be carefully managed. A company that is cash short will have difficulty with the day-to-day management of its liabilities. It may find it difficult to pay suppliers. It may also miss opportunities to develop the business. A new order may have to be refused if it has insufficient cash available. A business that has cash reserves that are too high will be missing out on opportunities to use that cash to generate additional business. The 'right' level of cash will depend on the nature of the business. The business may set itself a target of keeping cash at a percentage of turnover or as a stated amount.

## Return on capital employed (ROCE)

This is a measure of how well the company is using its assets to create profit. It is calculated by taking net profit or operating profit as a percentage of capital employed (see Chapter 59 on Financial ratio analysis).

Capital employed is all the long-term finance used to operate the business. Although this is a measure of profitability it concentrates on the use the business is making of its assets. Obviously, the business will want the highest possible return. It is important that the business should achieve a ROCE of more than the rate of interest that it is paying on borrowed funds. The ROCE can be improved by reducing capital employed or by increasing net profit.

## Shareholder returns

These can be expressed in terms of the dividend payments that will be given to shareholders, or in terms of maintaining or adding value to the share price. Shareholders hope to gain from their investment in the business in two ways.

1. Any increase in the value of their shares will mean that they can sell their shares at a higher price than they were bought at. This is a capital return.

2. Shareholders receive income on their shares through the payment of dividends by the business. Yearly profit made by the business can either be kept in the business for development (retained profit) or distributed to shareholders as dividends. These dividends are the income that the shareholders receive as a return on their investment. If the company is making insufficient profit to satisfy shareholders then shareholders will sell their shares and invest elsewhere. This is turn will cause the share price to fall.

A business that is seen as a poor investment by shareholders will find it very difficult to attract investment. It is therefore important that the level of profit and the level of dividends are kept at a level that satisfies shareholders. This in turn keeps the value of the share price high. Balancing the retained profit and dividend distribution is a difficult decision. If the business wants to expand or diversify it may wish to retain more profit and therefore risk upsetting shareholders by paying low dividends.

## 57.2 Making a profit: other considerations

### Ownership versus management

In a small business the management and the owners are often the same people. In large companies such as a public limited company (plc) the management (the directors) and the owners (the shareholders) are usually separate. The shareholders will want to see a healthy and immediate return on their investments but the directors may have other aims: they may be looking for growth or diversification, or may be content to just keep the business ticking along (satisficing). An increasing trend is for the bonuses of company directors to be related to the achievement of the financial objectives. Directors may therefore have an interest in setting targets that are achievable rather than challenging.

### Short term versus long term

Some business goals, such as growth or diversification, will need investment. This may mean a reduction in short-term profits with the hope of increasing returns in the future. If a business is in difficulty it will need to focus much more on survival, so increasing profitability will be a definite short-term goal.

### Stakeholders versus shareholders

In some businesses the pursuit of profit may cause conflict between the different groups with an interest in the business, as in the following examples.

● The rise of interest in the environment has meant that costs have increased for many firms and therefore profit has been reduced. However, many firms have also discovered that they can make huge savings, such as by limiting waste.

● Some firms, most notably supermarket chains, are accused of driving the prices of their suppliers to the lowest possible level. Low supply costs increase profits. Businesses need to ensure that there is a balance between keeping costs low and maintaining the quality of the supplies. In the food chain, tough bargaining by supermarkets may cause unacceptable welfare conditions for animals such as chickens and piglets; this, in turn, may backfire on the retailer's reputation.

- Taxation may be a consideration. Large multinational companies may deliberately reduce profit in one country in order to pay less tax, and increase profit in another where profits are taxed at a lower level. They are able to do this by charging differential prices between subsidiaries in different countries.

- Public image: a firm may choose to spend money on charitable concerns or sponsorship; this as a cost will reduce profit. However, it may well get a return on its investment through creating a better brand image or good public relations.

## 57.3 Internal and external influences on financial objectives

There are many factors that will influence the way a firm sets its financial objectives. These can be categorised as internal and external constraints.

'Objectives are not fate; they are direction. They are not commands; they are commitments. They do not determine the future; they are a means to mobilise the resources and energies of the business for the making of the future.' Peter Drucker, business author

## Internal constraints

### Financial

Although it may seem strange to talk about internal finance as a constraint on financial objectives, it can play an important part. The pursuit of higher profit might be constrained by lack of cash flow, especially at a time of rising or even booming demand.

### Labour force

Any business activity requires the co-operation of the workforce. It is also important that the business has the manpower with the necessary skills.

### Type of business

New or young businesses may set themselves financial objectives but because of inexperience or the difficulty in assessing a new market they may set unrealistic targets. Larger, more established businesses will find it easier to set and achieve their objectives because of the experience that they have. PLCs may be more constrained in their objectives, as they will have to satisfy the shareholders as well as the management.

### Operational

A firm that is close to full capacity may find that it has fewer opportunities for improving the profitability of the business, unless it has the confidence and the resources to increase capacity, perhaps by moving to bigger premises.

## External constraints

### Competitive environment

The plans of almost every business can be affected by the behaviour and reaction of competitors. A plan to increase profit margins by increasing prices may be destroyed if competitors react by reducing prices or by advertising their lower prices.

### Economic environment

The state of the economy plays a vital part in how well businesses can achieve their financial targets. A booming economy will help businesses to improve sales. However, high interest rates will reduce customers' disposable income and therefore spending, so financial targets may not be met. The effect will depend on the business. Supermarket own-brand producers may do better, whereas branded goods may suffer.

### Government

A firm may find its financial objectives limited by regulatory or legislative activity. Consumer watchdogs such as the Competition and Markets Authority have powers to fine businesses that they believe are not acting in the best interests of consumers. Legislation may also be introduced that increases business costs. A recent European Union environmental policy has forced producers of goods such as refrigerators to use lower-powered, more energy-efficient engines. This will help in meeting global targets for holding down greenhouse gas emissions.

## Building in the constraints

Good business planning involves being aware of the possible constraints. The internal constraints are easier to evaluate. External constraints will always be subject to more uncertainty as they are outside the power of the business. It is therefore important when setting financial objectives that the business includes a series of 'what if' scenarios when setting the objectives.

### Zara UK and financial objectives

From its base in Spain, Zara is the world's biggest clothing retailer. In 2013 Zara's UK business made a profit of £50 million and announced that its plan for 2014 was to 'strengthen profitability by increasing sales, controlling costs and increasing margins'.

In fact, when the 2014 figures came out UK sales were 3.4 per cent ahead at £458 million but profits had crashed by 34.5 per cent. Far from increasing margins,

Zara UK had allowed its gross profit margin to slip from 57.4 per cent to 54.7 per cent. This was compounded by a 7.2 per cent increase in expenses, which the company blamed on high store refurbishment costs.

Setting financial objectives is one thing; achieving them another.

'The trouble with not having a goal is that you can spend your life running up and down the field and never score.' Bill Copeland, athlete

## Five Whys and a How

| Question | Answer |
|---|---|
| Why might a business decide to set financial objectives? | As a way to encourage everyone in the business to try to achieve them, for example all working to save money if cost minimisation is the goal |
| Why may financial objectives cause conflict between a company's stakeholders? | Staff favour growth objectives (better promotion opportunities) and dislike a heavy focus on cost minimisation (their own jobs might be on the line) |
| Why may financial objectives backfire? | Because there may be too many external factors that make it impossible to achieve the goals management has set |
| Why is it important to bear in mind Peter Drucker's view that financial objectives 'do not determine the future'? | Because there's a risk that a boss who's set a goal will assume that staff will automatically work towards meeting it |
| Why is it important to monitor actual outcomes compared with the financial objectives/targets? | So that managers can learn from the experience – and hopefully get better at setting and meeting financial objectives |
| How many financial objectives should any business set at any one time? | Some companies use a model such as 5/5/50, so that staff can remember (5 per cent sales growth, 5 per cent cost reduction; 50 per cent profit increase); but there's a case for saying that a single target would be best |

## Evaluation: Financial objectives and constraints

Recent events have given a huge insight into the importance of financial objectives. On the one hand businesses such as Ocado and Amazon have made clear their lack of interest in short- or medium-term profit. They are both consciously pursuing growth – expecting that profit will come later. Because the stock market is in awe of online businesses, investors have allowed this to continue. At the other end of the spectrum comes

Apple – so desirous of profit that it supplements its $170 billion of cash with elaborate ways of avoiding paying its taxes.

In the long run, no business can survive unless its revenues cover all its costs – including the costs of capital. Financial objectives, therefore, are very important.

# Workbook

## A. Revision questions

(25 marks; 25 minutes)

1. Explain why financial objectives matter. (4)

2. Explain the conclusions investors might draw from Zara's problem in meeting its financial objectives (See Real Business on page 361). (6)

3. Explain why there may be differences in the financial objectives desired by the owners and the managers of a business. (6)

4. Explain two external constraints that should be taken into account when financial objectives are set by **one** of the following businesses.
   a) Fever Tree plc
   b) Zara UK
   c) Jack Wills. (6)

5. How can a private sector business such as Ocado ignore the need to make a profit? (3)

## B. Revision exercises
### DATA RESPONSE

**What a difference a book makes!**

Up until Spring 2014 Quercus Publishing plc was an independent publisher based in London. Founded by Mark Smith and Wayne Davies in May 2004, Quercus went on a rollercoaster in 2010 on the back of a publishing sensation. In June 2010 Quercus issued the following Press statement:

'The Board of Directors at Quercus Publishing Plc, the award-winning independent publisher, are pleased to report on trading for the six months ended 30 June 2010. The Company's interim results are expected to be issued on 27 September 2010.

Sales across all sectors have continued to be well ahead of management forecasts and, as a result, the Company's performance for the year ending 31 December 2010 is now expected to significantly exceed market expectations.

As a result of this strong trading, unaudited management accounts for the six months ended 30 June 2010 show:

- Revenue of £15.0 million (compared with revenue of £5.55 million in the same period in 2009).

- Group operating profit for the period rising to £3.40 million (against a loss of £0.10 million in the same period in 2009).

Improvement in Group margins, despite the continued decline in the UK book retail market and the wider economic and financial issues.

Mark Smith, Chief Executive of Quercus said: 'Our results continue to be driven by the continued success of Stieg Larsson's Millennium Trilogy, for which we own the global English language rights. These books represent the three bestselling fiction titles in the UK over the last six months, and Larsson is the first to have sold more than 1 million Kindle e-books through Amazon.'

Unfortunately for Quercus, by 2012 the Larsson boom (*The Girl with the Dragon Tattoo*) gave way to a new publishing phenomenon: *Fifty Shades of Grey*. In early 2014 Quercus announced that it had made significant trading losses in 2013, but before the annual accounts were published the company had been bought up cheaply by Hodder & Stoughton. Figure 57.2 shows the rollercoaster ride of their success and decline.

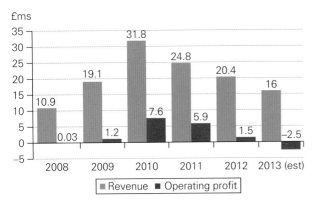

£ms

**Figure 57.2** Annual sales and profit for Quercus plc

Source: Quercus Publishing plc

## Questions (40 marks; 40 minutes)

1. Calculate the percentage rise in revenue and the percentage rise in operating profit between 2009 and 2010. (5)

2. Explain the problems a company would have in managing such a sales and profit rollercoaster. (6)

3. Analyse the factors the company would have had to take into account when setting financial objectives for the 2013 financial year. (9)

4. To what extent is it sensible for a business like a publisher to set financial objectives? (20)

## C. Extend your understanding

1. 'Shareholders should never allow a board of directors to stray from one simple objective: profit maximisation.' To what extent do you agree with this view? (25)

2. To what extent could any external factors constrain the ability of giants such as Apple to make the huge profits they seek? (25)

# Chapter

# 58

# Balance sheets and income statements

**Linked to:** Financial ratio analysis, Chapter 59; Value and limitations of financial ratios, Chapter 60; How to analyse data other than financial statements, Chapter 61

## Definition

The balance sheet shows an organisation's assets and liabilities at a precise point in time, usually the last day of the accounting year. An income statement shows a firm's sales revenue over a trading period and all the relevant costs generated to earn that revenue.

## 58.1 Introduction

The function of accounting is to provide information to various stakeholder groups on how a particular business has performed during a given period. The groups include shareholders, managers and suppliers. The period in question is usually one year. The key financial documents from which this information can be drawn are the balance sheet and the income statement.

By law, public limited companies must publish these accounting statements so that they can be investigated by journalists, competitors or staff. Late on 24 December 2014 City Link (a parcel delivery business) went into receivership. This was especially devastating for those of its drivers who had opted to be contractors, owning their own van and paying personally for it to be painted in City Link colours. They spent Christmas knowing not only that their income was at an end and that their investment in the van was wasted, but also wondering whether they would be paid any outstanding sums they were owed. If City Link had been a plc its financial position would have been open for staff to consider. In fact it was a private-equity-owned business so staff were completely in the dark right up until the Christmas Eve announcement.

For staff – or other interested parties – published accounts allow an analyst to find out:

- The amount of cash or near-cash the company holds in its bank accounts

- How that cash total compares with its short-term liabilities (the bills it needs to pay in the coming twelve months)

- How much of all the firm's long-term capital is in the form of debt – and therefore needs to be serviced with interest payments and eventually must be repaid

- How profitable the business is – both in absolute terms (the sum of money) and in relative terms, perhaps profit as a percentage of sales revenue. Between 2008 and 2014 operating profits at John Lewis rose from £394 million to £424 million. This seems less impressive when looked at as a percentage of sales: 6.5 per cent in 2008 down to 4.7 per cent in 2014. So in 2014 John Lewis made less than 5p profit per £1 of sales.

'The substance of the eminent socialist gentleman's speech is that making a profit is a sin, but it is my belief that the real sin is taking a loss.' Winston Churchill, UK politician and Second World War leader.

## Real business

Between 2008 and 2014 John Lewis Partnership pursued growth objectives. Despite the difficult economic circumstances at the time, both divisions of the business (John Lewis and Waitrose) opened new stores throughout the UK. Financing this growth required huge extra borrowings, pushing long-term debts over the £2 billion mark in 2014. The result of the extra debts was higher interest payments. Figure 58.1 shows the extraordinary growth in the net financing costs of John Lewis from £14 million in 2008 to £110 million in 2013 – and the slight improvement in 2014.

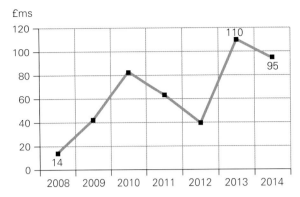

£ms

**Figure 58.1** John Lewis Partnership: net financing costs

○

## 58.2 Balance sheets

This accounting document looks at the question: 'How rich are you?' To find out how rich someone is, you would need to find out what they own (big house?) and what they owe (fat mortgage?). The balance sheet does this for a business, adding up the totals on the last day of the financial year. Balance sheets show the wealth, or the indebtedness, of the business – vital information for shareholders, managers, financiers and other stakeholders.

The balance sheet shows where a business has obtained its finances – its liabilities. It also lists the assets purchased with these funds. Therefore, the balance sheet shows what the business owns and what it owes. For bankers this is of vital importance when deciding whether or not to:

- invest in a business
- lend it some money
- buy the organisation outright.

---

'Debt is a prolific mother of folly and of crime.'
Benjamin Disraeli, nineteenth-century Prime Minister

---

### The composition of the balance sheet

The balance sheet is a 'snapshot' showing the position of a company at a given point in time. It shows what the business owns and owes on one day; in other words, it shows an organisation's assets and liabilities.

The foundations of the balance sheet (at the bottom) consist of the firm's capital. This may have come from shareholders, bankers or from reinvested profit. If Spark plc has £400,000 of capital invested, it follows that it must have £400,000 of assets. The top section shows the type of assets bought. Figure 58.2 shows a summarised and simplified version of this position.

| Spark plc: Simplified vertical balance sheet | |
|---|---|
| | £ |
| Long-term (non-current) assets | 300,000 |
| Short-term (current) assets | 100,000 |
| Total assets | 400,000 |
| Balancing with: Total capital | 400,000 |

**Figure 58.2** An example of a simplified balance sheet

'The accounts are a snapshot of the business at a moment in time. Take a picture the following day and the scene may look very different. As with many of us, companies like to look their best when they are photographed and sometimes dress for the occasion.' M.A. Pitcher, accounting author.

---

## Types of asset

### Long-term (non-current) assets

Non-current assets are long-term assets such as:

- land and buildings: property owned by the business, either freehold or leasehold
- plant/machinery/equipment: anything from specialised machinery used in manufacturing to computers or even furniture
- vehicles: all types
- patents/copyright: although patents are not physical assets such as a building, the exclusive rights to a technical advance can have huge long-term value.

### Current assets

Current assets are short-term assets that change daily, perhaps hourly. There are three main types of current asset:

1. *Inventories*: the value of all the stock the firm holds, either on shop shelves or in warehouses; all these stocks are valued at cost in a balance sheet. This is because it's more prudent to value stock at the lower cost figure instead of at the higher figure for selling price.

2. *Receivables* are the sums owed by customers who have bought items on credit; for some firms this can be a large sum of money; for example small suppliers to Boots the Chemist can be kept waiting for 105 days before Boots pays up. If customers are big and powerful, small suppliers may have to invest a lot of their own cash in the balance sheet item 'receivables' (also known as debtors).

3. *Cash* means all forms of bank account that can easily be accessed, for example the balance on a current account; in business, the term liquidity is used to

measure how able a business is to pay its bills and finance near-term spending; cash is the most liquid asset of all.

| Spark plc: Fuller version of the firm's balance sheet | |
|---|---|
| | £ |
| Property | 180,000 |
| Machinery and vehicles | 120,000 |
| Inventories | 80,000 |
| Receivables and cash | 60,000 |
| Current liabilities | (40,000) |
| Assets employed | 400,000 |
| Total capital | 400,000 |

**Figure 58.3** An example of a fuller version of a vertical balance sheet

## Capital on the balance sheet

Companies have three main sources of long-term capital: shareholders (share capital), banks (loan capital) and reinvested profits (reserves). Loan capital carries interest charges that must be repaid, as must the loan itself. Share capital and reserves are both owed to the shareholders, but do not have to be repaid. Therefore they are treated separately. Share capital and reserves are known as total equity.

Assuming Spark plc's capital came from £50,000 of share capital, £250,000 of loan capital and £100,000 of reserves, the final version of the vertical balance sheet would look like the one shown in Figure 58.3. Note that the two-column format allows sub-totals to be shown in the right-hand column.

| Spark plc: Balance sheet for 31 December last year | | |
|---|---|---|
| | £ | £ |
| Property | 180,000 | |
| Machinery and vehicles | 120,000 | 300,000 |
| Inventories | 80,000 | |
| Receivables and cash | 60,000 | |
| Current liabilities | (40,000) | |
| Total assets less current liabilities | | 400,000 |
| Loan capital | | (250,000) |
| Net assets | | 150,000 |
| Share capital | 50,000 | |
| Reserves | 100,000 | |
| Total equity | | 150,000 |

**Figure 58.4** An example of a final version of a balance sheet

## 58.3 Assessing financial performance using a balance sheet

Financial performance really means the level of success (or failure) achieved by a business. Typically this is measured by profit – perhaps the percentage growth in profit compared with the previous year. That can be found in a firm's income statement. The balance sheet gives a vital clue, though, to a company's real performance over time through the item known as reserves. This item shows the accumulated, retained profit ever since the business started trading. For a long-established business such as John Lewis, this should be a substantial figure. At the end of July 2014 the reserves figure for John Lewis was £1,861 million. If, in 2015, the business made an operating loss, that negative number would be added to the reserves total – bringing the accumulated figure down. If profits are made (and not all paid out to the owners in the form of dividends or bonuses), the reserves total will rise.

The value of this approach can be seen by a look at Tesco plc's performance over several years. As shown in the graph below, Tesco's reserves figure rose consistently in the period up until 2012. The decline in 2013 and 2014 tells the story of Tesco's financial problems. (Its 2015 figure – not yet out – will be especially interesting given the doubts about the accuracy of past Tesco profit figures.)

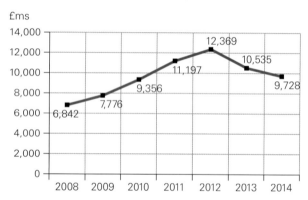

**Figure 58.5** Tesco reserves: retained profit

Source: Tesco Annual Report

## 58.4 Income statements

The income statement records all a business's revenues and costs within a given trading period. Income statements constitute a vital piece of evidence for those with interests in a company. For many stakeholders, profit is a major criterion by which to judge the success of a business:

- shareholders are an obvious example of those assessing profitability
- government agencies such as the tax authorities require data on profits or losses in order to be able to calculate the liability of a business to corporation tax
- suppliers to a business also need to know the financial position of the companies they trade with, in order to establish their reliability, stability and creditworthiness

- potential shareholders and bankers will also want to assess the financial position of the company before committing their funds to the business.

Making a profit is one of the most significant objectives for business organisations. It is this profit motive that encourages many people to establish their own business or expand an existing one. Without the potential for making a profit, why should individuals and companies commit time and resources to what may be a risky venture? Even charities must seek to generate revenues to at least match their expenditure, otherwise they cannot survive. Therefore the income statement is as important to a charity as it is to a company.

## The uses of income statements

The data within an income statement can be used for a number of purposes:

- to measure the success of a business compared with previous years or other businesses
- to assess actual performance compared with expectations
- to help obtain loans from banks or other lending institutions (creditors want proof that the business is capable of repaying any loans)
- to enable owners and managers to plan ahead; for example, for future investment in the company.

## 58.5 How an income statement shows a company's profit or loss

Figure 58.6 sets out the basic structure of an income statement for a public limited company.

|  |  | £m |
|---|---|---|
|  | Revenue | 26.0 |
| less | Cost of sales | (17.0) |
| gives | Gross profit | 9.0 |
| less | Overheads | (4.0) |
| gives | Operating profit | 5.0 |
| less | Financing costs | 1.5* |
| gives | Profit before taxation | 6.5 |
| less | Tax | (2.0) |
| gives | Profit after taxation for the year | 4.5 |

*In this case more interest was earned than paid out

**Figure 58.6** The basic structure of an income statement

The income statement comprises four main stages, as outlined below.

1. First, 'gross profit' is calculated. This is the difference between the income and the cost of the goods that have been sold. The latter is normally expressed simply as 'cost of sales'.

2. Second, 'operating profit' is calculated. This is done by deducting the main types of overhead, such as distribution costs and administration costs.

3. Next, profit before taxation is calculated, which is arrived at by the inclusion of interest received by the business and interest paid by it. These are normally shown together as a net figure labelled 'financing costs'.

4. The final stage of the income statement is to calculate profit after taxation. This is arrived at by deducting the amount of tax payable for the year and shows the net amount that has been earned for the shareholders.

## Calculating gross profit

This element of the income statement shows how much revenue has been earned from sales less the cost of goods sold. In other words, it calculates gross profit.

income (revenue) − cost of goods sold = gross profit

When calculating revenue, sales taxes such as VAT are excluded as they are paid directly to the tax authorities.

## Calculating operating profit

The next stage of the income statement sets out the net operating profit, or net operating loss, made by the business. The gross profit figure is necessary to calculate operating profit so this naturally follows on from calculating gross profit.

An important relationship to remember is that operating profit equals gross profit less expenses.

### Expenses

Expenses are payments for something that is of immediate use to the business. These payments include cash expenditures on labour and fuel, as well as non-cash items such as depreciation.

Examples of overhead expenses include:

- wages and salaries
- rent and rates
- heating, lighting and insurance
- distribution costs.

## Operating profit

Deducting expenses from gross profit leads to operating profit. Most firms regard this as the key test of their trading performance for the year. At the very least a firm would want operating profit to be:

- up by at least the rate of inflation compared with the previous year
- at least as high a percentage of capital employed as that achieved by rival companies
- high enough to reinvest in the future of the business while still paying satisfactory dividends to shareholders.

## Financing costs

Financing costs can add to or take away from the operating profit of a business. Most companies have relatively high borrowings and therefore can have to pay out a large proportion of their profit in interest charges. Japanese and German companies like to have substantial bank deposits earning interest, so this item can be a positive figure.

## Profit before and after taxation

All businesses pay corporation tax on their profits. In 2015 the rate of corporation tax paid by UK companies is 20 per cent. Once tax has been deducted, the final figure on the income statement is profit after taxation for the year. This figure is also known as the company's 'earnings'.

## Using profits

'Earnings' can be used in two main ways: it can either be distributed or retained. Usually businesses retain some profits and distribute the remainder. The balance between these two uses is influenced by a number of factors.

- *Distributed profit:* the company directors will decide on the amount to be paid out to shareholders in the form of dividends; if the shareholders are unhappy with the sum paid out, they can vote against the dividend at the annual general meeting.
- *Retained profit:* any prudent owner or manager of a business will use some of the profit made by the business to reinvest in the business for the future.

## 58.6 Assessing financial performance using an income statement

Public limited companies (plcs) are required by law to publish their accounts. This means that they are available for scrutiny not only by the owners (shareholders), potential investors and bankers, but also by competitors.

When a company draws up its income statement for external publication it will include as little information as possible. Public limited companies usually supply no more detail than is required by law. This format is illustrated below for the supermarket chain Morrisons plc. The income statement shows clearly that 2013/14 was a terribly difficult financial year for the company. In 2013 the business made £949 million of operating profit, but this figure collapsed into a £95 million loss in 2014.

| Summarised group income statement for Morrisons plc (year ended 4 February 2014) | 2014 (£m) | 2013 (£m) |
|---|---|---|
| Revenue (sales excluding VAT) | 17,680 | 18,116 |
| Cost of sales | (16, 606) | (16,910) |
| **Gross profit** | **1,074** | **1,206** |
| Administrative & other expenses | (266) | (257) |
| One-off losses (from write-offs) | (903) | – |
| **Operating profit** | **(95)** | **949** |
| Finance income | 6 | 5 |
| Finance costs | (87) | (75) |
| **Profit before tax** | **(176)** | **879** |
| Taxation | (62) | (232) |
| **Profit for the year** | **(238)** | **647** |

**Figure 58.7** A summarised income statement for Morrisons plc

To assess the financial performance of Morrisons' income statement, it makes sense to start at the top. In 2014 revenue fell from £18,116m to £17,680m, which is a fall of 2.4 per cent. This sparked an 11 per cent fall in gross profit. Administrative expenses rose, but not by much, leaving the real explanation for the collapse in operating profit coming from a one-off item: the £903 million 'write-off'. So although there are plenty of reasons to be disappointed at Morrisons' performance in 2014, the losses recorded at the bottom of the income statement are rather misleading. Morrisons didn't suddenly become a lost cause. As long as there are no more 'one-off' losses in 2015, Morrisons should return to profitability.

### Real business

#### *Profits and Candy Crush*

In March 2014 King Inc, the company behind the Candy Crush phenomenon, launched on to the US stock market. It sold just 10 per cent of its share capital for $500 million, valuing the company at $5,000 million. Many commentators were amazed that people were willing to buy shares in a business that relied on one game (Candy Crush) for 78 per cent of its revenue. But the startling growth figures shown below give an idea of the attractions of the shares. ⇒

| King Digital Entertainment Inc | | |
| --- | --- | --- |
| | Revenue ($s) | Operating (net) profit |
| 2011 | 64m | (1.3m) |
| 2012 | 164m | 7.8m |
| 2013 | 1,880m | 567.6m |

What happens when players get bored with Candy Crush, though? The share buyers hope that King will be able to come up with new products that work the same business miracle as Candy Crush.

## 58.7 Analysing the existing internal position of a business

At the beginning of 2015 no UK business had a better press than the John Lewis Partnership. It had become a cross between a national treasure and a business icon for the middle classes. Yet its accounts told a more complex story. Between 2008 and 2014 sales had risen by half, yet profits were stubbornly static. And the balance sheet was deteriorating. From successive John Lewis annual accounts it was possible to build up an analysis of the business through its strengths and weaknesses.

John Lewis strengths:

- Revenue up by half between 2008 and 2014; growth seems to have been the objective and was achieved
- Market share of Waitrose and John Lewis had risen substantially (according to data published alongside the accounts).

John Lewis weaknesses:

- Between 2008 and 2014 there was a remarkable decline in the John Lewis contribution to GB corporation (profit) tax. This was partly because of the government's policy of cutting corporation tax for big companies, but also because of the falling profitability of the business. In 2008 John Lewis made 6.5p profit per £ of sales; in 2014 the equivalent figure was 4.7p.
- There was a deterioration in the short-term financial position of the business, with current liabilities rising faster than the current assets needed to pay them.

As this brief analysis shows, published accounts can help analyse the internal position of a business – for the potential benefit of customers, staff and suppliers.

## Five Whys and a How

| Question | Answer |
| --- | --- |
| Why do plcs have to publish their accounts? | So that any member of the public can check on the company's progress, from investor to employee |
| Why is a balance sheet sometimes called a 'snapshot' of the finances of a business? | Because it's drawn up on a single day (usually the last day of the financial year). This restricts its usefulness |
| Why do firms need to publish both an income statement and a balance sheet? | Because the income statement shows the flow of revenue in and costs out, whereas the balance sheet shows the wealth at a point in time |
| Why might it be useful to look at a company's balance sheet reserves? | Because they show how much profit has been made (and kept) in the past – and changes in reserves give insight into company performance |
| Why might shares in King Digital (Candy Crush) be high risk? | Because the business is over-reliant on one game – and that game might be near or past its saturation point |
| How difficult is it to get the figures right? | Tesco showed in 2014 that it's possible to get the figures wrong by £260 million; this would not surprise professors of accounting who acknowledge that it's hard to achieve the accuracy shareholders' want |

Two evaluative themes can be considered in relation to published accounts. It is easy to make the assumption that a rising level of operating profit is evidence of a company that is performing well. There are a number of factors that need to be considered when making such a judgement. Has a new management pushed up prices, boosting profit for a year or so, but at the cost of damaged market share in the future? Is a company that pollutes the environment, uses materials from unsustainable sources, but makes a large profit, a successful business? Is profit necessarily the best measure of the performance of a business?

Even if we assume current profits are a good indication of how a company is performing, a number of other factors need to be taken into account. Is the market growing or declining? Are new competitors coming onto the scene? To what extent is the business achieving its corporate objectives? Is the profit earned likely to be sustained into the future. Information such as this is vital if a meaningful judgement is to be made about business success.

## Key terms

**Corporation tax:** a tax levied as a percentage of a company's profits.

**Cost of goods sold:** calculation of the direct costs involved in making the goods actually sold in that period.

**Creditors:** those to whom a firm owes money (for example, suppliers or bankers); these may also be called payables.

**Gross profit:** revenue less cost of goods sold; profit made on trading activities.

**Liability:** a debt (that is, a bill that has not been paid or a loan that has not been repaid).

**Liquidity:** a measurement of a firm's ability to pay its short-term bills.

**Operating profit:** gross profit minus expenses.

**Reserves:** a company's accumulated, retained profit; it forms part of the company's total equity.

**Revenue:** sales revenue (that is, the value of sales made); also known as income.

**Stock exchange:** a market for stocks and shares; it supervises the issuing of shares by companies and is also a second-hand market for stocks and shares.

# Workbook

## A. Revision questions

(40 marks; 40 minutes)

1. Give two possible reasons why a bank would want to see a company's income statement. (2)

2. Look at Figure 58.1.
   a) Calculate the percentage increase in the annual net financing costs for John Lewis between 2008 and 2013. (3)
   b) Explain one possible effect of this increase on the business. (4)

3. Outline two ways in which employees may benefit from looking at the income statement of their employer. (4)

4. Distinguish between gross and operating profit. (4)

5. Explain why even a charity such as Oxfam may want to make a profit. (4)

6. State two items that may be listed as current liabilities. (2)

7. Distinguish between non-current and current assets. (4)

8. Explain what may be included under the heading 'financing costs'. (4)

9. Look at the income statement for Morrisons shown in Figure 58.7.

   a) Calculate the percentage change in

   (i) its 2014 income and

   (ii) 2014 profit before tax. (5)

   b) Explain one conclusion that can be drawn from those findings. (4)

# B. Revision exercises
## DATA RESPONSE

### Whitbread plc

Whitbread plc was once a brewery, but is now focused on three markets: coffee bars (Costa), budget hotels (Premier Inn) and restaurants (Beefeater Grill). Costa has been a great success both in the UK and China. Study Figure 58.8 and answer the questions below.

### Questions (45 marks; 45 minutes)

1. a) Calculate Whitbread's cost of sales for both periods. (4)

   b) Calculate each figure as a percentage of the company's revenue for the corresponding period. (4)

   c) Explain the importance of this finding. (4)

2. a) Calculate the percentage increase Whitbread achieved in 2014 compared with 2013 in:

   (i) revenue (4)

   (ii) operating profit. (4)

   b) Analyse the data to suggest why the increase in operating profit was greater than the increase in sales revenue. (9)

| Whitbread plc group income statement (summarised) | | |
|---|---|---|
| | Year to 27/02/2014 | Year to 28/02/2013 |
| | £m | £m |
| Revenue (turnover) | 2,294 | 2,030 |
| Cost of sales | ? | ? |
| **Gross profit** | **458** | **403** |
| Central operating expenses | (27) | (26) |
| **Operating profit** | **431** | **377** |
| Net finance income | (19) | (24) |
| **Profit before taxation** | **412** | **353** |
| Taxation | (89) | (61) |
| **Profit for the year** | **323** | **292** |

**Figure 58.8** Adapted from Whitbread plc group income statement

Source: Whitbread Annual Report and Accounts, 2014

3. Whitbread's two main operating divisions are Hotels and Restaurants (mainly Premier Inn) and Costa Coffee. UK hotel profits rose by 10.9 per cent in 2014 and at Costa UK rose by 26.5 per cent. Evaluate how Whitbread's management might respond to that information. (16)

# C. Extend your understanding

1. People start businesses to make profits and from there to build a sellable asset. To what extent do the income statement and balance sheet capture that information? (25)

2. 'Profit is the most important thing and the way you get profit is through gross margins' says Arthur Snyder, businessman. To what extent do you agree with this view? (25)

**Linked to:** Balance sheets and income statements, Chapter 58; Value and limitations of financial ratios, Chapter 60; How to analyse data other than financial statements, Chapter 61.

## Definition

Ratio analysis is an examination of accounting data by relating one figure to another. This approach allows more meaningful interpretation of the data and the identification of trends.

## 59.1 Introduction

The function of accounting is to provide information to stakeholders on how a business has performed over a given period. But how is performance to be judged? Is an annual profit of £1 million good or bad? Very good if the firm is a small family business; woeful if the business is KFC and annual sales exceed £10 billion. What is needed is to look at the £1 million in relation to another variable, such as sales revenue, perhaps. This helps in judging a firm's financial performance in relation to its size and in relation to its competitors. The technique used to do this is called ratio analysis.

Financial accounts, such as the income statement and the balance sheet, are used for three main purposes:

1. financial control
2. planning
3. accountability.

Ratio analysis can assist in achieving these objectives. It can help the different users of financial information answer questions such as:

- Is this company/my job safe?
- Should I stop selling goods to this firm on credit?
- Should I invest in this business?

## 59.2 Interpreting final accounts: the investigation process

To analyse company accounts, a well-ordered and structured process needs to be followed. This should ensure that the analysis is relevant to the question being looked at. The seven-point approach shown in Figure 59.1 is helpful.

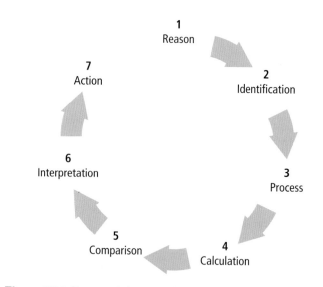

**Figure 59.1** Seven-point approach to ratio analysis

## 59.3 Types of ratio

The main classifications of ratios are as follows.

- *Profitability ratios:* measure the relationship between gross/net profit and revenue, assets and capital employed. They are sometimes referred to as performance ratios.
- *Liquidity ratios:* these investigate the short-term financial stability of a firm by examining whether there are sufficient short-term assets to meet the short-term liabilities (debts).
- *Gearing:* examines the extent to which the business is dependent upon borrowed money; it is concerned with the long-term financial position of the company.
- *Efficiency ratios:* these measure how efficiently an organisation uses its resources and controls credit.

The following sections look at each classification of ratios in more detail. An explanation of the seven-point approach to ratio analysis is given in Table 59.1.

**Table 59.1** An explanation of the seven-point approach to ratio analysis

| The investigation process | | |
|---|---|---|
| **Step 1** | Reason | The starting point for interpreting financial accounts is establishing why you are doing so. If you are considering supplying a company with a large order of goods, you want to try to establish its financial stability and ability to pay. |
| **Step 2** | Identification | Identify the relevant figures from the financial accounts. |
| **Step 3** | Process | Decide what method(s) of analysis will provide you with the most useful and meaningful results. |
| **Step 4** | Calculation | Make a comparison between data by calculating one figure as a ratio of another. For example, profit as a percentage of sales revenue or borrowings as a proportion of total capital. |
| **Step 5** | Comparison | Compare the figures from this period with the results from the last period, those of your competitors or other companies under investigation. |
| **Step 6** | Interpretation | Look at the results obtained and interpret them in relation to values that would be considered poor, average or good. |
| **Step 7** | Action | If certain results are worrying, initiate further investigation (maybe into areas which are not covered in the financial accounts), or take corrective action. |

## 59.4 Liquidity

The following ratio focuses on the short-term financial health of a business. It is concerned with the organisation's working capital and whether or not it is being managed effectively. Too little working capital and the company may not be able to pay all its debts.

Too much and it may not be making the most efficient use of its financial resources.

## Current ratio

This ratio looks at the relationship between current assets and current liabilities. It examines the liquidity position of the firm. It is given by the formula:

$$\text{current ratio} = \frac{\text{current assets}}{\text{current liabilities}}$$

This is expressed as a ratio such as, for example, 2:1 or 3:1.

### Example

Bannam Ltd has current assets of £30,000 and current liabilities of £10,000:

current ratio = current assets : current liabilities
= £30,000 : £10,000
= 3 : 1
current ratio = 3

### Interpretation

The above worked example shows that Bannam Ltd has three times as many current assets as current liabilities. This means that, for every £1 of short-term debts owed, it has £3 of assets to pay them. This is a comfortable position.

Accountants suggest the 'ideal' current ratio should be approximately 1.5:1 (that is, £1.50 of assets for every £1 of debt). Any higher than this and the organisation has too many resources tied up in unproductive assets; these could be invested more profitably (or the cash could be handed back to shareholders). A low current ratio means a business may not be able to pay its debts. It is possible that the result may well be something like 0.8:1. This shows the firm has only 80p of current assets to pay every £1 it owes.

The current ratios of a selection of public companies in 2014 are shown in Table 59.2. As this table shows, it would be wrong to panic about a liquidity ratio of less than 1. Huge firms such as Tesco have often had spells when their liquidity levels were less than 1.

**Table 59.2** The current ratios of a selection of public companies in 2014

| Company | Balance sheet date | Current assets £millions | Current liabilities £millions | Current ratio |
|---|---|---|---|---|
| French Connection plc | 31/01/2014 | £89,400,000 | £45,200,000 | 1.98 |
| Ted Baker plc | 25/01/2014 | £144,400,000 | £89,500,000 | 1.61 |
| Tesco plc | 22/02/2014 | £13,085,000,000 | £20,206,000,000 | 0.65 |
| Morrisons plc | 02/02/2014 | £1,430,000,000 | £2,873,000,000 | 0.50 |
| JD Wetherspoon | 26/01/2014 | £79,400,000 | £241,300,000 | 0.33 |

## Altering the ratio

If the ratio is so low that it is becoming hard to pay the bills, the company will have to try to bring more cash into the balance sheet. This could be done by:

- selling under-used fixed assets
- raising more share capital
- increasing long-term borrowings
- postponing planned investments.

## 59.5 Gearing

Gearing is one of the main measures of the financial health of a business. Quite simply, it measures the firm's level of debt. This shines a light onto the long-term financial stability of an organisation.

Gearing measures long-term liabilities as a proportion of a firm's capital employed. It shows how reliant the firm is upon borrowed money. In turn, that indicates how vulnerable the firm is to financial setbacks. The Americans call gearing 'leverage'. In boom times, banks and investors find leverage (debt) very attractive; but high gearing always means high risk.

Highly geared companies can suffer badly in recessions, because even when times are hard they still have to keep paying high interest payments to the bank.

'When you combine ignorance and leverage, you get some pretty interesting results.' Warren Buffett, investment guru

The formula for gearing is:

$$\text{gearing} = \frac{\text{non-current liabilities}}{\text{capital employed}} \times 100$$

This is expressed as a percentage.

## Interpretation

The gearing ratio shows the level of long-term risk in a company's balance sheet. If loans represent more than 50 per cent of capital employed, the company is said to be highly geared. Such a company has to pay substantial interest charges on its borrowings before it can pay dividends to shareholders or retain profits for reinvestment. The higher the gearing, the higher the degree of risk. Low-geared companies provide a lower-risk investment; therefore they can negotiate loans more easily and at lower cost than a highly geared company.

**Table 59.3** The gearing ratios of a selection of companies in 2014

| Company | Balance sheet date | Non-current liabilities (long-term loans) | Capital employed | Gearing (%) |
|---|---|---|---|---|
| Ted Baker plc | 25/01/2014 | £0 | £112,100,000 | 0 |
| Home Retail Group plc | 01/03/2014 | £326,900,000 | £3,000,400,000 | 10.9 |
| Morrisons plc | 02/02/2014 | £3,164,000,000 | £7,856,000,000 | 40.3 |
| Tesco plc | 22/02/2014 | £14,043,000,000 | £28,765,000,000 | 48.8 |
| JD Wetherspoon plc | 26/01/2014 | £655,724,000 | £890,191,000 | 73.7 |

### Real business

#### Carlyle Capital Corporation

During the credit crunch a US blogger with the fabulous name of Postman Patel warned that the Carlyle Capital Corporation (an American investment fund) was unable to pay its bills. Within a week it had collapsed, owing over $16 billion. It emerged that Carlyle Capital had a gearing level of 97 per cent. In other words, only 3 per cent of the money it invested was its own money; all the rest was borrowed. When times were good its shares were worth $20 each. Now they were worth nothing. High gearing means high risk. Ridiculously high gearing means ridiculously high risk.

## Altering the ratio

The gearing ratio can be altered in several ways, depending on whether the organisation wishes to raise or lower its gearing figure. Ways in which an organisation's gearing figure may be altered are shown in Table 59.4.

**Table 59.4** Altering an organisation's gearing ratio

| Raising gearing | Reducing gearing |
|---|---|
| Buy back ordinary shares | Issue more ordinary shares |
| Issue more preference shares | Buy back debentures |
| Issue more debentures | Retain more profits |
| Obtain more loans | Repay loans |

## 59.6 Profitability ratios

For private businesses, a key objective is to make a profit. But how much profit? Consider the following example.

### Example

Companies A and B operate in the same market. At the end of the year they report profits as follows:

|  | Profit |
|---|---|
| Company A | £100,000 |
| Company B | £1 million |

Which is the more successful company? Company B, surely. However, take into account the following additional information.

|  | Profit | Sales revenue |
|---|---|---|
| Company A | £100,000 | £200,000 |
| Company B | £1 million | £10 million |

This shows that company A's profit is terrific in relation to its sales; better, in fact, than company B. Profitability ratios allow comparisons such as this to be made in detail. The figures can be compared in percentage terms. This makes comparison easier.

|  | Profit | Divided by sales revenue | X 100 (to get a percentage) |
|---|---|---|---|
| Company A | £100,000 | £200,000 | 50% |
| Company B | £1 million | £10 million | 10% |

Company A's success can now be seen much more clearly.

Chapter 41 looked into profit margins in detail. It is worth re-reading that section, but here is a brief summary of what you need to know to answer A-level questions on profit margins:

**Table 59.5** Summary of profit margins and profitability

|  | Gross profit margin | Operating profit margin |
|---|---|---|
| Formula | Gross profit/Sales revenue x 100 | Operating profit/Sales revenue x 100 |
| What it shows | Gross profit per £ of sales | Operating profit per £ of sales |
| How to improve it | Price up Unit variable costs down | Boost gross margin Cut overheads per £ of sales Increase sales |
| Problem if it's too low | May not be enough gross profit to cover overhead expenses | May not be enough operating profit to reinvest into the business and so get growth |

## Return on capital employed (ROCE)

This is sometimes referred to as being the primary efficiency ratio and is perhaps the most important ratio of all. It measures the efficiency with which the firm generates profit from the funds invested in the business.

$$\text{ROCE} = \frac{\text{operating profit}}{\text{capital employed}} \times 100$$

Operating profit is profit after all operating costs and overheads have been deducted. Capital employed is all the long-term finance of the business (debt plus equity).

### Interpretation

The higher the value of this ratio the better. A high and rising ROCE suggests that resources are being used efficiently. ROCE measures profitability and no shareholder will complain at huge returns. The figure needs to be compared with previous years and that of other companies to determine whether this year's result is satisfactory or not.

A firm's ROCE can also be compared with the percentage return offered by interest-bearing accounts at banks and building societies. If bank interest rates are 6 per cent, what is the point of a sole trader investing money in his or her business, working very hard all year and making a return on capital employed of 4 per cent? The sole trader would be better off keeping the money in the bank, taking little risk and staying at home.

So what is the *right* level of ROCE? There is no clear answer, but most companies would regard a 20 per cent ROCE as very satisfactory. The returns achieved by a selection of public companies in 2014 are shown in Table 59.7.

### John Lewis Partnership

A difficulty with using the return on capital ratio is that modern balance sheets hide the figure for capital employed. The problem can be seen with these figures from John Lewis Partnership. In 2013 JLP made an operating profit of £453m; in 2014 the figure fell to £424m. To find the capital employed, it's necessary to understand a bit about the balance sheet. Capital employed is all the long-term finance within a business. It comes from three sources: share capital, reserves and long-term loans (known as non-current liabilities). In 2013, JLP had £1 million of share capital, £1,901 million of reserves and £1,828 million of long term debt. Note that although the non-current liabilities are in brackets on the balance sheet, I don't treat the figure as a negative number. It's simply in brackets because it's a liability not an asset. So JLP's capital employed in 2013 was £3,730m. Therefore its ROCE figure was £453/£3730m x 100 = 12.14%. In 2014 the figure was:

| 2014 share capital | £1m |
|---|---|
| 2014 reserves | £1,781m |
| 2014 non-current liabilities | £2,037m |
| Total 2014 capital employed: | £3,819m |

So 2014 ROCE was: £424m/£3,819m x 100 = 11.1%

**Table 59.6** John Lewis Partnership balance sheet (last day of January). All figures in £millions

| | 2014 | 2013 |
|---|---|---|
| Non-current assets | 4,385 | 4,116 |
| Inventories | 554 | 514 |
| Receivables | 226 | 192 |
| Cash | 360 | 542 |
| Current liabilities | (1,706) | (1,634) |
| Net current assets | (566) | (386) |
| **Non-current liabilities** | **(2,037)** | **(1,828)** |
| Net assets | 1,782 | 1,902 |
| **Share capital** | **1** | **1** |
| **Reserves** | **1,781** | **1,901** |
| Total equity | 1,782 | 1,902 |

**Table 59.7** The return on capital employed (ROCE) achieved by a selection of public limited companies in 2014

| Company (in Costa's case it is a Division of a company) | Annual operating profit | Capital employed | ROCE |
|---|---|---|---|
| Costa UK (coffee bars) | £109,800,000 | £271,100,000 | 40.5% |
| Burberry (clothing) | £39,600,000 | £112,000,000 | 35.4% |
| Tesco (retailing) | £2,631,000,000 | £28,765,000,000 | 9.1% |
| Mandarin Oriental (hotels) | £117,000,000 | £1,305,000,000 | 9.0% |

## Altering the ratio

The return on capital employed can be improved by:

- increasing the level of profit generated by the same level of capital invested, or
- maintaining the level of profits generated but decreasing the amount of capital it takes to do so.

## 59.7 Financial efficiency ratios

These three ratios are concerned with how well an organisation manages its resources - its working capital. They look at the management of inventories (stocks), receivables (credit periods taken by customers) and payables (credit periods given to suppliers). Ultimately, these three ratios are the ones that have the greatest impact on a firm's ability to pay its bills, that is its liquidity. Companies fall into administration when they can't find the cash to pay their bills, so financial efficiency ratios are hugely important.

## Inventory turnover

This ratio measures the number of times a year a business sells and replaces its inventory (stock). For example, if a market stall trader bought stock from wholesalers every morning and sold it all by the end of the afternoon, replacing the stock daily would mean an inventory turnover of 365 times per year. The formula for inventory turnover is:

$$\text{inventory turnover} = \frac{\text{cost of goods sold}}{\text{inventories}}$$

expressed as times per year.

## Interpretation

This ratio can only really be interpreted with knowledge of the industry in which the firm operates. For example, we would expect a local bakery to turn over its inventory virtually every day, as the bread has to be fresh. Therefore a suitable inventory turnover figure might be 250 to 300 times per year. This allows for the fact that some produce will last longer than one day. A second-hand car sales business could take an average of a month to sell the cars; therefore the inventory turnover would be 12 times.

### Altering the ratio

The inventory turnover ratio can be improved by:

● reducing the average level of inventories held, perhaps by a move towards just-in-time management

● increasing the rate of sales without raising the level of inventory.

Note that the inventory turnover ratio has little meaning for many service industries as they do not buy or sell stocks of goods.

## Receivables days (collection period from customers)

This particular ratio is designed to show how long, on average, it takes the company to collect debts owed by customers. Although you or I might pay for something in cash, business customers expect a credit period of perhaps 60 days. In other words a container-load of £50,000-worth of chocolate is received today by Waitrose, but the bill only needs to be paid to Cadbury in 60 days' time. Until the bill is paid, this £50,000 will be categorised by Cadbury as receivables. The formula for 'receivables days' is:

$$\text{receivables days} = \frac{\text{receivables}}{\text{annual revenue}} \times 365$$

expressed as days.

The accounts for the fashion clothing business Ted Baker plc make it possible to calculate the following receivables days' position (see Table 59.8).

---

'A pig bought on credit is forever grunting.' Proverb

---

## Interpretation

In other words, the average Ted Baker customer took 49 days to pay in 2013 and 40 days to pay in 2014. By collecting its money faster, Ted Baker would have improved its cash position. Better to have the cash than to be waiting for it.

### Altering the ratio

The receivables' collection period can be improved by reducing the amount of time for which credit is offered (for example, from 60 to 30 days), increasing the efficiency of the credit control department or by offering incentives for clients to pay on time, for example cash discounts. A common approach is to sort customers into the age of their debts to you – oldest first. This helps to focus upon collecting debts from the slowest payers. It may also encourage a firm to refuse to give credit in future to a persistent slow payer.

## Payables days (collection period for payables)

This particular ratio is designed to show how many days, on average, it takes the company to pay its suppliers. Payables are the bills owed to people and organisations that have supplied products or a service to the business, but haven't yet been paid. On public companies' balance sheets they are called 'trade payables'. The formula for this ratio is:

$$\text{payables days} = \frac{\text{trade payables}}{\text{cost of sales}} \times 365$$

The accounts for the fashion clothing business Ted Baker plc make it possible to calculate the following payables days' position (Table 59.9).

**Table 59.9** Information from the Ted Baker accounts: payables position

| | Cost of sales £ million | Payables £ million | Payables days |
|---|---|---|---|
| Year to 30 January 2013 | 95.7 | 40.8 | 156 days |
| Year to 30 January 2014 | 123.5 | 45.3 | 134 days |

**Table 59.8** Information from the Ted Baker accounts: receivables

| | Annual revenue | Receivables | Receivables days (collection period) |
|---|---|---|---|
| Year to 30 January 2013 | £254 million | £34 million | 49 days |
| Year to 30 January 2014 | £322 million | £35 million | 40 days |

## Interpretation

In other words, the average Ted Baker supplier had to wait 156 days to be paid in 2013 and 134 days to pay in 2014. Ted Baker is getting slightly better, but from a shockingly poor starting point. This would be important to know if your business was considering supplying Ted Baker for the first time (it's a long wait to get paid!). From Ted Baker's point of view, though, it's great to be able to hold onto the cash for ages before paying.

---

'Neither a borrower nor a lender be.'
William Shakespeare, author, *Hamlet*

---

## Altering the ratio

Payables days can be reduced by paying bills more promptly. This worsens the firm's short-term cash (and working capital) situation, but may provide long-term benefits if it helps build a strong business relationship with the supplier(s).

## Five Whys and a How

| Question | Answer |
|---|---|
| Why are financial ratios needed at all? | Because they cut through the huge amount of data in company accounts, allowing the user to focus on a few key pieces of analysis |
| Why is it sometimes said that ratios raise questions but don't answer them? | Because the ratio results don't tell you the thinking behind them, so a fall in inventory turnover might be due to stockpiling before a new product launch – rather than incompetence |
| Why is ROCE usually regarded as the single most important ratio? | Because it shows the real profitability of the business measured against all the capital invested, so it measures financial efficiency |
| Why do financial analysts like to see the same number for receivables days and payables days? | Because the credit periods cancel each other out, meaning no net drain on a firm's cash flow |
| Why do some business people and City analysts find gearing exciting? | Because high gearing means high risks but also high rewards if things go well |
| How many ratios do you really need to understand a company's performance? | The three most important ratios are ROCE (profitability), the current ratio (short-term financial health) and gearing (longer-term financial health) |

Ratio analysis is a powerful tool in the interpretation of financial accounts. It can allow for comparison between rival companies (inter-firm comparison), appraisal of financial performance and the identification of trends. It can therefore be of great help in financial planning and decision-making.

However, because of its usefulness and the range of possible applications, there is a tendency to attach too much importance to the results gained from this analysis. Other types of analysis exist, such as market share trends, and there are sometimes more important issues at stake than just financial performance. A changing society has seen a greater interest in social and ethical aspects of business performance. Although ratio analysis is useful, it is limited in the area it investigates.

**Key terms**

**Earnings:** for a company, earnings means profit after tax.

**Inter-firm comparisons:** comparisons of financial performance between firms; to be valuable, these comparisons should be with a firm of similar size within the same market.

**Liquidity:** the ability of a firm to meet its short-term debts; liquidity can also be understood as being the availability of cash or assets that can easily be converted into cash.

# Workbook

## A. Revision questions

(40 marks; 40 minutes)

1.  List four groups of people who may be interested in the results of ratio analysis. (4)

2.  State the key stages in conducting an analysis of company accounts using ratios. (7)

3.  Briefly explain the difference between efficiency ratios and profitability ratios. (4)

4.  Explain why the return on capital employed (ROCE) is regarded as one of the most important ratios. (3)

5.  Why may the managers of a company be pleased if its inventory turnover ratio is falling? (4)

6.  What could the figure for receivables days tell you about the way in which a business controls its finances? (4)

7.  Explain why a financial analyst might criticise a company for having a current ratio that's 'too high'. (4)

8.  Identify one advantage and one disadvantage of a company shortening its receivables collection period. (2)

9.  Outline two problems that a company could experience if its gearing ratio rose significantly. (4)

10. Explain one reason why investors might treat the results of ratio analysis with caution. (4)

## B. Revision exercises
### DATA RESPONSE 1

**Questions (75 marks; 75 minutes)**

1.  J. Orr Ltd makes garden gnomes. When analysing J. Orr's annual accounts, state and explain which three ratios you think would be of most use to:

    a)  a firm wondering whether to supply J. Orr with materials on credit (6)

    b)  the trade union representative of J. Orr's workforce (6)

    c)  a pensioner, wondering whether J. Orr will be a good investment (6)

    d)  the management of J. Orr's main rival, Gnometastic Ltd (6)

    e)  J. Orr's main customer, Blooms of Broadway garden centre. (6)

2. A garden furniture producer wants to buy a garden centre. It has identified two possible businesses and conducted some ratio analyses to help it decide which one to focus on. Look at the ratios for each business in Table 59.10, analyse which one you would recommend, and make a fully justified recommendation of which one to buy. (20)

**Table 59.10** Ratio analyses conducted for two garden centres

|  | Blooms of Cotswold | Broadway Carnations |
|---|---|---|
| Gross profit margin | 60% | 45% |
| Return on capital | 15.2% | 14.6% |
| Inventory turnover | 18 times | 24 times |
| Gearing | 52% | 35% |
| Sales growth (last 3 years) | +3.5% per year | +4.8% per year |

3. The balance sheet for GrowMax Co. as at 31 December is shown in Figure 59.2

|  | £000 |
|---|---|
| Non-current assets | 860 |
| Inventories | 85 |
| Receivables | 180 |
| Cash | 15 |
| Current liabilities | 200 |
| Non-current liabilities | 360 |
| Share capital | 160 |
| Reserves | 420 |

**Figure 59.2** Balance sheet for GrowMax Co. as at 31 December

a) Calculate the firm's net current assets and capital employed. (5)

b) Last year's revenue was £1,460,000 and operating profit margin was 10 per cent. Use this information plus your answer to 3a) to analyse the firm's profitability. (10)

c) GrowMax's main rival offers its customers 30 days' credit.

(i) How does this compare with GrowMax? (4)

(ii) Explain two further questions the GrowMax management should want answered before deciding whether their customer credit policy should be revised. (6)

## DATA RESPONSE 2

**Published accounts from three grocery retailers**

**Table 59.11** Income statements (year to Feb/March 2014). All figures in £millions.

|  | Tesco 2014 | Sainsbury's 2014 | Morrisons 2014 |
|---|---|---|---|
| Revenue | 63,600 | 23,950 | 17,700 |
| Cost of sales | (59,600) | (22,550) | (16,600) |
| Gross profit | 4,000 | 1,400 | 1,100 |
| Overheads and interest charges | (2,000) | (500) | (400) |
| Exceptional one-off profits/losses | 250 | - | (900) |
| Pre-tax (operating) profit | 2,250 | 900 | (200) |
| Tax | (350) | (180) | (50) |
| Profit after tax | 1,900 | 720 | (250) |
| Dividends | (1,200) | (320) | (280) |
| Retained profit | 700 | 400 | (530) |

**Table 59.12** Balance sheets (as at Feb/March date 2014). All figures in £millions.

| | Tesco 2014 | Sainsbury's 2014 | Morrisons 2014 |
|---|---|---|---|
| **Fixed (non-current) assets** | **34,600** | **12,200** | **9,300** |
| Stock (inventories) | 3,600 | 1,000 | 850 |
| Debtors (receivables) | 5,900 | 1,700 | 300 |
| Cash | 6,100 | 1,650 | 250 |
| Trade payables | (10,600) | (6,150) | (2,300) |
| Overdraft | (10,800) | (600) | (550) |
| **Net current assets** | **(5,800)** | **(2,400)** | **(1,450)** |
| Long-term (non-current) liabilities | (14,050) | (3,800) | (3,150) |
| **Net assets** | **14,750** | **6,000** | **4,700** |
| Share capital | 5,500 | 1,600 | 400 |
| Reserves | 9,250 | 4,400 | 4,300 |
| **Total equity** | **14,750** | **6,000** | **4,700** |

## Questions: 30 marks; 30 minutes

1. **a)** Calculate the current ratio for each of the three retailers. (4)

   **b)** Comment briefly on your findings. (6)

2. Compare the profitability of the three retailers using Return on Capital Employed. (8)

3. **a)** Calculate the gearing levels for each of the three grocers. (4)

   **b)** On the basis of this data, explain which is in the weakest position to raise extra loan capital. (8)

## C. Extend your understanding

1. 'The ability to assess the long- and short-term financial stability of an organisation is vital to every stakeholder.' To what extent do you agree with this statement? (25)

2. With the economy entering a recession, an investor wants to reassess her share portfolio. To what extent can she rely solely on the return on capital ratio, given the economic circumstances? (25)

# Chapter

# 60

# Value and limitations of financial ratios

**Linked to:** Balance sheets and income statements, Chapter 58; Financial ratio analysis, Chapter 59; Assessing short- and long-term performance, Chapter 62.

## Definition

Financial ratios can only be as accurate as the accounts they are based on. As Tesco showed when it overstated its profit by £260 million, published accounts are a matter of opinion rather than fact.

## 60.1 Introduction: giving a true and fair view?

The final accounts are usually the first point of reference for anyone interested in analysing a business's value or performance over a period of time. For instance, the year's revenue and expenses are reported in a firm's annual income statement. The balance sheet gives us information needed to calculate its book value (that is, the difference between its total assets and any liabilities it may have). Together these statements allow ratio analysis to be carried out. However, all this information may give an incomplete and possibly misleading view of what a business may actually be worth.

## 60.2 What accounts leave out

### Focus on quantitative data

Money acts as the language of accounting, allowing business transactions to be measured, compared and added together. This means that accounts focus on items that can be given a financial value. Yet a successful business depends on a lot more than the price paid for property and equipment, or the size of its outstanding debt. For example, a firm's culture and its attitude to risk-taking will be at the heart of its

performance. Similarly, a highly skilled, loyal and motivated workforce, a commitment to behaving in an ethical and environmentally friendly manner or a reputation for excellent customer service can increase a firm's ability to compete against rivals. These aspects of a business are likely to make it worth more, both to existing owners and potential buyers. However, such features are difficult to express in numerical terms and are therefore ignored by the main accounting statements.

## Using profit as a performance indicator

Profit is generally regarded as one of the most important indicators of performance. Yet the long-term success of a business may depend on a firm's willingness to sacrifice profits, in the short term at least. It may be useful, therefore, to also consider other indicators, such as growth in revenue and market share or investment in research and development and new product success.

## Real business

### R&D budget

Procter & Gamble (P&G) is one of the world's biggest household goods multinationals. Its long-term success came from creating markets for disposable nappies (Pampers), teeth-whitening toothpaste (Crest), stackable crisps (Pringles) and much more. In 2000 P&G spent more than 5 per cent of its sales revenue on research and development (R&D), compared with less than 2.5 per cent at rival Unilever. Yet by 2011 P&G's investment in R&D had fallen to below 2.5 per cent of sales. This was because a new chief executive believed the budget could be cut because decentralisation would make business-unit heads use the sums more efficiently. In fact this inadvertently slowed innovation because the unit heads tied research too closely to short-term profit concerns. By 2013 the company was increasing R&D spending again – and in 2014 P&G was responsible for seven of the ten most successful non-food launches in the US.

## The state of the market

The nature of accounts means that they are historical (that is, they reflect what has happened in the past, rather than commenting on the present or looking ahead to the future). No business can assume that the environment in which it operates will remain the same. The conditions that contributed to past performance, however recent, are bound to change at some point. For example, the number of competitors in a market may increase, or a healthy economy may suddenly descend into recession. Although most large companies produce a chairman's statement, which may speculate on future prospects, this document is not, strictly speaking, part of the accounts and may be deliberately written to create an overly favourable impression.

## 60.3 Analysing ratios over time

Most published accounts provide data covering the most recent two years. This allows a comparison between this year and last year, which is useful. Unfortunately there are risks with such limited comparisons. This year's profit of £10 million may look great compared with last year's £7 million. But what if the full story is as shown in Figure 60.1? Instead of being an impressive jump from 2014, the £10 million profit looks part of a downward profit trend.

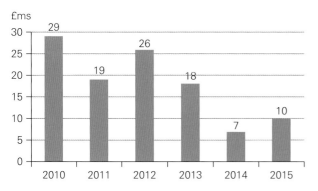

**Figure 60.1** Annual profit trends

Comparing ratios over time helps not only to get a sense of trends, but also to understand what a business is capable of. Accountants are said to believe that 1.5 is the right figure for the current ratio, but Sainsbury's has often had a figure of around 0.75. The fact that the business has coped with such a low level of apparent liquidity may suggest it would be no problem if Sainsbury's had a similar level in future.

The implications that may arise from ratio comparisons over time are shown in Table 60.1.

**Table 60.1** Ratio trends

| Ratio trend over time | Example | Implications |
| --- | --- | --- |
| Falling current ratio | 1.4 two years ago; 0.9 last year; 0.6 this year | Worryingly sharp fall in liquidity; needs to be tackled immediately, e.g. through a rights issue |
| Rising receivables days | 42 two years ago; 48 last year; 59 this year | Customers are taking significantly longer to pay, which will drain your own cash holdings and therefore hit liquidity |
| Falling gearing | 52% two years ago; 48% last year; 40% this year | Gearing has dropped from being a bit too high/risky to being normal/safer |
| Falling ROCE | 34% two years ago; 23% last year; 14% this year | Dramatic fall in profitability, perhaps because competitors have caught you up; you've lost your competitive advantage |

## 60.4 Analysing ratios in comparison with other businesses

When SuperGroup plc (SuperDry) floated onto the stock market in Spring 2010, it was a young company in need of yardsticks. It knew it was doing well, but how well? It made sense to compare its achievements with those of another independent, quirky fashion retailer Ted Baker plc. Were its gross margins high enough? (If not, perhaps prices could be pushed higher.) And was it getting long enough credit periods from suppliers?

**Table 60.2** SuperGroup vs Ted Baker inter-firm comparison

| Ratio | SuperGroup plc 26 April 2014 | Ted Baker plc 25 January 2014 | Conclusions |
|---|---|---|---|
| Gross margins | 59.7% | 61.7% | Very similar, with Ted Baker achieving slightly higher value added |
| Operating margins | 14.3% | 12.3% | SuperGroup's slight superiority suggests their overheads are lower than Ted Baker's |
| Return on capital | 21.0% | 35.3% | Ted Baker's remarkable figures show efficient use of its invested long-term capital |
| Inventory turnover | 2.23 times | 1.53 times | Both are remarkably slow (for fashion clothing firms) but SuperGroup is better |
| Payables (days) | 123.8 days | 133.9 days | Both very slow, again; suppliers have to wait 4 months+ to be paid |

Ultimately, as with a student's results in a test, figures need something to compare them with. In the above table, young SuperGroup plc can feel very pleased to be so similar to well-established Ted Baker plc. But SuperGroup's management can see that they should work hard to improve their return on capital employed.

'How do you explain to an intelligent public that it is possible for two companies in the same industry to follow entirely different accounting principles and both get a true and fair audit report?' M. Lafferty, banker and writer

## 60.5 Problems interpreting accounts

Although the purpose of a firm's accounts is to assign a value to the items contained within them, there are a number of reasons why such values should be treated with caution.

### Receivables

Firms are usually content to sell goods on credit to customers in order to generate sales; any outstanding payments are recorded as a current asset on the balance sheet. However, this figure tells us very little about the nature of the receivables themselves. Does the overall figure consist of regular customers who can be relied upon to pay on time, or long overdue amounts that are unlikely to ever be received? A high proportion of receivables made up of bad debts will result in an overvaluation of a firm's current assets on the balance sheet, increasing the chances of liquidity problems.

### Inventories

The value of inventory at the end of a trading period affects both the value of the business due to its inclusion on the balance sheet (under current assets) and the value of profit (due to its effect on cost of goods sold in the trading account). But how reliable is the value attached to it? The value of inventories can change rapidly, especially in industries subject to frequent changes in customer tastes. The traditional accounting practice is to value stock at cost or net realisable value, whichever is the lower. This means that the value of unsellable stock is potentially zero.

## Profit quality

The ability to generate profit is generally accepted as a key indicator of success. However, it is also worth checking the source of this profit in order to assess the likelihood of such profits continuing into the future. Selling off a piece of machinery at a price above its book value will generate a surplus, but this can only happen once and is, therefore, described as being of low profit quality. It is important that a firm's accounts separate 'one-off' low-quality profit from the high-quality profit that results from its normal trading activities.

## 60.6 Manipulating the published accounts

'Research evidence is consistent with the view that managers use latitude in existing financial reporting to benefit themselves.' Lawrence Revsine, US academic

There are a number of reasons why a business may decide to manipulate its accounts in order to flatter its financial position at a particular point in time. Such practices, known as window dressing or creative accounting, do not necessarily mean that fraud has been committed, but may nevertheless result in the users of accounts being misled. Window-dressing can create the impression that a business is financially stronger than it actually is. This can help to secure loans or support the sale of new shares. Common methods of window dressing include the following.

**Real business**

Autonomy, the British software company accused of large-scale fraud following a takeover by HP, misstated profits by a factor of more than five, according to revised accounts. In 2010, Autonomy Systems Limited, the subsidiary responsible for its European trading, reported profit after tax of £105.7m. In the restated version, the company's bottom line shows only £19.6m.

In the original accounts, audited by Deloitte, revenues were £175.6m. The restated turnover of £81.3m, signed off by HP's auditors Ernst & Young and filed on 3 February 2014 at Companies House, is less than half as much.

The revised accounts represent the first time HP has published financial details to support its fraud allegations. Autonomy's boss Mike Lynch, who denies wrongdoing, has said its claims are based on a misunderstanding of the difference between international accounting standards and US accounting rules. HP has dismissed his claims in turn. Mr Lynch founded Autonomy, which makes software for searching corporate databases, in Cambridge in 1996. It grew fast to report worldwide sales of $870m (£534m) in 2010, before HP outbid rivals to buy the business for £7.1bn.

Source: Adapted from *The Daily Telegraph* 3 February 2014

- *Sale and leaseback of fixed assets:* this allows a business to continue to use assets but disguises a poor or deteriorating liquidity position by generating a sudden injection of cash
- *Bringing forward sales:* a sale is recognised (and included in profit calculations) when an order is made, rather than when payment is received. Encouraging customers to place orders earlier than usual will mean that they are included at the end of one financial period rather than at the start of the next, giving an apparent boost to revenue and profit. (This is what Tesco admitted to doing in 2014.)

The Companies Act 2006 places a legal obligation on companies to provide accounts that are audited and give a true and fair view of their financial position. In addition, the Financial Reporting Council has the responsibility of providing a regulatory framework in order to create greater uniformity in the way company accounts are drawn up. Despite this, the pressure on plc chief executives is likely to mean that window dressing practices will persist.

## 60.7 Strengths and weaknesses of ratio analysis

### Strengths

Ratio analysis has stood the test of more than fifty years in use – worldwide. It is used widely by financial analysts and journalists, by trade unions (about to

negotiate on pay for their members) and by managers themselves. Among the key strengths:

- Focusing on specific areas of the accounts makes comparisons much quicker and easier to do, such as comparisons over time. In the workbook section is a question on John Lewis that includes seven years of accounting data – only with ratios would such a task be possible.
- Most users of accounts are interested in what rather than why; for instance they want to know what the gearing level is rather than why it's at that level; ratios give this information with stunning speed.
- Managements can gain huge insight from their rivals' performance as shown by ratios; perhaps Pepsi is managing to give shorter credit periods to customers (benefiting Pepsi's cash flow); Coca-Cola executives would want to know that.

### Weaknesses

The main single weakness is to take the figures from ratio analysis as if they are facts; the reality is that they are more like averages – and averages can be deceiving. The average temperature for the year in London and in Calgary, Canada is similar at around 10 degrees centigrade. But in London a typical range is from +2 to +24 centigrade. In Calgary it's from −12 to +29.

## Five Whys and a How

| Question | Answer |
|---|---|
| Why is it helpful to use inter-firm ratio comparisons? | Because comparing one firm's ratios to those of a rival helps in identifying strengths and weaknesses |
| Why may managers be tempted to window dress their accounts? | By making the accounts look better to outsiders, it may be easier to get credit and thereby keep the business going |
| Why might one firm's strength be another's weakness? | If a manufacturer takes a long time to pay a supplier, that's a strength for the manufacturer but a weakness for the supplier. |
| Why is Mr Lafferty puzzled? (see quote on page 384) | Because he struggles to believe that two very different accounting systems (and financial results) can both be right. |
| Why may a sale and leaseback be used for window dressing? | Because it turns a property asset into cash, which can help the business show stronger liquidity |
| How did Tesco window dress its profit statement in 2014? | By bringing forward 'sales' that had not yet been made |

## Evaluation: Value and limitations of financial ratios

Accounting information plays a key role in assessing the value and performance of a business. However, using such information alone, and failing to consider other relevant factors, will give an incomplete picture of a firm's current position and future potential. The quality of the workforce, investment in new technology and the state of the market in which it operates may be difficult to quantify but may be more accurate indicators of a firm's long-term success than an impressive set of final accounts.

## Key terms

**Bad debts:** when a firm decides that amounts outstanding as a result of credit sales are unlikely to be recovered, perhaps because the customer concerned has gone into liquidation.

**Going concern:** the accounting assumption that, in the absence of any evidence to the contrary, a business will continue to operate for the foreseeable future.

**Net realisable value:** this is the value given to an asset (usually stock) on the balance sheet if it is expected to be sold for less than its historic cost.

**Profit quality:** this assesses the likelihood of the source of the profit made by a business continuing in the future. High-quality profit is usually that which is generated by a firm's usual trading activities, whereas low-quality profit comes from a one-off source.

**Rights issue:** raising extra share capital by offering existing shareholders the right to buy extra shares at a price discount.

**Window dressing:** the practice of presenting a firm's accounts in a way that flatters its financial position (for example, selling and leasing back assets in order to generate cash and disguise a poor liquidity position).

# Workbook

## A. Revision questions

(30 marks; 30 minutes)

1. What is meant by the phrase 'a true and fair view' in the context of accounting? (3)

2. Identify three aspects of a business that may increase its value but are unlikely to be included in its accounts. (3)

3. Choose two ratios that can provide an interesting comparison between discount airlines easyJet and Ryanair. Explain why you chose each. (6)

4. Explain one weakness in using ratio analysis to assess the latest year's performance of Walls ice cream. (4)

5. Explain why it might be useful to analyse the trends in a firm's gearing level over the past 5 years. (3)

6. What is meant by the term 'window dressing'? (3)

7. Describe two reasons why a firm may window dress its accounts. (4)

8. Outline two ways in which a business could attempt to window dress its accounts. (4)

## B. Revision exercises
### DATA RESPONSE

**Is John Lewis the next Tesco?**

In the past ten years the John Lewis Partnership has become the national treasure of UK retailing. Both its John Lewis and Waitrose arms have been growing rapidly, in sales, in store numbers and via outstanding execution of online shopping. Both arms of the business have also been growing their market share: an especially fine achievement for Waitrose, as it's the only major retailer to withstand the market share pressure from discounters Aldi and Lidl.

As John Lewis announces each year's financial results, they are greeted with acclaim by the financial press. In 2014 *The Guardian* shouted: 'John Lewis overtakes Marks & Spencer as darling of the high street' and then went on to say 'Waitrose and John Lewis both experience record sales and the company's 91,000 staff are to share a £200 million bonus'. The latter statement was truth – but very incomplete truth. In fact the John Lewis staff were to get a 15 per cent annual bonus instead of the 17 per cent one they got the previous year. Unsurprisingly, because annual profits were down.

A possible explanation for the good press is that while banking scandals have damaged the reputation of bank plcs such as Barclays and Lloyds, John Lewis is employee-owned. It is a co-operative thanks to the amazing generosity of John Spedan Lewis who, in 1950, put all the shares in John Lewis into a partnership structure to be owned by the staff.

Without doubt John Lewis has been doing very well in terms of sales and consumer admiration. But not that long ago the same was true of Tesco. But when Tesco's ups turned down in 2014, the company had a degree of protection from a relatively strong balance sheet. Above all else, perhaps, it had overseas assets it could sell. But what of John Lewis?

So what has been going on during John Lewis's dynamic growth phase? How has it affected key stakeholders? And how does the balance sheet look today compared with 2008? Your task is to analyse the following data and build your arguments.

**Appendix A.** John Lewis Partnership income statements (year to end of January). All figures in £millions.

| | 2008 | 2009 | 2010 | 2011 | 2012 | 2013 | 2014 |
|---|---|---|---|---|---|---|---|
| Revenue | 6,052 | 6,267 | 6,735 | 7,362 | 7,759 | 8,465 | 9,028 |
| Cost of sales | (4,007) | (4,195) | (4,460) | (4,879) | (5,167) | (5,640) | (6,009) |
| Gross profit | 2,045 | 2,072 | 2,275 | 2,483 | 2,592 | 2,825 | 3,019 |
| Operating expenses | (1,651) | (1,751) | (1,885) | (2,052) | (2,199) | (2,372) | (2,595) |
| Operating profit | 394 | 321 | 390 | 431 | 393 | 453 | 424 |
| Net financing costs | (14) | (42) | (83) | (63) | (40) | (110) | (95) |
| Partnership bonus | (181) | (125) | (151) | (195) | (165) | (211) | (202.5) |
| Pre-tax profit | 199 | 281* | 156 | 173 | 188 | 132 | 126.5 |
| Tax | (60) | (48) | (49) | (46) | (52) | (31) | (25) |
| Profit for the year | 139 | 233* | 107 | 127 | 136 | 101 | 101.5 |

*Includes an exceptional one-off profit

**Appendix B.** John Lewis Partnership balance sheets (last day of January). All figures in £millions.

| | 2008 | 2009 | 2010 | 2011 | 2012 | 2013 | 2014 |
|---|---|---|---|---|---|---|---|
| Non-current assets | 3,120 | 3,329 | 3,568 | 3,775 | 4,005 | 4,116 | 4,385 |
| Inventories | 345 | 352 | 399 | 422 | 465 | 514 | 554 |
| Receivables | 212 | 139 | 168 | 211 | 223 | 192 | 226 |
| Cash | 135 | 221 | 574 | 538 | 554 | 542 | 360 |
| Current liabilities | (956) | (899) | (1,076) | (1,284) | (1,540) | (1,634) | (1,706) |
| Net current assets | (264) | (187) | 65 | (113) | (298) | (386) | (566) |
| Non-current liabilities | (1,172) | (1,419) | (1,928) | (1,590) | (1,697) | (1,828) | (2,037) |
| Net assets | 1,684 | 1,723 | 1,705 | 2,072 | 2,010 | 1,902 | 1,782 |
| Total equity | 1,684 | 1,723 | 1,705 | 2,072 | 2,010 | 1.902 | 1,782 |

**Appendix C.** John Lewis Partnership – other performance indicators.

| | 2008 | 2009 | 2010 | 2011 | 2012 | 2013 | 2014 |
|---|---|---|---|---|---|---|---|
| Staff levels* | 44,900 | 45,100 | 45,900 | 48,500 | 51,100 | 53,200 | 56,040 |
| Bonus as a % of pay | 20% | 13% | 15% | 18% | 14% | 17% | 15% |
| Number of John Lewis stores | N/A | 27 | 29 | 32 | 35 | 39 | 40 |
| John Lewis selling space (million sq ft) | 3.7 | 3.9 | 3.9 | 4.0 | 4.2 | 4.5 | 4.6 |
| Number of Waitrose stores | N/A | 198 | 223 | 243 | 272 | 290 | 305 |
| Waitrose selling space (million sq ft) | 3.6 | 4.0 | 4.2 | 4.6 | 4.9 | 5.2 | 5.4 |
| Total J. L. selling space (m. sq. ft.) | 7.3 | 7.9 | 8.2 | 8.6 | 9.1 | 9.7 | 10.0 |

* Full-time equivalents

## Questions (50 marks; 60 minutes)

**1. a)** Explain how three stakeholders might be interested in Appendix A and B: the John Lewis Partnership annual accounts. (6)

**b)** To what extent could it be said that John Lewis Partnership staff are the most important stakeholder group when appraising these accounts? (16)

**2.** Analyse Appendix C to show what light it sheds on the performance of the John Lewis Partnership over recent years. (9)

**3.** 'The financial health of a business is reflected in its liquidity and gearing.'

**a)** Explain why that is the case. (4)

**b)** Use relevant accounting ratios to evaluate the changes in John Lewis's financial health between 2008 and 2014. (15)

## C. Extend your understanding

**1.** When new Tesco boss Dave Lewis joined in Autumn 2014 he was advised to spend three months visiting stores and talking to customers. To what extent might he have benefitted rather more from a serious ratio analysis over time and between rival grocery chains? (25)

**2.** Window dressing has been described as 'flexibilities within accounting that provide opportunities for manipulation, deceit and misrepresentation'. To what extent would you agree that such actions should be illegal? (25)

**Linked to:** Corporate objectives, strategy and tactics, Chapter 54; The value of SWOT analysis, Chapter 56; Financial ratio analysis, Chapter 59; Value and limitations of financial ratios, Chapter 60; Assessing short- and long-term performance, Chapter 62; Different measures of assessing business performance, Chapter 63.

## Definition

Legally, public limited companies must publish a great deal of financial data that can be used to measure business performance. It may be that non-financial measures of employee, market and operations data are equally important.

## 61.1 Introduction

In 2013 Samsung was on a roll. Profits were booming and they were being touted as the most successful electronics company in the world. Profits of nearly $30 billion seemed to confirm this (see Figure 61.1). But actually there were problems. Samsung was the world market leader in Smartphones (with a 30 per cent market share) but in the world's biggest market – China – newcomer Xiaomi was growing dramatically. In the third quarter of 2014 Xiaomi's 5.2 per cent global market share compared with 1.5 per cent in 2013. Then in the West came the launch of the hugely successful iPhone 6 – and Samsung was floundering. In January 2015 Samsung warned that its 2014 profits would be 30 per cent down.

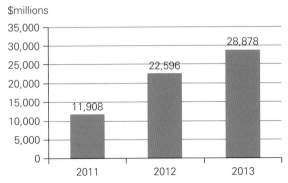

**Figure 61.1** Samsung's global profit for the year

To understand what 2014 was going to be like for Samsung, understanding the market was much more important than having the profit figures for the previous years. So what are the key non-financial pieces of data that companies should look at? To a great extent that depends on the company itself, especially its corporate objectives. But some general measurements of non-financial performance are gathered by almost every business. It is reasonable to start by looking at them under the headings:

● Markets and marketing

● People and the labour market

● Operations management.

'Measurement is the first step that leads to control and eventually to improvement. If you can't measure something, you can't understand it. If you can't understand it, you can't control it. If you can't control it, you can't improve it.' H. J. Harrington, business consultant

## 61.2 Marketing measurements of performance

Ultimately there are only two types of customer: new ones and old ones. The old ones may be actively loyal, they may admire and believe in the business; or they may be loyal solely due to inertia. In the latter case they may go to a specific sweetshop because it's on the way from school to home; they don't much like the owner or the prices – but hey, it's on the way. Therefore a new sweetshop opening five doors along may easily scoop up the business. Before opening that new shop, then, it would be wonderful to know if the customers of the existing sweetshop are loyal or passively inert.

And then there are the new customers. These are a delight but can be expensive to acquire. For example a business such as ASOS will know that its profits come from existing ('free') customers, whereas gaining a new customer may cost a lot of money in media and social media advertising.

Already, then, some key marketing measurements have been identified:

- What percentage of customers are repeat; what percentage are new?
- Of the 'old' customers, what percentage are committed and loyal? And what percentage are passive?
- What's the cost per head of gaining new customers (perhaps calculated as marketing expenditure divided by the number of new customers)?

In addition there are some standard – but important – ones:

- Market share – per brand and for the company as a whole, for example Cadbury's Twirl has a 2.2 per cent market share and the company as a whole has 35 per cent of the UK chocolate market
- Gross profit margin: the higher the better; this is highly secret information, but an indication of it comes with these figures for customer price per kilo for 2014 filled Easter Eggs:
  - Cadbury Creme Egg: £9.61
  - Cadbury Egg & Spoon: £16.42
  - Lindt Lindor: £19.37
- New product sales as a percentage of total sales; again, most companies would be delighted to see this figure as high as possible – if only because it proves the skills of the new product development arm of the marketing department.

## 61.3 Human relations measurements of performance

Whereas there would be widespread agreement among marketing professionals about performance measures, the same is not true in the management of people. Businesses such as Google or ooVoo would be very sceptical of measures that might assess the quality of input by their staff. Even if they accepted measurements, they would be to do with engagement, teamwork and non-conformity, whereas many other businesses focus on productivity, lateness and conformity. The differences largely revolve around hard and soft HRM, a topic covered in Chapter 45 of this book.

For a business with a hard HRM approach, suitable performance measurements might include:

- recruitment cost per new staff member
- graduate trainee retention rate
- overall employee retention rate
- customer calls handled per hour
- lateness for work as a percentage of days worked.

As you can see, all are relatively easily measured and reflect on quantities relating to staff rather than qualities.

For a business with a soft HRM approach, suitable performance measurements might include:

- annual ratings of job satisfaction
- diversity statistics at senior management levels compared with junior staff
- promotion data broken down into internal versus external (to see whether there is strong upward mobility within the organisation)
- training £s spent per employee.

It remains the case, though, that measurements such as these would rarely be used in the most dynamic workplaces, such as advertising agencies, investment banks or IT start-ups. In places where the organisational culture is dynamic and purposeful, staff are trusted to give of their best – and the key measurement is whether they succeed at their core job.

### Real business

In 2010 and 2011 Jaguar Land Rover was regarded as a backwards-looking, unprofitable carmaker. This was reflected in undergraduates' ratings of the company as a pretty undesirable employer. Top graduates looked elsewhere. Since then, the HR department has taken a great deal of pride from seeing the company jumping up the graduate league tables, as provided by *The Times* and *The Guardian* newspapers. It's clearly a valuable way of measuring HR success.

**Table 61.1** JLR's leap in being a desirable employer

|  | 2011/2 | 2012/3 | 2013/4 | 2014/5 |
|---|---|---|---|---|
| The Times Top 100 | 60 | 26 | 21 | 16 |
| The Guardian Top 300 | 127 | 30 | 20 | 8 |

'I have been struck again and again by how important measurement is to improving the human condition.' Bill Gates, founder, Microsoft

## 61.4 Operations management measurements of performance

Whereas there can be debate about the role of measurement in people management, there is none in operations. Everything that can be measured is measured – and always has been. This is partly because customers want their goods delivered to the exact specification at the right time – and partly because operations (making stuff) embodies the highest-cost part of the business process. In other words if costs are excessive here, the competitiveness and perhaps survival of the organisation will be put at risk. Quite simply, if you are Land Rover, making Land Rovers is the highest-cost part of the business!

All companies will measure the aspects of their operations set out in Table 61.2, though some will use more of the detailed measures (on the right) than others.

**Table 61.2** Measuring operational performance

| Areas of operations | Detailed measures |
|---|---|
| 1. Managing quality | Cutting customer returns from 5 per cent to 2 per cent<br>In 2014 the US JD Power survey of vehicle dependability placed Lexus first (by a large margin) and the BMW Mini last |
| 2. Managing waste | In 2013/14 Tesco counted its annual food waste at 56,580 tonnes; it plans to report each year on how well it is doing compared with that starting point |
| 3. Productivity | Sales per square ft. (Sainsbury's, sales per square foot down from £20.42 in 2010 to £18.93 in 2014)<br>Output per worker (at JLR, cars per worker per year have increased from 14 in 2011 to 15.53 in 2014) |
| 5. Managing time | At Panetteria Italiana the production time for making then baking bread has shortened from 5 hrs to 4 hrs<br>At Virgin Rail, 81.2 per cent of trains arrived within ten minutes of their scheduled arrival time in October-November 2014 |
| 6. Managing growth | Capital investment (at JLR, investment spending has jumped from £900 million in 2011 to £2,680 million in 2014) |

'If you can't measure it, you can't manage it…. Not true.' Liz Ryan, business writer, Forbes magazine

### Five Whys and a How

| Question | Answer |
|---|---|
| Why may it be hard to manage things you can't measure? | You may feel you can't be sure whether you're doing the right things or not |
| Why would Lindt be proud to have the highest Easter Egg price (see page 391)? | Because it shows the added value they've achieved with the Lindor brand (customers will pay twice what they'll pay for a Creme Egg) |
| Why may there be a problem if marketing managers have many different performance measures they can use to judge themselves? | They can pick and choose; this year choose one favourable statistic; next year choose another; so they must be forced to pick one or two and stick with them |
| Why are performance measures used especially within operations management? | Because productivity, quality and stock levels are facts that can be counted; arguably some HR measures may over-simplify |
| Why may Liz Ryan be right (see quote above)? | Because business stars such as Steve Jobs and Sergey Brin (Google) focused 100 per cent on creating great products – the performance measures were for junior managers to pick up later on |
| How should performance be measured at a hospital? | In many, many different ways, but perhaps 'Are you proud to work here?' might be the single most telling measure |

Measurement is hugely important, but involves many hazards. Above all else, the process of measurement can distort behaviour. When GPs are measured on the basis of treating a patient every 8 minutes, it should be no surprise that patients feel they're getting a less personal service (and perhaps signs of serious illness might be missed). In addition, those things that are not or cannot be measured may be treated more lightly. Some teachers know that, when observed, a 'starter' and a 'plenary' are on the observer's checklist; so they make sure those boxes are ticked – perhaps at the cost of a nicely quirky, interesting lesson.

Ultimately, everyone at work is being measured, whether they realise it or not. The key question is whether the right things are being measured. In his first season for then-Premier League side Fulham, centre forward Bobby Zamora scored only two goals in thirty-five games. Yet manager Roy Hodgson appreciated that Zamora's all-round play was important to the side, and he stayed as the number one striker. Other managers would have dropped Zamora for underperformance at scoring goals. The following year Zamora's great form took Fulham to the Europa League final.

# Workbook

## A. Revision questions

(25 marks; 25 minutes)

1. Explain why companies want actively loyal customers, not just regulars who are there due to inertia. (4)

2. Why might it be more expensive to gain a new customer than to keep an old one? (5)

3. Jaguar Land Rover went from 127th to 8th in *The Guardian* list of desirable employers. Explain how the business might benefit from this improvement. (5)

4. How might careful measurement of its diversity statistics lead to improved business performance by a company? (5)

5. Outline one way in which a retailer could measure the effectiveness of its waste management? (3)

6. How might small bakery Panetteria Italiana benefit from cutting its bread-making time from 5 to 4 hours? (3)

## B. Revision exercises
### DATA RESPONSE

2014 was an awful year for Morrisons supermarkets. It lost market share, went from profit into loss and eventually lost its boss, Dalton Phillips. It was widely believed that it was being squeezed by three forces that were hard to overcome in the short term:

- The growth of grocery discounters Aldi and Lidl from 5.2 per cent to 8.3 per cent market share between January 2013 and January 2015 (in the same period Morrisons market share fell from 12.4 per cent to 11.3 per cent)
- The growth of convenience retailing at the expense of big, traditional supermarkets
- The growth of online grocery selling at the expense of supermarkets.

Dalton Phillips was shown the door because he had been in charge of Morrisons for 5 years, yet all three of these problems had been tackled far too late.

In its 2014 annual report, Morrisons provided the following measurements of non-financial performance:

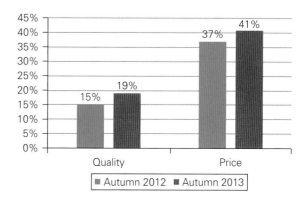

**Figure 61.2** Most important driver of product choice (Morrisons 2014)

Source: Morrisons Annual Report 2014

Use of on-the-spot price comparisons:

2010: 9 per cent of all Morrisons' shoppers

2013: 25 per cent of all Morrisons' shoppers

| Channel sales growth forecast 2013–2018 | | | |
|---|---|---|---|
| | **Sales 2013** | **Sales 2018** | **% change** |
| **Online** | £6.5bn | £14.6bn | +125% |
| **Convenience** | £35.6bn | £46.2bn | +30% |

## C. Extend your understanding

1. To what extent should the chief executive of a large company such as British Airways be judged on the basis of non-financial factors? (25)

### Questions (25 marks, 30 minutes)

1. Analyse how Morrisons might use two of the performance measures given above. (9)

2. To what extent should Dalton Phillips be blamed for the effects of external factors on the Morrisons business? (16)

# Chapter

# 62 Assessing short- and long-term performance

**Linked to:** Corporate objectives, strategy and tactics, Chapter 54; The value of SWOT analysis, Chapter 56; Financial ratio analysis, Chapter 59; Value and limitations of financial ratios, Chapter 60; How to analyse data other than financial statements, Chapter 61; Different measures of assessing business performance, Chapter 63.

## Definition

Short term means the timescale within which decisions can be reversed without causing much damage. Long term is a timescale in which resource commitments make it hard to back down.

## 62.1 Risks of confusing short- and long-term data analysis

In October 2009, two years into the life of his brainchild Fresh & Easy (Tesco USA) boss Terry Leahy dismissed the one year trading loss of $259 million by saying: 'We have been making good progress in developing the Fresh & Easy business'. Actually its 130 American stores were losing $2 million each per year. Oddly, Terry Leahy saw these facts as short-term problems that would seem unimportant in the long term. He hoped to create 1,000 Tesco stores in America and challenge WalMart (the world's Number 1 retailer). Now, with the benefit of hindsight, and the closure of the whole operation, it is clear that the £2 billion Tesco wasted on the whole venture was due to confusion between short- and long-term data analysis. Leahy thought the data was a short-term misreading of the long term. In fact it told the exactly right story: Tesco had nothing to offer the US grocery market.

## 62.2 Causes and effects of short-termism

Short-termism is when the actions of managers show an obsession with immediate issues rather than long-term

ones. Often such managers will use lots of long-term words such as mission, aims, strategy and legacy; but staff will soon learn when the real spur to action is this year or this month's budget. In a report on the topic, the Institute of Directors produced an interesting list of possible symptoms of short-termism:

● Inadequate expenditure on research and development

● Accounting adjustments that inflate current earnings

● A bias towards high dividend payouts and share buybacks, at the expense of investment

● Adoption of executive pay schemes that reward achievement of short-term financial goals

● Overly zealous cuts in employment levels, which destroy the company's stock of human capital

● A disregard for longer-term risks in the company's products, services or business strategy

● An excessive focus on acquisitions rather than organic growth.

### The causes of short-termism

The most commonly cited explanation of short-termism by UK companies is the relationship with financial markets; many people believe that the plc structure encourages short-termism. Many years ago Richard Branson's Virgin Group was a publicly quoted plc; he eventually took the group private because he hated the pressures to care more about immediate results than long-term strategy. The reason for these pressures is simple: City investors are more important today than private shareholders, and the City traders are measured on a quarterly basis. Pension funds controlling £billions judge their main advisors and investors every three months, to measure performance against stock market indices such as the FTSE 100. So if City investors are measured every three months, no wonder those investors care passionately about the short-term performance of the companies they've invested in.

Other important causes of short-termism:

● The widespread use in the City of short-term focused performance measures such as Earnings Per Share (EPS) as a way of judging the bonus level to be paid to the directors; EPS can be boosted by the ultimate short-termism measure: buying shares back from shareholders; this boosts a company's gearing yet creates a higher share price and therefore bonus level.

- The threat of takeover. When share prices are high there is usually a fashion for making takeover bids. So companies like to make it harder (and more expensive) by boosting their short-term profit.
- The bosses of UK firms are unusually likely to have had a career based in finance; therefore they have no inherent understanding of the long-term thinking that is more instinctive among engineers, scientists and marketing executives. In Germany and Japan, engineers often become the chief executive.

---

'The result of long-term relationships (with suppliers) is better and better quality and lower and lower costs.' W. Edwards Deming, quality guru

---

## The effects of short-termism

The most important effect of short-termism is underestimating or ignoring the opportunities that may exist in the long term. Companies such as Marks & Spencer, Morrisons, HMV, Game and Waterstones kept on believing in the profits to be made off-line despite all the evidence of the consumer move to online. By contrast Arsenal FC spent £400 million on the move from Highbury (35,000 capacity) to the Emirates stadium (capacity 60,000). This showed the board's ability to think about the long-term interests of the club. Interestingly this 'long-termist' example is from a private company, not a plc.

---

'Short-termism curtails ambition, inhibits long-term thinking and provides a disincentive to invest in research, new capabilities, products, training, recruitment and skills.' Sir George Cox, businessman

---

Other effects of short-termism:

- Reluctance to invest in capacity, training, R&D and perhaps also in image-building advertising
- Decisions that seem wise in the short term, but not down the line, such as when Waterstones sold off its loss-making online book sales division – to Amazon!
- Performance reward systems may over-focus on short-term gains, encouraging staff to achieve profit today even if it's at the expense of tomorrow; in the ten years to 2014 WH Smith constantly pushed their prices up; this was great for short-term profit but at the expense of the long-term market share of the business.

## 62.3 The tyranny of short-term reporting

In theory, the directors of a business are supposed to be looking ahead to the future while the managers get on with the day-to-day process of managing customer relations, suppliers and budgets. In an ideal world the chief executive would agree the overall budget for the coming year, and get on with long-term strategic thinking. Towards the end of the year key staff would come to the chief executive to say: yes, we've met our targets so the profit will be £x.

But short-term reporting makes this very difficult to achieve – especially because of the role of 'City analysts' (who are really representatives of the major share trading businesses). These analysts recommend whether to buy or sell shares, and expect to be given close guidance by plcs on current performance and therefore the profit that can be expected in this financial year. If a chief executive suggests a profit range of £100 – 105 million is likely, but the actual figure comes in at £92 million, the share price will fall sharply. Then analysts will talk about weak management (which business journalists will repeat).

So company bosses are trying to manage the expectations of the analysts by delivering the 'right' profit figure. Ideally this should be 10 per cent or so up on last year. But what a crazy world that implies! Just think of all the external factors that can blow a company's profit figures off course, from warm autumn weather (bad for clothing retailers) to a recession in a key market. Company bosses are in effect being encouraged to massage the figures to give the stock market what it wants. Perhaps it's surprising that scandals such as Tesco's 2014 profit overstatement occur so rarely.

---

### Real business

Sir Clive Thompson was once a stock market favourite. For ten years his company Rentokil Initial plc achieved profit growth of 20+ per cent a year. Thompson earned the title 'Mr Twenty Per Cent'. But after the ten years of success the business imploded in a series of profit collapses. Eventually he was sacked, with his successor saying: 'Sir Clive had become too obsessed with meeting short-term profit targets and had failed to invest in long-term top-line growth, a shortfall especially evident in staff recruitment and training'.

---

## 62.4 Plc Britain versus Mittelstand Germany

For many years big business in Britain has meant publicly listed companies, with shares bought and sold on the stock market. Generally the value of the British stock market is around 100-120 per cent of the value of annual GDP (the national income). Germany, by contrast, has a business sector dominated by world-class, medium-sized but family-owned and run businesses – the Mittelstand. The value of the German stock market is only about 40 per cent of the value of annual German GDP. So whereas the business pages of British papers are dominated by the latest results from plcs, in Germany there is more likely to be reporting on business issues and market opportunities.

When Germans are asked about their Mittelstand, they mention two things: family-ownership and humane management. Economists would add in two other features: long-term thinking and a focus on doing one thing well. The latter means that the typical Mittelstand firm is a world leader in a limited field, such as diesel car exhaust systems. A 2013 German government report showed that Germany had twenty times more 'world market leaders' than the UK – and strikingly more than America (see Figure 62.1). This is great for exports but also works well for employment, with the Mittelstand employing nearly 60 per cent of the German workforce, but 80 per cent of all trainees.

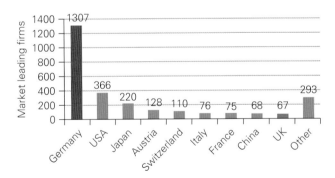

**Figure 62.1** World market leaders

The amazing success story of the German Mittelstand must be contrasted with the plc. First and foremost legal requirements force large plcs to report on profits and trading every six months. Then City analysts and the media will pore over the figures and declare the business a star or a dog. Tesco was unbeatable until it suddenly became untouchable. Every chief executive is in thrall to 'the market' and has to organise strategy and publicity accordingly.

The result is an excessive focus on the next set of results. This is rather more like the life of a Premier League manager than makes any sense. This helps to explain how a business such as Marks & Spencer can spend twenty years, under many different bosses, all failing to address the company's underlying problems. Long-term strategy can become empty words in the short-termist world of the plc.

In more recent years the importance of the plc in Britain has only been diluted by the arrival of private equity businesses. They may buy a plc (such as Boots the Chemist), make it private, load it up with debt, then run it as a combination of a cash cow and a tax-avoidance scheme. This can end up being even more short-termist than a plc structure. Needless to say private equity operations are much less significant in Germany than in Britain.

**Table 62.1:** The British versus the German business model

|  | **Plc** | **Mittelstand** | **Private equity** |
|---|---|---|---|
| **Typical financial structure** | Strong equity base Moderate gearing | Strong equity base Moderate gearing | High – very high gearing |
| **Typical ownership structure** | Owned by many, relatively small shareholders | Family-owned or majority family-owned with some shares listed on the stock market | Owned by a financially-focused business registered overseas (for tax reasons) |
| **Typical approach to spending on R&D and trainee staff** | Varies, but many will look for a low-spend model with high levels of outsourcing (and low investment in staff) | Desire for very long-term success and a sense of moral duty creates a culture of investment in people and technology | Again varies, but would tend to be even more short-termist than a plc |
| **Typical business objectives** | Maximise short-term share price to keep the market happy, and to enjoy a big bonus due to the high share price | Maintain a world-leading position to hand over a continuingly successful business to the next generation | Sell the business (or float it back onto the stock market) within 3 years |

'Any jerk can have short-term earnings. You squeeze, squeeze, squeeze, and the company sinks five years later.' Jack Welch, business super-leader

## 62.5 The importance of core competences

Germany's Mittelstand businesses are masters at building long-term, 'core competences'. This term was developed by Prahalad and Hamel in their 1990 Harvard Business Review article 'The Core Competence of the Corporation'. They were referring to 'collective learning across the corporation' that becomes the source of potential competitive advantages. At the time of writing, Apple is launching its first range of watches, with prices from $350 to $17,000. At the heart of the Apple business are core skills that mark the company out: design based on glamour plus simplification, skills at miniaturisation and a mastery of the interface between different functions. This enabled the business to move from computers to consumer electronics and then again to watches. Apple is already looking at the market for self-drive cars. Will its core competences enable it to succeed in that sector as well? Perhaps it will prove too great a stretch.

In everyday chat, most people would probably see Apple's success as marketing driven. The idea of core competences is that these are the fundamental learnings within the business that give it its inner strength within its particular expertise. As of 2015, no other car company has yet managed to make a real dent in the sales established by Toyota for its 'hybrid synergy drive' petrol/electric cars. Across Germany the same is true. The Mittelstand has developed its own expertise in very focused areas, and new competitors struggle to achieve the same mastery of product development and production. Core competences are at the heart of a long-termist approach to business.

### Five Whys and a How

| Question | Answer |
| --- | --- |
| Why is business short-termism a problem for the British economy? | Because it limits our ability to innovate and makes it hard for engineering and manufacturing to grow and thrive – stifling economic growth |
| Why doesn't a government change the rules, and allow financial reporting only once a year? Wouldn't that help? | Probably yes it would. Perhaps only allow an interim, 6-month report in exceptional circumstances. It would take a degree of short-term pressure off the back of plc bosses |
| Why doesn't the UK build a Mittelstand like Germany? | It's enormously difficult to change the national culture; in Britain, business is about making money; in Germany it's about building something great |
| Why might the board of Arsenal FC be capable of more long-term thinking than might be the case with other football clubs? | Some clubs are plcs, with outside shareholders who want profits now, because that boosts the share price; Arsenal is a private limited company |
| Why might 'short-termism curtail ambition' (quote from Sir George Cox, page 396)? | It's hard to have ambitions about the future when you're trying to cope with short-term pressures |
| How has the Mittelstand produced so many world market leaders for German business? | By focusing on the long term through strategies such as heavy investment in R&D and staff training |

Workbook

## Evaluation: Assessing short- and long-term performance

Given the level of pressure for short-term performance faced by many chief executives, it is interesting that City commentators admire most the plcs that sustain long-term success. In Britain a great example is Whitbread plc, which has built up its two key divisions (Costa Coffee and Premier Inn) to deliver huge growth in profits and dividends for more than ten years.

Ultimately what is wanted is a boss who can withstand short-term pressure while steadily delivering long-term success. To achieve this, many bosses like to start by 'kitchen sinking' the company

accounts in their first year. That means throwing every conceivable piece of bad financial news into the income statement, creating a dismal profit picture. From there, the only way is up. So as the business returns to normal profitability the comparison with an awful start makes the boss look impressive. This buys time to perhaps enable the boss to develop a worthwhile, long-term strategy. Needless to say, it would be better if such cunning was unnecessary, and that new bosses were simply given long enough to have a meaningful chance of getting the business onto a new growth path.

## Key terms

**Earnings per share:** company profits after tax divided by the number of shares issued; a rising EPS makes it easy to pay out rising dividends to shareholders.

**Mittelstand:** the family-owned small and medium-sized businesses that are the backbone of the German economy.

**Private equity:** a business set up to buy and sell other businesses, usually financed by debt and helped by active tax avoidance measures.

# Workbook

## A. Revision questions

**(20 marks; 20 minutes)**

1. Explain one possible reason why Terry Leahy wanted to 'challenge WalMart' (see Section 62.1). (4)

2. Explain why 'inadequate expenditure on research and development' might be a symptom of short-termism (see Section 62.2). (4)

3. Explain one possible benefit to a company if it appoints an engineer rather than an accountant to the role of chief executive. (4)

4. Explain why 'City analysts' play an important role in creating a business culture of short-termism. (4)

5. Explain why senior managers working for a plc might be concerned to hear that the business is to be taken into private equity ownership. (4)

## B. Revision exercises
### DATA RESPONSE

### Why strategy matters – Topshop, Zara and China

Back in 2002, when Philip Green bought Arcadia (Topshop), it and Inditex (Zara) were a similar size. By 2013/14 Inditex was making nearly twenty times

more profit than Arcadia. Topshop was and is a retail jewel, with the potential to be huge internationally. It is a retail brand suited perfectly to the emerging young middle classes in China. But by early 2015, Zara owned over 150 stores in China and its owner Inditex had become the world's biggest clothes retailer. Topshop has no stores in China and is a minnow globally. What went wrong?

Green appears regularly in lists of Britain's most admired businessmen. Yet a simple look at Arcadia's performance since 2002 makes it hard to see why. Britain needs business successes such as Zara, creating jobs and earnings from overseas. Why couldn't Topshop have achieved what Zara has? (In the graph of Zara vs Topshop, the actual figures are for Zara's owner Inditex vs Topshop's owner Arcadia Ltd.)

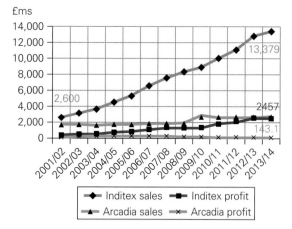

**Figure 62.2** Zara vs Topshop 2001–2014

Zara began in 1975 and has grown thanks to the desire by owner Amancio Ortega to create something of lasting value. At a time when his rivals were getting all their clothes made in the Far East, Ortega was proud that more than half his supplies came from Spain and Portugal. His company Inditex has been famous for its long-term approach to the clothing industry, with care taken over suppliers, staff and the environment.

Cleverly, Zara turned its Western European production into an advantage – being able to respond more quickly than others to changes in catwalk fashion. Today Zara delivers brand new designs twice a week to its stores worldwide, and can respond very quickly to any strong new trend. From early on, Zara adopted lean production as its way of working. Constant attacks on wastage suited Ortega's approach to business; as did minimising the amount of cash tied up in stock.

By contrast Sir Philip Green's business has stood still for ten years. Perhaps in part because of his famously

short-term way of looking at investment. His rule of thumb has always been a 12-month payback period – which is exceptionally rapid. Therefore only sure-fire, ultra-profitable investments work out. In the Table below, sales jumped in 2009 solely because Green decided to merge British Home Stores in with the rest of Arcadia. Excluding that, there has been no growth of significance.

**Table 62.2** Arcadia group sales and profits 2006–2014

|  | Arcadia sales (£millions) | Arcadia profits (£millions) |
|---|---|---|
| 2006/07 | £1,850 | £293 |
| 2007/08 | £1,840 | £275 |
| 2008/09 | £1,900 | £214 |
| 2009/10 | £2,800 | £213 |
| 2010/11 | £2,680 | £133 |
| 2011/12 | £2,679 | £167 |
| 2012/13 | £2,683 | £148 |
| 2013/14 | £2,707 | £143 |

It seems that owner Sir Phillip Green has been distracted by other priorities. In 2005, famously, Arcadia declared a £1,200m dividend to be paid out to the sole shareholder of the business: his wife Mrs Green. As a resident of Monaco, no tax would be paid on this. To find this huge sum, Arcadia needed to borrow £1,000m, which was not that hard to do in pre-crash 2005. Surely this sum would have been better invested taking Topshop to China. Ironically, it may have made Green more money in the longer term.

Is it too late for Topshop to make it in China? Perhaps not, though the middle-market positioning has been adopted in China by Zara, H&M, Gap and many others. Most striking, however, is the importance of focus on the long-term health of a business: Zara's Ortega had it; Arcadia's Green did not.

### Questions (25 marks; 30 minutes)

1. Analyse two reasons why Zara (Inditex) was so successful between 2002 and 2014. (9)

2. Using this business example together with any other businesses you're aware of, to what extent is short-termism a particular problem for British businesses and businesspeople? (16)

# C. Extend your understanding

1. How important do you think it is for a government to try to tackle short-termism in British business? Justify your answer. (25)

2. Some commentators think that it would be impossible to build an effective Mittelstand in Britain. To what extent do you agree? (25)

**Linked to:** Corporate objectives, strategy and tactics, Chapter 54; The value of SWOT analysis, Chapter 56; Financial ratio analysis, Chapter 59; Value and limitations of financial ratios, Chapter 60; How to analyse data other than financial statements, Chapter 61; Assessing short- and long-term performance, Chapter 62.

### Definition

Business performance means how well the company has done in relation to its objectives. The objective may purely be profit, but because that only records what *has* happened, it may be better to find a measurement that can also look to the future.

## 63.1 The value of different measures of business performance

In 2002 twenty-three per cent of accident and emergency (A&E) patients had to wait more than four hours to be seen. In 2003 a target was set that no more than 10 per cent should be left waiting four hours, and by 2004 only 5.3 per cent stayed that long. Here, then, is the point of targets. If the right measures are chosen, management and staff will focus on achieving them. Cutting from 23 per cent to 5.3 per cent in two years is an achievement indeed.

Nevertheless it is worth noting that the period 2002-2004 saw a substantial increase in government spending on the NHS. In January 2015, after several years of budget tightening on A&E departments, performance worsened. In the week ending 4 January 2015 13.3 per cent of visitors to A&E departments had to wait for four hours – the worst performance in years. In other words setting targets is not enough – the resources have to be there to make them achievable.

In its 2014 annual report Tesco includes various non-financial measures of business performance such as:

- Colleague retention: 90 per cent in the UK, 1 per cent down on 2013

- Colleagues being trained for their next role: 6.2 per cent, up 0.7 per cent on 2013

- Supplier agreement to the question 'I am treated with respect': 67 per cent, down 4 per cent on 2013

In addition Tesco provided some interesting data on employment diversity by gender, as shown in Figure 63.1, and this bar chart gives an idea of the purpose of measurement. Having seen this imbalance between female workers and women in senior management, Tesco is likely to try to address the situation – if only to reduce the embarrassment of publishing data such as this.

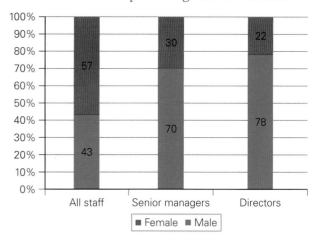

**Figure 63.1** Male/female split: Tesco plc 2014
Source: Tesco plc 2014 accounts

There are many methods for assessing overall business performance. For the AQA specification, two are required:

- Kaplan and Norton's balanced scorecard model
- Elkington's triple bottom line.

Fortunately they are very different from each other, so there should be no reason to confuse them.

## 63.2 Kaplan and Norton's balanced scorecard model

In 1992 Robert Kaplan and David Norton wrote an article criticising companies' fixation with profit as a performance measure. As profit is a statement of what happened *last* financial year, it fits in with the subtitle of a later book by Kaplan: *You Can't Drive a Car Solely Relying on a Rearview Mirror*. What Kaplan and Norton wanted was a 'balanced scorecard' with a broader view of the key performance measures for a business. Profit today is great, but what if it's being achieved at the cost of sales tomorrow?

---

'The balanced scorecard builds a feedback loop into strategy.' R.J. Bannister, management consultant

---

The balanced scorecard consists of four 'perspectives':

- The financial perspective: 'How do we look to our shareholders?' Kaplan and Norton acknowledged that shareholders would always want to know about profit growth, return on capital and cash flows; but they thought that the historic (backwards-looking) nature of the data was a huge flaw.

- The customer perspective: 'How do we look to our customers?' Measurements such as customer satisfaction, the rate of repeat purchase and market share are standard ways of checking whether your strategy is working for customers.

- The business process perspective: 'How effective are we internally?' This is primarily a check on operations management. The precise measures depend on the nature of the business. Service businesses are likely to use different measurements than manufacturers would use: perhaps speed of response to a customer query in a service business and inventory control in manufacturing.

- The learning and growth perspective: 'How can we change and improve?' This category points to the need to choose the right measurements. 'Training hours per employee' may seem a valid measure, but captures quantity without quality. 'Improvement suggestions per employee' might be a better measure (but still risks ignoring quality). Some companies place 'research and development spending per £ of revenue' in this category while others place it in the business process perspective.

To implement the balanced scorecard, a company should set out a clear strategy, then consult with managers about:

1. Main factors: the outcomes that need to be right for the strategy to succeed.

2. What to measure: how best to measure each of these factors.

3. How to measure: setting up measurements that are affordable and reliable.

In the example in Table 63.1, we look at Sainsbury's, with a new strategy to shift further upmarket – away from Tesco and Morrisons and towards Waitrose and M&S.

**Table 63.1:** Putting the scorecard into practice: Sainsbury's goes upmarket

| | 1. Main factors | 2. What to measure | 3. How to measure |
|---|---|---|---|
| Financial perspective | Revenue should at least stay stable as a result of the changes | Revenue per week compared with revenue in the same week last year | Use electronic till data adjusted by weather factors* for seasonal products *supplied by Met Office |
| | Gross profit margins rise as we move towards Waitrose pricing levels | Gross profit margins per department and for the store as a whole – compared with same week last year | Use electronic till data (at low/zero cost) |
| Customer perspective | Existing regular customers are happy | Change in £s spent this week per customer who came last week | Use Nectar (loyalty) card data (low/zero cost to us) |
| | New customers are attracted | Number of customers this week who haven't shopped with us for at least 8 weeks | Market researchers sampling stores daily (cost: £20,000 per week) |
| Business process | Install more manned counters, such as fresh fish and/or cheese | £s per customer spent in total on fish/cheese with and without the manned counter | Measure pre/post change and measure among stores with and without counters (using till receipts, so low/zero cost) |
| | Check that wastage rates aren't rising excessively now we're selling more fresh, unwrapped food | Average percentage of food sell-by date mark-down Average percentage of food thrown away | Measure pre/post change and measure among stores with and without counters (using till receipts, so low/zero cost) |
| Learning and growth | Staff need to develop a greater willingness to engage with and help customers | Customer feedback is needed on the degree and quality of staff engagement | Can use the same questionnaire process as above (sharing the £20,000 weekly cost) |
| | Encourage shop floor staff to put forward improvement ideas from customers | Measure the number of improvement suggestions per staff member | Store managers can record suggestions per staff member, rating their quality on a scale of 1–5 |

## Strengths of the balanced scorecard model

- Gives a more all-round view of the company and its achievements or failings. This can feed naturally into a SWOT analysis
- Encourages companies to find measures that look to the present and future, not the past
- Kaplan and Norton believe in the phrase 'measurement is management', that is, effective management only really occurs in relation to things that are measured.

## Weaknesses of the balanced scorecard model

- All systems based on measurements risk becoming targets that can distort behaviour (the Tesco profit problem in 2014); managers will find ways to 'hit targets', even if their actions cause unnoticed problems elsewhere. In other words targets cause their own problems (and, inevitably, things that are not included in the scorecard measures risk being ignored completely).
- Reports indicate failure rates of up to 70 per cent with balanced scorecard initiatives, usually because senior management relies too much on outside consultants and too little on their own staff – so performance measures end up being imposed on staff who don't believe in them (see the NHS as an example of this).
- As long ago as 2001 academic studies of the implementation of the balanced scorecard showed its downsides. In particular a study of the Swiss engineering company ABB stressed the risks of the balanced scorecard for 'companies which are facing increasing pressure due to rapid change and fierce competition' (Heinz Ahn, 2001). Implicitly, the balanced scorecard takes such a lot of time that it becomes inflexible, which is a major weakness.

'The metrics may improve, but all too often the underlying processes don't.' Arthur Schneiderman, author, *Why Balanced Scorecards Fail*

## 63.3 Elkington's triple bottom line

John Elkington was a long-established proponent of ethics in business when he first coined the term 'triple bottom line' in 1994. His idea was to encourage businesses to account for the full social cost of their activities (including, for example, pollution). The term 'bottom line' refers to the figure at the bottom of an income statement, that is, the profit for the year. His triple bottom line would include:

- financial accounts
- social accounts
- environmental accounts.

'The triple bottom line (TBL) consists of three Ps: profit, people and planet.' *The Economist* magazine.

In theory this might create a 'social income statement' such as:

|  | 2016 | 2015 | Notes on 2016 |
|---|---|---|---|
| Profit for the year: | £4.5m | £3.5m | Successful trading year |
| Social gain/loss | (£0.4m) | (£0.6m) | More jobs provided this year |
| Environment | (£0.8m) | (£0.4)m | Our April '16 river pollution crisis |
| Triple bottom line | £3.3m | £2.5m | Overall, a successful year |

The problem then is: what do we do with this information? Profit for the year forms part of a company's audited financial accounts and therefore has been independently checked on the basis of standard profit and loss calculations. But who exactly is to say what the right figures are for social or environmental loss or gain? Does the figure for the April '16 river pollution crisis really allow for every social cost involved? No outsider can be sure – therefore the triple bottom line figure cannot be relied upon.

John Elkington believed that properly audited figures for all three bottom lines would provide useful data that companies would want to provide to keep all their stakeholders happy. In fact the triple bottom line approach has been largely ignored by ordinary public companies – but sometimes used by companies with a public relations problem, or by non-governmental organisations hoping to get more funding. In other words it has tended to be used as a device rather than on principle.

A classic usage was by BP in its 2010 Sustainability Report. This was a business under huge pressure from its shocking 2005 Texas oil refinery explosion followed by the 2010 Gulf Oil spill. In the face of huge pressure because of clear compromises with safety in the pursuit of profit, BP wanted to show what a socially responsible company it really was. It didn't help!

So in practice the triple bottom line has been a real disappointment as a practical tool of business reporting. Above all else, it's done very little to change business behaviour. But what was the theory, in other words in an ideal world, what might be achieved if government passed legislation forcing all plcs to report using the triple bottom line? Quite simply, if all companies were forced to present their accounts in this way no one can doubt that behaviour would be affected. If a figure of *minus* £800,000 on the environmental reporting line could be eliminated by installing a £50,000 filtration system, companies would do that. In which case the £800,000 of environmental harm would have been fixed by £50,000 of the company's own money (instead of the local council picking up the bill).

'What is sound about the idea of a triple bottom line is not novel and what is novel about the idea is not sound.' Wayne Norman and Chris MacDonald, academics

## Strengths of the triple bottom line model

- The idea came from a man with a genuine desire to see increased social responsibility from businesses.
- If enforced by law (as financial accounts are), it would encourage firms to behave more responsibly towards social and environmental factors that currently are paid for by society as a whole.
- The measurement plus the publishing of those measurements annually would give incentives for managers to try much harder on issues such as workplace accidents and industrial pollution.

'In the industrial era, we used the language of profit. In this new era of sustainability, we need a common language for what we've done so far and what we want to do.' Laura Musikanski, executive director, Sustainable Seattle

## Weaknesses of the triple bottom line model

- Whenever measurement is introduced, one should worry about what else is important but unmeasurable (or unfashionable); so bullying in the workplace may go unnoticed, while gender equality gets measured. Is one more important than the other?
- In practice, the absence of political commitment to legislation has meant that the triple bottom line is an optional way to provide positive public relations to companies in need of some; so, perversely, the triple bottom line may be adopted most commonly by companies whose actions imply that their ethical standards are poor.
- Even fans of the triple bottom line worry that you can't really add profit and the damage caused by an oil spill as if they are both cash items, that is, the three lines don't really add up.
- It is an important business cliché to say that: not everything that can be measured matters and not everything that matters can be measured.

### Theory in 60 seconds:

*Triple bottom line*

- Written by Elkington in 1994
- Proposes that business performance should be measured by three 'bottom lines', i.e. calculations of net profit
- These are accounting profit/loss, social profit/loss and environmental profit/loss
- This would encourage firms to act with greater social responsibility
- But modern plcs have stayed focused on accounting profit and the interests of shareholders

## Five Whys and a How

| Question | Answer |
| --- | --- |
| Why may it be wrong to say that measurement is management? | Because so much in business cannot be measured directly, such as the warmth of a smile or the willingness to work weekends when it really matters |
| Why did the balanced scorecard theory take off as it did? | At a time when 'stakeholder theory' was a hot topic, the balanced scorecard fitted in. And management consultants need a new hot theory to sell to clients |
| Why has the balanced scorecard theory faded slightly? | In more recent times business survival has been the focus; when it's tough, business decisions will always focus on profit |
| Why have plcs never spent much time on the triple bottom line? | Directors are answerable to shareholders, so they can never be seen to be straying far away from concern for the bottom line: profit for the year |
| Why shouldn't a future government make the triple bottom line mandatory? | It could and perhaps one will, but it's unlikely to be in Britain, where company directors would lobby fiercely against it |
| How might a football club use a balanced scorecard to measure its success? | By looking at customer ratings of the food and the toilets and internal ratings of turnstile efficiency – but all the fans want is three points and some good football |

## Evaluation: Different measures of assessing business performance

No business has ever focused purely on the performance measures that stem from company accounts. Everyone has always cared about market share, customer loyalty and staff loyalty. The only question is how do you treat these measurements? Do you build them up into a huge document and make them the be-all and end-all of the management process? Or do you allow the measurements to be part of a bigger picture in which the organisational culture and ethical climate are the bedrock of the business. In 2014 Tesco had to admit overstating profit by more than £260 million because individual product and purchasing managers had been manipulating the figures to meet their performance measures. Not many years before, BP effectively fell into the same trap when compromising on safety standards.

It's hugely tempting for managers to look at the Premier League table and say 'I'd like to know whether we got three points this week'. But business is much more complicated than football and complex performance measures can cause their own problems. In Chapter 93 there's a quote that says 'Culture eats strategy for breakfast'. Organisational culture eats performance measures for breakfast too.

## Key terms

**Audited:** when figures are given an independent check by some sort of expert; in the case of accounts, the auditor is an independent accountant.

**Balanced scorecard:** measuring key activities broadly across the business to identify whether the chosen strategy is proving successful.

# Workbook

## A. Revision questions

**(30 marks; 30 minutes)**

1. Explain in your own words why 'setting targets isn't enough – the resources have to be there to make them achievable (see page 402). (4)

2. How should Tesco have interpreted this finding (see page 402): Supplier agreement to the question 'I am treated with respect': 67 per cent, down 4 per cent on 2013? (4)

3. Tesco accounts provided the data used in Figure 63.1 on gender diversity, but none on racial diversity. Outline two possible explanations for this. (4)

4. The balanced scorecard has two main features: breadth of performance measures and looking forwards instead of backwards. Which do you think is more important, and why? (6)

5. Outline the implication of a move to accounting annually for the triple bottom line in one of these companies:
   a) Shell Oil
   b) Rolls Royce Motors
   c) Walkers Crisps (6)

6. Explain what Sehneiderman may have meant in the quotation given on page 404. (6)

## B. Revision exercises
### DATA RESPONSE

### Churchill China plc: pottery manufacturer

**Figure 63.2**

Churchill China plc is a pottery company based in Stoke-on-Trent. It's shortly coming up to its 200th anniversary and is relatively rare in Stoke (once the world's leading pottery region) for still manufacturing locally. On the face of it, the company is going nowhere. Sales revenue is lower today than in 2006, and exports have changed little in the last ten years.

Yet there has been an interesting shift in strategy. In 2006 revenue came in a 55:45 ratio of Business to Business (B2B) sales to Business to Consumer (B2C) sales. In the first half of 2014 the ratio was 80:20. Churchill has switched to becoming overwhelmingly

a supplier of china plates, cups, etc. to hotels, restaurants and the catering trade generally. Indeed it is now the UK's market leader in supplying to the hospitality industry. This is a nice niche position to be in, because it's more to do with tailored batch or even job production than the mass market. This keeps Churchill's trade business away from direct competition from China. It also may give rise to a real growth path in the future, given that eating out remains a growth trend in Britain (and elsewhere in the West).

**Figure 63.3**

Even prior to 2006 Churchill had largely given up producing china for the retail market. Instead it designed tableware in the UK, but had it made elsewhere, notably China. So the fall-away in retail sales has quite a few economic positives. Churchill is now focusing on producing in the UK for the UK market – though it is also developing stronger export sales within the hospitality trade. In the first half of 2014 Churchill's B2B sales to continental Europe rose by 20 per cent.

The stock market has taken note of Churchill's more promising prospects. The share price has risen from 155p in early 2009 to 375p in November 2013 and 570p a year later. Perhaps now, at last, the business will start to deliver for all its stakeholders.

**Appendix A:** Share price, Churchill China plc November 2013–November 2014

**Appendix B:** Staffing and employee pay 2006–2014. Figures in £000s.

|  | 2006 | 2007 | 2008 | 2009 | 2010 | 2011 | 2012 | 2013 | 2014 |
|---|---|---|---|---|---|---|---|---|---|
| No. of staff | 596 | 635 | 599 | 510 | 555 | 540 | 535 | 520 | N/A |
| Staff cost | 13,991 | 16,592 | 15,817 | 14,258 | 14,421 | 15,128 | 14,991 | 15,844 | N/A |

**Appendix C:** Overall operational performance 2006–2014 (*1st half figures doubled up). Figures in £000s.

|  | 2006 | 2007 | 2008 | 2009 | 2010 | 2011 | 2012 | 2013 | 2014* |
|---|---|---|---|---|---|---|---|---|---|
| Revenue | 45,930 | 46,930 | 41,969 | 41,705 | 43,746 | 42,296 | 41,435 | 43,157 | 45,700 |
| Operating profit | 2,795 | 3,230 | 2,804 | 2,288 | 2,287 | 2,713 | 2,830 | 3,371 | 4,000 |
| Corporation tax | 1,631 | 1,147 | 938 | 567 | 504 | 530 | 571 | 609 | 800 |
| Profit for the year | 4,111 | 3,695 | 1,505 | 1,696 | 1,527 | 1,908 | 2,146 | 2,761 | 3,200 |
| Dividends | 1,217 | 1,375 | 1,531 | 1,526 | 1,529 | 1,530 | 1,529 | 1,564 | N/A |

**Appendix D:** Divisional performance 2006–2014: Revenue, profit and investment spending. Figures in £000s.

|  | 2006 | 2007 | 2008 | 2009 | 2010 | 2011 | 2012 | 2013 | 2014 |
|---|---|---|---|---|---|---|---|---|---|
| Hospitality revenue | 26,018 | 28,576 | 24,952 | 24,554 | 27,398 | 29,166 | 29,407 | 32,753 | 33,600 |
| Retail revenue | 19,912 | 18,354 | 17,017 | 17,151 | 16,348 | 13,130 | 12,028 | 10,404 | 8,200 |
| Hospitality profit | 3,623 | 4,330 | 3,668 | 3,289 | 4,055 | 4,710 | 4,161 | 5,055 | 5,400 |
| Retail profit | 725 | 877 | 1,709 | 1,726 | 755 | 1,008 | 1,420 | 1,234 | 450 |

### Questions (40 marks; 50 minutes)

**1.** From the information available and your understanding of how manufacturing works, set out a balanced scorecard for Churchill China based on Table 63.1. (10)

**2.** Analyse Churchill's strategy of focusing more on the hospitality sector. (10)

**3.** To what extent might the performance of a business such as Churchill China be affected by a boardroom decision to publish triple bottom line accounting from next year? (20)

## C. Extend your understanding

**1.** To what extent might the use of the balanced scorecard help Marks & Spencer achieve its desire to regain its position as the market leader in women's clothing? (25)

**2.** With global warming still being seen by many experts as the biggest threat to global economies in the coming decades, to what extent might Britain benefit from legislation enforcing the triple bottom line on all plcs? (25)

# Chapter
# 64 Changes in the political and legal environment

**Linked to:** The impact of government policy, Chapter 65; The impact of changes in the economic environment, Chapter 66.

## Definition

Every business will be affected in some way by laws passed by parliament, usually as part of government policy. For some, such as manufacturers of soft drinks or motor cars, the political and legal environment will be hugely important.

## 64.1 The scope and effects of UK and EU law

### Competition

#### What the law says

Competition law is designed to encourage competition within markets to ensure that consumers have choice. UK and EU laws exist in order to try to prevent the exploitation of monopoly power, whereby a single supplier in a market is able to charge over-inflated prices. Consumers may have to pay these prices if there is only one supplier. In addition, a company with a monopoly has little incentive to deliver good service or to innovate unless their market dominance is threatened.

There are other aspects to competition law, such as the need to:

- Prevent companies agreeing to work together to the detriment of consumers by operating a cartel, agreeing with supposed rivals to hold supply down in order to keep prices artificially high.
- Monitor the behaviour of any business with a strong enough position within its market to potentially be able to abuse that power. A recent example has been investigation of the major UK supermarkets to ensure that they are paying a fair price to farmers. Since so much of the output of farms is bought by the supermarkets, it is important to ensure that farmers are not forced to sell for less than the production cost.
- Ensure that takeovers and mergers do not break the rule of thumb, which is that 25 per cent should be the ceiling on any firm's share of a UK market.

### Effects

The most obvious way in which competition law affects business is when mergers or takeovers are proposed. In the UK, merger or takeovers that the government considers may have a detrimental effect on consumers are referred to the Competition and Markets Authority (CMA). This organisation, which is independent from the government, and therefore from political intervention, will investigate the likely impact of the proposed deal before reporting back to the government with recommendations on whether the proposed deal should be permitted. A similar arrangement exists whereby the European Union can investigate deals that might impact on the whole of the European market.

The impact of this legislation on strategic decision-making is that few companies would bother to pursue a takeover that would lead to a combined market share in excess of 25 per cent. At times, competition legislation will act as a major constraint on a firm's strategic plans, forcing them to enter new markets organically or through joint ventures that do not involve any change in ownership. It is notable that Chinese legislation currently forces major Western firms looking to enter the Chinese market to work with existing Chinese businesses, not take them over. These Chinese joint ventures have been spectacularly successful for Volkswagen and Jaguar Land Rover, but a washout for retailers Tesco and Kingfisher (B&Q).

## Law relating to the labour market

### What the law says

Employment law is designed to prevent the exploitation of employees by businesses. Therefore, the major areas covered include pay, working conditions such as entitlement to leave and holidays, physical working conditions and the right to trade union representation. The key area of the law governing payment is the need for employers to pay at least the National Minimum Wage. Up until September 2015 this was set at £6.50 an hour, with a lower rate of £3.79 an hour for under-18s. In addition to setting a basic minimum level of pay, legislation also exists to prevent discrimination in the workplace – a phenomenon that may present itself in women and men receiving different rates of pay for the same job. So legislation dictates that men and women must be paid equally for the same work. Meanwhile, anti-discrimination legislation also covers other scenarios in which discrimination can occur, such as when filling a job vacancy, choosing which staff are sent for training opportunities, dismissing staff or providing access to benefits such as sick pay or pensions. This leads us to other areas of employee protection such as legal entitlement to maternity and paternity leave and holiday pay.

### Effects

Tightening employment laws by, for example forcing companies to offer longer paternity leave to new fathers or increases in the National Minimum Wage may make firms adapt their operations strategies to reduce their reliance on UK-based human resources. Strategic options could include offshoring certain operations to countries where wage rates are lower or employment law less onerous, or, shifting to a more capital intensive approach, where machines and technology replace people. Certainly with technological changes advancing rapidly, many businesses are able to switch jobs out of the UK, or replace people with machines in areas previously unconsidered, such as data analysis and personal technical support.

Many employment laws have been influenced by European Union attempts to create a 'level playing field' among European countries. This ensures that competition between EU members cannot be based on one country offering particularly poor labour conditions. For many Members of Parliament, the EU's degree of intervention in UK labour laws has been a central reason for their desire that the UK should leave the EU. Others see these same laws as an essential part of a modern, civilised economy and society.

# Environmental laws

'Think about it...if we throw it away, we had to buy it first. So we pay twice, once to get it, once to have it taken away. What if we reverse that cycle? What if our suppliers send us less, and everything they send us has value as a recycled product? No waste, and we get paid instead.' Lee Scott, Chief Executive, WalMart

## What the law says

Environmental laws exist to try to minimise the negative impacts of business on the natural environment. Ways in which the law tries to do this include laws preventing pollution, determining the way that products are packaged, and recycling legislation. The nature of what is trying to be protected is so wide that there are many laws that govern the way in which businesses must work to protect the natural environment. The table below summarises a few of the areas covered by environmental protection legislation:

**Table 64.1** Environmental protection legislation

| Air pollution | Land pollution | Water pollution |
|---|---|---|
| Greenhouse gases and global warming | Waste disposal (Landfill Tax) | Recycling |
| Emission of 'particulate matter' from diesel cars | Planning permission for buildings | Waste treatment |
| Energy efficiency labelling | Building regulations | Water use |
| Energy use | Treatment of hazardous substances | Marine environment |

The Environment Agency is responsible for enforcing most environmental legislation within the UK. It operates at arm's length from politicians, yet is government-funded.

'A product which is unceremoniously wasted to landfill at end of life surely can't be considered good design!' Neil Tierney, Director, Lightweight Medical

## Effects

Traditionally, complying with environmental legislation was considered to be simply adding to the costs of a business. Recent research suggests, however, that countries with very high environmental standards are among the world's most competitive. Over the past twenty years or so, as legislation has tightened and focused on reducing, reusing and recycling as the basis of reducing long-term environmental damage, a growing number of firms have embraced greener ways

of doing business. First movers tended to benefit from a 'greener image' which allowed them to tap niche markets of environmentally conscious consumers. Nowadays, many of the effects of complying with environmental legislation centre on how reducing material and energy use can form part of a lean production programme to reduce costs.

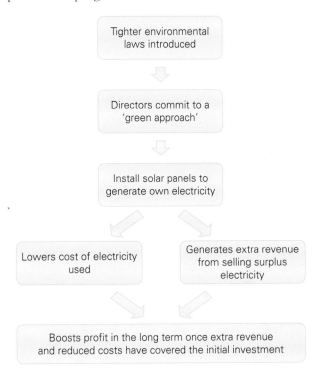

**Figure 64.1** The chain of logic

# Laws governing tax

## What the law says

Companies must pay tax. The two most significant taxes are Value Added Tax (VAT) and Corporation Tax. A business with a turnover above £81,000 (correct as at March 2015) must register for VAT with the UK's tax gathering organisation – HMRC. Registering for VAT means that customers must be charged VAT (currently 20 per cent). A VAT registered business can claim back VAT that they have paid on any supplies they have bought. Corporation Tax is a tax on profit. A limited company must pay tax on its profits, currently at a rate of 20 per cent. Profits generated in certain ways, including successful R&D, new patents or theatre, film or television production are exempted from corporation tax.

## Effects

The major effect of the VAT system is to create more work for accountants. Ensuring VAT is charged, recorded, handed over to HMRC and claimed back on items purchased keeps accounting departments busy all

**Table 64.2** Countries with low rates of corporation tax

| Country | Corporation tax rate 2014 (%) | Country | Corporation tax rate 2014 (%) | Country | Corporation tax rate 2014 (%) |
|---|---|---|---|---|---|
| Bahamas | 0 | Isle of Man | 0 | Cyprus | 12.5 |
| Cayman Islands | 0 | Jersey | 0 | Ireland | 12.5 |
| Guernsey | 0 | Qatar | 10 | Switzerland | 17.92 |

Source: KPMG

year round. However, the effect of corporation tax is more complex. There are plenty of tax advisors willing to show businesses how to find ways to reduce their stated profits (without lying – which would be fraud), thus reducing their corporation tax bill. Meanwhile, with corporation tax payable in most countries, multinational companies can take advantage of low tax rates in certain countries such as those shown in Table 64.2.

Although plenty of British companies pay corporation tax (FTSE 100 companies paid a total of £5.3 billion in 2014), the tax avoidance measures used by many large businesses act against the idea of a 'level playing field'. Small firms pay their tax, but some large businesses work hard to avoid doing so, giving them an unfair advantage. Apple, Starbucks, Google, Virgin and Amazon have all received negative press coverage in the UK for their aggressive approach to tax avoidance. It would be nice to think that they would follow the example of Ted Baker plc, which seems comfortable paying its 20 per cent contribution to British society.

## 64.2 Impact of the political and legal environment on strategic decision-making

Companies are inclined to threaten politicians and governments with calamity if they have the cheek to pass laws that may create costs for the companies. If companies had had their way, children would still be working in coal mines and petrol would still be full of poisonous lead.

The really impressive companies are those that look forwards – and see opportunities rather than threats. When China brings in a serious Clean Air Act (as it surely will), there will be huge new opportunities, perhaps for an electric version of the Evoque Land

Rover – and certainly for electric fires (coal fires would be banned). Strategic decision-making means looking ahead, not just months but years to see where the future is heading. Over the past hundred years the environment and the accident rates in countries such as Britain have been transformed by legislation. Good companies (and politicians) look forward instead of reminiscing about a misremembered past.

**Figure 64.2** A clean air act in China may lead to new opportunities

'Progressive companies regard climate change as an opportunity rather than a threat.' Tom Delay, Chief Executive, The Carbon Trust

## 64.3 Impact of the political and legal environment on functional decision-making

At a functional level, the need to ensure adherence to legal requirements tends to mean extra paperwork and administration for managers. Compliance is a key word for functional managers. Businesses will have formal administrative systems set up to ensure that the business complies with legislation such as employment or environmental laws; the role of functional managers will be to help design these systems. They must then spot-check the different departments to make sure that staff are following the set procedures. Part of the challenge at a functional level will be to ensure, initially through training, but then through ongoing communication, that staff at the lowest levels of the organisation understand the need to comply with the systems in place. This may not be as easy as it sounds, since staff may see sticking to the rules as a burden that makes their jobs harder. However, a decision made by a lowly production worker to pour hazardous waste materials down a drain, rather than stick to the proper company systems could cost the firm tens of thousands of pounds in fines.

'A sound man is good at salvage, at seeing nothing is lost.' Lao Tzu (500BC)

## Five Whys and a How

| Question | Answer |
|---|---|
| Why is competition such a good thing for consumers? | The argument here centres on choice ensuring that prices in a competitive market have to be kept low by individual firms needing to beat their competitors. In addition, there is a far greater incentive for firms in competitive markets to continually innovate in order to try to best competition. |
| Why do some employees need greater legal protection than others? | If a business has invested in training a member of staff over a long period after an expensive recruitment process, the firm is less likely to treat that employee poorly than a firm that employs unskilled, temporary staff. Although temporary staff may have fewer legal rights, they are more likely to need legal protection. |
| Why is the National Minimum Wage less than the Living Wage? | The Living wage is not part of the law, as created by politicians. Politicians who decide on the minimum wage must not only keep individual voters happy, they rely on keeping businesses happy to ensure their party funding. Therefore, businesses have significant influence over lawmakers in the UK – thus are able to keep rises in the National Minimum wage affordable to firms. |
| Why has environmental legislation been toughened in recent years? | As the planet's natural environment has degraded, the need for environmental legislation has become clearer. In addition, as living standards rise in more countries around the world, the environment becomes a more affordable concern for lawmakers. |
| Why is Ireland such an attractive location for multinational companies? | Ireland has one of the lowest corporation tax rates within the EU, meaning that a firm locating in Ireland will enjoy the benefits of being within an EU, indeed a Eurozone country, whilst also having a significantly lower corporation tax bill than would be faced in most other EU countries. |
| How can taxable profits be maximised in low tax countries and minimised in higher tax countries? | If a firm makes a component in a low tax country such as Ireland to be used to make a product in a high tax country such as France (33 per cent), their accounts may show that the finished product was sold in France at a very low profit margin, whilst the 'price' charged to the French assembly plant by the Irish component plant was high – generating most of the profit for that product in Ireland, where only 12.5 per cent of profits are taken as tax. |

## Evaluation: Changes in the political and legal environment

Legislation is designed to provide a level playing field for all businesses. However, in an increasingly global economy, differences between laws and tax rates from country to country mean that businesses in certain countries have a more favourable legal or taxation environment in which to operate. This can mean that companies based in countries where business activity is highly regulated face a loss of competitiveness in their global markets, with higher costs of staff or environmental protection. In addition, companies whose size allows them to operate in a range of different countries have the chance to select where in the world to perform certain tasks, allowing them perhaps to dodge strict environmental laws or high tax rates. In essence, the legal environment within which a business operates can provide a competitive advantage over other, international rivals, with multinationals perhaps best placed to take advantage of the variability of laws and tax rates around the world.

## Key terms

**Carbon footprint:** the net total of greenhouse gas emissions produced by an organisation.

**Joint ventures:** agreements between firms to collaborate on specific areas of common interest.

**Living wage:** the wage rate considered necessary for a household to have access to a minimum acceptable standard of living.

**Trade union:** an organisation funded by its members, who want the union to give them protection from rogue employers and, hopefully, a better standard of living.

## Workbook

### A. Revision questions

(35 marks; 35 minutes)

1. Explain two reasons why a market dominated by just one supplier may be bad for consumers. (4)

2. Explain one reason why consumers may benefit from a market being dominated by one huge firm. (4)

3. State three ways in which UK law protects employees. (3)

4. Analyse why a firm that offers pay rates and employment terms way above the legal minimum requirements may benefit from this policy. (6)

5. Explain why an above inflation increase in the National Minimum wage could create unemployment in the UK. (5)

6. Analyse two potential benefits to a major supermarket chain of replacing all its diesel powered delivery lorries with electric vehicles. (8)

7. Examine why bigger businesses may be better at avoiding corporation tax bills than smaller businesses. (5)

### B. Revision exercises
DATA RESPONSE

**Gender pay gap narrows, but still exists**

The Office for National Statistics Annual Survey of Hours and Earnings 2014 reports that weekly earnings decreased by 1.6 per cent for the year when adjusted for inflation – the sixth consecutive year that real earnings have fallen. Overall the gender pay gap has narrowed from 10 per cent in 2013 to 9.4 per cent in 2014 – the lowest since records began in 1997.

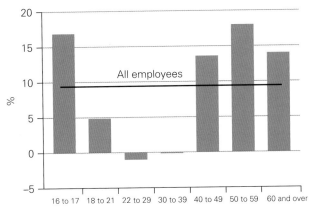

**Figure 64.3** Gender pay gap for median full-time gross hourly earnings (excluding overtime) by age group, UK, April 2014
Source: www.ons.gov.uk/ons/dcp171778_385428.pdf

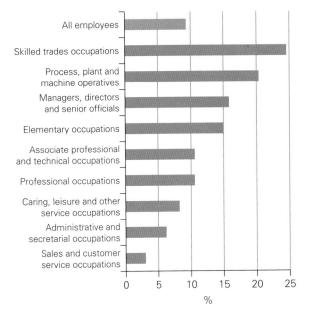

**Figure 64.4** Gender pay gap for median full-time hourly earnings (excluding overtime), by major occupation group, UK, April 2014
Source: Annual Survey of Hours and Earnings (ASHE) – office for National Statistics

### Questions (45 marks; 45 minutes)

**1. a)** Between what ages are women likely to earn more than men doing identical work? (2)

**b)** State three jobs in which the gender pay gap is likely to be widest in the UK. (3)

**2.** Explain two possible reasons why the gender pay gap widens as women get older. (6)

**3.** Explain two reasons why there are such great differences in the size of the gender pay gap according to the type of occupation being considered. (6)

**4.** Examine two reasons why closing the gender pay gap in the UK may be difficult to achieve. (8)

**5.** To what extent does six consecutive years of falling real earnings represent a problem for UK businesses? (20)

## C. Extend your understanding

**1.** New legislation provides strategic opportunities as well as threats for companies. To what extent do you agree? Justify your answer. (25)

**2.** 'It would be counterproductive for the British government to tighten tax regulations to force businesses operating in Britain to pay their full corporation tax bills.' To what extent do you agree? Justify your answer. (25)

**Linked to:** Changes in the political and legal environment, Chapter 64; The impact of changes in the economic environment, Chapter 66; The impact of social change, Chapter 68.

## Definition

The government policies covered in this unit are those that exclude economic policy. These government policies fall into four main categories: government initiatives to encourage enterprise; the role of industry regulators; laws and regulations that are designed to protect the environment; and government foreign policy towards international trade.

'The nine most terrifying words in the English language are, "I'm from the government and I'm here to help".' Former US president, Ronald Reagan

## 65.1 The role of regulators

In industries that were once state-owned, such as the railways, the government appoints regulators to try to stop firms from exploiting consumers. In markets where there is a lack of competition, the need for regulation is greatest. The government can protect consumers in two ways:

1. **Price controls**: industry regulators are sometimes asked to limit price increases, or set the price charged in an industry. This is most likely to be needed if the industry is a monopoly. A monopoly exists when a market is supplied by a single firm. A good example of a monopolist is Virgin Trains. They are the sole suppliers of passenger rail travel between London and Manchester. This means that there are no substitutes for Virgin's service, which reduces the price elasticity of demand for Virgin's rail tickets. Most monopolists will try to exploit their market power by raising price. This is because mathematically, raising the price of a price

inelastic product will always lead to an increase in total revenue. To prevent Virgin from exploiting its market power, the government has appointed a regulator: the Office of Rail Regulation (ORR). In 2014 the ORR imposed a maximum fare increase on train operating companies like Virgin equal to the rate of inflation, plus an additional 6 per cent.

2. **Regulating the product or service provided**: some train operators might be tempted to put profit before passenger safety. To stop this from happening the ORR also has the power to impose fines on train operators who break its safety regulations. The Department for Transport can also fine train operators for poor punctuality, or for cancelling too many trains.

## 65.2 Government policy related to infrastructure

Infrastructure is social capital. Examples of infrastructure include: transport networks, such as roads, bridges and railways; schools and universities; medical facilities to keep the population fit and healthy; and reliable national grids to supply essential utilities, such as broadband Internet, electricity, gas and running water to households and firms across the country.

The quality of a country's infrastructure is a very important factor affecting a country's international competitiveness. For example, UK manufacturers do not have to battle with an unreliable supply of electricity. In Nigeria this is not the case. Power outages occur frequently in Nigeria: when the power goes off, production stops. These stoppages cause productivity to fall, which increases unit costs. As a result of poor infrastructure, Nigerian firms are forced into charging higher prices for their products.

'A rising tide doesn't raise people who don't have a boat. We have to build the boat for them. We have to give them the basic infrastructure to rise with the tide.' Rahul Ghandi, Indian politician

According to many commentators, the UK suffers from a productivity gap. This means that output per worker in Britain is lower than in other countries. It could be argued that some of this productivity gap is caused by poor quality infrastructure: the two biggest problems being below par transport and education.

In Britain productivity is held back by our congested roads and railways. Long commutes to and from work contribute towards stress, which reduces efficiency. Production can also be disrupted when either people or products are delayed because they are stuck in traffic jams. In 2013 the government proposed building two high-speed train lines to help modernise Britain's rail infrastructure. This is important because German, French and Spanish firms already have access to such networks.

The quality of a country's schools and universities also contributes to the UK's productivity gap. According to OECD the standard of state education in Britain is poor by international standards. For example, in 2012 the UK was ranked 26th in the world for maths, 23rd for reading and 21st for science. Poor quality education adversely affects skills, which in turn, lowers productivity.

**Figure 65.1** Logic chain: the business significance of infrastructure

## 65.3 Government policy on the environment

Sometimes firms do things that are good for their profits but leave society worse off. For example, a paint manufacturer might choose to dump its waste in a local river because it is cheaper than investing in the expensive filtration equipment needed to prevent the pollution. Intervention is needed to stop a minority of unethical firms from causing damage to society.

Government policy can protect the environment in four ways:

**Green taxes**: Unlike theme park visits or goods sold in shopping centres, aspects of nature that bring pleasure to people's lives are not bought and sold in conventional markets. However, this does not mean that the government should not try to attach a monetary value to aspects of the environment that generate pleasure. If the government can estimate the monetary cost of pollution, they can impose green taxes of the same amount on the firm(s) that have created the pollution. If green taxes force firms to include the cost of pollution within their own accounts, they will have a financial incentive to reduce pollution.

**Subsidies**: a subsidy is a sum of money given by the government to producers. Normally, subsidies are paid per unit, according to the quantity produced. Subsidies increase the profitability of supply because they offset production costs. If firms can be persuaded to supply more, the price of the product being subsidised should fall. As a result of the lower price, consumers should respond by buying more of this product. The German government has used subsidies to achieve its environmental policy goals. In 2014 they spent €20 billion on subsidies for wind, solar and other renewable producers of electricity. The results have been spectacular. In the first quarter of 2014, 27 per cent of the electricity consumed in Germany came from renewables. This compares to just 9 per cent in Britain. German manufacturers operating in other industries have also benefited from cheaper power as a result of the subsidies. Thanks to the subsidies on renewable power, the supply of electricity in Germany has soared. As a result, wholesale electricity prices in Germany have fallen by over 60 per cent since 2008. Some of Germany's gas-burning power plants have been forced to close down because at today's prices, it is no longer profitable to produce electricity by burning imported Russian gas. This helps reduce greenhouse gas emissions.

**Laws and regulations**: a wide range of UK and especially EU laws govern issues as diverse as the materials that firms must use for certain products, the processes firms are allowed to use in manufacturing and making sure products are recyclable at the end of their lives. This is an area in which several EU directives have led to increased expectations of businesses in terms of environmental standards (see below). Companies often complain that it's hard to compete against firms outside the EU with less stringent environmental laws. Fortunately recent research shows that strict environmental standards within a country have no damaging effect on productivity.

'We know that our crumbling pipelines, roads and bridges are ticking time bombs – we can't have first-rate American communities with Third-World American infrastructure.' Christine Pelosi, political strategist

### WEEE

The Waste Electrical and Electronic Equipment (WEEE) Directive is an environmental law that applies across the whole of the European Union which forces manufacturers of electrical goods such as laptops, TVs and fridges to recycle their old products. The WEEE directive first came into force in 2002 and has proven to be a great success. For example, in Ireland the directive led to a five-fold increase in the amount of recycling. In 2014 the EU decided to make the WEEE directive targets for recycling even stricter. From 2016 manufacturers will have a legal obligation to recycle a minimum of 45 tonnes of electronic waste for every 100 tonnes of new electrical goods sold. The WEEE directive has improved Europe's environment, though possibly at a cost to developing countries. This is because Europe now exports its electronic waste to countries, such as Ghana, where children sort through electronic waste, looking for valuable metals that can be sold for recycling.

## 65.4 Government policy related to international trade

Like most other countries, the UK imports and exports a range of goods and services. The idea behind international trade is that countries pay for their imports by exporting some of the goods that they produce domestically to consumers abroad. The majority of economists and politicians favour greater foreign trade because it has the potential to lift living standards. This is because it can lower prices for consumers. It makes sense to import goods that can be made more efficiently abroad because they will tend to be cheaper than domestically produced alternatives. International trade enables countries to specialise: countries no longer need to produce everything that they would like to consume. By specialising, countries can enjoy economic growth by becoming more efficient. International trade is also popular with big business, because it provides the chance for firms to offer their services globally.

### The policy objective: promoting free trade

To encourage more trade between countries, governments sign free trade agreements. Free trade describes a situation where goods and services can move freely between countries without being impeded by either tariffs or quotas. Tariffs are taxes that are imposed on imports only. Quotas are physical restrictions on the volume of a particular imported good. Governments can choose to be more open to foreign trade by either signing a new trading agreement with another country, or more radically, by choosing to join a trading bloc, such as the EU.

## The European Union

The European Union (EU) is a trading bloc consisting of 28 European countries and over 500 million consumers. The goal of the EU is to create free trade between European countries, by passing laws to ensure that there is freedom of movement of people, goods, services and capital between EU member states. The UK joined in 1973. From that point onwards there was free trade between Britain and other European countries, such as Germany and France.

The European Single Act of 1992 was designed to promote even closer economic ties between member states by sweeping away hidden barriers to trade to create a European Single Market. An important aspect of the Single European Act was the harmonisation of product standards, so that the same rules apply across the whole of the EU.

The next step towards greater economic integration occurred when eleven members of the EU decided to adopt a single currency, called the euro. The euro was designed to create even closer economic ties between the countries that adopted it. Trade between countries using the euro would be a lot easier because firms would not have to worry any more about fluctuating exchange rates. Thanks to the euro, French firms would find it as easy to buy from a German supplier as from a French one.

At the time of writing (January 2015) there are ten EU countries that do not use the euro as their currency. Some of these countries would like to join the Eurozone, but they are not eligible because either interest rates, inflation or government debt levels are too high. An example of a country that is in this position is Poland. Other countries, such as Sweden and the UK have been eligible to join, but have decided not to for a variety of economic and political reasons. For example, critics of the single currency argue that our decision to keep control of our own currency and monetary policy helped the British economy during the financial crisis. This is because the Bank of England was able to unilaterally slash interest rates and engage in quantitative easing which helped to revive spending. Countries such as Greece and Spain have not been able to loosen their monetary policy in the same way because their monetary policy is set for them by the European

Central Bank (ECB). As a result, their economic recoveries have been less strong.

As a consequence of joining the EU, the pattern of the UK's international trade has changed - we now trade proportionately more with other European countries at the expense of the USA and Commonwealth countries.

'If you tell people, "That old banger of yours, we're going to tax the hell out of it", they'll rightly tell you to get lost. But if you tell people that when they next buy a car, the tax will be adjusted, so that the cleanest ones will cost less and the polluting ones will cost more, most people will say, "Fair enough".'
Zac Goldsmith

## Five Whys and a How

| Question | Answer |
|---|---|
| Why is it important for the government to invest in modern transport infrastructure? | Slow journeys and thus working time wasted cuts productivity, placing British firms at a competitive disadvantage |
| Why not scrap environmental pollution legislation ('red tape') and trust firms to be responsible? | Some firms might be tempted to ignore the environmental costs that they create and impose on society. Regulations regarding recycling and emissions force unethical firms to improve their behaviour |
| Why do some firms prefer free trade over protectionism? | Free trade (removing tariffs and quotas) makes it easier for firms to engage in international trade. This can boost revenues, by opening up new export markets |
| Why do some governments appoint regulators to cap price increases? | Some governments try to prevent the abuse of monopoly power. A monopoly exists when there is only one firm supplying a market. Some firms exploit this position by overcharging their customers |
| Why do firms lobby politicians about the quality of education provided in British schools? | Education is a matter of great concern to British business, because it affects the UK's international competitiveness. If educational standards are low, there will almost certainly be a productivity gap between us and our rivals overseas |
| How might a government encourage more new business start-ups, and greater enterprise within the economy? | Businesses call for less red tape (unnecessary rules and regulations) to make it easier for entrepreneurs to set up a new business. And they call for lower business taxes |

## Key term

**Quantitative easing:** when the Central Bank boosts the money supply to give banks the cash to be able to lend to companies or households.

Few things in business are more controversial than the impact of government policy, whether in relation to immigration, regulation or deregulation. Businesses often make wrong decisions, even though it should be relatively easy to decide what to do when measured against one criterion: profit. By contrast politicians have to make decisions that will be accepted by the press, social media, the electorate, business and the Treasury. So no wonder their decision-making processes tend to be slow and are often questionable.

In the lead-up to 2008/9 - the biggest global financial crisis since 1929 - the main causal factor was the deregulation of the financial services industry. In the UK a Labour government, egged on by the Conservatives, gave increasing operational freedoms to banks and bankers in the belief that 'the market' was a stronger and better source of decision-making than the government. Unfortunately the decisions made by bankers proved to be governed by what was best for bankers. They walked off with vast bonuses leaving the banks, the government and ordinary people much worse off. However weak governments may be at decision-making, the alternative is to leave everything to the market – and that can cause even greater problems.

# Workbook

## A. Revision questions

**(30 marks; 30 minutes)**

1. Explain two possible reasons why the UK government decided to set up the British Business Bank in 2012. (8)

2. Explain the benefits that businesses gain from being based in the European Union. (5)

3. Briefly describe the main aims of:
   **a)** government policy to promote enterprise
   **b)** industry regulators
   **c)** environmental protection policy. (6)

4. Explain two possible consequences of improved infrastructure for one of the following:
   **a)** a supermarket
   **b)** a chemical manufacturer
   **c)** a bank. (6)

5. Explain how a decision to reduce the rate of green taxation on fossil fuels might affect a car manufacturer. (5)

## B. Revision exercises

### DATA RESPONSE

**Has the government killed the pub?**

The UK pub industry has been in decline for well over a century. In 1905, there were nearly 100,000 pubs in Britain, by 2014 there were fewer than 50,000. However, the rate of decline has been unstable. Four days after the start of the First World War the government regulated the pub industry for the first time, due to concerns that consumption of alcohol would adversely affect the production of arms needed to fight the Germans. The Defence of the Realm Act of 1914 forced brewers into reducing the alcohol content of their beer, whilst the availability of beer was restricted by laws on pub opening hours. Most of these regulations were kept after the war ended. By 1935, the number of pubs in Britain had fallen by a quarter.

In 2005 the government helped the pub industry enormously by deregulating pub opening hours. At the time the government argued that allowing pubs to stay open for 24 hours a day would prevent binge-drinking, and instead establish a European 'café culture'. Unfortunately for pubs, deregulation did not stop the rate of pub closures. This was because at the same time, the government allowed supermarkets to stay open for longer. In addition the government made it easier for small shops to start selling alcohol, which increased competition for pubs.

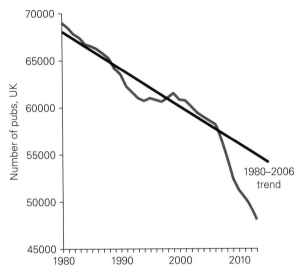

**Figure 65.2** Pub decline

Source: Institute of Economic Affairs: *Closing Time – Who's Killing the British Pub?* December 2014

The next big government policy change that affected pubs occurred in 2007 when smoking was banned in public places. Following the ban, pub beer sales crashed. This was unsurprising; according to research carried out by the pub industry*, over half of all pub goers were smokers. Non-smokers have clearly benefited from the smoking ban. According to the same survey carried out one year after the ban came into force, visits to the pub by non-smokers has

risen by 6 per cent. But net sales were sharply down because there was also a 74 per cent reduction in the number of pub visits made by smokers. In recent years pubs have also suffered because of a change in consumer behaviour: more and more people now prefer to drink at home rather than in the pub. This change is largely because beer prices in pubs have risen at a far faster rate than in supermarkets. Government policy has arguably contributed to this situation. For example, per square metre, city centre pubs tend to pay higher business rates than out of town supermarkets. Also, unlike supermarkets, pubs have to pay VAT on food.

*Federation of Licenced Victuallers' Association (FLVA) July 2008

### Questions (50 marks; 60 minutes)

1. Using Figure 65.2 explain what has happened to the rate of pub closures during the period shown. (6)

2. Analyse why the UK government wanted to deregulate pub opening hours. (12)

3. Some public health campaigners would like the government to regulate the drinks industry by imposing a minimum price of 50p per unit of alcohol. Evaluate the possible effects of this proposal for a pub chain such as JD Wetherspoon. (16)

4. The number of pubs in Britain has declined. To what extent can this decline be attributed to government policy? (16)

## C. Extend your understanding

1. Some politicians argue that stricter regulations and higher rates of taxation should be imposed on companies that create pollution. To what extent do you agree? Justify your answer. (25)

2. Would British businesses be better off if the UK left the European Union? Justify your answer. (25)

# Chapter 66

# The impact of changes in the economic environment

Linked to: Changes in the political and legal environment, Chapter 64; The impact of government policy, Chapter 65; Globalisation and emerging economies, Chapter 67.

## Definition

Economic change refers to fluctuations in national and international 'macroeconomic' variables, such as changes in exchange rates, inflation, unemployment and economic growth.

## 66.1 GDP (Gross Domestic Product)

GDP is the total value of all goods and services produced by an economy in a year. According to the World Bank, in 2014 the American economy produced $16,768 billion worth of goods and services, making it the largest in the world. China is very close behind. Its output in the same year was $16,149 billion. Rising GDP is normally seen as being good for business, because it indicates that the economy is growing. In the near future, most commentators expect Chinese GDP to overtake American GDP. This is because China has been achieving much faster rates of economic growth than the USA.

### What is economic growth and why does it matter?

Economic growth is the annual percentage increase in GDP. In the long run all economies tend to grow. This is due to technological advances that increase productivity. This means that more goods and services can be produced with the same population. Economic growth is important to a country because it improves the standard of living. If the UK economy produces more goods and services, there will be more for UK citizens to consume. Economic growth in Britain has

tended to average 2.5 per cent per year. This makes the average level of affluence double every 25 to 30 years.

Economic growth is very important to firms. A growing economy creates more opportunities as consumers' tastes change. It is easier to set up or expand a business in a country that has a rapidly growing economy. New gaps emerge in the market, creating more opportunities for budding entrepreneurs.

The economic growth rate of other countries will also be a concern for British firms. For example, the rapid growth in China has led to rising demand for Land Rovers. In 2014 Jaguar Land Rover (JLR)'s export sales to China increased by 72 per cent. To cope with the extra orders the company took on thousands of extra staff. The company also had to buy in more components. This benefited suppliers who also had to increase output and probably employment. The UK is a small country with a domestic market that is also quite small. Eighty-five per cent of the cars Jaguar Land Rover sells are for export. To achieve growth, UK-based firms like JLR depend, in part, on the economic growth rate in other countries.

## The business (economic) cycle

Unfortunately, the economy does not grow at an even rate over time. History shows that the British economy has experienced periods when the economy has grown rapidly. These periods are called booms. Booms are usually followed by recessions; during a recession economic growth grinds to a halt. Technically, a recession is defined as 'two successive quarters of falling output', but even a slowdown can be called a 'growth recession'. If matters do not improve, the economy could end up in a slump. A slump is a sustained period of negative economic growth. The Japanese economy experienced this situation during the period 1990 to 2003.

The UK economy has recently suffered from a very severe recession that many now refer to as the Great Recession. This recession was the deepest and the longest since the 1930s. By the end of 2009 the recession had caused the output of the British economy to fall by 6 per cent. The downturn lasted for a year and a half. The UK economy was helped out of recession by aggressive government action in late 2008 and in 2009. This included tax cuts, a dramatic cut in interest rates and an unorthodox monetary policy measure known as quantitative easing. This added £375 billion of cash to the UK's money supply. After recovery in late 2009 and early 2010, a new government policy of sharp spending cuts and higher taxes slowed the recovery. The economy only just managed to avoid slipping back into recession. Between 2010 and 2015 the UK's economy recovered – unusually slowly. The recovery was probably due to the Bank of England's decision to keep interest rates at record low level of 0.5 per cent for a sustained period. Low borrowing costs encouraged British households to use debt to finance extra spending. Without this increase in household debt,

demand would have stayed low because real wages declined between 2009 and 2014.

The Great Recession was felt by most countries. Only China and India went through this period unscathed.

'Globalisation and free trade do spur economic growth, and they lead to lower prices on many goods.' Robert Reich, political economist

## The impacts of the business cycle

The phases of the trade cycle are given in Table 66.2. The cycle affects firms in different ways according to the types of goods or services they sell. In general, luxury goods businesses like Ferrari benefit most from economic booms. On the other hand, firms like Lidl and Aldi benefit from falling incomes and rising unemployment. This is because cash-strapped

**Table 66.1** Annual percentage rates of economic growth 2008 to 2014

|         | 2008 | 2009 | 2010 | 2011 | 2012 | 2013 |
|---------|------|------|------|------|------|------|
| UK      | −0.3 | −4.3 | 1.9  | 1.6  | 0.7  | 1.7  |
| USA     | −0.3 | −2.8 | 2.5  | 1.6  | 2.3  | 2.2  |
| Germany | 1.1  | −5.6 | 4.1  | 3.6  | 0.4  | 0.1  |
| Greece  | −0.4 | −4.4 | −5.4 | −8.9 | −6.6 | −3.3 |
| Brazil  | 5.2  | −0.3 | 7.5  | 2.7  | 1.0  | 2.5  |
| Russia  | 5.2  | −7.8 | 4.5  | 4.3  | 3.4  | 1.3  |
| India   | 3.9  | 8.5  | 10.3 | 6.6  | 4.7  | 5.0  |
| China   | 9.6  | 9.2  | 10.4 | 9.3  | 7.7  | 7.7  |

Source: data.worldbank.org

**Table 66.2** The phases of the trade cycle

|                                    | Boom | Recession | Slump | Recovery |
|------------------------------------|------|-----------|-------|----------|
| **Consumer and business confidence** | Optimistic | Doubts emerging | Pessimistic | Gradually returning |
| **Consumer spending** | High. Low levels of saving. Spending supplemented by credit | Falling. Spending financed by credit starts to fall | Falling. Consumers save to pay off debts built up during the boom | Rising. Debts have now been paid off |
| **Economic growth** | Strongly positive | GDP begins to fall | GDP growth might now be strongly negative | Weak, but slowly improving |
| **Unemployment** | Close to zero | Low, but starting to rise | High | High, but starting to fall |
| **Inflation** | High, and possibly accelerating | Still positive, but falling. Firms now start to think twice about raising prices | Stable prices, or even some deflation (falling prices) is possible | Price stability |
| **Number of firms failing** | Low | Low, but rising | High | Falling |
| **Business investment** | Firms are optimistic about the future. Investment takes place for both replacement and expansion purposes | Falling. Expansion programmes may be postponed | Close to zero. Even replacement investment may have to be postponed to conserve cash | Slowly rising. Replacement investment projects previously postponed might now get the green light |

consumers respond to falling wages by trading down from more expensive alternatives. In 2014 in a UK grocery market that was barely growing, Aldi and Lidl saw their sales rise by 32 per cent and 17 per cent respectively. On the other hand, Tesco's sales fell by nearly 3 per cent.

Managers must appreciate that because no one knows what the future course of the economy will be, they have to set up their businesses to be able to survive good times and bad. Diversification helps; a business such as Unilever can cope with boom or recession, as its product portfolio includes brand essentials such as Persil plus brand luxuries such as Calvin Klein perfumes.

# The impact of economic change on corporate strategy and business functions

What actions should a producer of luxury goods take today if it predicts a recession in the near future?

## Business objectives and strategy

During a recession a producer of luxury goods might need to change its corporate objective from growth or profit maximisation to one of survival. During a recession revenue is bound to fall. The key to survival is to minimise losses, which can be achieved by introducing a package of cost-saving measures. Some of these changes could permanently damage the competitiveness of the business. For example, cutting back on expensive new product development may leave the product with an ageing product range in the future. However, if the firm does not cut costs now the business may not have a future to worry about! In a recession managers usually have to make difficult and unpopular decisions.

## Marketing

Some businesses react to a recession by changing their marketing strategy to emphasise value for money in an attempt to hold up revenue at a time when the market may be shrinking. Some companies may consider reacting to a recession by cutting prices to help boost sales. However, this may be risky because a price cut could cheapen the brand's image, resulting in a loss of sales once the economy recovers.

## Production

Sales of luxury goods fall during a recession; to prepare for this, producers of luxury goods should aim to cut production sooner rather than later. Cutting production cannot be achieved overnight. For example, suppliers of raw materials and components will probably have minimum notice periods written into their contracts.

If the firm waits until sales start to fall before cutting production the result is likely to be a build-up of stock; this is expensive to store and it also ties up cash. During recessions, expansion plans tend to be shelved because the extra capacity created by expansion will not be needed at a time when sales are expected to fall.

## Human resource management

During a recession a manufacturer of luxury goods might not need as many staff because fewer goods are being sold. One way of slimming down a workforce is via compulsory redundancy. Getting rid of staff because they are not needed any more is expensive, may create negative publicity and is bad for staff morale. A better option may be to reduce the wage bill via natural wastage. This involves suspending recruitment. By not replacing employees who leave or retire, the workforce will fall naturally without the need for redundancies.

Some firms use the job insecurity created by a recession to force through changes in working practices that are designed to reduce costs. During a recession job opportunities elsewhere tend to be scarce. Ruthless managers may use this to their advantage. They would argue that the whole business will be leaner and fitter as a result.

## Finance

Firms fail when they run out of cash (suppliers with unpaid bills take you to court). During recessions, producers of luxury goods leak cash because of low demand. Logically, the best chance of survival is for those businesses that started the period of recession with healthy balance sheets, low borrowing levels and high liquidity. To conserve cash during an unprofitable period of trading, a business could do the following:

- Carry out a programme of zero budgeting throughout the organisation to trim any waste from departmental budgets
- Restrict the credit given to customers and chase up debtors who currently owe the firm money
- Rationalise, that is, sell off any under-utilised fixed assets such as machinery and property. This will bring cash into the business.

# 66.2 Fiscal and monetary policy

## Fiscal policy

Governments collect taxes to pay for old age pensions and public services, such as the NHS, education, defence and law and order. Fiscal policy refers to the government's tax and spending plans for the year ahead. The British government normally runs a fiscal deficit. This means that the government spends more than its tax income. The government finances its fiscal deficit by borrowing.

'Education is the key to the future: you've heard it a million times, and it's not wrong. Educated people have higher wages and lower unemployment rates, and better-educated countries grow faster and innovate more than other countries.' Alex Tabarrok, economist

## Taxation

In Britain the main taxes collected by the government are:

- **Income tax:** this tax is paid by households on their incomes. The basic rate of income tax of 20 per cent is paid on any income earned above £10,000 per year. In most countries, income tax is progressive. This means that the rate of income tax paid rises as income rises. High rates of income tax reduce consumption because they lower household disposable incomes. Businesses normally prefer low rates of income tax.
- **National insurance:** is a tax on employment paid by both firms and households.
- **VAT (Value Added Tax):** this is a tax on goods and services paid by firms. Businesses pass VAT on to their customers by raising prices. Firms prefer lower rates of VAT, because it leads to lower prices and hence higher sales. In 2010 the government raised the rate of VAT to 20 per cent.
- **Excise duties:** in addition to VAT the government also imposes other taxes on some products, such as petrol, alcohol and tobacco. Usually the demand for these products is not very price sensitive, which allows the government to collect more in tax.
- **Corporation tax:** this is a tax on company profits. Businesses prefer lower rates of corporation tax because it increases the amount of post-tax profit available to either reinvest, or to pay to shareholders as dividends. The main rate of corporation tax in the UK in 2015 was 20 per cent.

'Government can wreck a business by confiscating its money by taxation.' Owen Paterson, politician

'The way to crush the bourgeoisie is to grind them between the millstones of taxation and inflation.' Vladimir Lenin, communist leader

## Government spending

Businesses like Virgin Care and BAE Systems benefit directly from government spending. Virgin Care supplies a range of health care services for the NHS. BAE Systems sells tanks, bombs and bullets that are used by the British Army overseas. If the government spends more on both health and defence, Virgin and BAE Systems capture additional revenue from taxpayers. Other firms benefit indirectly from government spending. For example, if the government increases pensions, older people will now have more money to spend. As a result demand for food and other essentials will rise. This helps companies that sell the goods and services bought by pensioners.

## Monetary policy

Monetary policy involves the Bank of England changing either interest rates or the money supply in order to influence the level of spending in the economy. During recessions, monetary policy is loosened to try to create a recovery by increasing demand. This is done by cutting interest rates and by creating more money. If interest rates are cut, the cost of borrowing falls. Households usually respond to lower interest rates by borrowing more (perhaps to buy a new car financed by credit). The increase in consumption created by lower interest rates enables firms to sell more of their products, which boosts revenue. Firms with big loans on their balance sheets also benefit from loose monetary policy. This is because a lower cost of borrowing reduces monthly loan repayments.

## 66.3 Exchange rates

In Britain goods and services are sold in our currency, the pound. In America goods and services are sold in dollars. The exchange rate measures the quantity of foreign currency that can be bought with one unit of another currency, for example, £1 buys $2. Movements in the exchange rate can dramatically affect profitability because the exchange rate affects both the price of imported and exported goods. Firms cannot influence the exchange rate. For example, the pound's rate of exchange against the US dollar is determined by the supply and demand for the pound on international currency markets. An individual firm is too small to affect the exchange rate; it is a good example of an external constraint that is beyond the control of any one manager. Exchange rates affect firms in different ways.

## The impacts of a high exchange rate

### On firms with large export markets

UK exporters such as Rolls Royce, Fever Tree and Bentley cars prefer a low exchange rate, that is, a weak pound. Why is this so? The best way of explaining is via a numerical example.

America is an important export market for Bentley. The company's most popular model is called the Flying Spur and is priced at £150,000 in the UK. To achieve the same profit margin in America, Bentley will have to charge a price in US dollars that will convert into £150,000. In January 2015 the exchange rate against the US dollar was £1: $1.50. To obtain £150,000 per export, Bentley charged its American customers:

$$£150,000 \times \$1.50 = \$225,000$$

If the pound's exchange rate rises to £1: $1.80, to generate the same £150,000 of export revenue Bentley will have to charge its American customers:

$$£150,000 \times \$1.80 = \$270,000$$

In other words, the rise in the pound would force Bentley to increase its US price by $45,000 dollars to maintain the current UK revenue (and profit) per car. If Bentley reacts to a rising pound by putting prices up in the US, demand for its cars will almost certainly drop, causing profitability to fall. On the other hand, if Bentley decides against raising its prices in America, the company will have to accept a lower profit on each car sold; either way Bentley loses out as a result of a higher pound.

In conclusion, exporters hate it when their currency rises in value; they like it to fall, not rise.

### On firms that import most of their raw materials or stock

Retailers that import most of their stock prefer a high exchange rate. A high exchange rate reduces the cost of buying goods from abroad. For example, Converse trainers are imported from America. If the US price of a pair is $45, the price paid by JD Sports:

If the exchange rate is £1: $1.50, will be $45/1.50 = £30.00

However, if the exchange rate goes up to £1: $1.80 the same trainers will now be £25 ($45/1.80 = £25).

A high exchange rate ('strong pound') benefits importers because the goods they import become cheaper in pounds. JD can then make more profit on each pair of Converse they sell to UK customers, or perhaps competition will force them to cut their UK prices.

## The impacts of a low exchange rate

The impacts of a weak exchange rate are the reverse of those from a strong exchange rate. Firms like Bentley that were damaged by a strong currency find life easier when the exchange rate falls. A weak pound makes their exports seem cheaper to foreign consumers, so Bentley should be able to sell more of its cars in America.

On the other hand, retailers like JD Sports will be damaged by a low exchange rate because it will now cost more in pounds to buy-in its imported stock. If JD reacts to the falling exchange rate by raising its prices the company could lose customers. If it leaves its retail prices unchanged, it will make less profit per imported item.

---

'One of the ways they (China) don't play by the rules is artificially holding down the value of their currency; China has been a currency manipulator for years.' Mitt Romney, U.S. politician and businessman

---

## 66.4 Inflation

### Introduction: what is inflation?

Inflation measures the percentage annual rise in the average price level. Inflation reduces the purchasing power of money within an economy. Between 2009 and 2014 the pay rises for most British workers weren't high enough to keep pace with inflation. Falling real wages caused a cost of living crisis.

The impacts of inflation on a firm's finances are mixed.

### Advantages of inflation to a business

#### Real assets become worth more

Inflation makes real assets become worth more. For example, the value of any property or stock that the firm might own will increase if prices are going up. A firm with more valuable assets will have a more impressive balance sheet. As a result the firm may find it easier to raise long-term finance from banks and shareholders because the business now looks more secure.

---

'Inflation is taxation without legislation.' Milton Friedman, economist

---

## The real value of money owed is eroded

Firms with large borrowings also benefit from inflation because inflation erodes the real value of the money owed. The fixed repayments on long-term loans become more easily covered by inflationary rises in income and profits. After, say, ten years the real value of a £1 million loan may be only £0.5 million by the time the borrower repays the loan. In the same way, some householders have trivial mortgage payments because they bought a house valued then at £80,000 (and perhaps worth £320,000 today).

## Drawbacks of inflation

### Damage to profitability

Inflation can damage profitability, especially for those firms that have fixed-price contracts that take a long time to complete. For example, a local building company may agree a £5 million price for an extension to a local school, which is expected to take three years to finish. If inflation is higher than expected, profit could be wiped out by unexpectedly high cost increases.

### Damage to industrial relations

Inflation can also damage industrial relations, that is, the relationship between the business and its staff. When making pay claims for the year ahead, staff representatives (perhaps a trade union) will estimate the likely inflation rate in the future. This estimate may be higher than that expected by management. Differences in inflationary expectations have the potential to cause costly industrial disputes that may damage a firm's reputation.

## 66.5 More open trade and protectionism

International trade can create opportunities for companies. In some cases international trade can help a firm to lower its costs. For example, unrestricted access to an overseas market might enable a manufacturer to replace an existing domestic supplier of raw materials with a cheaper foreign one. More open international trade can also help a firm to expand and grow via exporting. This is especially important for firms operating in countries with small populations. The population of Finland is just 5.5 million, which means that the domestic market for items such as clothing and consumer goods is quite small. Fortunately for Finnish companies Finland's membership of the European Union has enabled businesses there to have open trade access to the European Single Market of 500 million people.

Protectionism is the opposite of open international trade. Examples of protectionist trade barriers include:

- Tariffs: are taxes on imported goods. Tariffs are designed to increase the price of imported goods. Higher prices will hopefully divert demand away from imports towards domestically produced alternatives.

- Quotas: are annual physical limits on the quantity of specific goods that can be imported into a country. Once quotas have been filled, consumers will have no choice but to buy domestically produced substitutes.

Governments that use protectionist trade policies do so to try give a helping hand to inefficient domestic producers who would not otherwise be able to compete and survive.

## Evaluation: The impact of changes in the economic environment

When times are good companies tend to forget the economy. When recession hit in late 2008 it was clear that businesses such as Marks & Spencer were unprepared. No one can reliably forecast economic trends, but successful firms are prepared for any possible circumstances. They will have asked 'What if?' a specific economic trend depresses profitability. Firms can do nothing about the exchange rate and the economy. However, they can make internal changes to their businesses that are designed to minimise the worst effects of a possible economic problem.

For example, if Bentley believes that the pound will rise against the American dollar, the company could attempt to cut its costs by automating production. In short, it could aim to internalise external constraints.

To try to have some impact on government policy decisions on the economy, big companies such as Tesco and Unilever try to influence government decisions by lobbying and via donations to think tanks and political parties. Their goal is to create a favourable business environment where it is easier to make profit.

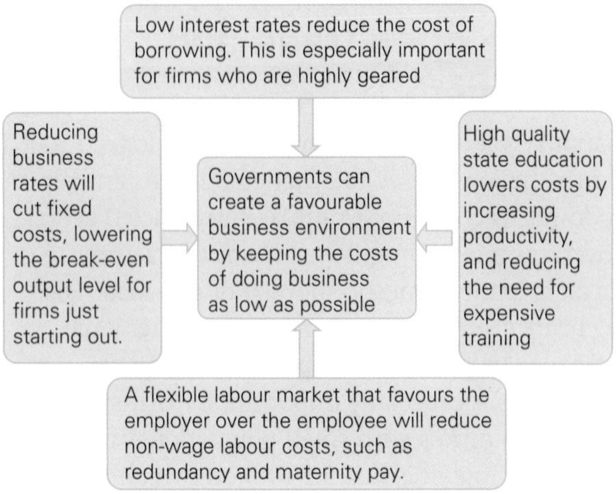

Low interest rates reduce the cost of borrowing. This is especially important for firms who are highly geared

Reducing business rates will cut fixed costs, lowering the break-even output level for firms just starting out.

Governments can create a favourable business environment by keeping the costs of doing business as low as possible

High quality state education lowers costs by increasing productivity, and reducing the need for expensive training

A flexible labour market that favours the employer over the employee will reduce non-wage labour costs, such as redundancy and maternity pay.

**Figure 66.1** Logic chain: companies lobby politicians to adopt policies design to create a favourable business environment

## Key terms

**Growth recession:** when economic growth slows to the point that businesses struggle and unemployment may start to rise.

**Inflation:** although often defined as the rate of rise in the average price level, inflation is better understood as a fall in the value of money.

**Natural wastage:** allowing staff levels to fall naturally, by not replacing staff that leave.

**Real wages:** changes in money wages minus the rate of change in prices (inflation), for example, if your pay packet is up 6 per cent but prices are up 4 per cent, your real wage has risen by 2 per cent.

**Recession:** two successive quarters of falling output (falling GDP).

## Five Whys and a How

| Question | Answer |
|---|---|
| Why might Tesco welcome a stronger currency? | A strong currency will reduce the price of the goods Tesco imports, leading to lower costs. An increase in the exchange rate will make UK exports more expensive. However, this will not affect Tesco because most of their customers live in Britain. |
| Why can inflation lead to lower levels of consumer spending? | If wage increases fail to keep pace with price increases, the purchasing power of household income will fall. If households are not able to buy as many goods and services as before, sales (measured in volume terms) will fall. |
| Why might car manufacturers welcome a fall in interest rates? | Like other expensive consumer durables, cars are typically bought on credit. When consumers make their decision on whether to buy or not, they look at the monthly repayment, rather than the full price of what they are buying. |
| Why do some private businesses benefit more from government spending than others? | Some businesses, such as Virgin Care and Capgemini, focus on government contracts, perhaps because they find it easier to make profits in this way. |
| Why do firms benefit when the rate of corporation tax is cut? | Corporation tax is a tax on company profits. If the government cuts the rate of tax, post-tax profits will rise. Firms can now invest more in efficiency or expansion – or may choose to increase dividends to shareholders (and boost the share price). |
| How can firms benefit from free trade areas, such as the European Union or the North American Free Trade Association? | Locating inside a free trade area enables a firm to gain tariff- and quota-free access to a much bigger export market. In addition, costs will fall with tariff-free imports of raw materials. |

# Workbook

## A. Revision questions

(35 marks; 35 minutes)

1. What is the business cycle? (2)

2. Explain why a business such as Chessington World of Adventures could be affected by a recession in America. (4)

3. Explain how a furniture manufacturer might benefit from a fall in the value of the pound. (4)

4. Explain how two features of a recession might affect an upmarket department store. (8)

5. Why may a firm respond to the threat of a recession by suspending recruitment, even before the recession actually arrives? (4)

6. What are inflationary expectations and why are they important? (4)

7. How could inflation benefit a small one-stop convenience store? (3)

8. Explain two reasons why staff morale can fall sharply during a recession. (6)

## B. Revision exercises

### DATA RESPONSE

**You've had your chips: award winning chippy closes doors**

In 2011, Ian Shaw ditched his day job and set up his own fish and chip shop. Using £15,000 of his own money, Shaw rented a bakery in Rochdale, converted it, and in early 2012, *The Best Cod in Town* opened its doors for the first time. The chippy proved to be a hit with customers. Shaw's business model was based on selling a top quality product at low prices. This meant buying in the best fish and changing the oil used for frying more often than usual.

Like many other entrepreneurs just starting out Ian worked very long hours, which helped to boost sales and keep staff costs down. Most of Shaw's customers who tried his fish and chips liked them, and came back for more, becoming regulars. Thanks to its popularity, the chippy generated good revenues. At the end of its first year, *The Best Cod in Town* was ranked in first place by *Trip Advisor* as Rochdale's best takeaway. Despite its substantial turnover the business struggled to make a profit. This was because fixed costs were too high, which created a high break-even point. The biggest fixed cost that he had to pay was business rates. Every month *The Best Cod in Town* had to pay Rochdale council £1,872. This was even higher than the £1,200 he paid per month in rent to lease the premises. When the council increased his rates again, and promised to do so in the years after, Shaw decided that there was no other option, the writing was on the wall: 'We had a break clause in our lease after 18 months and I've decided it's best to get out sooner rather than later.' *The Best Cod in Town* closed its doors for the final time in September 2013.

At the time Shaw said, 'The town centre is dying. Unless you want a pay day loan, a television on hire purchase or to go to a charity shop there just isn't a reason for people to come into Rochdale. With the changes that are coming in to the benefits system later this year people will have even less money to spend. We're the fourth business that is closing at this end of the high street and I can't see things getting any better.'

MP Simon Danczuk, Rochdale's MP was critical of the government, arguing, 'This government does not care about people like Ian; they are only interested in big business. Small businesses like Ian's are the lifeblood of the economy and if we're going to have a proper recovery then they need to be given a fighting chance of survival. Big business seems to get all the support and subsidies from the government and are being allowed to exploit tax loopholes. At the same time smaller firms are getting bigger and bigger business rate bills.'

The biggest employer in the town is Rochdale council. Due to government spending cuts, unemployment has soared and spending is sharply down. In December 2014, nearly a quarter of Rochdale's shops were vacant. The council reacted by offering new businesses who were prepared to move into an empty shop an 80 per cent discount on their business rates in the first year, and a 50 per cent cut in the second year.

## Questions (60 marks; 70 minutes)

1. Analyse the main factors that would have affected the break-even output level of *The Best Cod in Town*. (12)

2. Analyse how private businesses like *The Best Cod in Town* might benefit from government spending. (12)

3. When *The Best Cod in Town* made losses, Ian Shaw responded by closing the business down. To what extent do you agree with Ian Shaw's decision to shut his business down? (16)

4. *The Best Cod in Town*'s competitive advantage was based around selling a high quality product at low price. To what extent can this business model deliver long-run, sustainable, success? (20)

## C. Extend your understanding

1. In 2013, a number of high profile businesses such as Starbucks, Google and Amazon were criticised in the media for using creative accounting to legally avoid tax. How important do you think it is that the government should take action to close these tax loopholes? Justify your answer. (25)

2. A supermarket chain faces a combination of a recession, inflation and a falling exchange rate. Given the circumstances as described, to what extent would you agree that a fall in the supermarket's profit is inevitable? (25)

# Chapter 67

# Globalisation and emerging economies

Linked to: The impact of government policy, Chapter 65; Strategic direction: Ansoff's matrix, Chapter 75; Methods and types of growth, Chapter 80; Reasons for trading internationally, Chapter 84; China and India, Chapter 86; Targeting overseas markets, Chapter 87.

## Definition

**Globalisation:** the pressures leading to the world becoming one market, with the risk that national producers (and cultures) may be squeezed out. Emerging economies are those that have made a breakthrough to sustained, rapid (or quite rapid) growth – though average living standards may still be very low by Western standards.

## 67.1 Introduction

Globalisation is by no means a new force. In 1900 a quarter of the world's population lived under a British flag, bringing with it a 'culture' of tea, cricket and – from 1902 – Marmite. In the 1920s, American companies such as Ford and Coca-Cola started their moves to multinational status. By the 1960s Mickey Mouse, US films and British pop music were global forces. Yet the term globalisation only really started to stick in the 1980s. It was in this period that the huge growth of McDonald's and Coca-Cola made people start to question whether the world was becoming a suburb of America. Later, the growth of Microsoft, Starbucks, Google and Facebook brought the question further into focus. Figure 67.1 gives a sense of the extraordinary growth in world trade, but lends little support to any view that globalisation 'arrived in the year 2000'. Proportionately, the fastest growing decades were the 1960s and 1970s (see Figure 67.1).

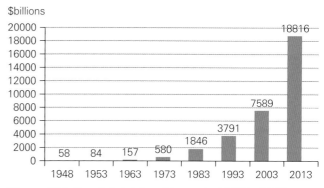

**Figure 67.1** Growth in total world exports, 1948 to 2013

Source: World Trade Organisation

The term globalisation encompasses many issues. Some are based on cultural questions, such as whether a language such as French can survive the onslaught of (American) English. Some are based on ethical questions that seem much starker when a rich Western company is getting its supplies from Cambodian labour paid 30p an hour. Others are more focused on the economic question, 'Are global giants wiping out national producers and restricting consumer choice?' Clearly these are all massive questions in a Business A-level course.

'Globalisation means that for a high-wage, developed economy like Britain's to compete we need to focus our efforts on the highly skilled, added-value sectors.' Lucy Powell, MP

## 67.2 Reasons for greater globalisation of business

Joseph Stiglitz, in his book *Globalization and its Discontents*, became the world's most famous critic of globalisation. Yet he identifies many important benefits from increasingly open world trade. To him, the biggest step forward by far is the increase in the number of people in less developed countries whose lives have been improved. He mentions the opening up of the

Jamaican milk market (allowing US competition in) as a huge benefit to poor children in Jamaica, even if it hurt the profits of the local farmers. It is also important to bear in mind that, however awful the figures may be for infant mortality in developing countries, they are incomparably better than they were 20, 40 or 50 years ago. Globalisation of health care is as important here as the globalisation of the economy.

Among the main reasons for globalisation are:

- a reduction in protectionism. After the World Trade Organisation (WTO) was formed in 1995 the proportion of global imports arriving tariff-free rose from 20 per cent to around 60 per cent today. Fewer taxes on international trade has helped spread trade globally

- increased competition forces local producers to be efficient, thereby cutting prices and increasing standards of living (people's income goes further)

- providing the opportunity for the best ideas to be spread across the globe (for example, AIDS medicines, water irrigation and mobile phones)

- if multinational companies open up within a country, this may provide opportunities for employment and training, and allow local entrepreneurs to learn from the experience of the more established businesses

- providing outlets for exports, which can allow a country to boost its standards of living by reducing dependence on subsistence farming (growing just enough to feed the family)

- it has provided the opportunity for a series of countries (for example, Bangladesh, Mexico and China) to break away from poverty to an extent. For example, average living standards in China rose by 1,700 per cent between 1993 and 2013 (measured in US dollars).

**Figure 67.2** Modern China

## Real business

### *Bangladesh*

In the 20 years until 1990, the annual growth rate in Bangladesh* was an extremely low 0.6 per cent. This left its under-5 mortality rate at 144 per 1,000 in 1990. Each year, more under-5s died in Bangladesh than all the under-5s living in Britain. By 1990 Bangladesh was developing a clothing industry based upon very low-wage labour, targeting Western companies. In the period 1990 to 2013 the growth rate rose to 3.3 per cent per person, helping the infant mortality rate to fall from 144 to 41 per 1000.

Bangladesh has by no means become a wealthy country. Many households have no access to clean water and, by 2013, only 14 per cent of the population had a fridge. But economic progress has made an impact, and should continue to do so.

* Bangladesh, with 160 million people, is the world's seventh most populated country

'We must ensure that the global market is embedded in broadly shared values and practices that reflect global social needs, and that all the world's people share the benefits of globalisation.' Kofi Annan, former head of the United Nations

**Figure 67.3** Logic balance: for and against globalisation

## 67.3 The case against globalisation

### The economic case against

Critics suggest that globalisation has made it harder for local firms to create local opportunities. In 2002 virtually no overseas car producer had a factory in

India; but, with the growth of the Indian economy, by 2014 Hyundai, Peugeot, Ford, Suzuki, BMW, Toyota, Nissan and Honda were present, with Kia of South Korea announcing a new factory in India by 2016. Amazingly, given that its ownership of Jaguar Land Rover has been a great success, Indian-owned Tata Motors struggles to make a profit in its home market. It may be that the bulk of India's car market will be captured by the big European and Far Eastern car producers.

There is also concern that new production in a country does not necessarily mean new wealth. Some multinational firms establish a factory locally, but use it in a way that could be called exploitation. In India there are many clothing factories that supply companies such as Gap, Primark and Asda. Wage rates are extremely low by Western standards, and working conditions are poor. Little of the value created by the sale of a £20 jumper in a London Gap outlet may seep back to India. If the clothing design, the branding and the packaging are all done in the West, all that is left is labour-intensive, low-paid factory work.

'Globalisation by the way of McDonald's and KFC has captured the hearts, the minds, and from what I can see through the window, the growing bellies of the folks here.' Raquel Cepeda, Latin American author

## The social and cultural case against

A French farmer once made headlines worldwide by bulldozing a McDonald's outlet. He was protesting about the Americanisation of France. Remarkably, even the French cosmetics powerhouse L'Oréal is inclined to show English-language television commercials in France. The increasing number of US outlets in French high streets was the farmer's main concern: KFC, McDonald's, Subway, Gap, Starbucks, and so on. Around the world, many agreed that their high streets were starting to look like those in America. Globalisation can be criticised for making our lives less interesting by reducing the differences between countries and cities.

Among the main disadvantages of globalisation are:

- that everywhere starts to look like everywhere else
- that globalisation is built on exploitation – the strong exploiting the poor
- that it may make it hard for local producers to build and grow in a way that is suited to local needs.

### Real business

#### Nigeria

There is probably no country in the world that has underachieved as severely as Nigeria. In the 20 years to 1990 its economy *shrank* by an average of 1.4 per cent a year. Its 1990 child mortality of 213 per 1,000 was among the world's worst. Since then, growth has averaged just 1.4 per cent a year; this is despite the fact that Nigeria is oil rich. Over the past 20 years more than £90 billion of oil has been exported from the country. This has been good for BP and Shell, but the people of Nigeria have little benefit to show for all this wealth. Corruption has been an important problem, but many Nigerians would point to the oil multinationals as well as their own leaders. The benefits of globalisation have passed them by.

## 67.4 The importance of globalisation for business

It is easy to forget that British business practice today has been shaped by two waves of globalisation. In the 1920s and 1930s the Americans came. Ford, Gillette, Mars, Vauxhall and Coca-Cola invested in brand new factories in Britain, employing tens of thousands. They also brought the American way of doing business – more evidence based and more based on F.W. Taylor's approach to scientific management. In the 1980s another inward investment wave occurred from Japan. In came Sony, Hitachi, Nissan, Toyota and Honda. In the case of the three car companies, they are very much still here. Before they arrived, British managements had heard of JIT and lean production – but they didn't believe it. Nissan UK, in particular, not only had business success but also shouted about the value of the new Japanese management approaches. British management in the twenty-first century owes a lot to the inward effects of globalisation.

Britain has also benefited more than most countries from outward globalisation – if one accepts that its origins can be traced back to colonisation, centuries ago. Today, few countries in the world have the 'brand' recognition Britain has. Whereas the German 'brand' means great engineering and the US brand spans 'innovative cool' and 'aspirational comfort' (McDonalds, Coca-Cola, Starbucks), Britain means 'traditional and classy'. So high-priced Fever-Tree tonic water – born in 2005 – can quickly have the brand credentials of Schweppes (born 1783). And Jaguar Land Rover can quickly catch up in China with

German car makers who had been in the country for more than twenty years.

Globalisation is important to British companies because:

- They have a natural advantage, especially in the luxury sector
- As economic activity has faltered in Europe (destination for half of all UK exports) it's invaluable to find fast-growing developing countries such as those in Asia and sub-Saharan Africa
- Having a substantial export market spreads costs and therefore helps keep down the prices UK consumers have to pay
- In November 2014 the government's statistical office ONS published a report showing that labour productivity at exporting firms grows nearly five times faster than at non-exporting firms. In effect, competing internationally toughens firms up. We can all benefit from that rising level of efficiency.

## 67.5 The importance of emerging economies for business

The most important thing is to realise that development happens. In 1981, 50 per cent of the world's population lived on less than $1.25 a day (about 80p). By 2015, a World Bank estimate puts the figure at 12 per cent*. Of course, that's still nearly a billion people living on extremely low incomes. But it is wrong to treat the issue of development with a shrug of the shoulders. There are hopeful signs. Table 67.1 shows the economic performance of a selection of less developed countries. Despite the figures in the right-hand column, the two central columns show that improvements are definitely occurring.

*Adjusted for inflation, so it's a real change.

Between 1980 and 2000, the big development wins were in China, in India, in South East Asia more generally, and in South America. Since 2000, China and India's success has been joined by sub-Saharan Africa. Without exception, these gains have come about as a result of economic development.

Does economic aid have much to do with this relative success? Not really, as governments and charities rarely do enough to make much impact throughout a country. In China, India and Mexico, for instance, the key factors have been:

- greater willingness to accept inward investment from multinational or other big, wealthy companies from the West or Japan
- greater enterprise on the part of the local business population
- more stable government than before
- easier access for exports to countries such as Britain, America and the rest of Europe, partly thanks to the World Trade Organization.

It would be wrong to complete a chapter on globalisation without mentioning the country with the most remarkable impact on the global economy for more than a hundred years – China. No single country has ever before moved so rapidly from nowhere to the world's leading exporter. It has also become the world's second largest importer of goods, after America. For many companies it's the Number 1 market; none more clearly than the car industry. In January 2015 car sales in China outstripped America by 75 per cent, even though the US market was buoyant. As Figure 67.2 shows, China has to be taken seriously as a focal point for global business in future.

'Globalisation has changed us into a company that searches the world, not just to sell or to source, but to find intellectual capital - the world's best talents and greatest ideas.' Jack Welch, former CEO, General Electric

**Table 67.1** Economic performance of selected countries

| | GDP at PPP 2013 | Average annual growth in GDP per head 1970–1990 | Average annual growth in GDP per head 1990–2012 | Percentage of population below $1.25 a day 2007–2011 |
|---|---|---|---|---|
| Bangladesh | $2,100 | 0.5 | 3.7 | 43 |
| Cambodia | $2,600 | 0.0 | 6.0 | 19 |
| China | $9,800 | 6.6 | 9.3 | 12 |
| India | $4,000 | 2.0 | 5.0 | 33 |
| Nicaragua | $4,500 | –3.7 | 2.0 | 12 |
| Nigeria | $2,800 | –1.3 | 2.1 | 54 |

Source: CIA Factbook 2015 and Unicef statistics 2015

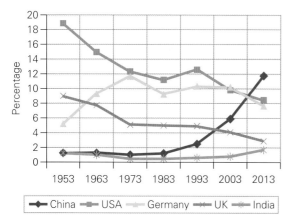

**Figure 67.4** World share of exports of goods, 1953-2013

Source: World Trade Organisation, January 2015

## Key terms

**Intellectual property:** new written, visual or technical material for which the originator may seek legal protection (for example, copyright, trademarks or patents).

**Protectionism:** government actions to protect home producers from competition from overseas (for example, by setting import taxes – tariffs; or imposing import quotas that place a cap on the number of goods that can enter a country).

**Tariff:** a tax placed only on imported goods.

## Five Whys and a How

| Question | Answer |
|----------|--------|
| Why do some poor countries struggle to kick-start sustained economic growth? | Perhaps because they are too willing to accept a continuing role as suppliers of raw materials; economic growth is associated far more with manufacturing (added value) output |
| Why do Western countries give aid to countries where corruption is so widespread? | Corruption is often a feature of developing economies (the mafia was hugely important in America until relatively recently) but there's not much evidence that it hinders economic growth |
| Why are British companies so poor, relatively, at exporting to developing countries? | Perhaps our timescales for business thinking are too short. The big winner in China is Germany's Volkswagen, which committed to the market when it was still tiny, more than twenty-five years ago |
| Why do some people worry that globalisation is a form of 'cultural imperialism'? | They dislike the thought that global Starbucks could wipe out the local individualism of cafes worldwide – making every high street look the same (American) |
| Why might Britain benefit from inward globalisation? | In the past Britain benefited from a wave of US investment in the 1920s and 1930s, then from Japan in the 1980s. Perhaps in the future the Chinese will open factories in Europe – if so, it'll be in Germany or the UK |
| How might a small British business today break into the global market for its products? | If the product has a distinctive positioning and brand, late arrival is no problem, as the Land Rover Evoque showed in China and as Fever-Tree tonic water has shown worldwide |

## Evaluation: Globalisation and emerging economies

The judgements involved in this area need to be especially subtle. Beware of poorly justified judgements that may suggest intolerance towards others, or ignorance of the extreme disparities between incomes in rich and poor countries. The more you read about different countries' successes and failures, the better rooted your judgements will be.

It is also valuable to take a critical look at all the evidence provided, questioning whether the claims made by businesses about their motives are the truth or just public relations. The same sceptical approach should be taken to any other form of evidence, whether from pressure groups such as Greenpeace or from government ministers or officials. Globalisation is a topic in which opinions are often clearer than facts.

# Workbook

## A. Revision questions

(40 marks; 40 minutes)

1. Reread the definition of globalisation at the start of the unit. Outline one advantage and one disadvantage of the world 'becoming one market'. (4)

2. **a)** Using Figure 67.1, calculate the percentage increases in world exports in the following periods.
   **(i)** 1983–1993
   **(ii)** 1993–2003
   **(iii)** 2003–2013. (5)
   **b)** How well do these figures support the idea that globalisation arrived in the 1990s? (3)

3. Outline two reasons why consumers may suffer as a result of a government policy of import protectionism. (4)

4. Outline two other factors that could affect a country's infant mortality, apart from economic development. (4)

5. Use Figure 67.1 to describe three major changes that occurred between 1948 and 2013. (6)

6. Should wealthy countries increase the rates of tax on their own populations in order to finance greater help to people living on less than $1.25 a day? (4)

7. Outline three possible reasons that may explain why China's growth rate is so much higher than that of India. (6)

8. Explain why a customer might worry that a £6 dress at Primark might be *too* cheap. (4)

## B. Revision exercises

### DATA RESPONSE

**Starbucks agrees to Ethiopian coffee branding**

In 2004, Ethiopian coffee farmers supported by Oxfam applied a trademark to some of their coffee brands in North America and other regions. These included the Sidamo, Harar and Yirgacheffe varieties.

This protection of their intellectual property would allow them to take better control of their brands and to earn more from the sale price of the coffee.

In 2007, following international pressure, Starbucks signed a distribution, marketing and licensing agreement with the coffee farmers. As a result, Starbucks could sell and market the branded varieties in accordance with the agreements signed with the farmers.

Evan O'Neil from the Fairer Globalization blog praised the agreement as an example of 'multi-stakeholder co-operation'.

**Questions (25 marks; 30 minutes)**

1. Explain what 'intellectual property' there can be in Ethiopian coffee. (5)

2. Explain how Ethiopian farmers could benefit from this initiative. (6)

3. Analyse the possible reasons why Starbucks may have decided to sign this deal with the Ethiopian coffee producers. (9)

4. Explain what the author means by the phrase 'this multi-stakeholder co-operation'. (5)

## C. Extend your understanding

1. To what extent might an online business such as ASOS benefit from setting an objective of becoming a fully global business? (25)

2. 'As long as the branding is right, we'll succeed globally.' To what extent is the managing director of a fast-growing luxury soft drinks business right to think this way? (25)

**Linked to:** The value of SWOT analysis, Chapter 56; Changes in the political and legal environment, Chapter 64; Globalisation and emerging economies, Chapter 67; The social environment including CSR, Chapter 69.

> **Definition**
>
> Social change refers to the fluidity of human behaviour and actions that affect demography and lifestyle.

## 68.1 Introduction

Businesses operate in an environment where external change is commonplace. Economic, environmental, political and legal changes all affect what businesses do and how they try to do it. This chapter focuses on three major social changes, considered both from a global and national perspective. Then it considers the impact of the social environment on strategic and functional decision-making.

## 68.2 Urbanisation and migration

'Immigration is not just compatible with but is a necessary component of economic growth.' Dave Reichert, US politician

### Urbanisation

Urbanisation tends to go hand in hand with economic development. As a country becomes increasingly wealthy people tend to move away from the rural areas that play host to agriculture towards better jobs in urban areas. The World Health Organization reports that in 2014, 54 per cent of the world's population lived in urban areas, up by 20 per cent since 1960, and forecast to rise by around 1.5 per cent per year for the next fifteen years. Table 68.1 gives this figure for several countries in both 2000 and 2014, and shows that the more economically developed a country is, the more urbanisation has occurred.

**Table 68.1** Percentage living in urban areas

| Country | Percentage of population living in urban areas 2014 | Percentage of population living in urban areas 2000 |
|---------|------|------|
| UK | 82 | 79 |
| USA | 81 | 79 |
| China | 54 | 36 |
| Brazil | 85 | 81 |
| India | 32 | 28 |
| Malawi | 16 | 15 |

Source: World Bank

Urbanisation means more concentrated geographical markets for businesses to serve. In the more highly urbanised countries, such as the UK, this can mean that it is no longer viable to maintain physical premises in rural areas. This has been a problem for UK banks, who have for years been closing branches in villages and small towns as the number of rural customers shrinks. Fortunately online banking and mobile technology are helping to make this less of a problem locally.

In developing countries such as China, where urbanisation has been rapid, the increased concentrations of population make it easier to identify large enough local markets to target. Whitbread plc has had a major success in China with its Costa Coffee brand, which has built a strong number two position behind Starbucks (see Figure 68.1). It is only profitable to open coffee shops in China because middle class people are clustered in urban areas.

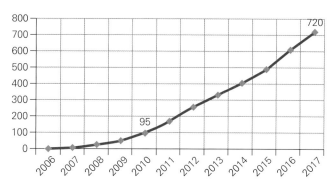

**Figure 68.1** Costa coffee shops in China (actual to 2014; Costa estimate for 2015–2017)

Source: Whitbread accounts

## Migration

Migration is the term used to describe people moving from one country to another. Inward migration (immigration) becomes politically important every time there is a recession. In the UK and elsewhere, an economic downturn stirs up hostility towards those born overseas, who get blamed for unemployment or for low wage growth.

For businesses, there is a primary concern regarding immigration: that it should be barrier-free. Companies want to be able to recruit specialist software engineers or surgeons from overseas, when necessary. For catering companies such as Pret A Manger, enthusiastic young migrants from Eastern Europe or Portugal or Spain are preferable to disaffected young Brits who may think that catering is beneath them. In the City of London especially the banking sector recruits overwhelmingly from Britain, but wants to be able to bring in a Yen specialist from Japan or a software genius from California as needed.

Migration to the UK has had a major impact on both the structure of consumer markets and the labour market. Most major supermarkets have introduced specialist sections in-store to cater for the needs of local migrant populations. Tesco has Eastern European, Irish, West and North African and Asian specialist sections in different stores around the UK. These migrants represent a perfectly viable market segment because they tend to be geographically concentrated.

Meanwhile, net migration into the UK has enabled UK businesses to keep wage costs down as the UK's available labour force has grown. Employment rates for migrants are significantly higher than for UK citizens. Although many migrants settle into low-paid, relatively unskilled jobs, migrant workers are more likely to fulfil professional jobs, such as lawyers or doctors. This is unsurprising given that nearly half of migrants in the UK possess a degree level qualification, as opposed to around one in four UK citizens. (Data from The Migration Observatory at the University of Oxford.)

It is also important to remember the potential value of emigration: 2.3 million Britons live elsewhere in the EU (2.4 million EU residents live in Britain). The European Union has free movement of labour, so any Briton is free to find job opportunities elsewhere: perhaps spending a year working in Ibiza in the summer and at a ski resort for the winter.

## 68.3 Growth of online business

'The entrepreneur always searches for change, responds to it, and exploits it as an opportunity.'
Peter Drucker, business guru

UK online retailing sales were reported in early 2015 to be £104 billion, representing a quarter of all sales. Twenty-five years ago they were zero. The rise in online shopping has caused major shifts in the way UK businesses sell their products. Fifteen years ago as online shopping began to take hold, analysts were suggesting that only certain types of product would be sold online. Books and music CDs were early examples of products where online sales took off early. Few predicted with certainty that fresh produce would be sold by supermarket online sites, nor that clothes would be sold online without the ability to try on before buying. These experiences suggest how hard it can be to forecast social changes far into the future. Several key enablers have allowed this growth in online sales:

- growth in the use of the Internet and accessibility via a wide range of devices, partly due to the rises in computing power embodied in Moore's Law

- new delivery services have enabled next-day delivery, and supermarkets have used technology to offer one hour windows for convenient delivery of online orders

- the growth of social media and apps such as Instagram have made it possible to enjoy a social shopping experience from your bedroom.

The online revolution is not confined to the UK, but the UK's online market is the biggest in Europe. A key to recent growth of online sales is purchasing on-the-go using mobile phones. In 2014, 37 per cent of online sales were made in this way. Whole sectors of retailing such as booking hotel rooms or flights are heading for 100 per cent online. These changes have forced businesses to consider how to harness the power of online retailing, as is explored further in Chapter 89 on uses of digital technology.

## Growth of online business: Analysis

Selling online has probably taken off because it offers tremendous convenience to consumers. Clicking from the comfort of your own home, then waiting a day or two for someone to deliver the product you have ordered is an attractive proposition for many. This has led to the amazing growth in demand for online purchasing as shown by the multi-billion pound sales figures already discussed. However, in addition to the chance of capturing new customers and therefore increasing revenues, online retailing has a second positive impact on profitability. Retailing online is generally cheaper than retailing in the high street. Without the need to have a physical presence, or at least to have fewer physical outlets, online retailers save money in two ways. First there is a saving on expensive high street rents; second there is a sharp fall in overall stock levels. Instead of stocking a full range of colours and sizes in, perhaps, two hundred separate stores, the online retailer needs only one warehouse. This cuts inventory levels sharply and therefore boosts the online trader's cash position.

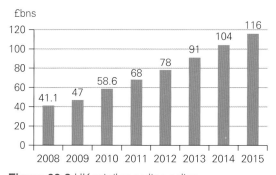

**Figure 68.2** UK retail spending online

### Real business

#### John Lewis – where in-store drives online

Some bricks and mortar retailers who have successfully added an online side to their operations have accepted the phenomenon of 'showrooming' – where customers browse for products in-store before making their purchase online at the lowest price they can find. ⇨

John Lewis Chief Executive Andy Street describes the role of the shop as being critical in terms of generating online sales. Reflecting on John Lewis' excellent Christmas 2014 performance, with online sales up by 19 per cent, he accepts that many customers will visit a John Lewis store to take advantage of the excellent advice offered by shop staff but go home to purchase online. John Lewis seems to have fared better than many at converting in-store browsing to online purchases from its own website. Nationally, 36 per cent of all John Lewis sales are online. Other retailers have done less well, notably Marks & Spencer. 'Showrooming' is unlikely to disappear in the near future – retailers will have to find a way to ensure that in-store browsers buy from their website. Perhaps John Lewis' success offers a model to follow.

## 68.4 Changes in consumer lifestyle and buying behaviour

An increased desire to buy online is just one example of how changes in lifestyle and buying behaviour have affected businesses in recent years. Broader changes in lifestyle such as an awareness of the importance of diet to health, an increase in the desire for convenience and a desire to use technology have all impacted upon businesses.

### Convenience

Despite sustained media focus on diet and body shape, the biggest trend by far in consumer lifestyles is the desire for greater convenience. We want to spend less time cooking and less time eating. So breakfast cereals are in decline because we'd rather eat a snack bar, and retail bread sales are down because we'd rather buy a sandwich. That's good for Greggs and Pret A Manger, but bad for Hovis and Kelloggs.

Today there are no end of business opportunities surrounding the concept of convenience (which overlaps with time saving). Some are already everywhere, others are still to develop fully:

- ready-meal sales in big supermarkets (a £2.5 billion market in 2014/15)
- home collection and return dry-cleaning
- baby meals in eat-on-the-go pouches (Ella's Organic 2014 sales: £41 million up 10.5 per cent on 2013)
- 'bagged snack' sales 2014: £2.7 billion up 1.1 per cent; bread sales 2014: £1.6 billion up 8.9 per cent.

### Inconvenience stores

2012 was the year that the number of smaller, convenience stores operated by Britain's Big Four grocers (Tesco, Asda, Sainsbury's and Morrisons) overtook the number of 'full-size supermarkets' they operated. Asda and Morrisons have been trying to catch up with Tesco and Sainsbury's who have far higher numbers of convenience outlets. The problem of this convenience store format battle is that convenience stores have been taking sales from larger stores. This is due to an increasing trend away from the idea of a 'weekly shop', where large supermarkets can capture shoppers and encourage them to pop a few extra items in their large trolleys. Instead, customers are now far more likely to buy for today and tomorrow, from a smaller convenience store – which stocks a far smaller range of items. It is estimated that it can take 10-15 convenience stores to match the sales of one traditional supermarket.

## A mobile connected world

The very existence of the Internet is a relatively new phenomenon, as is the mobile phone. With so much scope for technological research, the consumer electronics sector has frequently produced social change, from the introduction of the first radios and televisions. However, the pace of change has stepped up over the past 30 years and two exceptionally telling developments have changed the way people behave. The Internet has increased the availability of information to anyone with a connection to the web, and this increased availability of information, unconstrained by national borders, has had deep-rooted effects on how people use their leisure time, stay in touch with one another, or find out what everyone else thinks is fashionable, cool or trendy (imagine a world without YouTube, Facebook, Twitter, etc.). Meanwhile, at roughly the same time, the proliferation of the mobile phone, along with developments in the capabilities of mobile phone handsets, has meant that people are contactable almost wherever they are, as well as offering all the functions of the Internet in the palm of your hand.

## Social change and clothing

An increasingly wealthy population in the most economically developed countries have chosen to spend much of their extra wealth on what they wear. In the UK, clothing consumption has risen over 200 per cent by volume in the last 25 years. This is largely due to the rise in 'fast fashion' – low priced copies of high fashion garments that appear on the high street just days after the originals appeared on the catwalk. Also tied into the fast fashion revolution has been a side effect of another longer term social trend – a move towards a disposable culture. This replaced a 'make-do and mend' society that characterised the years of shortage that followed the World Wars of the twentieth century. Fast Fashion specialists – Zara and H&M are often quoted as examples – tend to focus more on reducing cost when actually manufacturing and choosing materials than on durability of garments. This has enabled these fashion firms to introduce new lines up to 52 times a year, compared to a fashion industry of 30 years ago which tended to only have two 'seasons' per year during which product ranges would be changed.

'In every school there are the cool and popular kids, and then there are the not-so-cool kids. Candidly, we go after the cool kids.' Mike Jeffries, former chief exec, Abercrombie & Fitch

## Changes in consumer lifestyle and buying behaviour: Analysis

What can be distilled from the changes discussed above is that social changes to consumers' lifestyles and buying behaviour can be split into two categories – changes to what is bought and changes to how it is bought. With adjustments to be made to both the product and place elements of the marketing mix, operational changes are needed to the range of products sold and methods of distribution. From the need to introduce click and collect systems to extra investment in R&D departments to develop new innovative products, these changes have deep-rooted effects throughout a business organisation. See the chain of logic below for an illustration of the chain of changes prompted by a decision by sandwich chain Subway to offer a delivery service.

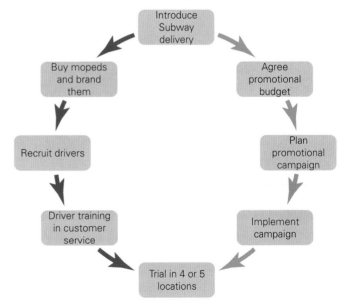

**Figure 68.3** Logic chain: Introduce Subway delivery service

## 68.5 The impact of the social environment on strategic and functional decision-making

Businesses that fail to respond to social changes will lose out to competitors who better adapt their offering to meet the changing needs of their markets. It is therefore likely that major social changes will lead to successful businesses adapting their corporate strategy to try to turn changes into opportunities. In fact several changes in strategic direction will be considered in greater depth within your A-level course:

● Urbanisation → creates opportunities for UK firms in developing markets

● Growth of online business → greater use of digital technology

● Convenience → innovation and/or greater use of digital technology.

Once a change in strategic direction has been decided, functional areas will need to adjust their methods to ensure that they can deliver on their part of the new corporate strategy. Social changes cause major changes within each functional area within the business, whether it be a new delivery system to cater for online selling, deciding how to enter a new foreign market or even developing a range of new products to cater for an emerging market niche at home.

### Five Whys and a How

| Question | Answer |
| --- | --- |
| Why is social change happening faster now than ever before? | Much of the answer to this is technology – a cynic might say we waste more time online and therefore demand more convenience; others see social media and online shopping as ways to give consumers more power |
| Why can social changes be a threat to business? | Social change may reduce the size of a traditional market – leading to declining revenues and perhaps threatening survival (such as HMV) |
| Why can social change create new markets? | Social changes may stimulate demand for new products and services that meet newly emerging needs, such as convenience or fast fashion |
| Why is social change hard to predict? | Although experts try to read early signs of change in social behaviour or lifestyle, it is impossible to accurately forecast the future |
| Why is net immigration good for most businesses? | Not only will immigration increase the range and variety of staff applying for jobs, an immigrant population may also represent a lucrative market segment to sell to |
| How can retailers with physical shops benefit from the trend towards online retailing? | As some retail sectors see an increasing amount of online trade, many retailers have been closing high street stores to save money. However, for those that remain, a physical presence can offer a point of differentiation in the eyes of consumers who still want to see, feel or try the products they want to buy |

## Evaluation: The impact of social change

Social changes represent a change in the external environment facing a business. These changes could be an opportunity or a threat – in many cases they are both. What matters is whether a firm can make the right strategic choice to turn a potential threat into an opportunity. For example, a company facing a downturn in demand caused by a move to healthier eating seizes the opportunity to reformulate their product into a healthy-eating option. This depends on the skill of the strategic management of the business.

In some cases, where huge firms dominate a national market, social changes could be argued to be the result of strategic decisions taken by the business. The death of the traditional high street-based grocery shop occurred in the UK mainly as a result of the growth of huge out-of-town supermarkets. The UK's big supermarket chains may be responsible for changes in the nature of the UK high street as a result of their decision to try to cut costs and prices by opening bigger and bigger stores.

## Key terms

**Urbanisation:** movement of population away from rural areas to live and work in cities.

**Demographic changes:** any change relating to the size, age distribution or make-up of a population.

**Moore's Law:** that computing power tends to double every two years (named after Gordon E. Moore, co-founder of Intel, who put it forward in 1965).

# Workbook

## A. Revision questions

(40 marks; 40 minutes)

1. Briefly describe how social change has affected the businesses operating in the following markets in the UK over the last 20 years:
   **a)** grocery retailing
   **b)** restaurants
   **c)** consumer electronics retailing. (12)

2. Give one example of how a social change can
   **a)** create a brand new market
   **b)** destroy an entire market. (4)

3. Explain two ways in which switching to online retailing can boost profits for a traditional high street clothing retailer. (6)

4. Explain what is meant by the following:
   **a)** showrooming
   **b)** bricks and mortar retailing
   **c)** fast fashion
   **d)** net migration. (8)

5. Using the example of either mobile phones or food manufacturing, explain why some commentators argue that some businesses create social change, rather than responding to it. (10)

# B. Revision exercises

## DATA RESPONSE

### Online retailing

**Table 68.2** Data on online retail sales in the UK – August 2014

| Category | Value seasonally adjusted year-on-year growth (%) |
|---|---|
| All retailing | 8.3 |
| All food | 12.5 |
| All non-food | 11.9 |
| Department stores | 20.1 |
| Textile, clothing & footwear stores | 27.3 |
| Household goods stores | 12.1 |
| Other stores | −13.1 |

Source: www.ons.gov.uk/ons/dcp171778_377638.pdf

**Table 68.3** Devices used to shop online

| | Percentage of online sales 2013 | Forecast percentage of online sales 2014 |
|---|---|---|
| Smartphone | 9 | 11 |
| Tablet | 4 | 7 |
| PC | 87 | 82 |

Source: www.retailresearch.org/onlineretailing.php

### Questions (35 marks; 40 minutes)

**1.** If total UK retail sales were £44.97 billion in 2014, calculate:

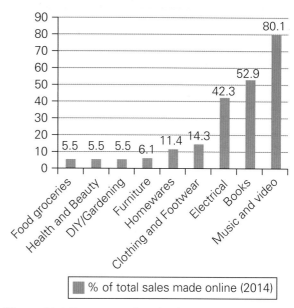

**Figure 68.4** Percentage of total sales made online by sector

**a)** the value of UK online music and video sales in 2014     (3)

**b)** the value of online sales made by department stores in 2013.     (3)

**2.** Analyse two possible implications of the data shown in Table 68.2 for a UK clothing retailer hoping to boost online sales.     (9)

**3.** To what extent does the data presented suggest that online retailing will never represent a major distribution channel for food retailers?     (20)

# C. Extend your understanding:

**1.** To what extent does UK net migration represent an opportunity for UK supermarkets?     (25)

**2.** 'Changes in consumer lifestyles and buying habits are easier to forecast than many other changes in the external environment'. Using industries that you have studied, to what extent would you agree with this statement?     (25)

# Chapter 69

# The social environment including CSR

**Linked to:** Understanding the role and importance of stakeholders, Chapter 10; Influences on the mission of a business, Chapter 53; Managing organisational culture, Chapter 93.

## Definition

The pressures on businesses that lead some to act with integrity towards society and others to only pretend to do so.

## 69.1 Introduction to the social environment

After many years in which businesses successfully put forward the notion that they operated to a self-imposed code of social responsibility, the period 2005-2015 called all this into question. BP's problems with safety and pollution, Shell's with pollution and political interference in Africa, and the UK arms industry's habit of giving bribes were all topped by the wretched performance of the UK's banking sector. Even though the evidence shows the UK to be among the least corrupt places to do business in the world, there is much that needs to be improved. British business needs to *talk* less about corporate social responsibility and *do* far, far more.

Among the important considerations of social responsibility in business are:

- dealing honestly and fairly with customers, (that is, the opposite of 'cowboy builders')
- protecting the environment through actions such as the use of sustainable sources of raw materials
- dealing with bullying, harassment and discrimination within the organisation
- the provision of accurate financial and other numerical information
- resisting anti-competitive practices

- whistleblowing on unethical practices within the business
- the ending of an attitude that 'business' and 'rich people' are one and the same – leading to the bankers' complicity in widespread tax avoidance

Two major influences shape the moral behaviour of businesses. First, an organisation is composed of individuals, who all have their own moral codes, values and principles. Naturally they bring these to bear on the decisions that they make as part of their working lives. Second, businesses have cultures that shape corporate ethical standards. The approach taken by the leaders of the business can have a big effect on both of these factors.

'There needs to be a balance between business and social responsibility... The companies that are authentic about it will wind up as the companies that make the most money.' Howard Schulz, boss of Starbucks

## 69.2 Corporate social responsibility

Corporate social responsibility (CSR) is – at its best – a form of self-regulation by which companies exceed legal minimum requirements in an attempt to be good social citizens. Such behaviour is claimed by businesses such as John Lewis, Unilever, Marks & Spencer and the Co-op. Critics, though, suspect that CSR is often no more than a branch of a company's public relations (PR) department – concerned with image, not substance. It may well be true that examples exist at both extremes, but that the majority of businesses are somewhere in between them.

What is undeniable is that these issues are complex. In 2005 Unilever plc came joint bottom of a ranking of corporate UK's ethical standards. Perhaps in response in 2010 the company launched its Sustainable Living Plan that it still claims to be the cornerstone of the business.

This helped Unilever move up to seventh in *The Guardian's* list of graduates' most-favoured employers. Yet in February 2015 an important health story broke showing evidence that 30 years of health advice was unfounded. Saturated fats were not a health problem and butter was no worse for your heart than margarine. Well, who had put out all this research into the evils of butter, years ago? Unilever, producers of Flora and many other margarines. Companies *may* adopt high standards, but it's wise to be sceptical of what they do and say. Their vested interest makes it harder than they realise for them to be objective.

---

'It's not good enough to do what the law says. We need to be in the forefront of these social responsibility issues.' Anders Dahlvig, CEO of IKEA

---

## 69.3 Reasons for and against corporate social responsibility (CSR)

### Reasons for CSR

Companies receive many benefits from behaving, or being seen to behave, in a responsible manner. John Lewis and its supermarket business Waitrose both gain from consumer affection based on the assumption that these employee-owned businesses behave better towards their stakeholders. Reasons for CSR include:

#### Marketing advantages

Many modern consumers expect to purchase goods and services from organisations that operate in ways that they consider morally correct. Some consumers are unwilling to buy products from businesses that behave in any other way. Some companies have developed their apparent ethical behaviour into a unique selling point (USP). They base their marketing campaigns on these perceived differences. Examples include Lush cosmetics, Innocent Drinks and Toyota (which, in January 2015, had the two top-selling cars in America – all based on the company's green image due to its Prius hybrid car).

#### Positive effects on the workforce

Firms that adopt strong CSR practices may experience benefits in relation to their workforce. They may be able to recruit staff who are better qualified and motivated, because larger numbers of high-quality staff apply. Innocent Drinks has had an unusually low labour turnover rate since its start-up. This cuts the employment costs associated with recruitment, selection and training. Creating a culture of social responsibility can also improve employee motivation.

In turn, that may boost the productivity and profitability of the business.

## Reasons for doubting CSR

Some shareholders criticise CSR as a distraction from the real business of making profits. For them the concerns are:

### Reduced profitability

Any business that really embraces corporate social responsibility faces higher costs. Exploiting cheap labour or very low-cost supplies from less-developed countries may be very profitable. If a business wants to act with responsibility, it must accept that principle may have to override profit. This is easier to do in a family-run business than in a public limited company, with its distant, profit-focused shareholders.

### Reduced growth prospects

It may also be that the company has to turn down the opportunity to invest in projects offering potentially high returns. This would limit the long-term growth potential of the business – which might allow competitors to become stronger on the back of their own high profits. Following the 2013 coup by the Egyptian army against a democratic leader, some travel agencies refused to carry on sending tourists to the country's Red Sea resorts. Others carried on, ignoring the moral issues. A true sense of corporate social responsibility has to include refusing business profits that are tainted morally.

The bigger critique of CSR comes from those who doubt its authenticity. Their reasons against include:

### Rejection of CSR as a tool of public relations (PR)

The actions of banks such as Barclays, Lloyds and HSBC have shown how hollow their CSR rhetoric can be. They pretended to be acting in the interests of the wider community as a cloak for some depressingly amoral, sometimes, immoral business behaviours.

---

'I often wince when companies talk too enthusiastically about their social or environmental responsibility. It often sounds like window dressing.' Gillian Tett, award-winning *Financial Times* columnist

---

### Rejection of CSR as a distraction from a truly moral purpose

During the period 2010-2014 Aldi and Lidl received praise for their low prices while Waitrose received praise for its socially responsible way of doing business. But surely not! During a time of heavily squeezed family budgets,

Waitrose was charging higher prices than any other food retailer. Surely Aldi and Lidl were being socially responsible by helping people survive the squeeze.

## 69.4 The pressures for socially responsible behaviour

In 2014, after nearly a decade of dreadful stories about how banks treat their customers, one million UK customers switched their bank accounts. Out of 50 million accounts that's a 'churn' rate of 2 per cent. How much pressure does that place on banks to clean up their act? Not a lot, surely. It is therefore arguable whether there is much pressure on firms to be socially responsible.

A separate but linked question is whether changes in consumer behaviour force firms to change their own behaviour? Here, there's a definite yes. Some people complained for years about sugary drinks – and Coke and Pepsi ignored them. Until falling sales started to hit them in their pockets. Nowadays the soft drinks manufacturers are trying all they can to keep up with changing tastes. Oddly, that forces them to do strangely contradictory things. Coca-Cola launches lower calorie Coke while also cashing in on the craze for 'energy' drinks. Its 'Monster' and 'Relentless' brands have successfully won market share from Red Bull. Energy drinks are higher in sugar and in additives than Coke – customer preferences allow Coca-Cola to offer social responsibility with one hand and take it away with another.

Fundamentally, real pressure on companies comes from real customers, rather than the media or the government. Customers need to be more consistent about their buying behaviour.

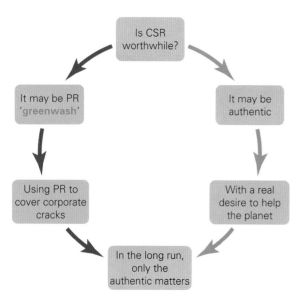

**Figure 69.1** Logic circle: Is CSR authentic or cosmetic?

## 69.5 The difference between the shareholder and stakeholder concept

A stakeholder is an individual or group that has an effect on and is affected by the activities of an organisation. Businesses can also be held to account for their impacts upon society at large.

All firms come into contact on a daily basis with suppliers, customers, the local community and employees. Each of these groups has an impact on the firm's success and at the same time is likely to be affected by any change in its activities. If, for example, the managers decide to expand the business, this may lead to:

- overtime for employees
- more orders for suppliers
- a wider range of products for consumers
- more traffic in the local community.

Groups such as suppliers, employees and the community are known as the firm's stakeholder groups because of their links with the organisation. A stakeholder group both has an effect on and is affected by the decisions of the firm. Each stakeholder group will have its own objectives. The managers of a firm must decide on the extent to which they should change their behaviour to meet these objectives. Some managers believe it is very important to focus on the needs of all the different stakeholder groups. Others believe that an organisation's sole duty is to its investors (that is, that decisions should be made in the best interests of shareholders alone).

This is known as the 'shareholder concept'. The logic is clear: the shareholders employ managers to run the company on their behalf and so everything the managers do should be in the direct interests of shareholders. The managers should not take the needs or objectives of any other group into consideration. If the owners want short-run profit, for example, this is what the managers should provide. If the owners want expansion, then this is what the managers should aim for. According to this view, the only consideration managers should have when making any decision is to meet their owners' objectives. Generally, this means maximising shareholder value (for example, increasing the share price and the dividends paid to shareholders).

The alternative view places emphasis on the need to meet the objectives of a wider group. This is known as 'the stakeholder concept' as opposed to 'the shareholder concept'. The stakeholder approach suggests that managers should take into account their responsibilities to other groups, not just to the owners, when making decisions. The belief is that a firm can benefit significantly from co-operating with its stakeholder groups and incorporating their needs into the decision-making process. Examples include:

- improving the working life of employees through more challenging work, better pay and greater responsibilities, so that the business benefits from a more motivated and committed workforce

- giving something back to the community to ensure greater co-operation from local inhabitants whenever the business needs their help; for example, when seeking planning permission for expansion

- treating suppliers with respect and involving them in its plans so that the firm builds up a long-term relationship; this should lead to better-quality supplies and a better all-round service; if, for example, your supplier has limited availability of an item, it is more likely you would still be supplied because of the way you have treated the supplier in the past.

The stakeholder approach is, therefore, based on an inclusive view in which the various groups that the firm affects are included in its decision-making rather than ignored. This, it is argued, can lead to significant advantages for the firm.

## 69.6 Carroll's corporate social responsibility pyramid

Professor Archie Carroll had been writing on CSR for many years before, in 1991, he sketched out a pyramid to show what he believed to be the chain of progress through which a business could develop to be a good corporate citizen. Unlike long articles that busy managers would set aside, here was a simple message about how to 'do' CSR.

**Figure 69.2** Carroll's corporate social responsibility pyramid

Source: Carroll (1996)

In order of priority he said a business should first make sure it had the economic base from which to act responsibly. No one wants an airline or a hospital to be struggling for cash and cutting corners. Here are Carroll's four steps to good citizenship:

1. *Economic responsibilities:* make sure to have the right balance between revenue and costs, and the right diversity of income streams, so that long-term financial viability is not in doubt.

2. *Legal responsibilities:* make sure to obey the different laws in the countries you operate in, prioritising consumer protection, employee protection, competition laws and environmental protection.

3. *Ethical responsibilities:* be willing to go beyond minimum legal requirements to meet moral duties (perhaps including the 'living wage' in the UK today). Create a culture in which bribery, collusion and exploitation are completely sidelined by honesty and integrity.

4. *Philanthropic responsibilities:* actively seek out ways to contribute to your section of society, such as a manufacturer based in Grimsby sponsoring the local football team or paying for a new arts centre.

## Critique of Carroll's pyramid

Business is far more complex than is implied by Carroll. Ethical responsibilities cannot be assumed to be 'sorted' as the company strides ahead to be philanthropic. Innocent Drinks boasts of giving 10 per cent of its profits to 'good causes', but it hides from its customers the fact that it is owned by Coca-Cola – and lobbies against doctors who warn against the sugar content in juices and smoothies. Big banks and oil companies can reasonably be accused of hiding their business ethics behind a cloak of philanthropic giving. Ultimately, what customers want is honest, open companies that provide high quality products labelled clearly. Carroll's pyramid follows the American model of seeing philanthropy as the highest corporate achievement; the European instinct is to see ethical behaviour as the ultimate test of a business.

'Businesses should be focused on business; social responsibility should be government responsibility.' Terry Gou, Taiwanese businessman

## Five Whys and a How

| Question | Answer |
| --- | --- |
| Why do some people believe that social responsibility is a modern trend? | It's a mystery. 100+ years ago companies such as Cadbury and Unilever focused far more on social factors than anyone does today |
| Why might a company choose to act with social responsibility – but without publicising it? | It might see more advantage in focusing on the good than in publicising the good, for example, knowing that staff like pursuing a goal other than shareholders' profits |
| Why is Marks & Spencer so proud of its 'Plan A'? | Because it was its own initiative for improving the company's environmental performance – and its employees and shareholders seem to value it |
| Why might CSR be handled by the PR department? | Because the company sees it as a tool for image-building, rather than a matter of substance |
| Why might a shareholder criticise 'over-focus' by a company on its wider stakeholders? | Because some shareholders buy purely with the intention of selling at a higher price; they want a focus on profits today rather than image-building for tomorrow |
| How might Carroll's stakeholder pyramid help a business with image problems? | If put on every employee's wall, it might help focus minds on the steady upward path needed to become a respected business again |

## Evaluation: The social environment including CSR

Evaluation involves making some sort of informed judgement. Businesses are required to make a judgement about the benefits of corporate social responsibility. Their key question may be whether social responsibilities are profitable or not.

This chapter has put forward arguments as to why CSR might be profitable. For example, responsible behaviour can give a clear competitive advantage on which marketing activities can be based. Every John Lewis Christmas commercial is designed to make customers feel warmer towards the business.

Operating an authentic policy of social responsibility gives a USP if none of your competitors has taken the plunge. Being first may result in gaining market share before others catch up. In these circumstances a CSR policy may enhance profitability. It can also be an attractive option in a market where businesses and products are virtually indistinguishable. In these circumstances a USP can be most valuable.

CSR policies may add to profits if additional costs are relatively small. Thus, for a financial institution to adopt such a policy may be less costly than for a chemical manufacturer. As many banking scandals have shown, the apparent ease with which a moral stance can be adopted seems to undermine the seriousness with which banks view the outcomes. For banks and social responsibilities, the years 2005-2015 represented easy come and easy go.

## Key terms

**Business culture:** the culture of an organisation is the (perhaps unwritten) code that affects the attitudes, decision-making and management style of its staff.

**Greenwash** is the environmental equivalent of whitewash, that is, painted on to cover the reality beneath – a business that dresses itself up to pretend to be environmentally conscious.

**Stakeholder:** stakeholders are groups such as shareholders and consumers who have a direct interest in a business. These interests frequently cause conflict (for example, shareholders may want higher profits while consumers want environmentally friendly products, which may be more costly to produce).

**Vested interest:** when a person or organisation stands to gain from a particular outcome they can influence.

# Workbook

## A. Revision questions

(45 marks; 45 minutes)

1. Explain why a company's corporate social responsibility programme might do little to change irresponsible behaviour within the organisation. (4)

2. Explain why a company's shareholders might be angry to see reports of bullying at a company's management level. (4)

3. Explain why a company in the public eye such as Next plc might find it difficult to pursue the shareholder concept. (4)

4. Outline two responsibilities a firm may have to:
   a) its employees (4)
   b) its customers (4)
   c) the local community. (4)

5. Explain how a firm could damage its profits in the pursuit of meeting its shareholder responsibilities. (4)

6. Outline why a firm's profit may fall as a result of meeting its stakeholder responsibilities. (3)

7. Some managers reject the idea of stakeholding. They believe that a company's duty is purely to its shareholders. Outline two points in favour and two points against this opinion. (8)

8. Briefly explain into which of the four layers of Carroll's Pyramid you might place each of the following business actions? (If you think it might fall into more than one, do say so).
   a) Tesco cutting costs by removing a layer of management (2)
   b) Red Bull sponsoring Formula 1 motor racing (2)
   c) In early 2015 Sainsbury's was selling an own-label 'Orange Energy Drink' that contained 40 teaspoons of sugar in its one litre bottle (159 grammes). (2)

## B. Revision exercises

### DATA RESPONSE

#### Marks & Spencer plc and Plan A

M&S has spent twenty years in a strategy vacuum. Bosses have come and gone, but nothing has altered the slide in the company's core business: women's clothing. It is curious, then, that the business has been consistent in one strategy for the past decade: 'Plan A': its corporate social responsibility plan. From its inception it has been remarkably wide in its scope, covering staff diversity through to health and safety and onto a series of environmental commitments. In some ways, it's hard to see how Plan A has helped. Today John Lewis can do no wrong while the reputation of Marks & Spencer is as low as it's ever been. But perhaps it has helped keep staff onside during such a turbulent period.

Plan A is supposed to keep M&S focused on a better tomorrow. Many of its targets are to be achieved by 2020. But it's surprising that some targets that are viewed as important one year disappear the next. The 2011/12 report boasts of an 'employee engagement positivity score of 75 per cent' (previous year 76 per cent), but this measure has been dropped by the time of the 2014 report. Other measurements are covered with more consistency, such as (Appendix A) the dramatic reduction in customer use of single-use (plastic) carrier bags since a 5p charge was levied in 2006/07.

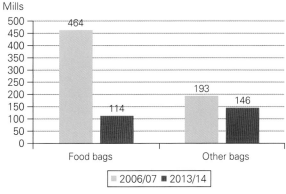

**Figure 69.3** Appendix A M&S Plan A: single-use carrier bags

Source: M&S Plan A report 2014

The same pattern of inconsistency occurs with the main environmental finding, showing an extraordinary change from 730,000 tonnes of $CO_2$ emissions in 2006/07 to zero in 2013/14, but dropping data for business travel.

**Table 69.1** Changes in $CO_2$ emissions

| | $CO_2$ emissions 2006/07 | $CO_2$ emissions 2011/12 | $CO_2$ emissions 2013/14 |
|---|---|---|---|
| Business travel | 10,000 tonnes | 14,000 tonnes | Not included |
| Total gross $CO_2$ emissions | 730,000 tonnes | 572,000 tonnes | 566,000 tonnes |
| Carbon offsets purchased | 0 | 131,000 tonnes | 566,000 tonnes |
| Net CO2 emissions | 730,000 tonnes | 441,000 tonnes | 0 tonnes |

Source: M&S reports 2011/12 and 2013/14

Amidst many other pieces of data, the figures for workforce diversity are interesting. It is a pity there is no data provided to cover the percentage of senior management occupied by ethnic minority employees.

## C. Extend your understanding

1. 'For a business such as Tesco, a strong commitment to social responsibilities is vital to the company's long-term success.' To what extent do you agree with that statement? (25)

**Table 69.2** Diversity data: UK figures as a % of the total UK workforce

| | 2011 | 2012 | 2013 | 2014 |
|---|---|---|---|---|
| Women employees | 76% | 74% | 74% | 73% |
| Women managers | 65% | 64% | 64% | 58% |
| Women in senior management | 32% | 35% | 35% | 39% |
| Ethnic minority employees | 12% | 13% | 12% | 11% |
| Ethnic minority managers | 11% | 12% | 13% | 14% |

Source: M&S reports 2011/12 and 2013/14

As mentioned above, it may be that Plan A has brought staff together, with a feeling of common purpose. From the outside, though, it is hard to see that it has achieved one of the goals M&S has set itself: 'To excite and inspire our customers at every turn'.

### Questions (40 marks; 50 minutes)

1. Analyse the data provided to examine two strengths and two weaknesses of Plan A so far. (12)

2. Examine whether Marks & Spencer is focusing most on its shareholders or its stakeholders. (8)

3. Do you think that Marks & Spencer should regard Plan A as a strategic success? Justify your answer. (20)

2. To what extent would you agree with the view that most businesses use CSR as a strategy for gaining a competitive advantage? (25)

# Chapter 70 Technological change

**Linked to:** Changes in the political and legal environment, Chapter 64; The competitive environment, Chapter 71; Economies and diseconomies of scale, Chapter 79; Digital technology, Chapter 89.

## Definition

The technological environment involves developments both in terms of what is produced and how it is produced.

## 70.1 Introduction

Technology is changing at an extremely fast rate. New products and new processes are being developed all the time. In markets such as computers, tablets, mobile phones and digital cameras, hundreds of new products are being launched every month. The moment you buy the latest laptop, tablet or mobile phone you know it is about to become outdated. Firms face similar problems. The welding robot brought out last month is already less efficient than the model being launched next month, probably at a lower price.

This rate of change is getting ever faster. Product development times are getting quicker and, consequently, more products are getting to market in less time. The result is that the typical life cycle is getting shorter. Naturally this creates serious problems for firms. With more and more products being developed, the chances of any one product succeeding are reduced. For many years, research showed that only one in five new products succeeds in the marketplace. Today the figure is one in seven; in other words six out of seven new products fail. Even if a new product succeeds, its life cycle is likely to be relatively short. Given the ever-higher quality demanded by customers, firms are having to spend more on developing products but have less time to recoup their investment. One of the main reasons for the rapid growth in technology is technology itself. The development of computer-aided design (CAD) and computer-aided manufacture (CAM) has enabled even faster development of new products and processes. Technology feeds off itself and generates even more ideas and innovations. The rapid rate of change creates both threats and opportunities for firms. The threats are clear; firms that do not adopt competitive technology will struggle to:

- keep their costs down…
- …or provide goods or services of sufficient quality and advanced specification

relative to their competitors.

Technology can certainly make life a lot easier for firms – generally by speeding up and removing human input from processes such as working out a full set of accounts for a large company without a spreadsheet. If one company avoids the latest technology while rivals adopt it, it is likely to suffer real problems with competitiveness. The rivals may be able to offer lower prices or substantially better or faster service standards.

'The computer can't tell you the emotional story… What's missing is the eyebrows'. Frank Zappa, musician and songwriter

## 70.2 Assessing the effects of technological change on business functions

Due to the costs involved it is not always possible for a firm to acquire the technology it wants. New technology can represent a significant investment for a firm and cannot always be undertaken as and when managers feel like it. This is particularly true when technology is changing at such a rate that any investment may be rapidly out of date. The difficulty is in knowing when to buy. Buy too late and you may well have lost the competitive advantage; your rivals will already be producing better quality and more cost-competitive work.

**Table 70.1** The impact of technological change on different functional areas

| | Internal technological change | External technological change |
|---|---|---|
| **Marketing** | Technological change can boost a firm's understanding of consumer behaviour with far greater computing power to analyse marketing data.<br><br>New product development is a critical function for firms competing in technology-driven markets. | New media have become available to widen the promotional options available, whilst the internet has brought new distribution channels.<br><br>Product developments that use technology can have a huge effect on markets – creating new ones or destroying long-standing markets for obsolete products such as non-digital cameras. |
| **Finance** | As computer software develops, financial information can be more easily recorded, processed and perhaps most powerfully shared within the business on an almost immediate basis.<br><br>Finance departments must be heavily involved in any decision to purchase new technology given the size of investment that is usually involved. | The internet has made financial information much more easily available – perhaps heightening one of the drawbacks of limited company status. However, the ability for public limited companies to share financial reporting data with shareholders and potential investors may be a benefit. |
| **Human Resources** | Firms adopting new technology may well find that staff need to be made redundant as technology takes over jobs previously filled by people. Not only is this likely to be in traditional contexts, where machines take over repetitive manual production tasks, but computers may now be able to assess information, such as X-rays to identify basic medical issues, taking over the role of medical staff.<br><br>Other significant implications are the need to provide training for staff who are expected to use new technology and/or the need to recruit staff skilled in the use of new technology. | Technology can lead to unemployment, which of course causes problems for government and society.<br><br>Technological change has also led to an increase in the amount of teleworking that can happen, with staff working from home. |
| **Operations** | Technology can have a revolutionary effect on operations management, not only in the way products are manufactured but also in the way that services are delivered. The drive to boost productivity is the underpinning factor behind the adoption of new technology – a constant desire to lower costs through finding technological solutions to the problem of how to lower unit costs. | Technological development in operations departments have had knock on effects on suppliers – with a greater ability to share information with suppliers, the chance to work in a genuine long-term partnership with customers has made many firms value the role played by their suppliers even more. |

Morrisons was the last of the UK's big four supermarkets to offer online shopping – a move that perhaps cost former CEO Dalton Phillips his job as the chain lost significant market share to its rivals. HMV's failure to adapt to online music purchasing led them into administration, whilst Kodak's decision to ignore the rise of digital photography led to the demise of a once market-leading company.

'The job market of the future will consist of those jobs that robots cannot perform. Our blue-collar work is pattern recognition, making sense of what you see. Gardeners will still have jobs because every garden is different. The same goes for construction workers. The losers are white-collar workers, low-level accountants, brokers, and agents.' Michio Kaku, theoretical physicist and futurist

## 70.3 Strategic choices and technology

The availability of technology plays a major role in the strategic choices made by businesses. Developing new products can offer the opportunity to enter, or even create, new markets. Technological change that offers new ways to do things can lead to opportunities to build a strategy around being the cheapest supplier, based on the cost advantages technology can bring. Meanwhile, for firms that choose not to adopt new technology, other strategic options are available. Some may look to build a business model around taking a 'traditional' or 'hand-made' approach – something which may offer them a successful future operating in a niche market. Others may be forced into a strategy based on off-shoring production or other functions where domestic rivals have a cost advantage due to adopting new technology.

'Once a new technology rolls over you, if you're not part of the steamroller, you're part of the road.' Stuart Brand, writer

## Five Whys and a How

| Question | Answer |
|---|---|
| Why does technological change affect product life cycles? | If technological change is rapid in an industry, any given product is likely to be surpassed by new innovations quickly. This means that products will have far less time between introduction and decline. |
| Why does technology need to be considered when devising strategy? | If business strategies basically focus on what to sell to whom and how to create those products or services, technological change can impact on overall corporate strategy in terms of what to sell, to whom and how to organise the production and delivery of those products and services. |
| Why might technological change represent an opportunity for businesses to reduce overheads? | Adopting methods such as teleworking can reduce the need for expensive office space. Meanwhile, with many administrative tasks now being automated, staff numbers can be drastically cut. Furthermore, communications technology can allow certain functions to be offshored to lower wage countries. |
| Why might technological change represent an opportunity for businesses to reduce production costs? | Technology can provide new ways to do things, through new processes or new materials. These may well reduce waste or faults in addition to speeding up production times and therefore productivity – thus lowering production costs. |
| Why might technological change lead to unemployment? | Technological innovations are frequently designed to find ways to replace people with machinery or computers. When this happens, most businesses, in order to cash in on the cost advantages enabled by this process will make job cuts. |
| How will a firm decide whether to buy new production technology? | The simple answer is using investment appraisal techniques (payback, ARR and NPV, see Chapter 73). To do so, it is necessary to forecast future cash flows. The initial investment is likely to be clear, whilst future running costs will be harder to forecast, but perhaps most tricky will be the need to accurately forecast the financial benefits of the technology, whether that be reduced production costs or enhanced revenues flowing from better quality. |

Whether new technology provides an opportunity or a threat for an organisation depends on the technology itself, the resources of the firm and the management's attitude to change. Used effectively new technology can reduce costs, increase flexibility and speed up the firm's response time. In all areas of the firm, from marketing to operations, technology can increase productivity, reduce wastage, and lead to better quality goods and services.

However, it may not always be possible for a firm to adopt the most appropriate technology (perhaps because it does not have the necessary finance). Even if it does adopt new technology the firm needs to ensure that the change is managed effectively. People are often suspicious or worried by new technology, and managers must think carefully about the speed of change and method of introduction if they are to avoid major resistance to change. Organisations must also monitor the technology of their competitors. If they fail to keep up they may find they cannot match their competitors' quality standards. However, they may be limited by their ability to afford the technology. Typically, managers will be faced with an almost constant set of demands for new technology from employees. Nearly everyone can think of some machine or gadget they would like in an ideal world. Managers must decide on priorities given their limited resources, and also look for the gains that can be achieved with existing equipment. As the kaizen approach shows (see Chapter 28), success can come from gradual improvements rather than dramatic technological change.

## Key terms

**Computer-aided design (CAD)** uses a software package to help draw and store new designs in digital form.

**Computer-aided manufacture (CAM)** uses software to specify speeds, accuracy and quantity to an automated production system.

# Workbook

## A. Revision questions

(30 marks; 30 minutes)

1. State three ways in which technological change can reduce costs for a business. (3)

2. Explain two possible reasons why a business may decide not to invest in the latest production robots. (4)

3. State three markets that did not exist 40 years ago that have been created by new technology. (3)

4. Explain one possible positive and one negative impact of the introduction of new production-line machinery for factory staff. (4)

5. Briefly explain three possible issues that a major retail chain might consider before deciding whether to upgrade their online store. (6)

6. Explain two possible reasons why the speed of technological change in the mobile phone handset market is so rapid. (10)

# B. Revision activities

## DATA RESPONSE

**Table 70.2** Annual revenues of companies

| Company | Annual revenue ($m) | | | |
|---|---|---|---|---|
| | **2001** | **2010** | **2013** | **2014** |
| **Google** | 440[1] | 29,320 | 59,830 | 66,001[2] |
| **Apple** | 5,360 | 65,230 | 170,910 | 199,800 |
| **Facebook** | 0[3] | 1,974 | 7,870 | 12,470 |
| **Ford** | 162,410 | 128,950 | 146,920 | 110,710 |
| **Nokia** | 27,800 | 56,940 | 17,550 | 16,050 |
| **Blockbuster** | 4,960 | 4,100 | 334[4] | n/a[4] |

[1]2002 figure – 2001 not available

[2]Unaudited

[3]Facebook only launched in 2004

[4]Figure for 2011, by 2013, Blockbuster had gone bust

### Questions (58 marks; minutes)

**1. a)** Calculate the percentage growth in Apple's revenue from 2001-2014. (3)

**b)** By what percentage did Nokia's revenue fall from 2010-2014? (3)

**2.** Using your own knowledge of these businesses, analyse:

**a)** Why Nokia's revenue fell so drastically from 2010 to 2014? (8)

**b)** Why Apple's revenue was sixteen times bigger than Facebook's despite Facebook having 1.37 billion subscribers and Apple selling just 175 million iphones, in 2014? (8)

**c)** Why technological changes caused Blockbuster's closure? (8)

**d)** Why Ford's revenue fell so significantly between 2001 and 2014? (8)

**3.** To what extent do the table and your answers to Question 2 suggest that technological change is now the most significant external factor that affects businesses' success? (20)

# C. Extend your understanding

**1.** 'Technological change is more likely to create markets than destroy them.' Using examples you have studied, consider to what extent this statement is true. (25)

**2.** Companies such as Nokia, HMV and Blockbuster all failed to keep up with major technological changes. To what extent would you blame the senior managers and to what extent would you blame the technology? (25)

**Linked to:** Changes in the political and legal environment, Chapter 64; Analysing strategic options, Chapter 72; Competitive advantage, Chapter 76; Strategic positioning, Chapter 77.

> **Definition**
>
> Competitiveness measures a firm's ability to shine in comparison to its rivals.

## 71.1 Introduction: What is a competitive market?

Markets used to be physical places where buyers and sellers met in person to exchange goods or to haggle over price. Street markets are still like that. In online or digital markets, there is no face-to-face negotiation, but the potentially huge number of buyers and sellers make transactions highly competitive.

A competitive market features intense rivalry between producers of a similar good or service. The number of firms operating within a market influences the intensity of competition; the more firms there are, the greater the level of competition. However, the respective size of the firms operating in the market should also be taken into account. A market consisting of 50 firms may not be particularly competitive, if one firm holds a 60 per cent market share and 40 per cent is shared between the other 49. Similarly, a market composed of just four firms could be quite competitive if they are of a similar size.

Consumers benefit from competitive markets. Not so, the firms themselves. In competitive markets, prices and profit margins tend to be squeezed. As a result, firms operating in competitive markets try hard to minimise competition, perhaps by creating a unique selling point (USP) or using predatory pricing.

'People of the same trade seldom meet together, even for merriment and diversion, but the conversation ends in a conspiracy against the public, or in some contrivance to raise prices.' Adam Smith, *The Wealth of Nations*, 1776

## 71.2 Porter's Five Forces

In 1980, with the publication of *Competitive Strategy,* Michael Porter became an instant business guru with his theory known as the Five Forces. Porter's target was to help businesses figure out how to achieve and sustain a competitive advantage. By this he meant establish a strength that rivals would struggle to copy. Coca-Cola has managed to stay the Number One soft drink for more than 125 years. It, of course, has branding on its side – and the benefits of scale. Porter's theory showed the main pressures on businesses that would determine their ability to compete and succeed.

Crucial to Porter's success was the simple and accessible diagram that shows the Five Forces he identified. See Figure 71.1

**Figure 71.1** Porter's Five Forces

Source: 'The Five Competitive Forces that Shape Strategy' by Michael E. Porter, *Harvard Business Review,* January 2008

## 71.3 Rivalry among existing competitors

### One dominant business

Some markets are dominated by one large business. Economists use the word 'monopoly' to describe a market where there is a single supplier, and therefore no competition. In practice, pure textbook monopolies rarely exist; even Microsoft does not have a 100 per cent share of the office software market (just 85 per cent). The UK government's definition of a monopoly is somewhat looser. According to the Competition and Markets Authority, a monopoly is a firm that has a market share of 25 per cent and above.

Monopolies are bad for consumers. They restrict choice, and tend to drive prices upwards. For that reason most governments regulate against monopolies that exploit consumers by abusing their dominant market position.

### Competition amongst a few giants

The UK supermarket industry is a good example of a market that is dominated by a handful of very large companies. This is known as oligopoly – competition between the few. The rivalry that exists within such markets can be very intense. Firms know that any gains in market share will be at the expense of their rivals. In markets made up of a few giants, firms tend to focus on non-price competition when designing the marketing mix. Firms in these markets are reluctant to compete by cutting price. They fear creating a costly price war where no firm wins.

Where oligopoly exists there is also a temptation towards collusion. Where this occurs, the competitive pressure is weakened.

### The fiercely competitive market

Fiercely competitive markets tend to be fragmented; made up of hundreds of small firms who each compete actively against other. In some of these markets, competition is amplified by the fact that firms sell near-identical products. These are products such as flour, sugar or blank DVDs that are hard to differentiate (and are usually termed commodities). In such markets firms have to manage their production costs very carefully because the retail price is the most important factor in determining whether the firm's product sells or not.

In fiercely competitive markets firms will try, where possible, to create product differentiation. For example, the restaurant market in Croydon, Surrey, is extremely competitive. There are over 70 outlets within a two-mile radius of the town centre. To survive without having to compete solely on price, firms in markets like this must find new innovations regularly because points of differentiation are quickly copied.

To Michael Porter, the single most important factor in rivalry between existing businesses is product differentiation. Even in an oligopoly market such as UK grocery, with a 74 per cent market share held by the top four companies (December – February 2015, Kantar Worldpanel), there has been scope for Waitrose, Aldi and Lidl to gain market share. Being big is great until others start chipping away at your market share. Ask Tesco.

'Competition is not only the basis of protection to the consumer, but is the incentive to progress.' Herbert Hoover, US President, 1929–33

## 71.4 Threat of new entrants

The number of firms operating within a market can change over time. If new competitors enter, a market will become more competitive. New entrants are usually attracted into a new market by the high profits or the rapid growth achieved by the existing firms. After the Europe-wide success of airlines such as easyJet and Ryanair, a huge number of imitators came into the airline business, including Air Berlin and Wizz Air. Although most of these have struggled to be profitable, their lower prices have unquestionably benefited the traveller.

The degree of threat from new entrants depends on the barriers to entry. Starting a new discount airline is relatively easy, as you can open one route at a time – and choose routes that no one else yet offers. In the long term you will need to build a brand name, but the Hungarian airline Wizz Air enjoyed its twelfth birthday in 2015, claiming at least that it was operating with record profitability. Contrast the low barriers to entry in airlines with the huge barriers in the manufacture of aircraft. The global market for large passenger planes is controlled 50/50 by America's Boeing and Europe's Airbus. Among the barriers to entry to this market are:

- Huge development costs; the new Airbus A350 cost at least £10 billion to develop
- Huge extra costs to build up the global engineering network to ensure that the planes are serviced properly

- Potential customer resistance based on lack of track record regarding quality and therefore safety (China's Comac aircraft makers wants to break into the market, but will face massive resistance from sceptical airline executives – and perhaps also from the travelling public).

Accordingly, the threat of new entrants may be an everyday one for some firms (pizza delivery firms, for example) but a distant one for others.

## 71.5 Changes in the buying power of customers

If you produce ready-meals that you sell to Morrisons, you are selling to a business that has an 11 per cent share of the UK grocery market. Morrisons is a big and powerful company. But if the buyers at Morrisons become too demanding of discounts and longer credit terms, you can negotiate with Sainsbury's or Asda (each with a 16.5 per cent market share). If the negotiations go well, you can tell Morrisons you no longer wish to supply them. So you, the producer, have some power in this relationship.

But what if Asda made a successful takeover bid for Morrisons? The combined business would have a 27.5 per cent market share (close to Tesco's 29 per cent) and your options would be restricted greatly. OK, Sainsburys might still be your saviour, but it's easy to see that Morrisons buying power is much greater when combined with Asda than when it's on its own. So changes in the buying power of customers can make a huge difference to a supplier's profitability, stability and long-term health.

## 71.6 Changes in the selling power of suppliers

A manufacturer of ready meals will have a wide number of suppliers, delivering food ingredients plus packaging materials. Most will be commodities such as chicken, which can be bought from a wide range of suppliers. But what if there's a range of premium ready meals that has special 'flavour-seal' qualities. This has been available from two packaging companies – but one has just gone into liquidation. So now you have to buy from the sole, monopoly supplier of the flavour-seal packs. Clearly the increase in the selling power of the supplier is going to mean higher prices and therefore higher costs for you. Your profit margin will be squeezed until you can find a solution – a completely different type of packaging perhaps.

## 71.7 Threat of substitutes

Whereas 71.4 looked at the threat of new entrants to a market, the threat of substitutes means new competition from outside the traditional industry. Twenty years ago BP competed with Shell and Esso. Arguably, today they compete also with wind power, solar power and liquefied petroleum gas. Technological development and innovation have brought new rivals to the market, giving customers some alternatives to traditional oil. This represents a new threat to the profitability of the oil companies, but is entirely in the best interests of consumers.

### Real business

In 2005, HMV was a highly profitable retailer. In the UK it made a profit of £93 million on sales of £986 million. Its success was built on its 25 per cent market share in sales of music and film CDs and DVDs. Virgin Megastores were the main retail rival, and there was a growing threat from online retailers such as Amazon. At the time, though, online retail had a 10 per cent share of sales of CDs and DVDs and although it was rising, it may not have seemed a huge threat.

Then came the digital deluge. New substitutes arrived in the form of iTunes, Spotify and many forms of illegal downloading. Within a few years analysts were questioning whether HMV could survive. Indeed in January 2013 the business went into receivership. Shareholders lost everything, though some of the shops were bought up and still trade today. For HMV, though, the threat of substitutes proved an existential one.

'Like many businessmen of genius he learned that free competition was wasteful, monopoly efficient. And so he simply set about achieving that efficient monopoly.' Mario Puzo, *The Godfather*, 1969

## 71.8 Implication of the Five Forces for strategic and functional decisions

When there was a change in the external forces it faced, HMV failed to adapt successfully. That might have been a management failure or it might possibly be that there was no escaping the impact of digital and online competition. Most bosses of most companies would believe that changes in external forces can be addressed successfully, given time and money.

## Implications for corporate, strategic decisions

### Find new markets

If a market suddenly becomes more competitive and less profitable, some firms react by trying to find new markets overseas with greater scope for a value-added, differentiated offer. In the UK New Look is at the lower end of the market for women's fashion. In China its new stores are more able to establish it as a Western, middle-market brand and therefore perhaps command higher pricing points than in the UK.

### Takeover

Some large firms react to changed external forces by buying their way out of potential trouble. In early 2015 Poundland made a £55 million bid for '99p Stores' – removing a direct competitor from the market. In addition it closed a possible regional entry point for new competitors, as Poundland was weak in London and the South East, whereas that was the regional strength of 99p Stores.

## Implications for functional decisions

### Increase product differentiation

Product differentiation is the degree to which consumers perceive a brand to be different, and in some way superior to other brands of the same type of product. If product differentiation can be increased, consumers will be less likely to switch to products supplied by the competition. To a degree, differentiation helps a firm to insulate itself from competitive pressure. Firms that want to increase differentiation can do so by improving:

- *Design*. An eye-catching design that is aesthetically pleasing can help a firm to survive in a competitive market. Good-looking design can add value to a product. For example, the Land Rover Evoque's quirky styling has allowed it to command a substantial price premium in the Chinese car market (the world's biggest).
- *Brand image*. Many products rely heavily on their brand image. When Jack Wills clothes and BMW 4x4 cars are purchased, the consumer hopes to share some of the brand's personality. Subconsciously they believe that some of the brand's image will rub off on them. A strong brand image can help a firm to fight off its competitors without having to resort to price cuts.

- *Unique product features*. In markets that are highly competitive, firms can redesign their products to ensure that they possess the latest must-have feature. In 2014 Apple gave its iPhone franchise a huge lease of life with the success of its iPhone 6 (so much so that in October-December 2014 69 per cent of all Apple's sales came from the iPhone – perhaps a worry in itself).

## 71.9 How the Five Forces might shape competitive strategy

Competitive strategy is the company's medium-long term plan for how to keep ahead of the competition. The Five Forces can be used as an analytic tool – in effect intertwined with SWOT analysis. Careful investigation of each of the forces might reveal one serious weakness on the part of the business. Perhaps if Marks & Spencer had done this, they would have realised that the threat of substitutes made it vital to invest more – and earlier – in a state-of-the-art online sales system.

It's important to tackle weaknesses, but perhaps even more important to build on strengths. Associated British Foods (owners of Primark) have done a remarkable job in identifying the potential for what was once a tiny (and rather odd) part of a huge food business. By the end of 2014 Primark had over 300 shops, made £662 million in profit and was generating a 33.2 per cent return on capital employed. The directors spotted that despite the apparently low barriers to entry in fashion retailing, rivals were struggling to achieve the Primark balance between design and price.

## 71.10 Critique of the Five Forces

Many academics have criticised the Five Forces theory, or suggested a sixth or seventh force. The single biggest weakness is that it is oddly static. It ignores completely the vast strategic importance of trends in market size. Implicitly Michael Porter would have missed the profitable opportunities that Costa Coffee, Burberry and Jaguar Land Rover found in China. It is also criticised for underestimating the forces of change. In the years since the FTSE 100 stock market index began in 1930 only two companies remain in existence today – BP and GKN. So that's two out of a hundred. Quite simply, the model understates the pace of change.

## Five Whys and a How

| Question | Answer |
|----------|--------|
| Why may it be hard for a business to sustain a competitive advantage? | Everyone copies successful products or processes, so it's hard to stay ahead, even if you've been the innovator |
| Why may the power of suppliers be a barrier to new businesses trying to enter a market? | If suppliers demand to be paid cash on delivery, it will add to the cash flow strains faced by a new, start-up business |
| Why may barriers to entry sometimes be psychological rather than real? | Time after time, new businesses have found ways to break into apparently rock-solid markets, such as Fever-Tree breaking the Schweppes hold on tonic water, and Lindt Lindor's successful competition with Cadbury Creme Eggs |
| Why may the threat of a new competitor keep prices down? | A business might choose to keep prices down to make it hard for a new business to enter the market |
| Why may some people critique the Five Forces? | Because they ignore a key market condition: whether the market size is expanding or declining |
| How effective might the Five Forces theory have been in spotting the deteriorating position of Tesco in 2013 and 2014? | Not well at all. It would have overestimated the importance of Tesco's power over suppliers and the strength of its market share. But then, no theory is perfect. |

## Evaluation: The competitive environment

As has always been the case, the best way a business can ensure its survival in a competitive world is to find something it is good at, and stick with it. Cadbury is great when it concentrates on making chocolate; Heinz is brilliant at making and marketing baked beans. Even if the massive Hershey Corporation brings its chocolate from America, Cadbury need not fear. Similarly, the launch of Branston's Beans made little impact on Heinz.

Sometimes, though, big judgements have to be considered, such as whether to risk launching a new product in a new country. When Tesco did this in 2007, launching Fresh & Easy stores in America, the questions were a) did they need to? and b) were they looking in the right direction? Wouldn't China or India have made more sense? In 2013 Tesco admitted their mistake by pulling out of America (losing $2,000 million). All too often, business leaders take actions that seem more to do with ego than logic. Models such as Porter's Five Forces are based on an assumption that business is about reacting to pressures, whereas a great deal of business decision-making is about choices and judgements.

## Key terms

**Collusion:** when managers from different firms get together to discuss ways to work together to restrict supply and/or raise prices. (See the Adam Smith quotation on page 456.)

**Oligopolies:** are markets dominated by a few large companies

# Workbook

## A. Revision questions

(35 marks; 35 minutes)

1. What is a monopoly? (2)

2. Explain how an increase in competition within the UK banking market might affect the shareholders of banks such as Barclays and HSBC. (4)

3. Analyse two factors which could decrease the level of competition within the car market. (8)

4. Explain which stakeholder group benefits most from new entrants joining a market. (4)

5. Explain why some companies decide not to respond to additional competition by cutting price. (4)

6. Outline two reasons why a supermarket such as Waitrose may be concerned if Mars and Cadbury merged into one business. (6)

7. How may product differentiation help a firm to cope with a more competitive market? (3)

8. Explain why many large firms prefer to buy out smaller rivals, rather than competing against them head to head. (4)

## B. Revision exercises

### DATA RESPONSE

#### Cadbury and Porter's Five Forces

In February 2015 Mondelez International (MI) reported a 44 per cent dip in 2014 net earnings, blaming 'developed market consumers responding negatively to chocolate price hikes'. MI (owners of Cadbury) stated that they would withdraw from certain retail customers in Europe that had refused to pay the price increases. In 2014 MI implemented price hikes in response to rising commodity costs, particularly cocoa. The main centre of resistance to the price rises was in France. Although Nestlé increased prices as well, Mars only increased prices in America and Lindt said it could weather cocoa cost increases without needing to increase prices. In Europe sales fell 1 per cent due to retailer resistance and in America growth was held to 1 per cent due to 'intense competition in biscuits and crackers'.

Only a few days earlier both MI and Mars were accused of 'exploiting small businesses' by extending payment terms to some UK suppliers from 60 to 120 days. The small business pressure group FPB declared that: 'At a time when the economic outlook remains uncertain it is fundamentally unfair that small

businesses are being used as a line of credit for larger organisations and propping up big business.'

Perhaps part of the pressure to act in the above ways can be blamed on competition. Although in the UK, Cadbury is giving big rivals Nestlé and Mars a hard time, the real stars in the UK market currently are Italian Ferrero and Swiss Lindt. In the 12 months to July 2014 sales by value for Ferrero rose by 22.1 per cent compared with 0.7 per cent for the market as a whole. Ferrero has only a 3.3 per cent market share in the UK, but it hopes that it will rise to 5.5 per cent by 2019. While Lindt's Lindor brand enjoyed sales of £80 million in 2014, up 13.6 per cent on 2013.

Source: various, including *The Grocer* 20 December 2014 and articles from www.confectionerynews.com

#### Questions (30 marks; 35 minutes)

1. Use Porter's Five Forces to analyse the external pressures faced by Cadbury (MI) at this time. (10)

2. To what extent would you agree that MI's strategy for dealing with external pressures is the right one for the long-term health of the business? (20)

## C. Extend your understanding

1. To what extent would the use of Porter's Five Forces help Marks & Spencer understand its continuing difficulties in clothes retailing? (25)

2. To what extent might Porter's Five Forces benefit from including a sixth force: 'change'? (25)

# Chapter

# 72 Analysing strategic options

**Linked to:** Decision-making: scientific and intuitive, Chapter 7; Decision trees, Chapter 8; The impact of strategic decision-making on functional decision-making, Chapter 55; Investment appraisal, Chapter 73; Strategic positioning, Chapter 77.

## Definition

Strategic options are the possible, long-term paths the business might take in pursuit of its goals.

## 72.1 Introduction

Strategic options are the long-term choices a business must decide between. If senior management has done its job, the directors of the business will be presented with several attractive options. If three top executives each had to make a presentation about a strategic option for the next 5-10 years, then the directors could choose the best of the best. So what might a strategic option look like? Here are a few:

● Ryanair deciding whether or not to start up the first mass-market, low-cost London-New York service

● Apple deciding whether to invest in a major extension strategy for the iPad, or instead to milk it while sales are still reasonably high

● Aldi deciding whether to buy Morrisons (the German group that owns Aldi is big and rich enough to buy Tesco, let alone Morrisons).

'Any approach to strategy quickly encounters a conflict between corporate objectives and corporate capabilities. Attempting the impossible is not good strategy; it is a waste of resources.' Bruce Henderson, CEO Boston Consulting Group

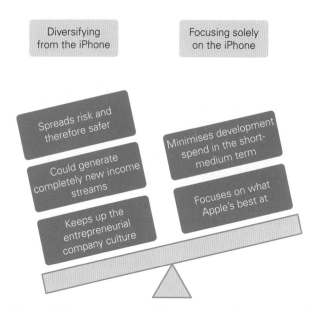

**Figure 72.1** Logic balance: 2015 strategic options for Apple Inc.

## 72.2. How are strategic options analysed?

Option examples such as those mentioned above are almost impossible to appraise using standard financial methods such as discounted cash flow. Big, one-off decisions are more likely to be the result of a process such as:

● Boardroom agreement about aims and possible objectives

● Independent management consultants brought in to bring fresh eyes to the company's future, perhaps recommending the closure of one division and the expansion of another

● A detailed account by the finance director of the sums available for a major strategic option; perhaps £2 billion or even £10 billion.

'Our view of strategy has changed from the classic Coca-Cola versus Pepsi market-share fight to how do you shape the emergence of new opportunity areas, whether it's branchless banking or genetic engineering.' Gary Hamel, business consultant

## Real business

Apple Inc, in the first quarter of its 2015 financial year, generated 69 per cent of its entire revenues from the iPhone. Usually large firms have highly diversified sources of income. Not Apple. The most valuable company on the planet was almost entirely dependent on one product. It would have been reckless for any management to regard this as normal or acceptable. Not long before, in 2013, Apple's products had been called into question by Samsung's skilful product development and marketing. Surely the same could happen again, leaving Apple vulnerable. So the senior management worked at developing new strategic options to reduce the company's dependence on the iPhone. Cue, in February 2015, stories from California that Apple was offering $250,000 signing-on fees to engineers willing to switch from Tesla Motors to Apple. The self-drive iCar was being seen as a strategic option.

## 72.3. Factors influencing strategic decisions

In early 2015 Kelloggs took a brave decision. After years as the world's main supplier of highly processed, sugary breakfast cereals, Kelloggs announced the launch in America of '*Origins* – real food prepared simply'. It was to be a range of muesli, granola and other 'healthy' cereals. The fact that Kelloggs had just suffered a 65 per cent decline in full-year profits might make such a strategic rethink seem obvious. But Kelloggs now only generates 25 per cent of its revenue in its traditional four markets: America, Canada, Britain and Australia. So it has chosen to make a move away from processed cereals, even though they generate the bulk of the company's revenue.

So what are the factors that influence strategic decisions such as this?

- The key factor is the reality of the marketplace, that is, what's selling and what isn't. Companies aren't very interested in what people say they'll do – only in what they actually do. In 2014 UK consumers spoke as warmly as they had in previous years about Fairtrade sourcing – but in fact Fairtrade sales slipped by 4 per cent. In the case of Kelloggs,

a serious slide in sales of Special K convinced managers that they had to try a radically new approach.

- Another factor is whether or not senior managers have the capacity for boldness. There are two key aspects of boldness: being willing to kill or sell off your weaker product categories or businesses (e.g. Whitbread selling David Lloyd Leisure Centres to focus on Costa Coffee); and the second is willingness to cannibalise. Starbucks has cannibalised successfully by opening new coffee shops close to their existing outlets – effectively freezing out the competition. In businesses such as Apple or Amazon, entrepreneurial, bold decisions are possible. In many big businesses they are not.

- Sometimes risks are taken because it seems even riskier not to. When online grocery shopping began, Morrisons opted to wait until it was clear that online grocery could be profitable. Others decided that they couldn't afford to be left behind, so companies such as Waitrose and Sainsbury's boldly went for online without knowing how it was to be made profitable.

## 72.4. How strategic decisions can go wrong

On its website, management consultancy McKinsey and Company tells the following story. A chief executive is trying to decide whether to proceed with a huge takeover bid. He gathers his top executives for a final discussion. The most vocal supporter for the deal makes a strong case – but he will be the one who heads up the combined, post-merger division. This will put him in pole position to succeed when the current chief executive retires. The chief finance officer argues that the forecasts are highly uncertain and the overall rationale for the bid is unconvincing. Worried about the takeover story leaking to the press, the chief decides not to wait for more financial evidence and agrees to the deal. It proves a disaster.

McKinsey suggests that there are two main problems here. The first is the inclination of top executives to overestimate their collective abilities. Most takeovers prove a disappointment, but bosses keep on imagining that their unique skills will enable them to beat that average. The second is the 'principal-agent problem'. In this case the most vocal supporter of the bid may not be aware of a subconscious motive based on self-interest. The common characteristic of these two problems is that they lie in human failings. People at the top of organisations may be earning millions yet still not be that good at making decisions in a coolly objective manner.

McKinsey has produced a list of seven sources of error when making strategic decisions; they form Table 72.1

'The strategist's method is very simply to challenge the prevailing assumptions with a single question: Why?' Kenichi Ohmae, Japanese strategy guru

**Table 72.1** Seven sources of error when making strategic decisions

| Factors that distort decision-making | Explanation |
| --- | --- |
| Over-optimism, i.e. high expectations of the unknown | This may be especially problematic for entrepreneurial leaders – automatically biased towards optimism |
| Loss aversion, leading to inaction | A cautious leader may fear a large loss more than a larger gain |
| Overconfidence, resulting in underestimation of challenges | Virgin started its Little Red internal UK airline in 2013, but never achieved beyond 40 per cent capacity utilisation (it closed in 2015) |
| Misaligned time horizons, i.e. focusing solely on time from a personal point of view | This includes a boss pursuing short-term profit targets to achieve a high personal bonus; good for the individual but not for the company |
| Misaligned risk aversion profiles, i.e. high career risk even though it's a low corporate risk | Cadbury launching a new chocolate bar entails virtually zero risk for the business (it can afford a flop) but perhaps a great deal of risk for the relevant product manager |
| Champion bias | A boss accepts an evaluation of a proposal more willingly when the proponent is a trusted colleague |
| 'Sunflower management', i.e. collective consensus around the boss's views | There may be an absence of debate over major issues, with everyone assuming that the boss has a right to make up his/her own mind |

## Key terms

**Cannibalise:** being willing to eat your own, for example, launching a new product that eats away at sales of your own existing brands (but therefore prevents others from doing the same).

**Principal-agent problem:** when the motives of the 'agent' (the business manager) are different from those of the 'principal' (the shareholder/owner). Managers look for more power or more income; shareholders want the business to make more profit.

## Evaluation: Analysing strategic options

Some bosses go through their period in office without ever needing to make a truly strategic decision. Between 1975 and 2015 running Primark has been a business dream, with steady growth in the UK and then continental Europe. Strategic decisions? I don't think so. By contrast Morrisons has needed a huge number ever since it bought the rival Safeway Stores in 2004. The company has been led upmarket, then back downmarket, while failing to get adequately involved in online or in convenience store retailing.

Understandably, bosses at Morrisons have made strategic mistakes.

It's reasonable to conclude that some bosses are simply lucky, either in the lack of decisions needed or in their good fortune when taking them. Fans of football clubs such as Arsenal, Tottenham and Liverpool have seen many strategic ups and downs over the years – and will know the relationship between the decisions made and performance (or lack of it) on the pitch.

## Five Whys and a How

| Question | Answer |
|---|---|
| Why may it be hard to reverse a strategic decision? | Because the decision may literally be final, such as when Tesco paid a local Chinese company to take Tesco China off its hands |
| Why are people such as Richard Branson so good at making these high-level decisions? | Well, he's not that good! He's made a huge number of big mistakes. In 2015 he closed down his Little Red internal UK airline that was started in 2013 – and flopped |
| Why might some top managers be better at strategic decisions than others? | Autocrats may make better decision-makers than democrats; the autocrat can coolly sieve the evidence; the democrat has to take account of the views of many others |
| Why might it be difficult to know who's best at making strategic decisions? | Most bosses are only in power for 5–8 years, so they may only have two or three big strategic decisions to make in that time; so even when an individual's decisions turn out well you can't be sure it's judgement rather than luck |
| Why may strategic decisions be easier for companies than for public sector organisations? | Ultimately, the criterion for private sector success is profit. In the public sector there's a far more complex mix of factors, from popularity to social value in addition to value for money |
| How do the best decision-makers make their strategic decisions? | By a mixture of cool objectivity and a bold willingness to anticipate what tomorrow's customers will want |

# Workbook

## A. Revision questions

(30 marks; 30 minutes)

1. Explain why it may be hard for a large, complex multinational business to shortlist its strategic options. (5)

2. Outline any reservations you might have about Apple's strategy of developing a self-drive iCar. (5)

3. Explain what Gary Hamel meant in the quotation shown on page 462–3. (5)

4. Explain 'loss aversion' (see Table 72.1) in relation to new product development. (5)

5. In the future Primark's owners (Associated British Foods) may have to decide whether to float or sell off the retailer (possibly for £20 billion), as it's now overwhelming the rest of the business. Analyse the possible benefits to Associated British Foods of selling Primark. (10)

## B. Revision exercises

### DATA RESPONSE

**Strategic thinking at P&G**

Even though Steve Jobs (Apple) and Howard Schulz (Starbucks) both did it, it remains rare for a boss to return. So when A.G. Lafley returned to US multinational Procter & Gamble, analysts expected it to be short and sharp.

Lafley's first term as chief executive coincided with a buoyant period for the company in the ten years to 2009. But since Lafley's 2013 return he's found it harder. His first action was to implement a structural reorganisation that appointed a 'president' to head each of its four new sector-based divisions. This was to provide clear accountability for employees at all levels of the organisation, as well as for shareholders.

Marketing magazine reported that: 'The quality that Lafley brings to P&G is focus - absolute, unwavering focus on consumers along with an unflinching ability to make strong decisions.' During his first spell he was renowned as a champion of innovation – though perhaps his biggest strategic move was buying Gillette for $57 billion.

In a 2013 interview to promote his book *Playing to Win: How Strategy Really Works*, Lafley said, '[P&G's] results came directly from focusing on our three most important strategic decisions – grow P&G's core, extend into beauty and personal care, expand into emerging markets. Fortunately, it worked. It shows just how powerful a few strategic choices can be.'

A major strategic shift needed by P&G is to move beyond traditional advertising media such as television and to enter the digital and social media age. Is 67-year-old Lafley the right person to lead this? Time will tell.

### Questions (35 marks; 45 minutes)

1. Since his 2013 return Lafley has found Proctor & Gamble harder to manage successfully. Analyse the difficulties in identifying the right strategic options in a multi-product business such as P&G. (10)

2. Lafley's successful first period as chief executive had a strategic heart based on 'grow P&G's core, extend into beauty and personal care, expand into emerging markets'. To what extent do you believe that would work for the business over the next five to ten years? (25)

## C. Extend your understanding

1. In a strong organisation, the chief executive should be spoilt for choice between attractive strategic options. To what extent do you think that creating such attractive options is more important than choosing between them? (25)

2. Military genius Napoleon Bonaparte once said, 'Never interrupt your enemy when he is making a mistake.' To what extent is that sufficient advice to enable a business to make the right strategic decisions? (25)

**Linked to:** Analysing strategic options, Chapter 72; Sensitivity analysis, Chapter 74.

## Definition

Using forecast cash flows to estimate the value of an investment decision based on quantitative criteria. Then backing up the calculations with an assessment of non-financial factors.

## 73.1 Introduction

Every day managers make decisions, such as how to deal with a furious customer or whether a cheeky worker needs a disciplinary chat. These can be regarded as tactical decisions because they are short-term responses to events. Investment appraisal applies to decisions that concern strategy rather than tactics (that is, the medium to long term). As they are significant in the longer term, they are worth taking a bit of time over; ideally, by calculating whether or not the potential profits are high enough to justify the initial outlay (the sum invested).

To carry out a full investment appraisal might take a manager several weeks, even months. The reason for this is not because the maths is so complex, but in order to find accurate data to analyse. For example, if trying to choose whether to launch new product A or B, a sales forecast will be essential. Carrying out primary market research might take several weeks until the results are received and analysed. Only then can the investment appraisal begin. Table 73.1 gives an idea of the data required to take effective decisions using investment appraisal.

**Table 73.1** The data required to take effective decisions using investment appraisal

| Decisions requiring investment appraisal | Information needed to make the decision |
|---|---|
| Should we launch new product A or B? | Sales forecasts, pricing decisions, and data on fixed, variable and start-up costs |
| Should we make a takeover bid for L'Oreal? | Forecast of future cash flows into and out of L'Oreal; compare the results with the purchase price |
| Shall we expand capacity by running a night shift? | Forecast of the extra costs compared with extra revenues |

## Financial methods of assessing an investment

Having gathered all the necessary facts and figures, a firm can analyse the data to answer two main questions.

1. How long will it take until we get our money back? If we invest £400,000, can we expect to get that money back within the first year, or might it take four years?

2. How profitable will the investment be? What profit will be generated per year by the investment?

To answer these two questions there are three methods that can be used:

1. Payback period

2. Average rate of return

3. Net present value

Two of these (methods 1 and 2) need to be used together; the third can answer both questions simultaneously. All three methods require the same starting point: a table showing the expected cash flows on the investment over time.

An example would be an investment of £60,000 in a machine that will cost £10,000 per year to run and should generate £30,000 a year of cash. The machine is expected to last for five years. The cash flow table would look like the one shown in Table 73.2.

**Table 73.2** Example cash flow table

|        | Cash in | Cash out | Net cash flow | Cumulative cash total |
|--------|---------|----------|---------------|-----------------------|
| NOW*   |         | £60,000  | (£60,000)     | (£60,000)             |
| Year 1 | £30,000 | £10,000  | £20,000       | (£40,000)             |
| Year 2 | £30,000 | £10,000  | £20,000       | (£20,000)             |
| Year 3 | £30,000 | £10,000  | £20,000       | 0                     |
| Year 4 | £30,000 | £10,000  | £20,000       | £20,000               |
| Year 5 | £30,000 | £10,000  | £20,000       | £40,000               |

*NOW = the moment the £60,000 is spent; can also be called the initial outlay or the sum invested.

The data can also be presented in the form of a graph or bar chart. The chart in Figure 73.1 shows the cumulative cash total based on the above figures.

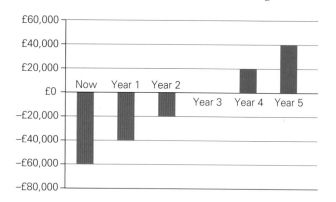

**Figure 73.1** Cumulative cash flows on an investment of £60,000

These figures will be used to explain the workings of each of the three methods listed above, which we will now look at in more detail.

## 73.2 Payback period

### Calculation

This method focuses on one issue alone: how long does it take to get your money back. In the above case, the £60,000 investment takes exactly three years to get back, as can be seen in the right-hand column: the cumulative cash total. All the £60,000 is recovered in three years because the business is generating £20,000 of cash per year.

If the annual net cash flows are constant over time, a formula can be used to calculate the payback period:

$$\text{payback:} \quad \frac{\text{sum invested}}{\text{net cash per time period}}$$

$$\text{for example:} \quad \frac{£60,000}{£20,000 \text{ a year}} = 3 \text{ years}$$

## What if the cash flows are not constant over time?

This can make it a little harder to work out a precise answer, though the principles are the same. For example, take the investment of £40,000 shown in Table 73.3.

**Table 73.3** Finding the payback period

|        | Cash in | Cash out | Net cash flow | Cumulative cash total |
|--------|---------|----------|---------------|-----------------------|
| NOW    |         | £40,000  | (£40,000)     | (£40,000)             |
| Year 1 | £20,000 | £5,000   | £15,000       | (£25,000)             |
| Year 2 | £30,000 | £10,000  | £20,000       | (£5,000)              |
| Year 3 | £36,000 | £24,000  | £12,000       | £7,000                |

In this case, payback has not yet occurred by the end of Year 2 (there's still £5,000 outstanding). Yet the end of Year 3 is well beyond the payback period. So payback occurred in two years and x months. To find how many months, the following formula will work:

$$\frac{\text{outlay outstanding}}{\text{monthly cash in year of payback}}$$

$$\text{for example:} \quad \frac{£5,000}{£12,000/12m} = 5 \text{ months}$$

In this case, then, the payback period was two years and five months.

### Interpretation of payback period

The word investment suggests spending money now in the hope of making money later. Therefore every investment means putting money at risk while waiting to make a surplus. The payback period is the length of time the money is at risk. It follows that every business would like an investment to have as short a payback period as possible. Company directors may tell their managers to suggest an investment only if its payback is less than 18 months. This yardstick is known as a criterion level.

Although managers like a quick payback, it is important to be beware of short-termism. If directors demand too short a payback period, it may be impossible for managers to plan effectively for the long-term future of the business. Quick paybacks imply easy decisions, such as for Primark to expand its store chain by opening its fifteenth store in London. A much tougher, longer-term decision would be whether Primark should open up stores in New Delhi. This could prove to be a clever move in the longer term, but the high costs of getting to grips with Indian retailing may lead to a minimum of a three-year payback.

The advantages and disadvantages of payback are set out in Table 73.4.

**Table 73.4** The advantages and disadvantages of payback

| Advantages of payback | Disadvantages of payback |
|---|---|
| Easy to calculate and understand | Provides no insight into profitability |
| May be more accurate than other measures, because it ignores longer-term forecasts (the ones beyond the payback period) | Ignores what happens after the payback period |
| Takes into account the timing of cash flows | May encourage a short-termist attitude |
| Especially important for a business with weak cash flow; it may be willing to invest only in projects with a quick payback | Is not very useful on its own (because it ignores profit), therefore is used together with ARR or NPV (see below) |

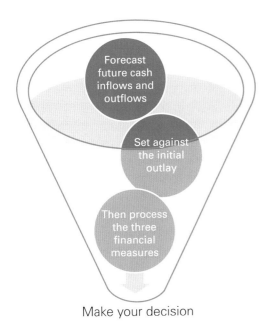

Make your decision

**Figure 73.2** Logic funnel: making the investment decision

World Cup and 2016 Olympic Games. In March 2013 the company announced a £40 million order from the Brazilian government for 1,000 of its backhoe loaders. JCB's prospects look good, even though they are playing catch up with the giant US construction company Caterpillar.

JCB hopes to repeat its amazing success in India, where it is market leader with a 50 per cent market share. It started in India in 1979, and kept going even though it took more than 15 years to make meaningful profits. Now it has four huge factories in India, with the latest opening in 2014.

**Figure 73.3**

## 73.3 Average rate of return

This method compares the average annual profit generated by an investment with the amount of money invested in it. In this way, two or more potential projects can be compared to find out which has the 'best' return for the amount of money being put into it in the first place.

### Calculation

Average rate of return (ARR) is calculated by the formula:

$$\frac{\text{average annual return}}{\text{initial outlay}} \times 100$$

There are three steps in calculating ARR, as follows.

1. Calculate the total profit over the lifetime of the investment (total net cash flows minus the investment outlay).

2. Divide by the number of years of the investment project, to give the average annual profit.

3. Apply the formula: average annual profit/initial outlay × 100.

For example, BJ Carpets is considering whether to invest £20,000 in a labour-saving wrapping machine. The company policy is to invest in projects only if they deliver a profit of at least 15 per cent a year (see Table 73.5).

**Table 73.5** Figures for BJ Carpets

| Year | Net cash flow | Cumulative cash flow |
|---|---|---|
| 0 | (£20,000) | (£20,000) |
| 1 | £5,000 | (£15,000) |
| 2 | £11,000 | (£4,000) |
| 3 | £10,000 | £6,000 |
| 4 | £10,000 | £16,000 |

Here, the £20,000 investment generates £36,000 of net cash flows in the four years. That represents a lifetime profit of £16,000 (see bottom right-hand corner of Table 73.5). To apply the three steps, then, proceed as indicated in Table 73.6.

**Table 73.6** BJ Carpets: applying the three steps

| Step 1 | Identify lifetime profit | £16,000 |
|---|---|---|
| Step 2 | Divide by number of years (4) | £4,000 |
| Step 3 | Calculate annual profit as a percentage of initial outlay | $\frac{£4,000}{£20,000} \times 100 = 20\%$ |

BJ Carpets can therefore proceed with this investment, as the ARR of 20 per cent is comfortably above its requirement of a minimum ARR criterion level of 15 per cent.

## Interpretation of ARR

The strength of ARR is that it is easy to interpret the result. Firms want as high a rate of profit as possible, so the higher the ARR the better. This makes it easy to choose between two investment options, as long as profit is the key decision-making factor. (It may not be, because some firms are pursuing objectives such as growth or diversification.)

Table 73.7 sets out the advantages and disadvantages of average rate of return.

**Table 73.7** The advantages and disadvantages of average rate of return

| Advantages of average rate of return | Disadvantages of average rate of return |
|---|---|
| Uses all the cash flows over the project's life... | ... but, because later years are included, the results will not prove as accurate as payback |
| Focuses upon profitability | Ignores the timing of the cash flows |
| Easy to compare percentage returns on different investments, to help make a decision | Ignores the time value (opportunity cost) of the money invested |

## 73.4 Net present value (NPV) of discounted cash flows

Useful though payback and ARR can be, they can work effectively only when used together. ARR provides information on average profitability, while payback tells you about the timing of the cash flows. It is better, surely, to have one method that incorporates profits and time. This is the third method of investment appraisal, which is based on 'discounted cash flows'.

Discounted cash flow (DCF) is a method that is rooted in opportunity cost. If a firm invests £10,000 in computer software, it is important not only to ask 'What is the rate of return on my investment of £10,000?', but also 'What opportunities am I having to give up as a result of this investment?' At its simplest, £10,000 tied up in software prevents the firm from enjoying a 5.75 per cent return on its money in the bank (when interest rates are 5.75 per cent).

From the idea of opportunity cost, businesses want to know the implication of the timing of cash flows on different projects. If one investment generates +£40,000 in Year 1, while another provides that inflow in Year 4, the firm must consider what it is missing out on by waiting three years.

In short, it is always preferable to have money now than the promise of the same quantity of money in the future. This is because money held at the present time has a greater value than the same quantity of money received in the future. In other words, £100 received in a year's time is worth less to a firm than £100 in the bank today. How much less? Well, if interest rates are 10 per cent, £100 in the bank for a year would become

£110. So £100 in a year's time is worth 10 per cent less than £100 today.

When considering potential capital investments on the basis of predicted future cash flows, it makes sense to ask, 'What will the money we receive in the future really be worth in today's terms?' These present values are calculated using a method called 'discounting'.

To discount a future cash flow, it is necessary to know:

● how many years into the future we are looking, since the greater the length of time involved, the smaller the present or discounted value of money will be

● what the prevailing rate of interest is likely to be.

Once these have been determined, the relevant discount factor can be found. This can be done by calculation, or looked up in 'discount tables'. An extract from a discount table is given in Table 73.8.

**Table 73.8** Extract from a discount table

| Table of selected discount factors | | | | | | |
|---|---|---|---|---|---|---|
| Years ahead | 4% | 6% | 8% | 10% | 12% | 15% |
| 0 | 1.00 | 1.00 | 1.00 | 1.00 | 1.00 | 1.00 |
| 1 | 0.96 | 0.94 | 0.93 | 0.91 | 0.89 | 0.87 |
| 2 | 0.92 | 0.89 | 0.86 | 0.83 | 0.80 | 0.76 |
| 3 | 0.89 | 0.84 | 0.79 | 0.75 | 0.71 | 0.66 |
| 4 | 0.85 | 0.79 | 0.74 | 0.68 | 0.64 | 0.57 |
| 5 | 0.82 | 0.75 | 0.68 | 0.62 | 0.57 | 0.50 |

The future cash flows are then multiplied by the appropriate discount factor to find the present value. For example, the present value of £100 received in five years' time, if the expected rate of interest is 10 per cent, would be:

$$£100 × 0.62 = £62$$

The higher the rate of interest expected, and the longer the time to wait for the money to come in, the less that money is actually worth in today's terms.

So how does a firm decide which discount factor to choose? There are two main ways.

1. The discount factor can be based on the current rate of interest, or the rate expected over the coming years.

2. A firm may base the factor on its own criteria, such as that it wants every investment to make at least 15 per cent; therefore it expects future returns to be positive even with a 15 per cent discount rate.

This book includes just one technique of discounting future cash flows to find their present value; this is the net present value method.

## Net present value (NPV)

### Calculation

This method calculates the present values of all the money coming in from the project in the future, then sets these against the money being spent on the project today. The result is known as the net present value (NPV) of the project. It can be compared with other projects to find which has the highest return in real terms, and should therefore be chosen.

The technique can also be used to see if *any* of the projects are worth undertaking. All the investments might have a negative NPV. In other words, the present value of the money being spent is greater than the present value of the money being received. If so, the firm would be better off putting the money in the bank and earning the current rate of interest. Projects are only worth carrying out if the NPV is positive.

For example, a firm is faced with two alternative proposals for investment: Project Z and Project Y (see Table 73.9). Both cost £250,000, but have different patterns of future cash flows over their projected lives. The rate of interest over the period is anticipated to average around 10 per cent. The calculation would be as shown in the table.

Despite the fact that both projects have the same initial cost, and they bring in the same quantity of money over their lives, there is a large difference in their net present values. Project Y, with most of its income coming in the early years, gives a much greater present value than Project Z.

**Table 73.9** Project Z versus Project Y

| Year | Project Z | | | Project Y | | |
|---|---|---|---|---|---|---|
| | Cash flow | Discount factor | Present value (£s) | Cash flow | Discount factor | Present value (£s) |
| 0 | (£250,000) | 1.00 | (£250,000) | (£250,000) | 1.00 | (£250,000) |
| 1 | £50,000 | 0.91 | £45,500 | £200,000 | 0.91 | £182,000 |
| 2 | £100,000 | 0.83 | £83,000 | £100,000 | 0.83 | £83,000 |
| 3 | £200,000 | 0.75 | £150,000 | £50,000 | 0.75 | £37,500 |
| | | NPV = | +£28,500 | | NPV = | +£52,500 |

## Interpretation

This method of appraising investment opportunities has an in-built advantage over the previous techniques. It pays close attention to the timing of cash flows and their values in relation to the value of money today. It is also relatively simple to use the technique as a form of 'what if?' scenario planning. Different calculations can be made to see what returns will be obtained at different interest rates or with different cash flows to reflect different expectations. The results, however, are not directly comparable between different projects when the initial investments differ.

Table 73.10 sets out the advantages and disadvantages of NPV.

**Table 73.10** The advantages and disadvantages of NPV

| Advantages of NPV | Disadvantages of NPV |
|---|---|
| Takes the opportunity cost of money into account | Complex to calculate and communicate |
| A single measure that takes the amount and timing of cash flows into account | The meaning of the result is often misunderstood |
| Can consider different scenarios | Only comparable between projects if the initial investment is the same |

## 73.5 Other factors affecting investment decisions

### Non-financial factors in investment appraisal

Once the numbers have been calculated there are decisions to be made. On the face of it, the numbers point to the answer, but they are only part of the decision-making process. For example, perhaps a board of directors can afford no more than £2 million for investment and must choose between the two alternatives shown in Table 73.11.

**Table 73.11** Investment A vs Investment B

| | Investment A | Investment B |
|---|---|---|
| Type of investment | New R&D laboratory | Relaunching an existing product with flagging sales |
| Investment outlay | £2 million | £2 million |
| Payback period | 4.5 years | 1 year |
| Average rate of return (over next five years) | 8.2% | 14.2% |
| Net present value | £32,000 | £280,000 |

Investment B is clearly superior on all three quantitative methods of appraisal. Yet there may be reasons why the board may reject it. Some of these are outlined below.

- *Company objectives:* if the business is pursuing an objective of long-term growth, the directors might feel that a relaunch of a declining brand is too short-termist; they may prefer an investment that could keep boosting the business long beyond the next five years.
- *Company finances:* if the £2 million investment capital is intended to be borrowed, the company's balance sheet is an important issue. If the business is highly geared, it may be reluctant to proceed with either of these investments, as neither generates an irresistible ARR.
- *Confidence in the data:* the directors will ask questions about how the forecasts were made, who made the forecasts and what was the evidence behind them. If the Investment B data came from the manager in charge of the product with flagging sales, might they be biased? Ideally, data used in investment appraisal should come from an independent source and be based on large enough sample sizes to be statistically valid.
- *Social responsibilities:* investing in recycling or energy-saving schemes may generate very low ARRs, but the firm may still wish to proceed for public relations reasons, to boost morale among staff or just because the directors think it is ethically right.

### Investment criteria

As explained above, company directors may set out minimum financial targets for investment, so that no boardroom time is wasted on projects yielding inadequate returns. If the directors' criteria say at least 10 per cent ARR and no more than 18 months' payback – there is clarity for all concerned.

### Risk and uncertainty

Every investment means putting money at risk in the hope of a satisfactory return. As the process includes estimates that will look years, or even decades into the future, every cash flow figure is subject to uncertainty. And the level of uncertainty grows the further ahead the figures are projected. Successful businesses never invest in a new project unless they can afford it to go wrong. In other words the firm's underlying liquidity and gearing must be satisfactory enough to withstand losing the initial outlay on an investment.

## Five Whys and a How

| Question | Answer |
|---|---|
| Why are all investment appraisals based on forecast cash flows? | Because cash is being spent on the outlay, so cash should be the measure of success |
| Why shouldn't payback be used on its own to appraise investments? | Because it says nothing about profitability and focuses too much on the short term |
| Why is NPV great in theory, but difficult to use in practice? | Because you can't easily compare investments of different sums or covering different timescales (which you can with ARR) |
| Why might all three appraisal measures be wrong? | Because they're all based on the same cash flow forecast; if the forecast's wrong, all three will give wrong answers |
| Why may it be necessary to set aside the findings from the financial methods of appraisal? | Sometimes principle is more important. In 2015 HSBC's Swiss bank was found to be at the centre of tax avoidance and the financing of drug deals; doubtless they had high ARRs |
| How might a long-termist business set its criterion levels? | They should accept high payback periods as long as the long-term ARR and NPV figures look attractive |

## Evaluation: Investment appraisal

Investment appraisal methods will often give conflicting advice to managers, who must be willing to make decisions based on a trade-off between risks and profit. This must be taken alongside the objectives of the business, which could well dictate which of the criteria involved is of most importance to the firm.

The size of the firm will also have an impact. Small firms will often have neither the time nor the resources to undertake a scientific approach to investment appraisal. They will often rely on past experience or the owner's hunches in making decisions such as these. In larger firms, the issue of accountability will often lead managers to rely heavily on the projected figures. In this way, should anything go wrong, they can prove they were making the best decision possible at the time, given the information available (and might keep their job).

## Key terms

**Criterion level:** a yardstick set by directors to enable managers to judge whether investment ideas are worth pursuing (for example, ARR must be 15 per cent+ or payback must be a maximum of 12 months).

**Cumulative cash:** the build-up of cash over several time periods (for example, if cash flow is +£20,000 for three years in a row, cumulative cash in Year 3 is +£60,000).

**Present values:** the discounting of future cash flows to make them comparable with today's cash. This takes into account the opportunity cost of waiting for the cash to arrive.

**Reward for risk:** calculating the difference between the forecast ARR and the actual rate of interest, to help decide whether the ARR is high enough given the risks involved in the project.

**Short-termism:** making decisions on the basis of the immediate future and therefore ignoring the long-term future of the business.

**Tactical decisions:** those that are day-to-day events and therefore do not require a lengthy decision-making process.

# Workbook

## A. Revision questions

(40 marks; 40 minutes)

1. Distinguish between non-financial and quantitative investment appraisal. (4)

2. Why should forecast cash flow figures be treated with caution? (4)

3. How useful is payback period as the sole method for making an investment decision? (3)

4. Briefly outline the circumstances in which:
   **a)** payback period might be the most important appraisal method for a firm (4)
   **b)** average rate of return might be more important than payback for a firm. (4)

5. How are criterion levels applied to investment appraisal? (3)

6. Explain the purpose of discounting cash flows. (4)

7. Using only non-financial analysis, would you prefer £100 now or £105 in one year's time, at an interest rate of 10 per cent? (3)

8. Outline two possible drawbacks to setting a payback criterion level of 12 months. (4)

9. What non-financial issues might a firm take into account when deciding whether to invest in a new fleet of lorries? (4)

10. Why is it important to ask for the source before accepting investment appraisal data? (3)

## B. Revision exercises

### DATA RESPONSE 1

Questions (30 marks; 30 minutes)

1. Net annual cash flows on an investment are forecast to be as shown in Table 73.12. Calculate the payback and the average rate of return. (6)

Table 73.12 Forecast of net annual cash flows on an investment

|  | £000 |
|---|---|
| NOW | (600) |
| End of year 1 | 100 |
| End of year 2 | 400 |
| End of year 3 | 400 |
| End of year 4 | 180 |

2. The board of Burford Ltd is meeting to decide whether to invest £500,000 in an automated packing machine or into a new customer service centre. The production manager has estimated the cash flows from the two investments to make the calculations given in Table 73.13.

Table 73.13 Estimated cash flows from two investments

|  | Packing machine | Service centre |
|---|---|---|
| Payback | 1.75 years | 3.5 years |
| NPV | £28,500 | £25,600 |

**a)** On purely quantitative grounds, which would you choose and why? (6)

**b)** Explain three other factors the board should consider before making a final decision. (6)

3. The cash flows on two alternative projects are estimated to be as shown in Table 73.14. Carry out a full investment appraisal to decide which (if either) of the projects should be undertaken. Interest rates are currently 8 per cent. (12)

Table 73.14 Estimated cash flows on two alternative projects

|  | Project A | | Project B | |
|---|---|---|---|---|
|  | Cash in | Cash out | Cash in | Cash out |
| Year 0 | £0 | £50,000 | £0 | £50,000 |
| Year 1 | £60,000 | £30,000 | £10,000 | £10,000 |
| Year 2 | £80,000 | £40,000 | £40,000 | £20,000 |
| Year 3 | £40,000 | £24,000 | £60,000 | £30,000 |
| Year 4 | £20,000 | £20,000 | £84,000 | £40,000 |

## DATA RESPONSE 2

Dowton's new finance director has decided that capital investments will be approved only if they meet the criteria shown in Table 73.15.

**Table 73.15** Criteria required for approval of capital investments

| Payback | 30 months |
| Average rate of return | 18% |
| Net present value | 10% of the investment outlay |

The assembly department has proposed the purchase of a £600,000 machine that will be more productive and produce a higher-quality finish. The department estimates that the output gains should yield the cash flow benefits shown in Table 73.16 during the expected four-year life of the machine:

**Table 73.16** Yield of cash flow benefits during expected life of the machine

| Year | £ |
| --- | --- |
| 0 | − 600,000 |
| 1 | + 130,000 |
| 2 | + 260,000 |
| 3 | + 360,000 |
| 4 | + 230,000 |

In addition:

1. The machine should have a resale value of £100,000 at the end of its life.

2. The relevant discount factors are: end of Year 1, 0.91; Year 2, 0.83; Year 3, 0.75; Year 4, 0.68.

### Questions (30 marks; 35 minutes)

1. Conduct a full investment appraisal, then consider whether Dowton's should go ahead with the investment on the basis of the quantitative information provided. (16)

2. Outline any other information it may be useful to obtain before making a final decision. (8)

3. Explain two sources of finance that may be appropriate for an investment such as this. (6)

## DATA RESPONSE 3

### 3D Sports

Altrincham Sports (AS) had been the only independent sports shop in town for more than ten years, surrounded by Sports Direct and other multiples. AS had kept itself going by great customer service, but sliding revenues recently suggested more was needed. Watching a news item on 3D printing made owner Jim Burn see a solution. Moulded trainers, made-to-measure and manufactured automatically in front of your eyes – surely that would be a real point of differentiation.

Jim found that the right grade of 3D printer would cost £12,000; with advertising, staff training and a few other fixed costs, the total investment outlay would be £20,000. The variable costs per pair would be about £10 and a selling price of £40 seemed realistic. Ongoing running (fixed) costs – including staffing - would be £1,000 a month.

But what was a realistic sales forecast? A Friday evening invite to the pub gave Jim the opinions of his staff. Most thought there'd be a great deal of interest at first, but that it would taper off. One said, 'But never mind, we need to get people out of Sports Direct and back to us. Even if you lose a bit on the printing we might more than make up for it with customers buying other things.' Jim accepted the logic, but explained that he needed the printer to pay for itself. He would have to borrow the money from HSBC and they wouldn't lend it on a vague promise of selling 'other things'. As HSBC would be charging an interest of 8 per cent he really needed an average rate of return of at least 10 per cent to be credible.

After a lot of thought, Jim produced this sales forecast for the '3D shoe':

| | Sales (pairs) |
| --- | --- |
| Year 1 | 1,000 |
| Year 2 | 600 |
| Year 3 | 400 |
| Year 4 | 200 |

Now, before going to see HSBC, he needed an investment appraisal to work out whether the proposition was realistic.

**Questions (40 marks; 45 minutes)**

1. From the above information, analyse two possible sources of inaccuracy in the underlying data being fed into the investment appraisal process. (12)

2. **a)** Turn the above data into a table showing cash inflow, outflow, net cash and cumulative cash. (5)
   **b)** Calculate the payback period. (3)
   **c)** Calculate the average rate of return. (4)

3. In the back of his mind, Jim has been wondering whether to drop the 3D idea altogether. To what extent do you agree with him? (16)

## C. Extend your understanding

1. 'Financial methods of assessing investment decisions are based on no more than educated guesses about future cash flows.' To what extent does that invalidate the use of these techniques? (25)

2. To what extent might making the wrong investment decision threaten the survival of a medium-sized company? (25)

# Chapter 74 Sensitivity analysis

**Linked to:** Break-even analysis, Chapter 38; Cash flow management and forecasting, Chapter 39; Profit and how to increase it, Chapter 41; Investment appraisal, Chapter 73.

## Definition

Sensitivity analysis, sometimes called 'what if' analysis, means testing models such as break-even to find out what happens if costs such as fuel prove 25 per cent or 50 per cent higher than expected.

## 74.1 The importance of sensitivity analysis

Sensitivity analysis is used when assessing the likely outcomes of a decision where quantitative techniques are used. Therefore it may be associated with any of the following:

- cash flow forecasting
- break-even analysis
- investment appraisal methods
- general profit and contribution calculations.

Its purpose is to allow managers to better understand the level of risk involved in decisions. It allows decision-makers to assess the likely consequences if their initial forecasts are inaccurate, as well as identifying which variables have the greatest impact on the outcome of decisions.

'Businesses use what if analyses to determine how different costs or investments will affect profit and other financial indicators.' Shelley Elmblad, financial software expert

## 74.2 How sensitivity analysis works

Table 74.1 Sensitivity analysis

| Variable | Pessimistic forecast | Expected | Optimistic forecast |
|---|---|---|---|
| Selling price | £8 | £10 | £12 |
| Variable cost per unit | £8 | £7 | £6 |
| Fixed costs | £12,000 | £10,000 | £8,000 |
| Predicted sales | 3,000 | 4,000 | 5,000 |

To carry out sensitivity analysis, change **one** variable at a time and see what happens to the outcome you are trying to measure – in this case profit.

Let's assume that things turn out as expected, except that tough competition means the selling price only averages £8:

Revenue = £8 × 4,000 = £32,000

Variable costs would be £7 × 4,000 = £28,000, plus fixed costs of £10,000 = total costs of £38,000

The firm would therefore make a loss of: £32,000 - £38,000 = £6,000

The following table shows the profit levels achieved if each of the above outcomes occur. As you can see, if things are exactly to plan, the business makes £2,000 in profit.

Table 74.2 Sensitivity analysis variations

| If we change: | Pessimistic forecast | Expected | Optimistic forecast |
|---|---|---|---|
| Selling price | (£6,000)* | £2,000 | £10,000 |
| Variable cost per unit | (£4,000) | £2,000 | £6,000 |
| Fixed costs | £0 | £2,000 | £4,000 |
| Predicted sales | (£1,000) | £2,000 | £5,000 |

NOTE: all figures shown in the table are the profit that would be generated in the event of one variable being changed, e.g. if selling price is at the pessimistic forecast level of £8 and variable costs, fixed costs and predicted sales are as expected, the profit would be (£6,000).

Having this information available is useful in itself; decision-makers can see the maximum expected loss that can occur in this scenario (given their pessimistic estimate) and decide whether they can afford to make such a loss. However, there is one further step that can be useful. In order to pinpoint the variable where changes make the most change to the overall outcome (profit), add a final calculation, showing the difference between the pessimistic and optimistic forecast levels:

**Table 74.3** Sensitivity analysis showing variables affecting profit

| If we change: | Pessimistic forecast | Expected | Optimistic forecast | Distance from optimistic value to pessimistic value |
|---|---|---|---|---|
| Selling price | (£6,000)* | £2,000 | £10,000 | £16,000 |
| Variable cost per unit | (£4,000) | £2,000 | £6,000 | £10,000 |
| Fixed costs | £0 | £2,000 | £4,000 | £4,000 |
| Predicted sales | (£1,000) | £2,000 | £5,000 | £6,000 |

This suggests that selling price is the key variable that needs monitoring since it is the one where the possible changes that the firm believes possible will have the biggest impact on the overall outcome. Therefore price has the greatest sensitivity (in this case) meaning that pricing decisions should be taken at the highest management level.

---

'Since there is no such thing as an accurate forecast, the best you can do — and should do — is to provide a forecast that reflects the impact of uncertainty.' Don Creswell, business analyst

---

## 74.3 Analysing sensitivity analysis

In many ways the skill behind sensitivity analysis lies in identifying which variables to adjust for. Note in the Table 74.4 that a sensitivity analysis on a cash flow forecast might adjust for different periods of credit. If this is the most likely variable to change (which it may well be if customers have a fluctuating record on paying their bills on time), it may be the most important to consider when forecasting cash flow. PLCs are expected to include the results of sensitivity analysis within their published annual accounts, as a form of risk assessment. Specifically, they are expected to show the possible impact of changes in external variables, most notably interest rates and exchange rates. This allows investors to assess the likely impact on profit and expected dividend levels of changes in these key external factors. For highly geared firms, changes in interest rates may make major changes to profit. Meanwhile, big exporters will find themselves vulnerable to changes in exchange rates.

These requirements are a further indication of the role that sensitivity analysis plays in managing risk. A key criticism levelled at the major banks that were badly affected by the sub-prime mortgage crisis of 2007-2008, was that they were guilty of poor risk management. Major banks such as RBS need to be aware of the scale of upside and downside risk involved in the financial assets they hold. Absurdly, they had failed to allow for the possibility of a fall in US house prices. More considered sensitivity analysis may have helped to prevent them holding so many high risk assets.

## Other sensitivity analysis scenarios

**Table 74.4** Other sensitivity analysis scenarios

| | Type of calculation | | | | |
|---|---|---|---|---|---|
| | Payback | ARR | NPV | Cash flow forecast | Break-even |
| Variables that can be adjusted | Cash in<br>Cash out<br>Initial investment | Cash in<br>Cash out<br>Initial investment<br>Estimated duration of project | Cash in<br>Cash out<br>Initial investment<br>Estimated duration of project<br>Discount rate used | Selling price<br>Expected sales<br>Credit period offered<br>Cash outflows<br>Credit period received | Selling price<br>Variable cost per unit<br>Fixed costs |

## Real business

### *Sensitivity analysis at Tesco*

As a UK-based plc, Tesco is required to carry out and publish a sensitivity analysis as part of its annual report. The 2014 report shows the effects on profit of changes in the value of a range of currencies including the US dollar, the euro, the Czech koruna and the Polish zloty. It also assesses the effect of a 1 per cent increase in UK interest rates. Also included in the report are details of the steps Tesco is taking to protect its profits from any future, negative changes in exchange rates.

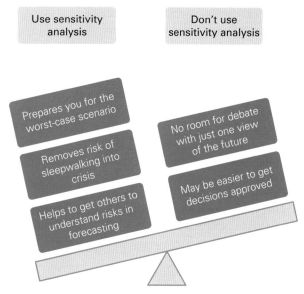

**Figure 74.1** Logic balance: Is sensitivity analysis worthwhile?

'The worst happens when you least expect it.' Dean Koontz, author

## Five Whys and a How

| Question | Answer |
|---|---|
| Why do external factors affect forecasts? | A whole range of unpredictable external factors, from interest rates to exchange rates, the weather to wars, can affect demand for a firm's products or services as well as the cost of their inputs |
| Why do firms benefit from sensitivity analysis? | Sensitivity analysis requires analytical thought as to likely future scenarios, it helps to quantify the risks involved in decisions and allows managers to focus on key, controllable variables |
| Why consider sensitivity analysis alongside investment appraisal? | As investment appraisal is based on the results of cash flow forecasts, inaccuracies affect the results generated by payback or NPV – so it's vital to check for a worst-case scenario |
| Why might some doubt the value of sensitivity analysis? | Full sensitivity analysis is a major job for forecasters and company analysts to carry out. The results could be argued to reduce the clarity of original forecasts, thus making decision-making harder rather than easier |
| Why are plcs legally required to conduct (and publish) a sensitivity analysis? | To ensure that those reading annual reports understand the likely effect of external changes on the firm's financial performance |
| How do firms reduce the risks identified by sensitivity analysis? | Many will try to 'hedge' against negative external changes, perhaps by holding a supply of dollars which they can sell if the value of the pound falls against the dollar, forcing up the cost of imported materials |

Sensitivity analysis helps with both the planning and monitoring functions of management. Asking 'what if' questions is something that all decision-makers need to do before reaching a decision. Although sensitivity analysis will not ensure that all forecasts are better understood, it will raise awareness of the levels of uncertainty involved when making decisions. Forecasting pessimistic outcomes helps managers to understand the possible downsides to their decisions. If Tesco plc had followed this approach, perhaps it would have avoided wasting £2 billion on an unsuccessful attempt to break into the American grocery market.

## Key terms

**Sensitivity analysis:** the process of assessing the impact of changed variables on the outcome of a forecast.

**Risk management:** a role within a business that aims to ensure that the possible effects of negative changes to variables are understood and where possible insured against.

# Workbook

## A. Revision questions

(20 marks; 20 minutes)

1. What is meant by sensitivity analysis? (2)

2. Identify three external factors that may cause forecasts to be inaccurate. (3)

3. Briefly explain how sensitivity analysis can reduce the risk involved in launching a new product. (5)

4. Explain how sensitivity analysis helps businesses quantify uncertainty when making investment decisions. (4)

5. Which variables may be key for a firm deciding whether to begin exporting fruit-based snacks from the UK to China? Briefly explain why for each variable you list. (6)

## B. Revision exercises

### DATA RESPONSE 1

#### A sensitive break-even analysis

Holly Nicholson is planning to open a clothes shop. As part of her preparation of a business plan, she has come up with the following forecasts:

Average selling price: £50
Average variable cost per unit: £20
Fixed costs: £12,000 per month

Holly has decided that most of the clothing she buys will be imported from India. She is aware that the sterling to rupee exchange rate is subject to change and may therefore affect the financial success of her business.

#### Questions (25 marks; 25 minutes)

1. Calculate the number of items the shop needs to sell per month to break-even if Holly's initial forecasts prove correct. (3)

2. Holly's business advisor suggests that exchange rate changes may increase variable costs by up to 20 per cent or cut them by up to 10 per cent. Calculate the distance between the optimistic and pessimistic break-even forecast if Holly's variable costs change. (6)

3. Complete the sensitivity analysis on her break-even point if Holly's selling price could vary between £45 and £55 and her fixed costs could vary between £10,000 and £15,000 per month. (10)

4. Explain which variable is likely to be the key determinant of Holly's break-even point. (6)

## DATA RESPONSE 2

Lidl is considering opening a new store. Before deciding, managers carry out an investment appraisal to see whether the store is likely to hit their minimum investment criteria of payback within 18 months and an ARR of 15 per cent. Their forecasts are shown below:

**Table 74.5** (Initial investment = £1.5m)

| Year | Cash inflow (£m) | Cash outflow (£m) |
|------|------------------|-------------------|
| 1 | 6 | 5 |
| 2 | 8 | 6 |
| 3 | 8 | 6.5 |

Their forecasters have suggested that cash inflows may be as much as 10 per cent below or above target in each year, whilst cash outflows may be between 5 per cent below and 10 per cent above target.

### Questions (25 marks; 25 minutes)

**1.** Calculate the payback based on the original forecasts. (3)

**2.** Calculate the ARR based on the original forecasts. (4)

**3.** Based on the original forecasts, should the store be opened? (2)

**4.** Use the following table to complete a sensitivity analysis for the store's ARR. (10)

| If we change: | Pessimistic ARR forecast | Expected ARR forecast | Optimistic ARR forecast | Distance from optimistic value to pessimistic value |
|---------------|--------------------------|-----------------------|-------------------------|------------------------------------------------------|
| Cash inflow | | | | |
| Cash outflow | | | | |

**5.** Based on the table above, explain whether managers should be more concerned with fluctuations in cash inflows or cash outflows. (6)

## C. Extend your understanding

**1.** 'The danger of sensitivity analysis is that it offers managers and investors a false sense of security.' To what extent does this mean that the cost of carrying out sensitivity analysis outweighs the benefits for a large plc? (25)

**2.** 'The value of sensitivity analysis is that it helps managers focus on the variables that matter.' To what extent do you agree with this statement? (25)

**Linked to:** Globalisation and emerging economies, Chapter 67; Competitive advantage, Chapter 76; Network analysis and strategic implementation, Chapter 95; Problems with strategy, Chapter 96.

### Definition

Igor Ansoff believed that businesses needed greater awareness of the risks involved in developing new products or new markets and, especially in the combination of the two: diversification.

## 75.1 What are the keys to finding the right strategic direction?

The term 'strategic' implies looking to the long-term future. It should be based on the company's strengths, but not simply derived from what is working well now. Apple Inc. set a good example in 2015. Just at the time it was launching its Apple Watch it was reportedly paying $250,000 starting bonuses to poach engineers from Tesla Motors (a producer of high-end electric cars). Apple was clearly thinking ahead to a possible iCar of the future. Doubtless this would be a self-drive car with fantastic entertainment features for the passengers.

'I begged, borrowed and stole concepts and theoretical insights from psychology, sociology and political science. And I attempted to integrate them into a holistic explanation of strategic behaviour.' Igor Ansoff, the 'father of strategic management'

## Strategy must be achievable

Strategy is concerned with what is possible, not just desirable. It must take into account market potential and company resources. The company needs to recognise its own limitations and potential. It also needs to consider economic and social circumstances. If the world economy is weakening, firms will be much more cautious about entering new export markets. If the home market is stagnating, businesses may well concentrate on lower-priced 'value' products.

## Strategy must be company specific

Each company will have a different strategic direction. The strategy selected will reflect the individual circumstances of the business. Different companies within the same industry may be pursuing different goals. The directions they choose will reflect those different goals. Within the same industry, one company may be aiming to increase market share while another looks for cost reductions in order to compete on price. The tyre industry is a good example of this. The market leaders were faced with increasing price competition from developing countries. They chose different strategic directions: Goodyear reduced costs; Michelin put its effort into innovation and widened its product range; Pirelli decided to concentrate on the market for luxury and speed.

## 75.2 Strategic direction and Ansoff's matrix

A useful way to look at the implications of changing strategic direction is to follow the approach taken by Igor Ansoff, who developed 'Ansoff's matrix'. Ansoff's academic background was in mathematics, so he believed all decisions should be based on extensive research, that is, gathering data.

In his 1965 book *Corporate Strategy*, Ansoff described strategy as a decision of medium- to long-term significance that is made in 'conditions of partial ignorance'. This 'ignorance' stems partly from the timescale involved. If you look three years ahead there are huge risks that marketplace changes will make your plans and forecasts look foolish. Such decisions are usually discussed and decided at board level.

Ansoff's matrix (Figure 75.1) is constructed to illustrate the risks involved in strategic decisions. These risks relate to the firm's level of knowledge and certainty about the market, the competition and customer behaviour – both now and in the future. The key issue is that risk becomes ever greater the further a firm strays from its core of existing products/existing customers (that is, the top left-hand corner of the matrix).

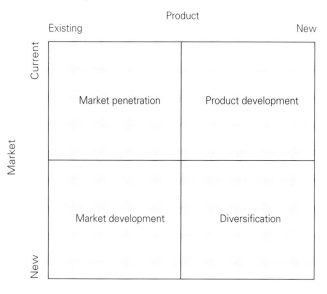

**Figure 75.1** Ansoff's matrix

Ansoff identified four types of strategy within his matrix; these are described below.

## Market penetration

This is about increasing market share by concentrating on existing products within the existing market. It is the most common and safest strategy because it does not stray from what the company knows best. If Tesco has opened 400 stores in towns all over Britain, and all are profitable, it is a simple matter of market penetration to open store 401 in a good-sized town that has not yet got its first Tesco.

Market penetration opportunities arise by:

- finding new customers, perhaps by widening the product's appeal to attract additional buyers

- taking customers from competitors; this may be achieved by aggressive pricing or by offering additional incentives to the customer

- persuading existing customers to increase usage; many food companies give recipes with their products to suggest additional ways of using the product; shampoo manufacturers introduced a frequent-wash shampoo to boost product usage.

## Market development

This is about finding new markets for existing products. It is more risky because the company must step into the unknown. For Cadbury to start selling chocolate in China requires a huge effort to learn to understand the Chinese consumer. Yet that is exactly what Cadbury is doing. Market development can be carried out by the following means.

- **Repositioning** the product: this will target a different market segment. This could be done by broadening the product's appeal to a new customer base. Land Rover's traditional market was farming and military use; it has now repositioned the product to appeal to town dwellers.

- Moving into new markets: many British retailers have opened up outlets abroad. Some, such as Tesco and Burberry, have opened up their own outlets. Others have entered into joint ventures or have taken over a similar operation in another country.

Moving Tesco into America was a major market development decision taken in 2006. Although backed by more than £1 billion of investment, Tesco 'Fresh & Easy' proved a disaster. In 2013 Tesco paid an American company to take the business off its hands. Even the mighty Coca-Cola has struggled to achieve success in India.

Why the difficulty? Surely market research can reveal whether customers in America want the same things as those in England? The answer to that is 'up to a point, perhaps'. But the skill with market research is to know what questions to ask and how to interpret the answers. This requires a degree of market knowledge that cannot always cross county boundaries, let alone national ones. This was why, over 80 years ago, the Ford Motor Company chose to set up a factory and offices in Britain, instead of relying on exporting from America. The rush of US firms that followed (for example, Heinz, Gillette and Mars) was followed much later by Japanese companies such as Sony and Honda. All took huge risks at the start, but believed they would only succeed in the long term by getting a deep understanding of local habits and needs. Famously, Sony budgeted for a 15-year payback period when it started up in Britain.

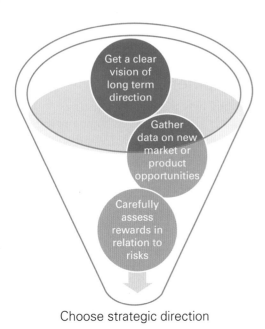

Choose strategic direction

**Figure 75.2** Implementing Ansoff's Matrix

## Product development

Product development means launching new products into your existing market (for example, L'Oréal launching a new haircare product). Hard though market development can be, it could be argued that product development is even harder. It is generally accepted that only one in seven new products succeeds; and that is a figure derived from the large businesses that launch new products through advertising agencies. In other words, despite their huge resources and expertise, heavy spending on R&D and market research, plus huge launch advertising budgets, companies such as Mars, Walls and L'Oréal suffer six flops for every success.

In highly competitive markets, companies use product development to keep one step ahead of the competition. Strategies may include those listed below.

### Changing an existing product

This may be to keep the products attractive. Washing powders and shampoos are good examples of this. The manufacturers are continually repackaging or offering some 'essential' new ingredient.

### Developing new products

The iPhone is a fantastic example of a new and successful product development, taking Apple from the computer business into the massive market for smartphones.

## Diversification

If it is accepted that market development and product development are both risky, how much more difficult is

the ultimate challenge: a new product in a new market, or diversification in Ansoff's terminology. This is the ultimate business risk, as it forces a business to operate completely outside its range of knowledge and experience. Virgin flopped totally with cosmetics and clothing, WH Smith had a dreadful experience in the DIY market with Do It All, and Heinz had a failed attempt to market a vinegar-based household cleaning product.

Yet diversification is not only the most risky strategy, it can also lead to the most extraordinary business successes. Nintendo was the Japanese equivalent of John Waddington, producing playing cards, until its new, young chief executive decided in the early 1970s to invest in the unknown idea of electronic games. From being a printer of paper cards, Nintendo became a giant of arcade games, then games consoles such as the Wii.

Ansoff emphasised the risks of diversification, but never intended to suggest that firms should fight shy of those risks. Risks are well worth taking as long as the potential rewards are high enough.

## 75.3 Ansoff's matrix in international markets

Entering into international markets carries the extra risk identified by Ansoff as market development. Naturally, the extent of the risk will depend on just how different the new market is from the firm's home country. For Green & Black's to start selling chocolate in France may not be too much of a stretch. French tastes are different and the distribution systems are very different from those in Britain, but there are many similarities in climate and affluence. But what about selling organic chocolate to Saudi Arabia? Or China? Or Sierra Leone? Figure 75.3 shows the way Ansoff would indicate the increasing level of risk involved.

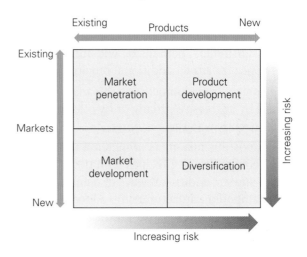

**Figure 75.3** Ansoff's matrix and risk

It is also possible that the product will need to be modified in order to be successful in the new market. International markets are littered with products and businesses that tried to shift their existing products and business models into overseas markets but failed. So even a business that plans to launch existing products into new overseas markets may find it has to adapt. In which case it will end up with a new product for the new market: diversification. More than twenty years ago Sony devised the corporate slogan: 'Think global. Act local.' It remains a valuable way to think.

'The thing is, continuity of strategic direction and continuous improvement in how you do things are absolutely consistent with each other. In fact, they're mutually reinforcing.' Michael Porter, theorist of competitive advantage

## Five Whys and a How

| Question | Answer |
|---|---|
| Why is it critical for a business to choose the right strategic direction? | Because a new direction is likely to tie up financial and human resources for several years – making the opportunity cost very high |
| Why is it hard for businesses to move away from their customer heartland? | Because customer understanding is at the core of every business success; move away and you've lost your competitive advantage |
| Why might a UK retailer struggle to transfer its business model to another country? | Why not? Why should the Americans, or French or Brazilians want exactly what the British want? |
| Why is diversification a word that must be used with great caution? | Because although Ansoff showed that it's the riskiest strategic direction, successful diversification reduces the risk of over-dependence on one product or market |
| Why might Ansoff's theory be of value to government as well as businesses? | Because governments often stray into territory they don't really understand, e.g. British foreign policy in Iraq and Libya |
| How should a business such as ASOS use Ansoff's matrix to help them evaluate their future strategic direction? | Ansoff would insist on the need for deep market knowledge before (for example) ASOS chose to move into the market for furniture – or to open a division in Africa |

## Evaluation: Strategic direction: Ansoff's matrix

Of all the business theories, none has been quite as illuminating as Ansoff's matrix. The huge financial crash of 2007-2009 can be attributed to high street banks developing products and entering markets that they didn't really understand. And past corporate failings at Tesco (USA and China) and at Greggs (trying to open Starbucks-style coffee shops) may not have happened if the managements were sufficiently alert to the problems of straying from the core of the business.

Yet one should not focus purely on risk when considering strategic direction. Ansoff could see the huge benefits that might accrue from successful diversification. Among the great diversifications remains Nintendo's path from a producer of playing cards to one of the world's most successful designers of games consoles and the accompanying software. Another famous diversification – Nokia going from producing car tyres to become the world's biggest mobile phone maker – has had a less happy ending.

## Further reading

Ansoff, I. (1965) *Corporate Strategy*. New York: McGraw-Hill.

# Workbook

## A. Revision questions

(30 marks; 30 minutes)

1. In the way business uses the terms, distinguish between 'strategy' and 'strategic'. (4)

2. How does strategic direction relate to the objectives of a business? (4)

3. Explain why strategic direction has to be company specific. (4)

4. Why is it important for a firm to examine its internal resources before deciding on a change of strategic direction? (3)

5. Explain the difference between market development and product development. (4)

6. Why is market research an important part of Ansoff's thinking? (4)

7. Why is market development more risky than market penetration? (4)

8. What might Ansoff mean by 'paralysis by analysis'? (3)

## B. Revision exercises

### DATA RESPONSE

**Morrisons' strategic direction**

In the 12 weeks to 30 March 2014 sales at UK grocery discounter Aldi rose by 35.3 per cent while at rival Morrisons they fell by 3.8 per cent. This compounded a wretched two-year period for Morrisons – the worst since Dalton Philips took over as chief executive in January 2010 (see the bar chart on page 487). On 8 May 2014 *The Independent* reported that:

'The supermarket chain slashed the price of 1,200 lines by 17 per cent last week to counter the rise of the discounters and to reignite its two-year attempt to report like-for-like sales growth. "I'm very confident we are doing the right things," Mr Philips said. "My job is to make big, bold decisions. The proof will be when there are more items in more baskets; how could it not be the right strategy to tackle this on price?"

Sainsbury's outgoing chief executive, Justin King, accused Morrisons of "playing catch-up" in lowering prices and said customers were enticed by ethically sourced products rather than simply price.'

Later, Phillips said that shareholders would 'hold our feet in the fire' if the price-cutting strategy proved unsuccessful, but he was convinced that this was the right long-term positioning for Morrisons.

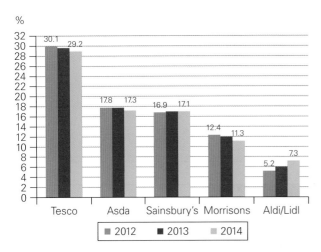

**Figure 75.4** UK grocery market share 2012–2014 (Dec to Feb data)

Source: data from Kantar Worldpanel

**Questions (30 marks; 35 minutes)**

1. Explain why price cutting in this case can be called a strategy rather than a tactic. (4)

2. Explain two factors that may determine whether Morrisons' 2014 strategy proves successful. (8)

3. Explain a possible weakness in the strategy as outlined in the data provided. (6)

4. In Morrisons' circumstances, analyse whether Ansoff would consider its new strategy to be 'market penetration' or 'market development'. (12)

## C. Extend your understanding

1. To what extent would Ansoff's matrix help to eliminate the risk involved in Cadbury launching a new range of crisps in the UK? (25)

2. Scoop is an ice cream business with a production unit, four shops and twenty-four ice cream flavours. Its owners are ambitious for the company's future. Do you think it would find the Boston matrix or Ansoff's matrix the more useful for its future development? Justify your answer. (25)

# Chapter 76 Competitive advantage

**Linked to:** The competitive environment, Chapter 71; Strategic direction: Ansoff's matrix, Chapter 75; Strategic positioning, Chapter 77.

## Definition

A firm is said to enjoy a competitive advantage over its rivals when it is able to grow its market share by offering consumers either lower prices, a better product quality or both simultaneously.

## 76.1 Types of competitive advantage

There are two types of competitive advantage. Differential advantage describes a situation where a firm can out-compete its rivals because they produce better quality products that are more highly differentiated. A good example of a company that enjoys a differential advantage is Mercedes-Benz. Drivers purchase 'Mercs' despite high prices because they want to buy into a brand image that screams exclusivity and personal achievement. The second type of competitive advantage is cost advantage. Low operating costs allow a firm to cut its prices without losing profit margin. A good example of a business with a cost advantage is Amazon. Unlike conventional bookshops Amazon does not have to pay for a chain of expensive high-street stores. As a result, Amazon can charge lower prices than bookshops and gain market share.

'If you don't have a competitive advantage, don't compete.' Jack Welch, author, and chairman and CEO of General Electric from 1981 until 2001

## Real business

In 2013 and 2014 the German discount supermarkets Aldi and Lidl enjoyed a clear competitive advantage over rivals such as Tesco and Sainsbury. Both supermarkets saw their share of the UK grocery market soar. In July 2014, a YouGov Brand Index survey showed Aldi to be the UK's favourite brand. When Aldi entered the UK in 1990, the company created a competitive advantage over rivals by offering customers lower prices. Since then both Aldi and Lidl have gone on to strengthen their competitive advantage by selling a wider range of products and by establishing a reputation for quality. Aldi's 'Specially selected' range of premium products includes products such as champagne and lobster that have won taste-test awards from magazines such as *Which*? The German discounters have created their competitive advantage by being more efficient. They can under-cut Tesco and Sainsbury because they operate with lower costs. In addition Aldi and Lidl benefit from being private rather than public limited companies. Unlike Tesco and Sainsbury's, who have shareholders to satisfy and dividends to pay, Aldi and Lidl can reinvest all of their profits into improved stores, even better food and new marketing campaigns.

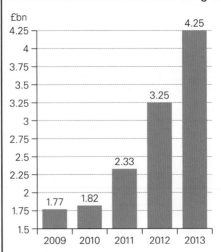

**Figure 76.1** Aldi's UK sales

Source: data from www.retail-week.com

## 76.2 The benefits of having a competitive advantage

### Higher profits

At its simplest, companies that produce better products than their rivals or who can under-cut their competitors' prices will generate higher revenues and profits. These higher profits can either be reinvested into developing new products or production processes to further strengthen the firm's competitive advantage. Alternatively, some of the profits made as a consequence of a competitive advantage could be distributed to shareholders as dividends. If a company pays higher dividends the demand for its shares will rise. This will push the company's share price up, increasing the company's market capitalisation. An increase in market capitalisation increases the cost of a hostile takeover making one less likely.

### Faster sales growth

China is the largest and the fastest-growing car market in the world. However, the rewards gained from operating in this market are not evenly distributed. Firms that have a competitive advantage will be more likely to achieve higher rates of growth than their rivals. A good example of a firm that has experienced rapid sales growth as a consequence of its competitive advantage is Jaguar Land Rover (JLR). The Indian owned company sold 122,000 cars in China in 2014, more than five times the figure achieved in 2010. As a result JLR was able to employ more than ten thousand extra staff – mainly in Britain. Sales growth is a popular corporate objective for senior managers because when it comes to executive pay, size matters more than profitability.

### High capacity utilisation

Capacity utilisation measures current output level as a percentage of maximum output. For example, due to low demand a brewery that can produce 1,000 barrels of beer per week might only be producing 600 barrels, implying a capacity utilisation of 60 per cent. A positive correlation exists between capacity utilisation and efficiency. This is because as capacity utilisation rises fixed costs will be spread across more units of output, causing unit costs to fall. Firms that offer consumers excellent value for money are more likely to operate with a high level of capacity utilisation because they will need to produce more to meet consumer demand. Other things being equal, this means that they are more likely to benefit from lower average costs, which make higher profit margins possible.

### Surviving recessions

During economic downturns most markets shrink in response to lower consumer spending. During recessions most firms just try to survive. In practice this means keeping sales above the break-even level. Firms with little or no competitive advantage are more likely to struggle in recessions than market leaders with a cost or value-added advantage over their rivals. For example, during the recent recession several of the restaurants along Croydon's Brighton Road were forced to close their doors. However, the recession barely touched the Galicia Tapas bar because of a strong local reputation for authentic Spanish food at low prices.

**Figure 76.2**

### Economies of scale

Economies of scale are factors that cause average cost to fall when a firm grows larger in the long run. To benefit from cost-saving economies of scale, firms have to grow by creating an increase in the demand for their product. The best way of creating a long-lasting increase in demand is to build a competitive advantage. In early 2014 Ryanair saw from its weak sales that rival easyJet was making a breakthrough with its offer of low prices plus good service. Ryanair felt forced to bring in a new friendly service policy, which seemed to be boosting demand by early 2015.

**Figure 76.3** Logic chain: Competitive advantage can be self-sustaining

## 76.3 The difficulties of maintaining a competitive advantage

Firms dislike competition and will do everything within their power to reduce the amount of competition that they face. To insulate themselves from the effects of competition firms try to develop a competitive advantage. However, their rivals will be doing the same thing at the same time. As a result, firms can struggle to retain a competitive advantage in the long term due to the following reasons.

1. **Product differentiation could be lost**

   Product differentiation measures the degree to which consumers believe that a particular brand is in some way unique and better than other brands of the same product. Firms that sell highly differentiated products that consumers like are likely to benefit from a competitive advantage. A good example of a product that was highly differentiated was the iPad. Since its 2010 launch companies such as Samsung have developed their own tablet computers that are very similar to the iPad. To keep this type of competitive advantage a company must keep on innovating in order to stay ahead of the competition. Apple has tried to do this by launching new and improved versions of the iPad that are smaller and lighter. Unfortunately these innovations have not been powerful enough to maintain its competitive advantage. In January 2015 the American company revealed that sales of the iPad had declined by nearly 20 per cent in the last three months as consumers switched towards cheaper Android tablets.

'The only sustainable competitive advantage is your organisation's ability to learn faster than the competition.' Peter Senge, MIT systems scientist

2. **New entrants to the market**

   Entrepreneurs who are able to identify gaps in the market before their rivals will typically go on to benefit from differential competitive advantage if their new product meets with customer approval. This competitive advantage will last until competition arrives. In 1988 Paul Cole and Jules Allen set up a business called Abel and Cole after spotting a gap in the market for home-delivered organic fruit and vegetable boxes. For many years the company's service was unique. They were the only supplier of their type. However, over time the market grew in response to a change in consumer tastes. Other entrepreneurs spotted the great profits that Abel and Cole were making and decided to cash-in by setting up their own home deliveries of organic fruit and vegetable boxes.

3. **Low productivity growth**

   Sluggish productivity growth can cause a firm to lose a cost-based competitive advantage. Productivity measures the output produced per worker. If productivity grows at a slower rate than wages, the labour cost of producing a unit of output will rise. The table below shows how a competitive advantage can be lost when pay outstrips productivity growth. The company concerned is a furniture manufacturer that in 2014 paid their staff £1,500 each per month. In 2015 the workers received a 10 per cent pay rise, at a time when productivity growth was only 5 per cent. The furniture manufacturer's pricing method is to apply a mark-up of 100 per cent to its unit labour costs. (See Table 76.1.)

   The increase in retail price is a result of productivity growing more slowly than wages. If this situation is allowed to persist consumers are likely to respond by buying a rival's product. Poor productivity growth can be caused by poor management and by a lack of investment in new machinery and in staff training.

**Table 76.1** Furniture manufacturer's costs, 2014 and 2015

|  | 2014 | 2015 |
| --- | --- | --- |
| Monthly output | 1,000 tables | 1,050 tables |
| Employees | 100 | 100 |
| Monthly wage bill | £150,000 | £165,000 |
| Unit labour cost | £150 | £157 |
| Retail price | £300 | £314 |

4. **Changes in fashion and consumer taste**

Some firms can lose their competitive edge as a result of a change in fashion or consumer tastes. This is what happened to the retailer Game which used to sell PC and console software on the high street. A longer-than-expected wait for the new Sony and Xbox products plus a switch to online purchasing dragged the business into administration in March 2012. Game lost its competitive advantage when consumer tastes and habits changed.

5. **New laws, taxes and government regulations**

Government intervention can cause a firm to lose its competitive advantage. A good example of this occurred in July 2014 when the Financial Conduct Authority proposed a cap on payday loan charges. Payday loans are a form of short-term credit that is targeted at borrowers who have a poor credit history. Payday loans are relatively risky for the lender because on average one in five loans made are never repaid. To make up for this the interest rates charged on payday loans are very high. The proposed cap on the interest rates threatens the competitive advantage of companies such as Wonga.com. In the future Wonga might struggle to compete head-on against credit card companies if they are no longer allowed to target sub-prime borrowers. Because payday loan companies have to compete against other financial institutions that supply other types of credit, government intervention in the payday loan market has adversely affected the competiveness of companies such as Wonga.

## 76.4 What can a company do to keep a competitive advantage?

The best way of keeping a competitive advantage is to embrace change, because most products have finite life cycles. According to the Boston Consulting Group's product portfolio matrix, technological advances and/or changes in fashion will result in firms losing their competitive advantage when cash cows age into dogs. To stay ahead businesses need to invest heavily in new product development in order to develop rising stars which will hopefully go and mature into new sources of competitive advantage.

If the advantage is based on a technical breakthrough there may be scope for patenting it. This can give up to twenty years' protection from direct competition. That may be long enough to develop other forms of competitive advantage, as James Dyson has done so successfully with his vacuum cleaners.

Strategic planning can also help firms to either develop new, or retain existing competitive advantages. This can involve studying the opposition's strengths and weaknesses before deciding what to do next. Monitoring market trends is also important because what might work today might not work tomorrow. A good example of a company that lost its competitive edge because it did not respond fast enough to a new market trend is the supermarket chain Morrisons. It was too slow establishing a home delivery service for online grocery shoppers.

**Figure 76.4** A payday loan company charges high interest rates as one in five loans are never repaid

## Five Whys and a How

| Question | Answer |
|---|---|
| Why is it important to have a competitive advantage? | Most markets are competitive. Therefore, in order to trade profitably firms need to offer consumers either a better product or a cheaper price, or preferably both |
| Why might a competitive advantage increase the probability of a firm surviving a recession? | Markets generally shrink during a recession, so only the most competitive firms in the market may be able to survive |
| Why might a firm lose its competitive advantage? | New firms may join the market, who offer consumers a cheaper or better product |
| Why do firms try to patent their innovative new products? | To prevent a competitor from launching a me-too product that might force the innovator into cutting price |
| Why is it important for companies to match the increases in productivity achieved by their rivals? | Low output per worker will mean that unit costs will be higher than they should be. To protect profit margins, higher costs usually force firms into raising their prices, which results in lost competitiveness |
| How might a firm go about creating a cost-based competitive advantage? | By becoming more efficient, quite possibly by ditching mass production in favour of lean production |

## Evaluation: Competitive advantage

### Complacency, the biggest challenge

Some firms that have developed a competitive advantage see no need to change, or are reluctant to do things differently for fear of wrecking a magic formula; the underlying philosophy being: if it ain't broke, don't fix it. This approach is usually very risky because in a competitive market standing still usually results in you moving backwards. One company that lost its competitive advantage due to complacency is Nokia. In 2006 the Finnish company that practically invented the mobile phone was still the market leader. However, Nokia was slow to react to innovations brought to the market by new entrants Samsung and Apple. Instead of adapting and changing, Nokia stuck rigidly to its 'candy bar' phones that had served the company so well in the past. An insistence that Nokia knew best led to a string of expensive new product flops. By the time the company accepted the need to change it was too late for them to catch up. In September 2013 Nokia's mobile phone division was sold to Microsoft.

'An organisation's ability to learn, and translate that learning rapidly, is the ultimate competitive advantage.' Jack Welch, author, and chairman and CEO of General Electric from 1981 until 2001

## Key terms

**Market share:** a company's or a brand's sales expressed as a percentage of total market sales.

**Market capitalisation:** is the current money value of a company's shares that have already been sold on the stock market. It is calculated by multiplying the number of shares that have been sold by their current share price.

**Patent:** a legal document that prevents a rival from copying a new product or production process for a limited amount of time. To be granted a patent a new product or production process must be new and inventive.

# Workbook

## A. Revision questions

(30 marks; 30 minutes)

**1. a)** Distinguish between a differential and a cost-based competitive advantage. (3)

  **b)** What type of competitive advantage does Aldi have over Tesco, Asda and Sainsbury? (4)

**2. a)** In Table 76.1, explain how the figures for unit labour cost and retail price were produced by reproducing the relevant calculations. Please show your working. (3)

  **b)** Explain one other way by which a firm might try to reduce its unit labour costs, other than by raising productivity. (2)

**3.** Identify and explain two ways in which a competitive advantage might help a car manufacturer to increase its profits. (4)

**4.** How might heavy investment in staff training help a fashion clothing retailer develop a competitive advantage? (4)

**5.** Explain how complacency can cause a firm to lose its competitive advantage. (4)

**6.** When Nokia first noticed that it was losing its differential competitive advantage, it responded by cutting its prices. Comment on whether price cuts are the best way of restoring a firm's competitive advantage. (6)

## B. Revision exercises

### DATA RESPONSE

**Nintendo Wii U**

Nintendo revolutionised the world of computer gaming in 2006 when it launched the Wii. The computer game market is highly competitive and product life cycles can be very short. To survive, games need a unique selling point. Before the Wii was launched the market for games was heavily skewed towards shoot-em-up games which mostly appealed to young men. Nintendo wanted to create a new games console that would appeal to a wider audience. To do this they designed games that would appeal to the whole family based on activities such as bowling, baseball, dancing and karaoke. However the Wii's key differentiating feature was a handheld remote controller that detected movement in three directions. The new remote controller made games more accessible by making them easier to play. There was no longer a need for players to invest hours of time learning how to operate a complex console. Instead, parents or even grandparents could play straight away

because Nintendo's hand-held remote controller was intuitive – move your hand to the left and your player on the screen moved in the same direction.

The Wii was an instant success, with 600,000 sold in the UK within a week of its 2007 launch as supply struggled to keep up with demand. Nintendo's TV advertising campaign for the Wii featured men, women and children of different ages playing the Wii happily together. Nintendo also benefited from favourable publicity, because unlike conventional computer games Wii players moved and expended energy whilst they played. Global sales of the Wii grew rapidly until 2009. From that point onwards sales fell steadily. This was partially due to a poor supply of new games from software specialists. For example, one of the most popular games of 2011 was *Call of Duty: Modern Warfare*. This game was available in formats that could be used on both the Xbox and PlayStation 3. However, unfortunately for Nintendo, the developers did not bother to produce a version for the Wii.

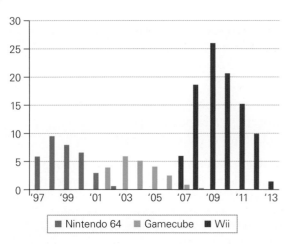

**Figure 76.5** The Nintendo Wii U (global unit sales in millions). Apr 1–Sep 30 2012

Source: data from www.statista.com

In 2012 Nintendo responded with an extension strategy, launching a new variant called the Wii U. The new version was different from the old in that the hand controller now included a HD touch screen. Unfortunately for Nintendo, the new console struggled to establish itself in the market. However, by July 2014 sales of the Wii U began to pick up. In the second quarter of 2014 Nintendo sold over 500,000 consoles, a rise of 300 per cent on the same period a year before. This was down to a cut in price from £300 to £240, making the Wii U considerably cheaper than either an Xbox or a PlayStation. Sales of the Wii U have also been assisted by the release of a new hit game, Mario Cars 8, which received strong reviews in gaming magazines.

**Questions (40 marks; 45 minutes)**

1. Analyse the competitive advantage Nintendo created when it first launched the Wii. (9)

2. **a)** Nintendo priced the Wii at £179 when it was first launched in Britain. Calculate the total revenue generated from the Wii in its first week of sales in the UK. (3)

   **b)** Explain two reasons why a competitive advantage can help a firm to increase its revenues. (8)

3. Explain two possible reasons why sales of the Wii declined rapidly from 2009 onwards. (8)

4. **a)** Study the chart that shows the Nintendo's worldwide sales of the Wii. Explain whether the pattern conforms to the product life cycle. (4)

   **b)** Explain two possible reasons why Nintendo's extension strategy took time to work. (8)

## C. Extend your understanding

1. In 2012 the UK government granted Virgin Trains the sole right to supply passenger rail travel on the highly profitable West Coast Mainline until 2017. In the light of this, to what extent do you think it is always necessary for a firm to develop a competitive advantage? (25)

2. Primark is a well-established retailer with more than 300 stores and a return on capital of 33 per cent. Other retailers such as New Look and Forever21 want a bigger share of Primark's profitability. To what extent do you believe Primark can sustain its competitive advantage? (25)

**Linked to:** Segmentation, targeting and positioning, Chapter 19; The impact of strategic decision-making on functional decision-making, Chapter 55; The value of SWOT analysis, Chapter 56; Strategic implementation, Chapter 94; Problems with strategy, Chapter 96.

## Definition

Strategic positioning is the high-level management thinking behind 'STEP analysis'. It is about defining where the business is going to park itself amidst the chaotic flows within the marketplace. Waitrose is parked on a road called 'posh'. Lidl and Iceland are parked at 'cheap'. Management guru Michael Porter believes either position can provide a sustained competitive advantage.

## 77.1 The strategic need to compete

A classic quote from investment sage Warren Buffet is that, 'It's only when the tide goes out that you see who's been swimming naked.' In the period 2008-2013 Morrisons seemed to be doing fine. Market share held up quite well and profit margins outstripped Sainsbury's. Yet when the pressure exerted by Aldi and Lidl forced Tesco to respond, Morrisons was the one that seemed stuck in the crossfire. As shown in Figure 77.1, Morrisons profits evaporated in 2014 and 2015.

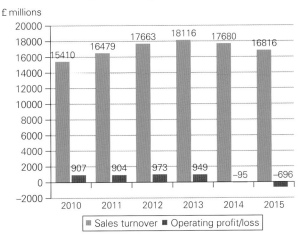

Source of data: Morrisons annual accounts

**Figure 77.1** Morrisons annual sales and profits 2010-2015

This example establishes the truism that companies need to think about their competitiveness even when things are going well. For a business such as Morrisons there is a balance to strike between customer benefits and price. They could offer free coffee to all customers, but would have to slip that cost onto prices somewhere along the line. In 2014, in the face of severe pressure, Morrisons decided to focus solely on price. It brought out a loyalty card that, it claimed, would reduce prices to the level found at discounters Aldi and Lidl. It was a major step away from the traditional Morrisons' positioning of good food for all. It had no alternative: it had to find a way to compete.

'Firms are often different but not differentiated, as they pursue forms of uniqueness that buyers do not value.' Michael Porter, author *Competitive Advantage*

## 77.2 Porter's generic strategies

If Morrisons had been able to afford Michael Porter as a consultant (his charges start at $100,000 a day) the message would have been clear – years ago. Porter consistently warns against taking up a position in the middle of a market. He believes that long-term success is best built on either a super-low price position or else a positioning based purely on product differentiation. So he would applaud Aldi, Lidl, Asda and (at the other end of the scale) Waitrose – but criticise Sainsbury's, Morrisons and Tesco. At the time of writing (early 2015) customer purchasing patterns are right with Porter.

Porter's **generic strategy** matrix suggests that all markets operate in the same way (hence the term 'generic'). They can be segmented in two ways: mass versus niche markets; and lowest cost versus highest differentiation strategies. In Figure 77.2 the example given is from the UK grocery sector. The bottom two quarters of the matrix represent niche markets (and low market shares). On the left are the two lowest-cost operators, Aldi and Lidl; their low costs enable them to charge low, everyday prices. According to *The Grocer* magazine, an Aldi shopping basket is usually 15 per cent cheaper than Asda, and 25–30 per cent cheaper than at Waitrose. In the top half of the matrix are the mass market businesses, with Tesco the market leader – and positioned squarely in the middle of the market.

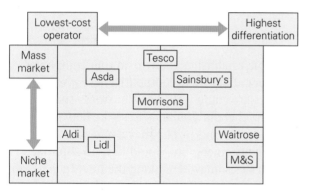

**Figure 77.2** Market positions

## Porter's low cost strategy

To Porter, there is no better position for long-term stability than to be the lowest cost operator, as long as you have an advantage that others cannot copy. Producing in China can be copied by anyone. But Aldi and Lidl both have very strong positions that are difficult to copy. Since starting in 1973, Lidl has grown to have 10,000 shops across Europe, with sales (in 2013) of more than €63 billion – that's more than Sainsbury and Morrisons combined. And Lidl operates with far fewer stock units than the main UK supermarkets. So vast buying power is focused on relatively few stock units, giving enormous bulk-buying leverage. Aldi operates in the same way. So not even Tesco has the same relative buying power as the German discounters.

As Porter makes clear, the joy of the lowest cost position is that you can choose to either charge the lowest prices or to charge relatively high prices but enjoy high profit margins. In another market, Ryanair is the unrivalled lowest-cost operator in Western Europe. But if you try to fly Ryanair at the last minute the price will be much the same as easyJet or British Airways.

## Porter's differentiation strategy

Porter is clear that differentiation works when it adds greater value than the cost embedded in the differentiation. Customers will be prepared to pay a price premium for a differentiated item, as long as the difference is something they value. In the market for cars, brands such as BMW (status; driver excitement) and Volvo (safety) each have their specific differentiating factors. In essence, if customers buy the brand rather than the price tag, not only is value added but also customer loyalty has been achieved.

In his book *Competitive Advantage*, Michael Porter emphasises that there are many ways to achieve differentiation beyond marketing. He believed that it could be derived from anywhere along the supply chain. Some businesses may be brilliant at purchasing, for instance a jeweller that keeps managing to obtain fantastic diamonds that can be turned into beautiful rings. Others may be brilliant at manufacture, producing the most reliable, durable cars on the market. As long as the consumer values the differentiating factor, the mission is accomplished.

One other factor is central to Porter's theme. Sustained advantage is only possible if the source of the differentiation can be protected. That's the wonderful thing about brand names. Coca-Cola has been able to sustain a price premium and some very loyal customers for more than a century based on its brand name and image. At the time of writing Coca-Cola is outselling Tesco Cola in Tesco stores even though Coke is priced at £1.83 for 1.75 litres while Tesco is 89p for 2 litres, that is, Coke is more than twice the price.

'Differentiation will lead to superior performance if the value perceived by the buyer exceeds the cost of differentiation.' Michael Porter, author *Competitive Advantage*

## Focused low cost

In the mass market the lowest cost producer will enjoy economies of scale that come from size; this may not be the case in a niche market. To be the lowest cost operator in the market for games Apps targeted at the under-9s will require a well-considered approach to management – perhaps with a very flat management structure based on almost total delegation of development and marketing decision-making. If your business can succeed at that, there will still be a threat that success creates its own threats to your way of working. Sustaining a focused low-cost position will be hugely challenging; but when successful, Porter says it's a strong place to be.

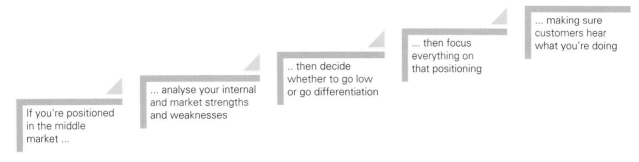

**Figure 77.3** Logic chain: Focus your strategic positioning

## Focused differentiation

Perhaps the most sustainable competitive position is focused differentiation, that is, within a niche market. Within the market for luxury goods, no brand is in a stronger position than Hermès of Paris. While companies such as Chanel sell bags for £3,000, Hermes is at £5,000 and upwards. It benefits from an exclusive image and can charge accordingly. In a different market the mobile phone brand Vertu charges upwards of £9,600 for a phone. 'Handcrafted in England from the finest rare materials', the Vertu phone doesn't want to compete with Apple's mass market dominance. It wants its own market positioning: focused differentiation.

'Strategy is about making choices, trade-offs; it's about deliberately choosing to be different.' Michael Porter, strategy guru

## 77.3 Influences on the choice of a positioning strategy

Every business should be clear on its main strengths and weaknesses. When easyJet and Ryanair were growing rapidly, British Airways decided to launch its own low-cost airline called Go (in 1998). Within two years it was struggling and in 2002 was sold to easyJet! It proved to be that British Airways was incapable of running an efficient low-cost airline. It had neither the management skills nor the history. British Airways, then, has little choice but to try to be a differentiated operator. In addition to the background and traditions of the business, there are other possible influences on the choice of positioning:

● *The positioning of others in the market.* No one today would start up a UK airline aiming to beat Ryanair as the lowest-cost operator. Ryanair has secured

that position for itself. But no European airline has managed to stand out as *the* airline of choice. So perhaps a newcomer would attempt to start with a positioning aimed at focused differentiation with the expectation, perhaps, of eventually becoming effectively differentiated in the mass market.

● *The operational skills within the business.* If there is a highly talented R&D department it may be that differentiation is a viable future. If the skills lie in automation and cost-reduction, then a low-cost strategy might be best.

● Another factor is the desire by some firms to operate only in markets where they have a market share high enough to put them in Number 1 or 2 position in their sector. So they may choose to withdraw from sectors where they're achieving little. This could be done by selling off underperforming divisions or simply by closing them down.

'The essence of strategy is deciding what not to do.' Michael Porter, strategy guru

## 77.4 The value of Porter's generic strategy matrix

In 2008 academics at Aston University carried out research among more than 1,800 former students from the Aston Business School. They wanted to find out the actual usage of the strategy theories taught at universities. Top by some margin came SWOT analysis. Bottom came Bowman's strategic clock. Porter's generic strategy matrix was not widely used, but was seen as of particular importance for 'strategy analysis' and 'strategic choice'. The most widely used theories were used for 'strategic implementation'.

**Table 77.1** Which business theories do managers really use?

| Strategy tool | Currently used % | Used, but not now % | Heard of, not used % | Never heard of % |
|---|---|---|---|---|
| SWOT analysis | 76 | 13 | 10 | 1 |
| Key success factors | 58 | 13 | 21 | 8 |
| Scenario plan | 45 | 19 | 29 | 7 |
| Porter's five forces | 39 | 25 | 30 | 6 |
| Industry life cycle | 36 | 21 | 33 | 10 |
| PESTLE analysis | 33 | 14 | 38 | 30 |
| Portfolio matrix, e.g. Boston | 29 | 20 | 40 | 13 |
| Porter's generic strategy matrix | 23 | 19 | 36 | 18 |
| Ansoff's matrix | 15 | 14 | 42 | 36 |
| Globalisation matrices | 6 | 7 | 26 | 63 |
| Bowman's strategic clock | 3 | 6 | 26 | 65 |

Source: adapted from Paula Jarzabkowski and Monica Giuletti, Aston University

www.egosnet.org/jart/prj3/egos/resources/dbcon_def/uploads/summer_workshop_papers/2007/W-019.pdf

## 77.5 Bowman's strategic clock

Cliff Bowman and David Faulkner wanted to develop further Porter's ideas on strategic positioning. They believed that the generic strategy matrix failed to capture all the possible options and therefore oversimplified. In what became known as Bowman's strategic clock (see Figure 77.4), differentiation and focused differentiation are somewhat submerged among many strategic possibilities.

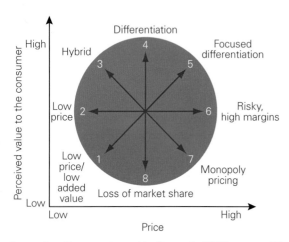

Source: from *Corporate Competitive Strategy* by Cliff Bowman and David Faulkner. © 1997

**Figure 77.4** Bowman's strategic clock

A key difference between Bowman and Porter is that the latter compares differentiation with low cost as strategic options. Bowman talks about price, not cost. For Porter, this misses the point. He emphasised that his strategy matrix was based on competitive advantage that could be generated anywhere within the value chain, from suppliers to after-sales service. So cost-minimisation in the classic Ryanair way (cutting back on time wasted between flights as much as

anything else) is lost on Bowman. The strategic clock is a statement of marketing positioning (e.g. pricing strategy) rather than a corporate strategic tool.

### Theory in 60 seconds

**Bowman's strategic clock**

● Compares price (high-low) with value to customer (high-low)

● Unlike Porter, it uses price as a variable, not cost

● Suggests eight strategic options

● Within these, the strong strategies are where 'value' is higher than 'price'

● Little used in business – perhaps because it's over-complicated.

## 77.6 The value of different strategic positioning strategies

Michael Porter is in no doubt that successful strategic positioning relies upon clarity. Be Lidl or be Waitrose; don't be a bit of each. This means that he appears to exclude some classically successful strategies. Who wouldn't want to be Wrigley, with more than a 90 per cent share of the UK market for chewing gum. Wrigley's approach is simple dominance of the chewing gum 'space'. But although one can find exceptions such as this, it is fair to view Porter's generic strategy matrix as a genuine insight into the business world. Low cost versus differentiation works perfectly as a way to analyse the grocery sector, the airline sector and the car market; but it means far less in the chocolate market where differentiation is far more important than low cost. Possibly Porter's strategy isn't quite as generic as he wishes it to be, but it's certainly of huge value in many industries.

Bowman's strategic clock, by contrast, attempts to do too much. It's suggesting so many different strategic positionings as to create confusion. In fact, the theory is trying to emphasise that some positions are inevitable losers, such as 'low price, low added value'. But the theory would be used more often if its conclusions were clearer.

## Five Whys and a How

| Question | Answer |
|---|---|
| Why is market positioning so important? | Because history shows that middle-market producers of weakly differentiated products struggle to survive |
| Why is Michael Porter associated most strongly with strategic positioning? | You could argue that he said little that was new, but his books brought the subject together in a way that no one had done before |
| Why might a business choose to take a central ('piggy in the middle') positioning? | Because that's where the bulk of the market is, that is, it's tempting to try to become the Tesco of your own marketplace |
| Why might focused differentiation be a more secure position than differentiation in the mass market? | Because it's easier to keep hold of a differentiated position when there's less competition (in a niche market, rivals often can't afford to spend big enough to catch up) |
| Why do differentiated businesses such as Nintendo ever struggle to be profitable? | Porter's matrix is sure of the value of a positioning such as Nintendo's, but doesn't alter the fact that the company needs to make the right strategy choices, for example taking its software brands into mobile platforms |
| How should a business react when it realises it's stuck in the over-competitive middle of the market? | It should choose either to go low cost or high differentiation depending on the strengths (and history) of the business |

## Evaluation: Strategic positioning

The strength of Porter's writings is the focus on three messages: manage your value chain with care; find your point of differentiation and hammer it home to the consumer and retailer; and then you'll have a basis for sustained competitive advantage. Critics of Porter accept his ideas, but worry that his views are too static in a fast-moving competitive world. Today's competitive advantage is tomorrow's slide into mediocrity, they say. So they want more uncertainty built into the theory.

That makes sense, but one still has to look at the reality of modern markets. Some work slowly enough for Porter's strategic positioning to make long-term sense. People were writing about the rise of Aldi and Lidl in 2008, when Tesco's market share started to slip. By 2015 the rise of the German discounters had become an everyday fact. But throughout the period 2008-2015 the simplicity of their lowest-cost positioning made Aldi and Lidl seem like a formula for strategic success: adopt the right positioning, then make sure to stay there – bringing customers to you.

## Key term

Generic strategy: a strategic position that will prove effective in every market (i.e. generically). Porter said lowest cost and highest differentiation were the perfect positions of strength.

# Workbook section

## A. Revision questions

(30 marks; 30 minutes)

1. Explain what is meant by 'a sustained competitive advantage' (4)

2. **a)** Use Figure 77.1 to calculate the change in Morrison's revenue (sales turnover) and the change in its operating profits between 2013 and 2015. (4)

   **b)** Briefly explain the implications of these changes. (4)

3. According to Table 77.1, what proportion of the sample had ever used Porter's strategic matrix? (1)

4. According to Table 77.1, which theory has had the highest rejection rate from those who have tried it out? (1)

5. Explain how effective focused differentiation might prove as a market positioning for one of the following:
   **a)** Porsche cars
   **b)** New Look retail
   **c)** Fat Face retail. (6)

6. Number 3 on Bowman's clock (Figure 77.4) is a hybrid that is part low-price and part differentiation. Explain how that might work as a strategic position for a brand of your choice. (6)

7. Explain why it is important to distinguish between Porter's focus on cost and Bowman's focus on price. (4)

## B. Revision exercises

### DATA RESPONSE

**Tesco signs deal to enter India's supermarket sector**

**Figure 77.5**

In the summer 2013 Tesco shocked analysts by paying $500 million to a Chinese grocery chain to take Tesco China off its hands. Nine years after buying into an established Chinese hypermarket chain, Tesco was giving up on the world's fastest-growing grocery market.

It was a slight surprise, then, that 20 March 2014 saw an announcement that Tesco had signed a deal to become the first foreign supermarket to enter India's $150 billion grocery market. If China was a complex, fragmented market, it was nothing compared with India, with its 8 million small, independent 'kirana' stores. Tesco was committing itself to invest £85 million into a joint venture with the Indian Tata group. Tesco would be the first Western retailer to venture into the Indian grocery market, implying considerable risks but perhaps the long-term benefit of first-mover advantage.

Until 2012, foreign retailers had been banned from investing in the country's retail sector. Now, following Indian government approval, Tesco would be investing about £85 million in the 50-50 deal to incorporate 12 supermarkets that already exist under the branding 'Star Bazaar'. Tesco has challenges but also amazing opportunities ahead. The eight million small grocers divide the market up into minute fragments, with an average annual revenue of $18,750, that is, about £12,000. In Britain a Tesco store might take £1 million in a week! It will be crucial to change people's shopping habits. Although 40 per cent of Indians' grocery spending is on 'wet' goods such as meat, fruit and vegetables, sales at groceries are heavily weighted towards 'dry', packaged goods.

Only 3 per cent of grocery sales are of wet goods, so Indians are buying their wet goods at markets or in specialist butchers/fishmongers/greengrocers. Another interesting feature of the grocery market in India is that only 14 per cent of the population had internet access in 2014, so online grocery selling was not yet developed.

International firms are now able to buy up to a 51 per cent stake in multi-brand retailers, but the decision has led to much opposition in the country. The move to relax the rules in September 2012 came after a similar decision, in November 2011, was scrapped following widespread protests. Rules stipulating that foreign supermarkets had to source 30 per cent of their products from local firms were eased in August 2013 amid fears the rule was blocking investment. The requirement remains, but foreign firms now have five years to hit the 30 per cent target, allowing them to import goods from overseas initially.

### Questions (40 marks; 45 minutes)

1. From the evidence available and your wider knowledge of China and India, to what extent would you agree with Tesco's strategic choices? (20)

2. In entering the Indian grocery market, Tesco can choose what market positioning to adopt. Michael Porter might recommend following a 'lowest-cost', mass-market strategy. To what extent would you agree that this is the best strategic positioning for the long-term future of Tesco in India? (20)

## C. Extend your understanding

1. To what extent does the success of a business theory depend on how widely it's adopted by businesspeople? (25)

2. To what extent would a high differentiation strategic position work for a business of your choice in an industry of your choice? (25)

# Chapter 78 Growth and retrenchment

**Linked to:** Corporate objectives, strategy and tactics, Chapter 54; Globalisation and emerging economies, Chapter 67; Economies and diseconomies of scale, Chapter 79; Problems with strategy, Chapter 96.

### Definition

Growth means expansion, while retrenchment describes a process whereby a firm slims down its operations. This will mean reducing capacity probably by factory or store closures, and usually redundancies.

## 78.1 Reasons why firms grow

Some firms can end up growing by accident. This is called unplanned growth. A good example is Baggit, who are now one of India's leading suppliers of luxury handbags. Nina Lekhi set up the business when she dropped out of university. Initially, Lekhi did not take her own business seriously, it was just a hobby. Fortunately, her brightly coloured bags proved to be very popular with Indian women, who loved her bold designs. More and more retailers wanted to stock Baggit, which meant that Lekhi had to take on more staff and expand.

**Figure 78.1** Baggit became a surprise success for its founder

On the other hand many firms grow in order to achieve an objective. This is called planned growth. The reasons for planned growth include:

1. **To increase profitability** Many firms choose to pursue growth because they hope that it will cause their profits to rise. In August 2014 Netflix, an American company that sells streamed films and TV series, announced its intention to grow by launching its service in France and Germany. In 2013 Netflix made a total profit of £80 million from 30 million subscribers. This implies that they made a profit of £2.67 per customer. Assuming that Netflix proves as popular in France and Germany as it has in America and Britain, an additional 10 million French and German subscribers would add £26.7 million to Netflix's bottom line.

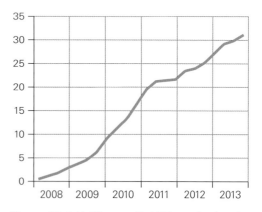

**Figure 78.2** Netflix growth: Millions of subscribers

Source: data from www.forbes.com/sites/markrogowsky/2013/12/19/hulus-billion-dollar-milestone-a-sign-of-just-how-far-behind-netflix-it-has-fallen/

2. **To become more efficient** A firm becomes more efficient when it is capable of producing more output from the same amount of physical space, raw materials or workforce. Increases in efficiency result in lower unit costs. Growth can help a firm to become more efficient in two ways. In the short run sales growth can help a firm to achieve higher capacity utilisation. If output moves closer to full capacity, fixed costs will be spread over more units of output, causing average cost to fall. Growth in the

long run can also cause cost per unit to fall due to economies of scale. A company that has to grow to realise a technical economy of scale is Hyundai. In July 2014 the Korean company launched the Tucson, the world's first zero-emission hydrogen fuel-cell car. Hyundai has great hopes for the car, explaining why they have already built a huge factory to mass produce the Tucson. In its first month on sale in America only 1,000 Tucsons were sold. To reduce unit cost to a manageable level, Hyundai will need to grow quickly in this new market segment.

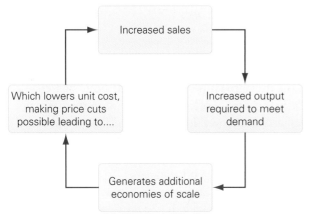

**Figure 78.3** Logic chain

3. **Market dominance** Colgate Palmolive is an example of a company that has achieved a position of market dominance via growth. The company leads the global toothpaste market with a share of over 40 per cent. Colgate has a broad product portfolio ensuring that all market segments are covered. If a firm can reduce the number of competitors that it faces it will be able to reduce substitutability in the market. This should make demand more price inelastic, making it possible to generate additional revenue by raising price.

4. **Managerial objectives** Big public limited companies are run by professional managers who run the business on behalf of the shareholders, who own the business. Pay, bonuses and psychological benefits such as status and ego often encourage managers to pursue growth, even if it comes at the expense of profit. The American economist Oliver Williamson criticises the conventional view that all firms pursue a goal of profit maximisation. According to him, managers try to make just enough profit to satisfy their shareholders so that they do not lose their jobs. They turn their attentions to pursuing growth, because this is more likely to give them pay rises and corporate luxuries like private jets.

## 78.2 Reasons why firms retrench

1. **To survive a recession** During recessions when consumers spend less, most markets tend to get smaller. As a result all but the most successful firms will suffer from falling sales. If sales fall below the break-even level losses will begin to mount up. In this situation some firms opt to retrench by slimming down their product range or by closing down underutilised factories. If fixed costs can be cut, and the break-even point lowered, the business should still be around when the economy finally recovers.

2. **Delayering to improve competitiveness** Delayering involves removing layers of management. It is normally done to reduce costs. In 2014 the German telecommunications company Telekom decided to retrench by making 750 of its middle managers redundant. In addition to lower costs, delayering can (in the long run) improve motivation because it forces managers into operating with a wider span of control, which encourages greater delegation.

3. **To prevent losses at the end a product's life cycle** Most products follow a life cycle of birth, growth, maturity and decline. During the decline phase sales gradually fall. It therefore makes sense to retrench before sales fall below the break-even level in order to avoid losses. The Internet has revolutionised the way we access media. This technology-driven change in consumer tastes has caused newspaper sales to decline. In 2012 the Daily Mirror retrenched by reducing its editorial staff by nearly one-fifth.

4. **A strategic change of direction** The BBC once had a TV series called *Troubleshooter* featuring Sir John Harvey Jones, former chairman of ICI. The BAFTA award-winning show featured Sir John visiting businesses that were in trouble. The advice offered each week did not tend to vary too much. He usually pointed out that the business featured was overly diversified. His advice invariably was that the business concerned must retrench. By selling off underperforming divisions of the business the owners would be able to raise the cash needed to invest in the parts of the business that Sir John thought offered the best long-run potential.

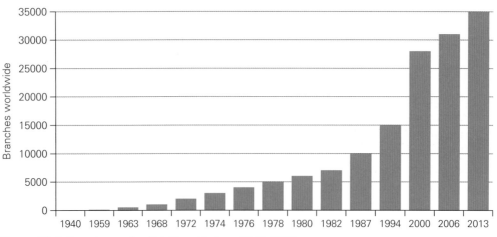

**Figure 78.4** Organic growth of McDonald's from 1940-2013

## 78.3 Types of growth

### Organic growth

Firms grow organically when they expand from within, rather than by taking over or merging with other businesses. Manufacturers grow organically by either enlarging existing factories or by opening new factories to supplement existing capacity. Service sector businesses like McDonald's grow organically by selling more products. This usually means that new branches will have to be opened. Figure 78.4 shows the organic growth achieved by the American fast-food retailer McDonald's.

To create organic growth, businesses like McDonald's must increase sales. McDonalds have used four tactics to create their phenomenal organic growth. Market penetration involves trying to sell more to existing consumers. This can be done via promotion or by price cuts. The second approach is called market development – which means selling your product to new customers in new places. McDonald's has also managed to increase its sales by launching new menu items. Opening restaurants early to serve breakfast is an excellent example of product development. The final method of generating the additional sales needed to make organic growth possible is diversification – which means launching new products into new markets. At one stage McDonald's tried unsuccessfully to diversify by setting up its own chain of McCafés (now they exist as a store-within-a-store).

### External growth

Firms can grow by takeover or merger. Companies are owned by their shareholders. Takeovers happen when a firm persuades the shareholders of another company to sell more than 50 per cent of their shares. In 2014 Apple Inc. wanted to grow and diversify by taking over a company called Beats Music, which had developed a

critically acclaimed subscription streaming service (and potential threat to iTunes). To persuade Beats' shareholders to sell their shares, Apple paid $3 billion. A merger is not the same as a takeover. It describes a situation where the shareholders and managers of two companies agree to bring two companies together. This is what happened in 2014 when electrical goods retailers Carphone Warehouse and Dixons merged. Unlike organic growth, external growth is extremely quick. If you take over a competitor their share of the market immediately becomes yours. See Chapter 80 for a fuller account of takeovers and mergers.

## 78.4 Problems created by growth and how they can be overcome

The most common type of problem created by organic growth is overtrading. This occurs when a business suffers from cash flow problems because it has tried to expand too rapidly with insufficient cash in the bank. When firms grow, cash flow can quickly become negative. This is because expansion creates additional cash outflows that start well before extra cash inflows. To resolve overtrading firms must forecast the cash flow implications of growth and raise the additional working capital required well before the expansion programme begins.

Takeovers and mergers can also backfire. Under Fred Goodwin's leadership the Scottish bank RBS grew rapidly by taking over other financial institutions. Unfortunately for RBS Goodwin bought badly because he failed to carry out due diligence and bought banks such as ABN Amro that had made risky loans to subprime borrowers who proved unable to repay their debts. This strategy led to the biggest annual loss in UK corporate history (£24.1 billion) in 2008. Cultural clashes between companies integrating can also cause problems. A company's culture is its shared values and ways of doing things. If companies have different cultures employees in the company that has been taken over may resent their new managers and their methods.

## 78.5 Problems created by retrenchment and how they might be overcome

When firms reduce the scale of their operations there are usually redundancies. Workers who are made redundant lose their jobs through no fault of their own. It happens because their employer has stopped or reduced production, so their job is no longer required. Redundancy does not just affect the workers who have lost their jobs; it also shatters the confidence of those that have survived the jobs cull. In 2009 when the recession was at its worst, the HR magazine

Personnel Today asked 266 firms about the effects of redundancy. Over half of them said that redundancy had damaged staff morale in their organisations. Falling morale matters because it can adversely affect both product quality and productivity. The best way to minimise this is to use natural wastage, rather than compulsory redundancy, to reduce a workforce.

## 78.6 Greiner's model of growth

When Larry Greiner introduced his growth theory in 1972, he suggested that there were five phases firms went through. Later, in 1988, he added a sixth. According to Greiner's theory, firms pass through six phases of growth when they expand. Each phase begins with a period of stable growth, which is then followed by a crisis. When one of these crisis events occurs the firm must reorganise if it is continue to grow and progress through to the next stage in the model.

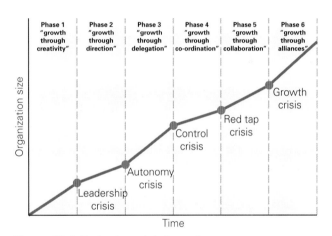

**Figure 78.5** Greiner's model of growth

Source: adapted from 'Evolution and Revolution as Organizations Grow' by Larry E. Greiner. Published by Harvard Business Review, May 1998

**Table 78.1** The impact of growth and retrenchment on the functional areas of business

| Functional area | Impacts of growth | Impacts of retrenchment |
|---|---|---|
| **Marketing** | To expand, firms operating in competitive markets might have to emphasise better value for money in the marketing mix. | A firm retrenching might opt to scale down their operations by reducing their product range, or by exiting from specific markets. Budgets for promotion and new product development might be reduced. |
| **Finance** | Price cuts used to increase market share will reduce profit margins. Over-rapid expansion can also cause cash flow problems. | Redundancy payments could cause additional cash outflows in the short run. However, in the longer term a smaller workforce should reduce the break-even output level by lowering fixed costs. |
| **Human resources** | Additional staff will probably have had to be hired to cope with the extra workload. | Redundancy programmes can cause morale to decline amongst the workers who survive the job cuts. Some of the company's more talented members of staff might decide to leave before the next round of redundancies. |
| **Operations** | Production methods might have to be adapted to ensure that the additional demand created by the marketing department can be supplied. | Investment in new machinery and equipment is likely to be halted. Poor staff morale is also likely to cause productivity to fall, making the firm less efficient. |

The phases are:

1. **Growth through creativity**. This describes the beginnings of a new business. Staff levels are low, so growth comes from longer working hours by the founders of the business. At the beginning of this stage the business is small enough to make informal face-to-face communication work. However, as the organisation expands, informal communication starts to fail which creates a **leadership crisis**. The business is now too big to be run on an ad hoc basis. To solve the crisis the founder has to accept the need to formally manage their business, or appoint somebody else who will do it on their behalf.

2. **Growth through direction**. The business is now being managed: communication within the business has now been formalised, for example regular meetings are held. Specialists in marketing, finance and other function areas have been appointed. However, all the major strategic decisions are still being made by the founder, creating an unmanageable workload for him or her, as the business grows larger. This phase ends with an **autonomy crisis**. To continue growing the founder must accept the need to delegate.

3. **Growth through delegation**. Middle managers have been appointed and empowered. These managers enable the business to grow by either spotting gaps in the market for new products, or by identifying new markets for existing products. This period of growth is ended by a **control crisis**. As the business grows bigger, empowered functional specialists are likely to make decisions that benefit their own department, but disadvantage the firm as a whole. To resolve this crisis a head office is required whose role is to oversee and co-ordinate the decisions made by the functional specialists.

4. **Growth through co-ordination and monitoring** has now begun. The business can start expanding again because previously isolated departments are now working together for the common good. Performance related pay is aligned to the achievement of company-wide corporate goals, rather than departmental goals. This phase of growth is ended by a **red tape crisis**: excessive paper-based monitoring and reporting leads to a wasteful and inefficient bureaucracy, which is slow to respond to external changes: growth opportunities are lost as a result.

5. **Growth through collaboration**. To grow again the firm must ditch its functional structure that encourages bureaucracy in favour of matrix management, where functional specialists from different areas work together in project teams.

6. **Growth through extra-organisational solutions**. According to Greiner, most organisations eventually stop growing because they run out of ideas. To grow again firms will need to form alliances with other businesses. This might be through merger or takeover, or joint ventures. In the latter case, two firms may agree to pool their management and resources within a limited area. Jaguar Land Rover operates in China under a joint venture with a local Chinese business.

## Critique of Greiner's theory

Although there's much to admire in Greiner's theory, it can be criticised for over-simplifying. Not every growing business will face these crises, as some will anticipate the need for change before the panic button needs to be pressed. More importantly, though, Greiner overstates firms' ability to overcome many of these problems. In some large businesses delegation remains a problem all the way through. People at the top continue to hold too much power and delegate too little. One final issue is that the theory ignores the pace of growth. A company such as Coca-Cola has grown steadily for more than a hundred years. So it has transitioned from Stage 1 to 6 without needing crises as the spur. For rapidly growing businesses the importance of crisis is far more plausible.

### Theory in 60 seconds

#### Greiner's model of growth

- To keep growing, businesses have to pass through the same six stages.
- The move from one stage to the next is usually triggered by crisis...
- ...which is only resolved by changes in leadership approach and organisational structure.
- Businesses that cannot make the adjustments get stuck in a difficult place that hinders or halts their growth.

## Five Whys and a How

| Question | Answer |
|---|---|
| Why do newly established firms need to grow quickly? | To hit their break-even sales level. Most start-ups are short of cash; therefore, they cannot survive for very long if they are losing money |
| Why might a firm opt for external growth over organic growth? | Organic growth can be very slow, because it takes time to steal market share and time to install additional capacity |
| Why is retrenchment more likely during recessions? | Spending levels fall during recessions, so most firms experience a fall in demand. To prevent losses from being made, firms retrench to reduce their break-even point by lowering fixed costs |
| Why might growth cause a firm to become more efficient? | Increasing output within existing facilities will cause capacity utilisation to increase. Fixed costs will be diluted over more units of output. Growth can also allow a firm to benefit from economies of scale |
| Why might the manager of a small business need to accept the need to delegate in order to grow their business? | According to Greiner's theory, delegation is required because the manager will suffer from information overload if they do not delegate. As a result, opportunities to grow may be overlooked |
| How might a firm reduce the risk of morale deteriorating during a programme of retrenchment? | By only using compulsory redundancy as a last resort. Where possible firms should try to reduce their headcount by natural wastage instead |

## Key terms

**Average cost:** this is the cost of producing one unit of output. It is calculated by dividing total cost by the current output level.

**Technical economy of scale:** larger firms have the output levels required to make it financially viable to purchase expensive new machinery, that, when used at high levels of capacity utilisation, will cause average cost to fall.

**Market dominance:** describes a situation when a firm sells a product that achieves a very high market share. This ascendancy over the competition enables the dominant firm to raise prices without losing too many customers. According to the EU firms that have a market share of more than 40-45 per cent are considered dominant.

**Outsourcing:** firms outsource when they subcontract work that used to be done in-house to other companies. Outsourcing can be done to improve product quality, or because the new external supplier is expected to deliver lower costs than the firm's own workforce.

**Due diligence:** is precautionary research carried out by a business before they decide to buy an asset or sign a contract.

**Natural wastage:** reducing the size of a workforce by not replacing workers who retire or leave for other jobs.

## Evaluation: Growth and retrenchment

The stock market is oddly inclined to ascribe companies' ups and downs to the quality of leadership. Often the real reason may be a combination of the business cycle (economic booms and slumps) and the degree of competition faced. Tesco's boom period from 2004-2008 coincided with a chaotic time for Sainsbury's. So the causes of growth may be fortuitous rather than genius.

But when growth hits, how can it best be handled? Greiner's theory suggests that growth is inevitably bumpy, with a series of crises that force managements to wise up to new realities. This fits in perfectly well with the widespread view of academics and consultants that growth is tough and rapid growth is among the biggest management challenges. If profit margins are as high as in the case of Google or Facebook, big money helps to water down big problems. For a business such as ASOS or SuperGroup, rapid Growth sometimes has to be slowed down – even if it means missing out on attractive opportunities.

# Workbook

## A. Revision questions

(35 marks; 35 minutes)

1. In your own words, explain the meaning of the term retrenchment. (3)

2. a) Using examples distinguish between external and organic growth. (3)

   b) Explain one problem a firm might encounter as a result of external growth. (4)

3. The iPad has been a very successful product for Apple. The table below shows the number of iPads sold and the revenues generated worldwide since launch.

   a) Calculate the percentage growth in the number of iPads sold between 2010 and 2011. (2)

   b) Describe what happened to sales growth in terms of the number of iPads sold in the years after 2011. (4)

   c) Using the information provided, calculate the average price of an iPad in each year shown. What conclusions can you draw? (4)

   d) In July 2014 Apple announced that in the last three months only 13.2 million iPads were sold, compared to 16.3 million the quarter before. Analyse whether Apple should be worried. (9)

4. Explain two difficulties that a sports retailer such as Sports Direct might face when attempting to grow organically. (6)

| Year | 2010 | 2011 | 2012 | 2013 |
|------|------|------|------|------|
| Units | 7.46 million | 32.4 million | 58.31 million | 22.86 million |
| Revenue | $4.96 billion | $20.36 billion | $32.42 billion | $10.67 billion |

## B. Revision exercises

### DATA RESPONSE

**Stagecoach**

Stagecoach is one of the biggest suppliers of public transport in the world, operating in eight countries, running 13,000 trains and buses, employing over 35,000 people. In 2014 the company's turnover was close to £3 billion, netting shareholders an operating profit of £223 million.

The business was not always this big. When Stagecoach was set up in 1980 they started with just three buses. The company's employees were the three founders, Brian Souter, who went on to be Chief Executive, did the driving, whilst his wife, Ann Gloag, made snacks to sell to their passengers. Robin, her brother, was the maintenance man.

Throughout Stagecoach's history, growth has always been the dominant corporate objective. In the early 1980s Stagecoach grew by buying out its local rivals. They also bought buses from local councils when they were privatised. In the 1990s there was a change in strategy as the company switched to organic growth. Instead of spending money on expensive takeovers, Stagecoach would expand their market share by stealing their rivals' passengers. The main method used to grow market share was low fares, which were designed to undercut the competition. On several occasions Stagecoach was found guilty of predatory pricing, which involves cutting prices below average cost with the deliberate intention of forcing a rival out of business.

In more recent times Stagecoach has grown by diversifying. For example in Sheffield they run trams and local train services as well as bus services. This allows Stagecoach to set timetables for different modes of transport in order to minimise waiting time for passengers who need to change from one mode of transport to another in order to complete their journey. The company would like to offer passengers the same type of 'integrated' transport service in other British towns and cities.

**Questions (30 marks; 35 minutes)**

1. Explain how growth might help a transport company like Stagecoach to increase its profits. (4)

**2.** Apart from a desire to generate higher profits, explain two other reasons why a company might choose growth as its corporate objective. (8)

**3.** Explain why predatory pricing is illegal. Why would the government want to stop bus passengers from benefiting from low fares? (6)

## C. Extend your understanding

**1.** With reference to Greiner's model of growth evaluate the problems that a rapidly growing company like Stagecoach might encounter during its expansion. (25)

**2.** In a recent year Barclays Bank declared an annual profit of over £3.5 billion. At the time the chief executive of Barclays revealed that the bank had cut 11,500 jobs in the previous year, and their

**4.** Analyse how Stagecoach's various stakeholder groups might be affected if Stagecoach is able to achieve its ambition of running all forms of public transport in certain towns and cities. (12)

intention in the coming year was to double this number of job losses.

**a)** Analyse the possible reasons that might explain why some highly profitable businesses like Barclays choose to retrench. (9)

**b)** To what extent should Barclays be criticised for shortcomings in its sense of corporate social responsibility? (16)

---

**Linked to:** Growth and retrenchment, Chapter 78; Methods and types of growth, Chapter 80; Reasons for trading internationally, Chapter 84.

---

### Definition

Economies of scale are factors that cause average unit costs to fall as the scale of output increases in the long run. Diseconomies of scale are factors causing average costs to rise as the scale of output increases.

---

## 79.1 Issues with growth

### Controlled growth

For posh soft drink mixer company Fever Tree, the first half of 2015 saw another huge leap in sales – they rose by 61 per cent. This was no problem because the company had planned for a continuation of the previous years' 50 per cent growth. It's also important to realise that Fever Tree outsources its production, so it effectively has no real capacity constraints. Another example of controlled growth comes from Costa Coffee, owned by Whitbread plc. In July 2015 the company announced that it was outgrowing its South London, 11,000 tonne coffee-roasting facility. A £36 million move to Basildon would allow a 45,000 tonne factory to open by mid-2017. This would ease future growth for the company.

### Uncontrolled growth

Soon after floating on the London stock market, Supergroup plc (trading as SuperDry) was motoring. The only concern among City traders was that the brand was becoming so popular that celebrity advocates such as David Beckham might walk away. Actually that didn't prove to be a problem. Supergroup's problems were all internal. In October 2011 it warned analysts of 'a warehouse and IT systems disaster' that would hit profits by £9 million. In 2012 things got worse when the company had to admit that 'arithmetic errors' had led it to overstate its forecast profit. The value of the shares fell by £170 million.

Supergroup's founder Julian Dunkerton said: 'We have grown incredibly fast and that brings itself challenges. This is an unfortunate day. It's not somewhere I want to be.'

As a generalisation it is fair to say that growing companies plan for economies of scale, but often get waylaid by diseconomies.

---

'The whole is greater than the sum of the parts.'
Aristotle, ancient Greek philosopher

---

## 79.2 Economies of scale

When a firm grows there are some things it can do more efficiently. The group term given to these factors is 'economies of scale'. When firms experience economies of scale their unit costs fall. For example, a pottery which could produce 100 vases at £5 each may be able to produce 1,000 vases at £4.50 per unit. The total cost rises (from £500 to £4,500) but the cost per unit falls. Assuming the firm sells the vases for £6 each, the profit margin rises from £1 per vase to £1.50. Economies of scale are, in effect, the benefits of being big. Therefore, for small firms, they represent a threat. If a large-scale producer of televisions can sell them for £99 and still make a profit, there may be no chance for the small guy. There are four main economies of scale.

### Purchasing economies

As a firm grows larger it will have to order more raw materials and components. An increase in the average order size the firm places with its suppliers leads to benefits from bulk buying. Large orders are more profitable to the supplier. Consequently, firms that can place large orders have significant market power. The larger the order the larger the opportunity cost of losing it. Therefore the supplier has a big incentive to offer a discount. Bulk buying reduces variable costs per unit.

### Technical economies of scale

When supplying a product or service there is usually more than one production method that can be used.

As a firm grows, it will find it more economic to invest in new technology. Switching the balance from labour towards new, high-tech machinery will generate savings in unit costs. Also, the new machinery may reduce wastage. Reducing the quantity of raw materials being wasted will cut the firm's variable costs.

These cost savings may not be available to smaller firms. They may lack the financial resources required to purchase the machinery. Even if the firm did have the money it may still not invest. Technology only becomes viable to use if the firm has a long enough production run to spread out the fixed costs of the equipment. Capital investment becomes more viable as a firm grows because fixed costs per unit fall as usage rises.

### Real business

#### The Airbus A380

The Airbus A380 is a true giant of the skies. As the size of a structure increases, the ratio of surface area to volume falls. In the case of an aircraft this ratio is very important. Fuel costs are heavily influenced by drag. Therefore it makes sense to minimise the surface area, because this will also minimise drag. The double-decker layout of the A380 has created an aircraft with a relatively low surface area to volume ratio. The unique design of the A380 means that the aircraft offers 50 per cent more floor area than its main rival – the Boeing 747-400. Airbus estimates that the operating costs of its aircraft are at least 15 per cent lower than its rivals. This economy of scale will become increasingly important if the price of oil and plane fuel increases.

## Managerial economies

When firms grow there is greater potential for managers to specialise in particular tasks. For instance, large firms have enough financial work to warrant employing full-time accountants. In many small firms the owner has to make numerous decisions, some of which he or she may have little knowledge of. This means the quality of decision-making in large firms could be better than in small firms. If fewer mistakes are made, large firms should gain a cost advantage. See Figure 79.1.

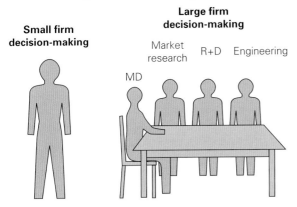

**Figure 79.1** Benefits of specialisation

## 79.3 Economies of scope

This theory proposes that average costs can be lower for a business producing two or more items than for two or three separate companies producing the same items. This sounds possible if one thinks of Cadbury producing Milk Tray and also producing Roses chocolates; and when Cadbury bought Green & Black's, they doubtless could produce the chocolate more cheaply than the previous, small business, owners.

However, the theory of economies of scope implies that there are always benefits from companies merging, which research shows to be untrue. Furthermore the theory seems to do no more than repeat the idea of synergy (that 2 + 2 = 5, or that the new whole is greater than the sum of the parts).

## 79.4 Diseconomies of scale

When firms grow, total costs rise. But why should costs per unit rise? This is because growth can also create diseconomies of scale. These are factors that push unit costs up as the scale of operation increases. Large organisations face three main types of diseconomy of scale.

### Poor employee motivation

When firms grow, staff may have less personal contact with management. In large organisations there is often a sense of alienation. If staff believe their efforts are going unnoticed a sense of indifference may spread. A falling level of work effort will increase the firm's costs. Poor motivation will make staff work less hard when they are actually at work. Absenteeism is also a consequence of poor motivation. This means that the firm may have to employ more staff to cover for the staff they expect to be absent on any given day. In both cases, output per worker will fall. As a result, labour costs per unit will rise.

### Poor communication

Communication can be a significant problem when a firm grows. First, effective communication is dependent on high levels of motivation. Communication is only effective if the person being communicated with is willing to listen. If growth has left the workforce with a feeling of alienation, communication can deteriorate alongside productivity. A second reason for poor communication in large organisations is that the methods chosen to communicate may be less effective. As a firm grows it may become necessary to use written forms of communication more frequently. Unlike verbal communication, written communication is less personal and therefore less motivating. Written messages are easier to ignore and provide less feedback. Relying too much on written forms of communication could result in an increase in the number of expensive mistakes being made.

## Poor managerial co-ordination

In a small firm co-ordination is easy. The boss decides what the goals are, and who is doing what. As firms grow, it becomes harder for the person at the top to control and co-ordinate effectively. The leader who refuses to delegate 'drowns' under the weight of work. The leader who delegates finds (later) that manager A is heading in a slightly different direction from manager B. Regular meetings are arranged to try to keep everyone focused on the same goals through the same strategy. But not only are such meetings expensive, they are also often poorly attended and lead to grumbles rather than insight. Co-ordination works well and cheaply in a small firm, but is expensive and often ineffective in large corporations.

'I feel that small, compact companies, are better run. That is partly because people feel more connected in small companies.' Richard Branson, founder and head, Virgin Group

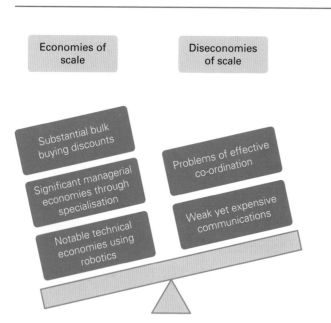

**Figure 79.2** Logic balance: Economies v diseconomies

## 79.5 Combining economies and diseconomies of scale

It is important to realise that growth normally creates both economies and diseconomies of scale. If growth creates more economies than diseconomies then

unit costs will fall. On the other hand, if the growth creates more diseconomies, the opposite will happen (see Figure 79.3).

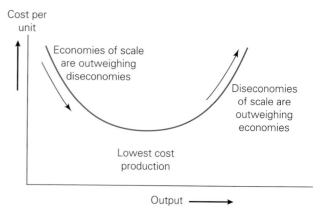

**Figure 79.3** Production costs and production scale

Normally, when a firm is small, initial bouts of growth will create more economies of scale than diseconomies. So growth pushes average costs down.

## 79.6 The experience curve

The experience curve shows the reduction in average costs that occurs when increased total output allows producers to learn from experience how to produce more efficiently. Proposed by the Boston Consulting Group in the 1960s, this theory implied that there was an effective economic law that would keep market leaders ahead of their competitors. See Figure 79.4.

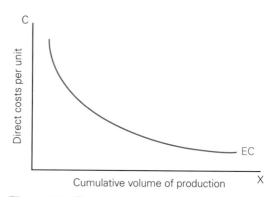

**Figure 79.4** The experience curve

Implicitly, then, the big producers would learn the most, produce the most economically – and stay in the lead for ever. Hm. Nokia, perhaps? Or Tesco?

Logically, it should be the case that experience leads to cost reductions; unfortunately size also tends to lead to complacency and a resistance to true innovation. So the benefits of the experience curve may be cancelled out – or outweighed – by the downsides of scale.

## 79.7 Synergy

The great American industrialist Harold Geneen once wrote a book called *Synergy and Other Lies*. The idea of synergy is simple: the sum is greater than the parts. This suggests that there are cost or revenue benefits from getting together, perhaps in a takeover or merger. Geneen suggests that this is rarely true. Experience taught him that fusing staff together creates problems, not benefits. Was there synergy when the Liberals went into coalition with the Conservatives? Or when Coca-Cola bought Innocent Drinks?

By contrast, some takeovers have such a strategic logic that synergies are inevitable. Prime among them was the Mars purchase of Wrigley gum. Even if diseconomies of scale emerge, there may be enough benefits from lower distribution and staffing costs for the overall synergies to prove worthwhile.

As a rule of thumb, though, it's wise to be sceptical if a chief executive tries to justify a takeover on the basis of 'cost synergies'. Strategic fit, yes maybe, but time after time companies have looked for synergies but ended up finding diseconomies of scale.

'Financial synergy is a will-o-the-wisp. It looks good on paper but it fails to work out in practice.' Peter Drucker, business guru

## 79.8 Overtrading

With careful planning, many diseconomies may be minimised or avoided completely. The key point is that diseconomies are more likely to arise either when growth is unplanned or when it is too rapid. Booming sales seems like an entirely good thing, but in fact it places huge strains on any management. Rapid growth makes it hard to manage cash flow at the very time when the management structure itself is being put under pressure.

Overtrading is the financial stress caused by expanding too rapidly from too narrow a capital base. When sales are static, this month's cash outflows are balanced by the cash inflows arriving from sales made two or more months ago (the average credit period taken by customers is 60–90 days). When growth is rapid (such as soft drinks maker Fever-Tree's 50 per cent annual expansion between 2007 and 2015), this month's expanding cash outflows outstrip the smaller cash inflows received from sales made a few months' ago. The longer the credit period demanded by customers, the greater this problem will be.

This underlying pressure on cash flow is worsened by the regular need to invest more to expand capacity: to build a new factory or warehouse, or open new sales operations overseas. In the meantime, the management structure is under pressure from the need to keep employing new staff. At first the new arrivals work under existing managers; but eventually spans of control get too wide, forcing the business to introduce a new layer of management into the hierarchy. This is highly disruptive, as staff get used to new bosses and a potentially more bureaucratic approach to decision-making as the hierarchy gets taller. Instead of focusing on cash flow management, there can be too great a focus on promotion opportunities or disappointments. A cash flow crisis may emerge suddenly – making the company a victim of overtrading.

'Avoiding the overtrading trap is just a case of finding a balance between enthusiasm for new sales and an efficiently-managed cash flow.' Mark Seemann, founder of Synety, cloud telephony business

## Five Whys and a How?

| Question | Answer |
|----------|--------|
| Why might a growing firm choose not to bulk buy? | Lean producers use Just In Time ordering and inventory systems, so bulk buying isn't appropriate |
| Why might managerial economies turn into diseconomies? | Companies assume that managerial specialisation will be a good thing, but managers can get bored with a narrowly defined job – just like anyone else |
| Why is co-ordination hard for large businesses? | Because communications are weakened by the extended vertical distance (and many intermediaries) between the bottom and top of the organisation |
| Why would any business be so unwise as to 'overtrade'? | If your product is suddenly in fashion, bosses naturally lap up the attention and may fail to see that success can be a threat as well as an opportunity |
| Why might synergy prove to be an illusion? | Because people resist enforced change, and therefore what might seem a nice fit to a boss looks an unpleasant threat to more junior staff |
| How might a big company overcome the problems of diseconomies of scale? | They can't be overcome, but could be minimised by a boss who can delegate effectively to local or more junior work teams; this requires very skilful management |

## Evaluation: Economies and diseconomies of scale

Three important issues should be considered:

1. Most diseconomies of scale are caused by an inability to manage people effectively. When firms grow, managers must be willing to delegate power in an attempt to avoid the problems caused by alienation. Enriching jobs and running training courses are expensive in the short term. The benefits of job enrichment and training are more long term – and harder to quantify financially. This means that it can be quite hard for the managers of a company to push through the changes required to minimise the damage created by diseconomies of scale.

2. Public limited companies may find this a particular problem. Their shares can be bought freely and sold on the stock market. This means that considerable pressure is put on the managers to achieve consistently good financial results. The penalty for investing too much in any one year could be a falling share price and an increased risk of takeover.

3. Do economies of scale make it impossible for small firms to survive? In highly competitive markets it is difficult for small firms to compete with large established businesses, especially if they try to compete with them in the mass market. In this situation, the small firm will lose out nine times out of ten. The small firm will not be able to achieve the same economies of scale. As a result, its prices will have to be higher to compensate for its higher costs. Yet the majority of firms within the economy have fewer than 200 employees. This proves that small firms do find ways of surviving, despite the existence of economies of scale.

## Key terms

**Capacity utilisation:** actual output as a proportion of maximum capacity.

**Capital investment:** expenditure on fixed assets such as machinery.

**Delegate:** hand power down the hierarchy to junior managers or workers.

# Workbook

## A. Revision questions

(35 marks; 35 minutes)

1. Identify three managerial motives for growth. (3)

2. State two possible benefits of specialisation. (2)

3. Explain why large companies are frequently able to command larger discounts from their suppliers than are smaller firms. (4)

4. Outline two diseconomies of scale that could harm the profitability of a night club that opens a chain of 12 other branches. (4)

5. Explain the likely consequences for a large business such as Cadbury of a failure to control and co-ordinate the business effectively. (4)

6. Many car manufacturers like Nissan are attempting to reduce the complexity of their designs by using fewer parts in different models. With reference to the concept of economies of scale, explain why this is happening. (4)

7. Give three reasons why employee morale can deteriorate as a consequence of growth? (3)

8. Outline three ways in which managers could tackle these morale problems. (6)

9. Explain how economies of scale could give a firm such as Ryanair a considerable marketing advantage. (5)

## B. Revision exercises

### DATA RESPONSE 1

Geoff Horsfield and his sister Alex are worried about whether they can compete effectively with their big local competitor, Bracewell plc. Alex believes that Bracewell's economies of scale mean that Horsfield Trading cannot compete head-on. Therefore she wants to switch the company's marketing approach away from the mass market towards smaller niches.

Geoff is not sure of this. He knows that Bracewell has a more up-to-date manufacturing technique, but has heard of inefficiencies in the warehousing and office staff. He doubts that Bracewell is as efficient as Alex supposes. Therefore he argues that Horsfield Trading can still compete in the mass market.

Fortunately the employment of an accountant from Bracewell plc has enabled direct comparisons to be made. The figures shown in Table 79.2 should help Geoff and Alex to decide on Horsfield's future strategy.

**Questions (35 marks; 40 minutes)**

1. Calculate the capital investment per employee at each company. What do the figures tell you? (6)

2. Explain two possible reasons for Alex's wish to aim at smaller market niches. (8)

3. a) Explain two possible reasons for the differences between the guarantee claims of each business. (8)

   b) Analyse the short- and long-term effects of these differences. (9)

4. Explain one other piece of evidence about diseconomies of scale at Bracewell plc. (4)

**Table 79.1** Comparisons of Horsfield Trading Ltd and Bracewell plc

|  | Horsfield Trading Ltd | Bracewell plc |
|---|---|---|
| **Capital investment** | £240,000 | £880,000 |
| **Factory employees** | 28 | 49 |
| **Other employees** | 7 | 21 |
| **Guarantee claims per 100 sales** | 1.2 | 2.1 |
| **Output per employee (units per day)** | 21 | 23 |

## DATA RESPONSE 2

### Burgers: big or small

Despite concerns about obesity, the UK market for fast food is still growing. The market leader in the UK is McDonald's, with 1,200 UK outlets. The sheer scale of McDonald's UK operation creates significant economies of scale. For example, by rolling out the brand across the UK, McDonald's has created substantial purchasing economies of scale. Such economies of scale enjoyed by large dominant companies can make life extremely tough for smaller companies, battling to make headway in the same market.

A new entrant to the UK fast-food market dominated by McDonald's is the Gourmet Burger Kitchen. The business was set up by three New Zealanders who spotted a gap in the UK market for premium quality gourmet burgers, freshly prepared to order. In addition to a standard burger and chips, the GBK menu also includes more esoteric items such as a chorizo spicy Spanish burger and a hot chicken satay sandwich. On average a burger at GBK costs from £8 to £10.

In 2014 GBK had 60 restaurants in the UK, most of which were located in the Greater London area. The company has already won several 'Best burger' and 'Best eats' awards in the capital. The management of the Gourmet Burger Kitchen has set an objective of growth. In five years' time they want to have 350 restaurants in the UK.

Business analysts believe that the GBK programme of growth could yield substantially more economies of scale than diseconomies of scale.

**Figure 79.5** Gourmet Burger Kitchen

### Questions (40 marks; 45 minutes)

1. Explain why economies of scale are important to companies such as McDonald's and GBK. (4)

2. Explain two reasons why McDonald's will be able to achieve more purchasing economies of scale than GBK. (8)

3. Explain one additional economy of scale that the GBK may be able to benefit from if they manage to achieve their objective of having 350 UK outlets. (4)

4. Explain two diseconomies of scale that could affect GBK if it manages to achieve its growth targets. (8)

5. Evaluate one strategy that a small company such as GBK could use to compete effectively against a larger firm, such as McDonald's. (16)

## C. Extend your understanding

1. Small firms are often said to have better internal communications than larger organisations. To what extent is it inevitable that rapid growth will create communication problems? (25)

2. MHK plc is a large manufacturer of bread and cakes. To what extent will communication and co-ordination problems be inevitable if it decides on a strategy of growth through centralising production? (25)

# Chapter 80

# Methods and types of growth

**Linked to:** Growth and retrenchment, Chapter 78; Economies and diseconomies of scale, Chapter 79; Reasons for trading internationally, Chapter 84; Managing organisational culture, Chapter 93.

## 80.1 Assessing methods and types of growth

Chapter 79 addressed organic growth, including its benefits and drawbacks. This chapter deals with external growth. This means finding ways to expand the organization by joining together with – or buying up – other businesses. The main methods include mergers, takeovers, joint ventures and franchising.

## 80.2 Mergers and takeovers: an introduction

Every time a company's shares are bought or sold on the stock exchange, there is a change in the ownership of that company. However, the significant changes occur when a majority of shares is bought by an individual or company. Any individual or organisation that owns 51 per cent of a company's shares has effective control over that company. To successfully take over a company, a firm (or individual) must

## Real business

### Rapid organic growth

In 2010 General Motors (GM) was number one in China, selling nearly 2 million cars. Despite the financial troubles in America that forced the US government to bail it out, GM chose to keep this growth going by building nine new factories in China. It announced that it expected its sales in China to rise to 3 million by 2015. In fact sales grew organically to 3.5 million by 2014, so it hugely outperformed. The rapid pace of growth in China should have been great news for the US taxpayer, but the government sold its GM shares in December 2013.

therefore buy 51 per cent of the shares. In America, this process is called mergers and acquisitions (M&A), acquisitions being another word for purchasing.

'It's far better to buy a wonderful company at a fair price than a fair company at a wonderful price.'
Warren Buffett, investment and takeover superstar

## Why do firms merge with or take over other companies?

Some examples of takeovers and the reasons for them are given in Table 80.1.

### Growth

The fastest way for any firm to achieve significant growth is to merge with, or take over, another company. The motives behind the objective of growth may be based on any of the reasons outlined below. However, as a basic motive behind mergers and takeovers, growth is often the overriding factor.

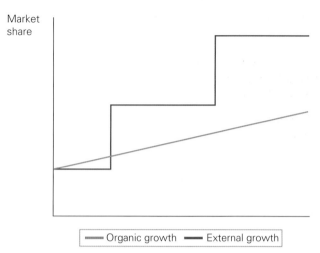

Market share

— Organic growth —— External growth

**Figure 80.1** Organic versus external growth

## Cost synergies

Cost savings are often used as a primary argument for corporate integration. It is suggested that economies of scale will arise from operating on a larger scale. If two businesses merge, output will increase. As a result, they are more likely to benefit from economies of scale, such as cheaper bulk purchasing of supplies. Synergies are the benefits from two things coming together. In this context, it is that the two firms together will have lower costs (and higher profits) than the two firms separately. In effect, synergy means that 2 + 2 = 5.

'Promises of synergy are rarely fulfilled.' *The Economist*, www.economist.com

## Diversification

This means entering different markets in order to reduce dependence upon current products and customers. Diversification is a way of reducing the risk faced by a company. Selling a range of different products to different groups of consumers will mean that, if any one product fails, sales of the other products should keep the business healthy. The simplest way to diversify is to merge with or take over another company. This saves time and money spent developing new products for markets in which the firm may have no expertise.

## Market power

When two competitors in the same market merge, the combined business will have an increased level of power in the market. It may be possible that this increased power can be used to reduce the overall competitiveness within the market. If prices can be increased a little, then margins will increase and the market will become more profitable.

**Table 80.1** Reasons for takeovers, and some examples

| Reasons for takeovers | Examples |
|---|---|
| Growth | Facebook pays $19 billion for mobile-messenger WhatsApp in 2014<br>Kraft's takeover of Cadbury in 2010 |
| Cost synergies | In May 2014 Carphone Warehouse and Dixons agreed to merge, saying they would enjoy annual cost savings of £80 million within three years<br>Co-op taking over Somerfield (it bid £1.7 billion in 2008); the result has been a disaster |
| Diversification | Tesco buying 49 per cent of Harris & Hoole coffee shops in 2013<br>Kellogg's buying Pringles crisps for $2.7 billion in 2012 |
| Market power | Indian car producer Tata (producers of the world's cheapest new car) bought Jaguar Land Rover for £1.3 billion in 2008<br>Holcim's planned merger with fellow cement giant Lafarge would give the combined group a 50 per cent market share in Canada, and not far short in Britain |

## 80.3 Types of business integration

There are four main types of merger or takeover (see Figure 80.2), as discussed below.

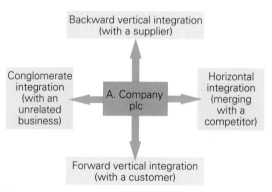

**Figure 80.2** Vertical and horizontal integration

## Vertical integration

Vertical integration occurs when one firm takes over or merges with another at a different stage in the production process, but within the same industry.

Backward vertical integration occurs when a firm buys out a supplier. In May 2014 advertising giant WPP bought Quirk, London – which had been supplying WPP with advice on digital and social media strategy. A key benefit of a backward vertical takeover is security of supply.

Forward vertical integration means buying out a customer, such as the purchase by Burberry of the franchisee that ran its shops in China. At the time Burberry made it clear that it wanted to be closer to its Chinese customers – to help develop the right product design and image for the rapidly developing Chinese market.

Table 80.2 explains the major advantages and disadvantages of backward and forward vertical integration for three important stakeholders: the company (and its shareholders), the workforce and the customers.

## Horizontal integration

Horizontal integration occurs when one firm buys out another in the same industry at the same stage of the supply chain. In 2014 the restaurant booking site Bookatable bought 2book – a direct competitor specialising in Sweden and Norway. This meant that Bookatable now represented more than 10,000 restaurants in 19 countries (and gave it a 90 per cent share of restaurants in Sweden and Norway). In the UK, if the market share of the combined companies is greater than 25 per cent, the Competition and Markets

Authority is likely to investigate before the integration will be allowed.

Of the four types of takeover, the most common by far is horizontal integration with a competitor. Typical examples include:

● Adidas buying Reebok
● Holcim Cement's 2014 merger with Lafarge Cement
● British Airways merging with Iberia Airways to form International Airlines Group.

For the purchaser, there are three major attractions:

1. Huge scope for cost cutting by eliminating duplication of salesforce, distribution and marketing overheads, and by improved capacity utilisation
2. Opportunities for major economies of scale
3. A reduction in competition should enable prices to be pushed up.

**Table 80.2** The advantages and disadvantages of backward vertical integration and forward vertical integration

| | Backward vertical integration | Forward vertical integration |
|---|---|---|
| **Advantages to the company** | Closer links with suppliers aid new product development and give more control over the quality and timing of supplies<br>Absorbing the suppliers' profit margins may cut supply costs | Control of competition in own retail outlets; prominent display of own brands<br>Firm put in direct contact with end users/consumers |
| **Disadvantages to the company** | Supplier division may become complacent if there is no need to compete for customers<br>Costs might rise, therefore, and delivery and quality become slack | Consumers may resent the dominance of one firm's products in retail outlets, causing sales to decline<br>Worries about image may obstruct the outlet, e.g. Levi stores rarely offer discounted prices |
| **Advantages to the workforce** | Secure customer for the suppliers may increase job security<br>Larger scale of the combined organisation may lead to enhanced benefits such as pension or career opportunities | Increased control over the market may increase job security<br>Designers can now influence not only how the products look, but also how they are displayed |
| **Disadvantages to the workforce** | Becoming part of a large firm may affect the sense of team morale built up at the supplier<br>Job losses may result from attempts to cut out duplication of support roles such as in personnel and accounting | Staff in retail outlets may find themselves deskilled. Owner may dictate exactly what products to stock and how to display them. This would be demotivating |
| **Advantages to the consumer** | Better co-ordination between company and supplier may lead to more innovative new product ideas<br>Ownership of the whole supply process may make the business more conscious of product and service quality | With luxury products, customers like to see perfect displays and be served by expert staff, for example at perfume counters in department stores<br>Prices may fall if a large retail margin is absorbed by the supplier |
| **Disdvantages to the consumer** | The firm's control over one supplier may in fact reduce the variety of goods available<br>Supplier complacency may lead to rising costs, passed on to customers as higher prices | Increased power within the market could lead to price rises<br>If the outlet only supplies the parent company's products, consumer choice will be hit, as in brewery-owned clubs or pubs |

Of course, no purchaser states publicly that the plan is to push prices up. But if you owned four consecutive motorway service stations covering over 190 km of driving, would you not be tempted to charge a bit more?

As horizontal mergers have particular implications for competition, they are likely to be looked at by the Competition and Markets Authority (CMA). If there is believed to be a threat to competition, the CMA has the power to refuse to allow the integration, or recommend changes before it can go through. For example, if Unilever (which produces Walls ice cream and much else) made a bid for Mars, the CMA would probably let the takeover through, on the condition that the Mars ice cream business was sold off.

## Conglomerate integration

Conglomerate integration occurs when one firm buys out another with no clear connection to its own line of business. An example was the purchase by the household goods giant Procter & Gamble of the Gillette shaving products business. Conglomerate integration is likely to be prompted by the desire to diversify or to achieve rapid growth. It may also be for purely financial motives such as asset stripping (breaking the business up and selling off all its key assets).

Although the achievement of successful diversification helps to spread risk, research shows that conglomerate mergers are the ones least likely to succeed. This is largely because the managers of the purchasing company have, by definition, little knowledge of the marketplace of the company that has been bought.

## Mergers

A merger occurs when two firms of approximately equal size choose to come together, perhaps by agreeing that shareholders will share ownership 50/50. This is therefore a friendly coming-together in which the directors are likely to have met often enough to know whether they can work together. It is therefore striking that research suggests that mergers have an even lower success rate than takeovers. Most researchers conclude that the reason is that there is no clear 'winner' and therefore leadership tends to be confused and weakened. There may even be an attempt at sharing leadership – which rarely works well. In a merger, both sets of staff expect their bosses to fight for them – to gain the plum jobs. So the infighting may be worse in a merger than in a takeover. It is striking that perhaps the two most expensive 'M&A' (mergers and acquisitions) flops in corporate history were both called mergers: Mercedes-Chrysler and AOL-Time Warner. Each has been estimated to have cost over $100 billion.

## 80.4 Takeover decisions and Ansoff's matrix

A useful way to analyse the risks and rewards from a takeover is to apply Ansoff's matrix (see Chapter 75). This considers the extent to which a business is keeping close to its core business (and knowledge/experience) or whether it is moving into new territory. For example, in February 2007 the US retail giant WalMart paid $1 billion to buy a Chinese business with 101 hypermarkets in China. In 2014 it announced the closure of 29 of these huge stores and a 'refocus' on smaller, local stores. In other words its big takeover was a mistake. On Ansoff's matrix, this radical move into a new market would have been represented as a major, high-risk move. If WalMart had bought a store chain in Canada (or Britain, where it owns Asda), it would have been much safer.

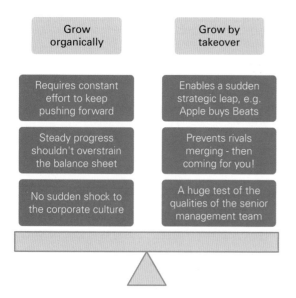

**Figure 80.3** Logic balance: takeover versus organic growth

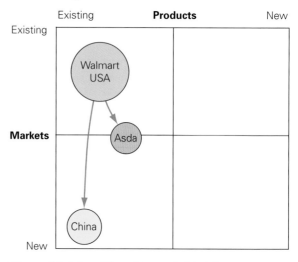

**Figure 80.4** Ansoff's matrix applied to takeovers

## 80.5 Other methods of growth: ventures and franchising

### Ventures

When a UK business looks to expand internationally, it faces a dilemma. Should it set up its own operation in – let us say – China, or should it rely on local people with local expertise? A joint venture is often the solution. This is usually a 50/50 agreement to co-operate in a specific venture within a specific country for a limited period of time (5 years, perhaps, or 10 years). When Burberry first went to China, this is exactly how it operated. Later, when it realised that its China operation could become the heart of its future strategy, it bought out its Chinese joint venture partners. The net effect has been hugely beneficial to the company. A joint venture has the advantage of local expertise plus clear financial incentives for the local partner, without the UK company risking losing control of this branch of its operations. As a method of growth, it is tried, tested and very widely used.

'Go for a business that any idiot can run, because sooner or later, they probably will.' Peter Lynch, businessman

### Franchising

The twin problems of growth are finding the finance for constant expansion and coping with the ever-rising management hierarchy, with more and more management layers to cope with the rising employee numbers. Much of this can be avoided if businesses choose to grow via franchising. Then it is the franchisee who finances the expansion. Buying into the Subway franchise network requires an outlay of between £86,000 and £233,000. After that franchisees pay Subway 8 per cent of sales revenue plus a further 4.5 per cent as a contribution to Subway's marketing spending. No wonder Subway has been able to expand globally to have 43,000 outlets by the end of 2014.

For entrepreneurs, it's easy to see the attractions of the franchising model. For example, if you start up an independent optician service, you have to:

- design and decorate a store that will create the right customer image
- create systems for staff training, stock control and accounting
- do your own advertising to bring in customers and to make them willing to pay the high prices charged by opticians.

Alternatively, you could start up your own, 100 per cent independent limited company, and then sign up for a Specsavers franchise. This would mean, for example, access to the specially written Specsavers store management software. From a scan of a sold pair of glasses, the software ensures that all the necessary stock ordering and accounting actions are taken. The franchise owner (Specsavers) also provides full training for the **franchisee** (the entrepreneur), plus advice and supplier contacts for store decoration and display and, of course, the huge marketing support from a multi-million pound TV advertising campaign. If you start up J. Bloggs Opticians, how many people will come through the doors? If you open up Specsavers, customers will trust the business from day one.

### Real business

#### Specsavers

Specsavers was started by Doug and Mary Perkins in Guernsey in 1984. They opened branches in Devon and Cornwall, each run by a manager within their own Specsavers chain. In 1988, the company decided to speed up its growth by getting individuals to open their own Specsavers franchise outlets. The finance needed to open each new branch (approximately £140,000) would come from the franchisee, not Doug and Mary. Also, the founders would no longer have to manage each store on a day-to-day basis. Each franchisee has every incentive to run his or her store well, because all the outlet's revenues are kept locally – apart from the royalty rate of 5 per cent that must be paid to Specsavers Head Office. Doug and Mary also receive a start-up fee from each new franchisee, which is a sum of between £25,000 and £50,000 depending upon the location.

This approach has allowed Specsavers to develop into the largest privately owned optician in the world, with more than 1,800 branches. Annual turnover for 2014 was more than £2,000 million.

### Founding a franchise

It only becomes possible to start selling franchises in your own business when its success is clear and quite long-established. Seventeen-year-old Fred deLuca borrowed $1,000 in 1964 to open a sandwich shop. He built his business up to a chain of successful stores and then, in 1975, started offering franchises to others who wanted to buy into his Subway business. By 1995 there were 11,000 Subway outlets and by 2014 there were over 43,000 (2,000 in the UK).

The franchise owner (also known as the **franchisor**) then needs to establish:

- a training programme so that franchisees learn to do things 'the Subway way'

- a system of pricing that is profitable without putting off potential franchisees; usually the franchise rights are bought for £10,000 to £100,000, then the franchisee must buy all store fittings and equipment via the franchise owner (this may cost £50,000 to £250,000) and then buy all supplies from the franchise owner; on top of this, a 5 per cent royalty is usually paid on all income and a fee of 3 per cent to 5 per cent to contribute towards the national advertising campaign
- a system of monitoring, so that poorly run franchises do not damage the reputation of the brand.

## Key terms

**Annual general meeting:** the once-yearly meeting at which shareholders have the opportunity to question the chairperson and to vote new directors to the board.

**Economies of scale:** the factors that cause average costs to be lower in large-scale operations than small ones.

**Organic growth:** growth from within the business (for example, getting better sales from existing brands, or launching new ones).

**Synergy:** this occurs when the whole is greater than the sum of the parts (2 + 2 = 5). It is often the reason given for mergers or takeovers occurring.

## Evaluation: Methods and types of growth

When looking at takeover bids, a key judgement is to see through the public relations 'hype'. Company leader A makes a bid for Company B, claiming that 'synergies will lead to better service and lower prices to our customers'. Really? Or will it mean factory closures, the elimination of small niche brands and – later – higher prices for all? Similarly, the leader may claim that the reason for a takeover is very businesslike, such as 'creating a world-leading company'. Yet the high failure rate of takeovers must imply that many claimed business benefits are a 'fig leaf'. The real reason for many takeovers is arrogance, and perhaps greed, on the part of the executives concerned.

An explanation for the problems firms may encounter after a merger or takeover is resistance to change. This will be especially true if the business cultures are widely different at the two companies. One may be go-getting and entrepreneurial; the other may be cautious and bureaucratic. Judgement is again required to consider whether a takeover is especially vulnerable to a clash of culture when the firms come together.

## Five Whys and a How

| Question | Answer |
|---|---|
| Why might a business be keen to make a horizontal takeover bid? | Quite apart from any economies of scale, there are bound to be profit gains from eliminating a competitor |
| Why might organic growth prove more successful than takeovers in the long term? | Because it comes from within the business, giving time for the culture to develop gradually; not get a sudden shock as two workforces merge |
| Why are so many takeovers unsuccessful? | Because bosses underestimate the significance of unquantifiable factors such as weakened motivation and clashes in culture |
| Why might a business choose to grow through a conglomerate takeover? | Because they have an objective of reducing dependence on one product or market |
| Why might a growing business choose franchising as a strategy? | Because the funding comes from the franchisees, and there's less of a need to build up a big management structure |
| How do takeovers actually work? | A cash bid means that one firm is buying up the shares in another for cash; a 'paper' bid means swopping shares in the bidder's company for those of the company being bought |

# Workbook

## A. Revision questions

(30 marks; 30 minutes)

1. What is horizontal integration? (2)

2. Explain one reason why a manufacturer might take over one of its suppliers. (5)

3. For each of the following outline two reasons why British Airways might like to make a takeover bid for:
   a) easyJet (4)
   b) high street retailer Flight Centre. (4)

4. Explain why diversification might be a bad idea for a fast-growing firm. (4)

5. Explain the meaning of the word 'synergy'. (3)

6. Explain why businesses should consider Ansoff's matrix before making a takeover bid. (4)

7. In March 2015 Philip Green's Arcadia retail business sold the BHS chain of 180 department stores for £1. Was the new buyer guaranteed to be able to make a profit on this deal? (4)

## B. Revision exercises

### DATA RESPONSE 1

**Apple buys Beats**

2014 saw the purchase of Beats Electronics by Apple Inc., which paid $3 billion for the headphones and music-streaming business. It would mean combining the 300 staff at Beats with the 80,000 employees at Apple. Some analysts saw this as a horizontal acquisition, with Apple putting its iTunes business together with Beats' subscription music streaming business to fight off Spotify (at the time of the takeover Beats had 110,000 subscribers; Spotify had 10 million). Others saw it as a vertical acquisition, with Beats headphones being put together with iPhone or iPad to create a compelling consumer proposition.

What was not in question was the valuation placed on Beats. In September 2013 Beats had raised extra capital at a price that valued the company at $1 billion. Six months' later Apple was paying three times that amount. Great for founders Jimmy Iovine, Dr Dre and Will.i.Am, with Forbes magazine estimating that Dr Dre alone held 20 per cent of Beats shares, but a curious comment on the heady valuations placed on companies when takeover bids are made.

**Questions (35 marks; 40 minutes)**

1. Calculate the value of Dr Dre's shares at the time of Apple's bid. (3)

2. Explain one possible motive behind Apple's purchase of Beats Electronics. (4)

3. Analyse the possible difficulties Apple may face following the takeover of Beats. (12)

4. Apple could decide to incorporate all the Beats staff and products into its own operations, or keep it at arms' length, that is, keep it operating as a separate business division. Evaluate which might be the better option. (16)

### DATA RESPONSE 2

**Dixons merges with Carphone Warehouse**

Carphone Warehouse and Dixons have agreed a £3.8 billion 'merger of equals' to create a retailing giant with 3,000 stores and sales of £11 billion.

Dixons Carphone, which brings Currys, PC World and Carphone Warehouse under one umbrella, will be an electrical retailer which will sell a multitude of gadgets (everything from fridges to phones) and offer service and support. The new structure anticipates a future 'Internet of things' in which domestic appliances are all Internet-enabled and controlled by mobile devices. As a result, the company plans to branch into domestic heating, lighting and security services – all controlled by mobile phone.

Carphone and Dixons anticipate annual synergies of at least £80 million within three years and expect to benefit from greater buying power and extra growth options.

Dixons and Carphone shareholders will each own 50 per cent of the combined group under the deal, and Carphone concessions will be built into every Dixons outlet.

Carphone's chairman and founder, Sir Charles Dunstone, will lead a 14-member board that includes two deputy chairmen, a chief executive, a deputy chief executive and a senior non-executive director. Dixons' boss, Sebastian James, will be chief executive, while Andrew Harrison of Carphone Warehouse becomes his deputy.

'This is a genuine merger of equals founded on core strategic principles rather than straight cost cuts,' according to Sebastian James. 'We do things that are so adjacent that it makes sense to come together. Our markets are converging, and we are converging.'

City analysts and investors remain unconvinced. According to Louise Cooper, an independent analyst at CooperCity: 'Two past-their-sell-by-date retailers merging does not an Amazon make.' She says the top-heavy leadership structure sends the wrong message to staff. 'The board is beginning to look as unwieldy as that of Co-op. Executives are not leading from the front. Mostly they are retaining their jobs.' Shares in both firms fell sharply after the announcement with Dixons down nearly 10 per cent to 46p a share, and Carphone down more than 7 per cent to 303p.

Source: adapted from *The Guardian* 15 May 2014

### Questions (30 marks; 35 minutes)

1. Is this a conglomerate or horizontal merger? Explain your answer. (5)

2. Explain the possible cost synergies that might form part of the £80 million annual savings forecast by Dixons Carphone. (5)

3. Based on the evidence in the case and your wider knowledge of mergers, do you think bringing together Dixons and Carphone is likely to be a business success? Justify your answer. (20)

## C. Extend your understanding

1. Do you think it's inevitable that people management problems will occur within a firm that has just been taken over? Justify your arguments. (25)

2. 'The high level of takeover activity in the UK leads to short-termism'. To what extent do you agree with this statement? (25)

**Linked to:** Technological change, Chapter 70; Becoming an innovative organisation, Chapter 82; Protecting innovative ideas, Chapter 83; Managing organisational culture, Chapter 93.

## Definition

Innovation means taking a brand new idea for a product or a process and making it happen in the marketplace or workplace.

## 81.1 The pressures for innovation

It is an old business saying that 'if you're not growing, you're shrinking'. Without new things to sell or new ways to make what is being sold, competitors will find a way to erode any differentiation that a business has managed to achieve. Arguably therefore, the background pressure for innovation is to ensure long-term survival. However, more immediate reasons can be identified in the shorter term.

- *Competition* –the need to constantly improve competitiveness is a key driver for business activity. Determinants of competitiveness such as product features, quality levels, production costs and speed of response to customer orders can all be helped by successful innovation. This might be through launching new products with unique features, in the way that Apple seeks to do with every new generation of iPhone; or finding new manufacturing processes that reduce unit costs or boost quality levels. Successful innovation helps any business in the race against competitors.

- *Market* – another pressure is from customers whose demands for ever-higher levels of product function or service can drive innovation. New methods of providing customer service, or delivering products ordered online may be developed following disappointing customer feedback. Here, the key is to be proactive; some businesses look at declining indicators and hope they'll not affect sales; others act promptly to tackle the problem area and try to move it from weakness to strength. In 2014 one of the criticisms of Tesco was that it bullied its smaller suppliers. In 2015 new Chief Executive Dave Lewis promised that small suppliers would be paid within 14 days.

- *Growth* – a further pressure to innovate comes from shareholders' expectations of continual growth in sales and profit. Stock markets can heavily influence plcs' strategic decision-making. If shareholders expect turnover to rise year after year, existing markets may be incapable of delivering the growth expected. In such cases, innovative new products may be necessary which allow companies to create brand new markets. A company with a product portfolio loaded with cash cows but no presence in high growth markets will certainly hope to innovate in order to ensure future cash flows. But no one should assume that this is easy. In March 2015 innocent Drinks announced that it was scrapping its Veg Pots product line. First launched in 2006 and relaunched in 2013, it was innovative, but never really struck a chord with consumers. As explained by Ansoff's Matrix (see Chapter 75), product development is easier to talk about than succeed with.

'Innovation is the specific instrument of entrepreneurship. The act that endows resources with a new capacity to create wealth.' Peter Drucker, business guru

## 81.2 Types of innovation

It is important to remember that innovations can be seen not only in products, but also in processes. While product innovation is more often obvious to us as consumers, new ways to get things done in businesses often have a profound effect on operational efficiency. Process innovation means finding new ways to make things, for example automating something that used to be done by hand.

## What is process innovation?

Designing and implementing new ways to do things can bring great rewards. In 1980 Marks & Spencer brought out Britain's first-ever range of ready-made sandwiches. It came about as a result of discussions with a supplier who suggested that conveyor-belt mass production of sandwiches could make them an affordable treat. This combination of process and product innovation has probably been worth £billions to M&S.

A new process may enable a firm to offer a product or service that was not previously available. Alternatively, a new way to do something may work out far cheaper – giving the innovative company a major cost advantage over its rivals. Designing a new process is often the result of a desire to remove wastage from a system – again a method of reducing costs. Process innovation can come from a range of sources used by innovative organisations, as detailed in Chapter 82. What is vital is to ensure that any innovation is protected, using a patent, as explained in Chapter 83.

## What is product innovation?

Many companies have found great success through product innovation – the development and successful launch of products that feature a genuinely new idea, or combine existing ideas in a new way. Product innovations can come from a range of sources including scientific and technical research, consumers' ideas and ideas of staff members. However, for the product to be classed an innovation, it must be successfully developed and used in the marketplace. See Chapter 82 for a fuller examination of how an organisation can try to become more innovative.

If in any doubt as to how valuable product innovation can be, consider the likely value of being the first company to effectively take the following ideas to the marketplace successfully:

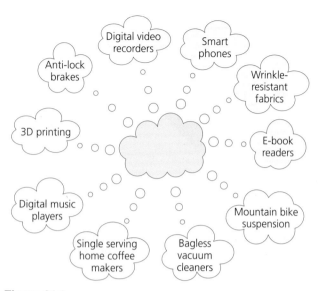

**Figure 81.1**

'Innovation is creativity with a job to do.' John Emmerling, innovation consultant and author

## 81.3 The value of innovation

The benefits of successful innovation can be huge:

- *Monopoly* – successful product or process innovation effectively creates a monopoly. Such a situation offers tremendous benefits to the successful innovator.

- *High price* – with no effective competition, the selling price can be set high to cream off revenue from customers who want to be the first to own the product (early adopters). This pricing strategy of skimming the market allows the firm to reduce its prices as it anticipates competitors arriving, perhaps as a result of finding an alternative way to make the product or the expiry of a patent.

- *Reputation* – innovators tend to have a positive reputation in the minds of consumers. Apple's development of its first MP3 player occurred over 15 years ago. Yet it has maintained the impetus that the innovative iPod brought by continuing to develop 'cutting edge' products and kept the benefit of being seen as a pacesetter in the consumer electronics market.

- *Cost reduction* – process innovation can bring cost savings to a business that can discover a new, more efficient method of production. These cost savings can either be passed on to customers as price reductions, or the selling price can be maintained to provide more profit per unit. The choice will depend mainly on the price elasticity of the product – price will be cut on price elastic products, but maintained for products that are price inelastic.

- *Quality improvement* – some process innovations will allow quality standards to improve, allowing the firm to use quality as a key competitive advantage in the marketplace.

## Real business

### *Toyota – Kings of Green*

In 1997, after ten years of development work, Toyota launched the Prius, with its innovative hybrid-drive system. This part electric, part petrol engine allowed dramatic reductions in CO2 emissions per mile. When petrol prices soared in 2004, so did Prius sales. By 2015 more than 3.5 million of the cars had been sold, making it by far the world's biggest selling electric or part-electric vehicle.

For Toyota, not only did the Prius become a profitable, big-selling car, it also served to sprinkle an environmental glow over the whole Toyota range. It helped Toyota become the world's biggest-selling carmaker – a crown it held in 2014, despite fierce competition from Volkswagen of Germany and General Motors, USA. The Prius has been especially important in the giant US car market (see Figure 81.2). In 2014 Toyota held a 14 per cent market share in America compared with VW's 3 per cent!

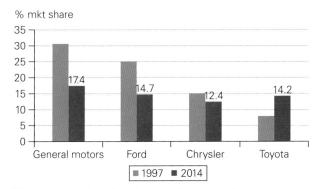

% mkt share

**Figure 81.2** US market share - selected producers

Source: www.wardsauto.com

## 81.4 The impact of an innovation strategy on the functional areas of the business

### Innovation and finance

Successful innovation is likely to require significant amounts of long-term investment. Therefore firms that are unwilling to accept long payback periods are unlikely to be innovators. Short-termist companies are far more likely to copy other firms' successes. In fact, much of the money spent by firms on innovation provides no direct payback. Ideas are researched and developed before discovering that they will not succeed in the marketplace, or it becomes clear that a new process is not going to be effective on a large scale. The result is that the goal of innovation can be a bit hit-and-miss. There are no guarantees, but the rewards, if they come, can be immense. As in the case of Toyota, successes can radically alter conditions in the marketplace, allowing an innovative company to claim a dominant position.

### Innovation and people

For many years, firms have considered that team-working provides many of the most successful innovations. Based on the principle that no single person is likely to have all the best ideas or answers to all the problems that arise when developing an idea, research teams are encouraged to share their ideas and breakthroughs. These research teams are often created by taking specialists in various different fields of operation from different departments within the organisation. This means that a team may consist of several scientists, an accountant, a production specialist and a marketing representative. This blend of expertise helps in identifying cost-effective, marketable new ideas that can be produced by the company.

### Innovation and production

New processes can revolutionise the way in which firms produce their product or service. These can lead to more efficient, cheaper or higher quality production. In pursuing a strategy of innovation, new processes may require the design and building of new equipment, machinery or materials. Operations management departments will need to ensure that new products can actually be manufactured in sufficient quantities and at a low enough cost to make launching the product feasible. This kind of innovation is likely to require the collaboration of partners within the supply chain, not only material and component suppliers but potentially logistics firms handling distribution, and retailers too.

'Business has only two functions - marketing and innovation.' Peter Drucker, business guru

## Innovation and marketing

Many would argue that the most important part of the marketing mix is the product itself. Successful product development keeps a firm one step ahead of the competition. This usually means keeping one step ahead in pricing as well. Whether you are introducing a new drug such as Viagra or a new football management computer game, you have the opportunity to charge a premium price. Innovative new products are also very likely to get good distribution. Tesco is reluctant to find space on its shelves for just another ('me-too') cola or toothpaste, but if the product is truly innovative, the space will be found.

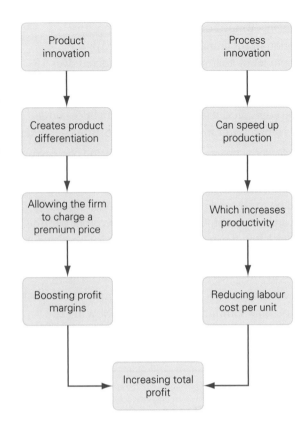

**Figure 81.3** Logic circle: Successful innovation brings significant benefits

## Five Whys and a How

| Question | Answer |
|---|---|
| Why does innovation have an impact on a firm's image? | Consumers notice firms such as Dyson or Apple who seem to regularly produce innovative products. This becomes a part of the image that consumers attach to these brands, adding value and lustre (and therefore justifying high price tags) |
| Why is process innovation so significant? | Finding new ways to do things can reduce costs, speed processes up, allow higher levels of quality or even allow the production of new products that could previously not be made |
| Why can innovative products perform poorly in market research? | Products which perform functions that have never before been possible may leave potential consumers unable to understand how the function will benefit their lifestyle |
| Why do new product development teams often feature staff from different parts of the business? | Great new ideas often come from combining developments from different areas of the business – Post-It notes were launched by 3M after a researcher showed a new unsticky glue to a colleague looking for a way to mark pages in his hymn book at church. |
| Why do innovative firms have higher profit margins? | Innovative products command a premium price, whilst innovative processes frequently mean lower unit costs – both outcomes which boost profit margins |
| How can a firm try to become more innovative? | Scientific and technical research (R&D) can be undertaken, while employees can be organised into kaizen groups to make small improvements. Firms can also encourage intrapreneurship. These methods are detailed in Chapter 82 |

Innovation, whether of product or process can be a major boost for a business, taking revenues and/or profits to unheard-of levels, as in the case of Apple Inc. which, in early 2015 was the most valuable company on the planet. However, innovation tends to be an expensive process, especially when heavy research and development spending is required. The problem with spending heavily on finding innovations is that there is no guarantee of a marketable return. The strategic question is therefore whether a firm feels it has sufficient resources, in terms of people and finance, to risk failing in the attempt to develop innovative products or processes. However, the challenge remains — to come up with innovations that will generate sufficient returns to outweigh the high cost of investing in a long-term strategy of innovation.

## Key term

**Research and development:** scientific and technical research aimed at producing innovative products or processes.

# Workbook

## A. Revision questions

(25 marks; 25 minutes)

1. Distinguish between product and process innovation. (3)

2. Briefly explain two potential benefits that might be enjoyed by Walls if its engineers design a new production process for manufacturing ice cream. (6)

3. Outline two examples of innovations that have created brand new markets. (4)

4. Explain the links between the concepts of innovation and short-termism. (4)

5. Explain the possible effect that a lack of innovation might have on the product portfolio of a confectionery business. (4)

6. Explain how a firm may try to market a brand new type of product developed from a scientific breakthrough. (4)

## B. Revision exercises
### DATA RESPONSE

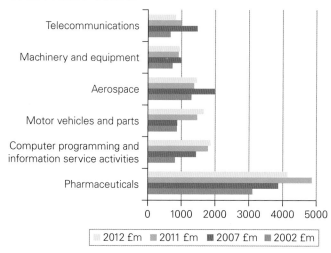

2012 £m    2011 £m    2007 £m    2002 £m

**Figure 81.4** R&D expenditure by businesses in the UK by product group

Source: ONS www.ons.gov.uk/ons/rel/rdit1/bus-ent-res-and-dev/2012/stb-berd-2012.html#tab-R-D-expenditure-by-product-group

**Table 81.1:** Percentage of GDP spent on R&D, selected countries, average figure over 2010-2014

| Country | Percentage of GDP spent on R&D Average figure over 2010-2014 |
|---------|------------------------------------------------------------|
| China   | 1.98 |
| Finland | 3.55 |
| France  | 2.26 |
| Germany | 2.92 |
| Sweden  | 3.41 |
| UK      | 1.72 |
| USA     | 2.79 |

Source: World Bank http://data.worldbank.org/indicator/GB.XPD.RSDV.GD.ZS

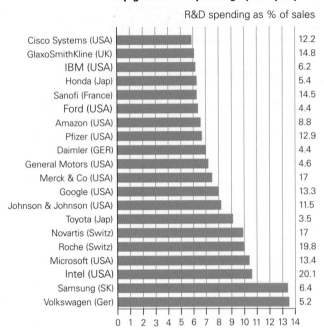

**Top global R&D spending by company**

R&D spending as % of sales

| Company | % |
|---|---|
| Cisco Systems (USA) | 12.2 |
| GlaxoSmithKline (UK) | 14.8 |
| IBM (USA) | 6.2 |
| Honda (Jap) | 5.4 |
| Sanofi (France) | 14.5 |
| Ford (USA) | 4.4 |
| Amazon (USA) | 8.8 |
| Pfizer (USA) | 12.9 |
| Daimler (GER) | 4.4 |
| General Motors (USA) | 4.6 |
| Merck & Co (USA) | 17 |
| Google (USA) | 13.3 |
| Johnson & Johnson (USA) | 11.5 |
| Toyota (Jap) | 3.5 |
| Novartis (Switz) | 17 |
| Roche (Switz) | 19.8 |
| Microsoft (USA) | 13.4 |
| Intel (USA) | 20.1 |
| Samsung (SK) | 6.4 |
| Volkswagen (Ger) | 5.2 |

0 1 2 3 4 5 6 7 8 9 10 11 12 13 14

**Figure 81.5** R&D spending by company

Source: Booz & Company

**Questions (35 marks; 45 minutes)**

1. **a)** Using Figure 81.5 calculate Samsung's annual sales for 2011. (3)

   **b)** Identify three UK industries in which R&D spending does not seem to have been harmed by recession. (3)

2. Analyse the implications of Table 81.1 on the international competitiveness of UK firms (9)

3. To what extent does the data in Figures 81.4 and 81.5 and Table 81.1 suggest that UK businesses are increasingly adopting a strategy of innovation? (20)

## C. Extend your understanding

1. To what extent does an innovative product guarantee success? (25)

2. In 2015 *The Grocer* magazine forecast that by 2025 all supermarket sandwiches will be made by robots. Evaluate the impact on the key stakeholders. (25)

**Linked with:** Technological change, Chapter 70;
Innovation, Chapter 81; Protecting innovative ideas,
Chapter 83; Managing organisational culture,
Chapter 93.

## Definition

An innovative organization is one that continually
develops and implements new ideas that help them to
achieve their goals.

## 82.1 Introduction

Businesspeople often use the word 'proactive' to sum
up a state of mind based on initiative and a desire to
be first. The opposite is 'reactive', where a business
hopes to be able to carry on as it is and will only
change if it has to. Needless to say an innovative
organisation is proactive, showing a willingness to
do things differently and to take risks in developing
new products, new management approaches and
new ways of operating. Government figures suggest
that investment in innovation accounts for 51 per
cent of productivity growth. This demonstrates the
importance of innovation to our economy, given
that productivity was the missing factor in the UK
between 2007 and 2015.

Many managements look in awe at innovative
companies such as Apple and Google. The question
posed by this chapter is: How can a business become
an innovative organisation?

'Creativity is thinking up new things. Innovation
is doing new things.' Theodore Levitt, author and
business academic

## 82.2 Ways of becoming an innovative organisation

### Kaizen

Kaizen is a Japanese term meaning continuous
improvement. The two fundamental principles behind
kaizen are:

- Most change comes from people and their ideas
  rather than technology.
- If hundreds of small changes are made, the
  cumulative effects can be significant.

Successful use of kaizen requires a positive culture that
is complex and focused on three basic characteristics:

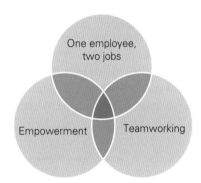

**Figure 82.1** The kaizen culture

*One employee, two jobs* – a belief behind kaizen is that
the real expert in any job is the person doing the job.
Therefore, the best source of improvements will be
from the expert – the person doing the job. For kaizen
to work effectively, each employee must believe that
they have two jobs to do – doing the job itself and
finding ways to improve the job and how it is done.

*Teamworking* – employees are split into teams composed
of staff in the same section of the business. The idea here
is that not only do individuals become experts, but small

groups of staff in one area come to understand their section of production better than anyone else. The team, known as a cell, is held responsible for their quality of work and meets regularly to discuss the causes of and solutions to problems occurring in their area.

For teamworking to be used to build an innovative company, though, it is not enough to encourage local cells to become teams. The teamwork has to be part of an overall attitude within the business that's built on a sense of common purpose. This is where mission comes in. People working for Google believe they are part of a business that's changing the world, that's empowering individuals (by giving them information) and making the world a better place. They also slip in a strong dose of patriotism, as it's *American* Google that's making the world a better place. So Googlers work together (while in other businesses 'turf wars' rage, with one department trying to outshine another).

*Empowerment* – the final component for successful kaizen is that teams are given the decision-making power to implement the solutions they come up with in their own cell. If their ideas are constantly ignored, or knocked back, the ideas will soon dry up. Therefore the cells must be empowered to make changes that affect their work.

Kaizen leads to small innovations, minor changes that it is hoped will have a huge cumulative effect. The majority of kaizen changes are likely to be examples of process innovation – new ways to organise machinery within a production cell, or ways to reduce materials wastage. This is usually the best way to boost long-term competitiveness. Between 2007 and 2015 labour productivity in Britain was unchanged. This would be inconceivable if most firms pursued a kaizen strategy – achieving regular improvements edging efficiency up by 0.5 per cent here and 0.75 per cent there.

---

'A new idea is delicate. It can be killed by a sneer or a yawn; it can be stabbed to death by a quip and worried to death by a frown on the right man's brow.' Charles Brower, US lawyer and judge

---

## Research and development

Committing financial, physical and human resources to research and development signals a clear commitment to innovation. Scientific and technical research can lead to breakthrough innovations in both product and process. The major snag with research and development is that costs are high and outcomes are uncertain. The frequency with which research and development leads to marketable new products or processes is low. This hit-and-miss nature means that

research and development spending can be hard to justify on financial grounds. In many ways, research and development requires a significant 'leap of faith' on behalf of directors, willing to commit resources with no promise of a return. But other countries seem to be clear that research and development is essential for long-term success. Just like investment in training – even though the benefits may be hard to measure, it's a necessity, not a luxury. Figure 82.2 shows recent trends across a wide range of countries. The picture is a disappointing one for the UK – especially as UK companies enjoyed rising profits and falling corporation tax levels during the period 2010 to 2013.

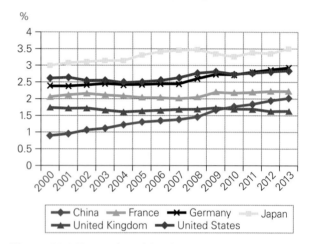

**Figure 82.2** Research and development spending as a percentage of GDP

Source: OECD March 2015

As shown in Figure 82.3, there is a risk of a downward spiral. As a result, the UK government has tried hard to encourage greater R&D spending. One initiative was publishing *The Innovation Report*, distributed free to company bosses by the Department for Business Innovation and Skills in March 2014.

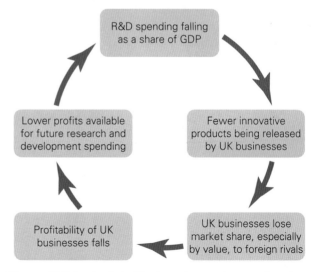

**Figure 82.3** Logic circle: The importance of research and development

## Intrapreneurship

This term describes the way some large firms encourage members of staff to act as entrepreneurs, spotting and developing new ideas for which the company will provide backing in terms of financial and other resources. Intrapreneurship has generated such products as Post-it notes and Gmail. The methods used to encourage intrapreneurship tend to revolve around programmes that allow staff to choose what they would like to work on for a set proportion of their working time. Google runs a 20 per cent programme, whereby staff are encouraged to work for the equivalent of one day per week on a problem of their own choosing – whether that be developing process or product innovation. This system is said to be responsible not just for the development of Gmail but also Google News and AdSense. Other businesses hold innovation days or run regular staff competitions for coming up with new ideas. The principle is to harness the creative power of staff and throw the full resources of a large organisation behind the best ideas. This might enable these large firms to experience the kind of spectacular growth of which small businesses are capable.

---

'Listen to anyone with an original idea, no matter how absurd it may sound at first. If you put fences around people, you get sheep. Give people the room they need.' William McKnight, 3M President

---

### Real business

#### *Facebook likes intrapreneurship*

Facebook's now famous 'like' button was the result of a collaboration between several Facebook employees, encouraged by the company's culture of sharing ideas and creativity. A few Facebook staff had begun discussing the initial idea of an 'awesome button' in 2007. They were able to discuss the idea face to face during one of Facebook's 'hackathons' – all-night sessions for staff to work on new ideas. The idea turned into a formal project but was rejected several times by Mark Zuckerberg. He was worried about whether the feature, by now known as the 'like button', would cannibalise Facebook's 'share' feature. The project did not go away and by the end of 2008, the project team used a data specialist to provide evidence that 'likes' would not reduce the number of comments. Finally, the 'like button' was launched in early 2009, and became a huge success.

## Benchmarking

Benchmarking means seeking out examples of outstanding ways other companies do things and then finding a way to implement these methods in your own business. (If that sounds like copying then, er, yes, that's right.) But why would any company allow another to copy them? The answer is that the companies may not be competitors. If a producer of car tyres has developed a brilliant new system of inventory control, the management may be happy to share their knowledge with Cadbury or Sainsbury's.

Alternatively, benchmarking may be carried out by consultants who persuade most or all the suppliers in a sector to hand over key pieces of information in exchange for anonymity plus a copy of the results. An example of the findings is as follows (anonymised):

**Table 82.1** Benchmarked data

|  | Worst | Lowest quartile* | Mean average | Highest quartile | Best |
|---|---|---|---|---|---|
| Inventory turnover (times a year) | 3.3 | 3.9 | 5.5 | 7.2 | 8.1 |
| Percentage of materials wastage | 11.4 | 7.8 | 5.0 | 2.1 | 0.3 |
| Productivity per worker per hour | 1.2 units | 2.0 units | 2.9 units | 3.8 units | 5.2 units |
| Lead time (hours between customer order and delivery) | 42.5 | 28.7 | 20.5 | 12.3 | 4.0 |

*lowest quartile is the average performance by the worst-achieving quarter of the sample

If a company received the above data together with a print-out of its own performance showing: Inventory turnover 6.2; wastage 2.2 per cent; productivity 3.4 units; lead time 28.9 hours – it would realise that it has to focus management efforts on customer lead time.

Examples of very common processes which may be benchmarked include:

**Table 82.2** Processes that may be benchmarked

| Most businesses | Manufacturers | Service providers |
|---|---|---|
| Motivating staff | Storing stock | Customer service training methods |
| Recycling waste | Planning production | How to run a call centre successfully |
| Analysing marketing data | Recycling waste | How computer networks are set up |
| Managing accounting information | Factory layout | Responding to complaints |

With so many processes and practices common to many types of business it is perhaps easier to understand how a toy manufacturer would be willing to show a bank how they analyse marketing data, with the bank, in return, allowing staff from the toy manufacturer to explore how the bank motivates its staff.

Once a business has identified an area in which it is underperforming, the benchmarking process is likely to follow a cycle similar to that shown below:

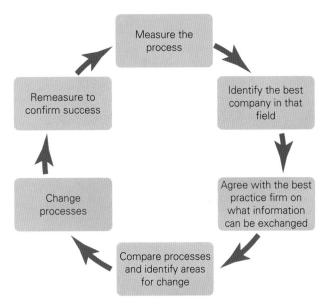

**Figure 82.4** Logic circle: benchmarking

Benchmarking has proved to be a useful exercise for many businesses. One of its major contributions has been to encourage businesses to recognise that they could do better. Having recognised that there may be a problem in the operation, it is easier to find solutions. Some businesses have found that they can usefully copy methods or processes used by other businesses. Others have discovered that 'bolting on' someone else's processes to their existing ways simply does not work. The concept of benchmarking is fairly simple, but the practice is often more complicated. Comparing processes may be a problem when it's not possible to compare like with like. Nevertheless companies have found that even if benchmarking does not provide a quick-fix solution, it does encourage people to think about the problem. This often leads to the discovery of alternative solutions.

'The difficulty lies not so much in developing new ideas as in escaping from old ones.' John Maynard Keynes, economist

## Five Whys and a How

| Question | Answer |
| --- | --- |
| Why does kaizen encourage change so effectively? | Small steps are easier for managers and employees to accept (as they're unlikely to threaten job security); with ideas coming from employees themselves they are more likely to make their ideas work in practice |
| Why can some firms survive without research and development? | In all markets there is room for a company that can efficiently, and legally, take ideas that others have developed and produce similar products or services a little more cheaply. Other firms use 'tradition' as a point of differentiation |
| Why can intrapreneurship be expensive? | Allowing employees time to come up with and develop their own ideas necessitates a drop in their productivity in their primary job. Google's '20 per cent time' implies just four days' work focused on the employee's primary task |
| Why would a leading company agree to be involved in a benchmarking exercise? | Leading companies are often those that are open to new ideas, and may therefore welcome the chance to share insights with another firm that wants to copy their successful methods. As shown above, benchmarking processes rarely needs two firms in direct competition to work together |

| Question | Answer |
|---|---|
| Why can the results of benchmarking be disappointing? | It may be hard to find a partner that is truly outstanding at the process you would like to improve; and in some cases the process may seem similar but prove quite different |
| How should a business start on a journey to become more innovative? | Leadership is crucial, to create a culture that supports policies designed to promote innovation |

## Evaluation: Becoming an innovative organisation

This unit has shown that there are a number of approaches that businesses can take to become more innovative. However, becoming an innovative organisation requires much more than simply choosing to spend money or implementing a new system for sharing ideas. Successfully innovative firms have a culture that clearly supports innovation and that values the ideas that come from mechanisms such as kaizen groups or benchmarking activities. The openness to change which is needed is not always found, even in firms that have committed to a new system or spent heavily on research and development. Read Chapter 93 for a fuller understanding of organisational culture.

## Key terms

**Intrapreneurship:** encouraging employees within a business to have and develop new business ideas whilst working for the business.

**Benchmarking:** the process of sharing best practice between businesses in the hope of improving areas of underperformance.

**Research and development:** scientific and technical research aimed at developing new products or processes through making scientific or technical breakthroughs.

# Workbook

## A. Revision questions

(30 marks; 30 minutes)

1. Explain two reasons why kaizen can boost productivity within a business. (8)

2. Briefly explain one reason why kaizen programmes can be hard to sustain in the long term. (4)

3. Explain how an online retailer may use benchmarking to improve its delivery times. (4)

4. Using a theory of motivation, analyse why intrapreneurial programmes such as '20 per cent time' at Google can boost motivation. (9)

5. In July 2015 Tesco announced that it would no longer stock sugar-added drinks such as Ribena and Capri-Sun. Explain how intrapreneurship within the producing companies might address this business problem. (5)

# Revision exercises

## DATA RESPONSE

### The world's 50 most innovative companies: only one UK firm listed

Unilever spends £1bn a year on R&D, but most UK firms don't see innovation as a top priority.

In a global ranking of the world's 50 most innovative companies, just one UK firm has made the list. Consumer goods giant Unilever, which spends almost £1 billion a year on new inventions and employs 6,000 people in R&D, is ranked 49. Virgin and BP, which made the list in 2013, dropped out this year as just 9 per cent of UK executives said they put innovation as their top business priority. Tech firms dominated the top 10. Apple tops the list for the ninth year in a row, followed by Samsung and Google in second and third place.

The list was put together by US-based Boston Consulting Group, which questioned 1,500 global senior innovation executives from companies with more than $100 million turnover annually about which companies they admire, and how they judge their own firm. Almost half of the companies on the list have generated more than 30 per cent of sales from innovations that occurred in the prior three years, the respondents said. Two-thirds added they are spending more on innovation this year than in 2013, while some revealed that their best ideas had come from analysing social media trends. The ones which are most successful put all their focus on one or two projects at a time, the report noted. 'Too many companies want to shoot for the moon while their innovation programs are barely airborne,' said Kim Wagner, a BCG senior partner and co-author of the report. 'Breakthrough innovators are especially effective at bringing together the pieces required for radical innovation and organising them for high impact.'

Since BCG's 2013 report, the biggest change has been in the automotive sector. Carmakers reported a 26 per cent decline in innovation priority as they look to cut costs, and there are just nine in the top 50, down from 14 a year ago. Tesla at number 7 is bucking the trend. The firm has recently announced a number of new innovations and has said it will not sue other electric-car makers that use its technologies 'in good faith'. It hopes that by removing obstacles, this will accelerate the growth of the electric car market, which currently accounts for around 2 per cent of cars sold overall. Last month, the ever-innovative Apple had its biggest product launch in recent history where it unveiled the iPhone 6 and iPhone 6 Plus, alongside the Apple Watch and Apple Pay, the company's take on a digital wallet.

Unilever, the only UK entry, has introduced innovations such as compressed deodorants in the last year, reducing carbon emissions by 25 per cent. BCG also praised Amazon, which has changed its business model many times since launching in 1994 and has become a one-stop shop for anything on the web. The company has built one of the biggest and most valuable databases of consumer information based on its 150 million customer accounts. 'It is the one retailer that all others in the retail and consumer-packaged-goods sectors must take into account when planning their future strategy,' the report noted. The most innovative firms use the company as a new-idea laboratory, it added. Apple under the late Steve Jobs is perhaps the best-known example. Google's policy of encouraging employees to spend 20 per cent of their time working on their own ideas is another.

### What makes an innovative company?

- Use of internal and external sources of knowledge, and a dedicated budget for venturing and testing concepts
- A focus on releasing products that customers need rather than pushing new technologies simply because they are novel
- They embrace and manage failure, leading to strong performance.

Source: telegraph.co.uk www.telegraph.co.uk/finance/businessclub/technology/11190526/The-worlds-50-most-innovative-companies-only-one-UK-firm-listed.html

| Top 20 innovative companies in the world | |
|---|---|
| 1. Apple | 11. HP |
| 2. Google | 12. General Electric |
| 3. Samsung | 13. Intel |
| 4. Microsoft | 14. Cisco Systems |
| 5. IBM | 15. Siemens |
| 6. Amazon | 16. Coca-Cola |
| 7. Tesla Motors | 17. LG Electronics |
| 8. Toyota | 18. BMW |
| 9. Facebook | 19. Ford |
| 10. Sony | 20. Dell |

**Questions (35 marks; 40 minutes)**

1. Describe how Amazon's database of consumer behaviour might help the company's attempts to innovate. (3)

2. Analyse two reasons why Tesla may be willing to allow other businesses to use its innovations without suing. (12)

3. To what extent does the article suggest the competitiveness of UK businesses is likely to fall in the next ten years? (20)

## C. Extend your understanding

1. 'Leadership is the key to creating an innovative organisation'. To what extent do you agree with this statement? (25)

2. Apple has shown that innovation is more about design than robots and technology. To what extent do you agree with that view? (25)

# Chapter 83 Protecting innovative ideas

**Linked to:** Technological change, Chapter 70; Innovation, Chapter 81; Becoming an innovative organisation, Chapter 82.

> ### Definition
>
> An idea cannot be protected, but patents and copyright are methods of preventing others from copying an actual invention or piece of creative work.

## 83.1 Intellectual property

Intellectual property (IP) is the general term for assets that have been created by human ingenuity or creativity. These would include music, writing, photographs and engineering or other inventions. Around the world, governments are keen to protect intellectual property because otherwise there would be no financial incentive to create anything. Why should J.K. Rowling spend years writing about Harry Potter if others could simply photocopy the books? She is protected by copyright. To get fully up-to-date information, go to www.ipo.gov.uk; this is Britain's Intellectual Property Office.

'If you didn't have patents, no one would bother to spend money on research and development.' James Dyson, billionaire founder of Dyson Appliances

## 83.2 Patent

The *Patents and Designs Journal* lists a series of patent applications that have recently been granted. One is by a British inventor Michael Reeves, for a 'lightning-protected golf cart'. It is easy to see that if this invention works (and can be produced at reasonable cost), it should sweep every other golf cart off the market.

The purpose of a patent is to provide a window of up to 20 years in which the work of an inventor cannot be copied by anyone else. The 20-year period starts from the moment the patent is applied for. The IPO itself admits that applications take at least two and a half years to process, and can take up to five years! In Michael Reeves' case, he probably has about 17 years after the patent has been granted to get his 'lightning-protected golf cart' to the market.

The patent system acts as an incentive to the inventor; nevertheless it can mean higher prices for the consumer. Mr Reeves' golf cart could prove to be significantly more expensive than its rivals, just because Mr Reeves has the monopoly power that comes from the patent.

For a small firm, obtaining a patent can be expensive, perhaps costing between £1,000 and £4,000 for the UK alone. Then, if the product has worldwide potential, patent applications will be required in America, Japan, China, and so on. The total cost could be £50,000+. Worse may come later, if a competitor breaks your patent. This is because breaking a patent is not a criminal offence, so you cannot call the police. It is a civil offence, so the patent owner has to sue the competitor. If a small firm is to take a giant such as Nike to court, there is a real risk that the cost of the court proceedings may ruin the minnow's finances.

'If you're a large corporation, you can afford to pay the money to register patents, but if you're an individual like me, you can't.' Larry Wall, inventor of computer programming languages

## Patents

Recently the Chief Executive of Sentec, a British company specialising in metering technology, said, 'If you go to court in a patent case, then effectively you need to have £1 million in your back pocket to be able to finance (the legal costs), which of course most small companies cannot afford to do.'

At the same time a partner in Notion Capital (venture capital firm) said, 'The process of filing for a patent is complicated, expensive, time-consuming and very frustrating. The whole area is not a level playing field … successfully protecting your IP is dependent on how much you can afford.'

'The under-funded and over-extended United States Patent and Trademark Office does not have the resources to adequately evaluate the burgeoning number of applications, and too many low-quality patents are being issued as a result.' Viet Dinh, former Assistant Attorney General for Legal Policy, USA

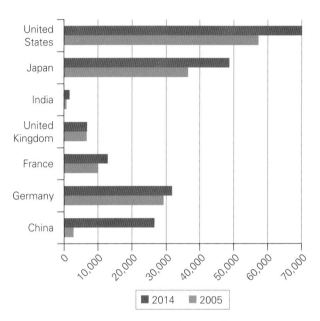

**Figure 83.1** European patent applications by country per year
Source: www.epo.org

Despite the shortcomings, the system of patents has proved to be an excellent way to give inventors the incentives they need. Globally, China now files more patent applications than any other country. As shown in Figure 83.1, even in Europe China's patent applications have grown dramatically. The same cannot be said of the UK.

**Table 83.1** Impact of patent rights

| | Impact on companies holding patents | Impact on competitors | Impact on customers |
|---|---|---|---|
| **Positive** | Giving monopoly power for up to 20 years<br>Prices can be higher and competition subdued<br>Creates incentives to develop new patentable opportunities | Makes it hard to enter the market competitively…<br>…which may force firms to be innovative in developing ways to get round the patent<br>Some patents may prove too tough to get round | Fosters product innovation which should benefit customers<br>But prices can be higher due to monopoly power, e.g. drug treatments priced at more than £10,000 a year |
| **Negative** | Taking out patents is expensive, perhaps costing £75,000 - £150,000 for global protection<br>Strong patent rights may lead to complacency | May lead to unethical business practices such as industrial espionage | Ordinary people in developing countries cannot afford life-preserving, patented drugs |

# 83.3 Copyright

Copyright applies to original written work such as books, newspaper articles, song lyrics, and so on. Unlike patents, it occurs automatically, so there is no need to spend time and money applying for it. Copyright in a literary work lasts for the lifetime of the author plus 70 years.

Clearly copyright is at the heart of the publishing and music industries. Less obvious is that it is also at the

heart of computing and the Internet. The imaginative prices charged by Microsoft for its Office software are bound up in the copyright protection it enjoys. If Microsoft catches anyone breaking its copyright it will sue immediately. As with patents, it can be argued that this is crucial to the development of the industry. Whereas the cost of developing a Playstation 1 game was around £500,000 and Playstation 2 around £5 million, the cost of creating a PS3 game was close to £20 million (Sony believes that developing a PS4 game is no more expensive than PS3). To justify such huge expenditure, the software producer needs to be confident that the game will sell millions of copies; if, instead, it is copied by millions there may be little incentive to create the games.

'Copyright infringement is often called piracy.' Wikipedia

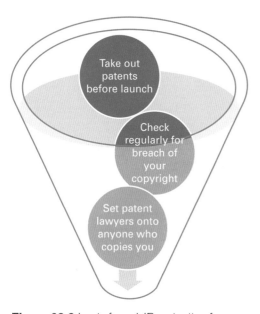

**Figure 83.2** Logic funnel: IP protection for a new product

## Key terms

**Copyright:** this makes it unlawful for people to copy an author's original written work.

**Monopoly power:** is the ability to charge high prices because you are the sole supplier of a product.

**Patents:** provide the inventor of a technical breakthrough with the ability to stop anyone copying the idea for up to 20 years.

## Five Whys and a How

| Question | Answer |
|---|---|
| Why do patent laws exist? | To ensure that inventors get the rewards their efforts deserve |
| Why do some people think they should be scrapped? | Because they guarantee a monopoly position for companies for as long as 20 years. Perhaps the rewards for successful new inventions are too high |
| Why are copyright rules easier for the IP owner than patent laws? | Because you don't have to register your copyright, so it's much cheaper for the IP owner |
| Why does Apple take so much care to protect its patents? | Because even for Apple, with its powerful brand name, it's great to be the only phonemaker offering specific features to customers |
| Why are patents especially controversial in the market for pharmaceuticals? | Because huge prices for treatments can make them entirely unaffordable in developing countries such as India |
| How come Dyson cleaners still command a price premium when the patents on their technology expired years ago? | James Dyson has given a lesson in how to maintain a price premium after the patent expires: great design, effective advertising messaging and great niche marketing (cleaners for pet owners) |

# Workbook

## A. Revision questions

(25 marks; 25 minutes)

1. Briefly explain why Mr Reeves should be able to build a very successful business based on the patent explained in Section 83.2. (4)

2. Explain why an entrepreneur may struggle if the success of new business relies on a patented invention. (4)

3. See Figure 83.1 and identify:
   a) Two countries where the number of patent applications rose by the largest number between 2005 and 2014. (2)
   b) Two countries where the number of patent applications rose by the smallest number between 2005 and 2014. (2)

4. Briefly explain why it may disappoint the British Government to see that the number of patent applications from Britain has hardly changed. (4)

5. For each of the following, identify whether the IP issue relates to patent or copyright.
   a) Galaxy has designed a new pack for its Celebrations brand. (1)
   b) Burberry has come up with a new way to get solar power from a tartan cap, sufficient to keep an iPod powered all day long. (1)
   c) Lacoste has developed a new, completely distinctive scent for men. (1)
   d) You have just copied a tennis game from your friend's Wii console. (1)

6. Why may intellectual property be more important today than 50 years ago? Briefly explain your answer. (5)

## B. Revision exercises
### DATA RESPONSE 1

#### Ladies and cycling patents

The transport sensation of the late Victorian period was the bicycle. A practical problem, though, was that 'ladies' wore long dresses, not trousers (or jeans). Therefore a bicycle was difficult to ride, with risks ranging from dirtied dresses to tangled spokes and sudden stops. British inventors set to work on this problem, with more than 50 patents registered with reference to 'ladies' and 'cycling'. An example of these patents includes 'a lady's rational or divided skirt for cycling', by Oretta Bywater of Glamorgan, in 1903. The main drawing is shown in Figure 83.3.

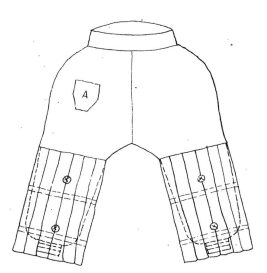 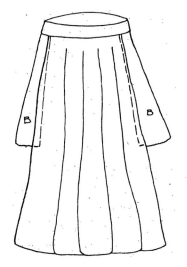

**Figure 83.3** A patent for a lady's rational or divided skirt for cycling

The drawings show the harness for bunched up skirts and the 'overdress' to protect the wearer's modesty. It is not known whether Bywater had a commercial success with the cycling skirt, because although a patent grants monopoly rights for up to 20 years, it does not guarantee that people will buy the product.

## Questions (30 marks; 35 minutes)

**1.** Explain in your own words the meaning of the word patent. (4)

**2.** Explain the likely reasons why Oretta Bywater applied for a patent on the technical innovations within the bicycle dress. (6)

**3.** Do you think Oretta is likely to lose out as a result of focusing on the patent application rather than her target market? Justify your answer. (20)

## DATA RESPONSE 2

### Getting started in business – the cronut craze

It's 5 a.m., Soho, Manhattan and dozens of people are already in line. Only 3 hours until the Dominique Ansel bakery opens. Are they looking for work? No, they're queuing for New York's food craze of 2013: the cronut. And when the shop opens they'll happily hand over $10 for a box containing just two of the pastries. It is said that they can be resold at 10 times the retail price, but as each customer is allowed just one box, this would be a hard way to make a living.

The cronut craze started in mid-May 2013 when bloggers spread the word about this new combination of donut and croissant at this new bakery. Baker-proprietor Ansel makes the flaky layers of a croissant into a ring shape, deep-fries it, then inserts patisserie cream and tops it off with a swirl of icing. Only 200 are made each day, so they sell out by just after 9.00 each morning. Ansel is trying to find a way to manufacture the cronut to meet demand throughout America. Until he does, the queues will persist.

Remarkably Ansel has been allowed to trademark the name 'cronut', so although he has many imitators already, the 'doissant', the 'zonut' and the 'dosant' have not been able to convince customers that they are the real thing. This has helped him keep the price at more than double the typical price for a New York pastry.

But are the cronuts any good? College students Danielle Owens and Camara Lewis clearly think so, as they've succeeded six times in queueing and eating the cakes. Each month Dominique Ansel changes the flavour of the pastry crème filling, to encourage repeat purchase. The *Financial Times* reports that, 'The deeply buttery pastry is wonderful, crispy and stacked high with greedy, messy-to-eat layers; the

lemon-maple cream is pleasingly sickly'. Visitors from around the U.S. make a beeline for the bakery.

Ansel has made a brilliant start so far to his business career. But can he turn the cronut into a nationwide success?

**Figure 83.4** The public are crazy about cronuts

## Questions (35 marks; 40 minutes)

**1.** Outline two entrepreneurial characteristics shown by Ansel in starting up his bakery. (4)

**2.** Explain the benefits to the Dominique Ansel Bakery of trademarking the cronut name. (6)

**3.** Analyse whether Dominique Ansel has spotted a gap in the market or developed an innovative product or process. (9)

**4.** Evaluate the factors that may determine whether Ansel succeeds in developing a profitable business nationally. (16)

## C. Extend your understanding

1. The prices charged for cancer drug treatments can be as high as £10,000 a month. The direct production costs would be no more than £10-£15. To what extent would you agree with critics who say it's time to scrap patent laws? (25)

2. As shown in Figure 83.1, the UK lags behind global rivals in its patent applications. To what extent do you agree that the government should work harder to encourage companies to apply for more patents as part of a strategy to boost manufacturing in the UK? (25)

# Chapter 84 Reasons for trading internationally

**Linked to:** Changes in the political and legal environment, Chapter 64; The impact of government policy, Chapter 65; The impact of changes in the economic environment, Chapter 66; Globalisation and emerging economies, Chapter 67; Competitive advantage, Chapter 76; Growth and retrenchment, Chapter 78.

## Definition

International trade occurs when a firm either buys goods or services from another business operating abroad, or sells its products to an overseas buyer.

## 84.1 The reasons for targeting, operating in and trading with international markets

The majority of firms in Britain are small, and may have no direct involvement in international trade. For example, corner shops, hairdressers, taxi-drivers and the local Indian restaurant sell all their output to customers living locally. Unsurprisingly, these services are not exported. These businesses are unlikely to directly import either. Even the Indian restaurant is more likely to buy from a British wholesaler than directly from a supplier in India.

Manufacturers, big retail chains and firms that sell specialised services such as law, accountancy, banking and management consultancy are more likely to consider international trade as a viable option. The motivations include:

1. **To improve profitability**

   Profits can be enhanced by either increasing revenues or by reducing costs. International trade can help a firm to achieve both of these things. For example, a supermarket chain might currently buy most of its meat from UK farmers. To reduce costs, the supermarket might consider replacing domestic suppliers with cheaper imported meat. If costs can be reduced, without consumers noticing a drop in product quality, profit margins will rise. Some firms that produce a high quality premium product might be interested in exporting because they believe that affluent consumers abroad will be willing to pay a higher price. For example, up to 90 per cent of the clams, cockles and shrimps harvested from Morecambe Bay (Lancashire) are exported to France, Holland and Spain where premium quality shellfish is highly prized and thus fetches a higher price.

2. **To grow**

   Some goods and services are bought regularly such as toothpaste, pints of beer and baked beans. Producers of these products can expect steady revenues once brand loyalty has been achieved because consumers need to repeat purchase. This is not the case for manufactured goods like cars, smartphones and tablet computers. When a successful must-have new product is launched sales will tend to grow quickly. However, the durability of most modern manufactured goods can work against the producer. Markets for manufactured products become saturated when all those who want a product already own one. When this happens sales fall as only those who need to replace their existing product will need to buy. If a firm wants to continue growing they may consider exporting their product to a country whose domestic market has yet to reach its saturation point.

3. **To reduce risk by diversifying**

   Economies do not grow at a steady rate. During booms demand rises as wages and incomes grow. During recessions the opposite happens and profits usually fall. Countries do not always experience booms and recessions at the same time; therefore it makes sense for firms to consider selling their product in different countries. If sales in the Eurozone fall they could be offset by rising demand from China, which may be enjoying a boom.

## 84.2 Influences on buying, selling and producing abroad

### Demographic factors

Demographic factors, such as the size of a country's population, can affect a firm's decision to trade internationally. For example, in countries such as Italy and Spain the population is declining, because the birth rate has fallen to a level that is not high enough to replace the number of people who die each year. To offset this adverse demographic trend an Italian company could try to export its product to countries such as India and Brazil which are experiencing population growth. The age distribution of a country's population can also affect willingness to engage in foreign trade. The UK's population is ageing, which means the market for health care in Britain looks set to grow. This explains why many American health care companies are keen to bid for NHS health care contracts.

### Exchange rates

Most countries have their own currency. So when these countries trade with each other they need to buy and sell each other's currency. For example, when a UK car dealer buys BMWs from Germany they have to sell pounds in order to buy the euros that they need to pay BMW. Exchange rates can affect a firm's willingness to engage in international trade because they can have a major bearing on profitability. The exchange rate measures the price of a currency in terms of another. For many years German companies benefitted from a weak euro, which made their exports seem relatively cheap. This encouraged German companies to grow by selling their product abroad.

**Figure 84.1** Logic chain: the effects of a weak currency on German exports

## 84.3 Methods of entering international markets

### Export

Some firms choose to enter an international market by exporting. An export is a product that is made domestically but sold abroad. The main advantage of exporting is that it does not require expensive new factories to be built in the overseas market that is to be supplied. Indeed, firms that are suffering from low capacity utilisation can use export markets to lower unit costs by raising capacity utilisation.

**Real business**

*Little Valley Brewery*

The Little Valley Brewery was set up in Hebden Bridge in West Yorkshire in 2005 by a Dutch immigrant, Wim van der Spek and his English partner Sue Cooper. The company brews a range of distinctive organic ales and lagers. Like many other small firms the biggest problem Little Valley has had to overcome has been poor distribution. These days, most beer in Britain is sold through the big five supermarket chains. To stand a chance of growing, Little Valley had to persuade one of the supermarkets to stock their product. For several years the brewery struggled because the only places that were prepared to stock its products were a handful of local pubs and specialist shops. In 2010 the business decided to change its distribution strategy. The partners approached an agent who had contacts with two of Finland's biggest supermarket chains. The beer sold well in a test market and both K-Market and S-Market agreed to stock their full range of beers in all their supermarkets. Little Valley's products continue to sell well in Finland. In more recent times the company has begun exporting to other Nordic countries. This required a new £250,000 plant which expanded capacity five-fold when it opened in 2014. Most of the beer produced by Little Valley is now shipped over 1,000 miles to be sold to beer enthusiasts in Finland, Sweden, Norway and Denmark. In 2013 the company's turnover rose by over 50 per cent to just under £500,000, helped hugely by export sales.

'JCB exports 75 per cent of our products...offering employees exciting opportunities to work in our international locations.' JCB website

**Figure 84.2** The Little Valley Brewery found success in exporting

## Direct investment

Direct investment enables a firm to supply an overseas market without the need to export to it. Instead of producing a product domestically and then transporting it to be sold overseas, the product in question is produced and sold abroad. A good example of direct investment was the decision by Tata (the Indian company which owns Jaguar Land Rover) to open up a giant new £1 billion factory near Shanghai in 2015 to produce its Evoque car. China is the world's biggest car market, and Jaguar Land Rover has been popular with China's huge emerging middle class. In 2014 the company sold 122,000 cars in China, an increase of 28 per cent on the previous year. By 2020 Tata expects the Chinese luxury car market to double to 2.5 million cars per year. Therefore, it makes sense to supply Chinese demand from a factory based in the same country, in order to minimise transport costs and to avoid paying China's high import tariffs (taxes).

## Licensing

A licence is a document that gives the holder the legal right to produce a patented or copyrighted product that was created by another firm in return for a royalty (an agreed percentage of the revenue, for example 5 per cent). Setting up a factory abroad to supply an overseas market domestically is usually expensive and will take time. A faster and cheaper option is to find a local supplier with spare production capacity that is willing to supply your product in their market under a local licensing agreement. This method has been used by Volkswagen to sell its famous 'Beetle' car in kit format, to be assembled under licence in countries such as Mexico and Brazil.

## Alliances

An alliance or joint venture is a strategic partnership between two companies. The companies that form the alliance agree to co-operate in a limited area of

their business for mutual benefit. Unlike a merger, the companies forming the alliance retain their own separate legal identity. In the aviation business a number of airlines have used strategic alliances to cut the costs of operating a broader network of less popular routes in Europe. A good example is Oneworld, an alliance between 15 airlines, including British Airways. Under the agreement members of the alliance agree to share maintenance facilities at airports, rather than each airline building and operating their own. This cuts operating costs. In addition members of the same alliance run flights in cooperation with each other. A passenger might book a flight to Helsinki with British Airways but end up on a Finnair flight to the same destination. This enables airlines to advertise a more frequent and hence attractive timetable of flights without reducing capacity utilisation to a level that is uneconomic.

'We built an 80-dealer network with very strong input from Chinese partners.' Bob Grace, president of Jaguar Land Rover China.

## 84.4 Reasons for producing more and sourcing more resources abroad

### Differences in operating costs

Some firms opt to relocate production to another country in anticipation of lower costs. This might be due to lower wages, rents, taxes or more relaxed environmental regulations that are cheaper to comply with. This is what James Dyson did with his vacuum cleaner business. The company began by making all its products in Britain from its factory in Wiltshire. Then in 2002 Dyson announced that it would close down this factory, making 800 British workers redundant. He wanted to transfer production to a new factory in Malaysia where costs were lower. At the time research by the Economist Intelligence Unit revealed the following:

**Table 84.1** Comparison of operating costs

|  | Cost of manufacturing labour per hour | Cost of office space per square metre a year |
|---|---|---|
| Britain | £9 | £114 |
| Malaysia | £3 | £38 |

### Distance

To make foreign trade viable the extra profits gained must be sufficient to offset transport costs. This is particularly true if the product being imported or exported is relatively bulky and hence expensive to transport relative to its price. This explains why soft drinks manufacturers usually decide against supplying foreign markets from domestic production facilities. Instead, the more profitable option is to avoid punitive transport costs by allowing the drinks to be produced under licence by a local partner.

## Trading blocs

Some countries try to encourage greater cross-border trade by agreeing to abolishing tariffs and quotas on each other's products. The establishment of new or the expansion of existing trading blocs can cause some firms to consider producing more, or sourcing more resources abroad. For example, American multinationals such as IBM, Pfizer, Dell and Intel all have factories in Ireland. It is doubtful that this inward investment into Ireland would have happened without Ireland being a member of the European Union. From their bases in Ireland these American-owned companies can supply the whole of Europe without having to pay the EU's external tariffs.

## 84.5 Offshoring and reshoring

Offshoring occurs when a firm transfers production, or a back-office function, such as IT, from a facility based in the company's home country to a new facility abroad. The motives for offshoring include minimising transport costs,

access to cheap labour and avoiding tax or expensive environmental or labour laws. Offshoring can cause bad publicity because it inevitably leads to job losses.

'This should not be about a race to the bottom.'
Alexis Herman, former US Secretary of State for Labour

Reshoring is an admission that offshoring has failed. It describes a situation where a business closes down its overseas facilities, bringing the work that used to be done abroad back home. There are several reasons why firms might choose to reshore. First, sales could be suffering due to declining product quality or customer service problems. Second, the decision to reshore might have been prompted by a desire to make a supply chain more compact in order to reduce lead time. Inditex, the Spanish company that owns the fashion retailer Zara, used to make most of its clothes in factories in Asia where wages were low. Then in the 1990s they changed strategy and began to reshore production back to Spain. The decision to reshore has worked well for Zara because the increase in labour costs has been more than offset by greater production flexibility which has enabled the company to operate on a just-in-time basis, reducing stock holding costs. Its new strategy helped Zara grow into the world's biggest clothing retailer.

## Five Whys and a How

| Question | Answer |
|---|---|
| Why might a domestic recession influence a firm's desire to trade internationally? | Countries are not always in recession at the same time. Falling domestic demand could be offset by rising demand from an export market that is enjoying a boom |
| Why might a firm consider the exchange rate before trying to export? | A strong currency makes it harder for firms to export because it makes the product more expensive to foreign buyers |
| Why might a firm choose to export a product, rather than selling it domestically? | Consumers abroad might be willing to pay higher prices, more than compensating for the shipping costs associated with exporting |
| Why might a firm choose to supply an overseas market by direct investment, rather than by exporting? | By operating inside a foreign market it should be possible to avoid import tariffs. Transport costs will also be lower |
| Why might a manufacturer have to consider exporting in order to maintain high rates of growth? | Domestic markets eventually become saturated when everybody who might want to buy your product already owns one. Exporting to a new unsaturated export market should help the firm to grow again |
| How might a firm decide whether it should outsource its production? | By comparing the various costs of operating at home and abroad. Once other factors, such as tax and transport costs, have been considered most firms will choose to manufacture in the lowest cost location |

## Evaluation: Reasons for trading internationally

It could be argued that the importance of international trade is affected by a company's location. Businesses based in countries that have relatively small populations need to sell their products abroad in order to operate at a scale that is big enough for the firm to be competitive. Alpro is a Belgian company that makes soy-based food and drinks that appeal to a niche market of health-conscious consumers. The population of Belgium is only 11 million, therefore, to achieve meaningful growth Alpro had to look outside Belgium for most of its growth. In 2014 Alpro sold £74 million of its soya milk in the UK alone.

For a country such as Britain, exports are also hugely important. Companies such as Rolls Royce aero-engines, JCB excavators and James Dyson cannot survive on the UK market alone. The income generated would not be enough to fund the investment in R&D needed to keep pushing technology forwards. Ultimately, then, the reason for trading internationally is survival. Without overseas sales few British manufacturers would survive for long.

## Key terms

**Disposable income:** is the amount of money that households have left for discretionary spending once fixed outgoings such as housing costs, debt repayments and other fixed outgoings are subtracted.

**Tariffs:** are taxes that apply to imports only. Tariffs increase the price of imports, diverting demand towards domestically produced substitutes that are now cheaper in relative terms.

**Quotas:** this is an annual physical limit on the volume of a particular good that is allowed to be imported into a country. Once a quota has been filled, consumers no longer have a choice: if they want to buy the product in question they must buy it from a domestic supplier.

**Royalty:** a payment received by the owner of a patent or copyright. Usually the royalty is a fixed percentage of sales revenue.

**Lead time:** the time taken by a firm to get a product into the customer's hands once an order has been placed.

## Workbook

### A. Revision questions

(45 marks; 40 minutes)

1. Identify two examples of British services that are sold abroad. (2)

2. Topshop recently opened two stores in America.
   a) Explain two possible reasons for this decision. (8)
   b) Explain why Topshop's international expansion might fail. (4)

3. The Little Valley Brewery recently began selling its range of beers in Hong Kong. Unlike many other brewers Little Valley decided to supply its new overseas market by exporting, rather than by seeking out a local partner who would produce their product under licence.
   a) What is meant by the term 'licence'? (2)
   b) Explain two possible reasons why Little Valley decided against licensing in favour of exporting to Hong Kong. (8)

   c) Little Valley sells its award-winning Hebden Wheat beer direct from its website to British consumers for £33 per case. Assuming that Little Valley want to generate the same revenue per unit in their export markets, calculate how much they would have to charge in Hong Kong assuming an exchange rate of £1:13 Hong Kong dollars. (3)

4. a) According to Table 84.1, in percentage terms how much lower were manufacturing wages in Malaysia than in Britain? (3)
   b) In addition to lower costs outline two other reasons that might explain Dyson's decision to offshore its manufacturing to Malaysia. (6)
   c) German manufacturers like BMW and Mercedes have decided against offshoring and continue to manufacture their products in Germany despite relatively high German wages. Analyse how firms such as BMW might manage to pay high wages but retain their international competitiveness. (9)

# B. Revision exercises

## DATA RESPONSE

### Reshoring: Bringing jobs back to the UK from abroad

A number of British firms are moving their production operations back to Britain, often from the Far East. One of the companies doing this is Symington's, who make Ragu pasta sauce and Pot Noodle. Both products used to be made in two factories in China. However, in 2013 the company cancelled its Chinese contracts and reshored both products to a brand-new British factory located near Leeds. According to a spokesman:

'We decided to do this because we knew that we could supply retailers more quickly if we produced noodles in Leeds. We are proud of the fact that we're creating manufacturing jobs in Leeds.'

The decision to reshore should enable the company to offer their customers greater flexibility – 'when retailers need more stock they do not want to wait weeks for a container ship to crawl across the sea, or to pay for the associated transport costs'. The resulting drop in lead time should enable retailers to operate with lower stock levels, without running the risk of losing out on sales due to stock shortages.

Low wages used to be a source of competitive advantage for Chinese firms. However wages in China have been rising at a rate of over 10 per cent per year over the last decade. Over the same period, once inflation has been taken into account, UK workers have seen their pay fall. According to Symington's business development manager, Henrik Pade:

'We can produce for roughly the same cost today in Yorkshire as we can out of China. If you go back in time, it would have been 30-35 per cent less in the heartland of China's factories in the Pearl River Delta.'

Some UK firms are still heading overseas to make the most of market opportunities in growing economies. However, if reshoring continues, more manufacturing jobs will be returned to Britain, meaning fewer imports, more exports and a stronger economy.

Sources: adapted from *Making it in Leeds* (14 March 2013) and *The Yorkshire Post* (7 March 2013)

### Questions (50 marks; 60 minutes)

1. Define the term reshoring. (2)

2. Explain two possible reasons why manufacturing wages in China have been growing more rapidly than in Britain. (8)

3. Explain how Symington's decision to reshore production might benefit the retailers who choose to sell the company's products. (4)

4. To what extent might Symington's decision to reshore production create a marketing advantage for the company? (16)

5. How important do you think the decision to reshore production might be for Symington's stakeholders? Justify your viewpoint. (20)

# C. Extend your understanding

1. To what extent would you agree with the proposition that: 'In today's globalised world all firms must engage in foreign trade if they are to grow and prosper'. (25)

2. By April 2015, despite its huge success in the UK, clothes retailer Primark had still not opened its first shop in China. To what extent do you think Primark's long-term success depends on trading internationally? (25)

**Linked to:** The impact of strategic decision-making on functional decision-making, Chapter 55; Changes in the political and legal environment, Chapter 64; The impact of government policy, Chapter 65; The impact of changes in the economic environment, Chapter 66; The impact of social change, Chapter 68; The competitive environment, Chapter 71; Strategic direction: Ansoff's matrix, Chapter 75; China and India, Chapter 86; Managing international business, Chapter 88.

### Definition

Market attractiveness describes the likely profits that might be available to a firm that is willing to enter a particular market or industry. An attractive market is one where it is relatively easy to make good profits and to achieve rapid rates of sales growth.

## 85.1 What is the point of assessing market attractiveness?

Well-managed firms are keen to assess a market's attractiveness before entering it: collecting the data needed to make an assessment of market attractiveness might be expensive. However, it is still cheaper to do the research rather than to enter a new market blind and suffer losses when the new venture fails. Companies often face a choice between big, established markets and less developed but faster-growing ones. In 2014, New Look chose to enter the fashion clothing market in China while Topshop opened stores in America. Both believed their chosen market to be attractive – but perhaps with different assessments of risk and reward.

Some firms who are already operating in an overseas market might also want to carry out regular evaluations of market attractiveness because things can change. A market that was once considered to be attractive might now be considered to be unattractive. This could be because new entrants have joined the market, making it more competitive than it used to be. Alternatively,

the problem could be that consumer tastes in this market have moved on, which has led to the good or service entering the decline phase of its product life cycle. In both cases the wise thing to do following the completion of the market attractiveness assessment might be for the firm to decide that it would be wise to exit this market to avoid losses.

### Real business

#### Russia

At the start of 2014 Russia seemed set to have another year of prosperity based on the country's buoyant oil industry. Then came a diplomatic row with its western neighbour Ukraine which led to economic **sanctions** from the West – followed by a startling collapse in the global oil price. This undermined the value of the rouble, which meant that imported goods were suddenly far more expensive to Russian shoppers. New Look responded by withdrawing completely from a country it had entered just two years before. The company decided that the short-term pain felt by the Russian consumer would last long enough to make it hard to make their stores profitable. Russia looked attractive in 2012, but not in 2014.

## 85.2 Factors that affect market attractiveness

### Market size and growth rate

The bigger the market the greater the potential profits available, making bigger markets more attractive to firms than smaller markets. An important factor that affects the size of a country's markets is population. There are over 320 million people living in America. According to Euromonitor International the average American spends £35 per year on chocolate, which means that the US chocolate market is worth £11 billion per year. If a new entrant can gain just a 1 per cent share of this giant market and achieve an operating profit margin of 10 per cent it would stand to make annual revenues of £110 million and a profit of £11 million. Per person, the British eat more chocolate than the Americans. However, despite this the British chocolate market is far smaller, and hence less attractive: in 2014 total UK chocolate sales were £2.5 billion. A firm achieving a 1 per cent share of the UK market, earning an operating margin of 10 per cent would generate a turnover of £25 million and a profit of £2.5 million.

Markets that are currently very small, but which are starting to grow rapidly, can also be viewed as attractive. They are potential 'rising stars'. Until recently, most people in China and India did not really eat chocolate. However, the emergence of a rapidly growing middle class in both countries has sent sales soaring from a low base. During the period from 2011 to 2014 sales of chocolate in India and China grew at annual rates of 17.6 per cent and 8.8 per cent respectively. In contrast, American chocolate sales only grew by 1.8 per cent per year over the same period. Companies such as Cadbury have been increasing factory capacity in India. They expect the Indian chocolate market to grow as the population adopts Western lifestyles, and thus Western per capita levels of chocolate consumption.

Table 85.1 Comparing the market size for chocolate

| Country | Annual per capita chocolate consumption (kg) in 2014 | Population in 2014 (millions) | Market size by volume (kg millions) |
|---|---|---|---|
| Brazil | 1.6 | 203 | 324.8 |
| Russia | 5.3 | 142 | 752.6 |
| India | 0.1 | 1,236 | 123.6 |
| China | 0.2 | 1,356 | 271.2 |

Source: www.confectionerynews.com/markets/chocolate-consumption-by-country-2014

How large will these markets become if chocolate consumption grows in Brazil, Russia, India and China, and reaches the UK average of eight kilograms per year?

'India offers exciting business opportunities owing to the growth in corporate travel and a significant middle-class population waiting to explore the world.' Lloyd Dorfman, founder, Travelex Group

## Economic factors

In addition to the size of a country's population, market attractiveness also depends on the purchasing power of the local population. This is determined primarily by average incomes, adjusted for differences in the costs of living. The best measure of this is GDP per capita (per person) at PPP (Purchasing Power Parity). The selected figures below give

a clear indication of the strong correlation between annual income and car purchasing, when you compare Column 1 with Column 4 in Table 85.2

Table 85.2 Purchasing power

| | GDP per capita at PPP US$s 2014 | New car purchases (market size 2014) | Population size 2014 | New car purchases per thousand people (2014) |
|---|---|---|---|---|
| USA | $53,000 | 16,400,000 | 318,892,103 | 51.43 |
| UK | $37,500 | 2,476,435 | 63,742,977 | 38.85 |
| Brazil | $12,100 | 2,504,161 | 202,656,788 | 12.36 |
| India | $4,100 | 2,570,531 | 1,236,344,631 | 2.08 |

There are other economic factors to consider, however, such as tax levels. In many Scandinavian countries taxes on both incomes and goods are relatively high. So despite high wages the domestic markets for non-essentials such as restaurant meals are smaller than they otherwise would have been. According to Euromonitor International the average person in Denmark spends less than £550 per year on restaurant meals. In Britain the same figure is £900 per year, even though average per capita income in Denmark is substantially higher than in Britain.

When assessing market attractiveness firms also try to predict the future state of a country's economy. Firms are particularly interested in forecasts of variables such as economic growth, inflation and unemployment that can have a major bearing on future spending levels, and hence market attractiveness. However, it is important to realise that these economic forecasts can sometimes be wrong.

In the lead-up to the financial crisis of 2008 many of Britain's markets must have looked very attractive. During this period Britons went on an unsustainable spending binge that was financed by cheap credit, rather than by wages. Many firms that based their assessments of market attractiveness on extrapolation were badly caught out, because the future is not always the same as the past. According to figures released by the charity Credit Action in January 2014, UK household debt now stands at £54,197 and is rising again. Markets in countries such as Hong Kong and Singapore that have relatively low levels of household debt will always look more attractive than markets in places like Britain where debt levels are high. In Hong Kong and Singapore only a very small proportion of income is wasted on paying debt interest, leaving more income available for spending.

'There are over 200 million illiterate women in India. This low literacy negatively impacts not just their lives but also their families' and the country's economic development.' Sachin Tendulkar, India's most-revered cricketer

## The regulatory environment

Governments use laws and regulations to try to dissuade firms from taking actions that are highly profitable but which might leave society as a whole worse off. For example, in the absence of environmental regulations some firms might be tempted to boost their profits by dumping their waste products into a local river, rather than paying for the expensive machinery needed to treat the waste. In the absence of labour market regulations some entrepreneurs might be prepared to use child labour to boost their profits. And, if there was no consumer protection legislation, other firms might try to increase their revenues by over-charging their customers, or by duping consumers into buying an unsuitable product using advertisements that make false product claims. Some firms prefer to operate in markets where there is minimal government intervention. They prefer to avoid minimum wages, maximum prices and environmental regulations that might require them to set up recycling or carbon offsetting schemes that may lead to lower short-run profits.

## Technological development

The attractiveness of a market can also depend on access to specialised components or infrastructure needed to supply a good or service. For example, the business model of a company such as Netflix which sells film downloads depends heavily on the number of people who have access to a high quality broadband Internet connection.

## Political and social factors

Some governments set out to make their markets more appealing by adopting business friendly policies. The goal is to attract foreign direct investment, which should help the economy to grow: a good example was the Irish government's decision to slash the rate of corporation tax (a tax on profits) from 32 per cent in 1998 to 12.5 per cent by 2003. This decision prompted American multinationals such as Dell and HP to pull out of Britain, where the rate of corporation tax was 40 per cent, and instead supply their European customers from a base in Ireland. The British government responded by cutting its corporation tax rate.

In 2013 the pressure group UK Uncut revealed that big corporations such as Vodafone, Amazon, Google and Starbucks had avoided tax in Britain. For example, in May 2013 the BBC reported that Starbucks has paid no corporation tax at all in the last year, despite achieving UK sales of £400 million. From the shareholders' point of view the opportunity to legally avoid tax in this manner has no doubt added to the appeal of doing business in Britain. However, the general public has suffered as a consequence, because public services

have had to be cut in line with lower tax revenue. Light-touch British banking regulations have also pulled foreign banks and hedge funds into the City of London because they can do things here that are illegal elsewhere.

The level of corruption within a country can also affect market attractiveness, though recent research has found no correlation between corruption and economic stagnation. It is important to recognise that all societies have a degree of corruption, but the scale varies notably in different countries, as shown in Figure 85.1.

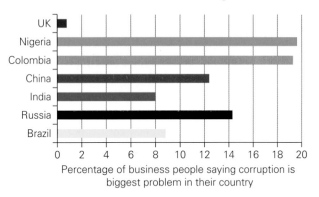

Source: World Competitiveness Report 2015

**Figure 85.1** Corruption: most problematic factor in doing business

'Corruption, embezzlement, fraud, these are all characteristics which exist everywhere. It is regrettably the way human nature functions, whether we like it or not. What successful economies do is keep it to a minimum. No one has ever eliminated any of that stuff.' Alan Greenspan, former U.S. Director of the Federal Reserve Bank

## Quality of local infrastructure

Infrastructure is a term that is used to describe the basic facilities needed by households and firms. Examples of this shared social capital include road and railways and reliable national systems for the supply of telecommunication, electricity, sanitation and fresh drinking water. The quality of a nation's infrastructure is an important factor that affects the attractiveness of that country's markets. For example, in Nigeria the supply of electricity is very unreliable. For firms that use modern machinery powered by electricity, regular power cuts result in regular production stoppages, which pushes productivity down and unit costs up.

The quality of a country's schools and universities also influences market attractiveness. In countries where educational standards are low, businesses will have to compensate for these shortcomings by spending more on staff training.

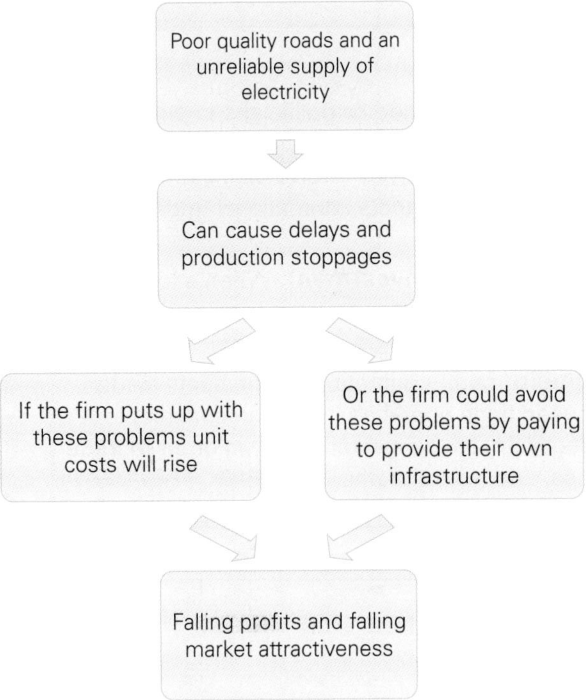

Poor quality roads and an unreliable supply of electricity

↓

Can cause delays and production stoppages

↓

If the firm puts up with these problems unit costs will rise

Or the firm could avoid these problems by paying to provide their own infrastructure

↓

Falling profits and falling market attractiveness

**Figure 85.2** Logic chain: impact of poor infrastructure on market attractiveness

## Evaluation: Attractiveness of international markets

Market attractiveness is determined by a host of factors. It can be difficult to assess market attractiveness because some variables, which influence attractiveness, such as corruption are extremely difficult to objectively measure. At the same time, in most markets some factors will be favourable, while others might be unfavourable, which could make it difficult to assess overall market attractiveness. For example, would the benefits of a bigger market make it more attractive than a smaller, but less competitive market? There is also a danger in viewing market attractiveness as an external factor that is beyond a firm's control. In practice big multinationals are not always put off from trading in markets that might be initially viewed as being unattractive. This is because some aspects of market attractiveness can be changed via political lobbying. In return for generous political donations, local politicians might make it relatively easy for a multinational which wants to set up in their country to water-down or to avoid taxes and regulations. Indeed, some of the most attractive markets of all are only accessible to firms who have cultivated close relationships with politicians who award lucrative public sector monopoly contracts to private suppliers.

## Five Whys and a How

| Question | Answer |
|---|---|
| Why might it be better to enter a developing market than a highly established one? | In established, saturated markets there is rarely room for new niches, whereas these emerge in growing, younger markets |
| Why might the combination of inflation and wage freezes compromise market attractiveness? | If wages do not grow in line with inflation living standards will fall. This will inevitably lead to falling spending levels, which will make it less attractive to sell luxury goods |
| Why might the level of competition within a market affect the attractiveness of the market? | As competition increases market attractiveness tends to fall because firms will probably have to offer lower prices, which may lower profit margins |
| Why does the quality of a country's infrastructure matter? | If the quality of infrastructure provided by the state is poor, firms will have to provide what is needed themselves at their own expense |
| Why is the UK an attractive market for American multinationals that want to export their product to the UK and other EU countries? | Britain is a member of the EU. By supplying from a base inside the EU the American firm can avoid tariffs. The British also speak American, making communication easier |
| How might a company set about assessing a market's attractiveness? | By using secondary market research, obtained from commercially available market intelligence reports published by companies such as Euromonitor International |

# Workbook

## A. Revision questions

(35 marks; 35 minutes)

1.  **a)** What is meant by the term 'market attractiveness'? (2)

    **b)** Briefly explain two factors that affect market attractiveness. (6)

2.  **a)** Using the data from Table 85.1, which BRIC country had the smallest chocolate market in 2012? (1)

    **b)** Calculate the size of the Chinese chocolate bar market in 2012. How big would it become if Chinese per capita consumption grew to British levels? (5)

    **c)** How much revenue would a chocolate manufacturer make each year if they managed to achieve a 5 per cent share of the Chinese

    chocolate market, assuming that the average price of a 50g chocolate bar sold in China is the equivalent of 50p? (4)

    **d)** Based on a 10 per cent operating profit margin, calculate how much profit the firm would make. (3)

3.  **a)** What is meant by the term 'brand loyalty'? (2)

    **b)** Explain how market attractiveness might be influenced by brand loyalty. (4)

4.  Explain two examples of how unreliable infrastructure might detract from a market's attractiveness. (8)

## B. Revision exercises
### DATA RESPONSE

**Will African Lions follow in the footsteps of Asian Tigers?**

Every year the accountancy firm Ernst & Young produces market attractiveness reports which are used by firms to assess whether it might be financially worthwhile to enter a new market. The country reports produced by Ernst & Young measure market attractiveness by considering factors such as: the quality of a country's infrastructure; the profitability of firms already operating in this country; and the degree of social and political stability.

According to Ernst & Young's 2014 report, the continent of Africa was the world's second highest recipient of foreign direct investment in the last year. Western multinationals are investing heavily in the facilities required to extract Africa's oil, gas and minerals. They have also been taking on lucrative government contracts to build new roads, bridges and rail networks. However, Africa's leading investor is China, who in 2012 bought African assets totalling $18.2 billion. Despite the on-going economic crisis in North America and Europe, many African countries have been able to achieve relatively high rates of economic growth. For example, in 2013 the Nigerian economy grew by 5.5 per cent. In 2014 Ernst & Young forecasted that even very poor African countries, such as Rwanda and Sierra Leone would grow by 7.5 per cent and 13.9 per cent respectively. A middle class is developing in richer African countries. A report produced by McKinsey in 2014 predicted that by 2050 there would be an additional 1.4 billion middle class Africans due to a six-fold increase in per capita incomes. In response to these predictions and rapidly growing consumer expenditure, American multinationals such as Domino's pizza, WalMart, Coca-Cola and Marriot hotels have also set up branches in Africa. However, rising demand will also create opportunities for local entrepreneurs who are prepared to compete head-on against the multinationals or more likely by filling market niches that multinationals have ignored or overlooked. In addition to huge untapped resources, an emerging middle class and unsaturated markets, Africa's attractiveness as a location for production is enhanced by improving standards of education and by its relatively young population: facts spotted by car manufacturers, such as Ford, BMW and Toyota who all have factories based in South Africa.

Ernst & Young's report also highlights issues which are detracting from African market attractiveness.

These include poor infrastructure, rising income inequality and conflicts.

## Questions (55 marks; 60 minutes)

1. Explain what a market attractiveness report is, who uses them and why companies like Ernst & Young produce them. (4)

2. Explain two reasons why American and Chinese firms are building roads, bridges and other types of transport infrastructure in Africa. (8)

3. Many African countries have unsaturated markets that are growing rapidly due to rising household incomes.
   a) Explain why unsaturated markets tend to be more attractive than markets that are saturated. (4)
   b) Analyse whether economic growth always increases market attractiveness. (9)

4. Many African countries have relatively young populations. Explain how this factor might add to the attractiveness of countries such as South Africa as locations for foreign direct investment. (6)

5. a) Using examples, explain what is meant by social and political instability. (4)
   b) Explain why social and political instability make markets less attractive. (4)

6. Evaluate whether African governments should relax environmental regulations and offer tax breaks to foreign multinationals that want to invest in their countries. (16)

## C. Extend your understanding

1. Evaluate the possible short-run and long-run implications of tax competitiveness on market attractiveness? (25)

2. Identify and explain the main factors that a soft drinks manufacturer might want to consider when assessing market attractiveness. Discuss which of these factors would be the most and least important. (25)

# Chapter 86 China and India

The specific examples of China and India don't form part of the AQA specification, but are included here in detail to supplement your understanding of international markets.

**Linked to:** The value of SWOT analysis, Chapter 56; Globalisation and emerging economies, Chapter 67; Analysing strategic options, Chapter 72; Attractiveness of international markets, Chapter 85; Managing international business, Chapter 88.

### Definition

As the world's most populous countries and fastest growing of the major economies, China and India are at the heart of the business opportunities offered by developing economies.

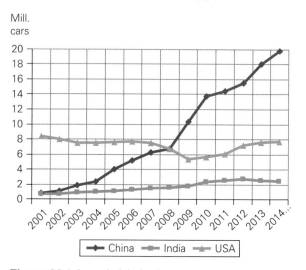

**Figure 86.1** Annual global sales: passenger cars

Source: www.OICA.net

## 86.1 China?

In 2001, investment banks coined the phrase BRICs to sum up the huge growth potential of Brazil, Russia, India and China. In fact the growth in China and India is far, far more significant than in the other two countries. In Brazil a growth rate of 3 per cent is applauded; China sees a growth rate of 7 per cent as a disappointment.

In 1997 the streets of every Chinese city were dominated by bicycles. The private car was still quite rare. Fewer than four households in one thousand owned a car. Yet in 2009 China overtook America to become the world's biggest car market. Since 2009 Jaguar Land Rover has benefited hugely, with sales in China rising from 15,000 in 2009 to over 100,000 in 2014 (at an average price of around £70,000 per car, that represents over £7 billion of sales in China). The boom in China has been incredible.

For more than 25 years the Chinese economy grew at around 10 per cent a year. That is faster than any other major economy in history. In Britain's Industrial Revolution the economy only grew at around 2 to 2.5 per cent a year. And, of course, China is not only remarkable for its rate of growth, but also its population size. This is a country with nearly one-quarter of the world's population. If 1,350 million people have economic wealth, even the United States will have to step back. China is set to become the world's superpower. Or is it…?

'Asia's rise to global economic pre-eminence could see China and India leading the world by 2050.' Price Waterhouse Coopers: *The World in 2050*, published in March 2015

**Figure 86.2** China has emerged as a strong contender for the title of world superpower

20 years there will be far more keen 20-year-olds entering the Indian job market than in China. This is because China has made huge efforts over the past 25 years to curb population growth by pressing its people to have only one child per family. Due to this policy, only 22 per cent of the Chinese population is 18 or under. In India the figure is 35 per cent. Details of the population figures for China and India are given in Table 86.1.

**Table 86.1** China and India: population figures

| | China | India |
|---|---|---|
| Population growth per year (2014) | 0.45% | 1.25% |
| Population level 2013 (UN data) | 1.39 billion | 1.25 billion |
| Population level 2050 (UN est.) | 1.38 billion | 1.62 billion |
| Population 18 and under (2013 data) | 302 million | 435 million |

## 86.2 Or India?

Some argue that India is in an even more powerful position. Although far behind China, its accelerating growth and population may make it the dark horse that eventually wins the prize. India has long been one of the world's poorest countries, yet one of the most populous. At 1,240 million, its position as the world's second-most populated country puts it way ahead of America (in third place with 'only' 320 million).

India's population has two features that China cannot match: it is rising and it is very young. Over the next

## 86.3 Which has been growing faster?

Here the answer is clear. As shown in Figure 86.1, since 1991 the Chinese economy has completely outstripped that of India and managed to overtake first Britain, then Germany and then Japan. This has largely been due to massive increases in 'fixed capital formation'. In the early 1990s the Chinese government started investing heavily in the economy, and started to encourage Western companies to invest as well.

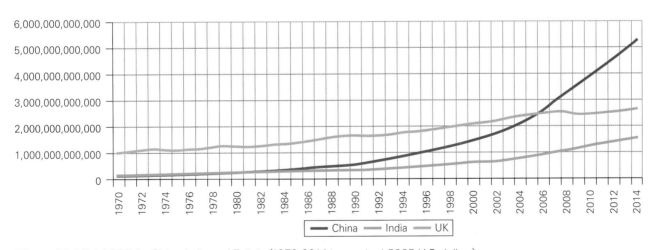

**Figure 86.3** Total GDP for China, India and Britain (1970-2014 in constant 2005 U.S. dollars)

Source: United Nations

Typically, the Western companies invested by building factories (taking advantage of extremely low-cost labour), while the government started building dams (for water and electricity), roads and other forms of infrastructure. Today that government investment is going into housing, railways, schools and hospitals. China is gearing up for continuing success. Figure 86.4 shows that China is now spending more than 40 per cent of its annual output on investing in its future (fixed capital formation). For many years India's investment spending was little higher than in the slow-growth, developed UK. But in 2004-2008 India pushed its capital formation rate up towards the level achieved in China. If India can keep its investment rate above 30 per cent of GDP it should be able to tackle its infrastructure weaknesses and achieve sustained economic growth.

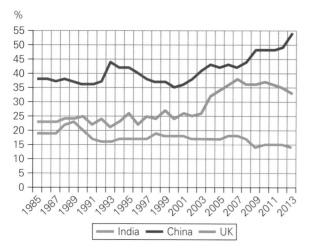

**Figure 86.4** Capital formation in China, India and the UK (1985 to 2013) as a percentage of GDP

Source: World Bank 2014

China's long-term success was largely built on export growth. Originally that was based on incredibly cheap labour (around 10p an hour in 1985-1990) and therefore outstanding cost competitiveness. In 2009, China's exports were seven times higher by value than India's. The recession that followed hit China's exports hard, as Western markets dried up during 2009 and 2010, but China remains the world's largest exporter of manufactured goods. Furthermore its exports contain a bigger proportion of high technology products than the UK, India or (amazingly) the United States (according to World Bank data 2014).

As the table shows, India is a relatively small-scale exporter of goods. At the heart of its commercial success are 'invisible exports' such as software

engineering and running English-speaking call centres. India has two important advantages over China: good English (the global language) and an education system that is excellent at the top end, so it produces many excellent managers and software experts.

**Table 86.2** Visible exports 2013

|  | **$bn** |
| --- | --- |
| China | 2,210 |
| USA | 1,575 |
| Germany | 1,493 |
| UK | 813 |
| India | 313 |

Source: CIA Factbook 2014

The big question now is whether India can sustain its recent success.

## 86.4 Can India grow rapidly and consistently?

India has three key weaknesses in its attempts to keep up with China.

### India's key weaknesses

India's key three weaknesses are set out below.

#### Its poor infrastructure

Underinvestment means that the road system lags behind China's, especially in motorway construction. It is possible that the reason is political. In China the government can dictate to the people that 40+ per cent of spending will be on investment. In India, there is a democratically elected government, and it may be that the public is unwilling to cut back too severely on today's spending, in order to invest in the country's future.

#### The narrow education system

Whereas the literacy level in China is 95 per cent, in India it is only 63 per cent (that is, 37 per cent of the population cannot read or write). Therefore if the growth rate led to job opportunities for a wider range of people, many would be unable to take up the jobs due to illiteracy. At the top end the Indian education system is very strong, but for the mass of the population it is shockingly poor.

#### International trade

Whereas in 2013 China had a current account surplus (more exports than imports) of $183 billion, India had a deficit of $75 billion. This implies that Indian consumers are overspending in relation to the goods foreigners want to buy from India. Balance of payments deficits make it hard for India to keep growing without an inflationary fall in the value of the rupee.

## Inevitable overheating?

This is not an issue of global warming, but of economic performance. In the past, accelerations in India's industrial production have triggered rises in inflation. This has made the Bank of India respond by pushing up interest rates. As a result the growth spurt is choked off. India has consistently had higher levels of inflation than China. Therefore there must be doubts about India's ability to match China's remarkable growth rates.

'While Chinese companies succeeded because of the government, Indian companies succeeded despite the government!' Girija Pande, Indian contributor to *Forbes* magazine

### Real business

#### Cat versus JCB

Thirty years ago, America's construction equipment giant Caterpillar (Cat) started investing heavily in China. Today its huge strength in China underpins its position as world number one. At much the same time, Britain's JCB chose to invest in India. Today its 50 per cent market share in India is crucial in securing JCB's 12 per cent share of the world market for construction equipment.

Now, both Cat and JCB are following similar strategies: build on strength, while dipping a toe in the weaker market. In 2014 Caterpillar announced that they had just opened their twenty-sixth factory in China, employing 15,000 staff. Caterpillar boss Doug Oberhelman said in March 2014 that 'in China we're in the lead position by a fairly nice margin'.

At the same time JCB announced that it would be opening a $100 million factory complex in Jaipur – the company's fourth factory in India. JCB is also investing cautiously in new capacity in China, just as Cat is doing the same in India.

As things stand, it looks as if Caterpillar made the better bet, 30 years ago. Happily for JCB, even if it never breaks into China, its strength in India guarantees it a strong position in the world market for the foreseeable future.

## 86.5 Can China outstrip America?

Some have expressed doubts about the sustainability of China's growth. They suggest that export growth must flatten out as Chinese wage rates incease. At present fast-food and factory workers in Beijing earn £1 – £1.20 per hour, so there is some way to go! In any case, this view assumes that China will remain a producer of low-cost items. In fact, in 2013 China was the world's biggest manufacturer of cars and produced 48.5 per cent of the world's steel (Japan came second with 6.9 per cent). Nevertheless, it is true to say that China will lose some low-cost production. For example, minimum wage rates in India are as low as 25p per hour. So India can already undercut China.

So can China's GDP overtake America's? Yes, without doubt. The CIA's figures show that China's total GDP for 2013 was 80 per cent of America's. Given China's more rapid growth, that implies that China should be the world's number 1 economy (at purchasing power parity, or PPP) by 2017. World Bank figures suggested in May 2014 that China might overtake the US GDP total by the end of the year. The differences are to do with the difficulty of setting the right figures for PPP adjustments.

What is not in doubt is that China's growth has serious environmental implications. There is no doubt that pollution is dreadful in industrial towns such as Linfen, and poor in cities such as Beijing and Shanghai. Nevertheless, China is investing heavily in cleaning up its rivers and air, and the country makes a relatively modest contribution to greenhouse gases (per capita). Table 86.3 shows the major contributors to global $CO_2$ emissions. Generally, the richer the country, the higher the total of $CO_2$ emissions.

**Table 86.3** Global carbon dioxide emissions

| | 2014 Tonnes of $CO_2$ per head per annum | 2014 Total $CO_2$ tonnes (millions) | Est 2019 Total $CO_2$ tonnes (millions) |
|---|---|---|---|
| India | 1.5 | 1,808 | 2,046 |
| China | 7.2 | 9,595 | 11,302 |
| Japan | 9.8 | 1,245 | 1,229 |
| USA | 16.5 | 5,261 | 5,441 |
| Russia | 11.5 | 1,633 | 1,732 |
| World | 4.7 | 33,186 | 35,998 |

Source: Energy Information Administration, 2014

As China grows, its emissions will continue to rise. This is why emissions in developed countries will have to be cut if there is to be a chance of stopping the global figure from growing further.

'New car sales in China are forecast to contribute 35 per cent of the world's car market growth until 2020. Still, car penetration (per household) will reach only about 15 per cent by 2020.' McKinsey & Company

## 86.6 What opportunities are there for British business?

Every director of every public company knows that she or he must have a strategy for China and India. Tesco has its investment in Chinese superstores and in 2014 invested £85 million in a joint venture into the grocery market in India. UK-owned Costa Coffee had 250 stores in China at the start of 2014 and plans to have 600 open by the end of 2016. Despite some successes in China, the value of German exports to China is more than five times the value of Britain's; even France outsells Britain by 2:1. Of all China's imports, Britain supplies little more than 1 per cent.

What about India? Britain ran India (as a colony) for 150 years, so there must be trade links remaining. Indeed in 2002 the British share of Indian imports was 4.96 per cent (about in line with Britain's share of world trade). By 2013, however, the British share had fallen to 3.2 per cent – half the level achieved by Germany. Despite this decline, Britain still has distinct advantages over France, Italy and Spain. The need is for British businesses to commit themselves to an effective strategy for India.

### Evaluation: China and India

China has been growing at a rate of over 7 per cent for 30 years and looks capable of doing the same in the future. It may be short of younger people, but it has over 400 million people working on the land, many of whom would be pleased to earn higher wages in a factory. India also has good prospects, though it is less clear that it will be able to deliver high growth year in year out. It needs huge investments in education and infrastructure, but the Indian government is unwilling, or unable, to provide this. In this two-horse race, the one to back is China.

Nevertheless, for an individual business, India may be the better bet. For a young British company lacking export experience, it would probably be easier to break into India than China, if only because there are fewer language and cultural barriers. Above all else, India lacks an effective manufacturing sector, so it may be a perfect place for British manufacturing exports or for setting up new factories. As always, each business case is different.

### Five Whys and a How

| Question | Answer |
|---|---|
| Why has China's growth not led to any world-leading brands? | Perhaps Chinese companies have focused mainly on their home market; or maybe it is struggling to move on from imitating Western products and processes |
| Why have UK firms been so slow to 'get' the China growth story – and therefore seize opportunities? | With impressive exceptions such as Costa, Land Rover and New Look, UK firms seem determined to see more risks than rewards. Lack of long-term thinking? |
| Why has India struggled to keep up with China? | It's been far less welcoming to foreign direct investment, and has had a series of dysfunctional, bureaucratic governments |
| Why doesn't China tackle its gross income inequalities? | For a supposedly communist government, it's odd – but perhaps the wealthy have as much power in China as elsewhere |
| Why has President Xi set lower growth targets for China in future (of 6.5–7.0 per cent)? | He says it's to allow greater priority for air quality and other environmental factors: the growth-at-all-costs phase is over |
| How might India try to boost growth to exceed that of China? | By heavy investment in mass education and in infrastructure |

# Workbook

## A. Revision questions

(34 marks; 35 minutes)

1. Outline two reasons why China's growth prospects may be greater than India's. (4)

2. Outline two reasons why India's growth prospects may be greater than China's. (4)

3. Explain the significance of the figures shown for 'capital formation' in Figure 86.4. (5)

4. Explain what Table 86.2 implies about the relative competitiveness of China vs India in 2013. (4)

5. Outline two reasons why a British retail firm such as Next may choose to invest in China rather than India. (4)

6. Look at Table 86.3 and answer the following questions.

   a) Explain why Russia's environmental record is sometimes criticised, given that its total carbon emissions are 'only' 1633 million tonnes. (4)

   b) America regularly criticises China for its impact on global warming. Analyse this view based on the data provided. (9)

## B. Revision exercises

### DATA RESPONSE 1

**Table 86.4** Grocery outlets in India and China

| Percentage of grocery sales by outlet size | | | |
|---|---|---|---|
| | **India** | **China** | **USA** |
| Hyper/supermarkets | 1.66 | 61.48 | 65.10 |
| Small grocery | 78.91 | 13.35 | 8.12 |
| Other grocery | 3.76 | 19.68 | 19.27 |
| Specialist food/drink | 15.67 | 5.49 | 7.51 |
| (Population) | 1,240 million | 1,350 million | 330 million |

Source: Euromonitor International 2014

Questions (20 marks; 25 minutes)

1. Outline two key differences between grocery distribution in India and China. (4)

2. Assume you are the boss of innocent Drinks, trying to decide whether to launch your fresh-fruit smoothie drinks into India or China. On the basis of the data given in Table 86.4, which country would you target first? Justify your answer. (16)

### DATA RESPONSE 2

#### The growth of the middle market

For many years the big business story in China was the growth of the luxury goods sector. Since late 2012 President Xi has made an impressive stand against corruption in China, which seems to have dampened down spending. This has allowed the biggest story of all to emerge: the rise of the middle market. Think shampoo, chocolate and toilet paper rather than Gucci bags and £50,000 watches. The table below tells the story: static demand for toilet paper in the West (with a little bit of inflation), but surging demand in China and India. In India, though, the 2008 starting point was 1.3 US cents per person per year, which makes it hard to make much of a 76.9 per cent growth rate.

Note that the populations of these four countries are: China 1.355 billion; India 1.24 billion; USA 320 million and the UK 64 million.

**Table 86.5** Growth in the toilet paper market

| $ per capita spending on toilet paper, 2008-2013 | | | | |
|---|---|---|---|---|
| | **China** | **India** | **USA** | **UK** |
| **2008** | 4.38 | 0.013 | 27.69 | 28.13 |
| **2009** | 4.81 | 0.015 | 28.69 | 28.90 |
| **2010** | 5.62 | 0.017 | 28.21 | 29.75 |
| **2011** | 6.81 | 0.020 | 29.24 | 30.12 |
| **2012** | 7.50 | 0.020 | 29.34 | 30.03 |
| **2013** | 8.33 | 0.023 | 29.74 | 29.85 |
| **2008-13 %** | +86.2% | +76.9% | +7.4% | +6.1% |

Source: Euromonitor Reports 2014

**Questions (35 marks; 40 minutes)**

1.  **a)** Calculate the market size for toilet paper in each country in 2008. (3)

    **b)** Calculate the growth in the market between 2008 and 2013 for China, India and the UK. (4)

    **c)** Analyse the conclusions that might be drawn from that data by the chief executive of a UK-based producer of a major brand of toilet paper. (12)

2.  Using extrapolation, evaluate whether India might have better growth prospects than China in the future market for toilet paper. (16)

# DATA RESPONSE 3

## Costa: a middle-market British success story

Perhaps Britain's most successful middle-market brand in China is Costa Coffee. Owners Whitbread took the decision to follow Starbucks into the market for coffee bars in 2006. Although they were many years behind Starbucks (who started in China in 1999, without joint venture partners, and had 250 outlets by 2006) Costa's coffee bars proved profitable from early on. By the end of 2013 Costa had 253 outlets spread over 28 cities, accounting for 10 per cent of all Costa coffee bars worldwide. Starbucks, in the meantime, had raced ahead to 1,017 shops across 60 Chinese cities. This still leaves cities with more than a million inhabitants (bigger than Manchester) with no Western-style coffee bars at all.

Whitbread plc seems careful to hide the turnover and profits of its Chinese outlets, perhaps in part at the behest of its joint venture partner the Yueda Group. The accounts of Starbucks, though, give an idea of the attractions of China as a market. Whereas the gross profit margin of running Starbucks outlets in America in 2013 ran at 21.5 per cent, in China Starbucks made a 35 per cent margin. This is, in part, because it is able to charge higher prices in China than America. As average incomes in China are about a fifth of those in America, this makes a visit to a Western coffee bar a luxury.

Partly because of the high prices, the Chinese drink – on average - only three cups of coffee a year. This compares with 240 cups per person per year globally, and around 600 cups in America. According to Mintel the market for coffee in China has been growing at 30 per cent a year. Rapid growth plus huge upward potential make this a marvellous market to be in.

**Questions (40 marks; 50 minutes)**

1.  With reference to your own research and the item above, evaluate the relative advantages and disadvantages of operating in China through organic growth as compared with opening up a joint venture with a Chinese company. (20)

2.  With reference to your own research and the item above, evaluate whether it is justifiable ethically for a British plc such as Whitbread to commit itself to major development in China. (20)

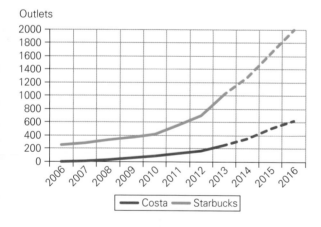

**Figure 86.5** Coffee bar outlets in China

Sources: various including company accounts and media reports

## C. Extend your understanding

1. Sainsbury is considering whether to open its first stores in China or India. To what extent would such a decision be down to intuition compared with scientific management? (25)

2. Having opened eighteen stores in China in 2014, low-cost fashion retailer New Look announced it would open 50 more in 2015. To what extent could it be said that long-term success for New Look in China is inevitable? (25)

# Chapter 87 Targeting overseas markets

**Linked to:** The impact of government policy, Chapter 65; Globalisation and emerging economies, Chapter 67; Strategic direction: Ansoff's matrix, Chapter 75; Methods and types of growth, Chapter 80; Reasons for trading internationally, Chapter 84; China and India, Chapter 86.

## Definition

A multinational is a firm which has its headquarters in one country and branches, manufacturing or assembly plants in others. In other words it is not just an exporter. It has business operations in many countries.

## 87.1 Introduction

Some multinationals are giants. Table 87.1 compares the turnover of several large multinationals with the total output of various entire countries.

**Table 87.1** Comparative size of top five multinational companies and selected national economies

| Country/Company | 2014 GDP/Sales ($ billion) |
|---|---|
| UK | 2,490 |
| Poland | 514 |
| 1. Walmart | 478 |
| 2. Shell | 451 |
| 3. Sinopec-China | 445 |
| 4. Exxon | 394 |
| 5. BP | 379 |
| South Africa | 354 |
| Pakistan | 237 |
| Kenya | 45 |

Source: *Forbes* magazine 2014 and *CIA World Factbook* March 2015

Traditionally, multinationals had their headquarters in Europe, the USA or Japan. Some of their branches or factories would also be located in highly developed economies, but with others in less-developed nations, especially in South America or Asia. Over coming years, an increasing number of multinationals will be based in India or China. Examples may include the Indian companies Tata (owners of Jaguar Land Rover) and Mittal, plus the Chinese giants Lenovo (owners of IBM computers) and Alibaba.

'Multinational corporations do control. They control the politicians. They control the media. They control the pattern of consumption, entertainment, thinking. They're destroying the planet and laying the foundation for violent outbursts and racial division.' Jerry Brown, former Governor of California

## 87.2 Advantages of operating in several countries

### Nearness to local markets

Many multinational expansions are driven by the desire to produce close to the market. Local production facilities will result in lower transport costs and probably more competitive prices. Multinationals may also set up local production facilities in order to avoid import tariffs or taxes. Producing in the country for which the products are required means that no products are being imported. The multinational is able to avoid any import restrictions imposed by the host country. During the 1990s far-sighted car manufacturers such as Volkswagen built factories behind China's high tariff walls. When the boom in China's car market began in 2004, the German multinational was in a great position to become the number one overseas brand (and the Chinese love brands).

Some other benefits from local production are as follows.

- It is far easier to tailor products to local customer preferences if senior managers live locally and therefore learn to understand local customs.
- In the long term it may be possible to become thought of as a local company. Many in Britain assume Ford and Vauxhall to be British rather than American, which may make them more inclined to 'buy British'.

## Low labour costs

Many multinationals shift production facilities to less economically developed countries where wage rates are low. Mass producers are able to set up production facilities in these countries and employ unskilled or semi-skilled workers to produce their products. If firms can reduce the labour cost per unit, they can either afford to drop prices, or they can keep price unchanged and accept a higher profit per unit – a pleasant choice to make!

## Low taxes

This may attract inward investment, as firms seek to find countries where their profits will be taxed at a lower rate than in their home country. This fact is used by many governments as a deliberate incentive to encourage investment by multinationals. The key tax is corporation tax, the percentage tax on company profits. This varies by country, as shown in Figure 87.1.

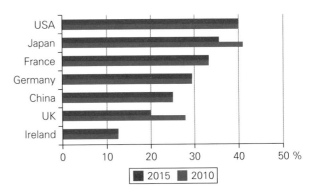

**Figure 87.1** Corporation tax in selected countries

The existence of different tax rates in different countries allows multinationals to practise transfer pricing. This is a way to boost profits by taking advantage of different tax levels in their countries of operation. It involves declaring high profits in countries where tax rates are low and minimal profits in countries where tax rates are high. For example, if Tesco UK sold goods cheaply to Tesco Ireland, its profits would rise in Ireland (where profit tax is low), and would fall in Britain. This would reduce Tesco's overall tax bill. The legality of transfer pricing tends to vary from country to country. As a result, it is difficult to clamp down on this practice, which many feel to be unfair.

An even more significant problem, in recent years, has been the increasing use of tax havens such as Bermuda or the Virgin Islands. Multinationals can register their businesses on these islands, where corporation tax may be 0 per cent. By channelling profits to these islands the multinational company can minimise its tax bill.

In 2014 the UK-based drinks multinational Diageo (Smirnoff, Baileys, Guinness) paid a corporation tax rate of 16.5 per cent. Local, probably smaller, British breweries would have had to pay the full 22 per cent tax. The scope for tax avoidance unfairly favours multinational companies.

## Government incentives

Governments of host countries are usually keen to attract multinationals. In order to do this, governments are prepared to offer a range of incentives to encourage multinationals to choose their country rather than any other. Among the methods for attracting this inward investment are reduced or zero tax rates, subsidies and reduced rate loans. These methods helped past British governments to attract foreign investors such as Nissan and Honda.

## 87.3 Ways of entering international markets

### Joint ventures

For a large UK-based business to set up a subsidiary in China, it needs government approval. It will only get this if it goes for a joint venture (JV) with a local business. This JV is set up with dual ownership and control, but focused on only one aspect of each company's activities. So Jaguar Land Rover UK (owned by Tata Motors of India) has a Chinese JV to operate its Jaguar Land Rover China business.

But joint ventures are not only set up to keep governments happy. In 2002 multinationals Nestlé and L'Oréal formed a JV to develop 'nutricosmetics' – in effect, pills with cosmetic benefits. They pooled their R&D and marketing efforts and launched several brands including Inneov – which had sales of 50 million Euros globally until it (together with the whole JV) was scrapped in 2014. The JV was dissolved, with a press announcement saying it had 'not met the expectations of both partners'.

### Franchising

As part of its early-stage growth, SuperGroup plc (Superdry) found franchise partners in Europe. For example a Dutch business became a franchise partner in 2008 and developed 29 stores in Holland and Belgium before, in 2011, SuperGroup bought them out. In 2008 SuperGroup had neither the cash nor the expertise to run shops in Holland. By 2011 the business had cash from its flotation and greater confidence that it could run shops outside the UK. Later, in 2014, it bought out a German franchisee as well. So it used the expertise of local franchisee/entrepreneurs to enter new markets successfully – then bought them out. A clever way to build a multinational presence.

### Organically

Most of the time, multinationals have no need for local help. They are experienced in placing managers in a desired new market, then letting them slowly build a presence. Coca-Cola struggles to make much profit at the moment in sub-Saharan Africa, but they are playing a long game. They want to make sure that the Coca-Cola brand is fully established when economic development allows it to become a mass market brand in the countries of Africa.

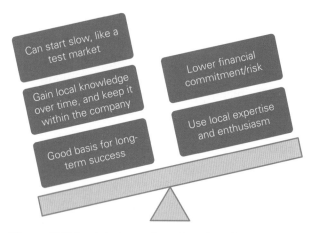

**Figure 87.2** Logic balance: Organic vs franchise expansion in countries of Africa

'The multinational corporation and international production reflect a world in which capital and technology have become increasingly mobile, while labour has remained relatively immobile.' Robert Gilpin, academic

## 87.4 Other ways to target overseas markets

A UK-based business does not have to become a multinational in order to sell overseas. Some rely purely on exports, with there being an increasing possibility of running an export business solely through an online sales outlet based in the UK. This is easiest to achieve with products that have a common footprint worldwide. A resident of Beijing might want to buy a Mulberry handbag because it's a British design and made in Somerset, in effect paying for the Britishness. So an export sale can take place without the UK business making any direct effort at all.

In addition to online, traditional exporting remains important. In 2014 £12.8 billion of food and non-alcoholic drinks were exported (73 per cent to EU countries). Many of the exporters (of salmon, perhaps) would have little by way of an overseas presence. But foreign supermarket buyers want salmon from Scotland, so track down the fisheries. Then the UK supplier just has to keep up its quality, delivery efficiency and value for money – and all will be fine.

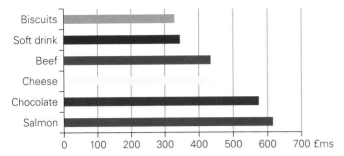

**Figure 87.3** UK's top six food exports, 2014 (£millions)

Source: Food and Drink Federation

## Key terms

**Subsidiary:** a company set up to be subordinate to another, for example Cadbury starting a sweet shop subsidiary business.

**Transfer pricing:** a way multinationals can minimise their worldwide tax liabilities by transferring their profits from high-tax to low-tax countries.

## Evaluation: Targeting overseas markets

Multinationals get a bad press. It is assumed that their lack of a solid connection to a single country weakens their sense of moral and social responsibility. It's difficult to see why that would be true. Many are so large that, as shown at the start of the chapter, they can rival nations in their size and wealth. So they can be expected to develop their own culture and their own sense of right and wrong. What's not in doubt is that a failing by McDonald's or Shell anywhere in the world can bite them all over the world. So in some ways multinationals may have to work harder at being 'good' than other companies. They have more to lose from bad publicity.

The use of extreme tax avoidance by several prominent multinationals such as Apple and Google is a reminder, though, that companies can allow themselves to lose sight of their moral responsibilities. They succeed thanks to the education and health of the people who work for them, so they should be *proud* to contribute to the tax base of the countries in which they operate. Sadly, their failure to do so affects many other companies as well. Richard Branson's Virgin Group even gets much of its income from UK government sources (rail income and operating outsourced health and social care businesses) – but it keeps its tax base in offshore havens such as the Virgin Islands.

## Five Whys and a How

| Question | Answer |
|---|---|
| Why might it be significant that Shell's sales revenue is ten times that of Kenya's GDP? (Table 87.1) | It might imply that Shell has the financial muscle to always get its own way when dealing with the Kenyan government |
| Why are workers at Jaguar Land Rover thrilled with their Indian multinational owner? | JLR was a poorly run business before Tata of India. Under British ownership and under American (Ford) ownership the workers' future looked very uncertain |
| Why do people get angrier with multinationals than badly-behaved national companies? | People believe that the sheer size of many multinationals gives those businesses a sense of entitlement – they can get away with whatever they want |
| Why do firms use transfer pricing? | To transfer their profits from high-tax to low-tax countries |
| Why might the data in Figure 87.1 tempt a French firm to move to the UK? | Corporation tax in France is about 33 per cent whereas here it's now 20 per cent. Surely that must be tempting! |
| How might a UK-China joint venture become a problem for the UK business? | The UK company may have the brand name and capital, but the Chinese have the local know-how and contacts; there may be temptations to trade unethically that could create bad publicity |

# Workbook

## A. Revision questions

**(45 marks; 45 minutes)**

1.  **a)** State four advantages to businesses of operating in several countries. (4)

    **b)** Which of the four would be the most important for each of the following businesses? Explain your reasoning:

    **i)** Rolls Royce Motors, if its management decided to open a factory overseas. (6)

    **ii)** Cadbury, if it wanted to open a factory in India. (6)

    **iii)** King Interactive, owners of the Candy Crush Saga, move half of its key software development team from London to Beijing. (6)

2.  Explain two potential problems for a British business opening up operations in more than one overseas market. (8)

3.  What is meant by the term 'transfer pricing'? (2)

4.  Explain how a multinational grocery business might seek to overcome the language barriers that might hamper internal communication. (5)

5.  Explain two advantages of producing in the country in which you are selling. (8)

## B. Revision exercises

### DATA RESPONSE

**Fever-Tree plc: the enterprising UK manufacturer**

Britain's biggest manufacturing sector is food and drink. Although the UK has a huge current account deficit in food and drink, we still sell plenty of food exports, often at very good profit margins. The sector is characterised by old, established firms such as Cadbury and Schweppes, plus lively newcomers such as Fever-Tree. Founded in 2005 by two experienced food marketing executives, the company was launched onto Britain's junior stock market (AIM) in early November 2014. Sixty per cent of the shares were floated raising £93 million. Almost all this cash was to reward the shareholders; only £4 million was to help finance growth.

But growth potential there certainly is. Fever-Tree's brand proposition is 'all-natural', from the quinine that goes in the tonic water to the ginger in the ginger ale. And no artificial sweeteners. This has helped it get 75 per cent penetration in the world's top restaurants, yet it has a market share of less than 0.5 per cent in the US retail market. Curiously, its highest market penetration is in Spain, with 5 per cent. Clearly there's plenty of scope for growth.

Although the Fever-Tree founders worked hard to source and test the recipes in their products, they saw no need to produce it themselves. They outsource production to a soft drinks factory in Shepton Mallet, Somerset. This provides English provenance, which lends credibility to the brand, especially as a mixer to as classically English a spirit as gin. Such has been the success of the brand that around 75 per cent of all sales come from abroad; 2014 saw a big push into India – Fever-Tree's fiftieth country in which it operates.

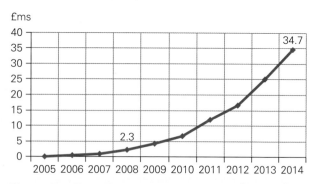

**Figure 87.4** Fever-Tree: annual sales turnover (£millions)

As the graph shows, sales have grown consistently and dramatically at an average growth rate of over 50 per cent a year. Profits have clearly been exceptional as well, judging by the company's ability to finance its own growth. In 2014 the company's stated operating profit was £8.1 million.

**Questions (45 marks; 50 minutes)**

1. Analyse why Fever-Tree may have chosen to target overseas markets. (9)

2. Evaluate whether Fever-Tree should continue to be based in England or should build more of a multinational structure? (16)

3. If financial constraints forced Fever-Tree to choose whether to focus on China or India, which do you think they should choose? Justify your answer. (20)

## C. Extend your understanding

1. 'To succeed in the long term, every car manufacturer has to develop a strong multinational presence'. To what extent do you agree with that statement? (25)

2. A Chinese electrical goods manufacturer is considering building a new plant in Britain to serve the European market. To what extent will this decision depend on the actions of the British government? (25)

# Chapter

# 88 Managing international business

**Linked to:** Globalisation and emerging economies, Chapter 67; Reasons for trading internationally, Chapter 84; China and India, Chapter 86; Targeting overseas markets, Chapter 87.

## Definition

Internationalisation means selling and/or operating in more than one country. The move to enter foreign markets allows firms to tap into new groups of customers.

## 88.1 The importance of internationalisation

As the global economy has become more interdependent, it has become easier for businesses to become international. Improvements in communication, reductions in transport costs and increasing global economic well-being mean that even relatively small businesses can consider selling abroad or outsourcing production to another country. This trend to internationalisation has implications on each functional area of the business.

### Internationalisation and marketing

A business that decides to sell in foreign markets must first start by ensuring that they understand the new market. It is one thing to understand that a foreign market differs from your home market, quite another to truly understand foreign markets as deeply as the home market. Foreign cultures differ tremendously, as outlined by Hofstede (see Chapter 93). Consumers want different things from products and services in different parts of the world. US consumers expect bigger food portions while Chinese consumers place great value on red as a lucky colour. To truly understand the way in which consumers in international markets think, market research may not be enough. It may be necessary to ensure that the firm consults with

or employs marketing specialists from that country. Hence the popularity of entering foreign markets using methods such as licensing or joint ventures with local firms. Of course, it is possible that firms may decide their marketing is strong enough to transcend national boundaries and they choose to make no major adaptations to what is being sold or how it is sold.

## Internationalisation and people management

The expertise provided by local staff can be invaluable in understanding how local business works. When KFC decided to try to enter the Chinese market, they formed a management team primarily from current staff who had been born and educated in Taiwan – one of China's closest neighbours. Their success is attributed to having a better understanding of the complexities of and the differences in Chinese culture than many of their Western rivals who entered the Chinese market with less success. This example contrasts with some companies who insist on flying in managers from their home country to ensure that the firm's organisational culture and methods of working are imposed on local staff. Although this can be an effective way of ensuring that the firm's procedures are followed in a new location, it can cause problems in understanding the local business environment, as well as being criticised by some as failing to aid in the development of the host countries' management cadre.

Of course, language differences will require staff to understand the local language – a clear encouragement to keep studying languages to further your business career.

## Internationalisation and operations management

Outsourcing production to lower cost countries can be an attractive option for any manufacturer. With lower labour costs linked with cheaper costs of land and materials being easier to source, manufacturing in less economically developed or developing countries can be the key to cost minimisation. However, decisions, such as that taken by Apple, to manufacture on the other side of the world, can lead to problems monitoring production. Not only do they need to keep an eye on their first level suppliers (companies such as Foxconn, who assemble most iPhones), but they are increasingly under scrutiny for the work done by second-tier suppliers – the firms that supply their suppliers. Criticisms of the way workers are treated can reflect on the company that has outsourced their production. In addition to this, there will be negative publicity when a firm decides to move manufacturing jobs away from the home country.

Managing supply chains within an international firm is also a massive logistical challenge. From the army of buyers who must find and assess potential suppliers of materials and components to those who are tasked with developing the computerised ordering systems to ensure that the right quantities of the right components and parts arrive in the right part of the world at the right time – everything must run smoothly if an internationalised business is to take full advantage of the increased efficiencies that are possible through internationalisation.

## Internationalisation and finance

A multinational organisation needs careful financial controls. This is likely to involve a complex budgeting system allowing managers of individual branches to work within constraints agreed with head office. However, the very largest firms will find it hard to monitor financial performance at the lower levels of the organisation.

Of course, much recent press coverage has been given to the ability of multinational companies to channel costs and revenues through their international subsidiary companies to ensure that profits are declared in the countries with the lowest rates of corporation tax – hence Amazon declaring so much profit from their Luxembourg operation where tax rates are notoriously low. Internationalisation makes internal financial systems incredibly complex – something which can be both a benefit and a drawback.

'The real voyage of discovery consists not in seeking new lands, but in seeing with new eyes.' Marcel Proust

## 88.2 Bartlett and Ghoshal's international strategies

Christopher Bartlett and Sumantra Ghoshal, working in the late 1980s and early 1990s distilled the strategic choices facing firms that choose to operate internationally into four choices, as shown in Figure 88.1.

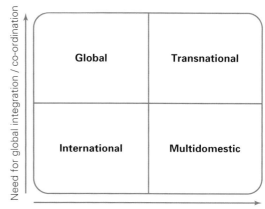

**Figure 88.1** Bartlett and Ghoshal's international strategies

Bartlett and Ghoshal identified two competing forces when selecting an appropriate strategy for 'going international'. Those forces are:

The need for local responsiveness – which represents the extent to which different countries' consumers expect products/services to be adapted to suit local tastes. These pressures are strong in industries such as food and beverages.

The need for global integration/co-ordination – this describes the extent to which the firm needs to standardise its offering to benefit from economies of scale and present an identifiably consistent image across the world. This force is strong for car manufacturers, perfume and other luxury goods makers and chemical companies.

The four strategies that emerge differ according to the extent to which the business chooses to recognise the importance of these conflicting forces.

*Global strategy* uses centralised operations to maximise scale advantages. Huge, centralised factories produce enough to supply on a global scale. For example all the wings for the Airbus A330 and A350 aircraft are produced in Broughton, Cheshire, then sent to Bremen in Germany for assembly. Local branches of the firm exist to implement the strategies devised by the parent company. There will be little sharing of knowledge and expertise with international branches. The centralised base of operations will be the heart of knowledge development for the business.

*International strategy* seeks to make the most of all benefits by maintaining a centralised approach to core activities but decentralising activities where scale provides little advantage. Each country of operation is encouraged to follow the parent company's strategy, but adapt it to suit local needs and tastes. Knowledge is developed at the centre of the business and then shared with local branches. This is the McDonald's approach, with centralised branding but localised menus.

*Multi-domestic strategy* is designed to maximise a firm's ability to suit local needs. Decision-making is decentralised and each local branch is seen as a separate business that does not rely on head office for anything. Strategies are devised and implemented on a country by country basis. In essence each individual country's branch is run on its own, with head office merely taking an overview of the firm's global activities.

*Transnational strategy* – this is perhaps the trickiest strategy to implement, with the goal being to harness both global size and local specialisation. Different branches in each country will be specialised in a particular area of competence, but work interdependently to ensure that global demand can be satisfied. This is perhaps best illustrated by global car giants, who may focus manufacturing of engines in just three or four countries. For example Ford's Dagenham factory produces more than half the company's global requirement for diesel engines. These plants feed assembly operations in many other countries, so that localisation of products can occur. In effect this uses the modern manufacturing approach known as mass customisation (see Chapter 33).

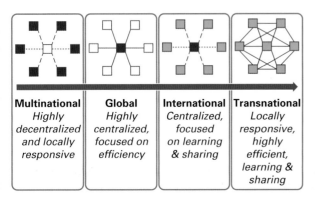

**Figure 88.2** Summary of the four strategies

Source: Adapted from Bartlett & Ghoshal

'Internationalisation is like creating a round-toed shoe that fits people with all types of feet. It is not as comfortable as a perfectly fitted shoe and doesn't fit snugly, but can be worn by many people.' David Debry, academic

## 88.3 Analysing international strategies

The trick to breaking down a firm's circumstances to identify an appropriate strategy lies in the assessment of the relative strength of Bartlett and Ghoshal's competing

forces – local responsiveness and global integration. When considering a particular business or industry, consider whether local market differences are more important than the need to bring down costs by producing on a global scale. This is true of cosmetics, where different skin tones in different countries call for slightly different products. At times, both forces will be high – at which point a transnational strategy is appropriate. Table 88.1 shows just a few examples of industries along with a generally acknowledged statement of their position on Bartlett and Ghoshal's grid:

**Table 88.1**

| | Weak forces for local responsiveness | Strong forces for local responsiveness |
|---|---|---|
| **Strong forces for global integration** | Consumer electronics (TV's, mobile phones) Engines | Cars and vans Pharmaceuticals |
| **Weak forces for global integration** | Paper Textiles Machinery | Food Drink Grocery retailing |

---

**Real business**

### *Kraft and Cadbury*

When Kraft bought Cadbury in 2010 they were buying a company that was already market leader in both the UK and India. Since the deal, although Kraft has integrated some of its brands such as Oreos with Cadbury's portfolio, Cadbury has been largely treated as a separate company in the markets in which it leads. Commentators saw Kraft's purchase of Cadbury as a long-term move, aimed at giving it ready-made access to the rapidly growing Indian confectionery market. Kraft sees Cadbury as part of a multinational strategy, in which its Indian subsidiary is allowed significant autonomy in deciding how to tackle the world's second most populous market.

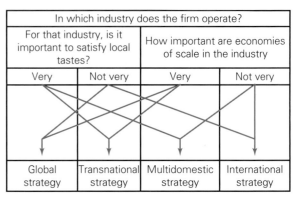

**Figure 88.3** Chain of logic

## Five Whys and a How

| Question | Answer |
| --- | --- |
| Why do firms expand internationally? | To increase the number of potential customers and hopefully gain economies of scale – all in a desire to boost profit through growing their business |
| Why can operating in different countries be a problem? | Diseconomies of scale, especially in terms of co-ordination and communication can damage efficiency, with quality problems and wastage levels rising |
| Why can internationalisation reduce costs? | If the firm can increase production of a standardised product, they may be able to bulk buy materials and components at far lower unit costs. In addition they may be able to buy and use specialist machinery that produces at lower unit costs |
| Why is a transnational strategy hardest to successfully implement? | Transnational involves trying to produce on a global scale, but tailor products to suit individual markets – therefore many product variants must be produced in 'national-sized' batches |
| Why do some firms succeed in global markets without adapting their products? | In some cases, products are commodities and simply cannot be differentiated. In others, there may be no major differences in what consumers expect from that type of product, whilst a few firms, such as Coca Cola, have convinced consumers to adapt their own tastes to fit the company's product |
| How should a firm decide which strategy to use? | Based on the industry in which the firm operates they should determine the extent to which they will need to try to gain global scale for cost reduction and the extent to which products will need to be adapted to suit local tastes |

## Evaluation: Managing international business

Since Bartlett and Ghoshal first published their work in 1989, many academics have taken a critical look at their findings. If there is one common theme to what has since been discovered, it is the recognition that the transnational strategy can rarely be successfully implemented. The problem is that the strategy requires the successful achievement of what seem to be two mutually exclusive goals – producing on a global scale, whilst catering to local differences – how can a firm manufacture enough standardised products to bring costs down whilst satisfying differing local needs?

However, that does not mean that firms no longer seek to pursue this strategy – in fact, with an increasingly interconnected global marketplace, more and more businesses are trying to scale up their production to benefit from previously unimaginable economies of scale, whilst wrestling with how to adjust their products to suit local tastes. In some ways, the most successful global firms have been those that have managed to adjust local tastes to suit their products – encouraging the whole world to believe that they need a McFlurry means that there is less need to respond to local tastes.

## Key terms

**Joint venture:** a temporary arrangement between two companies to work together on a specific limited area of operation, for example Jaguar Land Rover in China.

**Offshoring:** transferring a business function such as manufacturing to a foreign country.

# Workbook

## A. Revision questions

(30 marks; 30 minutes)

1. State which competing forces Bartlett and Ghoshal recommend that firms consider before choosing a strategy for internationalisation. (2)

2. State and briefly explain two types of economy of scale that a car manufacturer may hope to receive by manufacturing on a global scale. (6)

3. Explain why it is important to cater to local taste for a company producing branded food items such as ketchups and other sauces. (5)

4. Analyse why internationalisation may reduce the marketing effectiveness of a mobile phone retailer. (9)

5. Explain two reasons why multinational companies should not transfer profits to the countries in which they operate with the lowest tax rates. (8)

## B. Revision exercises

### DATA RESPONSE

**Heineken – A transnational brewer?**

**Figure 88.4** Heineken's global presence

Heineken is the third largest brewing group in the world. Selling in over 150 countries worldwide, the company has breweries in 70 countries – attempting to centralise their manufacturing in order to gain economies of scale in production. Their strategy is summarised as follows:

'Our brand strategy is to build a strong portfolio that combines the power of local and international brands and which has Heineken at its centre. The consistent growth of our brands requires solid creative brand management, which we co-ordinate centrally. By carefully balancing our brand's portfolios and achieving optimal distribution and coverage, we aim to build and sustain strong positions in local markets.'

From globally sold brands such as Heineken and Amstel beers, the company also adds smaller national brands, such as Zwyiec (Poland), Star (Nigeria) and Bintang (Indonesia). This allows beers and brands to be adapted to suit local tastes. However, the company also tries where possible to centralise purchasing of materials in order to benefit from purchasing economies of scale.

Upon the publication of financial results for the first half of 2014, CEO Jean-François van Boxmeer said,

'With revenue and profit growth in nearly all regions, this is a very good first half performance. This progress is the result of a continued disciplined strategic focus with sustained investment in our brands and strengthened commercial execution. Our emphasis on innovation has enabled us to exceed our target and deliver €682 million of revenues (extra revenues from new products). Heineken premium volume's grew 6.6 per cent, reflecting strong gains in key markets such as France, Nigeria, Russia, Brazil and China. We also delivered our three-year cost savings target of €625 million six months ahead of schedule.... We are confident that our strong brand portfolio, geographic breadth and focus on cost control will result in healthy top and bottom line growth in 2014 and beyond.'

Many of the cost savings mentioned above come from the 2010 creation of the company's Global Business Services Organisation – a division of Heineken which actively seeks to provide logistical and purchasing services centrally to the different regional operations of the firm. It is this part of the business, along with the work done by the marketing department on the global Heineken and Amstel brands that displays the firm seeking to benefit from its global size, whilst continuing to innovate with its local branding in the attempt to produce a genuine and successful transnational strategy.

**Table 88.2** Extracts from Heineken financial results for the first half of 2014

|  | First half 2014 (€m) | First half 2013 (€m) |
|---|---|---|
| **Group revenue** | 10,196 | 10,339 |
| **Group net profit** | 1,560 | 1,448 |

Sources: Transnational Strategies at Heineken? www.slideshare. net and www.theheinekencompany.com

## Questions (50 marks; 60 minutes)

1. Calculate Heineken's net profit margins for the first six months of both 2013 and 2014. (4)

2. Based on the information in the case study and financial data, is Heineken's CEO justified in suggesting the business is likely to see healthy growth in revenue and net profit? Justify your answer. (12)

3. Analyse the benefits that Heineken should achieve by centralising its purchasing function. (9)

4. Analyse the different approaches to marketing needed for Heineken's global and local brands. (9)

5. Using all the information provided, to what extent is Heineken correct to pursue a transnational strategy? (16)

## C. Extend your understanding

1. 'A switch to a more international strategy would force a UK-based business such as Sainsbury's to work hard to improve its functional efficiency'. To what extent do you agree with that statement? (25)

2. Using businesses with which you are familiar, to what extent do you think that Bartlett and Ghoshal's strategies imply that all businesses operating only on a national scale are doomed to lose out to multinationals? (25)

**Linked to:** Technology and operational efficiency, Chapter 30; Technological change, Chapter 70; Competitive advantage, Chapter 76; Economies and diseconomies of scale, Chapter 79; Innovation, Chapter 81.

## Definition

Digital technology includes any piece of equipment containing a computer chip. For Business A-level the key is how computer-based equipment and media affects the business functions: operations management, finance, marketing and human resources.

## 89.1 Pressures to adopt digital technology

The benefits of introducing more, or more up-to-date, digital technology involve boosting revenues by reaching more customers, by developing a better understanding of customers and by cutting costs. The drivers behind the introduction of digital technology can be traced through to its ability to improve profit for business.

**Table 89.1** How to achieve the underlying aim

| Underlying aim: To boost profit | | |
|---|---|---|
| Objective | How to do it | Digital technology that enables this |
| Boost revenue | Reach more customers Find out customer needs and address them Speedier, more accurate delivery | E-commerce Analysing data on consumer behaviour Enterprise resource planning |
| Reduce costs | Produce faster Lower overheads Less wastage | Computer aided manufacturing, enterprise resource planning, plus use of robots in production Teleworking Enterprise resource planning |

Digital technology brings its own problems, though. Introducing the technology in the first place is likely to involve a substantial initial investment that will cover design and purchase of hardware and software, training staff and reorganising physical systems. The purchase and implementation of new digital technologies will usually hinge on the results of investment appraisal methods (see Chapter 73). Not only will there be a significant financial cost to introducing new digital technology, but there will be other costs involved in making changes to the way in which the business operates. It is therefore important to consider the broader impact of introducing and managing change within the business, as explained in Chapters 90, 91 and 92.

## Real business

### A new operating system for John Lewis

Upgrading the operating system on your computer or phone can take an hour or two to get it working properly. Updating the operating system on 26,000 devices is a completely different type of challenge. As Microsoft announced the withdrawal of technical support for its Windows XP system, John Lewis knew that an upgrade to Windows 7 was needed. Indeed, they began planning for the project in 2011. The upgrading started in 2013 and by the late summer of 2014, IT staff were celebrating the completion, without too many hitches. The company discovered that changing the operating system was fairly straightforward – the bigger problem came in updating all the applications that ran on the John Lewis system. By the end of the project, the company benefited from happier staff with faster machines, the chance to get rid of some of their older applications and a clearer understanding of exactly what was on the hard drives of all the machines in John Lewis and Waitrose stores.

Source: adapted from www.eyeonwindows.com/2014/08/20/migrating-from-windows-xp-is-hard-john-lewis-explains/

## 89.2 E-commerce

E-commerce is the term used to describe the process of selling products or services online. The Internet has become a step in the distribution process, referred to as 'place' in the marketing mix. E-commerce has had a significant impact on the marketing function. Selling online means a radical shift in the place element of the marketing mix and with no physical environment to sell from, the electronic environment – that is, the website, must be carefully designed. This design process includes making the site look good, but more importantly ensuring ease of use for consumers. The need for expert webpage designers will increase within the marketing department, probably necessitating recruitment or training of new staff.

E-commerce also affects the operational side of the business. No longer do products need to be shipped to each individual store in sufficient quantity to ensure shelves are full and all sizes or colours are available. Now, the operational emphasis must be on the logistical challenge of ensuring that the product gets to customers quickly and conveniently without incurring excessive cost. This is where best practice is evolving, with many retailers now offering multi-channel distribution – a range of different ways to get the product from producer to consumer. Not just shopping, but also 'click and deliver' or 'click and collect'.

### Real business

#### Convenient eBay

Many eBay customers who have queued at their local post office to collect parcels or tried to arrange redelivery from a courier are beginning to discover that the convenience of buying online creates an inconvenience in trying to actually get hold of what they have bought. In an attempt to challenge Amazon's innovation of Locker delivery, to code-protected lockers in convenient locations such as shopping centres, eBay announced a trial of a click and collect service from Argos stores around the UK. A trial, involving some 50 major eBay sellers began in the autumn of 2013, with success leading to the inclusion of 650 Argos stores by early 2015. The move was just the latest in a range of innovations in distribution that have been triggered by the tide of e-commerce. Buying online is convenient, but still leaves the problem of how to physically get products to consumers.

## 89.3 Big data and data mining

'Big data' describes the vast amount of data generated by the technological devices that we use daily. This concept can be illustrated by considering the fact that your mobile phone tells your network provider where it is on a minute by minute basis (as your handset sends out a signal looking for the nearest usable mast). A firm with access to a few personal details relating to your purchasing habits and your movements during the day could find ways to use this combination of information about you to find better ways to sell its products to you. With so much data recorded about consumers and their daily lives, a business with access to sufficient computing power can sift through the data in order to try to find patterns in the buying behaviour of individuals. This process of sifting through data to try to identify trends and relationships is known as data mining or data analytics. The key skill is the ability to translate the patterns or relationships spotted into usable insights that boost profits.

### Big data and data mining in functional areas

#### Marketing

Big data is revolutionising market research. With so much information available about customers and potential customers and their behaviour, marketing departments' research insights can be vastly enhanced by harnessing the power of big data. Companies use computer software to identify useful customer profile types based on actual behaviour, rather than answering questionnaires. This does not change the benefits of qualitative market research in gaining a psychological understanding of customers, but it does replace much of traditional quantitative research.

Another impact is on promotional methods. Being able to process so much customer data and correlate customer attributes allows promotional offers and materials to be targeted more effectively. Cross promotions – where one product is offered at a reduced rate when another is purchased – can be selected to have the biggest impact on sales. And timings of promotional activities can be more precisely chosen given analysis of prior information about consumer purchasing habits. In addition, the effectiveness of promotional activities can now be measured on a customer by customer basis, rather than aggregating the overall impact on sales of a promotional offer. In the future, combining new advertising media with the personalisation allowed by big data may mean that your phone signal will trigger electronic billboard advertising aimed only at you.

#### Operations

Gathering digitally generated data throughout a production process can help strengthen a quality assurance system. With computer controlled machinery able to report data on each item being produced and the current state of the machine itself, malfunctions and faulty products are more easily prevented.

**Table 89.2** The impact of three digital technologies

| E-commerce | | Mining big data | | ERP | |
|---|---|---|---|---|---|
| Makes product more accessible to customers | | Can understand customers better | Increased cost of data analysis | Helps to spread information throughout the organisation | Substantial investment required in hardware and software |
| Boosts total size of potential market | | Allows customer needs to be met more closely | | Ensures decision-making is based on most reliable up-to-date information available | |
| Can increase revenues | Spend more on promotion trying to reach bigger market | May allow premium pricing and/or stronger customer loyalty | | Should improve decision-making and operational efficiency | |
| Need to invest in adjusting distribution network to service e-commerce, across a wider area | | Will increased revenues outweigh extra cost of data analysis? | | Ought to lower operating costs | |
| Will increased revenues outweigh extra costs? | | But there may be ethical issues involved when firms know 'too much' about customers | | How long will operating cost reductions take to outweigh initial investment in ERP? | |

## Human resources

Using varied pieces of data to spot correlations can allow more accurate workforce planning. For service providers, the number of staff available at any given time is a crucial decision – too few and waiting times for customers will be too long, too many and costs will be too high. Firms can schedule staffing more effectively by correlating recent data on customer sales with other factors such as the weather.

'Everything we do in the digital realm - from surfing the Web to sending an e-mail to conducting a credit card transaction to, yes, making a phone call - creates a data trail. And if that trail exists, chances are someone is using it - or will be soon enough.'
Douglas Rushkoff, Professor of Digital Economics

## 89.4 ERP - What it is and how it works

Enterprise Resource Planning (ERP) software is an integrated digital technology system used by businesses to collect, store, manage and interpret data from the different business functions. It helps to co-ordinate the operation of the business. This may be easiest to understand by considering the diagram below which shows the supply chain for a laptop computer.

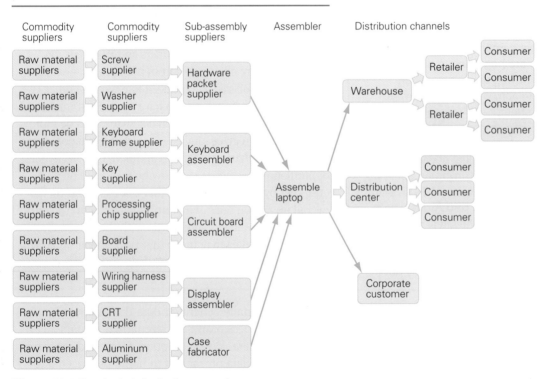

**Figure 89.1** Supply chain for laptop computers

Source: www.wright.edu

It is quite possible that every step in the process here is outsourced, but more likely that the laptop business will perform the role of assembler and handle the first stage of the distribution process. The ERP system will plan when supplies need to be available to the next stage of the process and when new supplies have to be ordered. ERP will:

- calculate how soon inventories will be used up and therefore need to be reordered from suppliers
- calculate what skills are needed to complete new orders and whether staff overtime is needed to complete the orders
- ERP systems are designed to enable all the right physical, human and information resources needed to be in the right place at the right time for the business to function effectively.

'Big data is not about the data.' Gary King, Harvard University, making the point that the real value is in the analytics

## Impact on functional areas

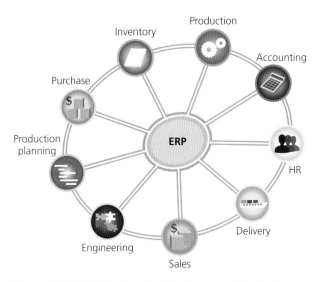

**Figure 89.2** ERP links the functional areas of the business

As can be seen from the diagram above, perhaps the most important role of ERP systems is to ensure that all functional areas are linked. This means ensuring that information generated or held in one area of the business can be communicated with or shared by other functional areas. For example, major car manufacturers' ERP systems should enable the following process to happen:

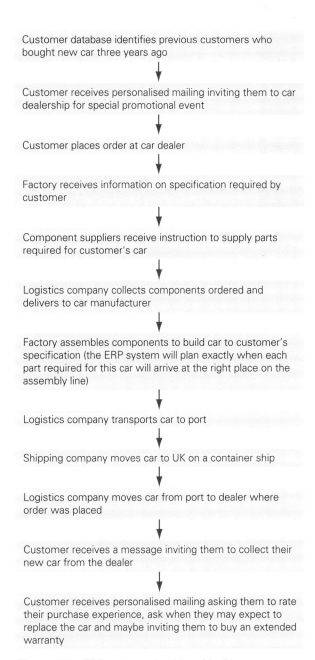

**Figure 89.3** ERP systems should enable this process

**Table 89.3** How ERP helps each functional area

| Marketing | Provides up to the minute sales figures via Electronic Point of Sale (EPOS) systems, such as the bar code scanners in supermarkets |
| --- | --- |
| | Gathers information on customer buying habits, often linked with a loyalty card system such as Tesco's Clubcard |
| | Can produce individually addressed promotional materials tailored to appeal to specific customers |
| **Finance** | Allows 'real-time' accounting information to be produced based on sales and costs incurred, generating financial information for individual profit centres or the whole business |
| | Allows budget variances to be analysed on a daily (or hourly) basis |
| | Some systems have the facility to conduct sensitivity analysis by pulling in data from other areas – such as how much profit would be generated from accepting a special order |
| **HR** | The payroll function (working out how much each staff member should be paid per month) can be an integrated component of an ERP system |
| | Staff rotas can be produced, based on predictions of demand that are generated by the analysis of past data on customer numbers for identical time periods |
| **Operations** | Production planning is perhaps the core function of a manufacturer's ERP system – working out how much to make of each type of product to satisfy demand and identifying the most efficient sequence of production for different orders to minimise both customer waiting times and time spent adjusting machinery |
| | ERP systems offer logistical functions which can plan for what supplies need to be transported from source to destination and the most efficient way to do this in terms of both time and cost |

Buying ERP systems is a complex matter costing millions of pounds. Major ERP suppliers, such as SAP, Oracle and Sage are not simply selling a piece of software, they install it, train staff and provide ongoing (but expensive) support for the system. All major suppliers offer cheaper, smaller, less tailored systems that can be used by small businesses to help their efficiency.

'I keep saying that the sexy job in the next 10 years will be statisticians, and I'm not kidding.' Hal Varian, chief economist, Google

### Real business

#### Churchill China and ERP

In 2008, as Britain was entering a sharp recession, 200-year-old pottery company Churchill China plc spent £800,000 on a brand new ERP system. It wanted the software as part of a strategy of faster response to customer orders, that is, shorter lead times. This was because the business wanted to reduce its commitment to the highly competitive retail market and focus instead on selling to the catering and hospitality trade. This goal was achieved by 2014, as 80 per cent of sales came from catering and hospitality – with retail sales becoming unimportant. Although it hadn't been a reason for the purchase, the business also benefited as the ERP system allowed inventory levels to be cut by more than £1 million.

### Evaluation: Digital technology

Adopting a strategy that increases the use of digital technology may or may not prove a source of competitive advantage. It is important to ask whether competitors are using digital technology as effectively as you are. If they are, the matter of whether to adopt digital technology boils down to the question of 'Can you afford not to?' The cost advantages linked with the added convenience to customers may mean that e-commerce is a given within your industry. Ideally a business would hope to use digital technology in a more sophisticated or effective way than others, perhaps creating a USP. Sadly, all rivals are trying to make sure that doesn't happen.

### Key terms

**Data mining:** the way digital technology trawls through vast amounts of data in order to spot patterns or correlations which can be used by a business.

**Correlation:** the identification of a relationship between two variables.

## Five Whys and a How

| Question | Answer |
|---|---|
| Why has e-commerce grown so rapidly? | E-commerce began with consumers buying at home through their desktop PC but has really mushroomed since the evolution of tablets and buying through mobile phones |
| Why is e-commerce more important in some markets? | In some markets, notably book, music and electronic game retailing, customers tend to buy on the basis of prior knowledge of products and then convenience, as offered by online purchase. Penetration is lower where customers want to see, feel or try before they buy |
| Why are people important in data mining? | Computers can process data and identify correlations, but need human interpreters to discover whether those correlations represent real causation. Only then will there be insight to enhance decision-making |
| Why can e-commerce require major operations management changes? | E-commerce offers the logistical problem, especially for traditional retailers, of needing to transport products to consumers, rather than letting consumers come to the store and take products home themselves |
| Why is ERP technology so expensive? | Top-end ERP technology is tailor-made for big clients, with programmers designing software and hardware systems that are used to pull together the data required. This requires a lot of man hours at very high pay rates |
| How can ERP help to reduce diseconomies of scale? | A fully integrated ERP system improves communication within a business. Different areas of the business will co-ordinate their activities more effectively as a result of this enhanced communication |

# Workbook

## A. Revision questions

(40 marks; 40 minutes)

1. Briefly explain two ways in which digital technology can reduce unit costs for a manufacturer. (4)

2. Identify three ways in which e-commerce customers may receive their orders from a major retail chain such as John Lewis. (3)

3. Explain how data mining makes big data useful. (4)

4. For each of the following combinations, explain how a major retailer could use this information provided by data mining:
   a) burger and ketchup sales rise together (4)
   b) customers who buy more fresh fruit tend to prefer wholemeal bread (4)
   c) buyers of nappies have a greater tendency to take advantage of 2 for 1 offers. (4)

5. Analyse how ERP could help to improve inventory availability at a clothing retailer. (9)

6. Explain why online-only retailers have major advantages over bricks and mortar-only shops. (4)

7. Explain why online food retailing may not have grown as quickly as online book retail. (4)

## B. Revision exercises

### DATA RESPONSE

**Netflix vs Amazon Prime**

The way we watch television and films at home is changing. This is why DVD rental store Blockbuster went out of business in 2013. Now, viewers expect TV shows and movies to be available on demand, through their TV boxes and via tablets and laptops. The two major players in this revolution are Netflix and Amazon (formerly LoveFilm), through their Amazon Prime service. When deciding what 'products to stock', in other words, what TV programmes to make or buy and stream to customers, both firms rely heavily on data mining. Having been trading for a longer period, Amazon has greater experience, and, as a more diversified company, a greater store of data on customers and potential customers. Netflix, however, is the clear market leader with a 57 per cent market share in mid-2014.

Much of the battle between the two is being fought via the making of exclusive TV series. With a TV series costing tens of millions of pounds to make, decisions over what shows to commission and film are major investment decisions for both firms. Their recent approaches have shown interesting differences in the way in which they have used data to help support decision-making. In 2013, looking for their next 'hit', Amazon commissioned 14 'pilot' episodes of different new series ideas and streamed these through their website. These were viewed by over 1 million people who rated the shows. Amazon was also able to monitor viewing habits – such as whether and when people stopped watching part-way through. The data gathered from these pilots was then distilled into a series of key variables, such as the proportion of viewers giving each a five-star rating, before Amazon executives decided which programmes to commission for a full series (*Alpha House* was the first to be commissioned).

At around the same time, Netflix used existing data to commission its most successful programme to date – *House of Cards*. Even before anyone had started filming, Netflix executives were confident they had a hit, since they identified three key points of popularity that they felt ensured that their customers would enjoy *House of Cards*. Actor Kevin Spacey's work was popular with Netflix viewers, whilst a high proportion of Netflix viewers were fans of the programme's director. In addition, the British version of *House of Cards* had performed well in the UK. In essence, Netflix skipped the primary research phase of their new product launch, based on what they considered to be the strength of their existing data and their ability to interpret this data effectively.

Netflix's method reflects what some technology analysts believe – that Netflix's data analysis is a little more sophisticated than older rival Amazon's. The methods by which Netflix tags films and programmes in order to offer customer recommendations (such a critical element to the success of streaming services) is said to be more sophisticated than Amazon's. Perhaps it is therefore a combination of the way Netflix gathers and mines data and interprets its results that gives it the edge. This is despite rival Amazon's total turnover for 2014 being 16 times the size of Netflix's $5.5 billion.

### Questions (40 marks; 45 minutes)

1. Explain what is meant by data mining. (4)

2. Calculate Amazon's total revenue for 2014. (4)

3. Explain why calculating the return on investment for a show such as *House of Cards* may be difficult for Netflix. (4)

4. Analyse two benefits for TV/movie streaming sites of the use of effective data mining. (12)

5. To what extent does the example above, and/or other examples you have studied, suggest that those with the most data will always understand their customers best? (16)

## C. Extend your understanding

1. To what extent is e-commerce an irrelevance for manufacturers such as Toyota and Nestlé? (25)

2. 'Data mining is nothing new. Firms have always carried out market research and analysed the results to help inform decision-making.' Using examples from businesses you have studied, evaluate the validity of this statement. (25)

# 90 Causes and value of change

**Linked to:** Methods and types of growth, Chapter 80; Barriers to change, Chapter 92; Managing organisational culture, Chapter 93; Strategic implementation, Chapter 94; Problems with strategy, Chapter 96.

## Definition

Change is a constant feature of business activity. The key issues are whether it has been foreseen by the company – and therefore planned for – and whether it is within the company's control.

## 90.1 Internal and external causes of change

Change arises as a result of various internal and external causes. The internal ones (such as a change in objectives) should at least be planned for. External causes may be unexpected, which makes them far harder to manage. Table 90.1 sets out some possible internal and external causes of change.

**Table 90.1** Examples of internal and external causes of change

| Internal causes | External causes |
|---|---|
| New growth objectives set by management | Rising consumer demand/the product becomes fashionable |
| New boss is appointed | Economic boom benefits a luxury product |
| Decision to open up new export markets | Closure/fire/strike hits competitor, boosting your sales |
| A decision to increase the shareholders' dividend makes it difficult to find the capital to invest in the business | New laws favour your product (for example new safety laws boost sales of first aid kits) |

'All great change in business has come from outside the firm, not from inside.' Peter Drucker, business guru (1909-2005)

Of all the issues relating to change, none is more crucial than when a business has to cope with a period of rapid growth. For example, in the first stage in the rapid growth of Instagram (the social photo site that launched in 2010 and was bought for $1 billion 18 months' later) the founders frequently found themselves working through the night when the site crashed through overuse. On the first day there were 25,000 users and within three months it hit 1 million.

'Change is inevitable; except from vending machines.' Anon

## 90.2 The pace of change: rapid vs incremental vs disruptive

### Business effects of forecast rapid growth

In certain circumstances managers can anticipate a period of rapid **organic growth**. This may be temporary (such as the effect of a change in the law) or may seem likely to be permanent (such as the growth in demand for a hot website). The most successful firms will be those that devise a plan that is detailed enough to help in a practical way, but flexible enough to allow for the differences between forecasts and reality.

When rapid growth has been forecast, firms can:
- compare the sales estimate with the available production capacity
- budget for any necessary increases in capacity and staffing
- produce a cash flow forecast to anticipate any short-term financing shortfall
- discuss how to raise any extra capital needed.

Timescales remain important, though. The forecast may cover the next three months; but increasing capacity may involve building a factory extension, which will take eight months, in which case there may be five months of excess demand to cope with (perhaps by subcontracting). In 2014 Center Parcs opened a new site near London. It opened exactly ten years after management made the decision to open it!

However accurate the forecast, there remains a lot of scope for error. The starting point is the increased workload on staff. Extra sales may put pressure on the accounting system, the warehouse manager and the delivery drivers. With everyone being kept busy, things can start to go wrong. Invoices are sent out a little later, unpaid bills are not chased as quickly and inventory deliveries are not checked as carefully. Suddenly the cash flow position worsens and costs start to rise. A strong, effective manager could retrieve this, but once they start to go wrong, plans are hard to sort out.

---

'No person will make a great business who wants to do it all himself or get all the credit.' Andrew Carnegie, businessman (1835-1919)

---

## Incremental change

From as early as 2005, John Lewis appreciated that its world was changing. From a purely physical ('bricks') high street retailer it saw that more and more people wanted to purchase online. Perhaps they might want to go to a store to choose which sofa or which TV to buy, but they would find it easier to make the transaction via a 'click' at home. To the operation's great credit it worked hard to create an easy-to-use e-commerce site and encouraged sales staff to see it as a complement, not a competitor to the stores. By 2015, with Marks & Spencer floundering in its wake, John Lewis was getting close to 30 per cent of all sales arising online, but with a clear strategy to open new stores within Britain to act as a shop window for the website.

This incremental change (steady and quite predictable) towards online shopping was intelligently managed by John Lewis, but botched by Marks & Spencer (and Morrisons). Quite simply, with years to look ahead and plan for this incremental change, there can be no excuses for the management failures of those who woke up to find they had missed the boat.

## Disruptive change

By contrast, disruptive change typically occurs within a timescale that makes planning almost impossible. In 2009, two years after the launch of the iPhone, Nokia held a 38.9 per cent share of the global market for smartphones. Two years' later its share was 8.2 per cent and dropping like a stone. Looking back, one could

point to the mistakes Nokia made; but it simply didn't have enough time to rethink the new world created by Apple (and Samsung). In the same timescale as Nokia's collapse, Samsung's global market share went from 3 per cent to 30 per cent.

The unusual aspect of Nokia's collapse is that the disruptive change came from Apple's marketing and design brilliance. Usually the causes of disruptive change are either technology or legislation, that is, external to the business. Banning smoking in public places meant that pubs had to adapt quickly – or die. Many died. The onset of online retailing finished off HMV, Blockbuster and Game retail chains.

The problem for businesses faced with dramatic change is that managers don't yet know the timescale and therefore do not know how disruptive the change will be. When General Motors launched its 'Volt' electric car in 2010 it forecast sales of 60,000 cars by 2012. In fact sales struggled to reach 24,000 units. The company had thought electric cars were the disruptive technology that would sweep petrol-based cars aside. Not yet. Now, as it plans its 2016 Volt, General Motors is trying hard to dampen down sales expectations.

---

'It isn't the changes that do you in, it's the transition.' Daniel Webster, U.S. politician (1782–1852)

---

## 90.3 The value of change

No one should doubt that most businesses, like most people, hate change. Just try persuading football supporters that it's time for a new home ground, or children that it's time to try a new type of food. So most business leaders drool over:

- Coca-Cola, born 125 years' ago, but still with 2014 retail sales of £1,178 million in the UK alone
- Cadbury's Dairy Milk, more than 100 years' old and with 2014 sales of £536 million in the UK.

Business people value lack of change, because it makes it easier to hang on to strong profits. For the consumer, though, change has potentially huge benefits. Although we may want Cadbury Dairy Milk unchanged, we benefit hugely when online retailers force shops to push prices down, or when Netflix starts paying for its own, high-quality programming to draw in more subscribers.

And when change comes, managements have to rethink their whole operation, to figure out how to be more efficient while simultaneously offering exciting new products or services to customers. It's at that point that change can be of value to many stakeholders: customers, shareholders, managers and perhaps the environment as well.

'Change is hard because people overestimate the value of what they have -and underestimate the value of what they may gain by giving that up.' James Belasco and Ralph Stayer, authors

## 90.4 Lewin's force field analysis

Writing in the 1940s, Kurt Lewin's interest in social psychology led him to consider why it was often so difficult to achieve change – even when change was needed. His research led in two directions: first in looking at change as a dynamic, continuing issue. He suggested that the absence of change occurs simply when the forces in favour of change are balanced by the forces against. He also found, though, that the reason why forces often seemed to be balanced against change

- Value each factor, using a scale such as 1-5, in line with its importance (5 = highest importance)
- Add up both sides to see which case is the strongest.

To show this in practice, let's take the early-2015 issue: the reformulation of the recipe for Cadbury's Creme Eggs. If Cadbury had chosen to use Lewin's approach, it might have looked as follows, with the case for change outweighing the case against by a score of 10:7.

For Lewin, the force field approach was not just about decision-making, it was also about identifying where effort needed to be focused. In the above example, the apparent need is to focus on customer resistance to a change in an iconic brand. That might mean hiring star social media names to post video clips of indulgent eating of the new Creme Eggs. In a human resource context, the resistance to change might be due to mistrust caused by the actions of previous, long-retired managers; it would then be necessary to show a united management front in favour of a new, open approach to consultation.

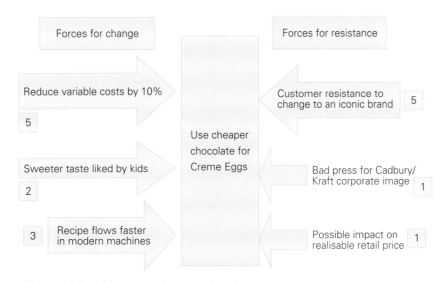

**Figure 90.1** Making a case for or against change

was because people's view of a situation had become 'frozen'. So successful change management required the skill to unfreeze a locked-in view – and then encourage a refreezing once the desired outcome had been achieved.

Lewin's force field analysis suggests the following management practice:

- Identify a problem or opportunity requiring change
- Through consultation, identify all the main factors suggesting change, and all those that make a case against that change

'If past history was all there was to the game, the richest people would be librarians.' Warren Buffett, investor extraordinaire

## 90.5 Planning for change

For managers who can foresee significant change, a strategic plan is needed. This should help in managing the change process, ensuring that the business has the personnel and the financial resources to cope. The strategic planning process is undertaken by an organisation's senior managers. The first decision they face is: 'How do we turn this change to our own advantage?'

Having established the strategic direction the organisation will adopt, the senior managers must next set the boundaries within which middle and junior management will take day-to-day decisions. A series of integrated actions must be set out. These will have the purpose of moving the organisation forward in the identified strategic direction. This plan will be introduced over a period of time known as a 'planning horizon'. This will commonly be between one and three years, but may vary depending on how stable the organisation's competitive environment is. The greater the stability, the longer the planning horizon will be.

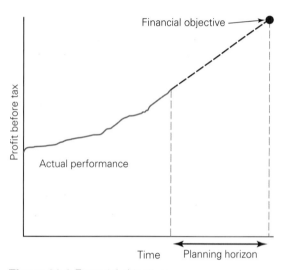

**Figure 90.2** Financial objectives

Strategic planning is only necessary because firms operate in a changing environment. If this was not the case then a single strategy, once designed, would bring success to the business on a permanent basis. However, changes in key variables such as technology, consumer tastes and communications make planning strategy increasingly important. The pace of change is intensifying, creating shorter product life cycles and encouraging increased competition. It is change that creates the '**strategic gap**' that must be closed by the second phase of the planning process.

Organisations that seek to achieve objectives such as the maximisation of long-term profits will set themselves financial targets. These will be influenced by shareholders' expectations and the personal and business ambitions of the company directors. These expectations will determine the financial objectives of the organisation over the forthcoming planning period.

The difference between the profit objective and the forecast performance of the business, is known as a strategic gap (see Figure 90.3).

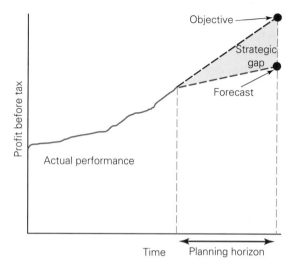

**Figure 90.3** A strategic gap

---

'Change is the law of life and those who look only to the past or present are certain to miss the future.'
John F. Kennedy, former US President

---

## Closing a strategic gap

Once a strategic gap has been identified it is necessary to devise a series of strategies to close it.

It may be possible to achieve this to some extent by performing existing operations more efficiently, in order to reduce costs and boost profit. However, this is unlikely to solve the whole problem. Only careful strategic planning can develop the means by which the organisation can increase its effectiveness in order to meet its financial objective.

The analysis of the strategic gap should reveal how difficult it will be to cope with the change. The future may look bright, such as for an organic farmer in a period of change towards more care and thought over healthy eating. Or it may look bleak, such as for Morrisons supermarkets in 2014 after a sustained loss in market share. Whether the gap is upwards or downwards (forcing the business to retrench), a careful planning process should make the transition easier.

---

'The entrepreneur always searches for change, responds to it, and exploits it as an opportunity.'
Peter Drucker, management academic and author

---

## Five Whys and a How

| Question | Answer |
| --- | --- |
| Why do plc bosses tend to blame poor results on external causes, but good results on internal causes? | Because external factors are outside the firm's control, whereas internal causes are down to the management |
| Why might a company's sales forecast prove inaccurate? | There are many possibilities, including that unexpected economic developments (such as a recession) could change the figures |
| Why might a business choose to use Lewin's force field analysis? | Because it's a model of how to assess and then overcome problems associated with workplace change |
| Why might disruptive change benefit a business? | Some long-established markets (such as for table sauces) see little change in yearly market shares, so the only chance for newcomers to break in is when there is disruptive change |
| Why might a business 'freeze', in relation to the views and attitudes of its staff? | Because a stable balance between change factors and forces for resistance can lock staff into a semi-permanent 'freezing' of behaviour |
| How might a small business effect major internal change among staff? | The key will be whether the business leaders have discussed the company's problems well enough to convince all important staff members to get involved |

## Evaluation: Causes and value of change

Change is normal, not abnormal. Therefore firms need to be alert to causes of change and quick to devise a strategic plan for coping. Many successful businesses do not have a formal strategic planning process. This does not mean that the issues raised here are not relevant to these organisations. The same problems must be dealt with when strategy emerges over time as when it is planned more systematically. The advantage of explicitly setting aside time for strategic planning is that managers' minds are concentrated on the key questions facing the firm in the future. Then the actions decided upon can be more closely integrated.

## Key terms

**Organic growth:** growth from within the business (for example, sales growing rapidly because a product is riding a wave of consumer popularity).

**Rationalisation:** reorganising to increase efficiency. The term is mainly used when cutbacks in overhead costs are needed in order to reduce an organisation's break-even point.

**Strategic gap:** the difference between where the business is and where it plans to be.

# Workbook

## A. Revision questions

(45 marks; 45 minutes)

1. Explain why rapid growth can cause problems for a company's:
   a) cash flow (4)
   b) management control. (4)

2. Distinguish between internal and external causes of growth, using examples. (5)

3. Identify three problems for a fast-growing firm caused by changes in the management structure. (3)

4. Explain one way in which your school/college could be affected by:
   a) incremental change (4)
   b) disruptive change (4)

5. Explain one advantage and one disadvantage to a business of using Lewin's force field analysis when considering bringing in new technology to modernise a production process. (8)

6. Explain why it may be hard for young, inexperienced managers of a successful business start-up to cope effectively with an unexpected, dramatic change. (5)

7. Explain one reason why change may be of value to an established grocery business. (4)

8. Explain why it may be hard for a struggling jewellery business to fill the strategic gap. (4)

## B. Revision exercises

### DATA RESPONSE

**Lush profits**

In 2014 the cosmetics producer and retailer Lush made annual profits of £23.3 million on sales of over £450 million. This was a wonderful reward for founders Mark and Mo Constantine, who still own 60 per cent of the shares. Founded in 1994 the business now has 900 stores in 49 countries. Growth has been dramatic and the business now supports over 4,000 jobs.

When Lush began, Body Shop was the store to beat. Now, Lush's indulgent, attractive cosmetics are starting to overshadow Body Shop. Lush also benefits from the enthusiasm of its staff for the company's backing for ethical causes such as banning fox hunting, or demanding legal representation for the Guantanamo Bay detainees. In 2014 Lush donated £3.8 million to charities.

Growing sales from £0 to £450 million in 20 years inevitably involves problems. When it had grown to £50 million of sales the manufacturing staff noticed that products made from essential oils (that can cost £3,000 per kg) were 'behaving' wrongly. After some weeks of panic Lush decided to get a chemist to analyse the oils. It emerged that suppliers had been adulterating the oils with as much as 70 per cent synthetic chemicals. This problem led to the establishment of a professional buying team, together with a quality control manager.

**Questions (35 marks; 40 minutes)**

1. a) Explain why Lush is likely to have had a significant increase in the number of layers of hierarchy within its business over recent years. (5)

   b) Analyse two ways in which an increase in the layers of hierarchy might harm operational performance at Lush. (10)

2. If Lush appointed a new chief executive, to what extent would the continuing success of the company be assured because its continued growth is based on incremental change? (20)

## C. Extend your understanding

1. The soft drinks company Fever-Tree has grown at a rate of 50 per cent per year for nearly a decade. To what extent is it inevitable that this pressure for change will cause serious setbacks for the business? (25)

2. Morrisons supermarket chain is thinking of removing two layers of management from its stores in order to save money. To what extent might Lewin's force field analysis be of help in succeeding with this plan? (25)

# Chapter 91 — The flexible organisation

Linked to: Competitive advantage, Chapter 76; Economies and diseconomies of scale, Chapter 79; Barriers to change, Chapter 92.

## Definition

A flexible organisation is one that is able to change rapidly without losing efficiency.

## 91.1 Introduction

To be flexible yet efficient involves developing and supplying new products rapidly in response to a change in consumer tastes. Flexible organisations are operationally flexible, being able to change methods of working, or production levels of existing products, to match the market's changing needs. In flexible firms the workforce is made up from two distinct groups: core and peripheral workers. The core workforce consists of employees who have permanent full-time contracts because they are difficult to replace quickly. This is because they have specific skills. To enhance their flexibility, core employees need to be multi-skilled so that they are capable of doing many different jobs. Those that make up the peripheral workforce are easily replaced and are employed on flexible contracts which mean that they are only employed when they are needed. This would be the only way to run a seaside hotel or a strawberry farm.

'An organization's ability to learn, and translate that learning into action rapidly, is the ultimate competitive advantage.' Jack Welch, former Chief Executive of the massive General Electric company of America

## 91.2 The value of a flexible organisation

Flexible organisations tend to be more profitable than less flexible organisations because faster rates of response and greater adaptability can lead to both higher revenues and lower costs.

## Higher revenues

To stay in business firms have to produce goods and services that consumers want to buy. However, due to changing fashions and technological advances consumer tastes can change quickly. Revenues from a product that has sold well for years might suddenly dry up as tastes move on or the product becomes outdated technologically. To stay in business the firm concerned needs to be flexible - able to respond rapidly to the change in consumer tastes.

The Spanish fashion retailer, Zara, is an example of a business that has benefited from improving its flexibility. Most clothes retailers operate on an inflexible predict and provide basis. This involves forecasting the type of clothes that consumers will want to buy before each fashion season. The clothes are then made in factories thousands of miles away in Asia, before being shipped over to Europe and North America to be sold. If the experts have predicted consumer tastes correctly the clothes will sell well. However, there is also a possibility that the retailers might be left with a lot of expensive stock on their hands that they cannot shift. Zara rejected this way of doing business and reshored manufacturing back to Europe. This decision enabled them to reduce delivery times, making their organisation more flexible. At the beginning of each fashion season Zara sends out relatively small amounts of stock to its stores. The company then responds to consumer demand, producing more of the items that have been selling well. The production of items that have not proved to be a hit with consumers is halted. This flexibility boosts the average selling prices, and hence revenues achieved by Zara because the company is less likely to be left with huge amounts of unsold stock that it has to clear at discounted prices.

Most products have finite selling lives in the market. Therefore it is vital that firms develop new products to satisfy new gaps in the market that they have identified via their market research. Flexible organisations are able to react faster than their rivals, taking less time to develop and launch their new products. This helps them benefit from **first mover advantage**. By being first into a market a company is able to charge consumers high prices until the competition arrives. In addition, revenues can hold up in the long run because brand loyalties once established are difficult to break. Originality can also be stressed in advertisements, creating a unique selling point that lowers price elasticity of demand, making premium prices possible.

## Lower costs

Most firms use their machinery to produce more than one product. In between batches, while the machinery is being cleaned and reset, production halts. Flexible organisations are able to keep this down-time to a minimum. This matters because the firm will be able to produce more from its resources, making it more efficient.

A firm that creates flexibility by creating a core and a peripheral workforce will also hope to benefit from lower costs by only paying for labour when it is needed.

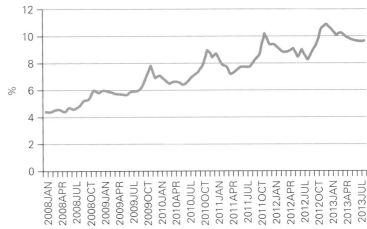

**Figure 91.1** Internet sales as a percentage of total retail sales

Source: ONS www.ons.gov.uk/ons/rel/rsi/retail-sales/august-2013/sty-patterns-in-retail-sles.html

---

### Real business

#### *Amazon's core and peripheral workforce*

The online retailer Amazon supplies its UK customers from a network of huge warehouses located throughout Britain. One of the largest of these warehouses is located in Rugeley in Staffordshire. The warehouse employs a core workforce of 950 workers who are employed on permanent contracts.

Retail sales are subject to sharp seasonal fluctuations. Demand is typically highest during the run-up to Christmas, as people buy each other presents. The chart below shows Internet sales as a percentage of all UK retail sales. During the period shown two trends can be observed. First, over time, more and more shopping is being done online. This is clearly good news for Amazon, and possibly explains decisions such as the one made in 2014 to double the size of the Rugeley warehouse from 700,000 to 1,400,000 square feet. The chart also shows that households are more likely to shop online during the run-up to Christmas.

---

To cope with this seasonal surge in demand Amazon uses a peripheral workforce, consisting of employees who have been hired on temporary contracts. This is far cheaper than employing extra permanent employees, who for most of the year will not be needed. At Rugeley the company took on 1,000 temporary seasonal workers in 2013; for 2014 the company intended to hire 2,500.

---

'Time is the scarcest resource and unless it is managed nothing else can be managed.' Peter Drucker, management guru

---

## 91.3 Examples of flexible organisation

### Restructuring

When a company's key product enters the decline phase of its life cycle it's time for the business to restructure. In other words reorganise its operations to reduce overall capacity and to reduce the break-even point. To achieve this flexibly might involve greater use of outsourcing. This involves transferring work that used to be done in-house to an outside company. More or less anything can be outsourced: IT support, marketing, credit control, customer service, etc. For example, in 2013 the electricity and gas supplier Npower closed down its UK call centres and outsourced its customer service to a specialist firm operating in India. The decision to outsource can make an organisation more flexible because it frees-up resources which can then be used to do other things. Even small firms can benefit from outsourcing in this way.

## Delayering

Delayering is a type of restructuring that involves removing layers of management from a firm's organisational chart. In other words a whole category of management is removed from a company's hierarchy. The work previously done by these middle managers can then be delegated to more junior staff. This type of restructuring has two benefits. First, costs should fall because the decision to make the middle managers redundant will reduce the company's wage bill. And second, removing middle managers will shorten the chain of command. This will make the organisation more flexible because it will take less time for information to pass from the top to the bottom of the hierarchy. This should reduce the amount of time needed to implement strategic changes made by senior management.

## Flexible employment contracts

An employment contract is a legal agreement that sets out matters such as a worker's responsibilities and duties; pay; entitlements to holidays and pensions; and in some cases, the duration of employment and/or weekly working hours. In the past most workers in Britain were employed on full-time, permanent contracts. Once they had been in their post for two years they were entitled to minimum periods of notice in the event of redundancy and the legal right to sue their employer for unfair dismissal. Over the last decade there has been a trend towards flexible employment contracts that enable the employer to alter the size of their workforce and wage bill more rapidly in response to changes in consumer demand. Examples of flexible employment contracts include **zero hours** and annual hours contracts. Annual hours contracts promise workers a set number of paid hours of work each year. However, unlike a conventional contract where employees work a fixed number of hours each week, under an annualised contract the employer can ask their workforce to do more hours than normal during busy periods, which results in shorter working hours during weeks when demand is below normal.

**Figure 91.2** Logic wheel: Flexible factors

## Organic structures versus mechanistic structures

A business with an organic structure has flexibility and fluidity – it is able to adjust to change because staff trust the management that change is necessary, and may even be for the better. According to Tom Burns and George Stalker (in their book *The Management of Innovation*, OUP 1994) firms that operate with an organic structure are more flexible than firms with mechanistic structures. This is because firms with organic structures favour informal verbal communication over more formal methods such as meetings and written memos which are more time-consuming. They also favour decentralised decision-making. Rather than waiting to follow orders, empowered teams are expected to spot either problems or external opportunities, and to make the right decision accordingly without having to wait for approval from the senior management team. In this type of business there is no attempt made to standardise tasks and procedures because the best way of doing things will be constantly changing due to either sudden changes in consumer tastes or rapid technological change. In fact the management *expect* the workforce to be constantly tinkering trying out new ways of working. The methods deployed by organic structures evolve constantly on a trial and error basis.

A mechanistic structure is the exact opposite of an organic structure. Firms operating with this type of business model favour centralised, top-down decision-making and formal communication and impose standardised ways of doing things. It is commonly used in firms led by autocratic managers who believe that they should make all the important decisions because they are more able and trustworthy than their employees. Businesses run along these lines are inflexible, with a workforce that is closely supervised to ensure that it always follows the procedures and policies laid down by management. According to Burns and Stalker, mechanistic structures are best suited to businesses that operate in markets that are relatively stable. With little need to change, flexibility is less important.

'Built into decentralisation is the age-old tug between autonomy and control: superiors want no surprises; subordinates want to be left alone.' Chris Argyris, business academic

## Information and knowledge management

Information management involves how best to cost-effectively collect and sift the data a firm believes it needs for its operations. This ranges from customer feedback questionnaires and collecting social media comments to data about production and delivery efficiency. A business can only operate flexibly if it understands fully the data that are at the heart of its business. For example, if the phone rings and it's a new customer asking for one thousand blue widgets to be delivered by 16:15 tomorrow afternoon, you have to have the data at your fingertips to say, 'Yes, that'll be no trouble. The price is £7,422.50.' or to say, 'Sorry, no can do.' The information can be available instantly if the firm's software system knows exactly which skills are needed to do the job, and the availability of staff to do it, even if they usually work from home.

Knowledge is useful information that may have been interpreted by others to make it even more valuable. This knowledge will need to be passed on to other employees within the firm. Knowledge management is all about creating the right learning environment within a firm so that vital knowledge can be disseminated quickly; this normally happens via training. Another important aspect of knowledge management is the preservation of knowledge. For example, firms should not allow valuable skills, contacts and insights to be lost when experienced workers walk out of the door to either retire or leave for another job. To prevent this from happening effective knowledge management is required. At its simplest this could mean making sure that the worker who is leaving provides adequate training to the worker(s) that will replace them. Effective knowledge management can make a firm more flexible and innovative because it encourages the free flow of ideas between employees in the same firm.

## Five Whys and a How

| Question | Answer |
|---|---|
| Why is it important for firms to be flexible? | Flexible firms are more adaptable, so they are more likely to be able to respond faster to adapt either their product range or production systems in response to technological changes or new fashions |
| Why do some firms employ a peripheral workforce in addition to their core workforce? | To create flexibility. The peripheral workforce is only used during peaks in demand. This means that the employer only pays for the labour that it needs |
| Why may a rapidly growing business choose to contract out activities that used to be done in house? | Outsourcing can free up capacity needed to allow the firm to keep customer waiting times low, so that customers do not go elsewhere, holding on to sales that would have otherwise been lost |
| Why might delayering shorten a firm's chain of command? | Delayering involves removing a layer from a firm's hierarchy. This will shorten the chain of command because a message sent from senior management directed at shop floor staff will now have to pass through one less layer of management |

| Why are organic structures better suited to unstable markets than mechanistic structures? | Because in unstable markets firms will need to be more adaptable and responsive. Therefore, an organic structure is better suited because this type of structure creates greater opportunities for empowered teamworking |
|---|---|
| How might a company go about improving its knowledge management? | By holding seminars and training workshops where older more experienced managers can pass on their wisdom and insights gained through experience to younger members of staff |

## Evaluation: The flexible organisation

Many markets are changing rapidly due to the accelerating rate of technological change. This will make it even more important for firms to be flexible, so that they will be able to respond quickly to a rapidly changing environment. It could be argued that therefore more firms will need to switch from a mechanistic towards an organic structure. Rising educational standards will also cause problems for firms that opt to retain a mechanistic culture. Future workers are unlikely to accept boring jobs with employers who expect them to just follow orders. Unenriched jobs are likely to create low morale, leading to low levels of productivity and high rates of labour turnover.

Unfortunately, many public and private sector organisations are reluctant to switch to organic structures because the people running these businesses lack trust in their staff. Over the last decade the culture within the British state education system has become less organic and more mechanistic. According to a report published by the Department for Education in 2014, two in every five newly qualified teachers leave the profession within five years of starting teaching. At a time when there's a stronger case than ever for flexible organisations, professions dominated by mechanistic attitudes must expect to lose staff.

## Key terms

**Chain of command:** describes the vertical line of power within a firm, which enables orders to be passed down through layers of hierarchy from senior managers to the final destination, which is the shop floor workforce.

**First mover advantage:** the advantages gained by a firm that is first to launch their new product into the market.

**Operational gearing:** measures a firm's fixed costs as a percentage of its total costs. Low operational gearing implies that a company's overheads are relatively low,

which will help to reduce risk by decreasing the break-even output level.

**Organisational chart:** a diagram that shows lines of responsibility and who is responsible and answerable to whom within the organisation.

**Unfair dismissal:** when an employer ends a worker's contract for a reason that is not permissible under employment law. An example of unfair dismissal would be ending a female worker's employment because she became pregnant.

# Workbook

## A. Revision questions

(45 marks; 45 minutes)

1. In your own words, explain the meaning of the term 'a flexible organisation'. (3)

2. **a)** What is meant by the phrase 'core workforce'? (2)

   **b)** Why are core workers more likely to be better skilled than peripheral workers? (2)

3. **a)** In 2013 Amazon took on 1,000 seasonal workers at their warehouse in Rugeley. In 2014 they plan to hire an extra 2,500 temporary staff before Christmas. Calculate the percentage change in the seasonal workforce. (2)

   **b)** Identify and explain two possible reasons that might explain Amazon's peripheral workforce at its Rugeley warehouse. (8)

4. In July 2014 the troubled Canadian mobile phone manufacturer BlackBerry announced that after three years the company's restructuring programme was at an end. The restructuring has seen the company's focus shift from hardware to software. The restructuring has also seen six in ten workers at the company lose their jobs. Analyse the possible effects of restructuring on BlackBerry: will it make the organisation more or less flexible? (9)

5. In 2014 the outsourcing company Capita announced that their profits had risen by 16 per cent to £238 million. The company has achieved most of its growth by winning contracts awarded by politicians to run public services on the tax payers' behalf, such as administering civil service pension schemes. The government also pays Capita to tag prisoners who have been released from jail but who still need to be monitored.

   **a)** Briefly explain two possible reasons why the government has chosen to outsource public services to companies like Capita. (6)

   **b)** Analyse the dangers of outsourcing public services to private companies? (9)

6. Distinguish between an annualised hours contract and a zero hours contract. (4)

## B. Revision exercises
### DATA RESPONSE 1

In 2011 Tim and Rachel Morris spotted a gap within Britain's rapidly growing bicycle market and began selling battery powered electric bicycles called ebikes for those that want to ride a bike, but who can't or won't pedal themselves. The business that they set up, eBikeShed grew so rapidly that the workload almost overwhelmed the owners. In 2014, to prevent sales being lost due to long waiting times, the pair decided to create the extra capacity they needed by outsourcing activities such as bike delivery and website development to specialist outside companies, which made the company more flexible. So the business kept the same level of fixed costs, yet had a greater capacity to meet customer orders.

Questions (30 marks; 35 minutes)

1. Explain one advantage and one disadvantage to eBikeShed of outsourcing in this way. (5)

2. Explain what the effect might be if Tim and Rachel developed a more mechanistic structure as eBike Shed grows. (5)

3. Ebikes have a strongly seasonal pattern of demand, with 60 per cent of the year's sales coming in April, May and June. To what extent does that make it essential that eBikeShed becomes a flexible organisation? (20)

### DATA RESPONSE 2

**Warning over zero hours contracts**

Citizens Advice Scotland (CAS) has spoken out against zero hours contracts claiming that some employees employed on zero hours contracts were going for long periods with little or no pay due to being offered few hours of work or none at all. It says the contracts make it impossible for employees to budget or make plans because they are unable to predict when or how much work they will be offered, with employers often making changes to agreed working at short notice. Some employers even failed to tell staff that their job would be on a zero hours contract when they were taken on, CAS said. In one case, a 19-year-old woman was interviewed for a job advertised as full-time by a clothes shop and was only told during training that it would be a zero hours post.

In addition workers employed on zero hours contracts often cannot claim benefits or tax credits, because they are not available for work, leaving them reliant on debt or food banks during quiet periods when they are not needed by their employer. According to CAS manager Keith Dryburgh:

'Zero hours contracts are meant to provide flexibility for employers and workers alike. They can be a useful option for some people. However, we see growing evidence that zero hours contracts are being abused by some employers'.

Some bosses have used drastic cuts to a worker's hours in order to force them to resign. The majority of zero hours workers in Scotland are aged under 25 or over 65. They are mostly women working in sectors such as catering, tourism, food and care. The benefits of zero hours contracts accrue mainly to the employer, not the worker.

Mr Dryburgh said the CAS hoped to change that situation by persuading employers that they should do right by their staff.

Source: Adapted from *The Herald* Scotland, 23 July 2014

### Questions (30 marks; 35 minutes)

1. Explain why staff might prefer full-time employment to a zero hours contract. (4)

2. Explain two reasons why a hotel might prefer to employ most of its staff on zero hours contracts, rather than on permanent full-time contracts. (6)

3. Mr Dryburgh would like to see all workers in Scotland on zero hours contracts have the legal right to request guaranteed hours from their employer without fear of dismissal. Scottish employers say that will damage their competitiveness. To what extent do you agree or disagree with Mr Dryburgh? (20)

## C. Extend your understanding

1. In 2013 *The Guardian* newspaper revealed that 90 per cent of the shop floor workers at Sports Direct are employed on zero hours contracts. The flexibility offered by zero hours contracts helped Sports Direct to make an annual profit of £240 million for the year ending July 2014. Zero hours contracts may add to a company's profits, but are they ethical? Justify your answer. (25)

2. Evaluate the reasons why most firms in the UK prefer to maintain a mechanistic organisational structure, rather than switching to an organic structure. (25)

# Chapter 92 Barriers to change

Linked to: Causes and value of change, Chapter 90; The flexible organisation, Chapter 91; Managing organisational culture, Chapter 93; Strategic implementation, Chapter 94.

## Definition

Factors within the organisation that make it harder to achieve change than might have been expected.

## 92.1 Introduction

The previous chapters explain the need for businesses to adapt their internal operations to meet a constantly changing external environment. This chapter considers the reasons why it may be difficult to navigate a period of change successfully. It also introduces the strategic approaches to managing the change process set out by the academics John Kotter and Leonard Schlesinger.

'There is nothing more difficult to take in hand, more perilous to conduct, or more uncertain in its success, than to take the lead in the introduction of a new order of things.' Niccolo Machiavelli, *The Prince (1532)*

## 92.2 Barriers to change

When individuals face any significant change in their work process, there is a tendency to resist the change. If businesses are to successfully overcome resistance to change, it is important that they understand why that resistance to change occurs. Kotter and Schlesinger's research identifies four major barriers to change:

Table 92.1 Kotter and Schlesinger's barriers to change

| Kotter and Schlesinger's four major barriers to change | |
|---|---|
| **Parochial self-interest** | Concern over how the change affects me, rather than the business as a whole |
| **Misunderstanding** | Of the details of the changes being implemented and how they will affect individuals |
| **Low tolerance** | Some individuals crave security and stability at work and will thus have a naturally low tolerance to change |
| **Different assessments** | From staff who may believe the change is unnecessary or believe the drawbacks of the changes will outweigh the benefits |

## Parochial self-interest

Changes within an organisation will often involve changes to the structure, or to the specific working conditions of groups of employees. Some will worry that their power within the business may be diminished. Others may suspect that their conditions of employment will change, perhaps from moving onto temporary contracts. Both reasons mean individuals would stand to lose out from the changes. These individuals will dislike the changes and may resist them.

## Misunderstanding

Kotter and Schlesinger note that misunderstanding and lack of trust of leadership combine to form a possible barrier to change. In many organisations there is a degree of mistrust between employees and managers – they often have conflicting personal objectives. Thus, when leaders introduce changes, there may be a natural tendency for employees to misunderstand the proposed changes in a negative way – expecting the worse – thus initially resisting change.

## Low tolerance

The ability of human beings to accept change is limited. People tend to crave stability and security – especially in their working lives. Change for them may mean the need to build new working relationships, or adjust their skills in order to perform new tasks. This fear of change, something that ties in well with Maslow's security or safety needs, can be a cause of those with a low tolerance to change resisting change, even if the change appears to be for the better.

## Different assessments

In some cases, staff may feel that a particular section of the business is doing well, or that a process is particularly efficient. If these areas are subject to change, they may believe that managers are wrong to change an area of strength. This assessment may be made without all the information available to management, who may be better placed to evaluate the competitiveness of that department. For example managers may have access to a benchmarking exercise. On the other hand, managements may themselves be the ones with the wrong view – partly because they are inclined to bring in outside management consultants, who inevitably lack the knowledge of the insider.

'If you want to make enemies, try to change something.' Woodrow Wilson, former U.S. President

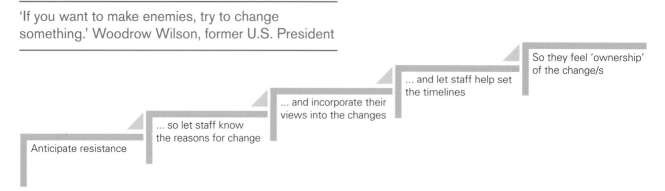

**Figure 92.1** Logic chain: Overcoming resistance to change

## 92.3 Overcoming resistance to change

Kotter and Schlesinger's work also identified six methods for dealing with resistance to change, which will have varying degrees of success depending upon the causes. Generally a mixture of methods will be used. They should be selected by carefully considering the methods that are most appropriate given the nature of the workforce and the nature and speed of the change. The six ways are explained below.

'The greatest danger in times of turbulence is not the turbulence; it is to act with yesterday's logic.' Peter Drucker, business guru

## Education and communication

A highly effective method for breaking down resistance to change is to successfully explain the need for change before it is implemented. This is especially effective where resistance is the result of misunderstanding or a different assessment of the firm's position before the change. However, this method relies on a level of trust between management and staff if the communication is to be believed by the staff whose resistance is to be overcome. Large scale presentations, or even corporate films can be used to try to provide the information and education needed for staff. Exactly these methods were used by British Airways, proving that trust is needed but not always forthcoming (partly because it isn't always deserved).

## Participation and involvement

Involving potential resistors in designing how the change will happen can be an excellent method of breaking down resistance before it becomes entrenched. The change managers here should listen carefully to the views of staff and seek to try to adapt changes where possible to take these views into account. This method tends to polarise opinion from managers, with Kotter and Schlesinger reporting that some managers believe participation of staff is vital, whilst others that it is highly dangerous. There is little doubt that if staff feel that change is based on their ideas, they are far more likely to commit to the changes – something which may be vital for the changes to work – instead of merely complying with new methods. It is worth pointing out that this method is likely to take time due to the amount of consultation needed, and therefore be unsuitable as a way of overcoming resistance when the speed of change is vital.

## Facilitation and support

This method works best when resistance is the result of fear of change – perhaps from those with a low tolerance to change. Extra training may be offered to staff to help prepare for the new situation or staff may be given time off after the changes are implemented. In addition, line managers can be supportive of staff and listen to their concerns. This can be a natural, organic method of overcoming resistance. However, it is time-consuming, so isn't suitable at a time of crisis.

## Negotiation and agreement

This involves offering some kind of incentive to resistors if they accept the change. Often used where resistance is led by a trade union, staff may be offered a pay rise for accepting changed working conditions, or perhaps offered the chance of early retirement. This method works particularly well when resistors are resisting due to parochial self-interest - since it is designed to reduce the extent to which the change will make them worse off. However, if this method is used, there is the danger that staff will feel that resisting future changes will always lead to compromise from managers. This would push up the costs of the next change programme (remembering that change is a constant in many firms).

## Manipulation and co-option

The manipulation referred to generally involves providing only limited information to those resisting change or the deliberate setting up of events to ensure that resistance weakens. This manipulation may involve appointing potential leaders of the resistance to positions within the change management team. However, the co-opted member of the team may not be listened to, merely put in place as an attempt to show that the views of the disgruntled are being heard. This manipulative, cynical strategy may backfire with long-term effects on relations with staff.

## Explicit and implicit coercion

Undoubtedly the least effective for maintaining workforce morale and effective employer-employee relations in the future, coercion means forcing by way of threats. Threats may include threatening the loss of jobs, reduced chances of promotion or training or actually firing or transferring staff from areas where change is required. This method for dealing with resistance to change will store ill will and negative sentiment in the workforce which is likely to continually hamper performance in the future. As Herzberg said, 'A remembered pain leads to a revenge psychology – they'll get back at you one day when you need them'. Despite this, there may be times when this is the only way to push through an essential change – such as a switch to robotic production by a loss-making company.

---

'Faced with the choice between changing one's mind and proving that there is no need to do so, almost everyone gets busy on the proof.' John Kenneth Galbraith, economist

---

**Table 92.2** Summary of methods for overcoming resistance to change

| | Advantages | Drawbacks | Use it when: |
|---|---|---|---|
| **Education and communication** | Builds commitment to the change once staff understand what is needed and why | Time consuming and expensive | Resistors lack information or understanding of the proposed change |
| **Participation and involvement** | The best way of building commitment as staff will feel ownership of changes they have had a hand in designing | Consultation is a time-consuming process; there is a danger of poor decision-making from staff who may not have all available information | Change designers lack information that staff could provide |
| **Facilitation and support** | Especially good at dealing with low tolerance change resistors | Can take time, be expensive and still fail | The major cause of resistance is difficulty in adjusting to new methods |
| **Negotiation and agreement** | Can be an effective way of gaining compliance of all who will be negatively affected | Can be expensive to make concessions and may alert others to the benefit of resisting | A powerful group will lose out from the change |
| **Manipulation and co-optation** | Can work quickly and be done cheaply | May leave staff feeling manipulated – damaging employer/employee relations going forward | Other methods will not work or are too costly |
| **Explicit and implicit coercion** | Can be done quickly and overcome any type of resistance in the short term | Leads to only grudging acceptance of changes and creates ill will which is likely to persist in the future | Speed is vital and those driving change are powerful |

## 92.4 Kotter and Schlesinger's theory – a critique

Ever since their article appeared in 1979, Kotter and Schlesinger's thoughts on change management have been implemented – largely unsuccessfully. Research right up to the present day shows a failure rate of 65-70 per cent on attempts at organisational change. This may simply be because it's such a difficult thing to get right (that is, perhaps the success rate would be even lower without Kotter and Schlesinger). It may also be because the theory seems based on the wrong premise. It seems to assume that just because change is inevitably necessary at some point, managements know which change is needed and when. The reality is that change is usually 'needed' when a new boss is appointed. When WH Smith bought Waterstones bookshops they centralised all buying decisions – effectively downgrading the role of store managers (it was a disaster). When the business was bought by a wealthy Russian who appointed James Daunt as the new boss – he decentralised the structure. Well, they couldn't both be right!

It is reasonable to suggest that the most important thing in change management is to identify the right change. When appointed boss of Tesco in 2014 Dave Lewis rightly spent months talking to staff throughout the business. He used consultation to be sure that he understood the problems, the staff attitudes and the possible solutions. Kotter and Schlesinger over-emphasise the *process* of change, forgetting that the *nature* of the change is what matters in the long run – which in turn affects the short-run staff response.

### Theory in 60 seconds:

#### Kotter and Schlesinger on barriers to change

- Written in 1979
- Suggests there are four major barriers to change: parochial self-interest, misunderstanding, low tolerance and different assessments
- …and six ways to overcome resistance to change, on a scale from education to explicit coercion
- Given the sustained high failure rate of change strategies (65 to 70 per cent) it might be felt that Kotter and Schlesinger's theory has proved a disappointment – perhaps because it ignores the management problem of identifying the right change.

'The rate of change is not going to slow down anytime soon. If anything, competition in most industries will probably speed up even more in the next few decades.' John P. Kotter, *Leading Change*

## Five Whys and a How

| Question | Answer |
|---|---|
| Why do people resist change? | Kotter and Schlesinger identified four main causes – self-interest, misunderstanding, low tolerance and different assessment |
| Why do organisations need to change? | Changes in the markets in which firms operate forces businesses to change in order to remain competitive |
| Why is it important to manage change? | Changes must be planned and then managed to ensure that staff implement those changes in the way that was planned |
| Why can some methods of overcoming change create future problems? | Manipulation and coercion will both create negative sentiments in staff who will feel they have been threatened, bullied or cheated by change managers. These negative feelings will breed a desire to get back at managers in the future |
| Why is commitment a key to successful change management? | Staff who feel that the changes are for the best will work harder to make new methods work – meaning the new methods are more likely to work as planned |
| How should managers choose the best method to overcome resistance to change? | Managers must assess the changes planned, the extent to which they have all information needed to make the changes, the speed with which change must take place, the importance of managing costs during the change and the main causes of resistance to the particular changes planned |

## Evaluation: Barriers to change

Even Kotter and Schlesinger – key academic figures in change management – qualify most of their work by stating that successfully managing change is one of the toughest jobs to complete in any organisation. Once people are working in an established way, for change to take place the status quo must be shattered and then adjusted before the new, desired, status quo can be established. This will take time, especially if the changes are resisted. Of course, changes which involve redundancies and changes to working conditions will distress some staff. This is why change is so difficult to manage.

The seriousness of the effects of change on staff make it inexcusable when bosses simply dodge real responsibility. Bringing in management consultants is a standard (and expensive – and not very effective) way to do this. The boss then steps aside while the consultants carry out their research and write their recommendations – and perhaps bring in the temporary managers who will carry out the redundancies and redeployments. Ultimately, a boss has the moral duty to accept the tough parts of the job as well as the glamorous ones. In July 2014 Forbes business magazine ran an article with the title: 'You can't outsource change management'. Quite right.

## Key terms

**Change management:** the business discipline of adjusting process or structure within an organisation.

**Barriers to change:** anything that represents a constraint on attempts to manage change within an organisation.

**Benchmarking:** using independently obtained evidence on the performance of a number of rival companies to find out what a good performance should look like, for example Jaguar Land Rover's labour turnover figure of just 1.8 per cent.

**Management consultants:** experienced outsiders who can look at a problem objectively and recommend a solution without concern for how tough it may be for certain individuals or groupings.

# Workbook

## A. Revision questions

(35 marks; 35 minutes)

1. Using your part-time job, school, or even home life, explain one occasion when you have resisted change for the following reasons:

   **a)** parochial self-interest

   **b)** misunderstanding

   **c)** different assessments. (9)

2. Explain why misunderstanding is more likely to cause resistance to change in branches of an international retailer. (4)

3. Briefly explain three issues that a change management team should consider when deciding which approach to take in overcoming resistance to change. (9)

4. Briefly explain which three methods of overcoming resistance to change are likely to avoid damaging employer/employee relations, and why. (9)

5. Explain why the presence of a trade union may be more likely to result in a negotiated route to overcoming resistance than manipulation and co-option. (4)

## B. Revision exercises

### DATA RESPONSE

Hemmings and Bennett Ltd is a medium-sized engineering firm that specialises in manufacturing cutting edge propulsion systems used in rockets. The firm has been established for over 25 years and has a loyal and exceptionally highly skilled workforce. Over recent years they have found it increasingly hard to generate the profit levels expected by shareholders as they have struggled to compete with emerging rivals from Europe and China. Chief Executive Andy Bennett has been convinced by his Finance Director that the firm needs to reduce costs in order to maintain competitiveness. In order for this to happen, they have identified a number of steps that can be taken without damaging the quality of output produced:

- Thirty per cent of the workforce to be made redundant.
- Staff holiday entitlement to be cut by 25 per cent.
- Several simple processes to be outsourced to a company in the Czech Republic.
- A 50 per cent cut in the training budget.

The shareholders agreed these proposals and gave Andy 12 months to make the changes. He and his directors held a series of planning meetings in order to decide how to proceed.

**Table 92.3** Hemmings and Bennett Ltd – selected data before the change programme

| | Hemmings and Bennett Ltd before the changes | Industry average |
|---|---|---|
| Capacity utilisation | 70% | 85% |
| Average age of staff | 46 | 32 |
| Index of unit cost | 124 | 100 |
| Labour costs as a per cent of total costs | 52% | 38% |
| Per cent of workforce who belong to a trade union | 17% | 12% |
| Net profit margin | 8% | 15% |
| ROCE | 6% | 16% |

### Questions (40 marks; 45 minutes)

1. Using the information from the case study and data table, analyse why change is needed at Hemmings and Bennett Ltd. (12)

2. Explain three possible causes of resistance to the changes proposed at Hemmings and Bennett Ltd. (12)

3. Recommend the best method(s) for Andy to use to overcome any resistance to change from staff. (16)

## C. Extend your understanding

1. 'Managing change is easier when change is being made in a successful business than one that is struggling'. To what extent do you agree with this statement? (25)

2. To what extent would it be difficult to change Marks & Spencer into a dynamic, young, fashion-conscious organisation? (25)

# Managing organisational culture

**Linked to:** Influences on the mission of a business, Chapter 53; Causes and value of change, Chapter 90; Barriers to change, Chapter 92; Strategic implementation, Chapter 94.

'The thing I have learned at IBM is that culture is everything.' Louis Gerstner, former Chief Executive, IBM

## Definition

Organisational culture sums up the spirit, the attitudes, the behaviours and the ethos of 'the organisation'. It is embodied in the people who work there via traditions that have built up over time.

## 93.1 Introduction

Culture is often described as 'the way we do things round here'. This will be built up over many years as a result of:

- **The aims or mission of the business**: if the aim is to be innovative, this will affect the business culture.

- **The behaviour of the company directors and other senior staff**: if they pay themselves huge bonuses and jump at chances to fly business class to questionable conferences, staff will pick up the idea that 'me, me, me' is at the heart of the business culture.

- **The attitude of senior management to enterprise and risk**: if an unsuccessful new product launch leads to the dismissal of the manager leading the project, this will send out a message to all staff to beware of taking on responsibility, which could be very damaging in the long term.

- **The recruitment and training procedures**: dynamic companies have a mixture of different types of staff: some organised, some creative but chaotic; some argumentative, some 'yes-men' and so on. Many HR departments use psychometric tests to recruit 'our type of person'. The culture could become quite passive – safe but dull – if new recruits have similar backgrounds, personalities and behaviours.

## Real business

### Cultural differences in India

A recent report on takeovers in India cites cultural differences as a high-risk factor in corporate deals. Twenty-nine different languages are spoken by at least 1 million Indian people and customs and working styles differ significantly between regions. Companies in northern India tend to have more assertive, Western cultures, while companies in the south are more traditionally Indian; that is, they have a more formal and subtle culture, emphasising protocol, seniority and indirect communication. Western predator companies often fail to understand these differences, seeing 'Indian' in a one-dimensional way. Indian companies have also come unstuck when trying to bring together two conflicting workplace cultures.

## 93.2 The importance of organisational culture

In recent years banks turned their backs on tradition and turned themselves into casinos. For centuries, a culture of caution had been at the heart of banking. The successful banker was one who went through a career without making any awful mistakes. Suddenly this approach was considered to be old-fashioned. The focus was no longer on building a career; it was on building a bonus. As that bonus might be from £100,000 to £10,000,000 (a year!), who would look any further ahead than the coming months?

Nor was it difficult to make the profits required to get the bonuses. With plentiful cheap money (low interest rates) the clever thing was to borrow lots and lend it out as fast as possible. Why check on whether 'sub-prime' borrowers were likely to default in a year or two, if this year's bonus could be boosted to £500,000?

The collapse of this house of cards in 2008 and 2009 led to a predictable collapse with huge losses within the banking sector (estimated by the World Bank at $1 trillion). The culture of recklessness and greed had been created by a crazy bonus system that gave people (non-returnable) rewards based on the short term. In the longer term, the shareholders, the bank customers and governments had to pay the bills.

This example shows that culture is at the heart (or *is* the heart) of every organisation. Unusually, the banking example shows that culture can be transformed quite quickly, in certain circumstances. More often, businesses find that 'the way we do things round here' is very resistant to change. When Newcastle United FC appointed manager Sam Allardyce to transform its underperforming stars, he brought his own results-orientated approach to St James's Park. He soon found himself swamped by the supporters' fury at his boring football. The 'Newcastle way' (the culture) had long been for bright, attacking, flair football. Big Sam did not last long.

Every organisation has its own culture. One school will have a staff room that is buzzing an hour before the start of the day; another's staff car park will still be empty. One clothes shop will have staff who take their time helping customers, while another's staff play and joke with each other. And one charity will be focused entirely on the people it is set up to help, while another will behave as if the charity itself is more important than its 'customers'.

Distinguishing between healthy and unhealthy cultures is not difficult. It can be summed up in the following:

- focus on customers' real needs (not just a script staff are supposed to follow)
- an attitude of 'can-do' rather than 'must we?'
- a real feeling for the organisation as 'us', as a long-term commitment
- a conviction among staff that the organisation is a force for good (that is, not just a money-making machine).

'Culture is one thing and varnish is another.' Ralph Waldo Emerson, nineteenth-century American sage

## 93.3 Handy's four types of culture

In his book *Gods of Management*, Charles Handy developed four ways of classifying business culture. These are discussed below and can be used to analyse business culture in more depth.

'Culture eats strategy for breakfast.' Richard Plepler, Chief Executive, HBO

### Power cultures

**Power cultures** are found in organisations in which there is one or a small group of power holders. In effect the boss can become the spider in the middle of the web, with everything going through him or her. There are likely to be few rules or procedures and most communication will be by personal contact. This encourages flexibility among employees. Decision-making is not limited by any code of practice. This can result in questionable, perhaps unethical, actions being taken in an attempt to please the boss. The leadership style in such a situation is clearly autocratic, and has been displayed in recent times by leaders such as Sir Alex Ferguson of Manchester United and Sir Alan Sugar (boss of Amstrad and notorious as the central character in BBC TV's *The Apprentice*).

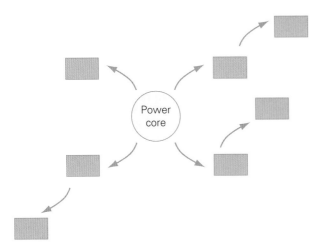

**Figure 93.1** In a power culture, a web of power grows from the centre of the organisation

## Role cultures

**Role cultures** are found in established organisations that have developed a lot of formal rules as they have grown. Power depends on the position an individual holds in the business, rather than the qualities of the person themselves. All employees are expected to conform to rules and procedures, and promotion follows a predictable pattern. This culture is bureaucratic, cautious and focused on the avoidance of mistakes. It may be appropriate when the competitive environment is stable; for example, in industries with long product life cycles. However, if the pace of change becomes more rapid, staff will struggle to adapt to new market conditions. This is the approach taken in businesses such as Microsoft, where the key thing is to preserve its huge share of the software market. The leadership style could be autocratic or paternalistic.

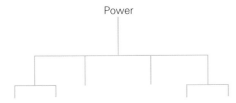

**Figure 93.2** In a role culture, power flows down from the top of the organisation

## Task cultures

**Task cultures** have no single power source. Senior managers allocate projects to teams of employees made up of representatives from different functional departments. Each group is formed for the purpose of a single undertaking and is then disbanded. Power within the team lies in the expertise of each individual and is not dependent upon status or role. This culture can be effective in dealing with rapidly changing competitive environments because it is flexible; for

example, in markets with short product life cycles. However, project teams may develop their own objectives independently of the firm. The approach to leadership in such organisations is a mixture of paternalistic and democratic.

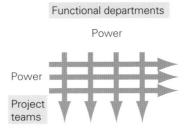

**Figure 93.3** In a task culture, power flows down from the functional departments at the top of the matrix, but also lies horizontally within project teams

## Person cultures

**Person cultures** are developed when individuals with similar training and backgrounds are encouraged to form groups to enhance their expertise and share knowledge. This type of culture is most often found within functional departments of large, complex organisations, or among professionals such as lawyers or accountants. It is largely associated with democratic leadership.

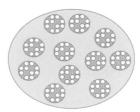

**Figure 93.4** In a person culture, power lies within each group of individuals, flowing from their common knowledge and skills

### Real business

#### River Cafe

At London's posh River Cafe restaurant, there's a friendly, chilled-out sense of teamwork among waiting and cooking staff. Perhaps uniquely, the waiters are incorporated fully into the business. They help prepare ('prep') the food before the lunch and dinner services and – like all the staff – enjoy at least one trip to Italy each year - to be taken to meet suppliers and to eat at some of the owner's favourite restaurants. All staff enjoy secure, permanent employment and wages that are far above the minimum-wage-norm in the catering trade. A waiter explains, 'We're paid well enough to not worry about tips: we can enjoy serving customers without needing to crawl to them.' The (privately-owned) River Cafe is noted in London for great service, and is rated among the top ten restaurants in Britain.

## 93.4 Hofstede's national cultures

The global guru of organisational culture is the Dutch psychologist Geert Hofstede. His research among more than 100,000 IBM employees led to important categorisations of the cultures of different nationalities. The categories can also be used to analyse the culture within different departments within a company. His original research (1960s-1970s) led him to suggest four important categories of culture that distinguish different peoples:

- power distance (the degree to which workers find it acceptable for there to be a big distance between them and those in power)
- individualism – collectivism (conviction in the power of the individual vs the power of the committee)
- uncertainty avoidance (being cautious vs being entrepreneurial)
- masculinity – femininity (rather uncomfortably, Hofstede used this terminology to distinguish between hard-edged, fact-based decision-making (supposedly male) and softer, more intuitive thinking (supposedly female).

Later, after work in China, he added a fifth: long-termism – short-termism.

Before adding this fifth dimension, Hofstede's research showed the differences between national cultures on his four main measures (Shown in Table 93.1).

## Implications

1. Power distance: greatest in Mexico and China, that is, people accept a wide gulf between bosses and workers; lowest in Denmark (and UK), where workers feel more equal to their bosses.

2. Individualism (as compared with collectivism). The most individualistic cultures are in America and the UK; the least individualistic in China and South Korea.

3. Uncertainty avoidance is highest in Poland, France and South Korea, that is, these cultures crave security. In Denmark, China, the UK and India there are more risk-takers.

4. Masculinity (defined as a focus on hard-edged decision-making) is highest in Mexico, the UK, Germany and China. Femininity prevails in Holland and Denmark.

## Other implications of Hofstede's work

- **Reasons for changes in organisational culture**: if a firm's research shows that uncertainty avoidance is higher among its staff than the UK national average, it might choose to tackle this risk-aversion head-on; in other words Hofstede's research gives a benchmark companies can measure themselves against.

- **Ways of changing organisational culture**: one way might be to shift the balance between staff of

**Table 93.1** Differences between national cultures using Hofstede's main measures

| | Power distance | Individualism | Uncertainty voidance | Masculinity/ Femininity |
|---|---|---|---|---|
| Canada | 39 | 80 | 48 | 52 |
| China | 80 | 20 | 30 | 66 |
| Denmark | 18 | 74 | 23 | 16 |
| France | 68 | 71 | 86 | 43 |
| Germany | 35 | 67 | 65 | 66 |
| India | 77 | 48 | 40 | 56 |
| Mexico | 81 | 30 | 82 | 69 |
| Netherlands | 38 | 80 | 53 | 14 |
| Poland | 68 | 60 | 93 | 64 |
| South Korea | 60 | 18 | 85 | 39 |
| United Kingdom | 35 | 89 | 35 | 66 |
| United States | 40 | 91 | 46 | 62 |
| Mean average | 58 | 49 | 65 | 50 |

Source: Geert Hofstede, *Culture's Consequences: International Differences in Work-Related Values,* 1980, Beverly Hills, CA

different national backgrounds, for example Marks & Spencer's growth strategy in China seems to have faltered; perhaps there are too many local (Chinese) managers in decision-making positions; it might be better to have more British middle managers.

- **Problems of changing organisational culture**: if national characteristics are such a constant as Hofstede's work implies, it may be very difficult to shift staff cultures, for example to make Chinese workers responsive to a democratic leadership style and ease them into a culture of staff suggestions or continuous improvement.

| Handy and culture | Hofstede and culture |
|---|---|
| Suggests four types: power, person, role and task | Five types: individualism, risk-taking, masculinity, power & long-termism |
| Takes a narrow view of culture, ignoring ethics and risk-taking | Based on an analysis of national cultures |
| Seems overly focused on leadership | Avoids stereotyping, apart from the awkward masculinity/femininity |

**Figure 93.5** Logic balance: Handy vs Hofstede

## 93.5 The influences on organisational culture

### Internal influences

**Leadership**: an organisation may have been moulded to the personality of the founder, for example Branson, Jobs, Zuckerberg or Bezos; if so the culture is derived from the founder/leader. And not just positive, entrepreneurial cultures; note the obsessive tax avoidance of Virgin, Apple, Facebook and Amazon, perhaps reflecting an insecurity summed up in the quote from Andy Grove of Intel, 'Only the paranoid survive'.

Some non-founder leaders have the personality (and longevity) to transform culture, such as Terry Leahy, whose fourteen years at the head of Tesco achieved profits but a flawed legacy. Most leaders, however, are not in post long enough to make much difference to 'the way we do things round here'.

**Real business**

### *GooglePerks*

Google has an unusual culture. Its U.S. Headquarters looks more like an adult playground than a place for work. Google's success can partly be attributed to this culture. Google has people whose sole job is to keep employees happy and maintain productivity.

Hence the 'GooglePerks':

- Free breakfast, lunch, and dinner. The organic food is chef-prepared
- Free health and dental care and haircuts
- Gyms and swimming pools
- Video games, foosball and ping pong.

**Figure 93.6** Google's HQ

And does it all add up to a profitable business? Well, in 2014 Google's global revenues of $66 billion yielded a pre-tax profit of $17.25 billion. The only cloud hanging over the company is its approach to tax avoidance which, in Britain at least, is starting to raise serious questions about Google's famous motto, 'Don't be evil'.

### Type of ownership

Public limited companies (plcs) have many external shareholders who seek 'shareholder value' (rising dividends and a rising share price) which derives from profit. In the UK, plcs produce half-yearly trading statements, giving a profit horizon of six months. Tight budgeting to meet profit forecasts can create its own narrow culture.

Some large, multinational limited companies such as JCB are family-owned and can take a longer-term view. JCB opened its first overseas factory in India in 1979; it took more than 15 years to break even, but it now has more than a 50 per cent share of the Indian construction vehicles market.

### Private ownership versus plc

In late 2014 and early 2015 the big retail flops were Tesco, Marks & Spencer, Sainsbury's and Morrisons (all plcs) while the successes were Waitrose, Aldi and Lidl. Aldi and Lidl are privately-owned companies while Waitrose is part of the John Lewis Partnership, effectively owned by its workforce. Aldi and Lidl boosted their combined grocery market share from 5 per cent in 2010 to 9 per cent at the start of 2015. Perhaps their ability to plan long term has helped them succeed against the supermarket plcs.

## Past recruitment policies

In middle and senior management, some firms represent a monoculture: perhaps stale, pale and male (old, white blokes). This may lead to a culture in which 'we' know best, even if 60 per cent of our customers are young women and 20 per cent non-white. Currently 7 per cent of FTSE 100 executive directors are women; non-white FTSE directors are in a tiny minority. Would the long-term weaknesses at Marks & Spencer, Game and HMV have persisted if the directors had been younger, and more online savvy?

## 93.6 Reasons for and problems of changing organisational culture

When a new chief executive joins a business, her first impressions will be of the culture. Is the customer embraced by the business, or kept at arm's length by voicemail and answerphone messages? Do staff enjoy Monday morning or only Friday afternoon?

If the new chief executive is unhappy about the culture, achieving change is unlikely to come easily. After all, some staff may have been working at the same place for 15 years, and will find it very difficult to change. Even more problematic is that staff collectively have a set of attitudes that may be tough to overcome. A manufacturing business may be dominated by middle-aged engineers who are sure they know best how to make a car or a caramel. Switching to a more market-orientated business may be very difficult.

The key to success in this process will be to ensure that all staff believe that the change is genuinely going to happen (and, preferably, that the change is the right one). There will be middle managers who are crucial to making things happen (for example, human resource managers or the finance staff who supervise the budget-setting process). If these people believe that the change is only skin-deep, they will hold back from supporting it. The engineers are likely to resist the change and perhaps they will prove right. Perhaps the new chief executive will be pushed aside by a board of directors who start to worry about whether a mistake is being made.

The key to cultural change, then, is to have a clear, consistent message. If everyone believes that the change is to be pushed through, they are far more likely to support it.

Not all cultural changes prove to be a success. Sometimes new leaders assume that a change in culture is essential, because they do not take the time to understand the strengths of the existing one. The Conservative governments of the 1990s swept away the tradition of NHS hospital wards being run by an all-powerful 'matron'. A failure to clean the ward properly would have meant risking the wrath of matron; cleaners cleaned. The new approach was to award contracts to outside cleaning companies, then check that agreed targets had been met. The matrons were pushed aside in favour of professional, 'can-do' managers. The managers were supportive of the new cleaning businesses; unfortunately, the cleaners were not so committed to cleaning. The later wave of MRSA-bug bacterial problems in hospitals can be put down to a management change based on inadequate understanding.

'In most organisational change efforts, it is much easier to draw on the strengths of the culture than to overcome the constraints by changing the culture.'
Professor Edgar Schein, academic and author

## Five Whys and a How

| Question | Answer |
|---|---|
| Why might 'culture eat strategy for breakfast'? (See the quote by Richard Plepler on page 604.) | Because you never know whether individual decisions or plans will turn out right, but with the right culture you'll keep being pleasantly surprised |
| Why is role culture said to be bureaucratic? | Because individuals have to conform to their roles and everyone checks things out with the next role up in the organisation (their boss) |
| Why do Handy and Hofstede's theories make no mention of ethics? | Indeed a mystery. The cultures of companies such as Barclays, Tesco and BP had ethical flaws at their heart. That will have soured every aspect of the culture |
| Why might Hofstede's 'masculine-feminine' category be important? | Because some great business decisions have been made intuitively rather than 'scientifically' (most famously, by Apple's Steve Jobs) |
| Why might culture be dominated by short-term thinking? | If a company is focused on short-term profit, that will prevent any positive culture traits emerging |
| How might a company measure the success (or otherwise) of a culture change programme? | By conducting regular research among customers – if positive change is happening among staff, customers will see or feel it |

## Evaluation: Managing organisational culture

Business leaders make many claims about the culture among their staff. They enjoy using words such as 'positive', 'can-do' and 'entrepreneurial'. Does the fact that the leader says these things mean that they are true? Clearly not. The leader cannot admit in public that the culture is 'lazy', 'negative' or 'bureaucratic'.

A well-judged answer to a question about culture will look beyond claims and public relations, and look for the evidence. Is there evidence that staff suggestions are welcomed and that they make an important contribution to the business? Is there evidence that mistakes are treated as learning experiences, rather than as reasons to be fired. Perhaps most important of all, is there evidence that staff love their jobs and look forward to coming to work? All these things are tests of an organisation's culture.

## Key terms

**Bureaucratic:** an organisation in which initiative is stifled by paperwork and excessive checking and rechecking of decisions and actions.

**Psychometric tests** are designed to test the psychological make-up of a candidate, that is, the personality and character of the individual.

# Workbook

## A. Revision questions

(40 marks; 40 minutes)

1. Explain why poor recruitment could lead to an ineffective business culture. (4)

2. Explain whether you think two of the following businesses would be likely to have an entrepreneurial or a bureaucratic business culture (that is, you choose two from four).
   a) Marks & Spencer
   b) Facebook
   c) L'Oréal
   d) Ryanair (8)

3. Explain why it is unlikely that a task culture could exist in a business with an authoritarian leadership. (4)

4. Explain why a role culture would be inappropriate for a new software company seeking to be more innovative than Google. (4)

5. Sir Alex Ferguson was manager of Manchester United for 25 years. Explain two problems in changing the culture at an organisation dominated by one person, as at Manchester United. (8)

6. There was an entrepreneurial culture within the UK banking sector in the lead-up to the crash of 2008/9. Does that prove that an entrepreneurial culture is a bad thing? Explain your answer. (6)

7. Recently a former quantity surveyor told the BBC that he had left the construction industry because he was so disillusioned by the problem of price fixing. Explain how a new leader of a construction firm might try to change the culture to one of honest dealing. (6)

## B. Revision exercises
### DATA RESPONSE

**Bakery culture**

Gianni Falcone had built his Italian bakery up over a 40-year period in Britain. He came to escape a life dominated in the 1960s by the Sicilian Mafia, and started a bakery in South London. For the first ten years his life had been hard and very poor. Baking only white rolls and white bread, he had to keep his prices low to compete with local supermarkets. He would get up at 1.30 a.m. every day to prepare and then bake the bread, and his working day would end 12 hours later. With a young family of four, he could not get to bed until 8.30 in the evening. Five hours' later he would be back at work.

Eventually he started to see ways of adding value to his dough. A half kilogram loaf of bread with 30p of ingredients would sell for 80p, but roll it flat, smear tomato, cheese and herbs on it (cost: 25p) and it became a £3 pizza. A series of value-added initiatives followed, all adding both to the popularity of the shop and to its profitability. By 2000 the queues on a Saturday morning were legendary. Gianni was able to finance houses for all his family and he started to dream of owning a Ferrari.

By 2005 the business employed all the family members plus six extra staff. All worked the Gianni way. All knew the principles behind the business: ingredients should be as natural as possible and of as high a quality as possible. The customer is not always right (rowdy schoolchildren will be thrown out if necessary) but the customer must always be treated with respect. A slightly over-baked loaf will be sold at half price and day-old currant buns are given away to regular customers. Above all else, Gianni wanted to be honest with customers; they knew that all the baked goods were baked freshly on the premises.

Then, in 2012, Gianni was taken ill. The problem was with his lungs; quite simply, 40 years of flour in the bakery air had taken its toll. He had to retire. As none of his family wanted to take on the commitment to the awful working hours, he had to sell up. The only person with the inclination and the money to buy was an experienced baker from Malta, Trevi Malone. He bought the business for £250,000. Gianni was able to retire to the substantial home he had built in Sicily (now relatively Mafia-free).

From the start, Malone's approach was dramatically different. While Gianni had been ill, all the baking had been done by his bakery assistant Carol. She had worked miracles by herself, so that the shelves were full every morning. Now, from the first morning, Malone showed his distaste for her ways of working. Why did she use organic yeast when there were perfectly good, cheaper ones? Why did she 'knead' the dough in batches of 5 kg when it would be better to do it by machine in 20 kg quantities? And when she suggested that it would be good to start making hot cross buns, Malone snapped, 'This crazy place already makes too many different lines; just concentrate on what you're doing.' In the past, Carol's ideas had led to successful new products such as a top-selling apricot doughnut. Now she was silenced.

In the shop, Malone's approach was also quite different. Instead of casual clothes, everyone would wear uniforms; customers would be addressed as 'Sir' or 'Madam', and every order must be followed by an 'upselling' suggestion. The person who bought only a loaf of bread should be asked, 'Would you like any doughnuts or cakes today?' The sales staff thought this was a daft idea, because – with so many regular customers – people would soon tire of being asked to spend more money. But they had quickly picked up the idea that Malone was not interested in discussion – he knew best.

Over the coming weeks things were changed steadily. The ham used on the meat pizza was changed from 'Italian baked ham' at £10 per kg to a much cheaper Danish one (with 20 per cent added water). As Malone said to Carol, 'Our customers don't see the ingredients label, so who's to know?' Malone noticed that doughnuts took longer to prepare than was justified by their 60p price tag, so he started to buy them in from a wholesale baker. Outsourcing was the sensible approach.

Within two months Carol began to look for a new job. She found it in another bakery, but soon left that as well, and went to college to retrain for a new career. Other staff steadily left, including all of Gianni's family. The newly recruited staff were accepting of Malone's rules, but none seemed particularly keen on the work. Perhaps that was fortunate, because sales started to slip after two months, and then fell at an increasingly rapid pace. Staff who left were not replaced, as they were no longer needed. Even more fortunate was the fact that Gianni was not well enough to travel back to England. He never knew how quickly 40 years of work fell apart.

### Questions (40 marks; 50 minutes)

1. Analyse why outsourcing the doughnuts may not have been 'a sensible approach' for Malone. (12)

2. Malone paid £250,000 for a business that steadily went downhill. Analyse why the problem was due to the change in culture within the workplace. (12)

3. To what extent does the example of Gianni's bakery prove that value added is at the heart of all business activity? (16)

## C. Extend your understanding

1. When he took over as boss of Barclays in 2012, Anthony Jenkins said that it would 'take five to ten years' to change the bank's organisational culture. To what extent might this be to do with the size of this multinational bank? (25)

2. To what extent will workplace culture be the key factor in your own choice of job when you leave education? (25)

# Chapter 94

# Strategic implementation

**Linked to:** The impact of strategic decision-making on functional decision-making, Chapter 55; The value of SWOT analysis, Chapter 56; Causes and value of change, Chapter 90; Problems with strategy, Chapter 96.

## Definition

Strategic implementation involves putting plans into action, so that the organisation can achieve its goals. A good plan will not automatically deliver success unless the plan can be put into practice and executed properly. Effective strategic implementation is as important to success as the plan itself.

## 94.1 The need for strategic change

To a certain extent, change is an unavoidable part of life, both for individuals and organisations. Existing markets decline and new products are developed. Experienced workers retire or leave, and are replaced by new employees with fresh ideas. According to recent research published by the Chartered Institute of Personnel Development (CIPD), organisations undergo major change once every three years on average, with smaller changes taking place almost continually.

The need for change can result from influences within and outside the business. Change is an inevitable part of business growth. For a firm that grows organically, this change may be relatively slow and steady, occurring over a prolonged period of time. However, managers will still need to have the skills and expertise required to anticipate and manage this change effectively. Change resulting from merger or takeover will be more sudden, and may be followed by a painful period of adjustment, even if careful planning has taken place beforehand.

Change may be anticipated, such as the introduction of a new marketing strategy, or unanticipated – for example, the collapse of an important supplier or a sudden deterioration in customer satisfaction. Changes may be beyond the control of individual businesses, such as the introduction of a national minimum wage or a ban on advertising during children's television programmes. A successful firm will see change as an opportunity to re-examine its operations and market conditions or, better still, anticipate changes before they occur and develop a competitive advantage over rivals.

## 94.2 How to implement strategic change effectively

Before a strategy can be implemented, the strategy itself must be understood. What is it that we are trying to achieve? Many firms use SWOT analysis to determine what their strategic goals should be. One option might be to base a new strategy on trying to exploit an existing strength in a new area. Other firms might base their strategies around a desire to overcome a weakness. For example, in 2014 the supermarket chain Morrisons decided to set up an online delivery service because the supermarket believed that this was one of their major weaknesses compared to their rivals. Strategic design should always precede strategic implementation. This is because firms will struggle to be successful if they do not even know what it is that they are trying to achieve!

A firm's ability to effectively implement strategic change is one of the most important factors that affects organisational success. To implement change firms must identify:

- What are the component activities or tasks that will need to be completed in order to implement the strategy?
- How will these tasks be carried out?
- Which employees will be assigned which tasks?

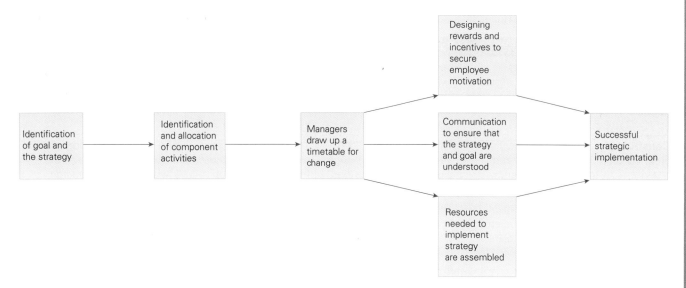

**Figure 94.1** Logic chain: Effective strategic implementation

● When will each task need to be completed? A timetable of change will need to be drawn up to ensure that the deadlines for the completion of strategic change are met.

To implement a strategy effectively managers will need to direct, and communicate and motivate their staff to ensure that the manager's plans are put into practice.

---

'Success doesn't necessarily come from breakthrough innovation, but from flawless execution. A great strategy alone won't win a game or a battle.' Naveen Jain, IT entrepreneur

---

## 94.3 The value of leadership in strategic implementation

In most cases, managers cannot successfully implement a new strategy on their own. They will need help from their employees. Therefore, one of the biggest challenges that leaders face when trying to implement strategic change is to convince workers that change is necessary. Like families, most organisations get set in their ways. So change is neither welcome nor easy. The job of a leader is to carry out the following:

● Ensure that the pressures for change are understood – first among board members and then throughout the organisation.

● Construct a clear vision about what the new future will look like and a narrative that explains the steps in getting from here to there.

● Appoint the right managers to handle each aspect of the change, ensuring that everyone knows that the leader has delegated full authority to them; then support the managers with necessary resources and backing.

● Keep going, even during the difficult short-term period in which the disruptions caused by change seem to outweigh any possible long-term gains.

If that sounds hard, it actually is an understatement of the difficulties. These arise when, in the middle of the change, senior managers realise that their original analysis of the problem was not 100 per cent right, that is, a change is needed to the change! Quite commonly this arises because junior staff or even the customers were not listened to in advance. Then the leader must decide whether to carry on as if nothing has happened ('It'll be better than it was') or to halt the process, rethink, and then change direction midstream.

Chapter 6 set out the four main styles of leadership: autocratic, paternalistic, democratic and laissez faire. When handling change, different leaders are likely to handle the process of change as shown in Table 94.1.

**Table 94.1** Leadership styles and the process of change

| | Autocratic | Paternalistic | Democratic | Laissez-faire |
|---|---|---|---|---|
| **Understand the scope of the change needed** | Leader hires a management consultant who reports directly to him or herself | Leader carries out an extensive consultation exercise among staff based on the known issues or problems | Discussion and consultation will be delegated to middle managers, taking care to include shop floor staff | A laissez-faire organisation may have been ahead of the external change, or may only react very late |
| **Construct a clear vision** | The management consultant writes a Vision Statement | This, again, will be done after consultation, though the leader will make the final decision | This should emerge, perhaps from suggestions from the shop floor | A laissez-faire leader may expect staff to grasp the vision as things emerge |
| **Appoint change managers** | Either management consultants or internal appointees who are used to doing what the boss wants | These will be appointed from among known 'team players', that is, those who buy into the vision decided by the leader | These will be selected from the brightest and best throughout the organisation | This is unlikely to happen; it will be expected that everyone will change over time |
| **Keep going through short-term problems** | Any internal critics may be sidelined or 'made redundant' | When things get tough, the leader will draw upon tough, family love and the need to stick together | If everyone shares the vision and has agreed the strategy, this stage should not be a real problem | Because the change will be less controlled and therefore slower and more organic, this problem may not occur |

The business writer Robert Townsend suggested that many newly appointed leaders 'disappear behind the mahogany curtain', and are rarely seen again by staff. He thought that 'finally getting to the top' made many leaders focus more on corporate luxuries ('Which jet shall we buy?') rather than on hard work. Yet he knew that great leaders can make a huge difference to long-term business performance. He advocated a leadership model based on extensive delegation within tight, agreed budgets. Many follow that model today.

Ultimately, judging a leader takes time. The media may find a new 'darling' – perhaps someone who looks and sounds great on TV. That person's achievements may be praised hugely, and they may win 'Business Leader of the Year' awards. Yet it will be several years before anyone outside the business can appraise the individual's performance. In most businesses it is easy to boost short-term profit: you push prices up here, and make redundancies there. This persuades the media and the shareholders that you are a fine leader. The real question, though, is whether your decisions will push the business forwards or backwards over the coming years. In an exam, therefore, hold back from rushing to praise (or condemn) a boss on the basis of short-term performance. Big business is a long game. Ninety minutes is a long time in football; a week is a long time in politics; five years is a long time in business.

'Actions speak louder than words.' Mark Twain, American author

## 94.4 The value of communication in strategic implementation

In big companies decisions on strategic change are usually made by senior managers, then passed down to middle managers who then explain it to their staff. No strategy fails at this point, though the seeds of failure may have been sown. This is usually due to poor communication: the management failed to make the new strategy fully understood by every employee in the organisation.

Managers need to break-out of the boardroom and begin communicating with the front-line staff who implement the plans. To do this they need to spell out their strategy clearly so that it is understood by all. This is obviously very important, because if the workforce does not understand the strategy they also probably will not know what is expected of them and what they are supposed to be doing. This error frequently occurs in team sports, such as football and netball, where a coach's strategy fails due to confusion. The cause of the confusion is poor communication: the players did not carry out the coach's instructions because they did not understand either what the coach was trying to achieve, or the methods to be used. To cascade strategy effectively down the firm's hierarchy senior managers should try to empower departmental managers, using their expertise to design their own implementation plans that will work best in their own functional areas.

## 94.5 Types of organisational structure: functional, product based, regional and matrix structure

A firm's organisational structure describes how a firm is set up and how it operates. Diagrams known as organisational charts provide a useful diagram of an organisation's structure. They show, for example, the different layers of management that collectively make up a firm's hierarchy. They can also show lines of authority, that is, who in the organisation is responsible for making which decisions, and internal channels of communication.

All firms have an organisational structure, but there are several different types.

### Functional structure

In a functional organisational structure the business organises employees by splitting them up into specialised departments, where each department has a specified role or task within the business. For example, in a company manufacturing biscuits, the business might be composed of the following specialised departments: senior management, production, sales and marketing, finance, and human resources.

**Figure 94.2** Organisational structure

The main advantage of a functional organisational structure is that it enables employees who have the same knowledge and skills to work in close physical proximity to each other. Junior functional specialists will have the opportunity to learn and hone their specialised functional skills by working closely with older more experienced colleagues from the same discipline. As a result of this type of organisational structure, productivity in each functional department should be high because workers with specialised skills should be able to complete their work faster and with fewer mistakes than generalists.

The main drawback of this structure is that it can lead to destructive departmental rivalries. These rivalries can lead to higher costs and product quality

problems. For example, a car manufacturer set out along functional lines might encounter a situation where a specialist engine design department creates an overly powerful and complex engine for a new car. The functional organisational structure tends to perform best in more stable markets, where there is less need for rapid change.

### Product based structure

The product based organisational structure is used by multi-product firms. In this type of structure a firm internally splits itself up into divisions, where each division specialises in producing a particular product. For example, Samsung produces smartphones, TV sets, laptop computers and microwave ovens. A product-based structure for Samsung would mean forming specialised division for each of the product lines sold. The smartphone division of Samsung would be specialised and entrusted to produce and sell all the company's mobile phones. Each division would then have its own specialised department that would deal with functional issues, such as marketing, human resources and production. In a product-based organisational structure, each business is in effect its own autonomous mini-business.

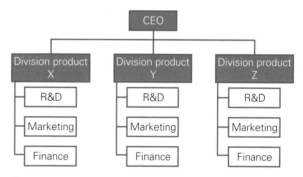

**Figure 94.3** Product-based structure

### Regional structure

The regional structure is similar to product-based structure in that the company is also sub-divided into divisions. However, in this case the divisions that collectively comprise the firm are geographical locations. Young Enterprise has a regional structure. This nationwide educational charity runs training courses across the UK by regional area. The North East regional office puts on training courses in schools in this part of the country, whilst the South East regional office carries out the same role for schools located in the Home Counties. Each office employs its own team of functional specialists.

The regional organisational structure works best when there are regional variations in consumer tastes and preferences. For example in Finland most people like eating rye bread, they prefer it to bread made from wheat. McDonald's operates with a regional structure. The flexibility created by this organisational structure led to the McRye Burger – a unique product developed specifically for the Finnish market by employees of the Finnish division of McDonald's.

## Matrix structure

In companies that are set out according to a matrix structure functional specialists from different specialisms work together in multi-disciplinary teams. For example, a construction company needs architects, structural engineers and draughtsmen. In a matrix management structure these different specialists work as a team on a particular building project. The main benefit of matrix management is that it enables the specialists to identify, negotiate and then overcome any functional trade-offs that could cause problems later. For example, architects working in isolation might design beautiful buildings that are not strong enough to withstand severe wind. In this case, it would make more sense to sit the architect next to the structural engineer so that a more collaborative approach could be taken.

In addition, matrix structures can help save time and money. If the construction company was set out along functional lines, specialists from different fields would rarely meet. They would work in isolation from each other. The business would be composed of three separate departments: an Architectural Department for the architects; a Structural Department for the engineers; and finally there would be a CAD department composed entirely of draughtsmen. Projects would be completed along a sort of design production line. All new projects would start with the architects. Once the architects had finished their work they would then pass the project on to the structural engineers. The problem with this approach is that the draughtsmen can only start work on the project once both the architects and the engineers have finished their work.

'The biggest risk is not taking a risk. In a world that is changing quickly, the only strategy that is guaranteed to fail is not taking risks.' Mark Zuckerburg, founder, Facebook

## 94.6 The importance of organisational structure in strategic implementation

The type of organisational structure adopted by senior management can have a significant impact on strategic implementation. For example, it will affect the day-to-day operational rules and policies used within the firm. In addition, a firm's organisational structure determines which employees get involved in making and carrying out key decisions.

Ultimately the key issue is the impact of structure on centralisation or decentralisation. McDonald's regional structure allowed the business to flourish globally, instead of being the equivalent of the Hard Rock Café – a tiny slice of America in cities worldwide – but numbered in dozens, not thousands.

## 94.7 Does effective strategic implementation sometimes require a new organisational structure?

A strategic change of direction can sometimes create a need to adopt a new organisational structure. For example, a business that is based around a regional structure might be better served by a matrix structure if there is an urgent need for a radical programme of new product development. An organisation's structure might also need to be changed because the current way in which the structure allocates the firm's scarce resources is not suited to the proposed strategic change of direction. For example, take a firm which is currently structured around geographical regions. If nothing is changed, resources will continue to be directed to the regional offices. This could mean that there are not enough resources available centrally to be used for much needed new product development.

'However beautiful the strategy, you should occasionally look at the results.' Winston Churchill, wartime leader

## Five Whys and a How

| Question | Answer |
|---|---|
| Why is strategic implementation as important as the formulation of the strategy itself? | A good strategy that makes sense on paper will not generate a favourable outcome for the firm unless it is successfully put into practice |
| Why do strategies need to be cascaded? | Strategy is normally devised at boardroom level. However, strategy needs to move out of the boardroom if it is to be implemented by the workforce |
| Why does effective strategic implementation depend on good communication? | If the strategy is badly communicated shop-floor workers will not know what is expected of them and what needs to be done |
| Why is resistance to change so common? | Most people do not like change, and are fearful of it because it could lead to a loss of status, pay, or worse still, their job! |
| Why might a firm need to change its organisational structure? | A change of structure might be needed to ensure that a new strategy is implemented successfully. For example, a supermarket creating a specialised new division to capitalise on the growth of online demand |
| How might a leader try to overcome resistance to change? | The leader could start the process of breaking down resistance to change by explaining why change is needed. For example, the company could be in decline. Redundancies might be needed now to prevent us all losing our jobs later |

## Key terms

**Multi-product firms:** businesses with a wide product portfolio.

**Vision:** a business aim expressed in evangelistic, super-motivational terms, for example 'connecting the world'.

# Workbook

## A. Revision questions

(40 marks; 40 minutes)

1. What is meant by the term strategic implementation? (2)

2. When implementing strategic change, why is it important to assign tasks to specific individuals? (4)

3. Resistance to change is one of the main barriers to effective strategic implementation.
   a) What is resistance to change? (2)
   b) Analyse how resistance to change might prevent effective strategic implementation. (6)
   c) What can leaders do to overcome resistance to change? Can it ever be completely overcome? (6)

4. Apart from overcoming resistance to change, explain one other reason why effective strategic implementation requires effective internal communication. (4)

5. In an organisational chart, explain why it might be important to avoid having a particular person reporting to more than one person above them in the chain of command? (4)

6. Distinguish between a product-based and a conventional functional organisational structure. (6)

7. Explain why it might be necessary for a firm to change its organisational structure before it begins implementing a new strategy. (6)

## B. Revision exercises

## DATA RESPONSE 1

### Strategic implementation at Tesco

In the past supermarkets only sold their products to consumers in one way. This way involved building a nationwide network of identikit, out-of-town superstores. Each of these superstores sold the same vast range of products, including clothes and electrical goods, as well as groceries.

By 2014 Tesco's old business model showed signs of weakness. Consumer behaviour had changed, partly due to the Internet and the rising popularity of online shopping. As a result big superstores were no longer attracting the customers needed to achieve the sales and profits expected by Tesco's shareholders. The company's board of directors decided that they should try to offer Tesco customers a choice of ways to buy their products. This is called multi-channel retailing. In Tesco's case the company would offer consumers more choice and convenience. Those who wanted to buy online could choose between collecting their purchases themselves from a nearby click-and-collect store, or they could opt for home delivery of their purchase instead. Tesco also sought to open more Tesco Metro and Tesco Express stores. These smaller branches of Tesco were located in town centres and sold a much narrower range of goods than conventional supermarkets. They were targeted at consumers who did not want to drive to big out-of-town superstores.

To implement this new multi-channel distribution strategy, Tesco needed to adjust its organisational structure. In Spring 2014 the company decided to adopt a regional structure for all its superstore and Tesco Extra formats. The UK was to be split up into three regions: North, Central and South. It was hoped that by switching to a more regional structure, Tesco would be able to increase sales by adapting what it sold in each region in order to better match local tastes and preferences.

In May 2014 one of Tesco's rivals also announced a major programme of restructuring. Asda removed an entire layer of middle management from their organisational structure. The middle managers were replaced by section leaders with highly specialised roles. For example, Asda now has a specialised e-commerce section leader in every one of its stores. The role of the e-commerce specialist is to help customers in store. For example, some products sold by Asda, such as TV sets and bicycles can be quite difficult to take home in a car. To overcome this problem the e-commerce section leader could encourage the consumer to make their purchase via Asda's online platform, there and then in store. The bulky TV set or bicycle could then be delivered direct to the customer's door via an Asda delivery vehicle.

### Questions (60 marks; 70 minutes)

1. Analyse why some supermarkets have decided to change their organisational structure, setting up specialised online sales divisions. (12)

2. According to market research carried out by Accenture in 2014, more than three-quarters of British shoppers said that consistency of pricing between a retailer's online and offline shops was crucial. Analyse why a retailer such as Tesco might allow different divisions of the business to charge customers different prices for exactly the same product. (12)

3. Using the example of UK supermarkets, to what extent is organisational structural change needed to ensure that the new strategy of multi-channel retailing is implemented effectively? (16)

4. To what extent is resistance to change inevitable when businesses such as supermarkets try to implement new organisational structures? (20)

## DATA RESPONSE 2

### Why a winning football formula can often get lost in translation

Alex Ferguson was probably the most successful manager ever in British football. After 26 seasons in charge of Manchester United, Sir Alex Ferguson went on to teach management at Harvard University, a move that led to an article in the Harvard Business

Review entitled 'Ferguson's Formula', listing the key attributes that brought him success.

Some of these related to practices now common among top clubs, which employ nutritionists, data analysts, physiotherapists, psychologists and others to eke out every last bit of performance from the players. Others were about structure, staff and ethos. At a recent talk to promote his autobiography, Sir Alex said he had been intent on building a club rather than just a team. 'My main interest was in getting the foundations right,' he stated. This meant building a scouting team almost from scratch, developing the youth system and, later, setting up a new training ground.

But most ingredients in 'Ferguson's Formula' concern people and how to deal with them – a skill many observers rate well above strategic and tactical acumen. Ian Maynard, Professor of Sport Psychology at Sheffield Hallam University, says, 'The really perceptive managers are those who recognise what motivates individuals.' Allied to this is the ability to find players who accept a manager's leadership style and who take the rest of the team with them. Describing the type of players he sought to have in his teams, Sir Alex constantly used words such as 'loyal', 'hard-working' and 'stubborn'. Yet one quality was paramount: they should be bad losers. 'I was after players with strength and resolve,' he says. 'I wanted to find out how they dealt with defeat.'

## C. Extend your understanding

1. To what extent is effective strategic implementation a matter of getting the organisational structure right, or are other factors, such as leadership and communication more important? Justify your view. (25)

Source: Adapted from *Financial Times* 1 December 2014

### Questions (40 marks; 45 minutes)

1. Analyse how the organisational structure created by Alex Ferguson contributed to Manchester United's success on the pitch. (12)

2. Using the example of Manchester United, to what extent do you think effective implementation of strategy depends on effective recruitment and training? (16)

3. In February 2014 Fulham FC appointed Felix Magath. In his native Germany Magath had used a combination of player rotation, high-intensity fitness-based training and a strict disciplinary code to create successful teams. Magath tried to implement the same strategy at Fulham, but failed miserably. By September he was sacked. Using the example of Felix Magath, analyse why the same strategy might be possible to implement in one situation, but not in another. (12)

2. Companies can adopt a range of organisational structures, including: functional, product-based, regional and matrix structures. Using examples of your choice from different industries, evaluate how the choice of organisational structure can affect the quality of a firm's strategic implementation. (25)

# Chapter
# 95 Network analysis and strategic implementation

**Linked to:** Corporate objectives, strategy and tactics, Chapter 54; Analysing strategic options, Chapter 72; Strategic direction: Ansoff's matrix, Chapter 75; Strategic positioning, Chapter 77; Strategic implementation, Chapter 94.

## Definition

Strategic implementation requires careful planning of how to carry out a project to ensure that it is completed quickly, cost-efficiently and on time. A network diagram helps to identify the critical path: the activities that require the most careful management scrutiny.

## 95.1 Strategic implementation

To implement a change of strategic direction, effective operations management is required. This involves many considerations, including quality, inventory management, information technology and effective management of time. Time is a critical competitive advantage, especially when two rivals are each trying to be first to market with a new product or business idea.

Well-run firms bring all these aspects into a single strategic plan. This is turned into a day-by-day plan to show supervisors and workers exactly what they should be doing: what, when and how. This kind of planning and control is fundamental to effective management. A useful model for planning an operational project is network analysis. It provides the basis for monitoring and controlling actual progress compared with the plan.

## 95.2 Network analysis and strategic change

Network analysis is a way of showing how a complex project can be completed in the shortest possible time. It identifies the activities that must be completed on

time to avoid delaying the whole project (the 'critical path'). Management effort can be concentrated on ensuring that these key activities are completed on time. This leaves greater flexibility in timing the non-critical items. The objectives are to ensure customer satisfaction through good timekeeping and to minimise the wastage of resources, thereby boosting the profitability of the project.

For example, suppose that a fish and chip shop wanted to change its strategic direction by diversifying into Chinese food. To complete this project a range of activities needs to be undertaken. Market research is needed to identify whether there is a viable gap in the market. Kitchen staff need to be retrained or new staff hired. New suppliers for raw ingredients are needed. A delivery vehicle must be bought and a driver hired.

Before going ahead the owner must think through which of these tasks should be undertaken first. It makes little sense to hire staff and to purchase kitchen equipment until the initial market research has been carried out. It is also helpful to identify tasks that can be undertaken at the same time. For example, it might take two months to hire and train kitchen staff. During this time, the new cooking equipment could be installed. The goal is to avoid wasted time. To minimise the time it takes to complete a project, managers construct network diagrams.

A network shows:

- the order in which each task must be undertaken
- how long each stage should take
- the earliest date at which the later stages can start.

If a housebuilding firm can predict with confidence that it will be ready to put roof beams in place 80 days after the start of a project, a crane can be hired and the beams delivered for exactly that time. This minimises costs, as the crane need only be hired for the day it is needed, and improves cash flow by delaying the arrival of materials (and invoices) until they are really required.

'In preparing for battle I have always found that plans are useless, but planning is indispensable.' Dwight Eisenhower, former U.S. General and U.S. President

## 95.3 Drawing critical path analysis diagrams

A Critical Path Analysis (CPA) network consists of two components.

1. An activity is part of a project that requires time and/or resources. Therefore waiting for delivery of parts is an activity, as is production. Activities are shown as arrows running from left to right. Their length has no significance.

2. A 'node' is the start or finish of an activity and is represented by a circle. All network diagrams start and end on a single node.

### Rules for drawing CPA networks

1. The network must start and end on a single node.

2. No lines should cross each other.

3. When drawing an activity, do not add the end node straight away; wait until you have checked which activity follows.

4. There must be no lines that are not activities.

5. Due to the need to write figures in the nodes, it is helpful to draw networks with large circles and short lines.

## 95.4 Case example: the need for networks

A chocolate producer decides to run a '3p off' price promotion next February. Any need for network analysis? Surely not. What could be easier? Yet the risk of upsetting customers is massive with any promotion. What if a huge order from Tesco meant that Sainsbury's could not receive all the supplies it wanted?

Think for a moment about the activities needed to make this promotion work smoothly. It would be necessary to:

- tell the salesforce
- sell the stock into shops
- design the 'flash' packs
- estimate the sales volume for one month at 3p off
- get 'flash' packs printed
- order extra raw materials (for example, a double order of cocoa)
- step up production
- arrange overtime for factory staff
- deliver promotional packs to shops…
- …and much, much more.

An efficient manager thinks about all the activities needed, and puts them in the correct time sequence. Then a network can easily be drawn up (see Figure 95.1).

Once the manager has found how long each activity is likely to take, she or he can work backwards to find out when the work must start. Here, the work must start 70 days before 1 February. This is because the longest path through to the end of the project is 70 (14 + 28 + 21 + 7).

Having drawn a network, the next stage is to identify more precisely the times when particular activities can or must begin and end. To do this, it is helpful to number the nodes that connect the activities. Figure 95.2 shows the '3p off' example with the activities represented by letters and the nodes numbered.

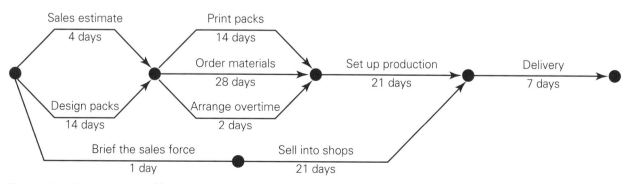

**Figure 95.1** '3p off' network (1)

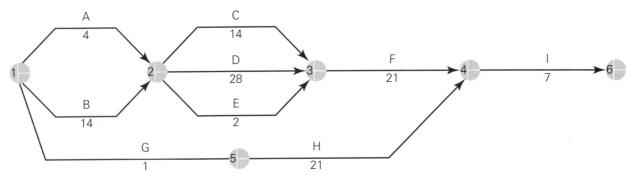

**Figure 95.2** '3p off' network (2)

## Earliest start times and latest finish times

Space has also been left in the nodes in Figure 95.3 for two more numbers: the earliest start time (EST) and the latest finish time (LFT). The EST shows the earliest time at which following activities can be started. On Figure 95.3, activities C, D and E can begin after 14 days, because that's when A and B are both finished.

Figure 95.4 shows the complete network, including all the ESTs. Note that the start of a project is always taken as 0 rather than 1. Therefore activities C, D and E can start on day 0 + 14 = 14. Activity F can start on 0 + 14 + 28 = 42. And the earliest the project can be completed is by day 0 + 14 + 28 + 21 + 7 = 70.

Calculating the ESTs provides two key pieces of information:

1. The earliest date that certain resources will be needed, such as skilled workers, raw materials or machinery; this avoids tying up working capital unnecessarily, for instance by buying inventory today that will not be used until next month.

2. The earliest completion date for the whole project (this is the EST on the final node).

The EST on the final node shows the earliest date at which the project can be completed. So when is the latest completion date that a manager would find acceptable? As time is money, and customers want deliveries as fast as possible, if next Wednesday is possible, the manager will set it as the latest acceptable date. This is known as the latest finish time (LFT).

The LFT shows the time by which an activity must be completed. These times are recorded in the bottom right-hand section of the nodes. The LFT shows the latest finish time of preceding activities. The number 42 in the bottom right-hand section of node 5 (Figure 95.4) shows that activity G must be finished by day 42 in order to give activities H and I time to be completed by day 70.

The LFTs on activities are calculated from right to left. In node 6 the LFT is 70, because that is the latest a manager would want the project to finish. Node 4 shows the LFT

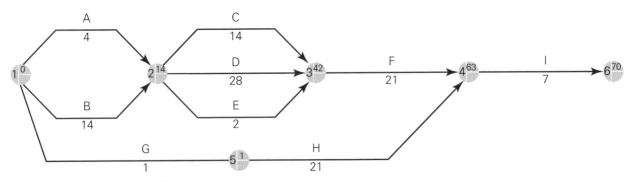

**Figure 95.3** '3p off' network (3)

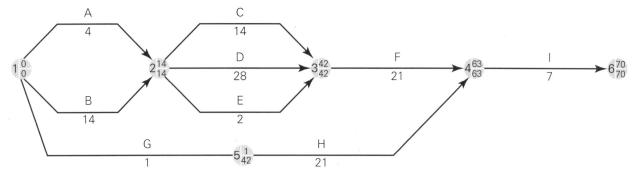

**Figure 95.4** '3p off' network (4)

for activities F and H. Both must be finished by day 63, to leave seven days for activity I to be completed.

Calculating the LFTs provides three main pieces of information:

1. It provides the deadlines that *must* be met in order for the project to be completed on time.

2. It helps to identify the activities that have 'float time' – in other words, some slack between the EST and the LFT; activity H can be started on day 1 and must be finished by day 63, but takes only 21 days to complete; so there is no rush to complete it.

3. It identifies the critical path.

## 95.5 The critical path

The critical path comprises the activities that take longest to complete. They determine the length of the whole project. In this case, it is activities B, D, F and I. These are the activities that must not be delayed by even one day. For then the whole project will be late. With C, a delay would not matter. There are 28 days to complete a task that takes only 14. But D is on the critical path, so this 28-day activity must be completed in no more than 28 days.

Identifying the critical path allows managers to apply management by exception; in other words, focusing on exceptionally important tasks, rather than spreading their efforts thinly. Of the nine activities within the '3p off' network, only the four critical ones need to absorb management time. The others need far less supervision.

If a supervisor sees a possibility that an activity on the critical path might overrun, she or he can consider shifting labour or machinery across from a non-critical task. In this way the project completion date can be kept intact.

To identify the critical path, the two key points are:

1. It will be on activities where the nodes show the EST and LFT to be the same.

2. It is the longest path through those nodes.

When drawing a network, the critical path is identified by striking two short lines across the critical activities (see Figure 95.5).

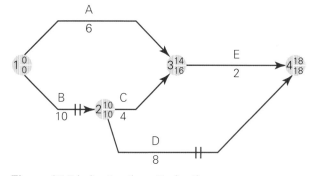

**Figure 95.5** Indicating the critical path

## 95.6 Float time (non-critical activities)

Float is the spare time available for the completion of any activity. If an activity that takes three days must be completed within a week, there are four days of float time. These can be used to complete the task in a leisurely way, perhaps switching half the staff to another task. Alternatively, the task could be started on day four.

There are different ways of measuring float time, but this A-level focuses solely on 'total float'. This measures the spare time available so that there is no delay to the overall project completion time. To work out the total float on any specific activity the following formula is required:

$$\text{LFT (this activity)} - \text{duration} - \text{EST (this activity)}$$
$$= \text{Total float}$$

Applying this formula to Figure 95.5 gives the following calculations for total float times:

| | LFT (this activity) | *minus* Duration | Minus EST (this activity) | = Total float |
|---|---|---|---|---|
| **Activity A** | 16 | 6 | 0 | 10 |
| **Activity B** | 10 | 10 | 0 | 0 |
| **Activity C** | 16 | 4 | 10 | 2 |
| **Activity D** | 18 | 8 | 10 | 0 |
| **Activity E** | 18 | 2 | 14 | 2 |

Note that the critical activities (B and D) have zero float time. This will always be the case. Once managers have calculated the total float on specific activities, they might

## 95.7 Amendment of CPA network diagrams

However carefully a network diagram is drawn up, real life can be different. A planned week for roofing turns into ten days because of foul weather. Or a disagreement among the marketing team means that a pack design that should take three days to complete takes eight. Therefore it can be necessary to amend network diagrams in the light of events.

For example, assume that some engineering work is to take place on the Leeds-London railway line. The work involves six activities that are to be tightly sequenced to get the job done in 14 hours. Start-time: 16.00 on

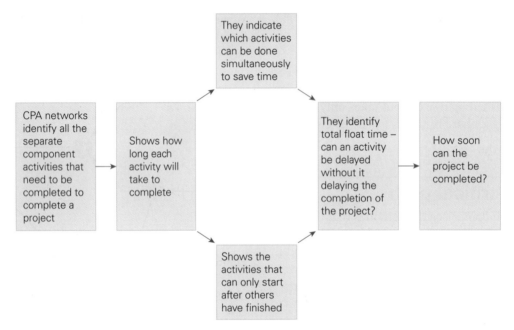

**Figure 95.6** Logic chain: what do CPA network diagrams show?

get the job done straight away, then switch staff to other activities. Or the managers may give staff the extra time to give more thought to the activity. For example, designing a new logo may need only two days, but it may well be that a better logo could be designed in five.

'Time is the only commodity that's irreplaceable: invest it, share it, spend it… never waste it.' Tracy Sherwood, author

Sunday; finish time: 06.00 on Monday, before the rush hour. The network is shown in Figure 95.7.

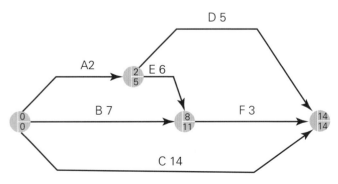

**Figure 95.7** Network diagram: renewing points on the Leeds-London railway line (1)

The work starts on time but at 17.00 a dreadful accident delays Activity A by five hours. Instead of D and E being able to start after two hours, they can only get going after seven. What would be the effect of this accident on the whole diagram?

As shown in Figure 95.8, these events will change the critical path, from activity C to A, E, F. And the overall project length is extended by two hours (eating into rush hour travel). The project manager may accept the two hour delay, or might attempt to make further amendments to the sequencing. After all, there is plenty of spare time on activity D – it has a total float of 16 - 5 - 7 = 4 hours. So perhaps staff could be switched from D to E or F, to try to cut down on the time taken on these critical activities. If staff from D could help cut E from six hours to five, an hour could be shaved off the overall project duration. And Leeds rail passengers will only face an hour's delay instead of two hours.

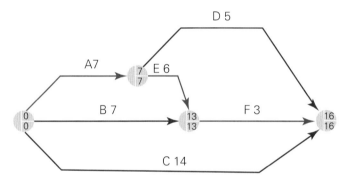

**Figure 95.8** Network diagram: renewing points on the Leeds-London railway line (2)

'The P in PM is as much about People Management as it is about Project Management.' Cornelius Fichtner, management consultant

## 95.8 Advantages and disadvantages of using network (critical path) analysis

### Advantages

The advantages of using network (critical path) analysis are set out below.

● It requires careful planning of the order in which events need to occur, and the length of time each one should take. This should improve the smooth operation of an important project such as a new product launch.

● By identifying events that can be carried out simultaneously, it shortens the length of time taken to complete a project. This is an important element in the modern business focus upon time-based management. For example, if a law is passed that allows 14-year-olds to ride motorbikes with engines of less than 40cc, the first company to design and launch a suitable product would do extremely well.

● The resources needed for each activity can be ordered or hired no earlier than their scheduled EST. Just such a focus upon careful planning of when stocks are needed is the heart of just-in-time production systems. In this way cash outflows are postponed as long as possible, and the working capital tied up in the project is minimised.

● If the completion of an activity is delayed for some reason, the network diagram is a good starting point for working out the implications and deciding on appropriate courses of action.

### Disadvantages

The disadvantages of using network (critical path) analysis are set out below.

● A complex project (such as the construction of the super-fast railway HS2) entails so many activities that a drawing becomes unmanageable. Fortunately, computers can zoom in and out of drawings, enabling small parts of the network to be magnified and examined.

● Drawing a diagram does not, in itself, ensure the effective management of a project. Network analysis provides a plan, but can only be as successful as the staff's commitment to it. This suggests that staff should be consulted about the schedule and the likely duration of the activities.

● The value of the network diagram is reduced slightly because the activity lines are not in proportion to the duration of the activities.

### Delays can cost billions

In April 2015 American Airlines (AA) took delivery of its first Boeing 787 Dreamliner. It was three years late. AA placed the order for forty-two 787s in 2008, with a promised delivery date of 2012. That slipped back steadily into 2014, then 2015.

The problem arose because of difficulties with the new lightweight materials being used in the plane. The most serious was a redesign announced in 2009 to 'reinforce an area within the side-of-body section' of the plane! The direct cost to Boeing has been estimated at more than £4 billion. The indirect effects are no less severe. Before Boeing admitted that its project was behind schedule, its European rival Airbus was struggling to sell its competitor A350 plane. After Boeing's production delays became clear, Virgin Atlantic announced it was cancelling its Boeing order to buy Airbus planes. In 2010, Boeing received net orders for the Dreamliner of 36 planes, while Airbus enjoyed net orders for 78 A350s. Three years later the same issue continued to dog Boeing, with the Airbus 350 outselling the Dreamliner.

When the design problem became the critical one for Boeing, management failed to find a successful way of coping. In this case, poor critical path analysis cost Boeing £billions.

Source: Airbus and Boeing websites: www.airbus.com and www.boeing.co.uk

## Evaluation: Network analysis and strategic implementation

The cliché 'time is money' has been around for years. Only recently, though, have systems such as just-in-time focused clearly on time-based management. Time is vital not only because it affects costs, but also because it can provide a crucial marketing edge. Primark's key advantage over Marks & Spencer is that it is much quicker at getting catwalk fashions into high street shops. So time can add value. Careful production planning can also help to get a firm's new product to the market before the opposition.

Network analysis is a valuable practical tool for taking time seriously. It involves careful planning and can be used as a way of monitoring progress. If critical activities are falling behind schedule, action can be taken quickly. This serves as a reminder that successful business management is not just about clever strategic thinking. Ultimately, success depends upon what happens at the workplace or at the construction site. Network analysis is a helpful way to ensure that strategies become plans that can be carried through effectively. Nevertheless, they guarantee nothing. Ensuring that the paper network becomes reality remains in the hands of the managers, supervisors and staff on the job. So effective people management and motivation remain as important as ever.

'Nothing is less productive than to make more efficient what should not be done at all.' Peter Drucker, management guru

## Key terms

**Critical path:** the activities that must be completed on time for the project to finish on time. In other words, they have no float time at all.

**Management by exception:** the principle that because managers cannot supervise every activity within the organisation, they should focus their energies on the most important issues.

**Network:** a diagram showing all the activities needed to complete a project, the order in which they must be completed and the critical path.

**Network analysis:** breaking a project down into its component parts, to identify the sequence of activities involved.

### Five Whys and a How

| Question | Answer |
|---|---|
| Why is it important to complete a project as soon as possible? | It's cheaper: if a project can be completed quickly it will carry a smaller share of the organisation's fixed costs. In addition, customers do not like waiting. The quicker the completion the greater the likelihood of repeat purchase |
| Why is it important to identify activities that lie along a project's critical path? | Because delays on critical activities put back the final completion date for the project |
| Why is it important to identify and calculate total float? | Activities that have float time are non-critical. They can be delayed without affecting the project's completion date. If a critical activity is delayed, resources can be transferred from other activities that have float time |
| Why is it important to identify activities that can be completed simultaneously? | The goal should be to complete the project as soon as possible. If two activities can be carried out at the same time, they should be. It'll speed up the whole project |
| Why is it important to calculate earliest start times and latest finish times? | This will help to ensure that specialist staff are only hired when needed. Don't hire bricklayers at the beginning of a project when they won't be needed for at least three weeks until the foundations are dug |
| How do firms go about drawing network diagrams? | They identify all the component activities and estimate how long each will take to complete. Then they decide on the correct order for tackling the activities. Then they decide which activities can be carried out simultaneously. Now the network can be drawn |

# Workbook

## A. Revision questions

(35 marks; 35 minutes)

1. Outline two objectives of network analysis. (4)

2. Distinguish between an activity and a project. (2)

3. State three key rules for drawing networks. (3)

4. Explain how to calculate the earliest start time for an activity. (4)

5. Explain why is it important to calculate the latest finish time on an activity? (4)

6. Explain what is meant by 'the critical path' and how you identify it? (4)

7. Explain why it would be useful to know which activities have float times available. (4)

8. Explain the value of network analysis for a small firm in financial difficulties. (5)

9. Explain how the use of critical path analysis could help a firm's time-based management. (5)

# B. Revision exercises

## DATA RESPONSE 1

**Table 95.1** Data for constructing a network

| Activity | Preceded by | Duration (weeks) |
|---|---|---|
| A | | 6 |
| B | | 4 |
| C | | 10 |
| D | A & B | 5 |
| E | A & B | 7 |
| F | D | 3 |

### Questions (40 marks; 40 minutes)

**1. a)** Construct a network from the information given in Table 95.1. (6)

**b)** Number the nodes and put in the earliest start times. (4)

**2. a)** Draw the following network:

Activity A and B start the project. C and D follow A. E follows all other jobs. (6)

**b)** Work out the earliest start times of the activities and put them in the nodes if, in the above question, A lasts 2 days, B = 9 days, C = 3, D = 4 and E = 7. (4)

**3. a)** Use the information given in Table 95.2 to construct a fully labelled network showing ESTs, LFTs and the critical path. (12)

**Table 95.2** Data for constructing a fully labelled network

| Activity | Preceded by | Duration |
|---|---|---|
| A | – | 3 |
| B | – | 9 |
| C | – | 2 |
| D | A | 5 |
| E | C | 3 |
| F | B, D, E | 5 |
| G | C | 9 |

**b)** If the firm was offered a £2,000 bonus for completing the project in 12 days, which activity should managers focus upon? Explain why. (8)

## DATA RESPONSE 2

**Every Friday needs managing**

Last Friday had been a washout. Claire, Bren, Alliyah and Ruth had dithered over what to wear, where to go and how to get there, and ended up watching a rotten film in Bren's bedroom. This week was going to be different. Bren had just been taught critical path analysis and she was determined to use it to 'project manage' Friday night. As it was Bren's birthday on Friday, the others had to agree.

They sat down on Tuesday to agree all the activities needed for a great night out. They started by focusing on the activities:

*Alliyah:* We have the best nights when we start at Harry's Bar for a couple of hours, then on to the Orchid at about midnight.

*Claire:* I like Harry's but prefer RSVP; no argument, though, we should go to the Orchid.

After half an hour back and forth, the agreement was Harry's at 9.00 and Orchid at 12.00.

Then they realised that there was a lot more to it than that. It would take half an hour to get to Harry's and they'd have to get ready beforehand: bath, hair, nails, make-up. And what about the preceding activities? Shopping for a new top… and shoes… and earrings… and getting some highlights done.

They argued about which came first, a top and then shoes and earrings to match? Or the other way round? It was time for Bren to set it all out. See Table 95.3.

**Table 95.3** Activities required for a night out

| Activity | | Preceded by | Duration |
|---|---|---|---|
| A | Booking a hair and nails appointment | – | 1 minute |
| B | Clothes shopping | – | 4 hours |
| C | Shopping for shoes | – | 3 hours |
| D | Shopping for earrings | B, C | 1 hour |
| E | Hair and nails appointment | A | 2 hours |
| F | Bath | D, E | 1 hour |
| G | Make-up and get dressed | F | 1 hour |
| H | Constant phone conversations | – | 24/7 |

**Questions (20 marks; 25 minutes)**

1. Draw up Bren's network, to help plan her birthday. (8)

2. How much float time is there on activities E and D? (2)

3. Examine why workers on a building site could benefit as much or more from critical path analysis as Bren and her friends. (10)

## DATA RESPONSE 3

### Slightly Mad delays Project Cars

The video games industry has grown enormously over the last decade. Slightly Mad Studios is a London-based company that produces video games for PS4, Xbox and Nintendo Wii.

Gamers are notoriously fickle. As a result, the typical video game tends to have a very short life cycle. This means that in order to survive, companies like Slightly Mad Studios must constantly innovate and come up with new games that excite the imagination.

In early 2013, designers at Slightly Mad began to develop a new driving game called Project Cars. The goal was to create the most authentic driving experience for gamers. Developing new games is usually a very expensive business. To help raise the finance needed to develop Project Cars, Slightly Mad Studios asked gamers to crowdfund the project. In return for their money gamers would receive a share of the profits generated from Project Cars. The crowdfunding project succeeded, and over £6 million was raised. The plan was for the new game to be available for Christmas 2014.

In October 2014 the news broke that the release date for Project Cars had been delayed until March 2015.

According to project director Andy Garton, 'This delay has come about because a couple of other big games are launching around the same time as our planned first date…. This would have had a very significant impact on our initial sales.'

The boss of Slightly Mad Studios, Ian Bell also tried to explain the delay by stating that, 'Our goal has always been to deliver a landmark title that encompasses the wishes and desires of racing fans from all around the world; something with features and content powered by the community, that provides a truly unforgettable and pioneering experience.'

**Questions (30 marks; 35 minutes)**

1. Analyse how video game companies, such as Slightly Mad Games, might benefit from network analysis and effective strategic implementation. (10)

2. To what extent do you agree with the view expressed by Andy Garton that delaying the launch of Project Cars until March 2015 will help the company to maximise its revenues? (20)

## C. Extend your understanding

1. 'Using network analysis to manage projects is as important to the finances and marketing of a business as it is to operations management.' To what extent do you agree? (25)

2. 'Almost all projects fail to meet their deadlines due to a combination of imperfect information and unexpected events, including unanticipated resource constraints. As a result they end up changing the original project specifications to meet deadlines. Network analysis is therefore an expensive waste of time and money.' To what extent do you agree with this statement? (25)

# Chapter 96  Problems with strategy

**Linked to:** Corporate objectives, strategy and tactics, Chapter 54; The impact of strategic decision-making on functional decision-making, Chapter 55; Analysing strategic options, Chapter 72; Strategic direction: Ansoff's matrix, Chapter 75; Strategic positioning, Chapter 77; Causes and value of change, Chapter 90; Strategic implementation, Chapter 94.

## Definition

Strategy is the way in which a firm attempts to achieve its objectives. The main problem is that the external business and economic environment is ever-changing. So today's thoughtful, well-considered strategy can become tomorrow's misfit.

## 96.1 Difficulties of strategic decision-making and implementation

Strategic decision-making implies a choice that will have an impact on the business for many years to come, and cannot easily be reversed. After many years of dithering, Morrisons responded to the growth of supermarket-run, high street convenience stores by opening its first M local convenience store in January 2013. That was the start of an expansion dash leading to more than 150 of these stores being opened by the end of 2014. The strategy was to catch up with rivals Tesco and Sainsbury's by pursuing ambitious targets for store openings. Then, in March 2015, the new boss of Morrisons declared that more than 30 per cent of the new 'M' stores were unprofitable; 23 would be closed immediately and the growth strategy put on hold. The cost of this was buried within a £792 million loss declared by the company for 2014/15.

So was the Morrisons problem a failure of strategic decision-making or implementation? Closing 23 stores

(not all 150) may suggest an implementation problem, perhaps related to store location. But going from one store at the start of 2013 to 150 within two years was surely such an ambitious growth rate that mistakes would be inevitable. In other words the decision makers on the board of directors were surely more to blame than the managers who tried to achieve what the board wanted.

## 96.2 Planned versus emergent strategy

In boardrooms, the 1980s and 1990s were dominated by Michael Porter's ideas on strategy and competitive advantage, exemplified most clearly by his '5 Forces' and 'generic strategy' theories. Porter's view was that strategy is 'owned' by business leaders. In other words it is consciously planned by the directors, who then expect their senior managers to implement the strategy laid down by the board. As Microsoft found out with the faltering launch of the Xbox One, life is not so simple. Microsoft's strategy had been to make the Xbox One the entertainment hub for family living rooms. This meant the product was over-equipped and overpriced. It took the business a whole year to simplify the product and cut the price. Then sales improved dramatically. The point, though, is that a planned approach to strategy may overstate the degree of control the business has over the marketplace it operates in.

By contrast with Porter's approach, Henry Mintzberg's writing had always emphasised the need for strategy to be flexible and responsive to changing circumstances. This is emergent strategy, that is, it emerges from the circumstances rather than being controlled and rigid. Of course, there is likely to be a plan at the outset, but Mintzberg emphasises that changing circumstances are likely to force the plan to change. To Porter, the best strategy comes from the best analysis of a company's situation; to Mintzberg the best strategy comes from managers with the speed of thought and the decision-making power to react to an ever-changing world.

For those who believe change is becoming ever-faster and ever-more ubiquitous, Mintzberg's theory of emergent strategy would be more convincing. In the case of Morrisons, mentioned above, it is quite clear that the development of convenience stores owes more to emergent than planned strategy.

'The world of deliberate strategy is one of strategy planning weekends at posh hotels in the English countryside discussing the 5 Forces in our particular industry.' Karl Moore, strategy academic

### Real business

In April 2015 Hotel Chocolat announced that its profits in the second half of its 2014/15 financial year had beaten those of Thorntons. As Hotel Chocolat was only ten years old compared with Thorntons' hundred years, this seemed notable. Thorntons has struggled due to shifting strategy. From a tight focus on developing its own shops, Thorntons switched to building up its distribution levels in supermarkets. This boosted sales in the short term at the cost of 'cannibalising' sales at its own stores. In 2014, 39 Thorntons stores were closed. Hotel Chocolat's founder, Angus Thirlwell, had a dig at this, saying, 'One of the things we have benefited from is taking a medium-term view of the business. Some of our competitors have suffered from having a revolving chair of different strategies.'

## 96.3 Reasons for strategic drift

Strategic drift means allowing a weak or failing strategy to carry on beyond its sell-by date. In April 2015 Marks & Spencer (M&S) announced with delight that sales of clothing and household had stopped falling (for the first time in 16 quarters!). This curious celebration was undermined by a less-publicised statement: the company's overseas division was faltering. Frankly, anyone who had ventured into a M&S store in Beijing or Budapest could have told them that. Rarely has the term strategic drift been more appropriate.

Clearly the effect of strategic drift is potentially damaging, so the only interesting question is how does it come about? What may be the causal factors?

The prime cause of strategic drift is likely to be management distraction. In other words directors have too many other, more important things on their plate. In the case of M&S, shareholders cared most

about stopping the slide in clothing sales. So boss Marc Bolland kept focused on that issue, allowing weak performance internationally to stumble on. Only when there was a clear profit downturn internationally did he start to address the problem. In effect strategic drift is an opportunity cost issue. It is the cost of what the company misses out on when bosses focus all their efforts in a different direction.

## 96.4 Divorce between ownership and control

In April 1999 shares in Lloyds Bank could be bought for 960p each. With talk of a booming City of London it might have seemed sensible to stock up on the shares. Many a pensioner would have seen Lloyds as a safe bet. In fact by 2005 their investment would have halved in value and by 2015 the share price had fallen by 90 per cent. Astonishingly, in most of those years Lloyds, like other banks, paid huge 'bankers' bonuses'. As an inner circle of bankers got spectacularly richer, shareholders (and often the customers) found themselves worse off. In Figure 96.1 it is understandable that the share price collapsed in 2009 – in the dramatic banking crisis – but astonishing that the shares did so badly in the 'good times' of 1999-2007.

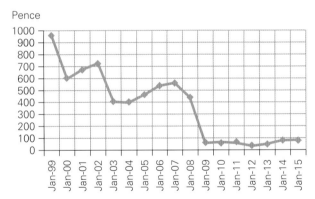

**Figure 96.1** Lloyds bank plc share price

Source: Google Finance

The explanation is simple. The shareholders have the *theoretical* power, because they can hold a vote of confidence in the Chair, and they elect the directors. The reality of most plcs, though, is that the shareholders own the company but the management controls it. The directors can get themselves on the remuneration committee. Then they can make sure that the 'independent' pay consultants who recommend pay levels are the 'right' people who 'understand' the sector. In 2007 the directors of Lloyds received a record £12.5

million between them. Staff at the bank continued to receive bonuses even after Lloyds' collapse forced the state to bail it out.

Shareholders would like to believe that the senior management is working hard to pursue the best interests of the business and therefore the shareholders. Banking has a long history, though, of showing a stark divorce between ownership and control. It is hard to understand why plc shareholders don't demand to be treated properly and fairly by managements, but sometimes they seem to be dazzled by the supposed excellence of the directors and senior staff. They would be wise to be rather more sceptical. In limited companies it is far less likely that control and ownership would be separated because in a family-owned business the owners and managers are likely to be the same people.

## 96.5 Corporate governance

In September 2014 a bombshell hit the stock market when Tesco announced that its half-year profit had been overstated by £250 million. As the profit had totalled £1,100 million, this was an admission that the half-year figures had been overstated by more than 25 per cent. Following this revelation – the result of an internal whistleblower – four senior managers at Tesco were suspended. And the recently appointed boss Dave Lewis told anyone he could that, 'Turning our business around will require change in our culture, as well as in our processes and our brand proposition. We want to work in a business which is open, transparent, fair and honest. We all expect Tesco to act with integrity and transparency at all times.' (*The Guardian*, 26 September 2014.) In the week after the announcement of the exaggerated profit, the value of Tesco's shares fell by 16 per cent (£3 billion). At the same time as this scandal unfolded, Tesco admitted investigating whether customer data had been sold by people within its South Korean operation.

So what went wrong with governance at Tesco? The man who should have been on top of this was the chairman, Sir Richard Broadbent. But he quickly upset investors by rather flippantly saying that, 'Things are always unnoticed until they're noticed' – as if it was OK to overstate profit by £250 million. As chairman of the board of directors, Broadbent had already presided over the unsatisfactory period with Philip Clarke in charge. If new boss Dave Lewis was pointing the finger at the Tesco culture, Broadbent must be partly to blame. Within a few weeks he was forced to stand down.

Serious though the technical issues were, regarding the profit overstatement, other commentators pointed

to a separate factor – that no one on the Tesco board had any experience of retailing. Given Tesco's financial embarrassment, it is ironic that the board was full of those with banking and financial experience. Incidentally among the ten board members, all were white; the reality of modern, diverse, Britain was nowhere to be seen.

'Good corporate governance is about "intellectual honesty" and not just sticking to rules and regulations.' Mervyn King, former Governor of the Bank of England

So what would ideal corporate governance look like? The starting point in the UK is that the posts of chairman and chief executive should be held by different people. Implicitly, no one person at the top should be too dominant. In fact, this doesn't solve the problem of individual dominance. Problems have arisen when the chief executive's reputation or charisma gives him (I can't think of a 'her' example) too much power; the chairman gives way to the person/s he is supposed to be supervising. This was the problem with several of Britain's biggest banks in the lead-up to the 2008 banking crisis. And, arguably, it was the problem for Tesco under the leadership of Terry Leahy.

In the long run, ethical and operational standards are helped if the board of directors is a robust debating chamber that scrutinises current performance and future plans. If it becomes a platform for a 'great' leader to receive monthly congratulation, the future prospects of every stakeholder in the business are weakened. Today's great leader often becomes tomorrow's embarrassment.

'The real mechanism for corporate governance is the active involvement of the owners.' Lou Gerstner, former boss of IBM

## 96.6 Evaluating strategic performance

Strategic performance means the outcomes of the strategic decisions. These can be evaluated using the measures chosen within the corporate objectives, probably amounting to a profit or a market share target. Needless to say, if profit has risen there will be an inclination to praise the strategic performance. A key factor to bear in mind, though, is timescale. At the time Terry Leahy retired as Chief Executive of Tesco plc, profits were at an all-time high and Leahy was being spoken of as an outstanding retailer. Four years' later, with Tesco in retreat operationally and hit by scandal financially, few still held that view. Strategic performance has to be evaluated over a long-enough time to enable a meaningful judgement to be made.

In 1979, at the time of the two-hundredth anniversary of the French Revolution, the Chinese Prime Minister Chou En-lai was asked his views on the French Revolution. He answered, 'It's too early to tell.' That's often true of business performance in the midst of change.

## 96.7 The value of strategic planning

Strategic decision-making means little without strategic planning. This is in two parts:

- planning how the strategic decision will be carried out, for example a takeover bid
- planning how to make the decision work, for example successfully integrating the two parties to a takeover bid.

Strategic planning is subject to the issue dealt with in Section 96.2: planned versus emergent strategy. Some businesses will set out a plan and demand that staff follow the plan to the letter. In other cases the plan will be more fluid, that is, an emergent strategy. In either case the important issue is to find what works for your company in its own unique circumstances.

## 96.8 The value of contingency planning

A strategic plan should outline the critical assumptions that have been made about the future competitive environment. If the success of the project depends on these judgements a 'fallback' position, or contingency plan, should be developed in case they prove wrong. As part of the planning process, 'What if?' questions should be asked. For example, a manufacturer of bicycles, thrilled about the sales boom in 2006–14 should ask the question, 'What if a slowdown in China forces oil prices back down again?' Lower oil prices would get people back into their cars, perhaps cutting demand for new bicycles. Contingency planning allows the firm to consider what actions it will take if particular opportunities or threats emerge. See the 'logic circle' in Figure 96.2 to see how contingency planning encourages managers to think ahead, as in the case of the bike manufacturer. Contingency planning reflects the business reality that the future is unknowable. Jaguar Land Rover's sales in China were booming, year after year, but suddenly fell 20 per cent in January–April 2005. This coincided with the opening of the company's first factory in China. It needed a plan to cope with this unexpected situation. A contingency plan would set out what to do – perhaps including diverting Chinese production from the Chinese market to India.

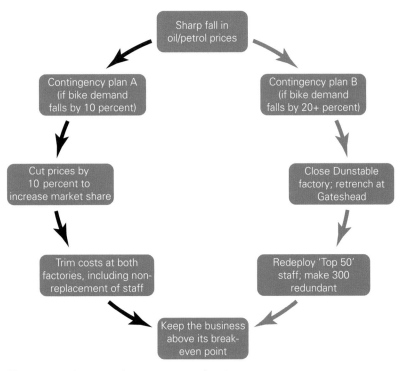

**Figure 96.2** Logic circle: contingency planning

## Five Whys and a How

| Question | Answer |
|---|---|
| Why is external change a problem when devising a strategy? | Because today's well-conceived strategy can become tomorrow's embarrassment (think Nokia) |
| Why might a planned strategy work well for a business such as Heinz? | Because its core brands have long, slow life cycles and dominant market shares, that is, there aren't too many surprises that could 'emerge' |
| Why might an emergent strategy be preferable for a young entrepreneur launching her first business? | All the uncertainties of business start-up make it better to respond flexibly to changes and disappointments, rather than plodding on with an unsuccessful (but brilliantly planned!) strategy |
| Why might corporate governance be more important today than ever before? | An online world gives huge scope for fraud (for example in crowdsourcing as a way of raising capital), so it's especially important to have people at board level who can be trusted |
| Why might divorce of ownership and control be a good thing? | For family businesses it can be a huge relief to have an outsider who will 'say it as it is' rather than just trying to keep everyone happy |
| How do contingency plans work out in practice? | A bit like corporate planning itself, they work best when they are emergent, that is, used flexibly to respond to a situation |

## Evaluation: Problems with strategy

Problems with strategy can stem from internal or external sources. External changes put pressure on strategy, but that can be tackled using the emergent approach as opposed to Michael Porter's more rigid methods. Internally-generated problems can stem from weak or cliquish leadership, but perhaps are most often a function of mismatched timescales.

In Spring 2015 QPR Director of Football Les Ferdinand claimed credit for the rise of Tottenham's Harry Kane. He pointed out that Kane had been loaned to four clubs, but was no closer to the first team until Ferdinand urged the new manager Tim Sherwood to give Kane a chance. As Ferdinand said to the BBC, 'The average lifespan at any club for managers now is 11-12 months maximum. They haven't got time to think about player development.'

The point is a simple one: short-termism gets in the way of a strategic approach to running any business, from a football club to a manufacturing giant.

## Key terms

**Contingency plan:** a Plan B in case Plan A goes wrong.

**Emergent strategy:** attempting to achieve corporate objectives in a way that is responsive to changing market and competitive circumstances, and therefore is a fusion of strategic and tactical choices.

# Workbook

## A. Revision questions

(25 marks; 25 minutes)

1. Explain why the success of a strategy rests as much on implementation as on the decision-making process. (4)

2. Choose **one** of these companies and decide whether a planned or an emergent approach to strategy would be more effective. Explain your reasoning.
   a) Heinz, in its management of its Tomato Ketchup brand
   b) Sony, in its management of its PS4 console. (5)

3. Outline two possible consequences for a business of being caught in a situation of strategic drift. (4)

4. Explain why divorce between ownership and control might be a particularly severe problem for a large multinational company. (4)

5. Good corporate governance relies on shareholders taking an interest in the long-term future of the business. Explain why that may not happen within a plc structure. (4)

6. Explain why contingency planning might be of particular value to **one** of these businesses:
   a) Primark
   b) Jaguar Land Rover
   c) Instagram. (4)

## B. Revision exercises

### DATA RESPONSE 1

#### JCB: one of the UK's most successful manufacturers

Late in 2014 JCB looks set to break the £3 billion turnover mark for the first time in its history. One of the country's biggest and most important engineering companies, JCB's yellow and black construction vehicles are among the top three bestsellers globally. In its UK heartland of Staffordshire and Derbyshire, JCB employs over 5,000 people in highly skilled, secure jobs.

One of JCB's secrets has been its willingness to invest. Its 1979 decision to start up in India has led to the achievement of a 50-per-cent market share in this huge, fast-developing country. India's new government is embarking on a huge programme of investment in roads and other infrastructure, which should be great for JCB. Just in 2014 the company has announced:

- a £25 million programme to double production in Germany
- a £45 million investment in a six-cylinder engine to slot into its fuel-efficient Dieselmax range
- a £150 million plan to expand production in the UK, with the expectation of creating 2,500 more jobs by 2018.

As the bar chart shows, not long ago – in the 2009 recession – the company's plans were thrown into turmoil by a collapse in sales. That year the company was saved by sales growth in India and China. Even so, with an estimated total capacity of 72,000 units in 2009, the rate of utilisation was very poor. To their credit, senior managers kept their heads and kept investing in the firm's future. From a struggle to break even in 2009 the company bounced back to make £365 million profit in 2012.

In 2014 JCB has been holding to its long-term plan for significant increases in its global capacity. Its factories in India and Brazil are getting greater investment and new factories are being built in Uttoxeter and Cheadle in Britain. JCB believes that developing countries will continue to plough funds into construction investment, and that JCB should be at the heart of this business. It shows no fear of its two huge global rivals: Caterpillar of America and Komatsu of Japan.

Another plan for the future is to improve the productivity of the JCB factories worldwide. In 2014 the 12,000-strong workforce was on course to produce 72,000 units. By 2018 the hope is to get annual productivity up to eight units per worker.

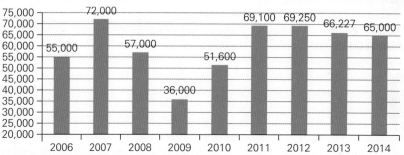

**Figure 96.3** JCB annual global sales (in units)

Source: JCB process reports

**Questions (40 marks; 45 minutes)**

**1. a)** Calculate JCB's capacity utilisation in 2009. (3)

   **b)** Explain how JCB might have set about rebuilding this figure. (4)

**2.** Analyse the problems JCB might face in implementing a new strategy that matches output to demand. (9)

**3. a)** Calculate JCB's labour productivity in 2014. (4)

   **b)** JCB's directors have asked managers to devise a new strategy to meet a productivity objective of eight units per worker by 2019. What internal and external factors might make it hard to achieve this? To what extent do those factors make failure inevitable? (20)

## C. Extend your understanding

**1.** 'In the long term, getting a strong link between shareholders and managers solves problems of governance and prevents a divorce between ownership and control.' To what extent would this ensure the success of a company's strategic decisions? (25)

**2.** After rumours that contracts had been won, in part, by bribery, in 2014 Rolls Royce plc (aero engines) brought out tough new anti-corruption guidelines for its staff summed up by the sentence, 'This means securing business fair and square in the countries where we operate'. Is this a sign of good corporate governance, or a sign that bureaucrats will dull the entrepreneurial flair of the company's staff? Justify your answer. (25)

In order to maximise the chances of launching a great new product, a business will use market research to discover just what the target market wants. In the same way, your answers are produced, by you, with a target market in mind – your examiner. This chapter explains the four key skills that you are expected to demonstrate when answering A-level Business questions.

## 97.1 Knowledge and understanding

Every question you are asked will test your knowledge of terms, concepts, theories, models and methods. In addition, the 'points' you make when answering a question are considered as knowledge. Your business knowledge must be seen as the foundation of every answer you write, even if answering a 25-mark essay-style question – it will be an opportunity to show what you have learned. Good answers are rooted in the knowledge gained during your business course. Use appropriate terminology whenever possible in your answers – just don't force it in where it does not belong.

The tougher challenge presented by A-levels is the expectation that you have not simply learned definitions and formulae like a parrot. Excellent A-level Business students understand the concepts and formulae that they have learned. In fact, understanding a term may help you to remember it. Knowing that gearing is about company indebtedness loans helps you to remember the formula.

Understanding is born of good study skills throughout your course. Never unquestioningly copy things a website or a teacher tells you. Think about the meaning of what is being explained – that will help you to develop a proper understanding of the subject.

## 97.2 Application

You need to apply your knowledge to the specific context provided by the text, numbers, graphs and bar charts within each question. To master this requires you to read and think about the material with care, writing your thoughts alongside the text and data. This skill is important because it forms the basis for good application and evaluation.

The way that you will show application will vary from question to question depending on which paper you are tackling. Some multiple choice and short answer questions expect you to show application by using numbers provided by the question to complete a calculation.

Data response questions require you to use information about the context provided within the data to develop your explanations and arguments when responding to questions. Where the data is mainly numerate, look to draw information from the material provided. Where data is provided in graphs and tables make sure that you:

- understand what the graph/table is showing
- use the appropriate units when quoting figures
- check the dates of the data you are using – note that sometimes accountants record the most recent year to the left of previous years' data.

In other instances, much more of the data provided will be text, about a company or perhaps industry. Read and annotate that carefully, looking to draw out the key issues raised by the data provided. Often you will need to infer (read between the lines) rather than expect to be explicitly told everything. Making notes in the margin next to the text helps you remember the key parts of the business story. The case study may well provide a mix of numerate and written information about the business. Combine the good habits described above to get the most out of the data provided.

Some questions will allow you to use businesses of your own choice to help illustrate your answers. This is why you have been reading around the subject for the whole of your A-level course. Knowing real business examples adds depth of application to your answers.

The final, perhaps most important hint provided for application may be in the question. Even without a case study or data to respond to, better students pick up on aspects of the question to show their ability to apply knowledge to different contexts, for example 'a business operating in a highly competitive market' or 'a small bakery'. Check the following to see if you can spot the context to which you need to apply:

1. Explain two methods of promotion that could be used by a firm trying to break into a highly competitive consumer goods market.

2. Analyse the benefits to a rapidly growing firm of using financial methods of motivation.

3. To what extent is greater use of digital technology an appropriate strategy for an established luxury goods manufacturer whose unique selling point is their 200-year history of unsurpassed customer service?

Good students will have picked up on the following features of each question to show their ability to apply knowledge to context:

| **Question 1** | Trying to break into a new market<br>The market is for consumer goods<br>The market is highly competitive |
| **Question 2** | The firm is rapidly growing |
| **Question 3** | The USP is customer service<br>The firm is traditional<br>Luxury goods are being sold |

Where possible, look to draw together several aspects of the information provided in order to help to build your arguments. This should help to ensure that your answer is fully rooted in the context provided.

## 97.3 Analysis

Analysis involves breaking information down into component parts. That generally means starting to show an awareness of cause and effect. The construction of a logical argument is also a vital component of strong analysis. So a key ability is building chains of logic that answer the question.

When building a chain of logic, the basic rules to consider are:

- start your chain from the question
- do not miss out links in the chain
- ensure every link is logical
- finish your chain back at the question.

A question such as 'Analyse the financial benefits of increased capacity utilisation' can be used to illustrate these four rules:

Start your chain at the question – in this case increased capacity utilisation is the starting point for your journey. From here you should begin to work through the consequences of increased capacity utilisation:

Increased capacity utilisation – more output without extra fixed costs – meaning fixed costs are spread over more units – so fixed costs per unit are lower – allowing a higher profit per unit.

Note that in the chain above there are no obvious steps forward within the chain that are illogical. In addition, there are no missing links in the chain. Finally notice the illustration of the fourth rule of analysis – the chain finishes back at the question – in this case, by showing the financial benefit that the question asked for.

**Table: 97.1** Question (command) words requiring analysis/evaluation

| **Analysis but NOT evaluation** | **Evaluation (in addition to the other Assessment Objectives)** |
| --- | --- |
| Analyse | Evaluate |
| Explain why | Justify |
| | To what extent |

## 97.4 Evaluation

Evaluation means making judgements, but they must stem from arguments (your analysis) that have been built on evidence from the scenario being considered, or from the real business examples you have provided.

The skill of evaluation can be thought of as making judgements. Ideally you should back up those judgements and arguments with evidence, explaining why. It is vital that when you make a judgement it flows logically from the arguments you have put forward. In the table above, you can see the three most commonly used evaluation command words. Each requires a subtly different form of judgement:

**Evaluate** – consider several issues before deciding on the most important. Explain why the issue is most important in this case.

**Justify** – this is where you will have been asked to make a decision. Your job is to explain why your decision is the most logical in this case.

**To what extent** – requires you to show a balanced judgement as to how likely something is to happen or its relative importance. It will therefore require you to consider alternatives before judging which is the most likely to be true.

What these have in common is the need to do something extra, beyond the knowledge, application and analysis you show within your answer. As your judgement should flow from your answer, it is sensible to offer your judgement at the end of your response to the question, that is, in your conclusion. Within the conclusion, you should ensure that you:

- make a clear judgement specific to the question asked
- explain why the judgement you have made is more appropriate than other judgements you could have made

- use the context of the question to show why your judgement is most appropriate.

The best judgements should show an element of weighing up alternatives before settling on a final decision.

## Five Whys and a How

| Question | Answer |
|---|---|
| Why must I learn key terms? | You will be asked to show knowledge of definitions of key terms, not only within multiple choice questions but also short answer sections |
| Why must I make sure I understand the theories I have learned? | Students with hazy understanding of key terms struggle to understand what the question is trying to ask. |
| Why is it helpful to stay abreast of current business news stories? | Not only will this deepen your understanding of business concepts, it will also help you enrich the quality and depth of the answers you give |
| Why is it so important to read the question carefully? | Fully addressing the question ensures that you have not missed a subtle clause within the question |
| Why is evaluation more than a summary? | Evaluation implies a judgement – some kind of weighing up of alternative arguments you have presented. That needs you to go beyond simply restating your arguments |
| How can I get a clearer idea of the assessment objectives? | Using the past papers* and mark schemes published on the Internet will allow you to see plenty of examples of what examiners expect to see to award good analysis, application and evaluation |

## Evaluation: Understanding assessment objectives

The single most important way to meet the Assessment Objectives is to answer the question. Take the time to think what *exactly* the question is asking you to do. Just because a question includes a piece of terminology such as training, does not mean that the answer should be 'all about training'. If the question wants to

know whether increased training is the best way to improve productivity, the question is really about how to increase productivity – a concept that must be at the heart of your answer.

Ultimately, exam technique can be summed up in one phrase: 'ANSWER THE QUESTION!'

# Chapter 98 Tackling data response questions

## 98.1 Introduction

A data response question requires you to do three things simultaneously:

1. Understand and use the data (perhaps an article).

2. Keep in mind the classroom/textbook theory.

3. Answer the precise terms of the question.

It would not be crazy to suggest that most human beings can do only one thing at a time; two at a push. But three? That is why data response papers are harder than they look.

For students who revise at the last minute, the problem is especially acute. Cramming focuses on knowledge, but tends to block out the other two factors. This makes the answers one-dimensional: full of knowledge, but lacking in application, analysis and evaluation.

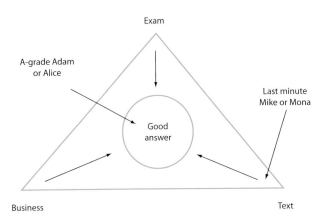

**Figure 98.1** The three-way answer

## 98.2 Using the data

The key is to find a way to get the guts out of the short passage of text; that is, to find the real business bits that matter. Many students use a highlighter pen, but seem to mark-up too much, turning the page from white to a lurid pink. That achieves little. It's better to jot down the key points as you go. These amount to:

- key points about the business context: competitors, consumer fashions, and so on
- key points about the business: its products, its image, its efficiency, and so on
- key points about the people running it: their experience, their enthusiasm, their judgement, and so on.

Below is a short piece of text on PD Ltd. Identify at least three key points that you could use to enrich the application shown in your answers. Give yourself a few minutes, then look at the suggestions given at the end of the unit.

> *PD Ltd*
>
> *Den and girlfriend Pam started PD Ltd with £15,000 borrowed from a friend and £15,000 from HSBC. Both keen surfers, their plan was to open the first surfing school in north-east England, on the coast above Newcastle. They were confident that they could persuade the Geordies to take up surfing, despite the cold weather.*

This exercise shows the enormous importance of reading the text with great care.

You can make use of every subtlety built into the text, but some of the more common issues worth looking out for are listed in Table 98.1.

Table 98.1 Some common issues to look out for

| Topic or issue | From one extreme ... | ... to the other |
|---|---|---|
| Seasonal sales | 70 per cent of the whole year's sales occur in the three-week run-up to Christmas (for example toys, posh perfume) | Sales vary little month by month (for example toilet paper) |
| Degree of competition | Fiercely competitive market in which customers care greatly about price | Few competitors, and they focus on giving high service levels to their own customers |
| Product life cycle | Very short product life cycles; a brand's sales can be ended by a technological breakthrough by another | Long life cycles protected by the conservatism of consumers (for example Heinz Ketchup – people won't try another) |
| Risk | A sole trader has started a new restaurant using borrowings secured against the family home | Tim started a limited company to run a small education business offering maths tutoring |

## 98.3 Using numerical data

Quite often, data response questions include numerical data such as budget statements or cash flow forecasts. These are very helpful.

The valuable thing about numbers is that they:

- give you a starting point for building an argument while…
- also ensuring that your answer is applied to the specific context having used the data given in the exam.

It can also be argued that numbers provide a good student with the opportunity to show both their knowledge of the course and provide a basis for making judgements. In other words, it can generate every one of the assessment objectives.

With numerical data (such as sales figures) it will always be valid to ask yourself certain questions (see Table 98.2).

Table 98.2 Questions to ask yourself about numerical data

| Valid questions about data | Example of good data | Example of bad data |
|---|---|---|
| Is the data actual or forecast? | Actual data on weekly sales over the last 18 months | A forecast of next year's sales made by a businessman wanting a loan |
| Is it based on a valid sample? | Based on a sample of 600 people within your target market, carried out by Gallup, an independent research company | Based on research carried out by the sales department |
| Is there a valid way to make comparisons? | The figures show sales of all our brands compared with the same period last year and the year before | The figures show the huge success of Brand P, which has seen a 70 per cent sales increase in the past two months |

## 98.4 Bringing it all together

The amount of data provided in a data response exam question may be quite substantial. It cannot, therefore, *all* be used to answer every question. Don't worry: the important thing is *not* to 'know it all'; the key is to have picked out enough key features to show that you're really trying to think for yourself. Having read the text and thought about the numbers, make sure to jot down the key points. If you don't, there's a risk that you'll forget the details by the time you tackle your third question. Every answer requires the context (that is, effective use of the case being looked at).

### Application points: PD Ltd

Things to look out for include the following.

- *The 'first' surfing school in north-east England.* This may mean that there is a fortune to be made, but it also suggests high risk (whereas being the fifteenth surfing school in Newquay, Cornwall, would probably not be a total disaster).
- *'They were confident that…'* The key here is what it does *not* say. It does *not* say: 'They'd done some market research, which gave them confidence that…'. Their confidence may mean nothing. Anyone who watches *The Apprentice* has seen no end of people with confidence but startlingly little ability. The key requirement in this case is evidence not confidence.

- '£15,000 borrowed from a friend and £15,000 from HSBC'. No bank would lend unless it has seen the owners invest at least half the start-up capital, so Den and Pam have probably not told the bank that they have borrowed it all. Having such high debts (relatively) must increase the riskiness of the investment.

Other possibilities include: the importance of the Ltd status (protection from unlimited liability); the importance of seasonality (especially in the north-east); the possible significance of the boyfriend/girlfriend relationship – how long have they been together?

# Chapter 99 How to revise for business exams

Studies have shown that good revision can add as much as two grades to a student's result at A-level. The aim of this unit is to help you to appreciate what makes up a quality revision programme.

## 99.1 Aims and objectives

A good revision programme should be aimed at achieving specific targets that will maximise your chances of success in the exam. How should these targets be set?

The basis for setting revision targets can be found in three places:

1. the specification (syllabus)
2. specimen Assessment Materials and (after a year or two) past papers
3. examiner's reports.

### The specification

The content of the course is set out in detail in the specification. As the questions in the exam are drawn from this document, you must ensure that you understand all the terms, especially the headings (which tend to be overlooked).

The specification also tells you what skills you need to show. As well as factual recall, there are a range of other qualities you must demonstrate if you are to score highly. These can be developed only through practice. So it is important to start your revision early and not leave it until the end. In fact, you should try to review your work every few weeks to make sure there are no gaps in your notes and that your files are well organised. This way it becomes easier to revise at the end of the course because everything is in place.

### What knowledge to revise

Every question is a race against the clock. So it's hugely helpful to know short, sharp definitions of key terms. They save time and make your answers stronger academically. Ideally you will have been collecting these definitions in a glossary notebook of your own – building it up over the two years. If not, you'll have to make sure that you can define the main terms that relate to each business function, plus the key, theoretical terms from the second year of study.

After gathering together the key terms, it's crucial to remind yourself of the main issues within the subject. This book helps hugely through the Five Whys and a How feature in every chapter. Go through each set of Five Whys and a How, and whenever you're not quite sure of what's being said, read the Evaluation section. If you're still puzzled ('I don't remember studying this at all!') you'll have to read the whole chapter.

### Specimen assessment materials and past papers

Before the first A-level exams in Summer 2017, the AQA's Specimen Assessment Materials are the only Board-approved indications of what an exam paper might look like. Make sure to access them at www.aqa.org.uk/subjects/business-subjects.

After 2017, previous exam papers will be very important in helping you to prepare for your exam. They show you what sort of questions you will face and the number of marks available. They also give you a feel for the type of words used in the question. It goes without saying that exam questions must be read carefully. However, there will be key words used in the questions that tell you how to answer them. There is, for example, a great difference in the answers expected for the following two questions.

1. Analyse New Look's 2015 objective of doubling its presence in China.
2. Evaluate New Look's 2015 objective of doubling its presence in China.

Unless you know what is expected from these two questions, you are unlikely to know how much detail is required or how your answer ought to be structured.

## Examiner's reports

These are available for each examination and can be obtained from your teacher. They are written by the principal examiner of each exam and provide an insight into what she or he found worked well or was not so successful. This provides another useful input when it comes to revising and knowing where to focus your efforts.

## 99.2 Other important resources

### Access to your teacher

Asking your teacher for help is vital. She or he is able to give you useful advice and insights, to quell sudden panics and suggest ways to improve your performance. Don't hold back – ask! Whenever you get a piece of work back where the mark is disappointing make sure you know what you need to do differently next time. Read any comments on your work and try to improve in the specific areas mentioned in the next piece of work. Remember, the journey to success is full of small improvements (this is, of course, the philosophy of *kaizen*).

### Other students

Talk to other students to help discuss points and clarify ideas. Learning from each other is a very powerful way of revising. Research shows that you remember something much better when you have to explain it to someone else. Why not agree as a group to revise some topics? Study them individually then get together to test each other's understanding. This works very well. There is no problem helping others to improve their performance and you will benefit from the explanations you give.

## 99.3 Learning the language of the subject

For revising business definitions you could use:

● definition cards
● past papers
● crosswords/word games
● brainteasers.

Your definitions should be written without using the word in question. ('Market growth is the growth in the market' is not a very good definition, for example!)

It is important, then, that you can produce high-quality definitions in an exam. This can be done only through learning and practice. Possible ways to achieve this are as follows.

### Definition cards

Take a pack of index cards or postcards, or similar-sized pieces of thick paper. On each one, write a particular term or phrase that you can find in the specification document. Remember to include things like 'motivation theories' where a clear definition or description can give an excellent overview. It is extremely unlikely that you will be asked to know a precise definition for any term that is not specifically in the specification.

On the back of each card write an appropriate definition. This could come from your class notes, a textbook or a dictionary. Make sure that the definition you write:

● is concise
● is clear
● does not use the word being defined in the definition.

Learn them by continual repetition. Put a tick or cross on each card to show whether or not you came up with an acceptable effort. Over time, you should see the number of ticks growing.

Shuffle the cards occasionally so that you are not being given clues to some definitions because of the words or phrases preceding them.

Try doing the exercise 'back to front', by looking at the definitions and then applying the correct word or phrase.

### Past papers

By using as many past papers as possible you can find the types of definition questions that are asked. More importantly, you can see how many marks are available for them, which will tell you how much detail you need to go into in your answer.

If possible, get hold of examiners' mark schemes. These will again give you a clear idea of what is being looked for from your answer.

### Business crosswords and brainteasers

You will be able to find many examples of word games in magazines such as *Business Review*. By completing these you are developing your business vocabulary and linking words with their meanings.

## 99.4 Numbers

In this A-level course 10 per cent of the marks are reserved for your numerical skills. There are two clear aspects to numbers:

1. calculation
2. interpretation.

The calculation aspects of business courses are one area where practice is by far the best approach. Each numerical element has its own techniques that you will be expected to be able to demonstrate. The techniques can be learnt, and by working through many examples they can become second nature. Even if maths is not your strong point, the calculations ought not to cause problems to an A-level student. Something that at first sight appears complex, such as investment appraisal, only requires multiplying, adding, subtracting and dividing. Going through the Workbook sections of this book will provide invaluable practice. Ask your teacher for a photocopy of the answers available in the *Answer Guide*.

Once calculated, all business numbers need to be used. It is all very well to calculate accounting ratios, for example, but if the numbers are then unused the exercise has been wasted. You must attempt to follow each calculation by stating what the numbers are saying and their implications for the business.

## 99.5 Final points on revision

1. Start early.
2. Know the purpose of your revision.
3. Work more on weaker areas.
4. Use past papers as far as is possible.
5. Keep a clear perspective.

Please don't revise on the night before the exam; it won't help and can only cause you anxiety. Eat well and get a good night's sleep. That way you will be in good physical shape to perform to the best of your abilities in the exam.

# Index

Page numbers in bold indicate a key term entry.